# CAMBRIDGE GREEK AND LATIN CLASSICS

GENERAL EDITORS

P. E. EASTERLING
*Emeritus Regius Professor of Greek, University of Cambridge*

PHILIP HARDIE
*Reader in Latin Literature, University of Cambridge*

RICHARD HUNTER
*Regius Professor of Greek, University of Cambridge*

E. J. KENNEY
*Emeritus Kennedy Professor of Latin, University of Cambridge*

# EURIPIDES

# MEDEA

EDITED BY

## DONALD. J. MASTRONARDE

*Melpomene Professor of Classics,*
*University of California, Berkeley*

CAMBRIDGE
UNIVERSITY PRESS

CAMBRIDGE UNIVERSITY PRESS

Cambridge, New York, Melbourne, Madrid, Cape Town, Singapore, São Paulo, Delhi, Tokyo, Mexico City

Cambridge University Press
The Edinburgh Building, Cambridge CB2 8RU, UK

Published in the United States of America by Cambridge University Press, New York

www.cambridge.org
Information on this title: www.cambridge.org/9780521643863

First published 2002
10th printing 2012

Printed in the United Kingdom at the University Press, Cambridge

*A catalogue record for this publication is available from the British Library*

ISBN 978-0-521-64365-8 Hardback
ISBN 978-0-521-64386-3 Paperback

# CONTENTS

v

# PREFACE

*Medea* is probably now the play of Euripides most widely known to the general public, from exposure to translations in classes in secondary schools and colleges and from performances either of translations of the Greek text or of looser adaptations of the plot. In the curriculum of programmes in ancient Greek, too, *Medea* is frequently an assigned text for study in the original language, and is sometimes the first Greek drama or first Greek poetry that a learner studies. In earlier generations, the play was equally studied but often frowned upon, for unAristotelian motivation and causation, for the extremity of Medea's action, and for the moral shock of its conclusion. In more recent times, the play has deservedly attained a better reputation, as critics and audiences have become more open to acknowledging the tensions and contradictions of classical Greek culture, to appreciating the chaotic as well as the harmonious and serene. Rather than seeing *Medea* as a realistic or psychological study, scholars now concentrate on issues like the problematics of the heroic code, the religious and ethical aspects of revenge, oath, and supplication, and the socio-political tensions reflected in the contest of genders and ethnicities evoked by the play.

The goal of this commentary is to make the play accessible in all its complication and sophistication to present-day students. It aims to provide, on the one hand, the linguistic and technical information that will support the task of translation and equip the student to appreciate the formal and artistic devices of Greek tragedy: hence, the sections Language and Style, and Prosody and Metre that follow the General Introduction. On the other hand, it is equally important to give an introduction to the major interpretive problems, with reference to some further discussions (mostly in English), and this purpose is addressed both in the Introduction and in the Commentary itself.

The aim has been both to replace, and not to replace, the famous commentary of Denys Page (Oxford 1938). Page's work contains many fundamental discussions of matters of tragic language and style and constitution of the text, but many of his notes are too technical for the modern student commentary, or concern matters on which later generations have not been in doubt, thanks in part to Page's work. In some respects, his work is, not surprisingly, outmoded, partly because of changes in critical approaches, and partly because of new evidence (papyri and vase-paintings) and new work on the textual tradition. But no one should doubt that the advanced student of Greek tragedy still has much to learn from Page's commentary.

My task in writing this book has been facilitated greatly by the recent work of high quality done on the text of the play, particularly that of James Diggle in the Oxford Classical Text Euripides (vol. 1, 1984) and David Kovacs for the new Loeb edition of Euripides (vol. 1, 1994). I have also benefited from reference to the Teubner edition of H. van Looy (Stuttgart and Leipzig 1992) and the edition with introduction, translation, and notes by V. di Benedetto and E. Cerbo (Biblioteca Universale Rizzoli, Milan 1997). I am grateful to the editors, Patricia Easterling and Richard Hunter, for the invitation to work on this play in this format and for their helpful advice and criticism, and to several other scholars for generously providing comments and corrections on various parts at various stages of their drafting: James Diggle, John Gibert, Luigi Battezzato, Mark Griffith. I owe advice on particular points to Michael Haslam, Andrew Garrett, Tony Long, Peter Parsons, and Henk Versnel, and I thank Ted Brunner, former Director of the Thesaurus Linguae Graecae at the University of California, Irvine, for his help. Among the students who have offered specific comments or discussed the play with me, I would like to acknowledge here Frank Cope, Melissa Mueller, and Mario Telò, as well as Alex Kozak, Donna Sy, and Kurt Lampe for bibliographic work, proofreading, and reference-checking. Two undergraduate classes and a graduate seminar also helped me make progress. The early stages of my work were supported by a sabbatical leave from the University of California, Berkeley, and a fellowship from the American Council of Learned Societies.

I am pleased to dedicate this book to my Classics colleagues and students at the University of California, Berkeley.

# ABBREVIATIONS

NOTE: 'Introd.' followed by a number refers to the numbered section of the General introduction, 'SE' refers to the section Structural elements of Greek tragedy, 'LS' refers to the section Language and Style, and 'PM' refers to the section Prosody and Metre. Fragments of Aeschylus and Sophocles are cited from the editions of Radt in *TrGF*, those of Euripides from Nauck. Other commentaries and secondary works referred to are listed in the Bibliography at the end of the volume.

Ast, *Lex. Plat.*    F. Ast, *Lexicon Platonicum sive vocum Platonicarum index* (Leipzig 1835–58)

Chantraine    P. Chantraine, *Dictionnaire étymologique de la langue grecque: histoire des mots* (Paris 1968–80)

*CGFPR*    C. Austin, *Comicorum Graecorum fragmenta in papyris reperta* (Berlin 1973)

*CMG*    *Corpus Medicorum Graecorum*

Dale, *MATC*    A. M. Dale, *Metrical analyses of tragic choruses* (BICS Suppl. 21.1–3, London 1971–83)

Denniston    J. D. Denniston, *The Greek particles* (2nd edn, Oxford 1954)

*EGM*    R. Fowler, *Early Greek mythography* (Oxford 2000)

Frisk    H. Frisk, *Griechisches etymologisches Wörterbuch* (Heidelberg 1954–72)

Goodwin    W. W. Goodwin, *Syntax of the moods and tenses of the Greek verb* (Boston 1890)

*FGrHist*    F. Jacoby, ed., *Die Fragmente der griechischen Historiker* (Berlin and Leiden 1923–54)

K–A    Rudolph Kassel and Colin Austin, eds., *Poetae Comici Graeci* (Berlin and New York 1983– )

K–G    R. Kühner and B. Gerth, *Ausführliche Grammatik der griechischen Sprache, 2. Teil: Satzlehre* (3. Aufl., Hanover 1898–1904)

*LIMC*    *Lexicon iconographicum mythologiae classicae* (Zurich and Munich 1981–97)

| | |
|---|---|
| LSJ | H. G. Liddell, R. Scott, H. S. Jones, *A Greek-English lexicon* (9th edn, Oxford 1925–40) |
| Nauck | A. Nauck, *Tragicorum Graecorum fragmenta* [2nd edn 1889]. Supplementum continens nova fragmenta Euripidea et adespota apud scriptores veteres reperta adiecit B. Snell (Hildesheim 1964) |
| OCD | S. Hornblower and A. Spawforth, eds., *The Oxford classical dictionary* (3rd edn, Oxford 1996) |
| PMG | D. L. Page, ed., *Poetae Melici Graeci* (Oxford 1962) |
| PMGF | M. Davies, ed., *Poetarum Melicorum Graecorum Fragmenta* (Oxford 1991) |
| Schwyzer | E. Schwyzer and A. Debrunner, *Griechische Grammatik* (Munich 1938–50) |
| Smyth | H. W. Smyth, *Greek grammar*, rev. by G. Messing (Harvard 1956) |
| TGFS | J. Diggle, ed., *Tragicorum Graecorum fragmenta selecta* (Oxford 1998) |
| TrGF | *Tragicorum Graecorum fragmenta*, ed. B. Snell, R. Kannicht, S. Radt (Berlin 1971–85) |
| TrRF | *Tragicorum Romanorum fragmenta*, ed. O. Ribbeck. (3rd edn, Leipzig 1897) |

# GENERAL INTRODUCTION

## 1 EURIPIDES: LIFE AND WORKS

For Greeks of the fifth century BCE there is very little biographical information that can be relied upon. Much of the information about Euripides extant in later antiquity[1] is based on plausible and (more often) implausible inferences from allusions in Old Comedy and from statements in the dramas themselves (according to the widespread, but false, assumption that various first-person statements may express the dramatist's own convictions). The doxographic tradition often constructed teacher-pupil relationships whenever a similarity was detected between two intellectuals. Anecdotes commonly transmitted stories based on traditional patterns of folktale and myth rather than on genuine biographical data.[2]

Eur. was probably born some time in the decade of the 480s, and no later than about 475. The first reliably recorded date in his life (from the *Marmor Parium*) is that of his first production of plays at the Great Dionysia in 455, when he was presumably at least 20 years old and may have been as old as 31 or 32. Different ancient traditions place his birth in 480/79 (in some sources, more precisely, on the very day of the Battle of Salamis) or in 485/4 (a coincidence with the first victory of Aeschylus) or one of the two previous years.

His father's name was Mnesarchides (or Mnesarchos) of the deme Phlya (Kekropid tribe), and anecdotes and later cult connect him with Salamis (for his birth, and for the cave in which he is supposed

---

[1] For the text of ancient and medieval sources for the life of Euripides (hereafter Eur.), along with English translation, see Kovacs (1994) 2–66. The major sources are the *Life* transmitted in some manuscripts of the plays, a long entry in the medieval encyclopedia known as the *Suda*, and papyrus fragments of a *Life* in dialogue form written by the Peripatetic grammarian Satyrus late in the third century BCE; other information comes from brief references in ancient writers, the scholia (marginal annotation) and hypotheses (plot summaries and other information prefaced to the plays in medieval texts), and the *Marmor Parium* (an inscription of 264/63 BCE recording by date key events in Attic history and general Greek history). For a fuller discussion of Eur.'s life and the reception of his dramas, see Kovacs' Loeb edition, 1 1–36.

[2] See Fairweather (1974), Lefkowitz (1979) and (1981).

to have isolated himself to compose).[3] In order to have received the extensive musical and poetic education implied by his career, he must have come from a family of ample means. The anecdote in one *Life*[4] about his training for athletic competition may also point to an upper-class background.[5] The jokes found in Old Comedy mocking his mother as a lowly seller of vegetables may be a distortion of some actual family connection with production of food for the Attic marketplace.

Eur. will have undergone the standard Attic military training and service in his youth and prime. He may have participated in deme activities and the Attic assembly, and may have served on juries or the Council, but nothing is recorded of this (nor is there any reason it should have been).[6] To become a dramatic poet, he presumably associated with and observed established poets, who in the early decades of the fifth century were also usually actors and chorus-trainers, and then attempted compositions on his own, preparing himself to 'request a chorus', that is, to ask the eponymous archon to include him among the competitors at a dramatic festival.

Eur. was obviously very much at home with the intellectual currents of his day, including developments in rhetorical training and the epistemological, political, and anthropological speculations of the Sophists.[7] To a greater degree than Sophocles, he presents us with characters who engage in intellectual and ethical speculations and who comment about language, the process of argumentation, and skill at speaking. Eur. uses these features, however, to dramatize the aspirations and frustrations of human knowledge and human

---

[3] The cave on Salamis where Eur. was believed to have worked has been identified and contains various dedications, showing it was a place of pilgrimage in post-classical times: one cup has Eur.'s name inscribed on it in lettering of the Roman period. See Blackman (1998) 16–17.

[4] Test. 1(3) in Kovacs (the *Life* that precedes the plays in some MSS).

[5] See Miller (2000) for the argument that not all Greek athletes came from wealthy families.

[6] Stevens (1956).

[7] This is too large and complex a subject to be dealt with in this context. On Eur. and the Sophists see Conacher (1998) and Allan (2000a), with the bibliography that they cite. On rhetoric and language see (e.g.) Croally (1994), Goldhill (1986) ch. 9, Lloyd (1992), Scodel (2000).

civilization, and in so far as one can speak of his attitude toward modern trends, it is neither uniformly positive nor negative.[8] The simplified claim made in the ancient *Life* that he was a 'pupil of Anaxagoras and Prodicus and Protagoras and an associate of Socrates'[9] should be greeted with scepticism, although such a belief has exerted a significant influence on Eur.'s posthumous reputation and modern reception.

When scholars in the fourth century examined the records of competitions in the Athenian state archives, they found that Eur.'s participation in the Dionysia began in 455. His last certain Athenian production during his lifetime was at the Dionysia in 408, and a final tetralogy was entered in the competition shortly after his death. His name was found in the list of competitions at the Great Dionysia 22 times (88 dramas), and ancient scholars catalogued 92 plays under his name, of which a few were of disputed authorship, and Eur. also produced at least a few plays for other venues.[10] Possibly his surviving *Andromache* is one such play, since it could not be found in the Attic production lists under Eur.'s name (although Callimachus thought it was the play listed under the name of Democrates).[11] At the end of his life he was writing plays in Macedonia at the court of the king Archelaos, including one about the king's mythological namesake, the lost *Archelaos*.[12] Eur. also wrote a praise-ode for the famous Alcibiades after his victory in the chariot-race at the Olympic Games of 416 (*PMG* 755–6), and Plutarch (*Nikias* 17.4) quotes as the work of Eur. a grave-epitaph for Athenians killed in the Sicilian disaster of 413.

---

[8] See (e.g.) Reinhardt (1957), Mastronarde (1986).

[9] Test. 1(4) Kovacs; a similar claim is made in the entry in the *Suda* (Test. 2(3) Kovacs).

[10] See Easterling (1994) and the more speculative discussion of Dearden (1999).

[11] On the uncertainties of the evidence see Allan (2000b) 149–52.

[12] See Revermann (2000) 454–5. Aelian *Var. hist.* 2.8 tells a story in which Eur. competes in a dramatic festival at Peiraeus; if this is true, it could have involved either a reperformance of a play also seen at the Great Dionysia or production of a play never staged in the city. On the number of Eur.'s plays see now Jouan and Van Looy (1998) XI–XVI.

The known dates in Euripides' theatrical career are as follows:

| 455 | first competition (included lost *Peliades*) |
| 441 | first victory in the competition |
| 438 | *Alcestis* (earliest surviving play of Eur.): fourth play in a tetralogy that won second prize (with lost *Kressai*, *Alkmeon A'*, *Telephos*) |
| 431 | *Medea*: first play in a tetralogy that won third prize (with lost *Philoctetes*, *Dictys*, and satyr-play *Theristai*) |
| 428 | second *Hippolytus*: part of a tetralogy that won first prize[13] |
| 415 | *Trojan Women*: third play of a tetralogy that won second prize, (with lost *Alexandros*, *Palamedes*, and satyr-play *Sisyphos*) |
| 412 | *Helen*, along with lost *Andromeda* |
| 408 | *Orestes* |
| 407/6 (winter) | death of Eur. in Macedonia |
| 405–400 | *Iphigenia in Aulis*, *Alkmeon B'*, and *Bacchae*, produced by Eur.'s son; posthumous first prize |

The other surviving plays and some of the lost plays are dated approximately on the basis of quotations in dated comedies, the proportion and type of resolutions allowed in the iambic trimeters, and (the least reliable criterion) possible allusions to contemporary events. Resolution in the trimeter has been studied in great detail,[14] and it has been shown that from the 420s to the end of his life Eur. gradually loosened the traditional form of the tragic trimeter by admitting a higher and higher percentage of resolved positions (see PM 19), by using more lines with multiple resolutions, and by extending the

---

[13] It is generally assumed that the second *Hippolytus* is the extant play; this is probably the case, but it must be conceded that ancient scholars may simply have had two Hippolytus plays and two dates on the production-lists and constructed what was to them a plausible story, that the play with the more shocking portrayal of Phaedra was the earlier and that criticism of it caused Eur. to write a new version. See Gibert (1997).

[14] See Cropp and Fick (1985).

word-shapes and positions in which the resolutions occur. The estimated dates based principally on resolutions in the trimeters are as follows:[15]

| | |
|---|---|
| c. 430 | *Heracleidae* |
| c. 425 | *Andromache* |
| c. 425–4 | *Hecuba* |
| c. 423 | *Supplices* |
| c. 420[16] | *Electra* |
| c. 416 | *Heracles* |
| c. 414 | *Iphigeneia in Tauris* |
| c. 414 | *Ion* |
| 411–409 | *Phoenissae* |

Although Eur. won only four first prizes during his life (441, 428, and two unknown dates), there was no question, once his career was established, that he was a tragedian of the highest rank, and clearly archons must have welcomed his participation in the contest of the Great Dionysia. It needs to be emphasized that it was not an individual play by itself that was ranked first, second, or last in a competition, but the entire tetralogy of which it was a part. Since we normally have no idea of the quality of the lost accompanying plays, the quality of the competitors' productions, or the technical competence of the direction and acting of any given tetralogy, it is idle to speculate on the reason for a particular prize based on the single surviving play. Many have nevertheless assumed that

---

[15] Omitted from this list is *Rhesus*, which is transmitted among the select plays of Eur. but seems to be a fourth-century tragedy by an unknown poet: see (in favour of Euripidean authorship) Ritchie (1964) and Burnett (1985); (against) Fraenkel (1965). The satyr-play *Cyclops* is also omitted, since it is uncertain whether the test of resolutions should apply in the same way to a satyr-play. Seaford in his edition of *Cyclops* argues that it should and dates the play to c. 410–408; others put the play in the 420s.

[16] Some scholars date *Electra* to 413 in the belief that lines 1347–8 allude to the Sicilian Expedition and that lines 1280–3 announce *Helen* of 412: see the counter arguments of Zuntz (1955) 63–71 and the additional remarks in Cropp's edition, l–li.

*Medea* so shocked or offended the Athenians that the judges were hostile.[17]

Aristophanes' *Frogs* shows that at his death Eur. could be regarded as one of the three giants of fifth-century tragedy. His popularity only increased after his death. Many features of the style and the projected world-view of his plays made them especially accessible and attractive to the developing panhellenic audience of the fourth century and the audiences and readers of the Hellenistic era and later: the relatively easier verbal style, the rhetorically-tinged self-presentation of his characters, the variety and complexity of plot mechanisms, the penchant for giving voice to marginalized groups, the emergence of personal themes less tied to civic identity, and the sense of abandonedness or even absurdity that often arises from the role of the divine and fortune (or Fortune) in the plays. His stature within the classical canon from the fourth century to the end of antiquity is evidenced by numerous quotations in ancient authors, the frequency of Euripidean lines in the anthology of Stobaeus and other similar collections, and inscriptions and papyri indicating performance and reading of his plays or of excerpts from them.[18]

Eur. has benefited during the past century from the remarkable recovery of ancient texts from scraps of papyrus rolls preserved in the sands of Egypt.[19] Along with fragments of summaries of several

---

[17] Nor is the assumption of a 'patriotic' reason for disapproval of *Medea* very cogent. The anecdote (Σ*Med.* 9) about Eur. being paid by the Corinthians to make Medea the killer of the children might go back to a joke in comedy about Eur. being 'unpatriotic' for treating the Corinthians (bitter enemies of Athens in the run-up to the full outbreak of the Peloponnesian War in 431) so well. On the negative side, Creon is depicted as an abettor of a perjuror, and the citizen-women of the chorus as acquiescing in the death of their own royal family. But the audience of *Medea* had more important things to be shocked about than the way the heroic-age Corinthians were portrayed.

[18] See the evidence in Csapo and Slater (1995) *passim*; for papyri, Pack (1967) is updated by the CD-ROM *Leuven database of ancient books* (1998), and the up-to-date database known as Mertens-Pack³ is to be made available on-line by the Centre de Documentation de Papyrologie Littéraire (CeDoPaL) of the University of Liège.

[19] Even before the age of discovery of Egyptian papyri, a substantial portion of *Phaethon* was recovered from some pages of an ancient book (fifth century CE) that had been reused (at some point after the sixth century) to repair

plays, the papyri have provided major gains in our knowledge of *Hypsipyle* (over 250 readable lines, and many additional scraps), *Antiope* (some 130 lines, most of which are readable), *Erechtheus* (about 80 readable lines to be added to two long book fragments from the orator Lycurgus and the anthologist Stobaeus), *Kretes* (about 60 lines), *Kresphontes* (50 lines, only half of which are complete), *Telephos* (about 40 full lines, plus scraps), *Melanippe Desmotis* (about 40 lines), *Archelaos* and *Phrixos A* (around 20 lines each). The more extensive fragments of lost plays are conveniently accessible in Diggle's *TGFS*, and in Collard, Cropp, and Lee (1995– ).[20]

## 2  THE PLAY: STRUCTURE, THEMES, AND PROBLEMS

Eur.'s play has been the object of intense scholarly study for over two centuries in all the languages in which classical scholarship is conducted, and even in English alone within the past few decades the bibliography is immense, and the pace of new contributions is accelerating. Similar ideas have been expressed many times over. The following discussion makes no claim to particular novelty, but attempts to deal with some major issues that are particularly germane at the beginning of the twenty-first century and to give some guidance to a selection of helpful bibliography. Many of the works referred to contain more exhaustive references to other contributions.[21]

---

another manuscript: we have portions of about 325 lines, with over 160 more or less complete. See Diggle's edition of *Phaethon*, 33–4.

[20] See also Jouan and Van Looy (1998) and (2000). For a full collection of fragments of Eur., we still await Vol. v of *TrGF* edited by R. Kannicht. In the meantime, the outdated collection to which reference is made is A. Nauck, *Tragicorum Graecorum Fragmenta* (2nd edn 1889, reprinted with Supplement by B. Snell, 1964).

[21] For recent lengthy bibliographies on *Medea*, see Van Looy's Teubner edition, xxix–lxiv; Clauss and Johnston (1997), McDermott (1989). Among the most influential and important English-language discussions of the interpretation of the play in recent decades are Burnett (1973), Easterling (1977), Knox (1977), Bongie (1977), Foley (1989) (revised in Foley (2001)), Boedeker (1991) and (1997), Rabinowitz (1993), Kovacs (1993), Burnett (1998).

## (a) Medea as revenge-plot

In terms of story-pattern, Eur.'s *Medea* may be analysed as a revenge-play.[22] In this variation of that common type, in place of the slaying of one antagonist by the other, the murder is transferred to the enemy's children[23] and his new kin, and a complete reversal of the antagonists' positions is accomplished. A revenge play commonly features such elements as grievance, overcoming of obstacles, deception, murder, and celebration of success, and these may easily be identified in Eur.'s play.

The grievance in *Medea* is Jason's abandonment of a marriage of several years' standing that has produced male offspring. In extant tragedy, the motif of the abandoned or wronged wife has its most famous parallel in Aeschylus' *Agamemnon* (458 BCE), although Agamemnon's sexual infidelity to Clytemnestra is only one aspect of a complex chain of causes culminating in his death at her hands.[24] Medea can usefully be read as a revision or extension of the model of Clytemnestra: both women are dominatingly persuasive and deceptive, both make use of the pretense of being a weak female, both use fabrics and woven material to entrap their victims, both can be identified with an Erinys, and Medea's scorning of military service as less fearful than childbirth challenges a motif of male superiority that Orestes and Athena used against Clytemnestra (248–51n.). The exact nature of Medea's grievance is the subject of dispute and ambiguity in the play, with the antagonists themselves and the observing characters (chorus, servants, Aegeus) offering shifting perspectives. Jason tends to reduce Medea's complaint to sexual jealousy, taking advan-

---

[22] See esp. Burnett (1973) and (1998); also Kerrigan (1996).

[23] Killing an enemy's children is a motif in many myths (notably, Atreus killing the children of Thyestes; in Eur. *Hec.*, Hecuba killing the children of Polymestor, and in *Her.* 970–1, 982–3, the mad Heracles threatening to kill the children of Eurystheus), and in a smaller subset the killer is also a parent of the victim (as in the story of Procne and Tereus).

[24] Sophocles' *Trachiniae* (which may possibly have been produced earlier than *Medea*: on the dating, see Easterling's comm., 19–23) also exploits this motif, but with the important qualification that the wife acts in ignorance of the harm she will cause and punishes herself with death upon realizing the truth.

tage of the Greek (male) stereotype of females' liability to sexual impulse, and thus he ignores the issues of status to which Medea herself often refers. On the one hand, Medea is a wife who has borne male children to Jason: by contemporary social norms and by the norms of 'heroic society' as depicted in the poetic tradition, she has fulfilled a vital familial role and is owed due consideration as a partner in the family. Medea's legitimate claim to such status is confirmed by the disapproval of Jason's remarriage expressed by the chorus and (significantly, because he is male and himself of high status) by Aegeus. On the other hand, Medea views herself as a heroic partner in Jason's adventures. She is not a normal citizen-woman, but a princess and a saviour, and she has formed her bond with Jason not as a subordinate in an exchange between her father and her husband, but as an equal (21–2n.). She and Jason exchanged the pledge of right hands and the oaths characteristic of *xenoi* of equal status, and again Aegeus serves importantly as an outsider who confirms Medea's status among the elite. Medea thus takes on the traits of the insulted chieftain. For her sense of outrage over the failure of her partner to abide by the heroic code of mutual exchange and loyal good will, she may be compared to the Achilles of the *Iliad* and the Ajax of Sophocles' eponymous play. Medea repeatedly refers to honour, dishonour, and the avoidance of being laughed at by her enemies (see section (*b*) below), and unlike Achilles, who for a time rejects the heroic code because he perceives it as flawed, Medea makes her tragic decisions because she gives precedence to her heroic status and to following the dictates of the heroic code of retaliation.

In order to get her revenge, Medea has many obstacles to overcome within the play, proceeding through more steps than is usual for extant Greek revenge-plays. These steps provide the structure of the plot in its linear aspect, although there are also parallel and symmetrical aspects that connect scenes through similarity and reversal (discussed below). Also remarkable in the structuring of this plot is the fact that so many separate decisions and intentions formed by Medea are brought successfully to fulfilment: this is unusual because for the actions attempted by the major characters in tragedy, the proportion of frustrated intentions and perverted outcomes is normally very high. The first obstacle Medea faces is her own distraction and despair, so vividly portrayed in the opening scenes. At the outset she seems not only totally isolated – a woman without a sponsor and a foreigner unwelcome back home and threatened by powerful enemies in the Greek world – but also inconsolable and self-destructive. Yet when she comes outdoors in the first episode, she has mastered herself and begins a series of persuasive and manipulative speeches. She solidifies the Corinthian women's sympathy and extracts their promise of silence in support of her hope to avenge her husband's insult. Creon's decision to exile Medea is the second obstacle, and structurally it is the precipitating plot-event that sets in motion this 'one day' of tragic action.[25] The audience has already learned of this decision through the conversation of the tutor and the nurse in the second scene of the prologue, but Medea herself is informed before their eyes, and in an immediate and supple reaction she uses supplication and gentle words to wrest from Creon the extra hours she needs to work toward her revenge. The third obstacle is her fear of being caught by her enemies, in the act of revenge or after the act, and subjected to their vengeance and mockery. This she overcomes in the Aegeus-scene, when she secures a place of refuge. The fourth obstacle, delivery of her poison, is surmounted in the fourth episode when she deceives Jason into taking the boys, with the poisoned gifts, to the princess. Medea's own divided feelings present another barrier to the completion of her scheme, and her temptation to save her sons is defeated in the famous monologue of the fifth episode. This internal obstacle is a brilliant deepening of the motif of hesitation that Aeschylus deployed in the confrontation of Orestes and Clytemnestra (*Choe.* 896–904), and this struggle with herself has had a long afterlife in Greek, Roman, and more modern literatures. Finally, the rapid arrival of Jason after the killing of the children lends urgency to the question of how Medea will actually escape from her house and make her way to Athens on her own, and the unexpected gift of her grandfather's winged chariot provides the solution.

The revenge, as often, depends on deception of the enemy, but there is considerable variation and complication in Eur.'s portrayal of Medea's deceptiveness. The most straightforward instance of de-

---

[25] On the tendency of Greek tragedy to present events in one day see Aristotle, *Poetics* 5 (1449b12–13).

ception in service of her stratagem is Medea's duping of Jason in the fourth episode. As in the plotting-scenes of Orestes-plays or the later so-called *mēchanēma*-tragedies (such as *IT* and *Helen*), Medea announces her scheme in advance to the chorus and audience and then carries it out. The audience is thus never in doubt about the insincerity (or hidden meaning) of Medea's words to Jason in this scene. The confrontation with Creon in the first episode reverses the sequence, for there the deception is unveiled after the fact: the chorus' anapaestic comment at 358–63 points to an unsuspecting reading of Medea's appeal, while Medea's following speech reveals its hostile intention. In the confrontation itself, Medea prepares for the wearing down of Creon's determination by minimizing her cleverness and diverting attention to the hostility of the clever person's social environment; she continues the process through a supplication that intensifies from a verbal to a physical form; and she finally attains her goal by conceding the main point and appealing to Creon as father of a child. This sequence makes possible a double-sided reception of Medea's words, both as the sincere expression of a wronged woman's reaction to new misfortune and as a carefully calculated manipulation.

The co-opting of the chorus of Corinthian women in the previous scene presents a similar potential for uncertainty and duality in the audience's reception of Medea. On the surface and on first hearing, Medea's speech may be accepted as an outpouring of genuine anxiety and resentment backed by acute social analysis and solidarity with ordinary women. A darker reading of the speech is invited by reflection and by retrojection of the audience's subsequent experience. Although it is possible to resist Medea's self-presentation at the very moment of her speaking (by noting, for instance, that Medea's marriage was not contracted in the same way as those of ordinary women, or that she has no 'anchorage' at home because she betrayed her father and murdered her brother), to do so is perhaps more characteristic of a reader than of a theatrical audience and in any case would require a rather narrow and uncooperative attitude of reception, unaffected by the emotional and thematic sequence of the prologue and parodos, with its emphasis on betrayal, injustice, and despair. It is rather the retrospective light of the following scenes that may make an audience feel that they too perhaps were duped by

Medea's initial appeal. The duping of the chorus is emblematic: they consent to keep silent so that Medea may punish Jason (but see 262n.), and in the first stasimon they look upon Medea's case as one that justifies an overthrow of authoritative misogynistic cultural discourse; but their promise slips into acquiescence in the extension of the revenge first to Creon and his daughter and then to the children.

A further variation on Medea's deceptive manipulation of friends occurs in the Aegeus-scene. The lyric on sincerity of friendship that precedes his entry turns out to have a double-edged reference, to Medea as well as Jason. Since the audience knows that Medea has suspended her plan while she awaits an idea about refuge from her enemies, it is able to formulate a split reading of the scene, appreciating both the surface level of Medea's persuasiveness for the unsuspecting Aegeus and the hidden agenda of her manipulation. The gap in understanding among the characters is reinforced by the juxtaposition of the naïve reaction of the chorus at Aegeus' departure with Medea's triumphant sense that her plan is now complete (759–63n.).

As revenger and victim, Medea and Jason naturally experience the major reversals in the play. The plot with double reversal (recovery of prosperity by the 'better' and fall from prosperity for the 'worse') is a traditional form well established in the *Odyssey* (cf. Arist. *Poetics* 13, 1453a30–3), but as often in tragedy the moral situation is much too complex for a comfortable ascription of 'good' to the triumphant party: violence directed to *philoi*, especially blood-relations, lends a charge of shock and revulsion even to a merited punishment. In this play, from Medea's physical neglect, emotional distraction, and isolation (heightened by her own withdrawal from contact with others: 27–9, 142–3, 187–9), she rises to complete triumph over her enemies and appears in the end physically raised above Jason, dispensing orders and predicting the future like the gods for whom the upper level and locomotion by the theatre-crane are normally reserved (1293–1419n.). From the 'blessedness' conventionally ascribed to newlyweds, from the wealth and power of the royal house, and from the expectation of a prosperous future with two sets of sons, Jason is cast down into total isolation and powerlessness, stripped of position, wife, and children, doomed (in mythical terms) to an empty future (as if prematurely aged and sterile). Jason's invocations of the gods, especially Zeus, in the final scene make him a mirror-image of the Medea of the opening of the play. The final confrontation also allows Medea to celebrate her revenge through direct taunting and rebuke of Jason, but as so often in the Greek literary tradition (where gloating over an enemy is not without risk), there are at least hints of the cost of the achievement to the successful revenger. Yet despite these pointers to Medea's grief for her children (1246–50, 1361–2, 1397), the predominant theatrical impression of the ending must be Medea's superiority and invulnerability, which are only with some effort to be moralized into a tragic loss of humanity.

In revenge-plays there are often additional details that emphasize reenactment, mirroring, and the similarity of opposites, or a special fittingness of the punishment to the offence. Eur. does much less than later authors to suggest reenactment of Medea's previous deeds in her present revenge: he does not dwell on the herb-gathering and magical processes at Colchis and Iolcus as precedents for her use of poison on the robe (indeed, he so downplays this element that he neglects to provide a mechanism for Medea to apply the poison: 789n.), nor does he evoke very strongly the analogy between killing Apsyrtus and killing her children (for he leaves unclear the details of the earlier killing, such as Apsyrtus' age). There is only the general analogy of multiple violations of ties of familial piety: Medea's against her father and brother, that of the daughters of Pelias against their father at her urging, the princess' against her father through her fatal grip instigated by Medea's poison, Medea's against her own sons, and (in the back of an informed audience's mind during the Aegeus-scene) Medea's future instigation of Aegeus against the un-recognized Theseus. In displaying the similarity of the opponents, the motifs of supplication, oath, and betrayal are prominent. Jason's supplication of Medea in Colchis (retroactively judged to be insin-cere) is echoed in Medea's deceptive use of supplication with Creon and Aegeus and in Jason's futile appeals to Medea at the end of the play (for more on supplication, see section (d) below). Jason's viola-tion of his oaths is direct and severe and the inferred cause of the cooperation of the gods in Medea's plan and escape, but Medea herself makes an underhanded use of an oath in the Aegeus-scene.

Jason's remarriage is described as a betrayal, but the term is also applied more than once to Medea's treatment of her father and fatherland (17n.).

Furthermore, when Medea espouses 'masculine' values (honour, courage, doing harm to enemies), she is assimilating herself to the heroic mould that Jason is supposed to personify. If Jason is open to condemnation as a *kakos* for his treatment of his family (a lack of proper behaviour toward *philoi*),[26] Medea ends up no better than he, for, as with Achilles in the *Iliad* or Ajax in Sophocles' play, her resentment sets in turmoil her whole system of friend-enemy relationships. Killing her children is the most extreme case of harming one's *philoi*. Medea's similarity to Jason also involves their shared intellectual qualities. Among the cluster of intellectual words such as σοφός, σοφία, βουλεύω, βούλευμα, τεχνάομαι, μηχανή, μηχανάομαι,[27] the 'contriving' terms are used of and by Medea, whose very name implies cunning intelligence (402n.). But 'cleverness' and 'planning' apply to both. In the *agōn*-scene Jason in fact suggests a competition, which he assumes he wins in terms of wisdom/cleverness and planning well, as he boasts of the calculations by which he determined to take a new wife to benefit his future prospects and those of his children. Medea, however, outdoes him in every way, until her *bouleumata* and contriving entrap their author herself. When in his concluding generalization the messenger criticizes 'those of mortals who seem wise and those who are practitioners of speeches/reasonings' (1225–7), the comment applies equally to Medea and Jason.

Medea's murder of the princess also demonstrates the symmetry or aptness typical of a revenge-story. The princess is in some ways a version of Medea's younger self, infatuated with Jason and ready to cooperate in his goals. Medea's gift of robe and crown marks the girl as a quintessential bride, since brides are specially dressed and crowned for their wedding. Moreover, the girl's use of a mirror associates her with the sexual allure of the bride and wife and with the concern for attractive appearance expected of a maiden on the threshold of maturity and betrothal (1161n.). Given the echoes of

[26] Schein (1990), McClure (1999b), Mueller (2001).
[27] The σοφ- root occurs 23 times in the play, βουλευ- 15 times, μηχαν- 5 times, τεχν- 4 times.

Hesiodic tradition in the first stasimon, it is also possible to think of the princess as a new Pandora, elaborately adorned with a deceptive surface beauty but in fact destructive.[28] In sending the gifts, Medea is virtually taking control of Jason's new wedding, and in killing the bride she symbolically kills her gullible former self and undoes, now on her own terms instead of on his, her marriage with Jason. The destruction of the children is likewise apt revenge, in two ways. Many conditional self-curses applied in oaths include destruction of off-spring as part of the punishment of the perjuror ('if I fail to keep this oath, may I be destroyed and my family with me'),[29] and since the production of children is the purpose of marriage, Jason's violation of that institution implies that he has no right to the benefits that arise from it.

### (b) Medea's motivations and decisions

Because of the success of Eur.'s play, the figure of Medea came to be identified most of all with the act of infanticide: the high point in the play, when she resists her maternal feelings and insists on the violent act, became crystallized in the popular mind as the essence of Medea's life and character. Concentration on this deed entailed ever increasing emphasis (in artistic depictions, in literary works, and in use of Medea as an example by Hellenistic and Roman philosophers: see section 6 below) on Medea's passionate emotions and violence. Furthermore, cultural assumptions about 'Greekness' and civilization in the centuries after Eur. encouraged the ascription of her extreme behaviour to her 'otherness' as Colchian and sorceress. Eur.'s own portrayal of Medea is complex and finely nuanced,[30] and it is important not to import into a reading of Euripides the assumptions derived from the later reception of the figure of Medea based on one part of this play.[31]

---

[28] McClure (1999a) 62–4, Mueller (2001).

[29] Watson (1991) 33–5.

[30] See esp. Gibert (1995) 66–84; Foley (1989). Additional bibliography is referred to in the Appendix.

[31] See Hall, Macintosh, and Taplin (2000), and in particular Hall (2000) and Macintosh (2000).

It is typical of the polyphony of dramatic voices in a Greek trag-edy, and also of Eur.'s conception of human action, that the play offers several perspectives on Medea's motivation. The divergent views are not to be judged as completely right or completely wrong or as mutually exclusive, but as elements to be weighed and eval-uated by the audience with due attention to speaker, context, and rhetorical purpose. The motif of sexual jealousy is given depth by allusions to the determining force of *eros* in Medea's initial contact with Jason and in her assistance in his quest: 8 (nurse), 433 (chorus), 526–31 (Jason). The chorus of Corinthian women cite the betrayal of the marriage-bed several times (155–9, 206, 436–8, 443–5), and in urging or praying for moderation they interpret Medea's strong emo-tion as a consequence of compulsive, excessive love (155–9, 627–44). Ultimately, they also connect the murder of the children to the be-trayed bed: 998–1001, 1290–2 (their last lyric statement in the play).[32] But in the chorus' perception, issues of status and justice are often as much involved with the marriage-bed as the question of sexual loyalty: 157 συνδικήσει, 208–9, 659–62, 1000 ἀνόμως. Jason, on the other hand, speaks more narrowly of the marriage-bed as the source of a woman's physical satisfaction and makes the loss of this the cause of hostility and violence (555–7, 568–73, 1338, 1367; there is a significant repetition of forms of κνίζω in 555 and 568). Finally, Me-dea herself echoes this language of the bed. In 1368 her reply 'do you think this is a small pain to woman?' accepts the premise of Jason's charge in 1367 λέχους ... οὕνεκα, 'for the sake of ⟨the pleasure of⟩ the bed'. Even earlier, in the finale of her speech to the women of the chorus, she generalizes 'when a woman has in fact been wronged with respect to her bed, no other heart is more murderous'. As is clear from the foil for this declaration ('in other respects a woman is full of fear and cowardly in the face of battle and unable to look upon weaponry'), Medea is here rhetorically tailoring her maxim to the ordinary women of the chorus (and to conventional Greek wis-dom), so that she portrays herself as like other women and implies that she too participates in the subordinate status posited by societal

---

[32] Gentili (1972). Note the witnessing presence of Aphrodite and Eros on the Policoro hydria (described in section 6 below), which shows the painter's interpretation of the violence as derived from scorned love.

norms. The maxim may also serve on another level to misdirect the audience somewhat, highlighting the motif of the angry spurned woman before Medea shows other aspects of her character and motivation in subsequent scenes.

The question of the importance, or primacy, of the sexual motive is complicated further by the parallel charge made by Medea against Jason – that he desires the princess as a younger woman. Does this point to a mixture of motivations in Jason, or should this charge be taken as a sign that Medea gives precedence to sexual motivation? In 491 τοῦδ' ἐρασθῆναι λέχους may be simply 'long for this new marriage', but the verb is probably chosen for its suggestion of real erotic desire. Later in the scene, Medea taunts Jason with 'longing for his new bride' (623), and Aegeus tellingly regards 'falling in love' with another woman as a possible cause of Jason's betrayal (697; so earlier the tutor at 88 εὐνῆς οὕνεκα). But although Medea seems at first to assent to this diagnosis (698 μέγαν γ' ἔρωτα), she soon defines the desire in terms that point to social climbing rather than sexual lust (700), thus echoing her earlier accusation of Jason's concern for public opinion (591–2). Jason himself vehemently denies desire for his new bride (555–7): his *agōn*-speech is aimed at showing the calculations of family wealth and status that motivated his new marriage, and he reasserts this in 593–7 (esp. 593 μὴ γυναικὸς οὕνεκα). Although there are hints that Jason may enjoy the compliance and adulation of the girl (945, 1146), nothing else in the play suggests that he regards his bride as any more than a means to the future he wants for himself, and Medea seems at times to be aware of this.

Another aspect of Medea's motivation is presented by reference to her strong will, unchecked emotion, and anger. The nurse begins this theme: 44 δεινή, 91–4 δυσθυμουμένηι ... ταυρουμένην ... χόλου, 99 κινεῖ κραδίαν, κινεῖ δὲ χόλον, 103–4 ἄγριον ἦθος στυγερὰν τε φύσιν φρενὸς αὐθάδους, 108 μείζονι θυμῶι, 109 μεγαλόσπλαγχνος δυσκατάπαυστος, 119 δεινὰ ... λήματα, 121 ὀργάς, 172 χόλον. The chorus exploits it early (133–4, 152, 156, 159, 176–7), remarks the vehemence of Medea's *agōn*-speech (520), rejects excess and strife in love and marriage in the second stasimon, and returns to such language at the idea of violence against the children (856–60 θράσος and δεινὰν ... τόλμαν in a corrupt passage, 865 τλάμονι θυμῶι). At the moment of the killing, in a strategy reflecting common Greek notions of the

mechanism of extreme violence, the chorus emphasizes mental aber-
ration, identifying Medea with an Erinys (1260) and comparing her to
'Ino rendered insane by the gods' (1284), and referring again to wrath
(1265–6 φρενοβαρὴς χόλος).[33] Jason is of course the character most
convinced that Medea acts without thought or control, but purely
from emotion: 446–7, 450, 457, 525, 590, 614, 621, 909, 1326, 1328,
1342–3, 1407. And Medea plays up to that belief when she adopts the
pose of the subservient female who has come to her senses (866–
975n.).

The explicit planning and deliberation (the display of *dianoia* in
the terms of Aristotle's *Poetics*) seen in Medea show her personality
and behaviour from a different angle. Only Creon, temporarily,
evinces awareness and fear of Medea's mental capacities. Jason is too
caught up in the competition of the *agōn* and in complacency with his
own plans to take Medea seriously as a plotting opponent, and the
guileless Aegeus has no idea in what circumstances Medea intends to
arrive as his guest. The chorus, too, finds it more comforting to fall
back on conventional beliefs and ascribe Medea's violence to divine
possession and madness rather than contemplate too closely the in-
tentionality of her acts. Even Medea herself draws back from full
commitment to the voluntariness of her acts: at 1013–14 she introduces the co-responsibility of the gods, and thereafter she manipulates her own image of the situation to emphasize the compulsion
exercised by an outside threat to her children (1059–61, 1238–41). It
is the ultimate irony of the play that her own skilful planning finally
entraps Medea herself, while her own manipulative rhetoric in the
end is applied to convincing herself that there is no way out for the
children.

Finally, there are the issues of status, reputation, and fame that
separate Medea from ordinary women (both the represented ordinary women of the chorus and the women living in the society of
Eur. and his audience) and assimilate her to Achilles, Ajax, and Jason
himself. Tragedy in general invites a fruitful confrontation between

---

[33] Such an interpretation of Medea's action is also conveyed in those vase-
paintings that show a demon (probably an Erinys) or Oistros (Frenzy) attending the scene of infanticide: see section 6 on vases (2), (3), and (5).

systems of value, especially between the heroic/aristocratic values transmitted in the authoritative epics of Homer and other mythological narratives carried in many forms of archaic poetry and the more polis-centred and more egalitarian values of contemporary society, which partly adapted and extended heroic values to a new context and partly defined its values against the inherited ones.[34] In *Medea* Eur. effects a very stark contrast between Medea's understanding of her mutual past with Jason and the assumptions made by Jason and Creon in the present moment. Binding herself to Jason through an exchange of oaths and the pledging of right hands, Medea acted as an equal partner in the heroic enterprise. Aegeus greets her as a friend, and she has somehow met the approval of the citizens of Corinth (11–12), not just the women. Her remarks on the behaviour of a stranger in a city (214–24) and the jealousy affecting the clever (292–305) present her as a public figure, a status open to a mythological figure but not to a contemporary Athenian woman. It is as though Medea is living in the world of Pindar's *Pythian* 4, where she is an authoritative and respected speaker, or *Olympian* 13, where she is worthy of mention as a famed figure casting glorious light on Corinth. Jason seems to live in a different world, more like contemporary Athens. He makes a unilateral decision about his future life and his children; he contracts his new marriage as an alliance between males, under the normal rules of betrothal (the father gives and the groom receives, while the bride has no say); and he clearly believes in the stereotypes that Medea exploits when she poses as the weak woman who has come to her senses and will now at last be σώφρων. Creon is clearly more alert to the dangers of Medea's power, yet in contracting the marriage before the start of the play he has treated Medea as a disposable foreign woman with no rights, not as the heroic partner and agent she has shown herself to be in the past.

Although Medea appeals to the opposition and competition between male and female, particularly in her first speech to the chorus of women (248–51, 263–6, 407–9), she arrogates to herself, and others

---

[34] Vernant (1981), Goldhill (1986), Griffith (1995).

occasionally use of her, terms from masculine spheres of action and modes of behaviour.[35] The honour-root, *tim-*, especially in its negated form in ἀτιμάζω and ἄτιμος, recurs at key points: 20n., 33, 438, 660, 696, 1354. 'Harming enemies' is conventionally paired with 'helping friends' as the action of a (male) person of significance, but the accent in this tragedy is particularly on harming enemies in return for ill treatment: 44–5, 93–5, 163–5, 398–400, 807–10, 1354–7. The other side of the coin of taking revenge is avoiding the gloating or mockery of the triumphant opponent, or not allowing the opponent to feel satisfaction with the results of an unrequited mistreatment: γέλως and γελᾶσθαι/ἐγγελᾶν recur in 383, 404, 797, 1049–50, 1355, 1362, and insistence on requital recurs in 44 οὔτοι ῥαιδίως, 398 (οὐ) χαίρων, 1050 ἀζημίους, and 1354–7 οὐκ ἔμελλες … τερπνὸν διάξειν βίοτον … οὐδ᾽ … ἀνατεί. Medea's references to ὕβρις also indicate her quasi-masculine concern for her status (255n.). Language drawn from the male provinces of athletic competition and warfare is also abundant in Medea's speeches or in reference to her (see section (*f*) below). Finally, despite her criticism of Jason's concern about his repute (591–2 οὐκ εὔδοξον; cf. 542–4) and her complaint about the cost of her own fame (292–305; cf. 539–41), glorious reputation (κλέος) turns out to be just as important to Medea, and even the chorus follows her lead in applying the concept to women: 218 δύσκλειαν (to be avoided), 236 οὐ … εὐκλεεῖς διαλλαγαί (to be avoided), 415 εὔκλειαν (now to be won by the female sex), 810 τῶν γὰρ τοιούτων [sc. avengers of their enemies] εὐκλεέστατος βίος.

There are thus many factors involved in Medea's motivations, and no simple interpretation of her behaviour or character is to be privileged. The indeterminacy extends to the formation of her central decision, her use of the death of the children to punish Jason. The idea develops naturally, in one sense, from the sequence of references to the importance of children, first for Creon (283, 327, 329, 344–5), then for Jason (562–7), and finally for Aegeus (669–71, 714–15, 721–2). It is open to a spectator to read Medea's plan, announced just after Aegeus' departure, as inspired by Medea's observation of Aegeus' eagerness to escape the misfortune of his childlessness. But

---

[35] See Bongie (1977), Knox (1977), Rehm (1989) and (1994).

the spectators have also heard and observed enough of Medea's ability to conceal her true purposes that they may be unsure whether the idea had not already formed itself before Aegeus' arrival.[36]

The intertwining of psychological motives is paralleled by an intertwining of mythological alternatives, and this mixture of elements accounts for the illogicality that critics have seen in Medea's great monologue. It is probable that versions in which the children of Medea were killed by the relatives of Creon or by the Corinthians in general were current before Euripides (see section 4 below). Although Medea worries in the first episode that she herself may be captured by her enemies in her attempt at revenge or after the act, she does not mention danger to the children until the monologue,[37] and the same concern later motivates Jason at 1301–5. The opening scene of the play introduces a different possible scenario, the murder of the children by a despairing and suicidal mother.[38] The third scenario – killing the children to hurt Jason – is revealed after Aegeus' departure, as just discussed, and may or may not be an innovation (see sections 4 and 5). Medea's monologue somewhat uncomfortably combines the first and third motifs, and the conflation has led many critics to postulate a textual confusion created by non-Euripidean revision of the scene (see Appendix). The view adopted here, however, is that Medea is not represented as being clear-headed and single-minded, but rather as combining forthright self-analysis with self-deception. The notion that she must protect her

---

[36] On this indeterminacy see Easterling (1977) 185–6. Manuwald (1983) argues that Medea has made her decision by 604 and that her claim to be a curse upon Jason's house (608) reveals that she has in mind to kill the children; but this puts far too much weight on the singular subject in 604 (as if ἐγὼ δ᾽ entailed exclusion of the children, when it is simply in rhetorical contrast to σοὶ μέν).

[37] Line 782, in which mention is earlier made of enemies treating her children with outrage, is best regarded as an interpolation.

[38] It would be fascinating to know whether such behaviour was well known in ancient Greek society, but this is not the sort of reality that is likely to leave a trace in our sources. Familial murder-suicide is known in modern Western culture, especially in the United States with the widespread availability of guns, although the majority of cases involve murderous husband-fathers rather than wife-mothers. See also Easterling (1977) 186.

children from the threat of mistreatment by her enemies by killing them first herself enters the equation suddenly and decisively at 1060–1 and recurs crucially at 1238–41. This motif is to be viewed in part as a device of the poet: he alludes to and partially appropriates a competing version of the story of the death of the children and manipulates the audience into regarding the infanticide as nearly inevitable. But a characterological explanation is also possible: in the service of her passion for revenge and her need to have the better of her enemies, Medea is redescribing her own situation in a forced manner, manipulating herself into completing her objective.

Medea's internal struggle is much more than a straightforward contest of reason and passion, as a common reading of the final lines of her great monologue has tended to make it (for fuller discussion see Appendix). If we import anachronistically the Platonic division of the soul, we may say that the emotional and spirited part of her soul is engaged on both sides of the struggle: on the one side, her maternal love, pity; on the other, her sense of heroic self and 'face', her wounded pride at sexual rejection, her anger at injustice and betrayal of oaths, her desire to make her enemies suffer as much as or more than she has or will. Medea uses her reasoning ability to weigh alternatives, develop plans, adjust her rhetoric to each situation, and perform a calculus of gains and losses, pleasures and pains. In the end, it is not a simple defeat of reason by emotion, but a display of the insufficiency of intellectual qualities to ensure a good outcome in the complex moral crises of human life.

### (c) Medea: barbarian, witch, woman

For several decades, one of the most frequently quoted and debated assessments of Eur.'s Medea and the Athenian audience's reception of her has been that of D. L. Page recorded in his introduction to his 1938 commentary (pp. xviii and xxi):

> She is a woman scorned, depicted at that stage of emotion in which her first torment of misery has passed into vindictive hatred. And here it is important to understand that the poet has described not a Greek woman but a barbarian. Though her emotions are natural to all women at all times in her posi-

tion, their expression and the dreadful end to which they lead are everywhere affected by her foreign origin.... Because she was a foreigner she could kill her children; because she was a witch she could escape in a magic chariot. She embodies the qualities which the fifth-century Athenian believed to be characteristic of Orientals.

This judgment crystallizes some essential problems: to what extent did Eur. want and expect his audience to understand and sympathize with Medea, despite her otherness, and to what extent did his portrayal (regardless of his intentions) reflect and reinforce his audience's ideological assumptions about Greekness and maleness?[39]

The first point to make is that Attic tragedy deliberately chooses to portray persons and events at a distinct remove from contemporary reality. The mythic past is, in some sense, a foreign country, to which contemporary categories are applicable only through a filter of difference. Kings and princely heroes like Jason and Creon represent to the audience 'the other' almost as much as Medea does. Moreover, the mythic past, as established by Homeric and Hesiodic poetry, is a world of permeable boundaries. The Greek gods beget children in other lands as well as in Greece, and heroic founders migrate from place to place. Cadmus and Pelops, for instance, come from the east, but their descendants are regarded as Greek. Homer's Trojans are credited with many of the same values, customs, and behaviours as his Greeks. Although it is clear that the Greeks' (and the Athenians') sense of distinction from, and even superiority to, other peoples became much more pronounced after the Persian Wars,[40] tragedy could look both ways, toward the epic model and toward contemporary assumptions, and this ambivalence is one source of tension in Eur.'s play.

Medea's foreignness certainly is made thematic in the play. At key points, allusions are made to the crossing of the boundary (Clashing Rocks or Bosporus) that divides the world of Medea from Greece (2, 210–12, 431–5, 1262–4). Upon entry, the chorus' first mention of

---

[39] On the audience's unreflective sociological assumptions and prejudices, see Hall (1997).

[40] Hall (1989).

Medea uses the periphrasis 'the unhappy Colchian woman' (133), and they refer repeatedly to her separation from her homeland (432, 442; cf. 645–53), as do Medea herself (253–5, 328, 502–3, 800–1), the nurse (35), and Jason (1332). The word βάρβαρος itself appears only four times in the play, uttered only by Medea (256, 591) or Jason (536, 1330), never by the chorus or other characters. Ethnic difference is cited especially in angry argument, by Medea in 509, 591, 801–2, and by Jason in 536–41, 1330–1, 1339–41: it is important to note that Jason's claims of Greek superiority in the *agōn* have been undercut by his own action (536–8n.), while his insistence in the finale that no Greek woman would have behaved as Medea did is a charge that would not stand up to reflection (Procne, Althaea, and the Lemnian women are all Greek women who killed their children). On the whole, then, Eur. has been rather restrained, and also partly ironic, in exploitation of the Greek–foreign contrast. This conclusion is borne out by two further points. First, within the play Medea is portrayed as worshipping and invoking the same gods as the Greek characters, and these gods second her plan. Although her progenitor Helios had no cult in classical Greece except in Rhodes, and although Aristophanes could cite sacrifice to Helios as distinguishing Persians from Greeks (Olson on Ar. *Peace* 406, 409–13), there is nothing exotic or unGreek in Medea's invocations of Helios in this play, nor any reason to regard his help with her escape as inconsistent with the will of Zeus. The only exotic religious feature is Medea's association of Hecate with the inmost centre of her house (397n.). Second, if Eur.'s treatment is compared to subsequent versions of the same story, one can see clearly how the motif of foreignness is intensified or exaggerated by later authors.[41] While it is likely enough that some segment of the original audience reacted as Page suggested, with smug confidence in the essential difference of Greeks and foreigners, the details and texture of Eur.'s text imply an audience, or audience segment, open to a different view.

Medea's skill in magic is a major aspect of her mythological personality, both before and after Eur., but again the restraint of Eur. in deploying this motif is noteworthy. In opposition to Page's sugges-

---

[41] See Dihle (1976) and (1977); Hall (2000); Macintosh (2000). See section 6 below.

tion that Medea's magical powers would be a defining trait that allowed the Greek audience to distance itself from her behaviour, and condemn it more strongly, Knox argued against applying the concept 'witch' to Medea and in favour of recognizing the ordinary humanity of her essential actions. Whatever the propriety of the term 'witch', it is implausible to minimize her magical powers to the degree that Knox attempted to do. The term φάρμακα appears six times in the play. Creon fears Medea because she is 'clever ... and knowledgeable in many means of harm' (285). Medea herself declares in a crucial decision that 'It is best to proceed on the direct path and, using the means in which I am most skilled, destroy them with poison drugs' (384–5n.), and she prays to Hecate as her special ally (395–7). On the other hand, Knox's critical instinct is essentially sound. Eur. passes up some opportunities of explicitly mentioning magic: for example, perhaps in Medea's winning the favour of the Corinthians (11n.), and in allusions to the protection of Jason from the fiery bulls, to the conquest of the guardian serpent, and to the death of Pelias (476–87). The act of applying poisons to the gifts, announced with the future χρίσω in 789, is not subsequently shown or narrated (more than that, it is neglected in the dramatic economy of the scenes), and Medea makes her plans with no expectation or hint that she will in the end have access to a winged chariot. The supernatural elements are thus downplayed, both in matters 'outside the drama' and those within the play, until the finale, apparently already a conventional locus for more open intervention of the divine or supernatural. The contrast with the presentation of Medea's magical powers in later versions of this plot is again striking. The motifs of herb-gathering and black-magic sacrifice and concoction are present in classical plays about other parts of Medea's history, in her instructions to Jason in Apollonius, *Argonautica* Book 3, and in Ovid's treatment of the rejuvenation of Aeson in *Metamorphoses* 7.159–293. Seneca incorporates these motifs into his *Medea*, where they are made typically prominent, and his portrayal had lasting influence from the Renaissance onward. Grillparzer, for instance, presents Medea's life in his *Medea* and in the preceding play of the trilogy as an ultimately futile struggle to put sorcery behind her and adopt the civilized life of an ordinary woman. And in this respect Robinson Jeffers' adaptation of Eur.'s play owes more to Seneca than to Eur., for sorcery and Colchian origin are emphasized in tandem as tokens of Medea's otherness and wildness.

Although the representation of women in Attic drama is too large and controversial a topic to be covered in much detail here, brief consideration must be given to Medea's status as female in regard to audience reception.[42] The dominant ideology of classical Athens was strongly exclusionary of women and distrustful of women's potentials and behaviours, and the legal status of women entailed many disadvantages. Respectable women of citizen families were ideally imagined as confined indoors, silent, and subservient. How far this ideal was actually lived out in the daily lives of women in Athens is a separate question, to answer which our evidence is largely deficient. It seems clear, however, that social and economic status, location of residence (city or village or isolated farmstead), political status (women of Athenian vs metic or foreign background), and age (premenopausal vs post-menopausal) played a significant role in determining the extent and kind of a female's freedom to appear outside the house, and that at least in some families women exerted informal influence in economic and familial matters through their relationships with husbands, sons, and brothers.[43] The conventions of tragic performance require the speaking female characters to appear outside the doors of their house, and some of the female choruses (as in *Medea*, *Hippolytus*, *Andromache*, and other plays, including Sophocles' *Trachiniae* and *Electra*) are women lingering in a public space *en masse* (without ritual or festival justification). The transgressiveness of this situation is thus partly softened by its theatrical conventionality, but the playwrights also deliberately point to the transgression when they wish to make some point. Euripides in particular is fond of noting the discontinuity between the impulse to conventional 'decency' and the desperate situations in which tragic women are enmeshed.

One mode of reception of Medea for a typical male member of the fifth-century audience would be to view Medea in the light of traditional assumptions and stereotypes inherited from the poetic

---

[42] See esp. Foley (2001), Rabinowitz (1993), Zeitlin (1996), Wohl (1998), McClure (1999a), Hall (1997), Griffith (2001), Mueller (2001); also Gould (1980), Foley (1981), Easterling (1987).

[43] See e.g. Just (1989), Cohen (1989), Fantham et al. (1994).

tradition, to regard her with fear and disapproval and interpret her actions as a confirmation of the need to distrust and tightly control all women in real life. Her marriage to Jason is abnormal, because formed without her father's consent, indeed against her father's interests. She is swayed (at certain points in the play, at least) more by emotion than reason, and her emotion is unrestrained and linked in particular to sexual satisfaction. She conceals her true intentions in many of her conversations and she uses the underhand method of poison drugs against her enemies, thus embodying the essential interiority and concealment that belongs to woman physically and mentally.[44] She manipulates unwary men to do her will through insistent and glib speech. On the other hand, Medea presents to such an interpreter (whom we might term the unreflective male chauvinist) the alarming image of a woman who engages in male activities, like Clytemnestra in Aeschylus' *Agamemnon*. She has exchanged oaths as an equal with Jason, she has a *xenia*-like relationship with Aegeus, she competes for honour, reputation, and revenge, and she lays claim to language and imagery from typically male spheres (military, athletic, political).

Why is such a mode of reception inadequate, even as a reconstruction of a fifth-century Greek's probable response? As has been mentioned before, the heroic world of tragedy is not a direct reflection of contemporary culture, and so the unusual actions or status of a female character may receive some degree of licence within the imagined different world. Medea's self-made marriage is more than a simple violation of norms, because it is also conditioned by a typical story-pattern of heroic quests (young hero succeeds in ordeal posed by older opponent with the help of opponent's daughter and with his success takes the daughter from her father). The very act of effective dramatic representation affords to almost all characters the possibility of persuading, seducing, or winning the sympathy of the audience: the captivation of the chorus of Aeschylus' *Agamemnon* when Clytemnestra makes such a vivid presentation of the journey of the fire-signal and of the capture of Troy and the sympathy and acquiescence of the chorus of *Medea* early in this play may be taken as internal indications of one aspect of audience response to these strong

---

[44] Zeitlin (1996) 55–86; Padel (1992).

female characters. In the evolving continuum of response that drama requires, an ideal audience-member will entertain a multiplicity of perspectives over time and even a split perspective at some individual moments.[45] Part of this process involves entering into the position and perspective even of a Clytemnestra or Medea, recognizing the analogies between their experiences of mistreatment and inequality and those in the audience-member's own life.

Medea's status as woman, therefore, should not have been a universal or insuperable obstacle to some degree of sympathetic engagement with her position. As often seems to be the case in Euripidean plays, the performance appears to be designed to evoke shifting and mixed reactions to the major figures and to leave little room for either moral certainty or moral smugness by the end of the play.

### (d) Medea *and Greek institutions*

In addition to the filtered scrutiny of the institution of marriage and of the culture's normative view of the place and potentialities of women, *Medea* also subjects other important Greek cultural practices to examination, revealing (as is typical of tragedy and other serious 'literature') their paradoxes and deficiencies. Of most significance in this play are oaths, supplication, and reciprocity, both beneficial and hostile, between elite peers.

Jason once pledged himself to Medea through an oath witnessed by gods and sealed with the pledge of the clasping of right hands. The ruin that overtakes him and deprives him of offspring is a typical recompense for his perjury. The nurse introduces this complex of ideas in 21–2: 'Medea ... shouts in protest about the oaths, and she summons back to memory the mighty pledge of the right hand, and she calls the gods to witness ...' The friendly clasping of hands is re-enacted on stage when the boys are told at 899 to take their father's right hand (on Medea's emotional reaction to this see 899n.). Later, Medea herself kisses and holds her children's hands in her ambiguous farewell (1069–73). Oaths and their patron gods (Themis and Zeus) are a repeated topic of Medea's distraught cries from indoors and the responses of nurse and chorus to them: 160–3, 169–70, 209.

---

[45] Griffith (1995); Griffith, comm. on Soph. *Ant.*, pp. 58–66.

The chorus' claim of reversal in the first stasimon stems from the failure of Jason's pledge in the name of the gods (412–13 θεῶν πίστις, cf. 422 ἀπιστοσύναν) and from the disappearance of 'the enchanting beauty/reciprocity of oaths' (439 ὅρκων χάρις), and the chorus also has Jason in mind when they reject the ungrateful man as friend (659–62; 659n. on ἀχάριστος). Medea repeats her charge in the *agōn* (492 ὅρκων δὲ φρούδη πίστις, 493 θεούς, 495 οὐκ εὔορκος), and in his reply Jason makes no defence on this point (since his position is indefensible). Medea cites Jason's faithlessness again before Aegeus (698 πιστὸς οὐκ ἔφυ φίλοις), and then insists on a pledge and oath from him (731 πίστις, 735 ὁρκίοισι ... ζυγείς, 737 θεῶν ἀνώμοτος), prompting a performance of oath-taking before the audience (745–55) – an oath that the audience understands Aegeus will keep faithfully. In the final confrontation, Medea alludes to the oath-breaking in 1352 (εἰ μὴ Ζεὺς πατὴρ ἠπίστατο) and 1364 (πατρώιαι νόσωι) and finally makes the devastating riposte 'What god or spirit gives ear to you, the oathbreaker and deceiver of a solemn friend (*xenos*)?'

The right hands of Medea and Jason are intrinsically connected to the institution of the oath in the play, but hands are also integral to the act of supplication.[46] In the past Jason clasped Medea's hands and knees (496–8 φεῦ δεξιὰ χείρ κτλ.), supplicating for her aid and laying himself under a lasting obligation to his protector – another duty that Jason is betraying.[47] Within the play,[48] we see Medea supplicating Creon, first simply through words and then with physical contact (324–51n.). This supplication is ultimately successful, after Medea reduces her request from remission of exile to a day's delay,

[46] Flory (1978); Szlezák (1990); Burnett (1998). My discussion of supplication is also indebted to conversation with and an unpublished paper of Frank Cope, esp. in regard to the double meaning of *Medea* 659–62.

[47] Compare the extra sting for both Adrestus and Croesus of the suppliant's responsibility for the death of his purifier's son, Hdt. 1.44–5.

[48] In all the references to marriage within the play, there is no hint of the idea of the bride as suppliant: Iamblichus *VP* 9.48 (cf. 18.84) reports as an element of Pythagorean teaching the notion that the bride is as if raised from a sacred hearth by the husband, but it is unclear how widely known this notion was. Eur. makes no allusion, moreover, to any supplication by Jason and Medea on their arrival in Corinth, although this is an element of the story in Seneca and others, as part of the effort to explain and justify Jason's betrayal by making clear his dependency on Creon's favour.

but Medea will use the favour against her 'benefactor', thus matching Jason's betrayal. Medea's next supplication is of Aegeus (709–13):
it too is successful and also involves some corruption of the institution, since she both conceals from Aegeus the planned circumstances
of her departure from Corinth and will in the distant future (as the
Athenian audience knows) threaten the life of her benefactor's son.
Medea also incorporates supplication into her plot against the princess and king, since the boys are to supplicate the girl and she is to
supplicate her father (971, 942–3). In the second half of the play,
Medea herself becomes the object of supplication and is relentless
in refusing appeals made to her. The chorus uses the language of
supplication in 853–5 to ask her not to kill her children, and they
imagine the children falling at Medea's knees as suppliants and successfully averting the murder (862–5): one may speculate that the
choreography at these corresponding passages of strophe and antistrophe perhaps reflected the theme through kneeling or outstretched
arms or both.[49] In the final tableau, Jason is virtually in the position
of a suppliant, below Medea's level, probably reaching up toward
her in his longing to touch his dead sons, as he makes his requests
(1377 πάρες, 1402 δός μοι πρὸς θεῶν – the phrase πρὸς θεῶν is a fos-
silized remnant of supplication) and is 'driven away' (1405 ἀπελαυνόμεθ') like a rebuffed suppliant. The reversal, and the undoing of
their previous relationship, are complete in this final refusal.

    While the peaceful, institutional uses of the right hand are per-
verted in the motifs of pledge and supplication, significant repetition
marks the hand also as the agent of violence, especially Medea's
hand, but occasionally that of her enemies: 857, 864, 1055, 1239, 1244,
1254, 1279, 1283, 1309, 1322, 1365. This violence overshadows the
fewer allusions to the affectionate use of touch, in embrace of the living or tender handling of the dead (939, 1034, 1070, 1141, 1378, 1412).

---

[49] Szlezák (1990), Wiles (1997) 125, and independently suggested to me by
Frank Cope. One may note as well 901–2 'children, will you, even living a
long time, thus stretch out your dear arm?', a gesture which makes visible,
though with the wrong object, the gesture imagined a few moments before by
the chorus in 863; and the use of προσπίτνει in 1205 and ἐξαναστῆσαι in 1212
and 1215, both words suitable to the ceremony of supplication, here used of
Creon's embrace of his daughter and inability to disengage from her grasp.

Hands are also evoked in allusions to gift-giving, ominously in the transfer of the gifts from Medea to the boys to the princess (784, 956, 973, 982, 1003), more innocently in Jason's offer of aid to his exiled family (612).

When Medea calls Jason 'deceiver of a solemn friend (*xenos*)', she points to Jason's failure to live up to the code of reciprocity that befits a Greek of elite status. A true relationship of *charis* between guest-friends has no temporal limit and does not admit of precise calculations of the balance of benefits.[50] Jason's abandonment of Medea is, from his own point of view, a denial of her status as an equal participant in an exchange-relationship. From the perspective of Medea (and Aegeus), however, his actions show that he is himself not an *agathos*, as his birth and adventures suggest, but a *kakos* (especially 465 παγκάκιστε, 488 κάκιστ' ἀνδρῶν, 498 κακοῦ πρὸς ἀνδρός, 518 τὸν κακόν, 618 κακοῦ … ἀνδρός, 690 κάκιστος, 699 κακός).[51] Jason frequently employs commercial and financial terms and metaphors (see (*f*) below), and he violates the 'rules' of aristocratic exchange (in which the participants are expected to misrecognize or overlook the precise economic value)[52] when he reckons up an account in which Medea has been adequately paid back once and for all. Medea, on the other hand, may be said to be reasserting her elite status by giving gifts: first, even as a suppliant of Aegeus, she offers him aid which he would greatly value – the promise of offspring; then, with Jason and the royal family, she offers what appears to be a splendidly honorific gift, ignoring the economic realities that Jason raises as an objection (she needs the wealth herself, the royal family already has ample gold and garments). Where Jason had abandoned the system (at least as far as his tie to Medea is concerned), Medea manipulates and corrupts the system both to underline its importance and to prove that she knows how to help friends *and* harm enemies.

---

[50] Mueller (2001).

[51] See McClure (1999b).

[52] As Glaucus correctly does in the famous exchange of armour with Diomedes in *Iliad* 6.230–6, whereas the narrative voice stands outside the elite exchange-system when it comments on the folly of accepting bronze in place of gold.

## (e) The gods

Most of Eur.'s plays feature gods[53] as characters at the margins of the dramatic action, in the prologue, or in a *deus ex machina* epilogue, or in both places. *Medea* has neither of these features, but instead leaves the intervention or operation of the gods to be inferred by those members of the audience who wish to detect it, in the same way that an audience is licensed to do in viewing plays like *Agamemnon* (in the safe and rapid arrival of Agamemnon home despite the storm that afflicted the Greek fleet) or *Oedipus Tyrannus* (in the timing of the plague and Polybus' death and the identities of the Corinthian messenger and the Theban herdsman). Zeus in particular and the gods in general have oversight over oaths and treatment of *xenoi*, and it has been shown above how Jason's suffering may be seen as the destruction that is expected to befall a breaker of oaths.[54] Apart from this, the references to Medea's descent from the sun-god Helios and the invocations of Helios (406, 746, 752, 764, 954) emphasize that god's twofold interest, as Medea's progenitor and as a witness of human action in general and of adherence to or violation of oaths in particular (cf. Garvie on Aesch. *Cho.* 984–6). The repeated naming of Helios prepares both for the prayer of the chorus to Helios in 1251–60 (which is not answered) and the provision of the winged chariot to Medea at the end (1320–2), which is a surprise to the audience and seems a spontaneous intervention, since there is no report of any prayer or request for this aid. The chariot on the crane allows Medea herself to take the position and perform some of the normal functions of the *deus ex machina* (1293–1419n., 1379–83n.). These features of the end of the play reveal clearly that the gods[55] are in some sense

[53] From antiquity there has been a strong tradition of regarding Eur. as an atheist or one who applies a caustic irony to his portrayal of the gods. Much work in recent decades rightly argues for the traditional basis of theological motifs in the plays and for the seriousness of allusions to ritual and religious practice, although some scholars go too far and slight the questioning and challenging element that coexists with the traditional. See e.g. Burnett (1971), Foley (1985), Mastronarde (1986) and (forthcoming), Kullmann (1987), Lefkowitz (1987) and (1989), Mikalson (1989) and (1991), Kovacs (1993).

[54] See Burnett (1973) and Kovacs (1993).

[55] For the question of the possible exoticism of Medea's connection to Helios and Hecate, see section (c) above.

on Medea's side in her struggle, and it is consonant with Greek religious thought to see the working of the gods, and not blind, random chance, in the arrival of Aegeus at just the moment Medea's plot needs him (663–823n.).

Once it is conceded that the frequent references to the gods and opportune events in the play point to a theological background that explains the disaster that befalls Jason, the question arises whether we should also interpret Medea's own downfall as a punishment brought upon her by the gods. Jason refers near the end of the play to an avenging demon (*alastor*) that pursued Medea from Colchis and brought suffering to him (1333–5). This demon was evoked by Medea's slaying of her own brother on the family hearth. This is a retrospective analysis by an interested party, so it is unclear how cogent it is to be felt to be. Medea herself laments at a crucial point that 'the gods and I have contrived' the situation that demands the death of her children (1013–14). Kovacs (1993) has suggested that when Medea plans her scheme of getting at Jason through the children and when she overcomes her own objections to it she may be understood to be mentally under the influence of the gods, who are bringing about her punishment at the same time as Jason's. Two objections may be made to such an inference. First, the tragedians normally explicitly reveal to the audience when a character is suffering a mental invasion that is controlling his or her perceptions and behaviour: so with Ajax in Sophocles' play, Phaedra in Eur.'s *Hippolytus*, and Pentheus in *Bacchae*. Such an indication is lacking in *Medea*. Second, tragedy frequently displays a dovetailing of a character's inclination and desire with the purposes of the god, and this dovetailing involves a rich double motivation rather than one that is reducible simply to divine influence or delusion (*atē*): so with Eteocles' decision to fight his brother, and Agamemnon's decision to tread on the tapestries at Clytemnestra's persuasion. In the case of Medea, the two sides of the causation are succinctly expressed in 1013–14, but this does not detract from the impression of freedom and voluntariness in Medea's previous development of her plan. This citation of the gods may in fact be interpreted as partly a rhetorical ploy by which Medea steels herself for the deed, just as in the *Iliad* Agamemnon's retrospective analysis of his *atē* is mainly a face-saving explanation that does not remove his obligation to make amends for his error. Accordingly, there is hardly a strong sense at the end of the play that Medea is being punished *by the gods*: she has their complicity, and she is on her way to enjoy years of safety and prosperity in Athens.

What this all means in terms of theodicy is that the polytheistic pantheon of traditional Greek religion and myth has a concern for the moral behaviour of men and upholds certain principles, but that the action of the gods is not entirely predictable to mortals or fully ethical by mortal standards. Gods choose when they will or will not act, and they are often more attentive to punishment of the guilty than to preservation of the weak or victimized, and the destructiveness of a punishment may seem, by human standards, to exceed by far what the offence demands. The futile prayer of the chorus for protection of the children underlines the discontinuity between human judgment and divine judgment. This discontinuity is often made blatant in Eur.'s plays, but it is not unique to him, since the same principles apply in tragedies like *Antigone* and *Agamemnon*. The final impression of this drama is morally disquieting, but this is not the result of a godless world.[56]

### (f) Imagery

As an heir and continuator of the high-style tradition of Greek poetry, tragedy makes ample use of figurative language. When the similes and metaphors of a tragedy present recurrent or related images, this feature provides one aspect of the texture of construction and reception, sometimes suggesting connections or contrasts that would not be obvious from overt features of character and action, and sometimes strongly reinforcing the literal meanings of a character's words. Aeschylus' *Oresteia* is famed for its extraordinarily rich and complex system of imagery,[57] but the same phenomenon can be observed, on a smaller scale, in works of Sophocles[58] and Eur.[59]

---

[56] In contrast, in the final couplet of Seneca's *Medea* Jason proclaims *per alta spatia vade sublime aetheris, | testare nullos esse, qua veheris, deos* ('Go to the height of heaven through the lofty expanses, give witness that where you fly there are no gods!').

[57] See e.g. Lebeck (1971).

[58] See e.g. Goheen (1951).

[59] See in general Breitenbach (1934), Barlow (1971), and Kurtz (1985).

The systems of figurative language deployed in *Medea* are drawn from areas that are common in much of classical Greek poetry: weather, the sea, and seafaring; disease and medicine; animals wild and domestic, along with hunting and agriculture. The imagery of storm and voyage is particularly suited to Medea's story, as she has travelled from one world to another across the sea, leaving behind the safe mooring of her childhood home and native culture. Medea's woes are like the water in the bilge threatening to make the ship founder (79) or are the rough seas themselves (362–3), and she lacks a place to anchor herself safely (258, 279, 442), until Aegeus offers her a harbour to moor in (769–70) after she sets sail (938 ἀπαίρομεν). Medea thus is figured as moving from helplessness and passivity to control of the vessel of her life. While Medea is still 'at sea', her enemies sail confidently, attacking her forcefully with full sails (278) and steering out of her stormy threats (523–4, Jason as skilled helmsman). For Medea is also like an unheeding wave of the sea (28–9) and a source of dark clouds and lightning (94, 106–8) and a storm of protesting language (524–5).

The medical imagery provides a similar mixture of perspectives. Medea is herself ailing in the first part of the play (60, 134, 197, 199, 473–4; perhaps 279 εὐπρόσοιστος). But she diagnoses Jason's 'disease' (471) and knows a way to heal herself (473 κουφισθήσομαι), and she is the mistress of φάρμακα (385, 789, 806, 1126, 1201, all of the poison used on the gifts; 718, of the drugs promised to cure Aegeus' childlessness). Medical metaphors also occur in 245 (the 'nausea' of the discontented husband), 283 ('incurable' harm), 520 (wrath 'hard to cure'), and 1138 (distress of the sympathetic household slaves).

Medea is also figured as a wild animal throughout the play. In her distress early in the play she is given the fierce glare of a bull or lioness (92, 187–8), and the nurse fears for the children because of Medea's 'wild character' (103 ἄγριον ἦθος). By the end Jason calls her a lioness and Medea exults in the name (1342–3, 1358, 1407), and she has 'a nature wilder (ἀγριωτέραν) than Scylla'. Although she is herself 'bitten' by her sufferings at the outset (110), later Medea 'bites' Jason (817, 1370) and he regards her as immune to the 'bite' of reproach (1345). The poison used by Medea devours and chews the princess: 1187 παμφάγου πυρός, 1189 ἔδαπτον, 1201 γνάθοις ἀδήλοις φαρμάκων.[60] The image of yoking for marriage (a commonplace) recurs in 242, 673, 804 (cf. 'new-tamed' in 1366), but it also applies to other close ties (735 of Aegeus' oath, 1017 of mother and children, 1145 of the pair of children). Bearing a yoke is also a trite metaphor for compliance (449, 1018, both recommendations to Medea). Medea also turns out to be a hunter of her victims, however, in the figure of the hunting net: 986 for the princess, 1278 for her sons.

Figurative language also contributes significantly to Medea's appropriation of masculine values and insistence on her claim to honour and revenge (see sections (a) and (b) above). Language of a military cast, both metaphorical and literal, is very frequent, almost all of it in reference to Medea or her actions or used in her own arguments: 183 ὁρμᾶται, 248–250 ἀκίνδυνον, μάρνανται δορί, παρ' ἀσπίδα, 263–4 φόβου, ἀλκήν, σίδηρον, 390 πύργος, 394 τόλμης δ' εἶμι πρὸς τὸ καρτερόν, 403 ἕρπ' ἐς τὸ δεινόν· νῦν ἀγὼν εὐψυχίας, 408 ἐσθλ', 466 ἀνανδρίαν, 597 ἔρυμα δώμασιν, 765 (cf. 45) καλλίνικοι, 852 φόνον αἴρηι, 938 ἀπαίρομεν, 1051 τολμητέον, κάκης, 1117 καραδοκῶ, 1185 ἐπεστρατεύετο, 1242 ἀλλ' εἴ' ὁπλίζου, 1244 λαβὲ ξίφος, 1246 μὴ κακισθῆις, 1322 ἔρυμα πολεμίας χερός. The same is true of the language of athletic contest (235 ἀγὼν μέγιστος, 366 ἀγῶνες, 367 πόνοι, 546 ἅμιλλαν, 585 ἐκτενεῖ, 1245 πρὸς βαλβῖδα λυπηρὰν βίου), although such terms also appear in other mouths (274 βραβεύς, 557 ἅμιλλαν, 1082 ἁμίλλας, 1181–2 runner and racecourse simile, 1214 παλαίσματα). The language of profit and commerce (which may be conceived of as in tension with aristocratic reciprocity in the form of χάρις and φιλία) is more commonly heard from Jason's mouth (454 κέρδος, 461 ἀχρήμων, 527 ναυκληρίας, 532 οὐκ ἀκριβῶς αὐτὸ θήσομαι λίαν, 535 εἴληφας ἢ δέδωκας, 542 χρυσός, 560 σπανιζοίμεσθα, 566 λύει, 611 χρημάτων, 612 ἀφθόνωι, 615 κερδανεῖς, 910 παρεμπολῶντος, 960 σπανίζειν, 963 χρημάτων), but Medea also employs it (369 κερδαίνουσαν, 516–9 χρυσοῦ, κίβδηλος, χαρακτήρ, 965, 968 χρυσός, 1362 λύει).

---

[60] Similar metaphors are found in Sophocles' descriptions of the poisoned cloak of Heracles: *Trachiniae* 769–71, 974–5, 979–81, 987, 1028–30, 1053–6, 1084, 1088.

## 3   PRODUCTION

The appearance of the theatre in the sanctuary of Dionysos Eleuthereus in Athens[61] in the year 431 BCE cannot be established with
certainty: at that date very little of the theatre was in stone; and since
the traces of fifth-century structures have been overlaid and largely
obliterated by later construction, the dating of what traces there are
is not certain. The theatre-building or *skēnē* in Eur.'s time was a temporary structure of wooden posts and panels (probably of fabric)
with a flat roof capable of supporting at least a couple of actors. The
background provided by this building was pierced by large central
double-doors, the only opening usually employed in tragedy,[62] where
it might represent the entrance to a temple, a palace, a humble
dwelling, a military tent, or a cave. The appearance of the background may have been modified by the use of painted panels with
*trompe-l'oeil* representation of architectural features or other scenery.

Before this background was a rectangular acting-space, where in-
teractions between the actors usually took place. The acting-area
may have been a wooden platform raised very slightly above the level
of the dancing-area or *orchēstra*; if so, the two spaces were still easily
accessible to each other by one or two steps. The dancing-area projected in front of the acting-area and into the hollow where the
audience was seated. In the fourth century the *orchēstra* was a
large circle, but it is a major issue of contention among scholars
whether this was true in the fifth century as well. Some architectural
traces of the honorary seating have been interpreted as indicating a
rectilinear dancing-area, and rectangular or trapezoidal dancing-
areas are proven in some small deme-theatres of the late fifth century. Many archaeologists are accordingly now convinced that the
circular dancing-area was introduced only in the fourth century to

---

[61] For fuller discussion and documentation of topics related to production
see Pickard-Cambridge (1968) and Csapo and Slater (1995). For a convenient
brief summary of the archaeological remains and their interpretation see
Moretti (2000).

[62] Secondary doors and window-openings may have been available *ad hoc*
or routinely, but are not exploited in most tragedies.

accommodate a vastly expanded *theatron* holding up to 30,000 spectators.[63] Whatever its shape, the chorus danced and stood in this area, probably spatially distinct (for the most part) from the actors, just as they were distinct in their mode of performance and their mode of experiencing the crucial events of the drama.[64] At either side, where the dancing-area and acting-area met, there was an entrance-ramp or path (*eisodos* or *parodos*), and by convention one side was often considered to lead to other parts of the city, the other to an exit from the city into the countryside.

In *Medea* the background represents the residence in which Medea and Jason have been living, while the acting-area and dancing-area represent the public street or plaza in front of this house. The city-side entrance leads to the place where the children have been taken to exercise before the play begins, to the marketplace and fountain-house where the tutor overhears the gossip about the decree of exile, and to the royal palace, into which Jason has moved to live with his new bride and father-in-law and where the deaths of Creon and his daughter take place. Thus all side-entrances and side-exits of actors except those of Aegeus occur on this side. The other side, used by Aegeus, leads to a gate in the city-wall and the roads giving access to other lands.[65] We cannot be sure from which side the chorus entered (possibly they even entered from both sides, as they are coming from the immediate neighbourhood).

Two mechanical devices were in use in the theatre during Eur.'s career. A crane (a counterbalanced swing-beam) behind the theatre-building, perhaps originally used for construction and dismantling of the building and transport of heavy props or painted panels, had been appropriated by the dramatists at some date earlier than *Medea*

---

[63] See most recently Moretti (2000) and Pöhlmann (1995a); recent advocates of the circular form include Wiles (1997) 46–53 and Scullion (1994) 3–66.

[64] This point too is controversial. For the distinct position and modes of the chorus, see Mastronarde (1998) and (1999). For the alternative view that the actors usually positioned themselves within a circle formed by the chorus, see Ley and Ewans (1985), Ewans (1995), Wiles (1997).

[65] Wecklein, however, has Aegeus come in on one side (from the harbour) and depart on the other (for a road leading to Troezen).

to show the flight of gods. Medea appears with the bodies of her two sons on a winged chariot suspended from this crane in the final scene of the play, and this theatrical coup depends for its effect on a pre-existing convention of a *deus ex machina* arriving suddenly to stop the human actors and make dispositions for the future.[66] A rolling platform (*ekkyklēma*) was available behind the central door: this could bring an interior scene (especially dead bodies) out before the chorus and audience. Jason's demand to see the bodies of his children and his call for the opening of the door would have suggested to the audience that the rolling platform was about to appear, but Eur. frustrates this expectation by his unusual use of the crane for Medea's escape and by her appropriation of the bodies.

Few props are required for this play. Creon's attendants are presumably armed, and Jason may also wear a sword, lending force to his threat of vengeance in line 1316 (but see n.). Creon probably has a royal staff or sceptre, and Aegeus either a sceptre or a traveller's staff. If one adopts an alternative reading in line 46 (see n.), then the children come on with hoops that they have been playing with before entering. The poisoned gifts are the most significant props, but it cannot be determined with certainty how they were treated in the original performance. The poisoned robe of Soph. *Trach.* is not seen when Deianeira gives it to Lichas: it has to be conveyed in a box or chest because sunlight activates the poison. A chest is depicted in a few South Italian vase-paintings showing the death of the princess, and it surely alludes to the carrying of the poisoned gifts, but whether this is a true reflection of stage-practice or simply a device of visual narrative is unknown. The poison used by Medea is apparently activated by the body-heat of the princess once the gifts are donned. Thus, they could perhaps be carried on open trays or in shallow boxes so that the servant and the boys may carry them but not in fact handle them directly, while the audience and Jason have some view of them. Jason refers to the two gifts in 960–1. If line 949 is correctly deleted as an iteration of 786, his ability to name them probably implies that they are visible to him (otherwise the audience is expected to assume that he knows these items well and recognizes the

---

[66] On the crane see Mastronarde (1990) and Lendle (1995).

containers – an unlikely technique for Greek tragedy).[67] The winged chariot attached to the crane has already been mentioned: see 1317n. for the question whether Euripides' own production showed winged serpents yoked to the chariot.

The speaking roles of a tragedy were performed during Eur.'s time by a troupe of three male actors. The leader of the troupe, who was eligible for a prize from 447 on, took the juiciest roles, and in *Medea* that would be the title character. Since Medea cries out from indoors while the nurse is onstage and the tutor is still in the process of guiding the children in from the stage (89–105), it appears that all three actors were used in the play (against the claim that it used only two actors, in imitation of a much older model). Guesses as to how the roles were divided between the second and third actor are inevitably arbitrary. The second actor, for example, could have played the nurse and Creon and Jason, while the third played the tutor, Aegeus, and the Messenger.[68] The actors wore an undergarment with sleeves and leggings, and over this they wore changeable tunics and robes to suit the different roles. The clearest mark of each role was the mask, a full head-covering including hair. Fifth-century masks were probably fairly realistic in style, without the gaping mouths and other exaggerated features that became the norm in the post-classical Greco-Roman theatre.

Medea will have been shown as a woman in her prime. If the Greeks bothered to think precisely about the age of mythical characters, they might have thought of her as in her late 20s (married at 16–18 and with two children under 10, perhaps under 7). There are several uncertainties about her costume and mask. First, when Medea initially appears, she has been distraught and fasting for some time (24n.; 25 τὸν πάντα ... χρόνον; 59–60, the tutor's expectation that she may have calmed down by this time), and her condition

---

[67] Some modern directors (as in the Broadway production of Robinson Jeffers' adaptation, available on video) have Medea handle and display the robe, emphasizing its similarity to the golden fleece that was in a sense Medea's own bridal gift. Such a gesture can probably be ruled out for the original performance of Euripides' script.

[68] Di Benedetto and Medda (1997) 223 suggest a similar division, except that the second actor takes the role of Aegeus as well. See also Pickard-Cambridge (1968) 145.

could also imply 'without bathing or changing clothes' (as in the case
of Orestes and Electra at the opening of *Or.*: see *Or.* 41–2, 225–6,
303, 387). Radical departures from normal dress and physical appearance are usually commented on in tragedy in the words of the
text. In Medea's case, we cannot expect Creon or Jason to show
much interest if she does look distraught and ill, but the behaviour of
Aegeus is probably telling: he hails Medea and converses with her
for 25 lines before commenting that her eyes and skin have a wasted
appearance. Thus the extent of 'realism' in Medea's appearance is
probably confined to the expression and skin-colour of the mask,
while her hair and costume are in normal condition. If this is correct,
then these physical aspects reinforce the unexpected self-control she
shows as soon as she appears.

A second uncertainty concerns the nature and significance of
Medea's costume. It has been argued that a change in the depiction
of Medea's dress in vase-paintings is a reflection of the costuming in
the Euripidean production of 431: before that date, Medea is shown
in paintings in 'Greek' dress; after it, there are paintings with ornate
'oriental' robes and 'Phrygian cap'; the 'oriental' dress of Medea is
then taken to be an innovation of Eur., visually marking her foreignness.[69] But the relationship of the conventions of tragic dress to the
conventions of vase-paintings is not at all clear, and through the course
of the fifth century ornate dress may have spread from the flute-
players and eastern kings to almost all tragic figures of elite status.[70]
It may be, then, that ornate dress signifies the otherness of the heroic/
tragic world and not the 'otherness' of being non-Greek. Related to
this problem is a theory about a change of dress for Medea within
the play itself. Following up on the variations in dress found in vase-
paintings of Medea, Sourvinou-Inwood (1997) 290–4 has suggested
that Medea in the chariot at 1317ff. wears a different costume than
she wore earlier. On this hypothesis, in 214–1250 she is in normal
Greek dress, but at the end she is fully distanced from the chorus,
Greeks, and the audience by representation in ornate oriental dress.
Without explicit guidance in the text signalling the significant gesture
of changed costume, however, one should be reluctant to assume it:

---

[69] Page, lxii n. 1; Hall (1989) 35 n. 110.
[70] Pickard-Cambridge (1968) 197–202.

most likely Medea is costumed in the same way throughout, probably in an ornate robe that marks her elite status.

Third, the Greeks sometimes thought of the Colchians as dark-skinned like the Egyptians and Ethiopians: Aia was originally thought of as a land at the far east of the world, visited by Helios (2n.). Herodotus (2.104) says that the Colchians are 'dark-skinned and curly-haired' like the Egyptians. It would be a significant visual mark of Medea's otherness if her mask were dark-skinned instead of whitish (the marker of femininity). Dark-skinned masks are attested in the words of the text for Aeschylus' *Suppliant Women* (70, 154–5, 719–20), and there were probably other cases in lost plays.[71] There is no hint of distinctive skin colour in the iconographic tradition of Medea, and it is noteworthy that Andromeda is shown as white-skinned even on vases which include dark-skinned Ethiopian slaves beside her, and Phaethon apparently inherits whiteness from his mother, although his father Merops may have been depicted as black (Diggle on *Phaethon* 4). It is most likely, therefore, that Medea's mask was white-skinned like those of other tragic women of elite status.

Jason is depicted as a man in his prime (again, if the audience bothered to think of chronology, they might think of him as around 30 years of age), thus with a full head of hair and a mature man's beard, but without traces of grey. Creon is an older man (1209) and presumably is shown with grey or greying hair and beard. Aegeus is probably shown as older than Jason (Medea is surprised he is still childless, 670) but younger than Creon, and his costume presumably included the cloak and broad hat characteristic of wayfarers. The humble characters are made distinct by the plainness of their robes and the shorter hair characteristic of slaves. The nurse and the tutor are both 'aged' (49, 53), while the servant who brings the report of the deaths at the palace is of indeterminate age.

The chorus-members represent ordinary wives of the neighbourhood and perhaps wear very plain costumes, in contrast to the elite figures, and the masks of mature matrons.

A number of silent extras are required for the stage action, and others may be present solely for the purpose of accompanying the

---

[71] See Friis Johansen and Whittle on Aesch. *Supp.* 154, 719; *LIMC* I 1.414 s.v. Aithiopes (Snowden); Carden (1974) 70–1 on Soph. *Inachos* fr. 269a.54.

major figures. Two child extras play the sons (who are perhaps to be imagined as around 7 years old). When the children's cries are heard from inside (1270a n.), one or two of the three actors provide the voices. In tragedy, most princely characters appearing from entrance-ramp or from central door and noble women emerging into the public from the door are attended by silent extras (see Stanley-Porter (1973)). We can clearly detect their presence only from the orders given to them at some point in the text. Medea must have at least one female attendant to receive the command given in 820–3, and this attendant should enter with Medea at 214. Probably there are two attendants, in imitation of the Homeric decorum seen in the formula οὐκ οἴη, ἅμα τῆι γε καὶ ἀμφίπολοι δύ᾽ ἕποντο (Il. 3.143 etc.). The attendant sent to fetch Jason returns with him at 866. An attendant fetches the gifts from indoors in the next scene (951n.). Some critics believe that Medea is alone with the children after the tutor is sent indoors without them at 1020;[72] but there is no logical point for the attendants present in the previous episode to depart (there is no reason for them to accompany the tutor to the palace earlier or to enter with him at 1020). Medea's attendants probably guide the children indoors at 1076 and from that point until 1250 she is alone on stage. A further problem related to the extras is whether one of them emerges at 214 wearing the mask and robe of the nurse, who would thus be converted from a speaking person to a silent extra. On the basis of the reference to loyalty and good will in 820–3, many commentators assume that the attendant addressed in 820–3 is the nurse. But the loyalty of a long-time slave is conventional (54n.), and there is no reason to believe that the nurse is the only servant who came from Colchis with Medea, that no other servant has been used by Medea for confidential activities, and that no other servant is well disposed to Medea. Moreover, it would be clumsy for a character who has been so well defined in the first 200 lines as a voice of moderation and who expressed such anxiety over the children's welfare to become a silent extra who is a tool of Medea's awful scheme.[73] The best

---

[72] See Battezzato (1991) 430 n. 1.

[73] There is nothing in extant Greek tragedy to match Seneca's habit of making his nurses and servants combine the function of philosophical warning figures opposing their vehement masters with the role of willing collaborator in their criminal schemes.

course is to have the nurse disappear once and for all after 203. She will have had a mask indicating age and anxiety, while the attendants who emerge at 214 should have a neutral and anonymous appearance.

Creon (269n.) and Aegeus surely have male attendants. Creon nearly orders his men to drag Medea away (335). Whether or not Jason has silent male attendants with him in any of his three appearances cannot be established from the text (see Stanley-Porter (1973) 74). In the *agōn*-scene, if he is attended, it is a scenic reflection of his status in the city and his sense of superiority to Medea. If he is not attended, his isolation might indicate confidence that he needs no support to deal with women. When he arrives at 866 in answer to Medea's summons, he would most logically be unaccompanied if he was unaccompanied in his first appearance; but if he was accompanied earlier, he might or might not have attendants at 866 (the carrying of the gifts by the boys later in the scene has its own reason and tells nothing about whether attendants are available or not). Finally, at 1293, if Jason is alone, this would be effective in showing the weak and isolated position in which Medea's vengeance has left him and it would indicate that he is alone in his hurried effort to rescue his sons from possible retaliation by Creon's kin. If he has retainers with him at this point, they must be loyal servants who are there to help accomplish his rescue of his sons. (See further 1314–15n. and 1317n.: the exact interpretation of those lines and the decision about staging are interrelated).

## 4   EURIPIDES' *MEDEA* AND THE MEDEA-MYTH

Attic tragedy almost always drew its plots from heroic myth, and the authors wrote with the expectation that their audience had a certain familiarity with poetic and oral traditions. At the same time, storytelling in poetry had always been a versatile and competitive skill, and the Greeks of archaic and classical times were aware that, depending on the location and the occasion of the telling as well as the identity of the teller, stories could be told in many different ways. Many members of the audience of tragedy thus had a large store of background knowledge to call upon (differing, of course, from individual to individual and not to be assumed to be universal), but also the ability to set much of the background aside while entering into the fictional world created on stage and awaiting references in the text that might activate some portions of their knowledge. In this way, the audience experiences a process of discovery even when confronted with familiar material.[74] For the modern interpreter interested in estimating the reception of a play within its original cultural context, it is useful to try to reconstruct the contemporary audience's possible background knowledge, since it was an important part of the horizon of expectations they brought to the experience of the play.

Medea had a significant role in a number of famous stories, but in archaic times and in the fifth century each episode was usually treated as relatively self-standing, and there was no compiled life of Medea in which all incidents had to be brought into logical harmony.[75] In his play Eur. refers or alludes to some earlier incidents, but was under no compulsion to provide a complete story. Nor does an audience attending to a drama in the immediate power of its performance divert its attention to a detailed reconstruction of all aspects of the past. While for modern students a lack of information may make uncertain the presence or the effect of an allusion to mythic details, for the ancient audience too there may also have been uncertainties that left their interpretation of allusions imprecise or open-ended. Nevertheless, it is worthwhile to review the evidence for various details of the background.

(1) The Argonautic expedition. We have no full Argonautic narrative extant earlier than Apollonius of Rhodes' epic of the third century BCE (which itself leaves gaps in the story, especially in its preliminaries), but the tale must be as old as the oral tradition from which the *Iliad* and *Odyssey* grew. Fairly extensive treatments were apparently present in two lost epics, Eumelus' *Corinthiaca* and the anonymous *Naupactia*;[76] allusions to characters or incidents of the story are seen in various archaic texts (*Il.* 7.468–9, 21.40–1, *Od.* 11.235–59, 12.69–72, Hesiod *Theog.* 992–1002); and some events are depicted in archaic and early classical art.[77] Pindar presented several parts of it

---

[74] Griffith (1990); Mastronarde (2000), esp. 24–6.

[75] See Graf (1997).

[76] See Huxley (1969) 60–73.

[77] See *LIMC* s.vv. Iason, Medeia.

in his unusually long lyric narrative in *Pythian* 4 (see also *Ol.* 13.49–54). The early prose writer Pherecydes also narrated the Argonautic voyage (*FGrHist* 3 F 105 = *EGM* 105).[78] By a normal epic device, the hero Jason has divine helpers (Athena for the building of the ship, Hera for passing through the Clashing Rocks, Aphrodite for the winning of Medea's favour) and the human princess as helper too. This divine and human assistance is debated in the *agōn* of the play (522–75n., 528n.). Other incidents alluded to are:

(a) Jason, using supplication and persuasion and erotic allure, induced Medea to help him and to betray her father (on this motif, 17n.), and promised to take her away as his wife (on this promise see section 2 (*c*) and (*d*)). See 496–7 'oh, my right hand, that you clung to so often, as also to my knees, how much in vain have I been touched by an evil man'; 801–2 'persuaded by the words of a Greek'; 8 'stunned in her heart with love for Jason'; 527–8 'Cypris alone of gods and men I deem to be the saviour of my voyage.' Earlier sources agree in putting emphasis on the erotic infatuation of Medea brought about by the will of the gods: Hes. *Theog.* 992–4; esp. Pind. *Pyth.* 4.213–19 'then for the first time the Cyprus-born goddess, mistress of keenest arrows, bound the many-coloured wryneck (*iunx*) to the four spokes of an inescapable wheel and brought it, bird of madness, down from Olympus to mankind, and she taught Aeson's wise son supplications that enchant, so that he could remove Medea's shame before her parents, and longing for Greece would whirl her under the whip of Persuasion as she burned in her heart'. In *Ol.* 13.49–54 Pindar praises Corinth for its excellence in heroic legend, referring specifically to Sisyphus as supremely clever and to Medea as 'saviour of the ship Argo and its crew'. Pindar's treatments show that it was possible to present Medea to a Greek audience as a figure of authority and as an important contributor to one of the glorious adventures of the heroic age.

(b) Jason had Medea's help to succeed in the tests imposed on him by Aeetes. These are alluded to in 476–9: 'I saved you ... when

---

[78] For fuller treatment of the Argonautic myths, see Hunter's edn of Apollonius' Book 3, pp. 12–21; Gantz (1993) 340–73; and esp. Moreau (1994), with full references to earlier treatments.

you were sent to control the yoke of the fire-breathing bulls and to sow the field with a deadly crop.' In fuller versions, we are told that Medea supplied a salve that protected Jason from the fiery breath of the bulls (Pindar, *Pyth.* 4.220–37; Ap. Rhod. 3.1026–62, 1278–1407). Although Apollonius provides the first extant detailed presentation of the battle of Jason with the Sown Men, it is a natural assumption that early versions included some magical means for Jason to overcome so many opponents and that Eur.'s audience knew some version in which Medea told Jason how to make the Sown Men turn their murderous fury against each other. In Sophocles' *Kolchides* (of unknown date), there was in fact a stichomythic dialogue in which Medea advised Jason on this ordeal (ΣAp. Rhod. 3.1040c, quoted *TrGF* iv.316).

(c) Jason had Medea's help in seizing the golden fleece, which was guarded by a great serpent. In 480–2 Medea states 'and by killing the dragon, which embraced and guarded the all-gold fleece with many-coiled loops, never sleeping, I held up for you the light of salvation'. Medea's use of κτείνασ' here may reflect an otherwise unattested older version in which Medea herself killed the dragon, or it may be an *ad hoc* invention by Eur. to magnify Medea's service to Jason. Less likely, 'having killed' could be meant as shorthand for 'gave you the means to kill': in Pindar, *Pyth.* 4.249 κτεῖνε μὲν γλαυκῶπα τέχναις ποικιλόνωτον ὄφιν, Jason is the subject, but τέχναις refers to Medea's role (in Ap. Rhod. 4.82–8, 123–66, the serpent is put to sleep by Medea's drug, but not killed). Early artistic depictions of the seizing of the fleece from the dragon show Jason being swallowed or disgorged by the dragon (often in the presence of Athena), and Medea is not present. Pictures with Medea present, often feeding the dragon drugged food or liquid, are found from *c.* 415 onward on South Italian vases, but Jason is there too with his sword (in a third series of images, Etruscan and Roman, Jason attacks the serpent with his sword, without Medea's presence). See *LIMC* s.v. Iason.

(d) Medea killed her brother Apsyrtus (167, 1334). The first allusion is vague, but in the second Jason reviles her for killing her brother 'by the hearth' (thus bringing pollution with her when she boarded the Argo to flee). This version is probably preferred here because it allows a heightening of horror, since the household hearth

is a sacred spot. Killing at home is also attested for Sophocles'
*Kolchides* (fr. 343). The version in which the boy was murdered and
dismembered at sea to slow down the pursuers (Apollodorus 1.133
and Roman authors) is also attested in the fifth century (Pherecydes
*FGrHist* 3 F 32a–c = *EGM* 32a–c).

(2) In Iolcus, after the return of the Argonauts, Medea caused the
death of king Pelias as a favour to Jason (9, 486–7, 504–8).[79] Medea's
identity as the killer of Pelias is emphasized in Pindar, *Pyth.* 4.250
'Jason stole away Medea, with her own consent, the slayer of Pelias'
(τὰν Πελίαο φονόν Wackernagel: τὰν Πελιαοφόνον codd.) and Pherecydes *FGrHist* 3 F 105 (= *EGM* 105) 'Hera put this idea [of recom-
mending to Pelias the fetching of the fleece] in Jason's mind so that
Medea would come to Greece as an evil for Pelias.' The wrath of
Hera against Pelias may have played a role in some early version
(Pelias had killed Sidero as she sought refuge at an altar of Hera),[80]
but Eur. makes no allusion to that. Medea 'persuaded' (9) the daughters of Pelias by demonstrating her magical power to rejuvenate,
either on Aeson or on a ram; the daughters then cut their father into
pieces, but Medea did not supply the magic to restore him.[81] The
story was put on stage by Eur. in his *Peliades*, a play from his very first
production in 455 BCE. Some conjecture that Sophocles' *Rhizotomoi*
told the same story, but the meagre fragments describing Medea
gathering magic herbs could easily come from some other part of her
life. It is significant that in *Medea* Eur. never names Acastus, the son
of Pelias who, in the mythographers, drives out Jason and Medea,

---

[79] Eur. is, characteristically, uninformative about the nature of Jason's
complicity in the scheme to kill Pelias. Some later versions insist on offering
more details, often exculpating Jason more or less entirely and emphasizing
Medea's wildness (cf. Sen. *Med.* 262–5, 496–503, followed closely by Corneille); Grillparzer not only makes the murder of Pelias a false rumour against
Jason (Act I), but also has Medea reveal that she was present in Pelias' cham-
ber only to fetch the fleece and that Pelias' death came about without her involvement (Act III). It is interesting that some vase-paintings apparently show
Jason assisting at the ruse: *LIMC* s.v. Pelias #11 (*c.* 510), #12 (*c.* 470), and s.v.
Peliades #5 (*c.* 480) – in two of these an unnamed mature male stokes the fire
under the cauldron and in the third he sits witnessing the deception.

[80] See Dräger (1993) 12–149, 357–60.

[81] *LIMC* s.vv. 'Peliades' and 'Pelias' (E. Simon).

and he even implies that Pelias had no son (487n.). In Seneca and some modern versions, in contrast, the threats of Acastus are used to extenuate the actions of Creon and Jason.

(3) Medea and Jason are outsiders in Corinth in the play, in exile from Iolcus, but this was not the only story told. Eumelus (fr. 5 Bernabé = fr. 3$^A$ Davies = Pausanias 2.3.10)[82] constructed the history of Corinth so that Aeetes was rightful ruler of Corinth by the gift of Helios, but migrated from there to Colchis, leaving Bounos as king; then, when Bounos and the succeeding royal line had died out, Medea was summoned from Iolcus by the Corinthians, and Jason, her husband, became king of Corinth. So too in Simonides (*PMG* 545 = Σ*Med.* 19), Jason ruled in Corinth (the quotation is corrupt, but may have said 'with his Colchian wife'). The *Naupactia* (fr. 9 Bernabé/Davies = Paus. 2.3.9), on the other hand, had Jason migrating from Iolcus to Corcyra after the death of Pelias.

(4) In the play, Medea and Jason have two sons, probably represented as under the age of seven, and no names are given (as is normally the case for children in tragedy). Hes. *Theog.* 1001 and Cinaethon (fr. 2 Bernabé/Davies = Paus. 2.3.9) give Medeios as the couple's son (Cinaethon adds a daughter Eriopis), a name intended to incorporate the Medes through their eponymous ancestor into Greek heroic genealogy.[83] According to the *Naupactia* (fr. 9 Bernabé/Davies = Paus. 2.3.9), Jason had sons named Mermeros and Pheres, and the poem told that Mermeros was killed by a lion while hunting on the mainland opposite Corcyra. The same two names are given for the victims of the Corinthians in the story told by Pausanias 2.3.6. Parmeniscus, a Hellenistic scholar and student of Aristarchus, cited by Didymus in Σ*Med.* 264, claimed that Medea and Jason had seven

[82] It appears that a prose epitome of Eumelus' epic was composed (perhaps in the early fourth century) and became the source of some later citations of Eumelus: see *FGrHist* 451 T 1 = Fowler, *EGM* 1 105.

[83] West on *Theog.* 1001 suggests that this genealogy should date from the middle of the sixth century at the earliest; Cinaethon's date is uncertain, but he may have written in the sixth century. Herodotus 7.62.1 says the name of the Medes came from Medea herself, who fled to their land from Athens. Pausanias 2.3.8 repeats this explanation, but says that she brought with her a son Medos sired by Aegeus; he quotes Hellanicus (*FGrHist* 4 F 132 = *EGM* 132) as saying the son she took with her was Polyxenus, sired by Jason.

boys and seven girls.[84] Diodorus Siculus 4.54.1 reports a version in which Jason and Medea lived in Corinth for ten years before Jason's betrayal and had three children, the twins Alkimenes and Thessalos and their younger brother Teisandros (with Thessalos surviving the disaster).

More important than the background events are the events of the plot itself. The most interesting and controversial aspect of the relation of *Medea* to the pre-existing traditions concerns the death of her children in Corinth. It is not possible to date the variants relative to each other except by guesswork, but several seem to be earlier than Eur.'s play.

(a) The children are killed by the Corinthians in a version told by Parmeniscus (in Σ*Med.* 264):

> Since the Corinthians did not want to be ruled by a woman who was a foreigner and a sorceress, they plotted against her and killed her children, seven male and seven female.... When the children were being pursued, they fled to the shrine of Hera Akraia and sought asylum there. But even so the Corinthians did not spare them, but they killed them all upon the altar. A plague beset the city and many were being killed by the disease. When they sought an oracle, the god replied that they should expiate the pollution of the children of Medea. From this origin the Corinthians have the annual practice right up to our own day of having seven boys and seven girls chosen from the most prominent families spend the year in the goddess' precinct and placate with sacrifices the wrath of the children and the anger of the goddess that originated because of them.

In lines 1378–83 Medea *ex machina* announces the burial of her two children in the same shrine of Hera Akraia and says that for all

---

[84] The number 14, with seven of each sex, is likely to be an inference from the number and sex of the Corinthian children participating annually in rituals propitiating the wrath of the children of Medea. Compare the ritual band of seven boys and seven girls sent by the Athenians to be victims of the Minotaur (Bacchylides 17.2–3). Thus one may doubt whether any archaic literary source specified this large number of children for Medea and Jason.

future time the Corinthians will perform rites in recompense for the killing. Since it is anomalous in cultic terms that the Corinthians are charged with the atonement of impious deaths for which Medea, and not they, was responsible, the most plausible inference is that such a cult practice did exist earlier than 431 and was previously explained as expiation for the killing of the children by the Corinthians themselves. Thus Parmeniscus is reflecting a tradition much older than the Hellenistic era.

(b) A story that combines the murder of Creon by Medea (now an outsider rather than queen) with the violence of the Corinthians themselves against her children is told by one Creophylus (in Σ*Med.* 264 = *FGrHist* 417 F 3 = *EGM* 3), whose date and identity are disputed:[85] 'the story is told that when Medea was living in Corinth she killed with drugs Creon, who was then ruler of the city, and that in fear of his friends and relatives she fled to Athens, but since her sons were rather young and unable to accompany her, she left them seated on the altar of Hera Akraia, convinced that their father would see to their safety. But the relatives of Creon killed them and spread the rumour that Medea had murdered not only Creon, but also her own sons'. The numerous allusions in the play (781, 1060–1, 1238–41, 1301–5, 1380–1) to the possibility that the relatives of Creon will kill the children to get their revenge on Medea have suggested to many that Eur. expected his audience to be familiar with the version in which the relatives were to blame. If this speculation is correct, then, whatever Creophylus' date, this detail of his narrative should be regarded as older than Eur. The detail about the rumour spread to shift the blame to Medea, however, is to be regarded as older than Eur. only if Creophylus was in fact an archaic author.

(c) In another story the children die when an attempt to make them immortal fails. Failed attempts of this kind are known from

---

[85] The two possibilities are that he is the archaic epic poet who is frequently mentioned as a host of Homer and as the author of *The capture of Oechalia* (about Heracles' conquest of Eurytus' kingdom and seizure of Iole) or – the more probable view – that he is the chronicler cited in an inscription from Priene (*FGrHist* 417 F 2). See Bernabé's apparatus for Creophylus fr. dub. 9 for refs. to supporters of each alternative (add Moreau (1994) 50, 76 n. 96, in favour of the epic author, and Davies, *fragmentum spurium*, pp. 152–3, and Fowler *EGM* I 64 in support of the chronicler).

other myths, such as Demeter's treatment of the royal baby De-
mophon of Eleusis told in the *Homeric Hymn to Demeter* (the baby dies
in the attempt in other versions, although he lives on in the *Hymn*),
and Thetis' attempt to make her children by Peleus immortal (told in
the epic *Aigimios*, Hesiod fr. 300 M–W). Eumelus (fr. 5 Bernabé =
fr. 3$^A$ Davies = Paus. 2.3.11) said that while ruling in Corinth with
Jason, Medea took each baby that was born to them to the temple of
Hera and 'hid it' (κατακρύπτειν: this could refer to burial or to 'hid-
ing in fire', as in the stories about Thetis and Demeter), thinking she
was making it immortal; but she found she was mistaken, and Jason
finally caught her doing it, and so they separated and left Corinth
for different destinations. A very brief narrative found in ΣPind. *Ol.*
13.74g reflects a closely-related version: 'in Corinth Zeus fell in love
with Medea, but Medea did not give her consent to him, seeking
to avoid the anger of Hera. For this reason Hera in fact promised
to make her children immortal. But they died, and the Corinthians
honour them, calling them "half-foreign".'[86]

(d) That Medea deliberately killed the children herself became
the canonical version after the fifth century, thanks to the influence
of Eur.'s play. A number of scholars have considered this to be an
innovation by Eur. himself. But this is hardly certain. As a general
rule, modern scholars tend to make too little allowance for the loss of
the vast web of competing stories that must have been told in archaic
and classical Greece and conversely tend to overestimate the innovations and originality of the authors who became 'classical'. Three
specific strands of evidence need to be considered. First, the story
told by Creophylus includes the motif of deliberate killing (as a false
allegation), but this author is likely to be post-Euripidean (n. 85), so
the question is whether the notion of Medea as deliberate killer is
one of the old elements in that version or is simply borrowed from
Eur. Certainly, in the competitive context of retold and refashioned
stories, the Corinthians would have been inclined to invent or wel-

[86] For interesting speculations on the beliefs, rites, and myths that may
have lain behind this story and the roles of Medea and Hera in connection
with protecting or threatening children, see Johnston (1997). See also Moreau
(1994) 101–15 and 191–217 on Medea as a form of mother-goddess displaced
by Olympian goddesses.

come a version that freed their forebears of the taint of murderous violation of asylum.[87] Second, the nurse's fears for the children (36, 90–5, 100–18) perhaps depend for their effect on the audience's awareness of a version or versions in which Medea killed them, although we can also detect here a typical dramatic *suggestio falsi* in the fact that the nurse fears harm motivated by suicidal despair (sometimes the motivation for infanticide and filicide in modern cultures) whereas the actual deed is done by logical planning of revenge against Jason.[88] Third, the pre-Euripidean origin of Medea as deliberate child-killer would be firmly established if we could be confident that the fragments ascribed to Neophron are really from a play produced earlier than 431. On this vexed problem, see the next section.

Eur.'s play also alludes to two future events, Medea's sojourn in Athens and Jason's death. The former must have been known to the original audience in one or more detailed versions. In various versions, either she flees to Athens from Corinth or she leaves Athens to go to Asia. The rise of Theseus as an Attic hero in the sixth century, with the resulting expansion of literary and artistic depictions, ensured that Eur.'s audience was familiar with the details of Theseus' life. What is not certain is how early Medea was given the role of the wicked stepmother trying to eliminate the newly arrived Theseus before Aegeus could discover his true identity. Attic vase-paintings show Theseus, Aegeus, Medea, and the Marathonian Bull from around 450. Some vases up to 50 years earlier show Theseus attacking an unidentified woman, who may or may not be Medea.[89] Vase-paintings

---

[87] Parmeniscus (ΣMed. 9) told a story that 'Euripides transferred the murder of the children to Medea after receiving five talents from the Corinthians' – unlikely to be true, but it illustrates the spirit in which a poet earlier than Eur. could have done so.

[88] For the argument that the effect of the nurse's fears depends on the pre-existence of the version in which Medea deliberately kills her children, see Manuwald (1983) 43–6, but also Easterling (1977) 181.

[89] The woman's name is not given on the vases, except for one where the name is that of Theseus' mother Aethra. See Sourvinou-Inwood (1979) for an argument that the name is a mistake for Medea and for the theory that the sixth-century *Theseid* featured a wicked stepmother in this role and that Medea displaced this stepmother shortly after the Persian Wars (her further argument for Alcmeonid and Cimonian involvement in these mythic developments is much more doubtful).

both earlier and later in date than Eur.'s *Medea* show scenes in which
Medea seems to be influencing Aegeus to send his as-yet unrecog-
nized son against the bull of Marathon, with suggestions of poison as
a backup should the bull fail to kill Theseus.[90] This failed attempt on
Theseus' life was the subject-matter of Eur.'s own *Aegeus*, the date of
which is unknown.[91]

If any members of the original audience of *Medea* tried to fit the
hints in the Aegeus-scene together with what they knew of traditional
Attic stories of Theseus, they may not have been able to arrive at any
definite harmonious combination. Clearly, they would assume that
Aegeus is shortly to sleep with Aethra in the house of Pittheus (683n.),
and so Aethra will conceive Theseus (perhaps with the co-paternity
of Poseidon). But how would they speculate about Medea's understanding of the oracle about the wine-skin (679n.)? Does she see the
obvious meaning and conceal it from Aegeus, believing that he will
not have intercourse until he returns to his wife in Athens and hoping
to make him think that her drugs are essential when they are not? (In
this case, the clever Medea is ironically outwitted by the cleverer
Pittheus.) If the notion that Medea herself bore children to Aegeus
was prevalent in Athens, it might seem that she hopes to marry
Aegeus as soon as she gets to Athens, but Aegeus' statement that he
already has a wife in Athens militates against that assumption. A possible composite story might be that after the potency promised by the
oracle was used up·on Aethra, Aegeus' barren wife was eventually
discarded and replaced by Medea, who bore children and then tried
to protect their interests by plotting against Theseus when he arrived

[90] U. Kron, *LIMC* s.v. Aigeus. In the version presented in Callimachus'
*Hecale*, the poisoning attempt and recognition precede the exploit of the bull:
Hollis on fragments 3–7.

[91] Many have assumed that Eur.'s *Aegeus* was produced earlier than *Medea*.
But the grounds for believing this are insecure: (1) the allusiveness of the
Aegeus-scene in *Medea* (this might presuppose general knowledge rather than
a particular play, and Sophocles also wrote an *Aegeus*); (2) the strict metrical
style of the fragments (but there are too few to judge reliably); (3) Attic vase-
paintings with Medea's poisoning attempt dated to 450–430. See Jouan and
Van Looy (1998) 1–13; Cropp and Fick (1985) 71. Sophocles' play (date unknown) apparently contained some of the same elements as Eur.'s, but there is
no evidence of Medea in the meagre fragments.

years later. But few audience members would bother to push their inferences so far. The only thing that seems clear is that the notion of Medea as future threat to Theseus is evoked for the audience: perhaps it casts an ironic light on Medea's promise to Aegeus of future children and lends poignancy to Aegeus' generosity to Medea.[92]

When Medea predicts the manner of Jason's death in 1387 ('struck on your head with a remnant of the Argo'), we cannot determine exactly what story Eur. expected his audience to recognize from this allusion, or whether it is an *ad hoc* invention. One scholion on the passage mentions a version in which Jason died when the *akrostolion* (stern- or prow-ornament) of the Argo, dedicated to Hera, fell off the temple wall to which it had been attached and struck him. A comparable motif is seen in the story of the statue of Mitys (Arist. *Poetics* 1452a7–10): 'the man responsible for the death of Mitys was killed by the statue of Mitys in Argos when it fell on him while he was looking at it (*or* attending a festival)'. Staphylus of Naucratis, a Hellenistic writer active before 150 BCE, recorded another version: 'Jason was killed in a certain sense by Medea. For she urged him to go to sleep like this under the stern of the Argo, when the ship was about to collapse because of the passage of time. At any rate, when the stern fell on Jason, he died' (*FGrHist* 269 F 11 Jacoby, from the Hypothesis to *Medea*). A similar motif is found in the tale of a sleeping hunter killed by the head of a boar he had suspended from a tree as an impious dedication to himself (Diod. Sic. 4.22.3, Pfeiffer (1934) 15–17). Another scholion tells this story more briefly: 'when Jason was sleeping beneath the Argo, which had grown rotten with the long passage of time, a piece of it fell off and struck him on the head'.

Let us turn finally to those features of the plot that might be innovations. Here too there is little certainty to be attained.

(1) The visit of Aegeus to Corinth looks like an innovation of Attic drama, whether by Eur. or by Neophron (see next section):

---

[92] Less probable is the view of Burnett (1998) 224 n. 130, who argues that the story of Medea's attempt to poison Theseus need not have been known to the audience in 431. Sfyroeras (1994) argues that the evocation of Medea's stepmotherly attack on Theseus provides a parallel for Medea being turned by Jason and herself into a virtual stepmother to her own sons, paving the way for her to kill them.

the oracle to Aegeus and the story of the conception of Theseus at Troezen did not require such a detour. It may also be observed that the synchronization of Aegeus' oracular inquiry with Medea's crisis in Corinth implies a chronology in which Medea spends about 18 years in Athens before being expelled, whereas if this synchronization is not present, then Medea's time with Aegeus can be more vaguely defined and felt to be shorter.

(2) The motif of Jason's betrayal and remarriage could have been present in earlier versions in which Medea caused Creon's death, although one may imagine other circumstances for that violence (such as a threat from the king to Jason and Medea, or to Medea alone).[93] Any story involving betrayal through remarriage would necessarily have included the princess.

(3) The specific means of killing Creon and his daughter with a poisoned robe delivered by the children could be a new feature, exploiting a motif known from the myth of Deianeira and Heracles; but the incorporation of this motif could have occurred earlier as well.

(4) The escape in the flying chariot is probably an invention for the theatre, as it exploits a device and convention specific to the theatre. (On the question whether the crane-prop used by Eur. showed winged serpents see 1317n.).

We know that Eur. (like the other tragedians, and other Greek poets) modified and extended Greek legends with great freedom and creativity. One may cite the apparent invention of Polymestor as killer of Polydorus in *Hecuba*, Electra's marriage to a poor farmer in *Electra*, the transposition of Heracles' murder of Megara and their children to the end of his career in *Heracles*, the journey of Orestes to the land of the Taurians and Iphigeneia's return from there in *Iphigeneia in Tauris*. The poets made their innovations more satisfying and 'convincing' by interlocking them with mythic events and details known from previous sources. So in *Medea* the allusions to the Argonautic adventure and the death of Pelias root this particular plot in the framework of the tradition, and the allusions to Medea's future

[93] So von Fritz (1959) 38–9 suggests a version in which Medea kills Creon because the king wishes to respond to the hostility of the Corinthians to her personally by exiling her.

sojourn in Athens and to future cult-practice in the precinct of Hera Akraia in Perachora demonstrate to the audience that, whatever may be new or surprising in the plot itself, the enacted events allow for reinsertion into the tradition and are validated by some connection to the present-day world (see 1379–83n.).

If one believes that the Neophron fragments are post-Euripidean, then the hypothesis involving the maximum of invention on Eur.'s part would be as follows: Eur. invented the princess, the new marriage, the involvement of Aegeus, the means of killing the princess and Creon, the deliberate murder of the children, and the means of escape by flying chariot. But given the lacunose nature of the evidence, it is prudent not to have too much confidence in every detail of this hypothesis. And if the Neophron fragments are pre-Euripidean, then almost all of these apparent innovations are anticipated there.

## 5  NEOPHRON'S *MEDEA*

### *Testimonia*[94]

**A.** *Hypothesis Eur. Medeae* 25–7 Diggle (II.138, 8–10 Schwartz = *TrGF* 15 T 2, Aristotle fr. 635 Rose = fr. 774 Gigon, Dicaearchus fr. 63 Wehrli)

τὸ δρᾶμα δοκεῖ ὑποβαλέσθαι παρὰ **Νεόφρονος** διασκευάσας, ὡς Δικαίαρχος ⟨ἐν ...⟩ τοῦ τῆς Ἑλλάδος βίου καὶ Ἀριστοτέλης ἐν ὑπομνήμασι.

'Euripides seems to have passed off the drama as his own, taking it from Neophron with modifications, as Dicaearchus says ⟨in Book

---

[94] A new piece of evidence that may or may not be relevant to Neophron is provided by a papyrus to be published in the Oxyrhynchus Papyri by Dr Daniela Colomo. Through the kindness of Peter Parsons this much may be reported here: 'a rhetorical declamation ... describes Euripides correcting and reworking a *Medea* so as to eliminate the on-stage murder of the children'; it is unclear from the fragments who was said to be the author of the version being reworked; Neophron is not named in the surviving scraps, and the author draws a parallel to the two Hippolytus plays. (Murdering the children 'on stage' is of course attested in Seneca's *Medea*, and he may have derived it indirectly from a Greek tragedy other than Eur.'s.)

One?⟩ of *The Life of Greece* and Aristotle in his *Commentaries* (*Hypomnemata*).'

**B.** *Suda* ν 218 (= *TrGF* 15 T 1)

**Νεοφρῶν** ἢ Νεοφῶν, Σικυώνιος, τραγικός· οὗ φασιν εἶναι τὴν τοῦ Εὐριπίδου Μήδειαν· ὃς πρῶτος εἰσήγαγε παιδαγωγοὺς καὶ οἰκετῶν βάσανον. ἐδίδαξε δὲ τραγωιδίας ρκʹ.

'Neophron or Neophon: from Sicyon, an author of tragedy; the one whose work they say the *Medea* of Euripides is; the one who was first to introduce to tragedy pedagogues and interrogation of slaves under torture; he produced 120 tragedies.'

**C.** Diogenes Laertius, 3.134 (= *TrGF* 15 T 3)

ταῦτα δ' ἐστὶν Ἀχαιοῦ ἐκ τῆς σατυρικῆς Ὀμφάλης· ὥστε πταίουσιν οἱ λέγοντες μηδὲν αὐτὸν ἀνεγνωκέναι πλὴν τῆς Μηδείας τῆς Εὐριπίδου, ἣν ἔνιοι **Νεόφρονος** εἶναι τοῦ Σικυωνίου φασίν.

(in life of Menedemus of Eretria, *c.* 350–278) 'These verses are by Achaeus, from his satyr-play *Omphale*. So they are in error who claim that Menedemus read nothing except Euripides' *Medea*, which some people say is the work of Neophron of Sicyon.'

*Fragments*

**1.** Σ[B] *Med.* 666 (= *TrGF* 15 F 1)

λέγουσι τὸν Αἰγέα εἰς Τροιζῆνα ἐληλυθέναι διὰ τὸ δεδοικέναι πεζῆι ποιεῖσθαι τὴν πορείαν, Σίνιδος κατ' ἐκείνους τοὺς χώρους ἐπιπολάζοντος. **Νεόφρων** δὲ εἰς Κόρινθον τὸν Αἰγέα φησὶ παραγενέσθαι πρὸς Μήδειαν ἕνεκα τοῦ σαφηνισθῆναι αὐτῶι τὸν χρησμὸν ὑπ' αὐτῆς [τῆς Μηδείας], γράφων οὕτω·

καὶ γάρ τιν' αὐτὸς ἤλυθον λύσιν μαθεῖν
σοῦ· Πυθίαν γὰρ ὄσσαν, ἣν ἔχρησέ μοι
Φοίβου πρόμαντις, συμβαλεῖν ἀμηχανῶ·
σοὶ δ' εἰς λόγους μολὼν ἂν ἤλπιζον μαθεῖν ...

'They say Aegeus travelled to Troezen because he was afraid to make the journey (to Athens) by land, since Sinis was active in those regions. But Neophron says that Aegeus came to see Medea in order to receive clarification of the oracle from her; Neophron writes: "Indeed I myself have come to learn some solution from you. For I am at a loss to interpret the Pythian oracle that the prophetess of Phoebus gave to me. By coming to speak to you I hoped that I would learn ..."'

**2.** Stobaeus, *Anthology* 3.20.33 (section περὶ ὀργῆς, 'on wrath') (= *TrGF* 15 F 2) **Νεόφρονος** ἐν Μηδείαι·

εἶέν· τί δράσεις, θυμέ; βούλευσαι καλῶς
πρὶν ἐξαμαρτεῖν καὶ τὰ προσφιλέστατα
ἔχθιστα θέσθαι. ποῖ ποτ' ἐξῆιξας, τάλας;
κάτισχε λῆμα καὶ σθένος θεοστυγές.
καὶ πρὸς τί ταῦτα δύρομαι, ψυχὴν ἐμὴν                    5
ὁρῶσ' ἔρημον καὶ παρημελημένην
πρὸς ὧν ἐχρῆν ἥκιστα; μαλθακοὶ δὲ δὴ
τοιαῦτα γιγνόμεσθα πάσχοντες κακά;
οὐ μὴ προδώσεις, θυμέ, σαυτὸν ἐν κακοῖς;
οἴμοι, δέδοκται· παῖδες, ἐκτὸς ὀμμάτων                    10
ἀπέλθετ'· ἤδη γάρ με φοινία μέγαν
δέδυκε λύσσα θυμόν. ὦ χέρες χέρες,
πρὸς οἶον ἔργον ἐξοπλιζόμεσθα· φεῦ,
τάλαινα τόλμης, ἢ πολὺν πόνον βραχεῖ
διαφθεροῦσα τὸν ἐμὸν ἔρχομαι χρόνωι.                    15

'So then: what will you do, heart? Consider it well before you make a mistake and before you consider what is dearest to be most hateful. To what extreme have you rushed, wretched heart? Check your emotion and a violence hateful to the gods. – To what purpose am I lamenting like this, when I observe that my life is deserted and neglected by those by whom it ought least to be? Am I going to prove to be soft when suffering such wrongs? Don't betray yourself, my heart, amidst these sufferings. – Alas, the decision is made. Children, go into the house. For now already murderous madness has entered my great heart. Oh hands, hands, for what a deed we are arming ourselves! Alas, I am wretched for my daring, who now go to destroy my long toil in a short moment.'

**3.** Σ^B *Med.* 1386 (= *TrGF* 15 F 3)
οἱ μὲν λέγουσι κατὰ Μηδείας [χόλον ἢ] κέλευσιν ὑπὸ τῆι πρύμνηι τῆς Ἀργοῦς καταδαρθέντα τὸν Ἰάσονα τελευτῆσαι ἐμπεσόντος αὐτῶι

ξύλου. **Νεόφρων** δὲ ξενικώτερον ἀγχόνηι φησὶ τελευτῆσαι· τὴν γὰρ
Μήδειαν παράγει πρὸς αὐτὸν εἰποῦσαν·

> τέλος φθερεῖς γὰρ αὐτὸν αἰσχίστωι μόρωι,
> δέρηι βροχωτὸν ἀγχόνην ἐπισπάσας.
> τοία σε μοῖρα σῶν κακῶν ἔργων μένει,
> δίδαξις ἄλλοις μυρίας ἐφ' ἡμέρας
> θεῶν ὕπερθε μήποτ' αἴρεσθαι βροτούς.

'Some say that at Medea's command Jason fell asleep beneath the
stern of the Argo and died when a piece of wood fell on him. But
Neophron, in a rather strange version, says Jason died by hanging
himself. For he brings on Medea saying to Jason: "For in the end
you will destroy yourself in the most shameful death, tightening the
knotted noose around your neck. Such a portion awaits you from
your evil deeds, a lesson for other men for countless days that mortals
should never raise themselves above the gods."'

It is clear that in the scholarly literature of the fourth and third centuries BCE the claim was made that Eur.'s *Medea* was heavily dependent upon another *Medea* that was believed to have been written by a
tragic poet named Neophron (**A**). This scholarly claim is carelessly
(or maliciously) reflected in the statements that Eur.'s play is actually
Neophron's work (**B**, **C**). It is the claim made by **A** that requires
serious evaluation.

Dicaearchus was a student of Aristotle (who died in 322) and
Theophrastus (*c.* 371–*c.* 287). His own dates of activity cannot be
more precisely specified. He was later respected as a very learned
scholar, and he wrote on philosophical topics as well as publishing
scientific, philological, and biographical works. His *Life of Greece* was
a treatise in three books on cultural history, based on biographical
researches on the poets, thinkers, and other writers of the past.[95]
Aristotle's *Commentaries* was apparently a collection of miscellaneous
historical observations and is elsewhere referred to as 'Aristotle's or

---

[95] It is also relevant that he wrote a work 'On the myths of Sophocles and
Euripides': for the controversy over whether this work is or is not to be identified with the ancient epitomes (dubbed by some moderns 'Tales from Euripides') see Mastronarde, comm. on *Phoen.*, p. 140 n. 1.

Theophrastus' Commentaries';[96] the work is generally regarded as a collection of notes by members of the Peripatos that may or may not reflect ideas or statements of Aristotle or Theophrastus himself. Since serious data-collection and archival research went on in the Peripatetic School, a citation in this source deserves some respect, even if its author is not identifiable.

The *Suda* reports that Neophron wrote 120 dramas. Entries in the *Suda* similarly report 160 dramas for Choerilus, 50 for Pratinas, 70 for Aristarchus of Tegea. These numbers, like the numbers given in ancient sources for Aeschylus, Sophocles, and Eur., appear to be based on the collection of official didaskalic data that took place in the fourth century and that formed the basis of the datings found in dramatic hypotheses and on inscriptions (see *TrGF* 1 3–16, 22–31). Therefore, it should be taken as established that there was a fifth-century tragedian named Neophron who competed very often at the Dionysia. For a reputable scholar to argue for the influence of Neophron upon Eur., there must have been not only very striking similarities in plot and conception between two plays entitled *Medea*, but also some reason to think that Eur.'s play came later than the other. It is a likely inference, therefore, that the didaskalic lists contained an entry for a *Medea* of Neophron in a year earlier than 431. Since there are such similarities between our fragments 1–3 and Eur., we may plausibly assume that Dicaearchus was indeed looking at the play from which these fragments come.[97] If these are actually from the fifth-century play, then we must accept that (1) the deliberate murder of the children by their mother was known or invented before Eur. treated the story in 431; (2) the connection of Aegeus to the critical events of Medea's departure from Corinth was also a pre-existing feature; (3) the whole conception of Medea as determined on revenge

[96] See Rose (1863) 561–3, and Aristotle fr. 631 Rose = fr. 772 Gigon (Athenaeus 173e–f), fr. 632 Rose = fr. 991 Gigon (654b–d). Gigon (1987) 214 notes that in cases of such alternative authorship the less 'spectacular' name is the more likely to be true.

[97] One may consider the possibility that the claim of borrowing or adaptation was based on a slander in comedy taken as historical truth. A number of ancient writers were guilty of such gullibility. But Dicaearchus seems to have been a scholar of higher quality.

but torn by her maternal feelings had been anticipated, at the minimum, by one earlier author.

The weakest link in the evidence is the identification of the play from which fragments 1–3 are drawn as the *Medea* of Neophron that was, on this reconstruction, recorded in the didaskalic lists before 431. For it is possible that the *Medea* on which Dicaearchus based his conclusion and from which our fragments come was not in fact a play written by Neophron earlier than 431, but a post-Euripidean play wrongly (or fraudulently) labelled as the work of Neophron.[98] There are three types of argument that have induced many to embrace this possibility.[99]

(1) The reputation of a classic author like Eur. creates among scholars an almost unconscious assumption of creativity and superiority. It is all too easy to assume that the process of canon-formation that led to the study and partial survival of the works of Aeschylus, Sophocles, and Eur. correctly winnowed out as inferior the work of other authors. Eur. himself is generally regarded as an innovator, so that scholars have been ready to assume that many mythical combinations and variants were his own invention, even though so much of the evidence for earlier versions is lost to us. It is in fact extremely unlikely that there were no plays at all written by other authors that approached the interest and quality of works of the great three. Moreover, it is likely that some assumptions about Euripidean originality are unjustified.[100]

(2) In studying variant sources, it is a common method to assess the probabilities of sequence and descent. One asks which version is

[98] On problems of attribution of works in the fourth century and in Alexandria, see Griffith (1977) 232–45.

[99] On the other side of the debate, some believe that *Medea* requires only two actors (unlike any other surviving tragedy of Eur., if we exclude *Alcestis* as 'prosatyric'; but that seems an arbitrary exclusion in this regard). They suggest that this is a result of imitating an older play from the time when two-actor plays were prevalent. It seems, however, that three actors are actually required in 96–105 (see section 3 above and 89n.), and one cannot assume in any case that the roles were played by two actors instead of three.

[100] Note the case of the survival of Jocasta in *Phoenissae* and her attempt to reconcile her quarrelling sons: Stesichorus' *Thebaid* (*PMGF* fr. 222b) shows that the reconciliation attempt is not wholly new and that Jocasta's survival might not be either (the name of the mother is not extant in the fragments): Mastronarde on *Phoen.*, pp. 25–6.

more likely to be the extension of or reaction to the other. The falli-
bility or inconclusiveness of this method is amply demonstrated by
the long debate over the chronological sequence of the *Electra*s of
Sophocles and Eur. Nevertheless, most critics have felt that the provision of an explicit motivation for Aegeus' arrival in fr. 1 is easily
understood as a reaction to Eur.'s lack of the same, especially if there
was in fact criticism of Eur. on this point in his lifetime or in the
fourth century (663–823n.). And fr. 2 may be seen as a shortened
version of Medea's monologue in Eur., depending for its effect on its
allusion to the fuller scene, but declining to imitate it too closely or at
equal length.[101] Indeed, if fr. 2 is post-Euripidean, one may detect
many allusions to Eur.'s play, and not just to the famous monologue
of Medea (line numbers in bold refer to Neophron): **1, 9** address to
θυμέ ∼ 1056; **2–3** τὰ προσφιλέστατα | ἔχθιστα θέσθαι ∼ 16 νῦν δ᾽
ἐχθρὰ πάντα καὶ νοσεῖ τὰ φίλτατα, 572–3 τὰ λῶιστα καὶ κάλλιστα
πολεμιώτατα | τίθεσθε; **3** τάλας ∼ 1057 τάλαν; **8–9** μαλθακοὶ ...
γιγνόμεσθα ∼ 1052 τὸ καὶ προσέσθαι μαλθακοὺς λόγους φρενί, 1246
μὴ κακισθῆις; **10** οἴμοι, δέδοκται ∼ 1236 φίλαι, δέδοκται τοὔργον; **13**
πρὸς οἷον ἔργον ἐξοπλιζόμεσθα ∼ 1242 ἀλλ᾽ εἶ᾽ ὁπλίζου, καρδία; **14**
τάλαινα τόλμης ∼ 1028 ὦ δυστάλαινα τῆς ἐμῆς αὐθαδίας; **13–14**
πολὺν πόνον ... διαφθεροῦσα τὸν ἐμόν ∼ 1029–31 ἄλλως ἄρ᾽ ὑμᾶς,
ὦ τέκν᾽, ἐξεθρεψάμην, | ἄλλως δ᾽ ἐμόχθουν καὶ κατεξάνθην πόνοις |
στερρὰς ἐνεγκοῦσ᾽ ἐν τόκοις ἀλγηδόνας.

(3) Page listed a number of linguistic and stylistic features of
fragments 1 and 2 that he judged unlikely to be found in a tragedy
written before 431. Thompson (1944) argued against Page's claims,
and there is in fact too little comparative evidence for tragic authors
other than Eur. and Sophocles for them to be cogent.[102]

---

[101] Michelini (1989) argues that in the monologue Eur. modified the simplicity of Neophron to his own technique of exaggeration and paradox and
that in his less motivated use of Aegeus Eur. deliberately emphasizes the surprise and arbitrariness of the end of the play.

[102] The story of the Corinthians' payment to Eur. for transferring the
blame for the children's deaths to Medea (ΣMed. 9) has as its premise the notion that Eur. was the first to do this. But it would be imprudent to rely on the
inventors of such an anecdote to guarantee either that Eur. really invented
the deliberate infanticide or that the Neophron fragments are post-Euripidean.
In later times, Eur.'s treatment was the famous one, and both the inventors of
the anecdote and its intended audience would not have been experts on literature outside the canon.

In conclusion, the evidence does not support a dogmatic conclusion and disagreement will no doubt continue. On the balance of probabilities, however, it seems more likely that the fragments ascribed to Neophron come from a post-Euripidean play.

## 6  MEDEA AFTER EURIPIDES AND THE INFLUENCE OF HIS *MEDEA*

Whether or not Eur. was preceded by any other poet (Neophron or unknown) in his depiction of Medea as the deliberate murderer of her children, it was evidently the growing authority of his depiction in the decades after his death that exercised the decisive influence on post-classical imaginings of Medea's character and of her most famous action. In the literary realm, *Medea* was a popular title for tragedies and comedies of the late fifth and the fourth centuries, and this may be due to the fame of Eur.'s play. But there are two reasons for caution. First, plays with this title are already ascribed to Epicharmus and Deinolochus, authors of Sicilian comedy who were active in the first half of the fifth century, decades before Eur.'s production. Second, the fragments or testimonia are so spare that we often cannot be sure whether such plays handled the Corinthian episode of Medea's life or her famous actions in Iolcus or Athens (where Eur.'s lost *Peliades* and *Aegeus*, or other plays, may have been influential). Of other fifth-century tragedians, a *Medea* is ascribed to another Eur. (*TrGF* 17) and Melanthius (*TrGF* 23) and the apparently fifth-century Neophron (see previous section); in the fourth century Dicaeogenes (*TrGF* 52), Carcinus II (*TrGF* 70), Theodorides (*TrGF* 78A), and Diogenes (or Philiscus) (*TrGF* 88) wrote under this title, as did later the undated Biotus (*TrGF* 205). If the fragments ascribed to Neophron are really post-Euripidean, they are probably from the fourth century. The close similarity of fr. 2 to Eur.'s play implies the fame and probably also the currency in performance of the older play in the fourth century, and the changed motivation of Aegeus' entry may perhaps attest to critical discussion of Eur.'s technique (see 663–823n.). Another fourth-century play (or the play of one of the authors named above) is presumably the source of the famous Apulian crater discussed below as no. (4) (cf. *TrGF* adesp. 6a). Finally, papyrus fragments of a play involving Medea, Jason, Creon, and a chorus of

Corinthian women may also be from a fourth-century tragedy (*CGFPR* dubia 350).[103]

Among comic treatments, the early examples by Epicharmus (test. 35 and p. 55 K–A) and Deinolochus (test. 3 and frr. 4–5 K–A) have been mentioned, and later in the tradition of Doric comedy the same title is found for Rhinthon (third century: fr. 7 K–A). The attested authors of *Medea* plays in Attic Old and Middle Comedy are Cantharus (late fifth century: fr. 1–4 K–A), Strattis (active end of fifth century into fourth: frr. 34–6 K–A), and in the fourth century Antiphanes (fr. 151 K–A) and Eubulus (fr. 64 K–A = fr. 64 Hunter). Strattis fr. 34 mentions gifts to a bride and so it is likely that this comedy exploited Eur.'s tragedy. A similar inference has been made from the mention of two kinds of chiton in Antiphanes fr. 151, but this is much less secure. The fragments of Cantharus and Eubulus are unrevealing.[104]

Roman tragedians also treated the theme. Some fragments of Ennius' *Medea exul* show an extremely close adaptation of Eur., and he wrote another *Medea* which took place in Athens and could have followed Eur.'s *Aegeus*.[105] Accius' *Medea*, however, took place in Colchis and had the alternative title *Argonautica* (*TrRF*, pp. 216–20). The later Roman versions may never have been performed as theatrical pieces, but still attest to the vogue of this classic story. Ovid's *Medea* met with great approval, but is lost to us (Quintilian 10.1.98, Tacitus *Dial.* 12.6). Seneca's *Medea* survives, but two or three others also from the first century CE are lost: those of Lucan (unfinished, according to Suet. *vita Lucani*), Curatius Maternus (Tac. *Dial.* 3.4), and perhaps Bassus (Martial 5.53.1: *Colchida quid scribis, quid scribis, amice, Thyesten?*).

By the late fourth century BCE, then, and probably somewhat earlier, Eur.'s treatment was a 'classic',[106] both the starting-point for adaptation or variation and the shared background that poets as-

---

[103] For the ascription to tragedy rather than satyr-play or comedy, as some have suggested, see Hunter (1981).

[104] For ingenious speculation connecting the Eubulus fragment to parody of Eur.'s *Medea*, see Schiassi (1955) 114.

[105] See Jocelyn's commentary on Ennius frr. CIII–CXVI.

[106] Hunter on Eubulus' *Medea* cites the casual quotation of famous lines from Euripides' play in Philemon fr. 82.1 K–A (*Med.* 57) and Machon 173, 407 Gow (*Med.* 1358, 1346).

sumed in most of their readers. Thus Apollonius' portrayal of both
Medea and Jason is to be read with the tragic Euripidean future
in mind,[107] and Ovid's *Epist. Heroidum* 12 likewise exploits the cul-
tured reader's familiarity with Eur.[108] Medea's vacillation between
maternal feelings and impulse for revenge was the feature of the
play that most impressed philosophers from the Stoic Chrysippus
onward, who quoted lines 1078–9 and analysed Medea's ethical
failure.[109]

The iconographic tradition tells a similar story of the development of 'classic' status for Eur.'s treatment.[110] Before Eur., illustrations of Medea in vase-painting relate to her magical actions in Colchis or Iolcus or her threat to Theseus in Athens. For the Corinthian
episode, there are no Attic vase-paintings either before or after the
production of 431 BCE. Some see this as indicative of the lack of success of Eur.'s play in Athens, others as not unexpected in view of the
rarity of fifth-century Attic vases that definitely can be tied to theatrical inspiration. But vases produced in South Italy from *c.* 400 onward show a pronounced openness to inspiration from the stories
featured in Attic tragedies, *Medea* among them.[111] In vase-paintings
theatrical inspiration may be inferred from the incidents portrayed
and the way figures are dressed, but the painters have their own way
of presenting a story synoptically, by inclusion of more characters
in one scene and by the interpretive addition of divine figures observing or guiding the action. The most telling examples involving
Medea herself are the following:

(1)  Policoro hydria, Museo Nazionale 35296, *c.* 400 [*LIMC* no. 35;
Taplin (1993) pl. 2.103]: Medea in foreign costume (ornate robe and
Phrygian cap) aloft in a chariot drawn by serpents, and below, the

---

[107]  See Hunter's comm. on Book 3, pp. 18–19.

[108]  See Bessone (1997). In addition, the first half of Book 7 of *Metamorphoses*
presents most incidents of Medea's life, but the episode at Corinth is abbre-
viated to only four lines (7.394–7).

[109]  See Appendix.

[110]  For previous and more detailed discussions, see Page's comm., pp.
lvii–lxviii; Séchan (1926) 396–421; Simon (1954); and M. Schmidt, *LIMC* s.v.
Medeia.

[111]  Taplin (1993) 6–8, 21–9; Simon (1954).

bodies of her children, mourned by a kneeling figure (the tutor), and Jason with drawn sword; at either side, Aphrodite[112] and Eros.

(2) Cleveland calyx-crater, Cleveland Museum of Art 91.1, *c.* 400 [*LIMC* no. 36 = Taplin (1993) pl. 1.101]: Medea in foreign costume (ornate robe and Phrygian cap) aloft in a chariot drawn by serpents (all within a nimbus of sun-rays), with a demon to either side; below the bodies of her children on an altar, mourned by an old woman and a man (the nurse and tutor), and Jason looking up.

(3) Naples amphora, Museo Nazionale 81954 (H 3221), *c.* 340 [*LIMC* no. 37]: Medea in Greek costume in a chariot drawn by serpents, with one child's body on the floor of the chariot, the other on the ground below; a fire-bearing demon in front of the chariot, between it and Selene; to the left, young men pursuing, one on horseback, two on foot.

(4) St Petersburg bell-crater, Hermitage Б 2083, second half of fourth century [*LIMC* no. 39]: Medea in Greek dress in a chariot drawn by serpents, holding the body of one child in each arm.

In (1)–(3), the correspondence to Eur. is inexact (body or bodies left behind, mourning figure(s); serpents unmentioned in the text – 1317n.), and this divergence may be due to the creativity of the painter (for compositional or iconographic reasons, or to give a more synoptic view of the event and its effects) or to inspiration by a different play (probably modelled on Eur.'s).[113] Nevertheless, theatrical inspiration seems secure because of the appearance of the chariot, not earlier associated with Medea. (4), in contrast, is easily taken as an illustration of Eur.'s own finale, or at least of a finale that followed his faithfully.

(5) Munich volute crater, Antikensammlung 3296 (J 810), *c.* 330 [*LIMC* no. 29]: in an upper band Creon clutching his dying daughter (collapsed on a throne) and other characters mourning or running to

---

[112] Less plausibly, this figure with a mirror is identified as the princess-bride in *LIMC* s.v. Kreousa II, no. 24 (Berger-Doer).

[113] Taplin (1993) 22–3 suggests as another possibility that the placement of the bodies might reflect a local staging of Eur.'s play in which his intention was overridden (for practical reasons). This seems less likely.

help;[114] in a lower band Medea in foreign costume about to stab one son while a serpent-drawn chariot steered by the demon Oistros (Frenzy) awaits her, and to the left a young armed man shields the eyes of the other son and apparently guides him away to safety,[115] and to the right the ghost of Aeetes looks on. The relation of this depiction to Eur.'s play has long been debated, but it seems clear that the painter was inspired by a treatment that was modelled on Euripides but introduced significant variations and complications (*TrGF* adesp. 6a).

(6) Paris rope-handled amphora, Cab. Méd. 876, *c.* 330 [*LIMC* no. 30]: Medea in foreign costume, reaching back to restrain a fleeing son by grasping his hair, while the other son already lies dead on an altar to her right, and with the mourning tutor at upper right.

(7) Paris rope-handled amphora, Louvre κ 300, *c.* 330 [*LIMC* no. 31]: Medea in Greek costume stabbing one son before a colonnade and a column topped with a statue of a god.[116]

All three of these, (5)–(7), show a quasi-theatrical interest in the moments of violence (though these would presumably have been

---

[114] There are one or two earlier depictions of the princess that do not include Medea. The definite case is a Naples crater, Museo Nazionale sa 526, *c.* 360–350 [*LIMC* s.v. Kreousa ii, no. 16]: the girl has slipped from her throne and struggles to remove her crown as the first flames appear; the pedagogue guides the children away, an Erinys looks on, Creon rushes toward his daughter, and a distraught woman (the mother?) runs away; also shown are the chest in which the gifts arrived and a mirror. This surely derives from Eur.'s version or a version very similar to it. The doubtful case is a Paris bell-crater, Louvre ca 2193, *c.* 390 [*LIMC* no. 1], which shows a robe being presented to a young bride by a female slave (who also holds a small chest) as an older man with a sceptre watches on the left (her father?) and a pensive or worried slave (pedagogue?) on the right. The stance and pensiveness of the figures suggest that the viewer was expected to supply the tragic story of the princess' death, and that story apparently owed its fame to Eur.

[115] M. Schmidt in *LIMC* s.v. Medeia (vi 1.396) speculates that this depiction need not entail that the second son escaped, but that the young man's gesture may simply be a solution to the problem of what to do with the other son while Medea is killing the first son. This is an unnecessary hypothesis.

[116] The god has been identified as Apollo, who has no connection to the story in the known versions. Theoretically, this could be some other child-killer, but the existence of other stabbing Medeas in fourth-century vase-paintings favours the hypothesis that this too is Medea.

narrated and not seen on stage in a tragedy).[117] The last two in particular point to the distillation of Medea's action to the horrible
moment of killing her children. The vase-painters do not, however,
respond to, or do not try to express, Medea's anguished indecision
before the deed. But just as her debate with herself became a topos
for Hellenistic and later philosophers, a Hellenistic painter in another medium seems to have depicted this effectively, and this lost
work is assumed to be the ultimate source of one type of the wall-
paintings from Pompeii that show Medea in a thoughtful pose, usually with the children nearby (*LIMC* nos. 7–14).[118] These are not so
much illustrations of Medea's monologue as depictions in purely visual form of the idea of her hesitation or anguish.

Since the re-emergence of Greek tragedy in the Renaissance,
*Medea* has inspired adaptations in stage-drama, opera, film, and the
visual arts.[119] Among stage versions by writers of some fame may be
mentioned Pierre Corneille's *Médée* of 1635, Franz Grillparzer's *Das
goldene Vliess* of 1821 (the third play of this trilogy is entitled *Medea* and
covers the Corinthian episode), Jean Anouilh's *Médée* of 1946 (first
performed in 1948 in Germany[120] and 1953 in France), and Robinson
Jeffers' *Medea* of 1947. Notable films inspired by the Medea story and
Eur. in particular are Pier Paolo Pasolini's *Medea* of 1969–70 and

---

[117] See, however, above n. 94, for the possibility of showing the murders
on stage.

[118] The type with standing Medea (and hands tensely intertwined) is believed to derive from an original of the third century; there is also a type with
Medea sitting. A famous Medea-painting by Timomachus of Byzantium was
purchased for a large price by Julius Caesar, and this painting inspired a
number of epigrams: see Gow and Page (1968) II 43–4 on Antipater 29. Pliny
(35.136) makes Timomachus a contemporary of Caesar, probably rightly,
while some scholars have wished to make him the master of the assumed
third-century original.

[119] For a lengthy tabulation see Reid (1993) II 643–50 s.v. Medea: the
treatments earlier than the mid-sixteenth century (when translations of Eur.
first became available) are inspired by Latin sources, especially Ovid.

[120] Reported by Simon (1954) 223 n. 4 ('der Erstaufführung von Anouilhs
Medea am 7. 11. 1948 in Heidelberg'), but not listed in Hall, Macintosh, and
Taplin (2000) 245–6. An English translation of Anouilh's play is printed in
J. L. Sanderson and E. Zimmerman, eds., *Medea: myth and dramatic form* (Boston
1967).

Jules Dassin's *A Dream of Passion* of 1978.[121] Mention may also be made of the 1996 novel *Medea* by the (East) German author Christa Wolf.[122] These and other adaptations attest to the enduring fascination of the classic story and usefully highlight the differences of the Euripidean version. Later authors often modify the motivations of both Medea and Jason, rendering them either more or less sympathetic. Moreover, as already in the Senecan version, ethnic difference is usually accentuated more forcefully than in Eur., and there is much more reference to the details of past events, which are to be read as indicators and determinants of present attitudes and actions. By contrast, Eur.'s play is noteworthy for the sparseness and indeterminacy of information about the past and leaves a more difficult and open-ended process of interpretation for its audience.[123]

## 7  THE TEXT

During the final decades of Euripides' career, copies of plays written on papyrus rolls were available not only to professionals working in theatrical production but also to a few interested amateurs (Ar. *Frogs* 52–3). As a book-based culture became better established in the fourth century, readers' copies became more prevalent, but the transmission was also affected by the copies used by troupes of actors, as is clear from the presence of additions to the text ('interpolations') that can plausibly be ascribed to actors.[124] Around 330, official copies of the works of Aeschylus, Sophocles, and Eur. were assembled in the Athenian state archives (Plutarch, *Mor.* 841F), and a story was told that about a century later Ptolemy III Euergetes (who ruled 247–221) borrowed these copies for his Alexandrian library and did not return them, instead forfeiting his deposit and sending back newly-made transcriptions (Galen 17a:607–8 Kühn = *CMG* 5:10:2:1.78–80).[125] It is

---

[121] See McDonald (1983) chs. 1–2.

[122] Translated by John Cullen as *Medea: a modern retelling* (New York 1998).

[123] On modern variations on the Medea story, see von Fritz (1959), Friedrich (1968), Dihle (1976) and (1977), Mimoso-Ruiz (1982), Caiazza (1989–93), McDonald (1992) and (1997), Kerrigan (1996), and esp. Hall, Macintosh, and Taplin (2000) with ample additional bibliography.

[124] Page (1934); Mastronarde on *Phoen.*, pp. 39–49.

[125] Fraser (1972) I 325; Pfeiffer (1968) 82.

unknowable how good the Athenian state copies were, whether the story in Galen is true, and (if true) how important these copies were to the subsequent textual tradition. In the fourth century Aristotle and his pupils studied tragedy extensively, and Hellenistic scholars followed their lead, cataloguing and writing commentaries and producing 'editions' based on comparison of a number of copies.[126]

The earliest books had almost no lectional aids: no space between words, no consistent punctuation, no explicit identification of the speakers (changes of speaker were marked with dots and horizontal strokes). The lyrics might have been written out with each stanza as one long paragraph. Aristophanes of Byzantium, active in the early second century, is credited with arranging the lyric passages in shorter lines – an arrangement that was transmitted thereafter with little change and thus forms the basis of the lyric layout in modern editions.[127] After the second century BCE copies of tragedies generally presented the form of text given authority by the Alexandrian scholars (which included doublets and lines judged by them to be of doubtful authenticity), but further corruption occurred in transmission, and additional 'interpolations' entered the text through the activities of readers and teachers, and possibly actors as well.

Between 200 and 400 CE tragedies, like other genres of classical literature, were assembled into collections that fit conveniently in codices (bound volumes of folded sheets), replacing transmission in rolls containing one play each. We have no idea who made the selections that survive and on exactly what grounds. Probably such factors as popularity in the educational system and with readers, availability of helpful annotations, and currency in the repertory of

[126] For fuller treatments of the history of tragic texts, see Barrett's edition of *Hippolytus*, 45–57, and Griffith (1977) 226–34.

[127] But it is not certain whether Aristophanes really deserves the credit. Although no early papyrus of tragedy has been identified that contains the familiar layout of lyric cola (and the Strasbourg papyrus of Euripidean lyrics, like the famous Timotheus papyrus, shows the absence of such layout), the lyrics of the Lille Stesichorus are set out in that way, apparently prior to the career of Aristophanes of Byzantium (see Turner (1987) plate 74 with discussion).

performers played a role.[128] For Eur. this selection included ten plays, one of which was *Medea*. During late antiquity and the early Byzantine period, excerpts from pre-existing separate commentaries were compiled in the margins of the pages of codices, and these annotations are the scholia (or *scholia vetera*, so called to distinguish them from revised, expanded, and added notes written in the thirteenth and fourteenth centuries).[129] In the medieval manuscripts short notes and definitions or synonyms (glosses) are often written between the lines in addition to the marginal annotation.

Whereas for Aeschylus and Sophocles we are limited to selections of seven plays, for Eur., by good fortune, we have nine additional complete plays to go with the selection of ten, because a portion of a complete collection of his plays in alphabetical order also survived to be copied in medieval times. Of the select plays of Eur., the three most frequently read and studied in Byzantine times (*Hecuba*, *Orestes*, *Phoenissae*) are transmitted in 100–350 handwritten copies dating from the tenth century to the sixteenth. The other plays of the selection survive in many fewer copies. For *Medea*, the 13 manuscripts that are not simply copies of other surviving manuscripts have been carefully studied by Diggle (1983), and reliable information about their readings may be found in his Oxford Classical Text (vol. 1 of 1984). The manuscripts fall into two groups, with H and B (the two oldest) joined by most of the others on one side, and L and P on the other. Medieval copyists and readers frequently compared texts with each other and so the tradition is characterized by contamination, that is, readings are shared 'horizontally' from one complete copy to another complete copy as well as 'vertically' from an exemplar to a new copy made from it, so that affiliations between surviving witnesses are inconsistent or impossible to establish and good readings may occasionally survive in isolation even in later copies. For *Medea* there are also over a dozen papyrus fragments dating from the third century

---

[128] See Easterling (1997b) 224–6. On the process of formation of corpora in late antiquity see Cavallo (1989). The speculations reported in Blanchard (1989b) about the formation of the selections of the dramatists are to be regarded with extreme scepticism.

[129] The *scholia vetera* of Eur. are published in E. Schwartz, *Scholia in Euripidem* (Berlin 1887–91); the scholia on *Medea* are in his vol. II, 137–213.

ʙᴄᴇ to the sixth century ᴄᴇ that give us glimpses of the text. In addition, quotations in ancient authors (testimonia) occasionally provide
variant readings of interest (as in 1078).

The text adopted here differs from the Oxford Classical Text of
Diggle in the following places: 5 ἀρίστων, 12 φυγὰς πολίταις, 43 line
retained, 106 δ᾽ ἀρχῆς, 159 εὐνάταν, 320 σοφός, 334 no obeli, 355–6
lines retained, 444 τῶν τε, 474 σε unemphatic, 549 σοὶ emphatic, 600
μετεύξηι (with question mark), 777 ταὐτὰ καὶ καλῶς γαμεῖ, 838 μετρίους, 850 μετ᾽ ἄλλων, 890 χρή, 910 obeli for last word only, 938
ἀπαίρομεν, 1012 κατηφεῖς, 1037 τ᾽ ἀεί, 1077 πρὸς σφᾶς, 1056–80 retained (but 1062–3 deleted), 1218 ἀπέστη, 1221 line retained, with
obeli, 1243 μὴ οὐ, 1316 line retained, 1359 line retained. In addition,
there are minor differences in punctuation or orthography in the
following lines: 37, 104, 120, 223, 380, 401, 414, 434, 452, 466, 496,
579, 581, 585, 678, 679, 820, 927, 933, 1084, 1111, 1214, 1242, 1259,
1280, 1353.

# STRUCTURAL ELEMENTS OF
# GREEK TRAGEDY

*1   Lyric vs dialogue and the registers of tragic utterance*

The alternation of song and speech was basic to the genre of tragedy
from its inception. The contrast between sung lyric metres and
spoken metres (iambic trimeter, or occasionally trochaic tetrameter)
parallels to a large extent the contrast between chorus and actor(s),
but crossover does occur. The head-man of the chorus (*koryphaios*)
speaks iambic trimeters, sometimes in a short dialogue with an actor
(as *Med.* 811–19) and sometimes (esp. in couplets) as a pause or articulation after a long speech by an actor (as *Med.* 520–1, 576–8, 906–7,
1231–2). On a few occasions, other individual members of the chorus
speak iambic lines to indicate indecision (as in Aesch. *Ag.* 1346–71,
Eur. *Hipp.* 782–5). Actors sometimes sing either short exclamatory
lyrics (as Medea in 96–167) or an extended aria (as Hippolytus in
*Hipp.* 1347–88). A lyric exchange or lyric dialogue (*amoibaion*) may
involve two actors or the actor(s) and chorus. Both participants in
such an exchange may be lyric voices (esp. in a *kommos*, a quasi-ritual
lament, as at the end of Aesch. *Pers.*), or one voice may be confined to
iambic trimeter to provide a calmer counterpoint to the emotion expressed in the other voice's lyrics (as Soph. *Ant.* 1261–1346; Eur. *IT*
827–99, *Helen* 625–97). Sometimes the relative emotional levels of
the two voices vary during the scene, as Aesch. *Ag.* 1072–1177 (where
Cassandra's emotion infects the chorus), 1406–1576 (where Clytemnestra first responds in trimeters, then joins in the lyrics). A similar
contrast of registers is conveyed in the juxtaposition of Medea's
singing with the nurse's chanting in *Med.* 96–172.

The main dialogue metre is the iambic trimeter, discussed below
in PM 16–20. In some plays, trochaic tetrameters function as a byform of dialogue. This metre is based on a fifteen-syllable pattern
that is closely similar in rhythm to the shorter, twelve-syllable pattern
of the iambic trimeter. Trochaic tetrameters seem to have been used
frequently in early tragedy (some blocks of dialogue in Aesch. *Pers.*

are in tetrameters: 155–75, 215–48, 697–758), then were very little used in the mature period of tragedy, and were revived in many plays of Eur.'s last decade. In ethos the tetrameter was regarded as more dance-like and potentially less serious; it often accompanies more agitated action or emotion than is found in adjacent iambic scenes.

Another metre that may express an emotional register between the level of spoken trimeters and sung lyric is 'marching' anapaests, discussed below in PM 22. In *Medea* these are used by actors: by the nurse both in response to Medea's (lyric) cries from within in the scene leading up to the entrance of the chorus and in her exchange with the chorus; and by Jason and Medea in their final expostulations and insults. Sometimes anapaests chanted by a chorus serve as a long prelude to an entrance-lyric (Aesch. *Ag.* 40–103) or as a short prelude or transitional form leading to choral song (Aesch. *Ag.* 355–66), or announce an entrance at the end of a choral song (Aesch. *Ag.* 783–809). In *Medea* brief choral anapaestic passages accompany the departure of Creon and Aegeus from the stage (358–63, 759–63), and an extended anapaestic interlude serves in place of an act-dividing lyric at 1081–1115. At the end of a play, a transition to anapaests often provides a modulation in pace and rhythm to accent the conclusion of the play.

Formally, the lyric portions of the plays, particularly choral songs, are normally written in *antistrophic composition*. That is, stanzas are grouped in pairs (each pair being of unique form): the first stanza of a pair is called a *strophe*, the corresponding stanza with the same metrical pattern is called the *antistrophe*. It is unfortunately uncertain how the dance movements accompanying a strophe and antistrophe corresponded or contrasted with each other. The number of pairs is variable, but in mature tragedy the majority of choral songs have two or three pairs (the stasimons of *Medea* all have two pairs). Usually the antistrophe follows immediately after its strophe, but occasionally a short stanza called a *mesode* appears in between, or responsion occurs over a distance (as with *Hipp.* 362–72 = 669–79), or some unusual order occurs (as in the kommos in Aesch. *Cho.*). Sometimes a choral ode will end with an additional stanza not in correspondence (not paired), called an *epode* (*Med.* 205–12 is formally an epode).

## 2   *Divisions of a play*

The basic structure of a tragedy may be viewed as one of acts and act-dividing songs, the beginning of a new act normally being apparent from the entry of a new character after a song.[1] There is also a traditional terminology that has been used since antiquity in the description of Greek plays.

*Prologue*: in its wider sense, the part of the play preceding the entry of the chorus, usually two scenes (sometimes three, rarely one). The first of these scenes may be a *prologue-monologue* (or prologue in its narrower sense), especially common in Eur. and rare in Sophocles. The monologue-speaker may be a god, a minor character, or a (the) major character. Such a speaker normally addresses the audience more or less directly (though not quite so informally as in comedy, and full dramatic illusion does not take hold until the conclusion of the speech. In a few plays there are no prologue-scenes and the exposition begins immediately with the entrance of the chorus (Aesch. *Pers.*).

*Parodos*: entry of the chorus and the name of the song they sing as they enter (or of the chanted anapaests plus following song). Often the chorus enters with the stage empty of actors, but in some plays an actor is present and may or may not be acknowledged in their song. In *Medea* and in several late fifth-century tragedies, the parodos takes the form of an amoibaion involving the actor(s).

*Episode*: the scene(s) between the parodos and the first act-dividing song or between two act-dividing songs. In fifth-century tragedy the length and the number of episodes vary with considerable freedom. During the fourth century the structure of five dialogue-acts (μέρη, 'parts') divided by four choral interludes (including what had been called the parodos) apparently became standard: it can be seen in Menander's comedies (since New Comedy apparently assimilated its structure to that of fourth-century tragedy) and in the Hellenistic literary theory reflected in Horace, *Ars Poetica* 189–90. An episode may contain lyric elements such as aria or amoibaion as well as dialogue-scenes.

*Stasimon*: any extended song of the chorus after the parodos; al-

[1]  See Taplin (1977).

most always in antistrophic form. The stasimons tend to get shorter as the play proceeds. In late fifth-century tragedy, with the diminution of the dramatic weight of the chorus, the interval between stasimons is sometimes very long, and the number of true antistrophic stasimons may be small (as in Eur. *Helen*, Soph. *Phil.*).

*Exodos*: the scene(s) following the final stasimon. In many plays of Eur. (and in Soph. *Phil.*) there is a divine epiphany in the exodos, with the god appearing on the crane (Introd. 3) or emerging on the *skēnē*-roof from below. Medea's appearance on a winged chariot exploits this convention in a striking way (1293–1419n.).[2]

### 3  Formal elements of dialogue-scenes

#### a. Extended speeches

*Rhesis*: a rhesis is an extended speech in trimeters (or, rarely, tetrameters), often formally organized in its rhetoric. Long speeches are always dramatically noteworthy and may serve a variety of functions: self-justification, revelation of values and character, persuasion, invective, lamentation, bidding farewell, reviewing one's life and misfortune, critique of the conditions of society or human life, etc. In *Medea* Eur. gives Medea a remarkable series of speeches, climaxing in the great speech expressing her divided impulses (1021–80). Two special varieties of extended rhesis deserve attention:

*Agōn logōn*: the 'contest of speeches' is a recognizable form in both Sophocles and Eur. Generally, there are two speeches, each followed by a couplet from the koryphaios. The two debaters may be performing in front of a third actor who serves more or less as 'judge' (sometimes the 'judge' closes the scene with his or her own rhesis). In many cases the rheseis of the debate are followed by argumentative short dialogue which sharpens the opposition and shows that nothing positive has been accomplished. See 446–626n.

*Messenger-rhesis*: critical news from offstage (inside the building or at a distant location) is usually conveyed in a scene of reporting to

---

[2] Ancient scholars also used the term *epiparodos* to describe the scene in which and song with which a chorus returns after, exceptionally, leaving the stage in the middle of the action: Aesch. *Eum.* 244ff., Soph. *Ajax* 868–960, Eur. *Alc.* 861ff., *Helen* 515ff. (where, extraordinarily, the chorus had gone into the palace).

the chorus alone or to an appropriate character along with the chorus. The messenger-scene usually appears about two-thirds to four-fifths of the way through the play, but earlier messenger-scenes are found (Aesch. *Pers.*, *Ag.*) and some plays have two messenger-scenes (Eur. *IT*, *Bacch.*). Typically, the messenger conveys the essential news and relieves the tension in a short dialogue and then is asked to give the whole story, which he does in a leisurely rhesis extending up to 80 or even 100 lines. See 1116–1250n.

### b. Dialogue in shorter speeches

For short stretches the actors (or actor and koryphaios) may converse in speeches of varying lengths. The formality of the genre normally requires that each speech end at the end of a full trimeter. *Antilabe*, the breaking of a line between two speakers, is not found in Aeschylus (there is a possible case in *Prom.*) and is used only for special effect in most of Sophocles and Eur. (in some of late Sophocles antilabe seems to produce only informality or 'naturalness', not a shock effect). For the one instance in *Medea*, see 1009n.

Another aspect of the formality of tragedy is that very commonly dialogue in shorter speeches is arranged in regular patterns.

*Stichomythia* is line-for-line dialogue, sometimes lively and compressed, sometimes casual, gradual or roundabout. Syntactic ellipsis and suspension are frequent (see LS 29). Any extended exchange between actors usually tends toward the regular pattern of stichomythia. An extended stichomythia often begins or ends (or has its transitions marked) with an irregularity such as a couplet. Stichomythia is found in trochaic tetrameters as well as iambic trimeters.

*Distichomythia* is an extended sequence of two-line speeches in alternation.

*Continuous antilabe* presents a series of trimeters in which each is divided between the two speakers (A:B :: A:B :: A:B :: etc.). This usually occurs within or at the end of a stichomythia to quicken the pace and heighten the excitement. In some passages one can see a subtle artistic effect in the gradual shortening of speaker A's portion of the line (Soph. *OT* 1173–6). Continuous antilabe is not usually carried on for long; but in late Eur. it may be extended more easily when used in the longer trochaic tetrameters (e.g. *Orestes* 774–98).

*4   Analysis of the structure of Eur.'s* Medea

PROLOGUE 1–130

   (1)  prologue-monologue of nurse 1–48
   (2)  iambic dialogue of nurse and tutor 49–95 (irregular, with short distichomythia 74–81)
   (3)  anapaests of nurse and Medea (indoors) 96–130

PARODOS 131–213
   actors' anapaests (nurse and Medea) interspersed with choral song (astrophic entry-stanza, one pair of corresponding stanzas, and an astrophic stanza (epode) sung after nurse's departure)

FIRST EPISODE 214–409

   (1)  Medea and the chorus 214–70 (major rhesis 214–66)
   (2)  dialogue-scene, Medea and Creon 271–356 (supplication stichomythia 324–39)
   (3)  Medea and chorus 357–409 (choral anapaests 357–63; major rhesis 364–409)

FIRST STASIMON 410–45: two pairs of stanzas

SECOND EPISODE 446–626
   *agōn logōn* of Medea and Jason: opening rhesis of Jason, paired debate-rheseis 465–575, followed by irregular dialogue

SECOND STASIMON 627–62: two pairs of stanzas

THIRD EPISODE 663–823

   (1)  dialogue of Medea and Aegeus 663–763 (stichomythia 667–707, followed by irregular dialogue; choral anapaests 759–63)
   (2)  Medea and chorus 764–823 (major rhesis 764–810, followed by irregular dialogue)

THIRD STASIMON 824–65: two pairs of stanzas

FOURTH EPISODE 866–975
   Medea and Jason (children brought out by tutor at 894) (irregular dialogue; major rhesis 869–905)

FOURTH STASIMON 976–1001: two pairs of stanzas

FIFTH EPISODE 1002–80

  (1) tutor and Medea 1001–20 (irregular dialogue)
  (2) Medea's great monologue (rhesis) 1021–80

ANAPAESTIC INTERLUDE 1081–1115: in place of a stasimon

SIXTH EPISODE 1116–1250
  messenger-scene (irregular dialogue, messenger-rhesis 1136–1230, short rhesis of Medea 1236–50)

FIFTH STASIMON 1251–92: two pairs of stanzas with incorporated trimeters

EXODOS 1293–1419

  (1) dialogue of Jason and chorus 1293–1316 (stichomythia 1308–13)
  (2) iambic dialogue of Medea (*ex machina*) and Jason 1317–88 (major rhesis of Jason 1323–50, stichomythia 1361–77)
  (3) anapaestic dialogue of Medea and Jason 1389–1414 [choral exit-tag (anapaests) 1415–19]

# INTRODUCTION TO LANGUAGE
# AND STYLE

The Attic tragedians wrote in an artistic literary language which deliberately set itself apart in many ways from colloquial Attic and
formal Attic prose, although the language used in the dialogue portions of tragedy is relatively closer to ordinary Attic than that of the
lyric portions. When considering the language and style of Euripides,
one must be aware of three main levels of differentiation from 'normal' (non-poetic) speech. First, in many respects the tragedians are
continuing the traditions of high-style poetry and thus they inherit or
share forms and constructions found in epic, choral lyric, and other
archaic genres. Tragedy's debt to various lyric genres is especially
heavy in the choral odes, while messenger speeches tend to feature
more prominently certain epicisms. Second, there are distinctive elements of tragic style that seem to be common to all its practitioners,
features that one might find in Aeschylus or Sophocles or other tragedians of the fifth century (or even later). Finally, there are the features and mannerisms specific to Euripides himself, some of which
represent simply extensions or greater frequency of stylistic features
already found in the tradition (such as various forms of verbal repetition), and some of which are more clearly innovative or idio-
syncratic (such as the admission of more colloquialisms[1] and the
extension of tragic vocabulary through the allowance of additional
word-shapes within the iambic trimeter and through greater openness to contemporary intellectual and technical vocabulary).[2] In
contrast to Aeschylus (especially) and to Sophocles, Euripides was
regarded by ancient readers as simpler and clearer in style.[3]
Although this comparative assessment is valid, particularly for the

---

[1] On colloquial expressions see Stevens (1976).

[2] On Euripidean vocabulary see Breitenbach (1934), Clay (1958–60), Lee
(1968) and (1971), and Schmid (1940) 792–5. For the relation of Euripidean
vocabulary to that of Thucydides see Finley (1967). For developments in the
vocabulary of Sophocles, whose career overlapped with Eur.'s for almost 50
years, see Long (1968).

[3] Note already Aristophanes, *Frogs* 907–79, 1056–8, 1119–79, 1434.

dialogue portions, where the language is plainer and metaphor much less prevalent, it must be emphasized that Euripides' language is still poetic and in many ways artificial, sometimes straining the normal semantics of common words, word-order, and syntax.

The following presentation is intended for the student who has been trained in the morphology and syntax of Attic prose and who may be reading poetry or tragedy for the first time. Examples are drawn from *Medea* whenever possible (with citation by bare line number).

# MORPHOLOGY

*Dialectal peculiarities*

**1.** In those aspects in which the everyday Attic dialect is most 'provincial' (different from common Greek or Ionic), tragedy favours a common Greek or Ionic (or old Attic) colouring in the dialogue.

a. Common Greek -σσ- appears instead of Attic -ττ-. E.g. ἀπαλ-λάσσουσα (27), θαλάσσιος (28), φυλάσσεσθ' (102), κρεῖσσον (123), πράσσοιτε (313), ἧσσον (318).

b. Common Greek -ρσ- is used instead of Attic -ρρ-. E.g. ἀρσένων (428), θάρσει (926), Τυρσηνίδος (1342).

c. Certain sequences of long vowel and short vowel found in common Greek (e.g. λᾱός) are replaced in Attic by similar vowels in the sequence short–long (e.g. λεώς). In tragedy Attic forms showing this shift (quantitative metathesis) are either avoided or coexist with the non-Attic forms. 'Temple' is νᾱός (*Andr.* 162), not νεώς. For λᾱός/λεώς 'men, army, people' (*Andr.* 1089 vs *Andr.* 19) and for proper names such as Ἀμφιάρᾱος, -άρεως, Μενέλᾱος, -έλεως both forms are used (for metrical convenience). The Doric forms of the gen. sing. and pl. of ναῦς occur in both dialogue and lyric (νᾱός, νᾱῶν, 523, *Tro.* 122), while the Attic forms are seen in dialogue only (νεώς, νεῶν, *Tro.* 1049, 1047).

d. Open, uncontracted forms of adjectives and nouns may be used as well as the contracted forms: (1) adjs. with contraction: χρύ-σεος (632) as well as χρυσοῦς (1160, 1186); (2) sigma-stem nouns and adjs.: gen. sing. (in lyric) τείχεος (*Phoen.* 116) vs λέχους (491), ξίφους (1278); neut. nom./acc. pl. (in lyric) τείχεα (*Hel.* 1162) vs τείχη (*Hec.* 11). The gen. pl. of sigma-stems is written in the open form and the ending is sometimes counted as two syllables (in lyric ἀχέων 647, παθέων 658, in trimeters τειχέων *El.* 94) and sometimes as one by synizesis (PM 5) (τειχέων in *El.* 615).[4]

e. In verb forms, the epic-Ionic contraction of εο or εου to ευ (instead of Attic ου) is found very rarely, as in 423 ὑμνεῦσαι (<ὑμνέουσαι), *Hipp.* 167 ἀύτευν.

**2.** In the lyrics of tragedy, the language is given a superficial Doric colouring by the use of ᾱ for η when the η represents an original ᾱ of early Greek. E.g. 96b δύστανος = δύστηνος, 98 ὀλοίμαν = ὀλοίμην, 111 τλάμων = τλήμων, 113 ματρός = μητρός, 131 φωνάν, βοάν, 144 κεφαλᾶς, 146 καταλυσαίμαν, 147 βιοτάν, 162 ἐνδησαμένα.

**3.** Words which are not native to Attic may appear exclusively in their Doric form, even in dialogue: e.g. ὀπᾱδός (53), ἕκᾱτι (281), κυνᾱγός (*Hipp.* 1397), λοχᾱγός (*Tro.* 1260).

**4.** For metrical convenience an epicism like πτόλις (*Andr.* 699) for πόλις may be admitted (also ἀπτολέμους (643) = ἀπολέμους).

*Inflection*
**5.** Nouns and adjectives

a. α-declension: in lyric, the gen. sing. of masc. nouns or compound adjs. in -ᾱς/-ης is -ᾱ (<-αο, Doric), as in Ἄιδα (981), Οἰδιπόδα (*Phoen.* 813), χιλιοναύτα (*IT* 141); in lyric, the gen. pl. of nouns (all types) and adjs. is -ᾶν (<-άων, Doric), as in καθαρᾶν (660), ἱκετᾶν (863), ἀναδεσμᾶν (978); in dialogue and lyric, the dat. pl. is, according to metrical convenience, -αις, -αισι, or -αισιν, as in θαλίαις (192), νάπαισι (3), ἐκπονουμέναισιν (241). (In Aeschylus, the old Attic -ῃσι/-ᾱσι is also found.)

b. o-declension: in lyric, the gen. sing. is sometimes -οιο, as διγόνοιο (*Hipp.* 560); in dialogue and lyric the dat. pl. is, according to metrical convenience, -οις, -οισι, or -οισιν, as in γάμοις (18), φίλοισι (521), τέκνοισιν (11).

c. consonant-declension: πόλις has for gen. sing. both πόλεως and πόλεος (*Hcld.* 94, 95); sigma-stems (neuter nouns in -ος, adjs. in -ης,

---

[4] Note that tragic texts often have the open spelling even when the metre shows that a contraction is necessary: thus χαλκέοις (*Phoen.* 1359) and ἄχεα (*Phoen.* 1513) may be disyllabic.

-ες) may have open forms along with contracted forms (see **1**.d above). Some nouns show variation between a stem ending in a consonant and a shorter stem that lacks the consonant: just as in normal Attic one may find o-stem comparative forms like μείζω (43, 534), μείζους (1083) (alongside nu-stem forms μείζονα, μείζονες), so in tragedy one may find acc. γέλων (383, 1041) as well as γέλωτα (404, 1049); acc. εἰκώ (1162) instead of prosaic εἰκόνα (also gen. sing. εἰκοῦς (*Hel.* 77) and acc. pl. εἰκούς (*Tro.* 1178)); gen. χροός (*Hipp.* 1359) as well as χρωτός (1403), dat. χροΐ (787, 1175) as well as χρωτί (*Andr.* 259), acc. χρόα (*Alc.* 159) as well as χρῶτα (*Hec.* 406). A similar phenomenon may be seen with the acc. sing. of dental stems varying with i-stems: χάριτα (*El.* 63) and normal χάριν (186, 227), ὄρνιθα *Hel.* 1109 and ὄρνιν *Hipp.* 733.

d. Adjs. may show variation between declension with two endings (with a common form for masc. and fem.) and with three endings (with separate fem. form). E.g. fem. μῶρος (61) vs μώραν (Soph. *El.* 890), fem. δῆλος (1197), φονίαν (1260) vs φόνιον … δίκην (*Andr.* 1002), and probably μετρίους … αὔρας (839–40n.). Some poetic compound adjs. regularly have three endings (fem. ἐναλία as in *IT* 255, 1240), and others may be used either with common masc./fem. or with separate fem. (διανταία Aesch. *Septem* 894, but fem. διανταῖος *Ion* 766; ζαθέα *Hipp.* 750, but fem. ζάθεοι *Tro.* 1075).

**6.** Pronouns

a. Article: rarely, the nom. pl. masc. and fem., when used in a demonstrative sense, take the alternative epic forms τοί (Aesch. *Pers.* 18) and ταί (*Andr.* 284).

b. The forms of the article which have initial tau are occasionally used as relative pronouns, when this form is metrically convenient. In Eur. this usage is almost confined to lyric passages (as *Hipp.* 747 τὸν Ἄτλας ἔχει) and rare in dialogue (*El.* 279, *Bacch.* 712).

c. Gen. sing. of first and second pers. personal pronouns may be ἐμέθεν (lyric only, as *Tro.* 260) or σέθεν (lyric or dialogue, as 65, *Hipp.* 826).

d. Dual personal pronouns are found: first person nom./acc. νώ (*Hel.* 981), gen./dat. νῶϊν (871); second person nom./acc. σφώ (*Alc.* 405), gen./dat. σφῶϊν (1021).

e. Third person pronoun: in addition to oblique forms of αὐτός, there are gen. sing. ἔθεν (Aeschylus only); dat. sing. οἷ or enclitic οἱ (Aeschylus and Sophocles only; indirect reflexive use in Eur. *El.* 924) (and possibly σφιν is sing. in Soph. *OC* 1490, Aesch. *Pers.* 759); acc. sing. (any gender) νιν (92, 180) or σφε (33); dat. pl. σφίσι(ν) (Soph. *OC* 69) or σφιν (399); acc. pl. enclitic σφας (1378) or (any gender) νιν (1312) or σφε (394).

**7.** Verbs

a. In lyrics and anapaests (as in epic or archaic lyric) augment is sometimes omitted, both syllabic (χόρευσε *Alc.* 583, τέκετο *Phoen.* 649) and temporal (ἄιον 205, ὄφελον 1413, ἀύτευν *Hipp.* 167). Much more rarely, the syllabic augment is omitted in dialogue, where omission is confined mainly to extended narratives like messenger-speeches and to the initial position in the line: in Eur. only in *Bacchae* (767 νίψαντο, 1066, 1084, 1134).

b. For metrical convenience, the personal ending of the first pl. mid.-pass. may be either -μεσθα (78, 315) or -μεθα (334, 338).

c. The shorter (epic) third pl. active secondary personal ending -ν replaces -σαν in a very few cases: (in lyric or anapaests) ἔβαν for ἔβησαν (e.g. *Andr.* 287) and ἀπέδραν for ἀπέδρασαν in Soph. *Ajax* 167; in dialogue only ἔκρυφθεν for ἐκρύφθησαν in *Hipp.* 1247 and ἔσταν in *Phoen.* 1246 (both messenger-speeches).

d. In the optative the third pl. mid.-pass. ending is sometimes -οιατο or -αιατο instead of -οιντο or -αιντο (metrically convenient at line-end). E.g. οἰχοίατο *IT* 1341, ἀντιδωρησαίατο *Hel.* 159.

**8.** Prepositions

a. Both εἰς (82, 362) and ἐς (2, 56) are used according to metrical need; where metrical need does not decide, editors differ in their practice (in the OCT Diggle always prints ἐς unless εἰς is required by the metre, and the same convention is followed in this book). Same variation in compound verbs in εἰσ- (41, 264) and in adverb ἔσω/εἴσω (89, 100).

b. Both ξύν (11, 240, 463) and σύν (25, 71, 114) are found; where metre does not decide between the forms, editors usually follow the manuscripts, which are inconsistent.

c. All three tragedians use ὑπαί for ὑπό (but rarely; Eur. only in *El.* 1188); Aeschylus alone uses διαί for διά a few times.

**9.** The dual number: as in colloquial Attic and in Aristophanes, the dual number of both nouns and verbs survives in Attic tragedy. Examples: 370 χεροῖν, 1289 παίδοιν, 1073 εὐδαιμονοῖτον. Note that the authors feel free to combine dual subject with plural verb form, and to shift back and forth between dual and plural in reference to the same persons or things (Smyth §1045): for example, in one sentence at 969–72 vocative τέκνα, participle εἰσελθόντε, imperatives ἱκετεύετε, ἐξαιτεῖσθε, participle διδόντες.

## SYNTAX

*Case usage*

**10.** Genitive

a. Various adnominal genitives (i.e. relating one noun to another) are much more frequent than in prose: for instance, the defining gen., as in 1 Ἀργοῦς ... σκάφος, 174–5 μύθων ... αὐδαθέντων ... ὀμφάν, *Hipp.* 802 βρόχον ... ἀγχόνης.

b. The gen. may depend on compound adjs. or substantives, in an objective or separative sense (esp. with adjs. formed with alpha privative). E.g. 673 εὐνῆς ἄζυγες γαμηλίου, *Hipp.* 743 ὁ ποντομέδων πορφυρέας λίμνας, *Phoen.* 324 ἄπεπλος φαρέων λευκῶν, *Supp.* 810 τέκνων ἄπαιδα.

c. The gen. of cause (Smyth §1407), rare in prose, is more common in poetry, esp. with an exclamation, as in 96 δύστανος ἐγὼ μελέα τε πόνων, 358 φεῦ φεῦ, μελέα τῶν σῶν ἀχέων.

d. The gen. of separation may be used directly with a verb of motion, without a preposition (an early Greek usage maintained in high-style poetry; Bers (1984) 99–101): 70–1 παῖδας γῆς ἐλᾶν Κορινθίας ... μέλλοι, 166 ὧν ἀπενάσθην.

**11.** Dative

a. The dative may be used in a locative sense without a preposition more freely than in prose (another old usage inherited from earlier poetry; Bers (1984) 86–99): 397 μυχοῖς ναίουσαν, 440 Ἑλλάδι τᾶι μεγάλαι.

b. The dat. is used (rarely) with a verb to express the direction or goal of motion: e.g. *Ion* 1467 ἀελίου ἀναβλέπει λαμπάσιν, 'looks up toward the torchlight of the sun'.

c. The dat. may depend on a noun (adnominal dative), sometimes expressing interest (advantage, possession) and sometimes by analogy to the use of the dat. with a verb of related meaning (Smyth §1502): 478–9 ἐπιστάτην ζεύγλαισι, 597 ἔρυμα δώμασιν.

**12.** Accusative

a. The internal accusative is very frequent in tragic style (e.g. *Hipp.* 32 ἐρῶσ' ἐρῶτ' ἔκδημον; 571 τίνα θροεῖς αὐδάν; 587 γαμεῖν γάμον τόνδ'). 'The acc. in apposition to the sentence' (or in fact to any verbal phrase) is a form of internal acc. and is typical of tragic style: e.g. 645–8 μὴ δῆτ' ἄπολις γενοίμαν τὸν ἀμηχανίας ἔχουσα δυσπέρατον αἰῶν', οἰκτρότατον ἀχέων, 'may I not become cityless, having the life of helplessness, hard to live through – [a fate (sc. being cityless and helpless) that is] most pitiful of woes'; *Hipp.* 756 ἐπόρευσας ... κακονυμφοτάταν ὄνασιν, 'you brought ... [and this bringing was] a benefit that was no more than ill fortune in marriage'; also 1035 ζηλωτὸν ἀνθρώποισι, 1341 κῆδος ἐχθρόν (both in apposition to infinitive phrases).

b. The acc. without a preposition (εἰς, πρός, ἐπί) expressing the goal or direction of motion (Smyth §1588) is common in tragedy as in other high-style poetry (Bers (1984) 62–85): 7 πύργους γῆς ἔπλευσ' Ἰωλκίας, 668 ὀμφαλὸν γῆς θεσπιωιδὸν ἐστάλης, 771 μολόντες ἄστυ καὶ πόλισμα Παλλάδος, 920–1 τέλος μολόντας.

*Verbal aspect*

**13.** The 'dramatic' or 'tragic' or 'instantaneous' aorist (Smyth §1937). Usually in dialogue, but also sometimes within a connected speech, the aor. of the first person may be used in what is called a 'performative' utterance (in which the pronouncing of the words itself performs an action): for instance, 791 ᾤμωξα is a performative utterance replacing exclamation οἴμοι. In English translation the present tense is usually appropriate. This usage has traditionally been explained as denoting an instantaneous reaction or sudden access of new emotion, as the event is considered from the point of view of its sudden inception. Lloyd (1999) has offered a new explanation, emphasizing the pragmatic distancing effect of using the performative aor. rather than a present or an exclamation: such aors. connote greater emotional control or greater 'politeness' or concern for the effect on others present. This is an important new observation, but in some particular cases there is still room to dispute how emphatic such an aor. may be, and the notion of instantaneous reaction may still be relevant (the speaker slightly distances himself or herself from the action by *representing* it as just performed). Other examples in *Medea* include 223 ἤινεσ᾽, 272 ἀνεῖπον; elsewhere words like ἀπέπτυσα (see Barrett on *Hipp.* 614). Another idiomatic use of the aor. seen in dramatic dialogue has sometimes been included with the 'dramatic' aor. of the type just described, but is in fact not performative, but descriptive, indicating an action that has just been (perhaps very quickly) completed (see Lloyd (1999) 43–4): so 64 μετέγνων.

**14.** The aor. participle (in the nom.) is sometimes used with a main verb in the aor. (or future) to express *coincident* action. There is no cause-and-effect relation between the action of the part. and the action of the main verb; rather the two verb-forms describe the same action or different ingredients of the same action. E.g. 432–5 ἔπλευσας ... διδύμους ὁρίσασα Πόντου πέτρας, 650–1 δαμείην ... ἀμέραν τάνδ᾽ ἐξανύσασα.

**15.** The gnomic aor. (Smyth §1931) is used in generalizations and is to be translated into English as a present: 130 ἀπέδωκεν, 235 ἔπαυσε, 629 παρέδωκαν.

**16.** Historical present: in narrative (e.g. prologues, messenger-speeches) the historical present is often used side by side with the aor. to denote factual occurrences in the past: e.g. (in the messenger-speech) 1141, 1161, 1163.

**17.** Registering present (or imperfect): permanent facts of kin-relationship, naming, and the like are often expressed in the present (less often the imperfect), although the English translation will normally use a simple past tense. E.g. τίκτει, γαμεῖ, ἔτικτεν, ὠνόμαζε.

*Infinitive*
**18.** The epexegetic infinitive ('added to explain'), expressing purpose or result (without ὡς or ὥστε), is common in tragedy. E.g. 257–8 οὐ μητέρ᾽, οὐκ ἀδελφόν, οὐχὶ συγγενῆ μεθορμίσασθαι τῆσδ᾽ ἔχουσα συμφορᾶς, 316 λέγεις ἀκοῦσαι μαλθάκ᾽, *Hipp.* 78–81 (λειμῶνα) αἰδὼς ... κηπεύει ... τούτοις δρέπεσθαι.

**19.** The inf. of indirect discourse is used somewhat more widely than in prose (e.g. it is found with the active of λέγω). Compare also 594n. for inf. with οἶδα.

**20.** Sometimes the acc. of the articular inf. is used where prose would use a simple complementary inf. (e.g. Soph. *OC* 442–3 τὸ δρᾶν οὐκ ἠθέλησαν) or an inf. with ὥστε (e.g. *Hipp.* 49 τὸ μὴ οὐ παρασχεῖν).

*Verbal periphrasis with the participle*

**21.** With εἰμί: a present participle is sometimes used periphrastically with εἰμί, esp. when the participle is quasi-adjectival: *IT* 1368 πυγμαὶ δ' ἦσαν ἐγκροτούμεναι, *Phoen.* 66 ζῶν δ' ἔστ' ἐν οἴκοις. See Aerts (1965) 5–26.

**22.** With ἔχω: a nom. act. participle periphrasis with ἔχω is used to emphasize a permanent result for the object (in contrast, the perfect tense of classical Greek normally serves to emphasize a permanent result for the subject). E.g. 33 ἀτιμάσας ἔχει, 90 ἐρημώσας ἔχε, *Hipp.* 932 διαβαλὼν ἔχει. See Aerts (1965) 128–60.

*Article*

**23.** Tragedy follows the tradition of the earlier language and of established poetic genres in frequently preserving the original force of the article as a demonstrative pronoun. The pronominal use is common when ὁ, ἡ, τό is followed by μέν or δέ (as in 140, 216–17, 303–5, 1141, 1215–16) and is also seen with prepositions (πρὸ τοῦ 696, ἐκ δὲ τῶν *Alc.* 264, πρὸς δὲ τοῖσι *Supp.* 207). Aeschylus and Sophocles occasionally use this pronoun before γάρ or without a following particle. In its articular use, the article is much less common than in prose or everyday speech, being optional when a noun is particularized or generic.

*Prepositions*

**24.** Anastrophe: In prose anastrophe is sometimes found with περί (the noun precedes the preposition). In tragedy all two-syllable prepositions except ἀντί, ἀμφί, διά can follow their noun, and in that case the accent is thrown back to the first syllable. E.g. 34 συμφορᾶς ὕπο, 66 τῶνδε ... πέρι, 224 ἀμαθίας ὕπο. Note that in dialogue the preposition in anastrophe is normally at the end of the trimeter.

**25.** The word-order noun–preposition–adjective (210 Ἑλλάδ᾽ ἐς ἀντίπορον, *Hipp.* 30 πέτραν παρ᾽ αὐτὴν Παλλάδος) or adjective–preposition–noun (69 σεμνὸν ἀμφὶ Πειρήνης ὕδωρ, *Hipp.* 17 χλωρὰν ἀν᾽ ὕλην) is quite common, and in the former case the preposition is not treated as if in anastrophe.

**26.** πάρα (1347, 1408), ἔνι (*Hipp.* 966), μέτα (*Hipp.* 876) are used for πάρεστι (πάρεισι), ἔνεστι (ἔνεισι), μέτεστι. The shift of accent marks this special use of these prepositions.

*Conjunctions and particles*
**27.** Particles are very heavily used, singly and in combinations, especially in close dialogue and stichomythia. Many express a colloquial liveliness or a vehemence that would be unusual in formal prose and oratory, but is at home in comedy as well as tragedy and in the dialogues of Plato. Here are listed some of the livelier and less prosaic uses, with references to notes containing further details and citation of Denniston.

ἀλλά, in addition to the common uses, has an elliptical use in the sense 'at least' (912n.); also noteworthy are the elliptical combination ἀλλὰ γάρ (1085n.) and the similar ἀλλὰ ... γάρ (252n., 1301n.), and δ᾽ ἀλλά (942n.) and ἀλλ᾽ οὖν (619n.), which mark an alternative or fall-back position.

ἄρα (postpositive) expresses lively realization (78n.) and is used idiomatically with past tenses to express recognition of a fact previously unacknowledged (703n.).

ἆρα introduces questions (901, 1294).

ἀτάρ, 'but', is a poetic conjunction (80n.).

γάρ (postpositive) has in tragedy a variety of uses other than the explicit explanatory use: anticipatory γάρ (80n.); imprecise connections involving understood intermediary thoughts (59n., 122n., 689n.); clauses that give the reason for uttering the previous phrase (234n., 1370n.); γάρ in stichomythia implying assent or dissent with what has just been said (329n.); γάρ introducing the content of a statement (656–7n.); the so-called progressive use in stichomythia (1312).

γε (postpositive) often adds emphasis, especially to personal or demonstrative pronouns (80, 88, 500, 1361) and adjectives (1250; with adjs. used ironically, 504n.); it is also commonly added in close dialogue to phrases in which one speaker adds an element to the syntax begun by the other (6, 1397, 1398). In other uses γε is limitative (867, 1247, 1369). Also noteworthy are combinations with other conjunctions and particles, such as εἰ ... γε (88n., 512), ἐπεί ... γε (495), καὶ ... γε (608, 687, 944), δὲ ... γε (818n.), γε μέντοι (95n.), οὔτοι ... γε (44, 1365), ἤτοι ... γε (1296–7n.).

γοῦν (postpositive) is a stronger alternative to limitative γε (123n., 1408).

δαί (postpositive) is a colloquial particle (common in comedy, rare in tragedy) added to interrogatives to express emphasis or connection (1012n.; cf. 339n.).

δή (postpositive), 'indeed', adds emphasis especially to verbs, adjs. of quantity, and relative and interrogative pronouns, and also combines with other particles as in καὶ δή (386n., marking imaginary realization of a proposed action, cf. 1107; 1118n., marking sight of entering character), γὰρ δή (722, 821, 1067, 1334).

δῆτα (postpositive) commonly intensifies negatives ('indeed', 336, 1048, 1056, 1378) and expresses logical connection with interrogatives ('then', 674, 678, 929, 1290). In stichomythia it may be used to emphasize a repeated word cast back at the interlocutor (1373, see 1361–78n.).

ἦ introduces a strong asseveration (579; reinforced with μήν in 1032).

καίτοι, 'and yet', is an adversative that is somewhat abrupt and combative, at home in lively speech (187, 199, 1049).

μέντοι (postpositive) may be emphatic (703n.) or very strongly adversative, often replacing δέ (72, 790, 1147, 1167). An even stronger adversative is γε μέντοι (95n.).

μήν (postpositive) occurs in the combination ἦ μήν (see above) and in καὶ μήν, which marks argumentative reversal (1375, 1361–78n.)

μῶν (a contraction of μὴ οὖν) lends a tone of incredulity or reluctance to questions (567n., 606, 733, 1032).

νυν (enclitic, emphatic or logical rather than temporal in force) often accompanies imperatives (105n.).

οὐδέ and μήδε are used in tragedy (unlike Attic prose) as sentence connectives even when the preceding clause is not negative (36, 93, 638, 1091).

οὖν (postpositive) exhibits, in addition to normal logical uses, an idiomatic use in questions of the type πῶς οὖν; (1376n.), and combinations such as δ' οὖν (breaking off and concentrating on what is essential, 306n.), ἀλλ' οὖν (see above), γε ... οὖν conveying irony (504n.), and γὰρ οὖν (533n.).

που (postpositive) is idiomatic in questions with οὔ που (incredulous, 695n.) and with ἦ που (sarcastic or bewildered, 1308n.).

τοι (postpositive), a frozen form of the so-called ethic dat. of the second-person sing. pronoun, often marks a direct appeal for agreement or understanding, 'you see', 'you know' (344n.; 1116n.); but it also combines with other particles, usually adding emphasis, as in οὔτοι and μήτοι and ἤτοι.

τοιγάρ, 'therefore', is a poetic particle inherited from epic (458, 509, 622).

*Stylistic features*

**28.** Asyndeton is the absence of connective words between individual terms or clauses. Since Greek in general favours constant connection of clauses, asyndeton stands out more in Greek and normally has a stylistic or rhetorical effect. Adjs. in groups of two or three in asyndeton usually express pathos or vehemence: 255n. Paired verbs in asyndeton likewise have heightened intensity (1258–9 κάτειργε κατάπαυσον): see Diggle (1994) 99–100 (lyric exx.), Mastronarde on *Phoen.* 1193 (verbs expressing violent action paired at the start of a trimeter). When one clause follows another in asyndeton, the second is often explanatory of the first, equivalent to a γάρ-clause (Smyth §2167b): 157n., 413n., 717n.; cf. 698n. (equivalent to a result-clause). Or the asyndeton may reflect emotion or vehemence, especially in combination with other rhetorical effects like anaphora (765–7n.).

**29.** Suspended, borrowed, and elliptical syntax: in stichomythia (or rapid lyric exchanges) the grammatical construction may be suspended across the intervening comment, or one speaker may complete the syntax of the other (680n.), or a line may be internally incomplete in syntax because some elements of the sentence are understood to be carried over from the other speaker's line (606–7n., 698n., 748n.). See Mastronarde (1979) ch. 4.

**30.** Tragic style uses more nouns and adjs. (particularly compound adjs.) than a formal prose style. This makes the language more concrete and descriptive. In addition, there is more frequent use of the 'nominal sentence', that is, a sentence with subject noun and predicate term with no copula expressed. According to some linguists, this form tends to express timeless truths or the ascription of a settled, intrinsic quality to a subject (as perhaps in 824–30), but in Eur. it is also sometimes used with no such implication.[5] The omission of the copula may be extended even to subordinate clauses (as in 72, 82, 200–1, 332), and occurs in first- or second-person sentences as well (first pers. as in 612; second pers. as in *Hipp*. 949).

**31.** The vocabulary of tragedy has several distinctive features. (1) There are words and forms that are 'poetic', such as 2 αἶα. This aspect of vocabulary is already described by Aristotle in *Poetics* 21 and is classed as 'defamiliarization' by moderns. (2) Greek vocabulary is naturally extensible by many types of word-formation, and tragic authors frequently coin new words (or seem to do so to us, who are able to look only at the literature that has survived) (e.g. 4 ἐρετμῶσαι, 423 ἀπιστοσύναν). (3) A word with a standard everyday meaning may be used (especially in lyric passages) in an unusual sense (e.g. 19 αἰσυμνᾶι, 109 μεγαλόσπλαγχνος, 434–5 ὁρίσασα), or a word's meaning may be stretched in figures of speech that are characteristic of poetry (for instance, synecdoche (use of whole for part or part for whole), as in 1 σκάφος = ναῦς; or metonymy (use of a word for another that it suggests in any way), as 651 ἡμέρα, 'daylight' for 'life'). (4) The use of abstract formations to refer to a person is a favourite device: e.g. λάτρευμα = servant; λέχος = wife; λόχευμα = child. (5) Many compound and double-compound verbs are used for greater expressiveness; but at the same time some simple verbs which have died out in Attic prose (replaced by compounds) are retained in tragedy (e.g. ἧκα, στέρομαι, θνήισκω, κτείνω). (6) Variety is obtained by using τίθημι in many places where prose would use ποιέω (e.g. 66 σιγὴν ... θήσομαι); δράω supplements ποιέω and πράσσω; πίτνω alternates with πίπτω; τρέφω is often used more or less synonymously with ἔχω.

**32.** Tragic style usually favours circumlocution, fullness, even redundancy. Especially in lyric, but also in iambics and anapaests,

---

[5] See Guiraud (1962), but also Lanérès (1994).

an element of a compound epithet may be almost synonymous with the modified noun, and sometimes a gen. of related meaning will be added: e.g. 200–1 εὔδειπνοι δαῖτες, 204 ἀχὰν ... πολύστονον γόων (for fullness in lyric in general see Breitenbach (1934) 186–96). Often when a fuller expression is used, there is a deliberate variation of positive and negative statements of the same idea (412–13n.). Finally, related items may be grouped in a series of increasing length or weight. Thus, with two elements, 27–8 οὔτ' ὄμμ' ἐπαίρουσ' οὔτ' ἀπαλλάσσουσα γῆς | πρόσωπον; but most commonly with three elements (rising or ascending tricolon), as in 21–3 (half-line clause, one-line clause, one-and-a-half-line clause) and 257 (οὐ μητέρ', οὐκ ἀδελφόν, οὐχὶ συγγενῆ).

**33.** The 'poetic' plural is used for the singular with various effects (see Bers (1984) 22–61). The plural may connote dignity or generalization or may simply be convenient for variation or metrical fit (e.g. 244 τοῖς ἔνδον, 308 ἐς τυράννους ἄνδρας, 367 τοῖσι κηδεύσασιν). When a woman uses a first person plural verb of herself, the modifiers too may be plural and also masculine (see 314–15n.).

**34.** The relation of sentence structure to the structure of the iambic trimeter is worth noting. In a high proportion of lines a major or minor punctuation occurs at line-end: this tendency is most pronounced in Aeschylus and is reduced in the more supple sentence structure of Sophocles and Eur. Enjambment may be classified in much the same way as for the Homeric hexameter: (1) no enjambment (e.g. 16, 36); (2) periodic enjambment (that is, a subordinate structure is complete at line-end, and another subordinate structure or the main clause begins the next line: e.g. 17, 26); (3) optional enjambment (that is, the sense is apparently complete with the end of the line, but dispensable modifying elements are added in the next line: e.g. 7, 10, 14, 18); and (4) integral enjambment (that is, the sense is incomplete at line-end and what follows is indispensable to the completion of the sense: e.g. milder versions at 1, 22, stronger versions at 4, 5, 9, 21, 28). Within a line, there is often at least a mild break in phrasing at the caesura (e.g. 2, 5, 16, 19). When a syntactic unit carries over into the next line, there is often punctuation at the caesura of the next line (e.g. 3–4, 5–6, 21–2, 31–2). Almost 90 per cent of major punctuations occur either at line-end or at one of the two caesura positions; the next commonest positions after these are after the third or the second element of the trimeter (e.g. 28, 44, 47, 48, 234, 263).

**35.** Although Greek word-order is highly flexible even in prose and the everyday spoken language, poetry is characterized by even more varied order and by more frequent (and at times artificial) separation of elements that would tend to be adjacent outside of poetry.[6] For instance, an adj. or dependent gen. may be separated from its noun: in 7 γῆς ἔπλευσ᾽ Ἰωλκίας the verb intervenes (cf. 70, 71, 76), while in 8 there is the more artful separation of ἔρωτι at line-beginning and Ἰάσονος at line-end (cf. 240, 340). The postponed second element of a phrase may in fact be relatively unemphatic, an optional or easily anticipated addition or specification (as in 714–15 ἔρως ... παίδων, 1309 παῖδες ... σέθεν; more complex pattern in 1294–5 ἄρ᾽ ἐν δόμοισιν ἡ τὰ δείν᾽ εἰργασμένη | Μήδεια τοισίδ᾽, where both enjambed words are predictable). Occasionally there is a more elaborate interlacing of elements, as in 362–3 (see n.), 391 δόλωι μέτειμι τόνδε καὶ σιγῆι φόνον, 473–4 ἐγώ τε γὰρ λέξασα κουφισθήσομαι | ψυχὴν κακῶς σὲ καὶ σὺ λυπήσηι κλύων (double chiasmus and strong enjambment: see n.). Sometimes the word-order is chosen in order to produce an expressive juxtaposition of terms (as in 76 παλαιὰ καινῶν, 79 νέον παλαιῶι). Another exception to routine word-order is the placement of words belonging to a subordinate clause in front of the subordinating conjunction, as in 72–3 ὁ μέντοι μῦθος εἰ σαφὴς ὅδε | οὐκ οἶδα, or postponement of a conjunction (as with ἤ in 847). Similar is the promotion of emphatic words in an interrogative sentence to the front of the clause, before the interrogative word, as in 309 σὺ γὰρ τί μ᾽ ἠδίκηκας; and 701 δίδωσι δ᾽ αὐτῶι τίς; (also 500, 502, 565, 682); on this topic see in general Thomson (1939).

---

[6] Certain kinds of separation, or apparent displacement ('hyperbaton'), also occur in classical Greek prose, but the instances in poetry differ in frequency (since adjectives are in general more densely present in poetry) and in kind. Poetry allows in hyperbaton all kinds of adjectives, including those that are descriptive or non-contrastive, as in 1148 λευκήν τ᾽ ἀπέστρεψ᾽ ἔμπαλιν παρηίδα. For technical discussion, see Devine and Stephens (2000) 112–15, 202–3, and also 88–140 for a survey of typical types of hyperbata.

**36.** Various forms of repetition provide rhetorical emphasis or emotional intensification. These are more common in lyric passages, but occur in trimeters as well. Anaphora may be heightened by placement of the repeated words at the opening of successive metra or cola (in lyrics) or as first word of a trimeter and first word after the caesura (lyric: 99 κινεῖ κραδίαν, κινεῖ δὲ χόλον, 131 ἔκλυον φωνάν, ἔκλυον δὲ βοάν, 978–9 δέξεται νύμφα χρυσέων ἀναδεσμᾶν | δέξεται δύστανος ἄταν; trimeter: 467 ἦλθες πρὸς ἡμᾶς, ἦλθες ἔχθιστος γεγώς). Note also polyptoton or paregmenon (475 ἐκ τῶν δὲ πρώτων πρῶτον, 513 μόνη μόνοις, 579 πολλὰ πολλοῖς, 1165 πολλὰ πολλάκις) and anadiplosis (650 θανάτωι θανάτωι, 111 ἔπαθον τλάμων ἔπαθον, 1273 ἀκούεις βοὰν ἀκούεις τέκνων, 1282 μίαν δὴ κλύω μίαν τῶν πάρος). On this topic see in general Fehling (1969).

# INTRODUCTION TO PROSODY AND METRE

**1.** Greek metre is quantitative, that is, it is based on a pattern of 'long' (or 'heavy') and 'short' (or 'light')[1] syllables. To determine the quantity of the syllables within a given metrical line, one must treat the words as continuous and divide into syllables that are either 'open' or 'closed' (a syllable is *closed* if it ends in a consonant, *open* if it ends in a vowel). For metrical purposes,[2] a single consonant between vowels goes with the following vowel. Most double consonants between vowels are divided between the two syllables (likewise triple consonants).[3] The first line of *Medea*, Εἴθ᾽ ὤφελ᾽ Ἀργοῦς μὴ διαπτάσ-θαι σκάφος, is to be divided into syllables for metrical purposes as follows:

| 1 | 2 | 3 | 4 | 5 | 6 | 7 | 8 | 9 | 10 | 11 | 12 |
|---|---|---|---|---|---|---|---|---|----|----|----|
| Εἴ | θώ | φε | λ᾽Ἀρ | γοῦς | μὴ | δι | απ | τάσ | θαισ | κά | φος |

In this example syllables 1, 2, 3, 6, 7, and 11 are open, while syllables 4, 5, 8, 9, 10, and 12 are closed.

**2.** A syllable is *metrically short* only if it is open and contains a short vowel. The open syllables in positions 3, 7, and 11 above contain short vowels and thus scan as short. A syllable is *metrically long* if it is

---

[1] The terms 'heavy' and 'light' avoid confusion between the quantity of the vowel within a syllable and the metrical weight of the syllable; but the terms 'long' and 'short' are so firmly established, esp. for describing metrical patterns and for reading the symbols – and ∪, that it is convenient to retain them. For a key to the metrical symbols used in this book, see the final page of this section. For a fuller introduction to Greek metre see West (1987) or West (1982). For more technical treatment of prosody see Devine and Stephens (1994).

[2] The articulation of words and elements of words for morphological or phonological purposes is not necessarily the same as the articulation implied by metrical practices.

[3] For this purpose the double consonants ζ, ξ, ψ are treated as σδ, χσ, φσ.

closed or if it is open but contains a long vowel or diphthong.[4] Of the open syllables in the above example, those in positions 1, 2, and 6 contain long vowels and thus scan as long. The pattern of long and short in the example is thus: long, long, short, long, long, long, short, long, long, long, short, long (or $- - \cup - - - \cup - - - \cup -$).

**3.** Complications are introduced into the basic scheme just described (1) by the treatment of certain combinations of consonants and (2) by the conjunction of consecutive vowels in certain circumstances.

**4.** In ordinary Attic (and in Aristophanes except when he is being paratragic), when a plosive (π, τ, κ, β, δ, γ, φ, θ, χ) is followed by a liquid or nasal (λ, ρ, μ, ν), the two consonants cohere and together begin the following syllable, leaving the preceding syllable open unless another consonant precedes. Thus πατρός is usually divided πα|τρός and the first syllable is short. In epic the two consonants usually do not cohere and thus a closed (long) syllable is created (πατ|ρός). In tragedy either scansion may be used for metrical convenience (and sometimes the alternatives appear in the same line, as Soph. *Phil.* 296 ἀλλ' ἐν πέ|τροισι πέτ|ρον ἐκτρίβων μόλις). There are limitations on this freedom of choice: (a) voiced plosives δ and γ followed by μ or ν are always treated as double, not cohering (δ|μ, δ|ν, γ|μ, γ|ν); with voiced β and γ, the liquid λ usually forms a double consonant, not cohering (β|λ, γ|λ); (b) *initial* plosive and liquid normally cohere and leave a preceding syllable open (the exceptions in tragedy are all in lyric passages: 246n.); (c) conversely, if the plosive and liquid are in separate words (or separate parts of a compound), they cannot cohere and must be treated as double (ἐκ λόγων and ἐκλιπεῖν must be scanned $- \cup -$).

**5.** Certain adjoining vowels in the same word (esp. εω in gen. -εως or -εων) may contract in pronunciation to form one long vowel. Such contraction is called *synizesis*. Thus in *Med.* 1200 ὀστέων is disyllabic by synizesis (but in 1207 the same word is trisyllabic); and forms of

---

[4] For the purpose of metrical scansion final αι or οι counts as long, just as other diphthongs do; this differs from the phenomenon of accentuation, for which final αι or οι usually counts as short.

θεός may be monosyllabic (*Med.* 493, 528, 670, 879, 919) instead of disyllabic.

**6.** Within certain words *internal correption* (shortening) of αι or οι before a following vowel is found: in dialogue, the οι of τοιοῦτος and ποιεῖν is sometimes shortened (thus *Med.* 626, 810 τοιοῦτ- scanned ∪−); in lyric or anapaests, the αι of δείλαιος and γεραιός may be shortened (*Med.* 134 γεραιά scanned ∪∪−).

**7.** Shortening of a final long vowel or diphthong before the initial vowel of the next word is termed *epic correption* (because this is a regular practice in the Homeric dactylic hexameter). In tragedy this is found in lyric metres that feature double-short movement (dactyls, anapaests, ionic, aeolic, dochmiac): thus, in *Med.* 427 -τωρ μελέων ἐπεὶ ἀν(τάχησ’), final ει is shortened before initial α in a dactylic element −∪∪−∪∪−(−−).

**8.** The features just described are not normally reflected in the spelling of the text, but some other prosodic peculiarities are usually reflected graphically. In Attic poetry there is a general avoidance of *hiatus* ('gaping'), the conjunction of a final vowel and an initial vowel in which both vowels retain their full pronunciation. In tragedy, hiatus is found within a metrical line only in the sequence τί οὐ/οὖν and rarely after ἤ (no instance of either in *Med.*).

**9.** With a final short vowel other than ῠ hiatus is avoided by *elision* (indicated by an apostrophe: ὄμμ’ = ὄμμα).[5] Elision is common in inflectional endings,[6] disyllabic prepositions, and various adverbs, conjunctions, and particles (examples in the opening lines of *Med.* include εἴθ(ε), ὤφελ(ε), μηδ(έ), δέσποιν(α), ἔπλευσ(ε), ἐκπλαγεῖσ(α), ἤισθετ(ο)).

**10.** Much less common is *prodelision* (elision from in front), whereby the initial epsilon of a preposition is suppressed after a final long vowel (*Med.* 754 μὴ ’μμένων = μὴ ἐμμένων).

---

[5] Final αι in middle-passive endings is sometimes elided in comedy and other Greek poetry, but apparently not by any of the three tragedians (a few possible examples seem to be the result of corruption of the text).

[6] In tragedy elision of dative singular ending -ι is avoided. Thus there is no ambiguity in elisions such as τιν’ = τινα or μητέρ’ = μητέρα (257).

**11.** Where elision is impossible, hiatus is avoided by contraction of the vowels across the boundary between the words. This is called *crasis*, 'mixing'. In familiar combinations the syllable is written to show the contraction,[7] with a coronis (identical in appearance to a smooth breathing) over the contracted vowel: *Med.* 39 ἐγῷδα = ἐγὼ οἶδα; 43 κἄπειτα = καὶ ἔπειτα; 686 ἁνήρ = ὁ ἀνήρ.[8] Poets are also able to avoid hiatus (and take advantage of alternative word-shapes) by adding the optional nu (nu movable, paragogic nu, nu ephelkustikon) to various inflectional endings: e.g. εἷλε/εἷλ'/εἷλεν, κακοῖς/κακοῖσι/κακοῖσιν.

*Verse structures: period and synapheia*

**12.** Within the metrical unit known as a *verse* or *period*, the prosody is continuous, that is, the determination of metrical syllables and metrical length is independent of punctuation or even at times change of speaker. This condition is called *synapheia*, 'continuity'. At the end of a verse or period synapheia ends, and there is a metrical pause (symbol ‖), which allows the final syllable of the sequence to count as long no matter whether it is open or closed or its vowel long or short (pause also makes hiatus allowable). There is a tendency for metrical pause to coincide with semantic or syntactic pause, but it is no more than a tendency, and it is also possible for words that belong together to be separated by metrical pause.

**13.** A larger metrical composition is constructed of a series of verses or periods. When a speech or a scene or a whole poem is built up from an arbitrary number of repetitions of the same metrical line, with each line being a period, ending in metrical pause, the metre is termed *stichic* (from στίχος, 'row, line'). Stichic composition is found

---

[7] Sometimes the crasis is not indicated typographically: for instance, in *Med.* 35 μὴ ἀπολείπεσθαι must be pronounced and scanned as five syllables, μἠπολείπεσθαι.

[8] If the first vowel in crasis has rough breathing, then only a rough breathing is shown over the contracted vowel, and the coronis is omitted. This is the convention in modern typography, based on the practices of some medieval scribes (in MSS instances of crasis are often corrupted or indicated in various other ways or not at all).

in the Homeric epics and other poetry written in dactylic hexameters. Tragedy has two stichic metres used in its dialogue scenes, the common iambic trimeter and the much less common trochaic tetrameter catalectic (not found in *Medea*).

**14.** A uniform rhythm in variable lengths is seen in the chanted anapaests of tragedy, in which an arbitrary number of anapaestic metra are strung together to form a period, with the period-end normally marked by *catalexis*, a contrasting modification of the final metron (most often by the omission of an element at the end: the Greek term implies 'ending early'). The adjective corresponding to catalexis is 'catalectic' (see below, 22 and 24).

**15.** Lyric compositions, on the other hand, are structured in strophes or stanzas containing one or more periods; the periods within a stanza are rarely all identical, and most stanzas written for tragedy are unique combinations of elements. Some lyric stanzas are self-standing, without responsion (*astrophic*), but most are arranged in corresponding (*strophic*) pairs in which a strophe and antistrophe share the same metrical pattern. A typical choral ode in Euripides consists of two strophic pairs (thus all five stasimons in *Medea*).

*Iambic trimeter: the verse of tragic dialogue*

**16.** The iambic metron is $\times - \cup -$ (where $\times$ represents an element that may be long or short, termed *anceps*, 'doubtful'); verses may be built from various numbers of iambic metra (esp. 2, 3, or 4). The trimeter ('three-metron length') is found in archaic poetry from Archilochus and Semonides to Solon and became the most important dialogue metre of tragedy and comedy.[9]

$$\times \quad - \quad \cup \quad - \quad \times : - \quad \cup (:) - \quad \overline{\cup} \quad \overline{\phantom{-}} \quad \cup \quad - \parallel$$

scheme  1  2  3  4  5  6  7  8  9  10  11  12

**17.** *Caesura*, 'cutting', is a regular position of word-break (and often also a mild or strong semantic or syntactic break) within the line, dividing it into unequal subunits. In iambic trimeter caesura is most

---

[9] For the associations between ἰαμβεῖον (iambic metre) and ἴαμβος (lampoon, invective) see West (1974) and Rosen (1988).

common after the fifth element (penthemimeral, indicated by ⋮ in the scheme), but if no word-break occurs there, then there will be caesura after the seventh element (hepthemimeral, (⋮) in the scheme).[10]

**18.** *Porson's law* (also known as law of the final cretic or Porson's bridge) concerns a constraint upon the third anceps of the trimeter, the ninth element. This constraint applies to the more formal uses of the iambic trimeter, so that it is observed in tragedy, but not in comedy. Unless the ninth element is a monosyllabic word, it may be long only if it belongs to the same word or word-unit as the following long (element 10) – hence the union symbol joining the long of 9 to the long of 10 in the above scheme. Stated conversely, this means that if the final 'cretic' (long, short, long) of the line is realized in a trisyllabic word, the preceding syllable must be short (unless it is a monosyllable). See, e.g., *Med.* 45, 239, 255, 264 for 'final cretic' preceded by a polysyllabic word with short final syllable; 16, 21, 40, 44, 54 for 'final cretic' preceded by a monosyllable; 1, 2, 4, 5 for long elements 9 and 10 belonging to the same word.[11]

**19.** The iambic trimeter is in theory a 12-syllable line, but a higher number of syllables may appear in tragedy because of *resolution*, the substitution of two shorts for a long element (position 2, 4, 6, or 8; in later Eur. also 10) or for the first anceps.[12] To accommodate a proper name, the second or third anceps (positions 5 and 9) may be resolved, or two shorts may be substituted for the single short at positions 3 and 7 ('anapaestic substitution'). In most of Attic tragedy, including the plays of Euripides written before *c.* 425,[13] resolution is not very common, and there is usually no more than one resolution in any

---

[10] In a very few lines in tragedy, the verse has no penthemimeral or hepthemimeral caesura but is instead bisected by word-end (with elision) after the sixth element (see *Med.* 237, 470, 1014); even more rarely, in Aeschylus and Sophocles, such mid-line division is not accompanied by elision (e.g. Soph. *OT* 738).

[11] For a technical discussion of the theoretical basis of this rule see Devine and Stephens (1984).

[12] Comedy is even freer in resolution and other substitutions.

[13] After that date, resolutions become more common in Euripides, and he also becomes freer in their positioning and in the word-shapes in which they are admitted: see Cropp and Fick (1985). See also above, Introd. 1.

given line. There are about 75 resolutions in about 1030 iambic trimeters in *Medea*, for an average of one resolution every 14 lines. Three lines contain two resolutions each (324, 710, 1322: the first two of these occur in earnest supplication, but the third is probably spoken without particular agitation). More than half of the resolutions occur at position 6 (e.g. 18, 21, 31), less than a quarter at position 8 (e.g. 9, 75, 224), the rest at positions 2 and 4 (e.g. 10, 273, 324, 375) or at position 1 (e.g. 6, 397, 486). There are no cases of anapaestic substitution in *Medea*.

**20.** Here is a sample of scansion, *Med.* 483–7 (with commas added to the scheme to help the beginner perceive the three metra):

‒ ‒ ∪ ⏖ , ∪ ⫶ ‒ ∪ ‒ , ∪ ‒ ∪ ‒ ‖

αὐτὴ δὲ πατέρα καὶ δόμους προδοῦσ' ἐμοὺς   (resolution of position 4)

‒ ‒ ∪ ‒ , ∪ ⫶ ‒ ∪ ‒ , ∪ ‒ ∪ ‒ ‖

τὴν Πηλιῶτιν εἰς Ἰωλκὸν ἱκόμην

‒ ‒ ∪ ‒ , ‒ ⫶ ‒ ∪ ‒ , ∪ ‒ ∪ ‒ ‖

σὺν σοί, πρόθυμος μᾶλλον ἢ σοφωτέρα·

⏖ ‒ ∪ ‒ , ‒ ⫶ ‒ ∪ ‒ , ‒ ‒ ∪ ‒ ‖

Πελίαν τ' ἀπέκτειν', ὥσπερ ἄλγιστον θανεῖν,   (resolution of first anceps)

‒ ‒ ∪ ‒ , ‒ ⫶ ‒ ∪ ‒ , ‒ ‒ ∪ ‒ ‖

παίδων ὕπ' αὐτοῦ, πάντα τ' ἐξεῖλον δόμον.

*Anapaests*

**21.** The anapaestic metron in Greek is basically ∪∪ ‒∪∪‒, but ‒ may regularly be substituted for ∪∪ and ∪∪ for ‒ within certain limits, producing anapaestic metra of the forms ‒∪∪‒‒ and ‒‒∪∪‒ and ‒‒‒‒ and ‒∪∪‒∪∪ (the rarer forms ‒‒‒∪∪ and ∪∪‒‒∪∪ are not found in *Medea*). Many passages in Greek tragedy consist of extended chains of various numbers of anapaestic metra. There are two kinds of anapaestic passages: (1) 'marching' anapaests and (2) sung anapaests.

**22.** Marching anapaests were probably chanted rather than sung,[14] and derive their name from the fact that they often accompany the entrance or exit of the chorus and some other entrances and exits,

---

[14] Compare the contrast between recitative and aria in classical and romantic opera.

although they are also found in other passages which in emotion and
ethos fall between the spoken trimeter and fully lyric rhythms. In this
type of anapaests, the substitutions of ∪∪ and − are limited by the
avoidance of a sequence of four shorts. In addition, there is regularly
word-break (*diaeresis*, 'division') after every metron (symbol |), and
Attic eta is usually retained. Marching anapaests run continuously in
'systems' which are by convention presented in texts as dimeters
(sometimes with occasional monometers), but an anapaestic period
has no standard length. Period-end in an anapaestic period is usually
signalled by a concluding shortened (catalectic) dimeter, called a
*paroemiac*. The paroemiac is ∪∪−∪∪−∪∪−− (substitutions are
possible in the first metron, not in the second, and word-break may
be absent between these metra): cf. *Med.* 110 (no diaeresis), 130, 143,
170, 172. In some longer chains, it is possible that there is also period-
end at a full metron (so certainly in conjunction with change of
speaker at 1396, and perhaps at other points − see 184−204n.).

Here is a sample passage scanned (*Medea* 105−10):

∪ ∪ −    −  − |  −    ∪  ∪  − − |
ἴτε νυν, χωρεῖθ' ὡς τάχος εἴσω.

−   −   −   − |− −   ∪ ∪  − |
δῆλον δ' ἀρχῆς ἐξαιρόμενον

∪ ∪  − −   − |  −   ∪ ∪  − − |
νέφος οἰμωγῆς ὡς τάχ' ἀνάψει

−   ∪ ∪  −  − |∪ ∪    −   ∪ ∪ − |
μείζονι θυμῷ· τί ποτ' ἐργάσεται

∪   ∪  −   −   −  |  −  ∪ ∪   −   − |
μεγαλόσπλαγχνος δυσκατάπαυστος

−   −   −   ∪  ∪ − − ‖
ψυχὴ δηχθεῖσα κακοῖσιν;              (catalectic dimeter or
                                     paroemiac; no diaeresis)

**23.** Sung anapaests (also called melic, threnodic, or lyric anapaests)
belong to a higher emotional register and unlike the chanted variety
admit sequences of four shorts, may feature the Doric long alpha
in place of eta, occasionally omit word-break between metra, and
more frequently use catalectic lines and lines with many long elements.[15] Not all of these features need be present. In contrast to the
chanted anapaests of the nurse in 98−110, 115−30, etc., the anapaests

[15] See Dale (1968) 47−52.

of Medea in 96–7, 111–14, etc. are presumably sung: although they lack the other diagnostic features, they do have Doric long alpha and sung anapaests would suit the representation of Medea as emotionally distraught and out of control.

*Lyric verse*

**24.** A lyric stanza consists of one or more lyric periods (stretches of verse featuring synapheia within and metrical pause at the end). In order to understand fully the structure of a stanza and of its musical accompaniment, it is necessary to determine the division into periods, but unfortunately this division cannot always be established. Two indicators of period-end are hiatus (final vowel ending one period followed by initial vowel at the start of the next period) and *brevis in longo* (in full, *syllaba brevis in elemento longo*, 'short syllable in a position that is long in the metrical scheme'). A third indicator is catalectic structure (see above 14 on catalexis), and the end of a stanza is also always a period-end (symbol |||). For convenience of layout on the page and often to display parallelisms of partial internal structure within a period, periods are divided into shorter units called *cola* (singular *colon*, 'limb'). There does not have to be word-end at colon-end, and between cola within a single period there is synapheia.

**25.** Many of the cola found in tragic lyric are common and have well-established names; others are unique or rare and nameless. Cola are generally classified according to the general character of the rhythm: iambic ×–∪–; trochaic –∪–×; dactylic –∪∪; anapaestic ∪∪–∪∪–; ionic ∪∪––; choriambic –∪∪–; dochmiac ×––×–; aeolic (...–×) –∪∪– (×–...). Some cola have a tendency to appear at period-end because, within a given family of cola or a particular sequence of cola, they provide a sense of conclusive contrast (*catalexis* in the broadest sense). A colon with this character may be called a *clausula*. The paroemiac (anapaestic dimeter catalectic) is a good example – it is the clausula in systems of marching anapaests, as seen above.

As a sample of a simple lyric period, here is the scheme for the final period of the second pair of stanzas in the first stasimon of *Medea* (435–8 = 442–5). The period is built of cola that are familiar units of aeolic verse. The telesillean may be viewed as a glyconic with a shortened beginning and the pherecratean as a glyconic with a shortened end (that is, catalexis: see next paragraph). The division of the period into cola serves to highlight the familiarity and the similarity of the subunits of the period:

> ⏑̄ – ∪∪ – ∪ –| telesillean
> – – ∪∪ – ∪ – telesillean
> – – – ∪∪ – ∪ – glyconic
> – ⏑̄ – ∪∪ – ∪ – glyconic
> – ∪ – ∪∪ – –||| pherecratean (clausula)

Most of the lyrics in *Medea* fall into three categories: aeolic, dactylo-epitrite, and dochmiac.

**26.** *Aeolic verse* features a mixture of double-short and single-short movement (in contrast to the purely double-short movement of dactyls or anapaests and the single-short movement of iambic and trochaic). Aeolic cola all contain a double-short choriamb (– ∪∪ –) as kernel. Attached to this kernel are various lengths of different form (similar to a short piece of single-short movement, but including elements that feature successive longs, like the spondee – – or the bacchiac ∪ – –). Some of the more familar aeolic cola are shown here (∘∘ means two syllables that can be realized as – – or – ∪ or ∪ –, but not as ∪∪). It is not important for a beginner to master the recondite names, but rather to recognize the affinity of the many variations of aeolic.

| | | |
|---|---|---|
| glyconic (gl) | ∘∘ – ∪∪ – ∪ – | 8-syllable symmetric |
| hagesichorean (hag) | × – ∪∪ – ∪ – – | 8-syllable asymmetric |
| hipponactean | ∘∘ – ∪∪ – ∪ – – | 9-syllable |
| pherecratean (ph, pher) | ∘∘ – ∪∪ – – | 7-syllable (= catalectic glyconic, usually clausular) |
| telesillean | × – ∪∪ – ∪ – | 7-syllable |
| aristophanean | – ∪∪ – ∪ – – | 7-syllable |
| reizianum | × – ∪∪ – × | 6-syllable (= catalectic telesillean, usually clausular) |

Aeolic cola are found in the parodos and in the second halves of the first three stasimons.

**27.** *Dactylo-epitrite* is a somewhat different strain of rhythm mixing double-short and single-short movement. This verse-form seems to have originated in the great mythological lyric poems of Stesichorus and was much used in the epinicians of Pindar and Bacchylides. *Medea* is the surviving tragedy with the greatest concentration of dactylo-epitrite elements. Dactylo-epitrite verse may be analysed as built of certain familiar units of dactylic and iambo-trochaic structure. The most common dactylic unit is $-\cup\cup-\cup\cup-$, which in isolation is called a hemiepes (because it is the shape of the first half of an epic hexameter up to one of the common points of caesura in that line – the 'masculine' caesura); within a larger structure this unit is represented by the symbol D. The common iambo-trochaic pieces are $-\cup-$ (symbol e), the extensions of this made by adding anceps before and/or after $\times-\cup-$, $-\cup-\times$, $\times-\cup-\times$, and the paired unit $-\cup-\times-\cup-$ (symbol E). Dactylo-epitrite periods can be built up by an accumulation of these units, with or without a 'linking' anceps element between them: for instance, the opening lines of the first pair of the fourth stasimon may be denoted by the symbols $-D-e(\|?)e-D-\|$. Dactylo-epitrite cola are featured in the parodos and the first four stasimons.

**28.** *Dochmiac verse* is a form virtually unique to Attic drama and is the verse-form most clearly expressive of a consistent ethos, that of extreme agitation or excitement, whether resulting from grief or fear or joy. The basic scheme of the dochmiac metron is $\times--\times-$. Because of the frequency of resolution of the longs (esp. the first) and the various permutations of the two anceps elements, there are theoretically 32 possible versions of the dochmiac metron, but some do not occur at all, and several are quite rare. The most common variations include: $\cup--\cup-$, $\cup\widehat{\cup\cup}-\cup-$, and $-\widehat{\cup\cup}-\cup-$. The fifth stasimon is largely written in dochmiacs.

## KEY TO METRICAL SYMBOLS

| | |
|---|---|
| – | long element |
| ∪ | short element |

| $\overset{\frown}{\cup\cup}$ | two short elements resulting from resolution in a long position |
| × | anceps element (position allows long or short) |
| $\wedge$ | element suppressed in syncopation |
| ○ ○ | the paired initial elements in many aeolic lines, which may be $--$ or $-\cup$ or $\cup-$, but not $\cup\cup$ |
| ⋮ | mark of caesura in the iambic trimeter |
| \| | mark of diaeresis between anapaestic metra or word-end coinciding with colon-division within a period |
| \|\| | period-end (previous element counts as long, regardless of vowel-length) |
| \|\|[h] | period-end accompanied by hiatus (if in the scheme for a pair of stanzas, in one or both of the pair) |
| \|\|[b] | period-end accompanied by *brevis in longo* (if in the scheme for a pair of stanzas, in one or both of the pair) |
| \|\|[?] | period-end possible, but not certain |
| \|\|\| | end of lyric stanza |
| anap | anapaest ($\cup\cup-\cup\cup-$) |
| ba | bacchiac ($\cup--$) |
| cr | cretic ($-\cup-$) |
| D | $-\cup\cup-\cup\cup-$ (in dactylo-epitrite) |
| d[1] | $-\cup\cup-$ (in dactylo-epitrite) |
| d[2] | $\cup\cup-$ (in dactylo-epitrite) |
| da | dactyl ($-\cup\cup$) |
| dochm | dochmiac ($\times--\times-$) |
| E | $-\cup-\times-\cup-$ (in dactylo-epitrite) |
| e | $-\cup-$ (in dactylo-epitrite) |
| ia | iamb ($\times-\cup-$) |
| sp | spondee ($--$) |
| tro | trochee ($-\cup-\times$) |

When one symbol of metrical length is placed over another, this indicates that the upper symbol applies to the strophe of a corresponding pair and the lower symbol applies to the antistrophe. Thus, $\overline{\cup\cup}$ indicates a long syllable in the strophe corresponding to a pair of short syllables in the antistrophe.

# A NOTE ON THE CRITICAL
# APPARATUS

The apparatus criticus for this edition is extremely brief. Those requiring specific information about individual manuscripts, papyri, and testimonia should consult the Oxford Classical Text of Diggle; fuller information about testimonia may be found in H. van Looy's Teubner edition. Here medieval witnesses are not specifically identified. Readings of papyri are mentioned only when a variant is of interest, and no inference should be made from silence (specific identification of papyri may be found in the OCT, except for the papyrus cited at lines 1056a–87, published by Luppe (1995)). Variants are recorded only where they make some difference to the sense or receive discussion in the notes. All emendations accepted here are recorded, but otherwise only the most important of those discussed in the notes are listed. Orthography has tacitly been adjusted to the form established for tragedy by modern research.

Symbols in the apparatus:

**o**   reading of all the manuscripts
**p**   reading of one or more of the manuscripts
Π   reading of a papyrus
Σ   reading attested by a scholiast
ᵞᵖΣ   reading mentioned as variant (γράφεται = 'is read') by scholiast

Abbreviations in the apparatus:

add.      addidit
coni.     coniecit
del.      delevit
om.       omisit
s.l.      supra lineam
transp.   transposuit
trib.     tribuit

# ΜΗΔΕΙΑ

## ΤΑ ΤΟΥ ΔΡΑΜΑΤΟΣ ΠΡΟΣΩΠΑ

ΤΡΟΦΟΣ

ΠΑΙΔΑΓΩΓΟΣ

ΜΗΔΕΙΑ

ΧΟΡΟΣ ΓΥΝΑΙΚΩΝ

ΚΡΕΩΝ

ΙΑΣΩΝ

ΑΙΓΕΥΣ

ΑΓΓΕΛΟΣ

ΠΑΙΔΕΣ ΜΗΔΕΙΑΣ

# ΜΗΔΕΙΑ

## ΤΡΟΦΟΣ

Εἴθ' ὤφελ' Ἀργοῦς μὴ διαπτάσθαι σκάφος     1
Κόλχων ἐς αἶαν κυανέας Συμπληγάδας,
μηδ' ἐν νάπαισι Πηλίου πεσεῖν ποτε
τμηθεῖσα πεύκη, μηδ' ἐρετμῶσαι χέρας
ἀνδρῶν ἀρίστων οἳ τὸ πάγχρυσον δέρος     5
Πελίαι μετῆλθον. οὐ γὰρ ἂν δέσποιν' ἐμὴ
Μήδεια πύργους γῆς ἔπλευσ' Ἰωλκίας
ἔρωτι θυμὸν ἐκπλαγεῖσ' Ἰάσονος·
οὐδ' ἂν κτανεῖν πείσασα Πελιάδας κόρας
πατέρα κατώικει τήνδε γῆν Κορινθίαν     10
ξὺν ἀνδρὶ καὶ τέκνοισιν, ἁνδάνουσα μὲν
φυγὰς πολίταις ὧν ἀφίκετο χθόνα
αὐτῶι τε πάντα ξυμφέρουσ' Ἰάσονι·
ἥπερ μεγίστη γίγνεται σωτηρία,
ὅταν γυνὴ πρὸς ἄνδρα μὴ διχοστατῆι.     15
νῦν δ' ἐχθρὰ πάντα καὶ νοσεῖ τὰ φίλτατα.
προδοὺς γὰρ αὑτοῦ τέκνα δεσπότιν τ' ἐμὴν
γάμοις Ἰάσων βασιλικοῖς εὐνάζεται,
γήμας Κρέοντος παῖδ', ὃς αἰσυμνᾶι χθονός.
Μήδεια δ' ἡ δύστηνος ἠτιμασμένη     20
βοᾶι μὲν ὅρκους, ἀνακαλεῖ δὲ δεξιᾶς
πίστιν μεγίστην, καὶ θεοὺς μαρτύρεται
οἵας ἀμοιβῆς ἐξ Ἰάσονος κυρεῖ.
κεῖται δ' ἄσιτος, σῶμ' ὑφεῖσ' ἀλγηδόσιν,
τὸν πάντα συντήκουσα δακρύοις χρόνον     25
ἐπεὶ πρὸς ἀνδρὸς ἠισθετ' ἠδικημένη,
οὔτ' ὄμμ' ἐπαίρουσ' οὔτ' ἀπαλλάσσουσα γῆς

---

5 ἀρίστων o: ἀριστέων Wakefield     12 φυγὰς πολίταις Pierson (πολίταις
Barnes): φυγῆι πολιτῶν o     13 αὑτῶι Sakorraphos: αὐτή o

πρόσωπον· ὡς δὲ πέτρος ἢ θαλάσσιος
κλύδων ἀκούει νουθετουμένη φίλων,
ἢν μή ποτε στρέψασα πάλλευκον δέρην            30
αὐτὴ πρὸς αὑτὴν πατέρ᾽ ἀποιμώξῃ φίλον
καὶ γαῖαν οἴκους θ᾽, οὓς προδοῦσ᾽ ἀφίκετο
μετ᾽ ἀνδρὸς ὅς σφε νῦν ἀτιμάσας ἔχει.
ἔγνωκε δ᾽ ἡ τάλαινα συμφορᾶς ὕπο
οἷον πατρῴας μὴ ἀπολείπεσθαι χθονός.          35
στυγεῖ δὲ παῖδας οὐδ᾽ ὁρῶσ᾽ εὐφραίνεται.
δέδοικα δ᾽ αὐτὴν μή τι βουλεύσῃ νέον,
[βαρεῖα γὰρ φρήν, οὐδ᾽ ἀνέξεται κακῶς
πάσχουσ᾽· ἐγᾦδα τήνδε, δειμαίνω τέ νιν
μὴ θηκτὸν ὤσῃ φάσγανον δι᾽ ἥπατος,            40
σιγῇ δόμους ἐσβᾶσ᾽ ἵν᾽ ἔστρωται λέχος,
ἢ καὶ τύραννον τόν τε γήμαντα κτάνῃ]
κἄπειτα μείζω συμφορὰν λάβῃ τινά.
δεινὴ γάρ· οὔτοι ῥᾳδίως γε συμβαλὼν
ἔχθραν τις αὐτῇ καλλίνικον ἄσεται.            45
ἀλλ᾽ οἵδε παῖδες ἐκ τρόχων πεπαυμένοι
στείχουσι, μητρὸς οὐδὲν ἐννοούμενοι
κακῶν· νέα γὰρ φροντὶς οὐκ ἀλγεῖν φιλεῖ.


ΠΑΙΔΑΓΩΓΟΣ

παλαιὸν οἴκων κτῆμα δεσποίνης ἐμῆς,
τί πρὸς πύλαισι τήνδ᾽ ἄγουσ᾽ ἐρημίαν          50
ἕστηκας, αὐτὴ θρεομένη σαυτῇ κακά;
πῶς σοῦ μόνη Μήδεια λείπεσθαι θέλει;
Τρ.   τέκνων ὀπαδὲ πρέσβυ τῶν Ἰάσονος,
χρηστοῖσι δούλοις ξυμφορὰ τὰ δεσποτῶν
κακῶς πίτνοντα καὶ φρενῶν ἀνθάπτεται.        55


38–42 del. Barthold (38–43 Dindorf; 41 Musgrave, 42 Valckenaer et Pierson)   42 τύραννον **o**: τυράννους Hermann   45 αἴσεται Muretus: οἴσεται
**o**   46 τρόχων **o**: τροχῶν Trypho apud Ammonium

ἐγὼ γὰρ ἐς τοῦτ' ἐκβέβηκ' ἀλγηδόνος
ὥσθ' ἵμερός μ' ὑπῆλθε γῆι τε κοὐρανῶι
λέξαι μολούσηι δεῦρο δεσποίνης τύχας.

Πα.  οὔπω γὰρ ἡ τάλαινα παύεται γόων;
Τρ.  ζηλῶ σ'· ἐν ἀρχῆι πῆμα κοὐδέπω μεσοῖ.          60
Πα.  ὦ μῶρος, εἰ χρὴ δεσπότας εἰπεῖν τόδε·
ὡς οὐδὲν οἶδε τῶν νεωτέρων κακῶν.

Τρ.  τί δ' ἔστιν, ὦ γεραιέ; μὴ φθόνει φράσαι.
Πα.  οὐδέν· μετέγνων καὶ τὰ πρόσθ' εἰρημένα.
Τρ.  μή, πρὸς γενείου, κρύπτε σύνδουλον σέθεν·          65
σιγὴν γάρ, εἰ χρή, τῶνδε θήσομαι πέρι.

Πα.  ἤκουσά του λέγοντος, οὐ δοκῶν κλύειν,
πεσσοὺς προσελθών, ἔνθα δὴ παλαίτεροι
θάσσουσι, σεμνὸν ἀμφὶ Πειρήνης ὕδωρ,
ὡς τούσδε παῖδας γῆς ἐλᾶν Κορινθίας          70
σὺν μητρὶ μέλλοι τῆσδε κοίρανος χθονὸς
Κρέων. ὁ μέντοι μῦθος εἰ σαφὴς ὅδε
οὐκ οἶδα· βουλοίμην δ' ἂν οὐκ εἶναι τόδε.

Τρ.  καὶ ταῦτ' Ἰάσων παῖδας ἐξανέξεται
πάσχοντας, εἰ καὶ μητρὶ διαφορὰν ἔχει;          75
Πα.  παλαιὰ καινῶν λείπεται κηδευμάτων,
κοὐκ ἔστ' ἐκεῖνος τοῖσδε δώμασιν φίλος.

Τρ.  ἀπωλόμεσθ' ἄρ', εἰ κακὸν προσοίσομεν
νέον παλαιῶι, πρὶν τόδ' ἐξηντληκέναι.

Πα.  ἀτὰρ σύ γ', οὐ γὰρ καιρὸς εἰδέναι τόδε          80
δέσποιναν, ἡσύχαζε καὶ σίγα λόγον.

Τρ.  ὦ τέκν', ἀκούεθ' οἷος εἰς ὑμᾶς πατήρ;
ὄλοιτο μὲν μή· δεσπότης γάρ ἐστ' ἐμός·
ἀτὰρ κακός γ' ὢν ἐς φίλους ἁλίσκεται.

Πα.  τίς δ' οὐχὶ θνητῶν; ἄρτι γιγνώσκεις τόδε,          85
ὡς πᾶς τις αὑτὸν τοῦ πέλας μᾶλλον φιλεῖ,
[οἱ μὲν δικαίως, οἱ δὲ καὶ κέρδους χάριν,]

68 παλαίτεροι Pierson (cf. Chr. pat. 1181): παλαίτατοι o          87 del. Brunck
(cf. Σ)

εἰ τούσδε γ᾽ εὐνῆς οὕνεκ᾽ οὐ στέργει πατήρ;

Τρ.   ἴτ᾽, εὖ γὰρ ἔσται, δωμάτων ἔσω, τέκνα.

σὺ δ᾽ ὡς μάλιστα τοῦσδ᾽ ἐρημώσας ἔχε          90
καὶ μὴ πέλαζε μητρὶ δυσθυμουμένηι.

ἤδη γὰρ εἶδον ὄμμα νιν ταυρουμένην
τοῖσδ᾽, ὥς τι δρασείουσαν· οὐδὲ παύσεται
χόλου, σάφ᾽ οἶδα, πρὶν κατασκῆψαί τινι.

ἐχθρούς γε μέντοι, μὴ φίλους, δράσειέ τι.          95

ΜΗΔΕΙΑ (ἔσωθεν)

ἰώ,
δύστανος ἐγὼ μελέα τε πόνων,
ἰώ μοί μοι, πῶς ἂν ὀλοίμαν;

Τρ.   τόδ᾽ ἐκεῖνο, φίλοι παῖδες· μήτηρ
κινεῖ κραδίαν, κινεῖ δὲ χόλον.

σπεύδετε θᾶσσον δώματος εἴσω          100
καὶ μὴ πελάσητ᾽ ὄμματος ἐγγὺς
μηδὲ προσέλθητ᾽, ἀλλὰ φυλάσσεσθ᾽
ἄγριον ἦθος στυγεράν τε φύσιν
φρενὸς αὐθάδους.

ἴτε νυν, χωρεῖθ᾽ ὡς τάχος εἴσω.          105
δῆλον δ᾽ ἀρχῆς ἐξαιρόμενον
νέφος οἰμωγῆς ὡς τάχ᾽ ἀνάψει
μείζονι θυμῶι· τί ποτ᾽ ἐργάσεται
μεγαλόσπλαγχνος δυσκατάπαυστος
     ψυχὴ δηχθεῖσα κακοῖσιν;          110

Μη.   αἰαῖ,
ἔπαθον τλάμων ἔπαθον μεγάλων
ἄξι᾽ ὀδυρμῶν. ὦ κατάρατοι
παῖδες ὄλοισθε στυγερᾶς ματρὸς
     σὺν πατρί, καὶ πᾶς δόμος ἔρροι.

94 τινι Blomfield: τινα o      100 σπεύδετε p: σπεύσατε p      106 δ᾽ p: δ᾽ ἐξ p:
ἀπ᾽ Diggle

Τρ.  ἰώ μοί μοι, ἰὼ τλήμων.                                    115
τί δέ σοι παῖδες πατρὸς ἀμπλακίας
μετέχουσι; τί τούσδ᾽ ἔχθεις; οἴμοι,
τέκνα, μή τι πάθηθ᾽ ὡς ὑπεραλγῶ.
δεινὰ τυράννων λήματα καί πως
ὀλίγ᾽ ἀρχόμενοι, πολλὰ κρατοῦντες,                          120
χαλεπῶς ὀργὰς μεταβάλλουσιν.
τὸ γὰρ εἰθίσθαι ζῆν ἐπ᾽ ἴσοισιν
κρεῖσσον· ἐμοὶ γοῦν ἐπὶ μὴ μεγάλοις
ὀχυρῶς γ᾽ εἴη καταγηράσκειν.
τῶν γὰρ μετρίων πρῶτα μὲν εἰπεῖν                            125
τοὔνομα νικᾶι, χρῆσθαί τε μακρῶι
λῶιστα βροτοῖσιν· τὰ δ᾽ ὑπερβάλλοντ᾽
οὐδένα καιρὸν δύναται θνητοῖς,
μείζους δ᾽ ἄτας, ὅταν ὀργισθῆι
δαίμων οἴκοις, ἀπέδωκεν.                                    130

ΧΟΡΟΣ

ἔκλυον φωνάν, ἔκλυον δὲ βοὰν
τᾶς δυστάνου Κολχίδος· οὐδέπω
ἤπιος; ἀλλ᾽, ὦ γεραιά, λέξον.
ἀμφιπύλου γὰρ ἔσω μελάθρου γόον                           134-5
ἔκλυον, οὐδὲ συνήδομαι, ὦ γύναι,
ἄλγεσι δώματος,
ἐπεί μοι φιλία κέκραται.
Τρ.  οὐκ εἰσὶ δόμοι· φροῦδα τάδ᾽ ἤδη.
τὸν μὲν γὰρ ἔχει λέκτρα τυράννων,                         140
ἡ δ᾽ ἐν θαλάμοις τήκει βιοτὴν
δέσποινα, φίλων οὐδενὸς οὐδὲν
παραθαλπομένη φρένα μύθοις.
Μη.  αἰαῖ,

123 ἐπὶ μὴ μεγάλοις Barthold: εἰ μὴ μεγάλως o   124 γ᾽ Reiske: τ᾽ o   135
ἀμφιπύλου Weil: ἐπ᾽ ἀμφιπύλου o   γόον Elmsley: βοὰν o   138 φιλία
κέκραται Porson: φίλον κέκρα(ν)ται o

Μη. διά μου κεφαλᾶς φλὸξ οὐρανία
βαίη· τί δέ μοι ζῆν ἔτι κέρδος; 145
φεῦ φεῦ· θανάτωι καταλυσαίμαν
βιοτὰν στυγερὰν προλιποῦσα.

Χο. ἄιες, ὦ Ζεῦ καὶ Γᾶ καὶ φῶς, [στρ.
ἀχὰν οἵαν ἁ δύστανος
μέλπει νύμφα; 150
τίς σοί ποτε τᾶς ἀπλάτου
κοίτας ἔρος, ὦ ματαία;
σπεύσεις θανάτου τελευτάν;
μηδὲν τόδε λίσσου.
εἰ δὲ σὸς πόσις καινὰ λέχη σεβίζει, 155
κείνωι τόδε μὴ χαράσσου·
Ζεύς σοι τάδε συνδικήσει.
μὴ λίαν τάκου δυρομένα σὸν εὐνάταν. 158-9

Μη. ὦ μεγάλα Θέμι καὶ πότνι' Ἄρτεμι, 160
λεύσσεθ' ἃ πάσχω, μεγάλοις ὅρκοις
ἐνδησαμένα τὸν κατάρατον
πόσιν; ὅν ποτ' ἐγὼ νύμφαν τ' ἐσίδοιμ'
αὐτοῖς μελάθροις διακναιομένους,
οἳ' ἐμὲ πρόσθεν τολμῶσ' ἀδικεῖν. 165
ὦ πάτερ, ὦ πόλις, ὦν ἀπενάσθην
αἰσχρῶς τὸν ἐμὸν κτείνασα κάσιν.

Τρ. κλύεθ' οἷα λέγει κἀπιβοᾶται
Θέμιν εὐκταίαν Ζῆνά θ', ὃς ὅρκων
θνητοῖς ταμίας νενόμισται; 170
οὐκ ἔστιν ὅπως ἔν τινι μικρῶι
δέσποινα χόλον καταπαύσει.

Χο. πῶς ἂν ἐς ὄψιν τὰν ἁμετέραν [ἀντ.
ἔλθοι μύθων τ' αὐδαθέντων

149 ἀχὰν Elmsley: ἰαχὰν o 151 ἀπλάτου Elmsley: ἀπλάστου vel ἀπλήστου
o 153 σπεύσεις Blaydes: σπεύσει p: σπεύδει p τελευτάν; o: τελευτά·
(cum σπεύσει) Weil 159 εὐνάταν p, Tyrwhitt: εὐνέταν p 165 οἳ' ἐμὲ
Kaibel: οἵ γέ με o

δέξαιτ' ὀμφάν, 175
εἴ πως βαρύθυμον ὀργὰν
καὶ λῆμα φρενῶν μεθείη;
μήτοι τό γ' ἐμὸν πρόθυμον
φίλοισιν ἀπέστω.
ἀλλὰ βᾶσά νιν δεῦρο πόρευσον οἴκων 180
ἔξω· φίλα καὶ τάδ' αὔδα,
σπεύσασά τι πρὶν κακῶσαι
τοὺς ἔσω· πένθος γὰρ μεγάλως τόδ' ὁρμᾶται.

Τρ.  δράσω τάδ'· ἀτὰρ φόβος εἰ πείσω
δέσποιναν ἐμήν· 185
μόχθου δὲ χάριν τήνδ' ἐπιδώσω.
καίτοι τοκάδος δέργμα λεαίνης
ἀποταυροῦται δμωσίν, ὅταν τις
μῦθον προφέρων πέλας ὁρμηθῆι.
σκαιοὺς δὲ λέγων κοὐδέν τι σοφοὺς 190
τοὺς πρόσθε βροτοὺς οὐκ ἂν ἁμάρτοις,
οἵτινες ὕμνους ἐπὶ μὲν θαλίαις
ἐπί τ' εἰλαπίναις καὶ παρὰ δείπνοις
ηὕροντο βίωι τερπνὰς ἀκοάς·
στυγίους δὲ βροτῶν οὐδεὶς λύπας 195
ηὕρετο μούσηι καὶ πολυχόρδοις
ὠιδαῖς παύειν, ἐξ ὧν θάνατοι
δειναί τε τύχαι σφάλλουσι δόμους.
καίτοι τάδε μὲν κέρδος ἀκεῖσθαι
μολπαῖσι βροτούς· ἵνα δ' εὔδειπνοι 200
δαῖτες, τί μάτην τείνουσι βοήν;
τὸ παρὸν γὰρ ἔχει τέρψιν ἀφ' αὑτοῦ
δαιτὸς πλήρωμα βροτοῖσιν.

Χο.  ἀχὰν ἄιον πολύστονον γόων,
λιγυρὰ δ' ἄχεα μογερὰ βοᾶι 205
τὸν ἐν λέχει προδόταν κακόνυμφον·

---

182 σπεύσασά Schöne: σπεῦσαι **p**: σπεῦσον **p**    τι πρὶν **p**: πρίν τι **p**    194
βίωι Page: βίου **o**    204 ἀχὰν Dindorf: ἰαχὰν **o**

θεοκλυτεῖ δ' ἄδικα παθοῦσα
   τὰν Ζηνὸς ὁρκίαν Θέμιν, ἅ νιν ἔβασεν    208–9
   Ἑλλάδ' ἐς ἀντίπορον    210
   δι' ἅλα νύχιον ἐφ' ἁλμυρὰν    211–12
   Πόντου κλῇδ' ἀπεράντου.

## ΜΗΔΕΙΑ

Κορίνθιαι γυναῖκες, ἐξῆλθον δόμων
μή μοί τι μέμψησθ'· οἶδα γὰρ πολλοὺς βροτῶν    215
σεμνοὺς γεγῶτας, τοὺς μὲν ὀμμάτων ἄπο,
τοὺς δ' ἐν θυραίοις· οἱ δ' ἀφ' ἡσύχου ποδὸς
δύσκλειαν ἐκτήσαντο καὶ ῥαιθυμίαν.
δίκη γὰρ οὐκ ἔνεστ' ἐν ὀφθαλμοῖς βροτῶν,
ὅστις πρὶν ἀνδρὸς σπλάγχνον ἐκμαθεῖν σαφῶς    220
στυγεῖ δεδορκώς, οὐδὲν ἠδικημένος.
χρὴ δὲ ξένον μὲν κάρτα προσχωρεῖν πόλει·
οὐδ' ἀστὸν ᾔνεσ' ὅστις αὐθάδης γεγὼς
πικρὸς πολίταις ἐστὶν ἀμαθίας ὕπο.
ἐμοὶ δ' ἄελπτον πρᾶγμα προσπεσὸν τόδε    225
ψυχὴν διέφθαρκ'· οἴχομαι δὲ καὶ βίου
χάριν μεθεῖσα κατθανεῖν χρῄζω, φίλαι.
ἐν ὧι γὰρ ἦν μοι πάντα, γιγνώσκω καλῶς,
κάκιστος ἀνδρῶν ἐκβέβηχ' οὑμὸς πόσις.
πάντων δ' ὅσ' ἔστ' ἔμψυχα καὶ γνώμην ἔχει    230
γυναῖκές ἐσμεν ἀθλιώτατον φυτόν·
ἃς πρῶτα μὲν δεῖ χρημάτων ὑπερβολῆι
πόσιν πρίασθαι δεσπότην τε σώματος
λαβεῖν· κακοῦ γὰρ τοῦτ' ἔτ' ἄλγιον κακόν.
κἂν τῶιδ' ἀγὼν μέγιστος, ἢ κακὸν λαβεῖν    235
ἢ χρηστόν. οὐ γὰρ εὐκλεεῖς ἀπαλλαγαὶ

---

212 ἀπεράντου Milton: ἀπέραντον **o**: ἀπέρατον Blaydes    215 μέμψ- **p**:
μέμφ- **p**    224 πολίταις **p**: πολίτης **p**    228 γιγνώσκω Canter: γιγνώσκειν **o**    234 τοῦτ' ἔτ' Brunck: τοῦτ' **p**: τοῦδ' ἔτ' **p**: τοῦτό γ' **p**

γυναιξὶν οὐδ' οἷόν τ' ἀνήνασθαι πόσιν.
ἐς καινὰ δ' ἤθη καὶ νόμους ἀφιγμένην
δεῖ μάντιν εἶναι, μὴ μαθοῦσαν οἴκοθεν,
οἵωι μάλιστα χρήσεται ξυνευνέτηι.                           240
κἂν μὲν τάδ' ἡμῖν ἐκπονουμέναισιν εὖ
πόσις ξυνοικῆι μὴ βίαι φέρων ζυγόν,
ζηλωτὸς αἰών· εἰ δὲ μή, θανεῖν χρεών.
ἀνὴρ δ', ὅταν τοῖς ἔνδον ἄχθηται ξυνών,
ἔξω μολὼν ἔπαυσε καρδίαν ἄσης                           245
[ἢ πρὸς φίλον τιν' ἢ πρὸς ἥλικα τραπείς]·
ἡμῖν δ' ἀνάγκη πρὸς μίαν ψυχὴν βλέπειν.
λέγουσι δ' ἡμᾶς ὡς ἀκίνδυνον βίον
ζῶμεν κατ' οἴκους, οἱ δὲ μάρνανται δορί,
κακῶς φρονοῦντες· ὡς τρὶς ἂν παρ' ἀσπίδα                 250
στῆναι θέλοιμ' ἂν μᾶλλον ἢ τεκεῖν ἅπαξ.
ἀλλ' οὐ γὰρ αὐτὸς πρὸς σὲ κἄμ' ἥκει λόγος·
σοὶ μὲν πόλις θ' ἥδ' ἐστὶ καὶ πατρὸς δόμοι
βίου τ' ὄνησις καὶ φίλων συνουσία,
ἐγὼ δ' ἔρημος ἄπολις οὖσ' ὑβρίζομαι                      255
πρὸς ἀνδρός, ἐκ γῆς βαρβάρου λεληισμένη,
οὐ μητέρ', οὐκ ἀδελφόν, οὐχὶ συγγενῆ
μεθορμίσασθαι τῆσδ' ἔχουσα συμφορᾶς.
τοσοῦτον οὖν σου τυγχάνειν βουλήσομαι,
ἤν μοι πόρος τις μηχανή τ' ἐξευρεθῆι                     260
πόσιν δίκην τῶνδ' ἀντιτείσασθαι κακῶν
[τὸν δόντα τ' αὐτῶι θυγατέρ' ἥν τ' ἐγήματο],
σιγᾶν. γυνὴ γὰρ τἄλλα μὲν φόβου πλέα
κακή τ' ἐς ἀλκὴν καὶ σίδηρον εἰσορᾶν·
ὅταν δ' ἐς εὐνὴν ἠδικημένη κυρῆι,                       265
οὐκ ἔστιν ἄλλη φρὴν μιαιφονωτέρα.
Χο.   δράσω τάδ'· ἐνδίκως γὰρ ἐκτείσηι πόσιν,

240 οἵωι μάλιστα Musgrave: ὅτωι μάλιστα fere ο: ὅπως (Meineke) ἄριστα Barthold     245 καρδίαν ἄσης p: καρδίας ἄσην p     246 del. Wilamowitz     262 del. Lenting     264 τ' Tyrwhitt: δ' ο

Μήδεια. πενθεῖν δ' οὔ σε θαυμάζω τύχας.
ὁρῶ δὲ καὶ Κρέοντα, τῆσδ' ἄνακτα γῆς,
στείχοντα, καινῶν ἄγγελον βουλευμάτων.　　　270

## ΚΡΕΩΝ

σὲ τὴν σκυθρωπὸν καὶ πόσει θυμουμένην,
Μήδει', ἀνεῖπον τῆσδε γῆς ἔξω περᾶν
φυγάδα, λαβοῦσαν δισσὰ σὺν σαυτῆι τέκνα,
καὶ μή τι μέλλειν· ὡς ἐγὼ βραβεὺς λόγου
τοῦδ' εἰμί, κοὐκ ἄπειμι πρὸς δόμους πάλιν　　　275
πρὶν ἄν σε γαίας τερμόνων ἔξω βάλω.
Μη.　αἰαῖ· πανώλης ἡ τάλαιν' ἀπόλλυμαι·
ἐχθροὶ γὰρ ἐξιᾶσι πάντα δὴ κάλων,
κοὐκ ἔστιν ἄτης εὐπρόσοιστος ἔκβασις.
ἐρήσομαι δὲ καὶ κακῶς πάσχουσ' ὅμως·　　　280
τίνος μ' ἕκατι γῆς ἀποστέλλεις, Κρέον;
Κρ.　δέδοικά σ', οὐδὲν δεῖ παραμπίσχειν λόγους,
μή μοί τι δράσηις παῖδ' ἀνήκεστον κακόν.
συμβάλλεται δὲ πολλὰ τοῦδε δείγματα·
σοφὴ πέφυκας καὶ κακῶν πολλῶν ἴδρις,　　　285
λυπῆι δὲ λέκτρων ἀνδρὸς ἐστερημένη.
κλύω δ' ἀπειλεῖν σ', ὡς ἀπαγγέλλουσί μοι,
τὸν δόντα καὶ γήμαντα καὶ γαμουμένην
δράσειν τι. ταῦτ' οὖν πρὶν παθεῖν φυλάξομαι.
κρεῖσσον δέ μοι νῦν πρός σ' ἀπεχθέσθαι, γύναι,　　　290
ἤ μαλθακισθένθ' ὕστερον μεταστένειν.
Μη.　φεῦ φεῦ.
οὐ νῦν με πρῶτον ἀλλὰ πολλάκις, Κρέον,
ἔβλαψε δόξα μεγάλα τ' εἴργασται κακά.
χρὴ δ' οὔποθ' ὅστις ἀρτίφρων πέφυκ' ἀνὴρ
παῖδας περισσῶς ἐκδιδάσκεσθαι σοφούς·　　　295

---

272 Μήδει', ἀνεῖπον Harrison: Μήδειαν, εἶπον **o**　　　284 τοῦδε δείγματα Wieseler: τοῦδε δείματος **o**: τῶιδε δείματι Schöne　　　291 μεταστένειν gnomolo-
gium Escorialense (coni. Nauck): μέγα στένειν **o**

χωρὶς γὰρ ἄλλης ἧς ἔχουσιν ἀργίας
φθόνον πρὸς ἀστῶν ἀλφάνουσι δυσμενῆ.
σκαιοῖσι μὲν γὰρ καινὰ προσφέρων σοφὰ
δόξεις ἀχρεῖος κοὐ σοφὸς πεφυκέναι·
τῶν δ' αὖ δοκούντων εἰδέναι τι ποικίλον          300
κρείσσων νομισθεὶς ἐν πόλει λυπρὸς φανῇ.
ἐγὼ δὲ καὐτὴ τῆσδε κοινωνῶ τύχης·
σοφὴ γὰρ οὖσα, τοῖς μέν εἰμ' ἐπίφθονος,
[τοῖς δ' ἡσυχαία, τοῖς δὲ θατέρου τρόπου,]
τοῖς δ' αὖ προσάντης· εἰμὶ δ' οὐκ ἄγαν σοφή.      305
σὺ δ' οὖν φοβῇ με· μὴ τί πλημμελὲς πάθῃς;
οὐχ ὧδ' ἔχει μοι, μὴ τρέσῃς ἡμᾶς, Κρέον,
ὥστ' ἐς τυράννους ἄνδρας ἐξαμαρτάνειν.
σὺ γὰρ τί μ' ἠδίκηκας; ἐξέδου κόρην
ὅτωι σε θυμὸς ἦγεν. ἀλλ' ἐμὸν πόσιν              310
μισῶ· σὺ δ', οἶμαι, σωφρονῶν ἔδρας τάδε.
καὶ νῦν τὸ μὲν σὸν οὐ φθονῶ καλῶς ἔχειν·
νυμφεύετ', εὖ πράσσοιτε· τήνδε δὲ χθόνα
ἐᾶτέ μ' οἰκεῖν. καὶ γὰρ ἠδικημένοι
σιγησόμεσθα, κρεισσόνων νικώμενοι.                315

Κρ.   λέγεις ἀκοῦσαι μαλθάκ', ἀλλ' ἔσω φρενῶν
ὀρρωδία μοι μή τι βουλεύῃς κακόν,
τοσῶιδε δ' ἧσσον ἢ πάρος πέποιθά σοι·
γυνὴ γὰρ ὀξύθυμος, ὡς δ' αὔτως ἀνήρ,
ῥάιων φυλάσσειν ἢ σιωπηλὸς σοφός.                320
ἀλλ' ἔξιθ' ὡς τάχιστα, μὴ λόγους λέγε·
ὡς ταῦτ' ἄραρε κοὐκ ἔχεις τέχνην ὅπως
μενεῖς παρ' ἡμῖν οὖσα δυσμενὴς ἐμοί.

Μη.   μή, πρός σε γονάτων τῆς τε νεογάμου κόρης.
Κρ.   λόγους ἀναλοῖς· οὐ γὰρ ἂν πείσαις ποτέ.      325
Μη.   ἀλλ' ἐξελᾶις με κοὐδὲν αἰδέσηι λιτάς;
Κρ.   φιλῶ γὰρ οὐ σὲ μᾶλλον ἢ δόμους ἐμούς.
Μη.   ὦ πατρίς, ὥς σου κάρτα νῦν μνείαν ἔχω.

---

304 om. **p**, del. Pierson    309 σὺ γὰρ τί **p**: τί γὰρ σὺ **p**    317 βουλεύῃς
Elmsley: βουλεύσηις **o**    318 δ' **p**: γ' **p**    320 σοφός **o**: σοφή Diggle

Κρ.  πλὴν γὰρ τέκνων ἔμοιγε φίλτατον πολύ.

Μη.  φεῦ φεῦ, βροτοῖς ἔρωτες ὡς κακὸν μέγα.  330

Κρ.  ὅπως ἄν, οἶμαι, καὶ παραστῶσιν τύχαι.

Μη.  Ζεῦ, μὴ λάθοι σε τῶνδ' ὃς αἴτιος κακῶν.

Κρ.  ἕρπ', ὦ ματαία, καί μ' ἀπάλλαξον πόνων.

Μη.  πονοῦμεν ἡμεῖς κοὐ πόνων κεχρήμεθα.

Κρ.  τάχ' ἐξ ὀπαδῶν χειρὸς ὠσθήσῃ βίαι.  335

Μη.  μὴ δῆτα τοῦτό γ', ἀλλά σ' ἄντομαι, Κρέον.

Κρ.  ὄχλον παρέξεις, ὡς ἔοικας, ὦ γύναι.

Μη.  φευξούμεθ'· οὐ τοῦθ' ἱκέτευσά σου τυχεῖν.

Κρ.  τί δ' αὖ βιάζῃ κοὐκ ἀπαλλάσσῃ χερός;

Μη.  μίαν με μεῖναι τήνδ' ἔασον ἡμέραν  340
καὶ ξυμπερᾶναι φροντίδ' ἧι φευξούμεθα
παισίν τ' ἀφορμὴν τοῖς ἐμοῖς, ἐπεὶ πατὴρ
οὐδὲν προτιμᾶι μηχανήσασθαι τέκνοις.
οἴκτιρε δ' αὐτούς· καὶ σύ τοι παίδων πατὴρ
πέφυκας· εἰκὸς δέ σφιν εὔνοιάν σ' ἔχειν.  345
τοὐμοῦ γὰρ οὔ μοι φροντίς, εἰ φευξούμεθα,
κείνους δὲ κλαίω συμφορᾶι κεχρημένους.

Κρ.  ἥκιστα τοὐμὸν λῆμ' ἔφυ τυραννικόν,
αἰδούμενος δὲ πολλὰ δὴ διέφθορα·
καὶ νῦν ὁρῶ μὲν ἐξαμαρτάνων, γύναι,  350
ὅμως δὲ τεύξῃ τοῦδε. προυννέπω δέ σοι,
εἴ σ' ἡ 'πιοῦσα λαμπὰς ὄψεται θεοῦ
καὶ παῖδας ἐντὸς τῆσδε τερμόνων χθονός,
θανῆι· λέλεκται μῦθος ἀψευδὴς ὅδε.
νῦν δ', εἰ μένειν δεῖ, μίμν' ἐφ' ἡμέραν μίαν·  355
οὐ γάρ τι δράσεις δεινὸν ὧν φόβος μ' ἔχει.

Χο.  φεῦ φεῦ, μελέα τῶν σῶν ἀχέων,  358
δύστηνε γύναι,  357

---

336 ἄντομαι Wecklein: αἰτοῦμαι **o**   339 δ' αὖ **p**; δ' οὖν **p**: δὴ Elmsley, δαὶ
Housman   χερός Wilamowitz: χθονός **o**   345 δέ σφιν Vitelli: δ'
ἐστὶν **o**   355–56 del. Nauck   357 post 358 trai. Barthold; om. **p**, del.
Matthiae

ποῖ ποτε τρέψηι; τίνα πρὸς ξενίαν
ἢ δόμον ἢ χθόνα σωτῆρα κακῶν                    360
[ἐξευρήσεις];
ὡς εἰς ἄπορόν σε κλύδωνα θεός,
Μήδεια, κακῶν ἐπόρευσεν.

Μη. κακῶς πέπρακται πανταχῆι· τίς ἀντερεῖ;
ἀλλ' οὔτι ταύτηι ταῦτα, μὴ δοκεῖτέ πω.          365
ἔτ' εἰσ' ἀγῶνες τοῖς νεωστὶ νυμφίοις
καὶ τοῖσι κηδεύσασιν οὐ σμικροὶ πόνοι.
δοκεῖς γὰρ ἄν με τόνδε θωπεῦσαί ποτε
εἰ μή τι κερδαίνουσαν ἢ τεχνωμένην;
οὐδ' ἂν προσεῖπον οὐδ' ἂν ἡψάμην χεροῖν.        370
ὁ δ' ἐς τοσοῦτον μωρίας ἀφίκετο
ὥστ', ἐξὸν αὐτῶι τἄμ' ἑλεῖν βουλεύματα
γῆς ἐκβαλόντι, τήνδ' ἐφῆκεν ἡμέραν
μεῖναί μ', ἐν ἧι τρεῖς τῶν ἐμῶν ἐχθρῶν νεκροὺς
θήσω, πατέρα τε καὶ κόρην πόσιν τ' ἐμόν.        375
πολλὰς δ' ἔχουσα θανασίμους αὐτοῖς ὁδούς,
οὐκ οἶδ' ὁποίαι πρῶτον ἐγχειρῶ, φίλαι·
πότερον ὑφάψω δῶμα νυμφικὸν πυρί,
ἢ θηκτὸν ὤσω φάσγανον δι' ἥπατος,
σιγῆι δόμους ἐσβᾶσ' ἵν' ἔστρωται λέχος;        380
ἀλλ' ἕν τί μοι πρόσαντες· εἰ ληφθήσομαι
δόμους ὑπερβαίνουσα καὶ τεχνωμένη,
θανοῦσα θήσω τοῖς ἐμοῖς ἐχθροῖς γέλων.
κράτιστα τὴν εὐθεῖαν, ἧι πεφύκαμεν
σοφοὶ μάλιστα, φαρμάκοις αὐτοὺς ἑλεῖν.          385
εἶέν·
καὶ δὴ τεθνᾶσι· τίς με δέξεται πόλις;
τίς γῆν ἄσυλον καὶ δόμους ἐχεγγύους
ξένος παρασχὼν ῥύσεται τοὐμὸν δέμας;
οὐκ ἔστι. μείνασ' οὖν ἔτι σμικρὸν χρόνον,

359 πρὸς ξενίαν p: προξενίαν p      361 ἐξευρήσεις del. Elmsley      373 ἐφῆκεν
Nauck: ἀφῆκεν o      385 σοφοὶ Tate, Dalzel: σοφαὶ o

ἦν μέν τις ἡμῖν πύργος ἀσφαλὴς φανῆι,     390
δόλωι μέτειμι τόνδε καὶ σιγῆι φόνον·
ἢν δ' ἐξελαύνηι ξυμφορά μ' ἀμήχανος,
αὐτὴ ξίφος λαβοῦσα, κεἰ μέλλω θανεῖν,
κτενῶ σφε, τόλμης δ' εἶμι πρὸς τὸ καρτερόν.
οὐ γὰρ μὰ τὴν δέσποιναν ἣν ἐγὼ σέβω     395
μάλιστα πάντων καὶ ξυνεργὸν εἱλόμην,
Ἑκάτην, μυχοῖς ναίουσαν ἑστίας ἐμῆς,
χαίρων τις αὐτῶν τοὐμὸν ἀλγυνεῖ κέαρ.
πικροὺς δ' ἐγώ σφιν καὶ λυγροὺς θήσω γάμους,
πικρὸν δὲ κῆδος καὶ φυγὰς ἐμὰς χθονός.     400
ἀλλ' εἶα φείδου μηδὲν ὧν ἐπίστασαι,
Μήδεια, βουλεύουσα καὶ τεχνωμένη·
ἕρπ' ἐς τὸ δεινόν· νῦν ἀγὼν εὐψυχίας.
ὁρᾶις ἃ πάσχεις; οὐ γέλωτα δεῖ σ' ὀφλεῖν
τοῖς Σισυφείοις τοῖσδ' Ἰάσονος γάμοις,     405
γεγῶσαν ἐσθλοῦ πατρὸς Ἡλίου τ' ἄπο.
ἐπίστασαι δέ· πρὸς δὲ καὶ πεφύκαμεν
γυναῖκες, ἐς μὲν ἐσθλ' ἀμηχανώταται,
κακῶν δὲ πάντων τέκτονες σοφώταται.

Χο.   ἄνω ποταμῶν ἱερῶν χωροῦσι παγαί,     [στρ. 410–11
καὶ δίκα καὶ πάντα πάλιν στρέφεται·
   ἀνδράσι μὲν δόλιαι βουλαί, θεῶν δ'
   οὐκέτι πίστις ἄραρεν·
τὰν δ' ἐμὰν εὔκλειαν ἔχειν βιοτὰν στρέψουσι
     φᾶμαι·     415–16
ἔρχεται τιμὰ γυναικείωι γένει·     417–18
οὐκέτι δυσκέλαδος φάμα γυναῖκας ἕξει.     419–20

μοῦσαι δὲ παλαιγενέων λήξουσ' ἀοιδῶν     [ἀντ. 421–2
τὰν ἐμὰν ὑμνεῦσαι ἀπιστοσύναν.

405 τοῖσδ' Herwerden: τοῖς τ' **o**     413 δ' **o**: τ' Elmsley     416 στρέψουσι
Elmsley: στρέφουσι **o**     421 ἀοιδῶν **p**: ἀοιδᾶν **p**

οὐ γὰρ ἐν ἀμετέραι γνώμαι λύρας
ὤπασε θέσπιν ἀοιδὰν                                      425
Φοῖβος ἀγήτωρ μελέων· ἐπεὶ ἀντάχησ' ἂν ὕμνον    426–7
ἀρσένων γένναι. μακρὸς δ' αἰὼν ἔχει              428–9
πολλὰ μὲν ἀμετέραν ἀνδρῶν τε μοῖραν εἰπεῖν.   430–1

σὺ δ' ἐκ μὲν οἴκων πατρίων ἔπλευσας              [στρ.
μαινομέναι κραδίαι, διδύμους ὁρίσασα Πόντου    433–4
πέτρας· ἐπὶ δὲ ξέναι                                     435
  ναίεις χθονί, τᾶς ἀνάν-
  δρου κοίτας ὀλέσασα λέκ-
  τρον, τάλαινα, φυγὰς δὲ χώ-                        438a
  ρας ἄτιμος ἐλαύνηι.                                     438b

βέβακε δ' ὅρκων χάρις, οὐδ' ἔτ' αἰδὼς            [ἀντ.
Ἑλλάδι τᾶι μεγάλαι μένει, αἰθερία δ' ἀνέπτα.   440–1
σοὶ δ' οὔτε πατρὸς δόμοι,
  δύστανε, μεθορμίσα-
  σθαι μόχθων πάρα, τῶν τε λέκ-
  τρων ἄλλα βασίλεια κρείσ-                          445a
  σων δόμοισιν ἐπέστα.                                  445b

ΙΑΣΩΝ

οὐ νῦν κατεῖδον πρῶτον ἀλλὰ πολλάκις
τραχεῖαν ὀργὴν ὡς ἀμήχανον κακόν.
σοὶ γὰρ παρὸν γῆν τήνδε καὶ δόμους ἔχειν
κούφως φερούσηι κρεισσόνων βουλεύματα,
λόγων ματαίων οὕνεκ' ἐκπεσῆι χθονός.            450
κἀμοὶ μὲν οὐδὲν πρᾶγμα· μὴ παύσηι ποτὲ
λέγουσ' Ἰάσον' ὡς κάκιστός ἐστ' ἀνήρ·

432 πατρίων editio Aldina: πατρώιων o    434 διδύμους p: διδύμας
p    435 ξέναι editio Aldina: ξείναι o    444 τῶν τε Elmsley: τῶνδε o: σῶν
τε Porson    452 Ἰάσον' Elmsley: Ἰάσων o

ἃ δ' ἐς τυράννους ἐστί σοι λελεγμένα,
πᾶν κέρδος ἡγοῦ ζημιουμένη φυγῆι.
κἀγὼ μὲν αἰεὶ βασιλέων θυμουμένων                    455
ὀργὰς ἀφήιρουν καί σ' ἐβουλόμην μένειν·
σὺ δ' οὐκ ἀνίεις μωρίας, λέγουσ' ἀεὶ
κακῶς τυράννους· τοιγὰρ ἐκπεσῆι χθονός.
ὅμως δὲ κἀκ τῶνδ' οὐκ ἀπειρηκὼς φίλοις
ἥκω, τὸ σὸν δὲ προσκοπούμενος, γύναι,                    460
ὡς μήτ' ἀχρήμων σὺν τέκνοισιν ἐκπέσηις
μήτ' ἐνδεής του· πόλλ' ἐφέλκεται φυγὴ
κακὰ ξὺν αὑτῆι. καὶ γὰρ εἰ σύ με στυγεῖς,
οὐκ ἂν δυναίμην σοὶ κακῶς φρονεῖν ποτε.
Μη. ὦ παγκάκιστε, τοῦτο γάρ σ' εἰπεῖν ἔχω                    465
γλώσσηι μέγιστον εἰς ἀνανδρίαν κακόν,
ἦλθες πρὸς ἡμᾶς, ἦλθες ἔχθιστος γεγώς
[θεοῖς τε κἀμοὶ παντί τ' ἀνθρώπων γένει];
οὔτοι θράσος τόδ' ἐστὶν οὐδ' εὐτολμία,
φίλους κακῶς δράσαντ' ἐναντίον βλέπειν,                    470
ἀλλ' ἡ μεγίστη τῶν ἐν ἀνθρώποις νόσων
πασῶν, ἀναίδει'. εὖ δ' ἐποίησας μολών·
ἐγώ τε γὰρ λέξασα κουφισθήσομαι
ψυχὴν κακῶς σε καὶ σὺ λυπήσηι κλύων.
ἐκ τῶν δὲ πρώτων πρῶτον ἄρξομαι λέγειν·                    475
ἔσωσά σ', ὡς ἴσασιν Ἑλλήνων ὅσοι
ταὐτὸν συνεισέβησαν Ἀργῶιον σκάφος,
πεμφθέντα ταύρων πυρπνόων ἐπιστάτην
ζεύγλαισι καὶ σπεροῦντα θανάσιμον γύην·
δράκοντά θ', ὃς πάγχρυσον ἀμπέχων δέρος                    480
σπείραις ἔσωιζε πολυπλόκοις ἄυπνος ὤν,
κτείνασ' ἀνέσχον σοι φάος σωτήριον.
αὐτὴ δὲ πατέρα καὶ δόμους προδοῦσ' ἐμοὺς
τὴν Πηλιῶτιν εἰς Ἰωλκὸν ἱκόμην
σὺν σοί, πρόθυμος μᾶλλον ἢ σοφωτέρα·                    485

468 del. Brunck          480 θ' p: δ' p

Πελίαν τ' ἀπέκτειν', ὥσπερ ἄλγιστον θανεῖν,
παίδων ὕπ' αὐτοῦ, πάντα τ' ἐξεῖλον δόμον.
καὶ ταῦθ' ὑφ' ἡμῶν, ὦ κάκιστ' ἀνδρῶν, παθὼν
προύδωκας ἡμᾶς, καινὰ δ' ἐκτήσω λέχη,
παίδων γεγώτων· εἰ γὰρ ἦσθ' ἄπαις ἔτι,                    490
συγγνώστ' ἂν ἦν σοι τοῦδ' ἐρασθῆναι λέχους.
ὅρκων δὲ φρούδη πίστις, οὐδ' ἔχω μαθεῖν
εἰ θεοὺς νομίζεις τοὺς τότ' οὐκ ἄρχειν ἔτι
ἢ καινὰ κεῖσθαι θέσμι' ἀνθρώποις τὰ νῦν,
ἐπεὶ σύνοισθά γ' εἰς ἔμ' οὐκ εὔορκος ὤν.               495
φεῦ δεξιὰ χείρ, ἧς σὺ πόλλ' ἐλαμβάνου
καὶ τῶνδε γονάτων, ὡς μάτην κεχρώισμεθα
κακοῦ πρὸς ἀνδρός, ἐλπίδων δ' ἡμάρτομεν.
ἄγ', ὡς φίλωι γὰρ ὄντι σοι κοινώσομαι
(δοκοῦσα μὲν τί πρός γε σοῦ πράξειν καλῶς;            500
ὅμως δ', ἐρωτηθεὶς γὰρ αἰσχίων φανῆι)·
νῦν ποῖ τράπωμαι; πότερα πρὸς πατρὸς δόμους,
οὓς σοὶ προδοῦσα καὶ πάτραν ἀφικόμην;
ἢ πρὸς ταλαίνας Πελιάδας; καλῶς γ' ἂν οὖν
δέξαιντό μ' οἴκοις ὧν πατέρα κατέκτανον.              505
ἔχει γὰρ οὕτω· τοῖς μὲν οἴκοθεν φίλοις
ἐχθρὰ καθέστηχ', οὓς δέ μ' οὐκ ἐχρῆν κακῶς
δρᾶν, σοὶ χάριν φέρουσα πολεμίους ἔχω.
τοιγάρ με πολλαῖς μακαρίαν Ἑλληνίδων
ἔθηκας ἀντὶ τῶνδε· θαυμαστὸν δέ σε                    510
ἔχω πόσιν καὶ πιστὸν ἡ τάλαιν' ἐγώ,
εἰ φεύξομαί γε γαῖαν ἐκβεβλημένη,
φίλων ἔρημος, σὺν τέκνοις μόνη μόνοις·
καλόν γ' ὄνειδος τῶι νεωστὶ νυμφίωι,
πτωχοὺς ἀλᾶσθαι παῖδας ἥ τ' ἔσωσά σε.               515
ὦ Ζεῦ, τί δὴ χρυσοῦ μὲν ὃς κίβδηλος ἦι
τεκμήρι' ἀνθρώποισιν ὤπασας σαφῆ,

487 τ' **p**: δ' **p**    δόμον **p**: φόβον **p**    493 εἰ Reiske: ἢ **p**: ἦ **p**    509 ἑλληνίδων **p**: καθ' (vel ἀν') ἑλλάδα **p**    514 τῶι ... νυμφίωι **p**: τῶν ... νυμφίων **p**

ἀνδρῶν δ' ὅτωι χρὴ τὸν κακὸν διειδέναι
οὐδεὶς χαρακτὴρ ἐμπέφυκε σώματι;

Χο.  δεινή τις ὀργὴ καὶ δυσίατος πέλει,                    520
ὅταν φίλοι φίλοισι συμβάλωσ' ἔριν.

Ια.  δεῖ μ', ὡς ἔοικε, μὴ κακὸν φῦναι λέγειν,
ἀλλ' ὥστε ναὸς κεδνὸν οἰακοστρόφον
ἄκροισι λαίφους κρασπέδοις ὑπεκδραμεῖν
τὴν σὴν στόμαργον, ὦ γύναι, γλωσσαλγίαν.    525
ἐγὼ δ', ἐπειδὴ καὶ λίαν πυργοῖς χάριν,
Κύπριν νομίζω τῆς ἐμῆς ναυκληρίας
σώτειραν εἶναι θεῶν τε κἀνθρώπων μόνην.
σοὶ δ' ἔστι μὲν νοῦς λεπτός· ἀλλ' ἐπίφθονος
λόγος διελθεῖν ὡς Ἔρως σ' ἠνάγκασεν         530
τόξοις ἀφύκτοις τοὐμὸν ἐκσῶσαι δέμας.
ἀλλ' οὐκ ἀκριβῶς αὐτὸ θήσομαι λίαν·
ὅπηι γὰρ οὖν ὤνησας οὐ κακῶς ἔχει.
μείζω γε μέντοι τῆς ἐμῆς σωτηρίας
εἴληφας ἢ δέδωκας, ὡς ἐγὼ φράσω.             535
πρῶτον μὲν Ἑλλάδ' ἀντὶ βαρβάρου χθονὸς
γαῖαν κατοικεῖς καὶ δίκην ἐπίστασαι
νόμοις τε χρῆσθαι μὴ πρὸς ἰσχύος χάριν·
πάντες δέ σ' ἤισθοντ' οὖσαν Ἕλληνες σοφὴν
καὶ δόξαν ἔσχες· εἰ δὲ γῆς ἐπ' ἐσχάτοις      540
ὅροισιν ὤικεις, οὐκ ἂν ἦν λόγος σέθεν.
εἴη δ' ἔμοιγε μήτε χρυσὸς ἐν δόμοις
μήτ' Ὀρφέως κάλλιον ὑμνῆσαι μέλος,
εἰ μὴ 'πίσημος ἡ τύχη γένοιτό μοι.
τοσαῦτα μέν σοι τῶν ἐμῶν πόνων πέρι        545
ἔλεξ'· ἅμιλλαν γὰρ σὺ προύθηκας λόγων.
ἃ δ' ἐς γάμους μοι βασιλικοὺς ὠνείδισας,
ἐν τῶιδε δείξω πρῶτα μὲν σοφὸς γεγώς,
ἔπειτα σώφρων, εἶτα σοὶ μέγας φίλος
καὶ παισὶ τοῖς ἐμοῖσιν· ἀλλ' ἔχ' ἥσυχος.       550

531 τόξοις ἀφύκτοις **p**: πόνων ἀφύκτων **p**     543 κάλλιον **p**: βέλτιον **p**

ἐπεὶ μετέστην δεῦρ' Ἰωλκίας χθονὸς
πολλὰς ἐφέλκων συμφορὰς ἀμηχάνους,
τί τοῦδ' ἂν εὕρημ' ηὗρον εὐτυχέστερον
ἢ παῖδα γῆμαι βασιλέως φυγὰς γεγώς;
οὔχ, ἧι σὺ κνίζηι, σὸν μὲν ἐχθαίρων λέχος          555
καινῆς δὲ νύμφης ἱμέρωι πεπληγμένος
οὐδ' εἰς ἅμιλλαν πολύτεκνον σπουδὴν ἔχων·
ἅλις γὰρ οἱ γεγῶτες οὐδὲ μέμφομαι·
ἀλλ' ὡς, τὸ μὲν μέγιστον, οἰκοῖμεν καλῶς
καὶ μὴ σπανιζοίμεσθα, γιγνώσκων ὅτι          560
πένητα φεύγει πᾶς τις ἐκποδὼν φίλον,
παῖδας δὲ θρέψαιμ' ἀξίως δόμων ἐμῶν
σπείρας τ' ἀδελφοὺς τοῖσιν ἐκ σέθεν τέκνοις
ἐς ταὐτὸ θείην καὶ ξυναρτήσας γένος
εὐδαιμονοίην· σοί τε γὰρ παίδων τί δεῖ;          565
ἐμοί τε λύει τοῖσι μέλλουσιν τέκνοις
τὰ ζῶντ' ὀνῆσαι. μῶν βεβούλευμαι κακῶς;
οὐδ' ἂν σὺ φαίης, εἴ σε μὴ κνίζοι λέχος.
ἀλλ' ἐς τοσοῦτον ἥκεθ' ὥστ' ὀρθουμένης
εὐνῆς γυναῖκες πάντ' ἔχειν νομίζετε,          570
ἢν δ' αὖ γένηται ξυμφορά τις ἐς λέχος,
τὰ λῶιστα καὶ κάλλιστα πολεμιώτατα
τίθεσθε. χρῆν γὰρ ἄλλοθέν ποθεν βροτοὺς
παῖδας τεκνοῦσθαι, θῆλυ δ' οὐκ εἶναι γένος·
χοὔτως ἂν οὐκ ἦν οὐδὲν ἀνθρώποις κακόν.          575
Χο.      Ἰᾶσον, εὖ μὲν τούσδ' ἐκόσμησας λόγους·
ὅμως δ' ἔμοιγε, κεἰ παρὰ γνώμην ἐρῶ,
δοκεῖς προδοὺς σὴν ἄλοχον οὐ δίκαια δρᾶν.
Μη.      ἦ πολλὰ πολλοῖς εἰμι διάφορος βροτῶν·
ἐμοὶ γὰρ ὅστις ἄδικος ὢν σοφὸς λέγειν          580
πέφυκε πλείστην ζημίαν ὀφλισκάνει·
γλώσσηι γὰρ αὐχῶν τἄδικ' εὖ περιστελεῖν

561 φίλον Driver: φίλος o

τολμᾶι πανουργεῖν· ἔστι δ' οὐκ ἄγαν σοφός.

ὡς καὶ σύ· μή νυν εἰς ἔμ' εὐσχήμων γένηι
λέγειν τε δεινός· ἐν γὰρ ἐκτενεῖ σ' ἔπος·            585
χρῆν σ', εἴπερ ἦσθα μὴ κακός, πείσαντά με
γαμεῖν γάμον τόνδ', ἀλλὰ μὴ σιγῆι φίλων.

Ια.  καλῶς γ' ἄν, οἶμαι, τῶιδ' ὑπηρέτεις λόγωι,
εἴ σοι γάμον κατεῖπον, ἥτις οὐδὲ νῦν
τολμᾶις μεθεῖναι καρδίας μέγαν χόλον.       590

Μη.  οὐ τοῦτό σ' εἶχεν, ἀλλὰ βάρβαρον λέχος
πρὸς γῆρας οὐκ εὔδοξον ἐξέβαινέ σοι.

Ια.  εὖ νυν τόδ' ἴσθι, μὴ γυναικὸς οὕνεκα
γῆμαί με λέκτρα βασιλέων ἃ νῦν ἔχω,
ἀλλ', ὥσπερ εἶπον καὶ πάρος, σῶσαι θέλων     595
σέ, καὶ τέκνοισι τοῖς ἐμοῖς ὁμοσπόρους
φῦσαι τυράννους παῖδας, ἔρυμα δώμασιν.

Μη.  μή μοι γένοιτο λυπρὸς εὐδαίμων βίος
μηδ' ὄλβος ὅστις τὴν ἐμὴν κνίζοι φρένα.

Ια.  οἶσθ' ὡς μετεύξηι καὶ σοφωτέρα φανῆι;     600
τὰ χρηστὰ μή σοι λυπρὰ φαίνεσθαί ποτε,
μηδ' εὐτυχοῦσα δυστυχὴς εἶναι δοκεῖν.

Μη.  ὕβριζ', ἐπειδὴ σοὶ μὲν ἔστ' ἀποστροφή,
ἐγὼ δ' ἔρημος τήνδε φευξοῦμαι χθόνα.

Ια.  αὐτὴ τάδ' εἵλου· μηδέν' ἄλλον αἰτιῶ.       605

Μη.  τί δρῶσα; μῶν γαμοῦσα καὶ προδοῦσά σε;

Ια.  ἀρὰς τυράννοις ἀνοσίους ἀρωμένη.

Μη.  καὶ σοῖς ἀραία γ' οὖσα τυγχάνω δόμοις.

Ια.  ὡς οὐ κρινοῦμαι τῶνδέ σοι τὰ πλείονα.
ἀλλ', εἴ τι βούληι παισὶν ἢ σαυτῆι φυγῆς     610
προσωφέλημα χρημάτων ἐμῶν λαβεῖν,
λέγ'· ὡς ἕτοιμος ἀφθόνωι δοῦναι χερὶ

---

584 post σύ punctum habent **p** (coni. Witzschel): om. **p**      588 οἶμαι Nauck:
οὖν **p**: οὖν μοι vel οὖν σὺ fere **p**      594 βασιλέων **Π** (coni. Elmsley): βασιλέως
**o**      600 μετεύξηι **o**: μέτευξαι (sine interrogationis signo) Elmsley      601–2
φαίνεσθαί ... δοκεῖν Reiske (cf. Σ): φαινέσθω ... δόκει **o**      610 σαυτῆι φυγῆς
**p**: σαυτῆς φυγῆι **p**

ξένοις τε πέμπειν σύμβολ', οἳ δράσουσί σ' εὖ.
καὶ ταῦτα μὴ θέλουσα μωρανεῖς, γύναι·
λήξασα δ' ὀργῆς κερδανεῖς ἀμείνονα.    615
Μη.  οὔτ' ἂν ξένοισι τοῖσι σοῖς χρησαίμεθ' ἂν
οὔτ' ἄν τι δεξαίμεσθα, μηδ' ἡμῖν δίδου·
κακοῦ γὰρ ἀνδρὸς δῶρ' ὄνησιν οὐκ ἔχει.
Ια.  ἀλλ' οὖν ἐγὼ μὲν δαίμονας μαρτύρομαι
ὡς πάνθ' ὑπουργεῖν σοί τε καὶ τέκνοις θέλω·    620
σοὶ δ' οὐκ ἀρέσκει τἀγάθ', ἀλλ' αὐθαδίαι
φίλους ἀπωθῆι· τοιγὰρ ἀλγυνῆι πλέον.
Μη.  χώρει· πόθωι γὰρ τῆς νεοδμήτου κόρης
αἱρῆι χρονίζων δωμάτων ἐξώπιος.
νύμφευ'· ἴσως γάρ, σὺν θεῶι δ' εἰρήσεται,    625
γαμεῖς τοιοῦτον ὥστε θρηνεῖσθαι γάμον.

Χο.  ἔρωτες ὑπὲρ μὲν ἄγαν ἐλθόντες οὐκ εὐδοξίαν    [στρ. 627–8
οὐδ' ἀρετὰν παρέδωκαν ἀνδράσιν· εἰ δ' ἅλις
ἔλθοι    629–30
Κύπρις, οὐκ ἄλλα θεὸς εὔχαρις οὕτω.    631–2
μήποτ', ὦ δέσποιν', ἐπ' ἐμοὶ χρυσέων τόξων
ἀφείης    633–4
ἱμέρωι χρίσασ' ἄφυκτον οἰστόν.    635

στέργοι δέ με σωφροσύνα, δώρημα κάλλιστον
θεῶν·    [ἀντ. 636–7
μηδέ ποτ' ἀμφιλόγους ὀργὰς ἀκόρεστά τε
νείκη    638–9
θυμὸν ἐκπλήξασ' ἑτέροις ἐπὶ λέκτροις    640–1
προσβάλοι δεινὰ Κύπρις, ἀπτολέμους δ' εὐνὰς
σεβίζουσ'    642–3
ὀξύφρων κρίνοι λέχη γυναικῶν.

626 θρηνεῖσθαι Dodds: σ' ἀρνεῖσθαι o    634 ἀφείης Naber: ἐφ(ε)ίης o

ὦ πατρίς, ὦ δώματα, μὴ                              [στρ. 645
  δῆτ' ἄπολις γενοίμαν
  τὸν ἀμηχανίας ἔχουσα δυσπέρατον αἰῶν',            647-8
  οἰκτρότατον ἀχέων.
  θανάτωι θανάτωι πάρος δαμείην                     650
  ἀμέραν τάνδ' ἐξανύσα-
  σα· μόχθων δ' οὐκ ἄλλος ὕπερ-
  θεν ἢ γᾶς πατρίας στέρεσθαι.

εἴδομεν, οὐκ ἐξ ἑτέρων                             [ἀντ.
  μῦθον ἔχω φράσασθαι·                              655
  σὲ γὰρ οὐ πόλις, οὐ φίλων τις οἰκτιρεῖ παθοῦσαν   656-7
  δεινότατα παθέων.
  ἀχάριστος ὄλοιθ' ὅτωι πάρεστιν
  μὴ φίλους τιμᾶν καθαρᾶν                           660
  ἀνοίξαντα κλῆιδα φρενῶν·
  ἐμοὶ μὲν φίλος οὔποτ' ἔσται.


                    ΑΙΓΕΥΣ

        Μήδεια, χαῖρε· τοῦδε γὰρ προοίμιον
        κάλλιον οὐδεὶς οἶδε προσφωνεῖν φίλους.
Μη.     ὦ χαῖρε καὶ σύ, παῖ σοφοῦ Πανδίονος,        665
        Αἰγεῦ. πόθεν γῆς τῆσδ' ἐπιστρωφᾶι πέδον;
Αι.     Φοίβου παλαιὸν ἐκλιπὼν χρηστήριον.
Μη.     τί δ' ὀμφαλὸν γῆς θεσπιωιδὸν ἐστάλης;
Αι.     παίδων ἐρευνῶν σπέρμ' ὅπως γένοιτό μοι.
Μη.     πρὸς θεῶν, ἄπαις γὰρ δεῦρ' ἀεὶ τείνεις βίον;   670
Αι.     ἄπαιδές ἐσμεν δαίμονός τινος τύχηι.
Μη.     δάμαρτος οὔσης ἢ λέχους ἄπειρος ὤν;

645 δώματα Nauck: δῶμα o    648 αἰῶν' o: αἰῶ Wilamowitz    649 οἰκτρότατον Musgrave: οἰκτροτάτων o    655 μῦθον Nauck: μύθων o    657
οἰκτιρεῖ fere Wieseler: ὤικτειρε(ν) o: ὤικτισεν Musgrave    658 δεινότατα o:
δεινότατον Triclinius    660 καθαρᾶν Badham: καθαρὰν o

Αι. οὐκ ἐσμὲν εὐνῆς ἄζυγες γαμηλίου.
Μη. τί δῆτα Φοῖβος εἶπέ σοι παίδων πέρι;
Αι. σοφώτερ᾽ ἢ κατ᾽ ἄνδρα συμβαλεῖν ἔπη.               675
Μη. θέμις μὲν ἡμᾶς χρησμὸν εἰδέναι θεοῦ;
Αι. μάλιστ᾽, ἐπεί τοι καὶ σοφῆς δεῖται φρενός.
Μη. τί δῆτ᾽ ἔχρησε; λέξον, εἰ θέμις κλυεῖν.
Αι. ἀσκοῦ με τὸν προύχοντα μὴ λῦσαι πόδα
Μη. πρὶν ἂν τί δράσῃς ἢ τίν᾽ ἐξίκῃ χθόνα;               680
Αι. πρὶν ἂν πατρῴαν αὖθις ἑστίαν μόλω.
Μη. σὺ δ᾽ ὡς τί χρῄζων τήνδε ναυστολεῖς χθόνα;
Αι. Πιτθεύς τις ἔστι, γῆς ἄναξ Τροζηνίας.
Μη. παῖς, ὡς λέγουσι, Πέλοπος, εὐσεβέστατος.
Αι. τούτωι θεοῦ μάντευμα κοινῶσαι θέλω.               685
Μη. σοφὸς γὰρ ἁνὴρ καὶ τρίβων τὰ τοιάδε.
Αι. κἀμοί γε πάντων φίλτατος δορυξένων.
Μη. ἀλλ᾽ εὐτυχοίης καὶ τύχοις ὅσων ἐρᾷς.
Αι. τί γὰρ σὸν ὄμμα χρώς τε συντέτηχ᾽ ὅδε;
Μη. Αἰγεῦ, κάκιστός ἐστί μοι πάντων πόσις.               690
Αι. τί φής; σαφῶς μοι σὰς φράσον δυσθυμίας.
Μη. ἀδικεῖ μ᾽ Ἰάσων οὐδὲν ἐξ ἐμοῦ παθών.
Αι. τί χρῆμα δράσας; φράζε μοι σαφέστερον.
Μη. γυναῖκ᾽ ἐφ᾽ ἡμῖν δεσπότιν δόμων ἔχει.
Αι. οὔ που τετόλμηκ᾽ ἔργον αἴσχιστον τόδε;               695
Μη. σάφ᾽ ἴσθ᾽· ἄτιμοι δ᾽ ἐσμὲν οἱ πρὸ τοῦ φίλοι.
Αι. πότερον ἐρασθεὶς ἢ σὸν ἐχθαίρων λέχος;
Μη. μέγαν γ᾽ ἔρωτα· πιστὸς οὐκ ἔφυ φίλοις.
Αι. ἴτω νυν, εἴπερ, ὡς λέγεις, ἐστὶν κακός.
Μη. ἀνδρῶν τυράννων κῆδος ἡράσθη λαβεῖν.               700
Αι. δίδωσι δ᾽ αὐτῶι τίς; πέραινέ μοι λόγον.
Μη. Κρέων, ὃς ἄρχει τῆσδε γῆς Κορινθίας.
Αι. συγγνωστὰ μέντἄρ᾽ ἦν σε λυπεῖσθαι, γύναι.
Μη. ὄλωλα· καὶ πρός γ᾽ ἐξελαύνομαι χθονός.
Αι. πρὸς τοῦ; τόδ᾽ ἄλλο καινὸν αὖ λέγεις κακόν.               705

678 κλυεῖν West: κλύειν o   695 οὔ που Witzschel: ἢ που fere o   703
μέντἄρ᾽ Hermann: μὲν γὰρ p: γὰρ p

Μη.   Κρέων μ' ἐλαύνει φυγάδα γῆς Κορινθίας.
Αι.   ἐᾶι δ' Ἰάσων; οὐδὲ ταῦτ' ἐπήινεσα.
Μη.   λόγωι μὲν οὐχί, καρτερεῖν δὲ βούλεται.
      ἀλλ' ἄντομαί σε τῆσδε πρὸς γενειάδος
      γονάτων τε τῶν σῶν ἱκεσία τε γίγνομαι,                    710
      οἴκτιρον οἴκτιρόν με τὴν δυσδαίμονα
      καὶ μή μ' ἔρημον ἐκπεσοῦσαν εἰσίδηις,
      δέξαι δὲ χώραι καὶ δόμοις ἐφέστιον.
      οὕτως ἔρως σοι πρὸς θεῶν τελεσφόρος
      γένοιτο παίδων καὐτὸς ὄλβιος θάνοις.                      715
      εὕρημα δ' οὐκ οἶσθ' οἶον ηὕρηκας τόδε·
      παύσω γέ σ' ὄντ' ἄπαιδα καὶ παίδων γονὰς
      σπεῖραί σε θήσω· τοιάδ' οἶδα φάρμακα.
Αι.   πολλῶν ἕκατι τήνδε σοι δοῦναι χάριν,
      γύναι, πρόθυμός εἰμι, πρῶτα μὲν θεῶν,                     720
      ἔπειτα παίδων ὧν ἐπαγγέλληι γονάς·
      ἐς τοῦτο γὰρ δὴ φροῦδός εἰμι πᾶς ἐγώ.
      οὕτω δ' ἔχει μοι· σοῦ μὲν ἐλθούσης χθόνα,
      πειράσομαί σου προξενεῖν δίκαιος ὤν.
      [τοσόνδε μέντοι σοι προσημαίνω, γύναι·                    725
      ἐκ τῆσδε μὲν γῆς οὔ σ' ἄγειν βουλήσομαι.]                 726
      ἐκ τῆσδε δ' αὐτὴ γῆς ἀπαλλάσσου πόδα·                     729
      αὐτὴ δ' ἐάνπερ εἰς ἐμοὺς ἔλθηις δόμους,                   727
      μενεῖς ἄσυλος κοὔ σε μὴ μεθῶ τινι·                        728
      ἀναίτιος γὰρ καὶ ξένοις εἶναι θέλω.                       730
Μη.   ἔσται τάδ'· ἀλλὰ πίστις εἰ γένοιτό μοι
      τούτων, ἔχοιμ' ἂν πάντα πρὸς σέθεν καλῶς.
Αι.   μῶν οὐ πέποιθας; ἢ τί σοι τὸ δυσχερές;
Μη.   πέποιθα· Πελίου δ' ἐχθρός ἐστί μοι δόμος
      Κρέων τε. τούτοις δ' ὁρκίοισι μὲν ζυγεὶς                  735
      ἄγουσιν οὐ μεθεῖ' ἂν ἐκ γαίας ἐμέ·

---

717 γέ F. W. Schmidt: δέ **o**      725–6 om. **Π**, del. (una cum 727–8) Kirchhoff      725 τοσόνδε **p**: τοσόνγε **p**      728 μεθῶ τινι **o**: προ]δῶ ποτ[ε
**Π**      729 ante 727–8 hab. **Π**, post 727–8 **o**      736 μεθεῖ' **p**: fere μεθεῖς **p**

λόγοις δὲ συμβὰς καὶ θεῶν ἀνώμοτος
φίλος γένοι᾽ ἂν κἀπικηρυκεύμασιν
τάχ᾽ ἂν πίθοιο· τἀμὰ μὲν γὰρ ἀσθενῆ,
τοῖς δ᾽ ὄλβος ἐστὶ καὶ δόμος τυραννικός. 740

Αι. πολλὴν ἔδειξας ἐν λόγοις προμηθίαν·
ἀλλ᾽, εἰ δοκεῖ σοι, δρᾶν τάδ᾽ οὐκ ἀφίσταμαι.
ἐμοί τε γὰρ τάδ᾽ ἐστὶν ἀσφαλέστερα,
σκῆψίν τιν᾽ ἐχθροῖς σοῖς ἔχοντα δεικνύναι,
τὸ σόν τ᾽ ἄραρε μᾶλλον. ἐξηγοῦ θεούς. 745

Μη. ὄμνυ πέδον Γῆς πατέρα θ᾽ Ἥλιον πατρὸς
τοὐμοῦ θεῶν τε συντιθεὶς ἅπαν γένος.

Αι. τί χρῆμα δράσειν ἢ τί μὴ δράσειν; λέγε.

Μη. μήτ᾽ αὐτὸς ἐκ γῆς σῆς ἔμ᾽ ἐκβαλεῖν ποτε,
μήτ᾽ ἄλλος ἤν τις τῶν ἐμῶν ἐχθρῶν ἄγειν 750
χρήιζηι μεθήσειν ζῶν ἑκουσίωι τρόπωι.

Αι. ὄμνυμι Γαῖαν φῶς τε λαμπρὸν Ἡλίου
θεούς τε πάντας ἐμμενεῖν ἅ σου κλύω.

Μη. ἀρκεῖ· τί δ᾽ ὅρκωι τῶιδε μὴ ᾽μμένων πάθοις;

Αι. ἃ τοῖσι δυσσεβοῦσι γίγνεται βροτῶν. 755

Μη. χαίρων πορεύου· πάντα γὰρ καλῶς ἔχει.
κἀγὼ πόλιν σὴν ὡς τάχιστ᾽ ἀφίξομαι,
πράξασ᾽ ἃ μέλλω καὶ τυχοῦσ᾽ ἃ βούλομαι.

Χο. ἀλλά σ᾽ ὁ Μαίας πομπαῖος ἄναξ
πελάσειε δόμοις ὧν τ᾽ ἐπίνοιαν 760
σπεύδεις κατέχων πράξειας, ἐπεὶ
γενναῖος ἀνήρ,
Αἰγεῦ, παρ᾽ ἐμοὶ δεδόκησαι.

Μη. ὦ Ζεῦ Δίκη τε Ζηνὸς Ἡλίου τε φῶς,
νῦν καλλίνικοι τῶν ἐμῶν ἐχθρῶν, φίλαι, 765

---

737 ἀνώμοτος **p**: ἐνώμοτος **p**    738 κἀπικηρυκεύμασιν **o**: -ματα Σ    739
τάχ᾽ Wyttenbach, fort. Σ: οὐκ **o** et Σ alter    741 ἔδειξας Sigonius et Valckenaer: ἔλεξας **o**    ἐν λόγοις **p**: ὦ γύναι **p**    743 ἀσφαλέστερα **p**: ἀσφαλέστατα **p**    751 ζῶν **p**: γῆς **p**    752 φῶς τε λαμπρὸν Ἡλίου Page: λαμπρὸν
ἡλίου τε φῶς **p**: λαμπρόν (θ᾽) ἡλίου φάος **p**: ἡλίου θ᾽ ἁγνὸν σέλας **p** (coni.
Musgrave): Ἡλίου θ᾽ ἁγνὸν σέβας Porson e scholio

γενησόμεσθα κἀς ὁδὸν βεβήκαμεν,
νῦν ἐλπὶς ἐχθροὺς τοὺς ἐμοὺς τείσειν δίκην.
οὗτος γὰρ ἀνὴρ ἧι μάλιστ᾽ ἐκάμνομεν
λιμὴν πέφανται τῶν ἐμῶν βουλευμάτων·
ἐκ τοῦδ᾽ ἀναψόμεσθα πρυμνήτην κάλων, 770
μολόντες ἄστυ καὶ πόλισμα Παλλάδος.
ἤδη δὲ πάντα τἀμά σοι βουλεύματα
λέξω· δέχου δὲ μὴ πρὸς ἡδονὴν λόγους.
πέμψασ᾽ ἐμῶν τιν᾽ οἰκετῶν Ἰάσονα
ἐς ὄψιν ἐλθεῖν τὴν ἐμὴν αἰτήσομαι. 775
μολόντι δ᾽ αὐτῶι μαλθακοὺς λέξω λόγους,
ὡς καὶ δοκεῖ μοι ταὐτὰ καὶ καλῶς γαμεῖ
γάμους τυράννων οὓς προδοὺς ἡμᾶς ἔχει,
καὶ ξύμφορ᾽ εἶναι καὶ καλῶς ἐγνωσμένα.
παῖδας δὲ μεῖναι τοὺς ἐμοὺς αἰτήσομαι, 780
οὐχ ὡς λιποῦσ᾽ ἂν πολεμίας ἐπὶ χθονὸς
[ἐχθροῖσι παῖδας τοὺς ἐμοὺς καθυβρίσαι],
ἀλλ᾽ ὡς δόλοισι παῖδα βασιλέως κτάνω.
πέμψω γὰρ αὐτοὺς δῶρ᾽ ἔχοντας ἐν χεροῖν,
[νύμφηι φέροντας, τήνδε μὴ φεύγειν χθόνα,] 785
λεπτόν τε πέπλον καὶ πλόκον χρυσήλατον·
κἄνπερ λαβοῦσα κόσμον ἀμφιθῆι χροΐ,
κακῶς ὀλεῖται πᾶς θ᾽ ὃς ἂν θίγηι κόρης·
τοιοῖσδε χρίσω φαρμάκοις δωρήματα.
ἐνταῦθα μέντοι τόνδ᾽ ἀπαλλάσσω λόγον. 790
ὤιμωξα δ᾽ οἷον ἔργον ἔστ᾽ ἐργαστέον
τοὐντεῦθεν ἡμῖν· τέκνα γὰρ κατακτενῶ
τἀμ᾽· οὔτις ἔστιν ὅστις ἐξαιρήσεται·
δόμον τε πάντα συγχέασ᾽ Ἰάσονος
ἔξειμι γαίας, φιλτάτων παίδων φόνον 795

767 νῦν Lenting: νῦν δ᾽ o	777 ταὐτὰ Barnes et γαμεῖ Bolkestein: ταῦτα ... ἔχει o	778-9 del. Porson (778 Reiske)	779 ἐγνωσμένα p: εἰργασμένα p	781 λιποῦσ᾽ ἂν Elmsley: λιποῦσα o	782 del. Brunck	785 om. p, del. Valckenaer	τήνδε o: δῆθεν ʸᵖΣ

φεύγουσα καὶ τλᾶσ᾽ ἔργον ἀνοσιώτατον.
οὐ γὰρ γελᾶσθαι τλητὸν ἐξ ἐχθρῶν, φίλαι.
[ἴτω· τί μοι ζῆν κέρδος; οὔτε μοι πατρὶς
οὔτ᾽ οἶκος ἔστιν οὔτ᾽ ἀποστροφὴ κακῶν.]
ἡμάρτανον τόθ᾽ ἡνίκ᾽ ἐξελίμπανον                    800
δόμους πατρῴους, ἀνδρὸς Ἕλληνος λόγοις
πεισθεῖσ᾽, ὃς ἡμῖν σὺν θεῶι τείσει δίκην.
οὔτ᾽ ἐξ ἐμοῦ γὰρ παῖδας ὄψεταί ποτε
ζῶντας τὸ λοιπὸν οὔτε τῆς νεοζύγου
νύμφης τεκνώσει παῖδ᾽, ἐπεὶ κακὴν κακῶς                    805
θανεῖν σφ᾽ ἀνάγκη τοῖς ἐμοῖσι φαρμάκοις.
μηδείς με φαύλην κἀσθενῆ νομιζέτω
μηδ᾽ ἡσυχαίαν ἀλλὰ θατέρου τρόπου,
βαρεῖαν ἐχθροῖς καὶ φίλοισιν εὐμενῆ·
τῶν γὰρ τοιούτων εὐκλεέστατος βίος.                    810
Χο.    ἐπείπερ ἡμῖν τόνδ᾽ ἐκοίνωσας λόγον,
σέ τ᾽ ὠφελεῖν θέλουσα καὶ νόμοις βροτῶν
ξυλλαμβάνουσα δρᾶν σ᾽ ἀπεννέπω τάδε.
Μη.    οὐκ ἔστιν ἄλλως· σοὶ δὲ συγγνώμη λέγειν
τάδ᾽ ἐστί, μὴ πάσχουσαν, ὡς ἐγώ, κακῶς.                    815
Χο.    ἀλλὰ κτανεῖν σὸν σπέρμα τολμήσεις, γύναι;
Μη.    οὕτω γὰρ ἂν μάλιστα δηχθείη πόσις.
Χο.    σὺ δ᾽ ἂν γένοιό γ᾽ ἀθλιωτάτη γυνή.
Μη.    ἴτω· περισσοὶ πάντες οὑν μέσωι λόγοι.
ἀλλ᾽ εἶα χώρει καὶ κόμιζ᾽ Ἰάσονα·                    820
ἐς πάντα γὰρ δὴ σοὶ τὰ πιστὰ χρώμεθα.
λέξηις δὲ μηδὲν τῶν ἐμοὶ δεδογμένων,
εἴπερ φρονεῖς εὖ δεσπόταις γυνή τ᾽ ἔφυς.

Χο.    Ἐρεχθεῖδαι τὸ παλαιὸν ὄλβιοι                    [στρ.
καὶ θεῶν παῖδες μακάρων, ἱερᾶς                    825

---

798–9 del. Leo    802 τίσει **p**: δώσει **p**    805 κακὴν κακῶς **p**: κακῶς κακὴν
**p**    816 σὸν σπέρμα **p**: σὼ παῖδε **p**: σὸν παῖδα **p**    822 λέξηις Elmsley:
λέξεις **o**

χώρας ἀπορθήτου τ' ἄπο, φερβόμενοι        826–7
κλεινοτάταν σοφίαν, αἰεὶ διὰ λαμπροτάτου        828–9
βαίνοντες ἁβρῶς αἰθέρος, ἔνθα ποθ' ἁγνὰς        830–1
ἐννέα Πιερίδας Μούσας λέγουσι        832–3
ξανθὰν Ἁρμονίαν φυτεῦσαι·

τοῦ καλλινάου τ' ἐπὶ Κηφισοῦ ῥοαῖς        [ἀντ. 835
τὰν Κύπριν κλήιζουσιν ἀφυσσαμέναν
χώρας καταπνεῦσαι μετρίους ἀνέμων        837–8
ἡδυπνόους αὔρας· αἰεὶ δ' ἐπιβαλλομέναν        839–40
χαίταισιν εὐώδη ῥοδέων πλόκον ἀνθέων        841–2
τᾶι Σοφίαι παρέδρους πέμπειν Ἔρωτας,        843–4
παντοίας ἀρετᾶς ξυνεργούς.        845

πῶς οὖν ἱερῶν ποταμῶν        [στρ.
    ἢ πόλις ἢ φίλων
    πόμπιμός σε χώρα
    τὰν παιδολέτειραν ἕξει,
τὰν οὐχ ὁσίαν μετ' ἄλλων;        850
σκέψαι τεκέων πλαγάν,
σκέψαι φόνον οἷον αἴρηι.
μή, πρὸς γονάτων σε πάνται
πάντως ἱκετεύομεν,
    τέκνα φονεύσηις.        855

πόθεν θράσος †ἢ φρενὸς ἢ        [ἀντ.
    χειρὶ τέκνων σέθεν†
    καρδίαι τε λήψηι
    δεινὰν προσάγουσα τόλμαν;
πῶς δ' ὄμματα προσβαλοῦσα        860

835 ἐπὶ p: ἀπὸ p        ῥοαῖς p: fere ῥοᾶς vel ῥοῶν p        837–8 χώρας Reiske:
χώραν o        μετρι]ους Π: μετρίας o        850 μετ' ἄλλων o: μέταυλον Lueck
852 αἴρηι Elmsley: αἱρῆι o        853–4 πάνται πάντως post Herwerden
Diggle: πάντες πάντως vel πάντως πάντες fere o        855 φονεύσηις Brunck:
μὴ φον- o

τέκνοις ἄδακρυν μοῖραν
σχήσεις φόνου; οὐ δυνάσῃ
παίδων ἱκετᾶν πιτνόντων
τέγξαι χέρα φοινίαν
τλάμονι θυμῶι. 865

Ια.  ἥκω κελευσθείς· καὶ γὰρ οὖσα δυσμενὴς
οὔ τἂν ἁμάρτοις τοῦδέ γ', ἀλλ' ἀκούσομαι·
τί χρῆμα βούληι καινὸν ἐξ ἐμοῦ, γύναι;

Μη.  Ἰᾶσον, αἰτοῦμαί σε τῶν εἰρημένων
συγγνώμον' εἶναι· τὰς δ' ἐμὰς ὀργὰς φέρειν 870
εἰκός σ', ἐπεὶ νῶιν πόλλ' ὑπείργασται φίλα.
ἐγὼ δ' ἐμαυτῆι διὰ λόγων ἀφικόμην
κἀλοιδόρησα· Σχετλία, τί μαίνομαι
καὶ δυσμεναίνω τοῖσι βουλεύουσιν εὖ,
ἐχθρὰ δὲ γαίας κοιράνοις καθίσταμαι 875
πόσει θ', ὃς ἡμῖν δρᾶι τὰ συμφορώτατα,
γήμας τύραννον καὶ κασιγνήτους τέκνοις
ἐμοῖς φυτεύων; οὐκ ἀπαλλαχθήσομαι
θυμοῦ; τί πάσχω, θεῶν ποριζόντων καλῶς;
οὐκ εἰσὶ μέν μοι παῖδες, οἶδα δὲ χθόνα 880
φεύγοντας ἡμᾶς καὶ σπανίζοντας φίλων;
ταῦτ' ἐννοηθεῖσ' ἠισθόμην ἀβουλίαν
πολλὴν ἔχουσα καὶ μάτην θυμουμένη.
νῦν οὖν ἐπαινῶ σωφρονεῖν τέ μοι δοκεῖς
κῆδος τόδ' ἡμῖν προσλαβών, ἐγὼ δ' ἄφρων, 885
ἧι χρῆν μετεῖναι τῶνδε τῶν βουλευμάτων
καὶ ξυμπεραίνειν καὶ παρεστάναι λέχει
νύμφην τε κηδεύουσαν ἥδεσθαι σέθεν.
ἀλλ' ἐσμὲν οἷόν ἐσμεν, οὐκ ἐρῶ κακόν,
γυναῖκες· οὔκουν χρή σ' ὁμοιοῦσθαι κακοῖς, 890

862 φόνου **p**: φόνον p    864 χέρα φοινίαν Triclinius: χεῖρα φονίαν fere
**o**    867 οὔ τἂν Porson: οὐκ ἂν **o**    882 ἐννοηθεῖσ' **p**: ἐννοήσασ' **p**    887
ξυμπεραίνειν **p**: ξυγγαμεῖν σοι p    890 χρή **p**: χρῆν **p**

οὐδ' ἀντιτείνειν νήπι' ἀντὶ νηπίων.
παριέμεσθα καί φαμεν κακῶς φρονεῖν
τότ', ἀλλ' ἄμεινον νῦν βεβούλευμαι τάδε.
ὦ τέκνα τέκνα, δεῦρο, λείπετε στέγας,
ἐξέλθετ', ἀσπάσασθε καὶ προσείπατε                    895
πατέρα μεθ' ἡμῶν καὶ διαλλάχθηθ' ἅμα
τῆς πρόσθεν ἔχθρας ἐς φίλους μητρὸς μέτα·
σπονδαὶ γὰρ ἡμῖν καὶ μεθέστηκεν χόλος.
λάβεσθε χειρὸς δεξιᾶς· οἴμοι, κακῶν
ὡς ἐννοοῦμαι δή τι τῶν κεκρυμμένων.                    900
ἆρ', ὦ τέκν', οὕτω καὶ πολὺν ζῶντες χρόνον
φίλην ὀρέξετ' ὠλένην; τάλαιν' ἐγώ,
ὡς ἀρτίδακρύς εἰμι καὶ φόβου πλέα.
χρόνωι δὲ νεῖκος πατρὸς ἐξαιρουμένη
ὄψιν τέρειναν τήνδ' ἔπλησα δακρύων.                    905

Χο.   κἀμοὶ κατ' ὄσσων χλωρὸν ὡρμήθη δάκρυ·
      καὶ μὴ προβαίη μεῖζον ἢ τὸ νῦν κακόν.

Ια.   αἰνῶ, γύναι, τάδ', οὐδ' ἐκεῖνα μέμφομαι·
      εἰκὸς γὰρ ὀργὰς θῆλυ ποιεῖσθαι γένος
      γάμους παρεμπολῶντος ἀλλοίους †πόσει†.            910
      ἀλλ' ἐς τὸ λῶιον σὸν μεθέστηκεν κέαρ,
      ἔγνως δὲ τὴν νικῶσαν, ἀλλὰ τῶι χρόνωι,
      βουλήν· γυναικὸς ἔργα ταῦτα σώφρονος.
      ὑμῖν δέ, παῖδες, οὐκ ἀφροντίστως πατὴρ
      πολλὴν ἔθηκε σὺν θεοῖς σωτηρίαν·                   915
      οἶμαι γὰρ ὑμᾶς τῆσδε γῆς Κορινθίας
      τὰ πρῶτ' ἔσεσθαι σὺν κασιγνήτοις ἔτι.
      ἀλλ' αὐξάνεσθε· τἄλλα δ' ἐξεργάζεται
      πατήρ τε καὶ θεῶν ὅστις ἐστὶν εὐμενής·
      ἴδοιμι δ' ὑμᾶς εὐτραφεῖς ἥβης τέλος              920
      μολόντας, ἐχθρῶν τῶν ἐμῶν ὑπερτέρους.

---

894 δεῦρο Elmsley: δεῦτε **o**    910 γάμους ... ἀλλοίους **p**: γάμου ... ἀλλοίου
**p**    πόσει **o**: ἐμοῦ histriones secundum Σ: δόμοις Diggle    915 σωτηρίαν **p**: προμηθίαν **p**

αὕτη, τί χλωροῖς δακρύοις τέγγεις κόρας,
στρέψασα λευκὴν ἔμπαλιν παρηίδα,
κοὐκ ἀσμένη τόνδ' ἐξ ἐμοῦ δέχηι λόγον;
Μη. οὐδέν. τέκνων τῶνδ' ἐννοουμένη πέρι.　　925
Ια. θάρσει νυν· εὖ γὰρ τῶνδ' ἐγὼ θήσω πέρι.
Μη. δράσω τάδ'· οὔτοι σοῖς ἀπιστήσω λόγοις·
γυνὴ δὲ θῆλυ κἀπὶ δακρύοις ἔφυ.
Ια. τί δῆτα λίαν τοῖσδ' ἐπιστένεις τέκνοις;
Μη. ἔτικτον αὐτούς· ζῆν δ' ὅτ' ἐξηύχου τέκνα,　　930
ἐσῆλθέ μ' οἶκτος εἰ γενήσεται τάδε.
ἀλλ' ὧνπερ οὕνεκ' εἰς ἐμοὺς ἥκεις λόγους,
τὰ μὲν λέλεκται, τῶν δ' ἐγὼ μνησθήσομαι·
ἐπεὶ τυράννοις γῆς μ' ἀποστεῖλαι δοκεῖ
(κἀμοὶ τάδ' ἐστὶ λῶιστα, γιγνώσκω καλῶς,　　935
μήτ' ἐμποδών σοι μήτε κοιράνοις χθονὸς
ναίειν· δοκῶ γὰρ δυσμενὴς εἶναι δόμοις)
ἡμεῖς μὲν ἐκ γῆς τῆσδ' ἀπαίρομεν φυγῆι,
παῖδες δ' ὅπως ἂν ἐκτραφῶσι σῆι χερὶ
αἰτοῦ Κρέοντα τήνδε μὴ φεύγειν χθόνα.　　940
Ια. οὐκ οἶδ' ἂν εἰ πείσαιμι, πειρᾶσθαι δὲ χρή.
Μη. σὺ δ' ἀλλὰ σὴν κέλευσον ἄντεσθαι πατρὸς
γυναῖκα παῖδας τήνδε μὴ φεύγειν χθόνα.
Ια. μάλιστα· καὶ πείσειν γε δοξάζω σφ' ἐγώ,
εἴπερ γυναικῶν ἐστι τῶν ἄλλων μία.　　945
Μη. συλλήψομαι δὲ τοῦδέ σοι κἀγὼ πόνου·
πέμψω γὰρ αὐτῆι δῶρ' ἃ καλλιστεύεται
τῶν νῦν ἐν ἀνθρώποισιν, οἶδ' ἐγώ, πολύ
[λεπτόν τε πέπλον καὶ πλόκον χρυσήλατον]
παῖδας φέροντας. ἀλλ' ὅσον τάχος χρεὼν　　950
κόσμον κομίζειν δεῦρο προσπόλων τινά.

926 τῶνδ' ἐγὼ θήσω **p**: τῶνδε θήσομαι **p**: τῶνδε νῦν θήσομαι **p**　　929–31
post 925 transp. Ladewig　　929 δῆτα λίαν **p**: δὴ τάλαινα **p**　　930 ἐξηύχου
Scaliger: -χουν **o**　　938 ἀπαίρομεν **o**: ἀπαροῦμεν Elmsley　　942 ἄντεσθαι
Weidner: αἰτεῖσθαι **o**　　945 Iasoni continuant **p**: Medeae trib. **p**　　949
del. Bothe

εὐδαιμονήσει δ' οὐχ ἓν ἀλλὰ μυρία,
ἀνδρός τ' ἀρίστου σοῦ τυχοῦσ' ὁμευνέτου
κεκτημένη τε κόσμον ὅν ποθ' Ἥλιος
πατρὸς πατὴρ δίδωσιν ἐκγόνοισιν οἷς.          955
λάζυσθε φερνὰς τάσδε, παῖδες, ἐς χέρας
καὶ τῆι τυράννωι μακαρίαι νύμφηι δότε
φέροντες· οὔτοι δῶρα μεμπτὰ δέξεται.

Ια.   τί δ', ὦ ματαία, τῶνδε σὰς κενοῖς χέρας;
δοκεῖς σπανίζειν δῶμα βασίλειον πέπλων,          960
δοκεῖς δὲ χρυσοῦ; σῶιζε, μὴ δίδου τάδε.
εἴπερ γὰρ ἡμᾶς ἀξιοῖ λόγου τινὸς
γυνή, προθήσει χρημάτων, σάφ' οἶδ' ἐγώ.

Μη.   μή μοι σύ· πείθειν δῶρα καὶ θεοὺς λόγος·
χρυσὸς δὲ κρείσσων μυρίων λόγων βροτοῖς.          965
κείνης ὁ δαίμων, κεῖνα νῦν αὔξει θεός,
νέα τυραννεῖ· τῶν δ' ἐμῶν παίδων φυγὰς
ψυχῆς ἂν ἀλλαξαίμεθ', οὐ χρυσοῦ μόνον.
ἀλλ', ὦ τέκν', εἰσελθόντε πλουσίους δόμους‚
πατρὸς νέαν γυναῖκα, δεσπότιν δ' ἐμήν,          970
ἱκετεύετ', ἐξαιτεῖσθε μὴ φεύγειν χθόνα,
κόσμον διδόντες· τοῦδε γὰρ μάλιστα δεῖ,
ἐς χεῖρ' ἐκείνην δῶρα δέξασθαι τάδε.
ἴθ' ὡς τάχιστα· μητρὶ δ' ὧν ἐρᾶι τυχεῖν
εὐάγγελοι γένοισθε πράξαντες καλῶς.          975

Χο.   νῦν ἐλπίδες οὐκέτι μοι παίδων ζόας,          [στρ. 976
οὐκέτι· στείχουσι γὰρ ἐς φόνον ἤδη.
δέξεται νύμφα χρυσέων ἀναδεσμᾶν
δέξεται δύστανος ἄταν·
ξανθᾶι δ' ἀμφὶ κόμαι θήσει τὸν Ἅιδα          980–81
κόσμον αὐτὰ χεροῖν.

963 ἐγώ p: ὅτι p    970 δ' Elmsley: τ' o    976 ζόας Porson: ζωᾶς o    978
ἀναδεσμᾶν Elmsley: ἀναδέσμων o    982 χεροῖν Nauck: χεροῖν λαβοῦσα o

πείσει χάρις ἀμβρόσιός τ' αὐγὰ πέπλον     [ἀντ.
χρυσότευκτον ⟨τε⟩ στέφανον περιθέσθαι·
νερτέροις δ' ἤδη πάρα νυμφοκομήσει.     985
τοῖον εἰς ἕρκος πεσεῖται
καὶ μοῖραν θανάτου δύστανος· ἄταν δ'     987-8
οὐχ ὑπεκφεύξεται.     989

σὺ δ', ὦ τάλαν ὦ κακόνυμφε κηδεμὼν
τυράννων,     [στρ. 990-1
παισὶν οὐ κατειδὼς
ὄλεθρον βιοτᾶι προσάγεις ἀλόχωι
τε σᾶι στυγερὸν θάνατον.
δύστανε, μοίρας ὅσον παροίχηι.     995

μεταστένομαι δὲ σὸν ἄλγος, ὦ τάλαινα
παίδων     [ἀντ. 996-7
μᾶτερ, ἃ φονεύσεις
τέκνα νυμφιδίων ἕνεκεν λεχέων,
ἅ σοι προλιπὼν ἀνόμως     1000
ἄλλαι ξυνοικεῖ πόσις συνεύνωι.

Πα.   δέσποιν', ἀφεῖνται παῖδες οἵδε σοι φυγῆς,
καὶ δῶρα νύμφη βασιλὶς ἀσμένη χεροῖν
ἐδέξατ'· εἰρήνη δὲ τἀκεῖθεν τέκνοις.
ἔα.
τί συγχυθεῖσ' ἕστηκας ἡνίκ' εὐτυχεῖς;     1005
[τί σὴν ἔτρεψας ἔμπαλιν παρηίδα
κοὐκ ἀσμένη τόνδ' ἐξ ἐμοῦ δέχηι λόγον;]
Μη.   αἰαῖ.

983 πέπλον Elmsley: πέπλων **p**: πέπλου **p**     984 χρυσοτ- **pΣ**: χρυσεοτ- **p**
τε add. Reiske     989 ὑπεκφεύξεται **p**: ὑπερφ- fere **p**     993 ὄλεθρον **p**:
ὀλέθριον **p**   βιοτᾶι **p**: βιοτὰν fere **p**     1005 ἔα paedagogo continuat **p**
(coni. Kirchhoff): Med. trib. **p**     1006-7 del. Valckenaer

Πα. τάδ' οὐ ξυνωιδὰ τοῖσιν ἐξηγγελμένοις.

Μη. αἰαῖ μάλ' αὖθις. Πα. μῶν τιν' ἀγγέλλων τύχην
οὐκ οἶδα, δόξης δ' ἐσφάλην εὐαγγέλου; 1010

Μη. ἤγγειλας οἷ' ἤγγειλας· οὐ σὲ μέμφομαι.

Πα. τί δαὶ κατηφεῖς ὄμμα καὶ δακρυρροεῖς;

Μη. πολλή μ' ἀνάγκη, πρέσβυ· ταῦτα γὰρ θεοὶ
κἀγὼ κακῶς φρονοῦσ' ἐμηχανησάμην.

Πα. θάρσει· κάτει τοι καὶ σὺ πρὸς τέκνων ἔτι. 1015

Μη. ἄλλους κατάξω πρόσθεν ἡ τάλαιν' ἐγώ.

Πα. οὔτοι μόνη σὺ σῶν ἀπεζύγης τέκνων·
κούφως φέρειν χρὴ θνητὸν ὄντα συμφοράς.

Μη. δράσω τάδ'· ἀλλὰ βαῖνε δωμάτων ἔσω
καὶ παισὶ πόρσυν' οἷα χρὴ καθ' ἡμέραν. 1020
ὦ τέκνα τέκνα, σφῶιν μὲν ἔστι δὴ πόλις
καὶ δῶμ', ἐν ὧι λιπόντες ἀθλίαν ἐμέ
οἰκήσετ' αἰεὶ μητρὸς ἐστερημένοι·
ἐγὼ δ' ἐς ἄλλην γαῖαν εἶμι δὴ φυγάς,
πρὶν σφῶιν ὀνάσθαι κἀπιδεῖν εὐδαίμονας, 1025
πρὶν λουτρὰ καὶ γυναῖκα καὶ γαμηλίους
εὐνὰς ἀγῆλαι λαμπάδας τ' ἀνασχεθεῖν.
ὦ δυστάλαινα τῆς ἐμῆς αὐθαδίας.
ἄλλως ἄρ' ὑμᾶς, ὦ τέκν', ἐξεθρεψάμην,
ἄλλως δ' ἐμόχθουν καὶ κατεξάνθην πόνοις, 1030
στερρὰς ἐνεγκοῦσ' ἐν τόκοις ἀλγηδόνας.
ἦ μήν ποθ' ἡ δύστηνος εἶχον ἐλπίδας
πολλὰς ἐν ὑμῖν, γηροβοσκήσειν τ' ἐμὲ
καὶ κατθανοῦσαν χερσὶν εὖ περιστελεῖν,
ζηλωτὸν ἀνθρώποισι· νῦν δ' ὄλωλε δὴ 1035
γλυκεῖα φροντίς. σφῶιν γὰρ ἐστερημένη
λυπρὸν διάξω βίοτον ἀλγεινόν τ' ἀεί.
ὑμεῖς δὲ μητέρ' οὐκέτ' ὄμμασιν φίλοις
ὄψεσθ', ἐς ἄλλο σχῆμ' ἀποστάντες βίου.

φεῦ φεῦ· τί προσδέρκεσθέ μ' ὄμμασιν, τέκνα;　1040
τί προσγελᾶτε τὸν πανύστατον γέλων;
αἰαῖ· τί δράσω; καρδία γὰρ οἴχεται,
γυναῖκες, ὄμμα φαιδρὸν ὡς εἶδον τέκνων.
οὐκ ἂν δυναίμην· χαιρέτω βουλεύματα
τὰ πρόσθεν· ἄξω παῖδας ἐκ γαίας ἐμούς.　1045
τί δεῖ με πατέρα τῶνδε τοῖς τούτων κακοῖς
λυποῦσαν αὐτὴν δὶς τόσα κτᾶσθαι κακά;
οὐ δῆτ' ἔγωγε· χαιρέτω βουλεύματα.
καίτοι τί πάσχω; βούλομαι γέλωτ' ὀφλεῖν
ἐχθροὺς μεθεῖσα τοὺς ἐμοὺς ἀζημίους;　1050
τολμητέον τάδ'· ἀλλὰ τῆς ἐμῆς κάκης,
τὸ καὶ προσέσθαι μαλθακοὺς λόγους φρενί.
χωρεῖτε, παῖδες, ἐς δόμους. ὅτωι δὲ μὴ
θέμις παρεῖναι τοῖς ἐμοῖσι θύμασιν,
αὐτῶι μελήσει· χεῖρα δ' οὐ διαφθερῶ.　1055
ἆ ἆ.
μὴ δῆτα, θυμέ, μὴ σύ γ' ἐργάσηι τάδε·
ἔασον αὐτούς, ὦ τάλαν, φεῖσαι τέκνων·
ἐκεῖ μεθ' ἡμῶν ζῶντες εὐφρανοῦσί σε.
μὰ τοὺς παρ' Ἅιδηι νερτέρους ἀλάστορας,
οὔτοι ποτ' ἔσται τοῦθ' ὅπως ἐχθροῖς ἐγὼ　1060
παῖδας παρήσω τοὺς ἐμοὺς καθυβρίσαι.
[πάντως σφ' ἀνάγκη κατθανεῖν· ἐπεὶ δὲ χρή,
ἡμεῖς κτενοῦμεν οἵπερ ἐξεφύσαμεν.]
πάντως πέπρακται ταῦτα κοὐκ ἐκφεύξεται·
καὶ δὴ 'πὶ κρατὶ στέφανος, ἐν πέπλοισι δὲ　1065
νύμφη τύραννος ὄλλυται, σάφ' οἶδ' ἐγώ.
ἀλλ', εἶμι γὰρ δὴ τλημονεστάτην ὁδὸν

1043 φαιδρὸν **p**: τερπνὸν **p**　1044 χαίρετω **p**: ἐρρέτω **p**　1052 προσέσθαι Badham (cf. Σ): προέσθαι **o**　φρενί **p**: φρενός **p**　1054 θύμασιν **p**: δώμασιν **p**　1056a ἆ ἆ om. **Π**　1056–80 del. Bergk, Reeve; 1056–64 del. Kovacs　1056 μὴ σύ γ' **p**: μή ποτ' **p**　1062–63 om. **Π**, del. Pierson　1064 πέπρακται **p**, **Π** in linea: πέπρωται **p**: δέδοκται **Π** s.l.　1065 καὶ δὴ **o**: ἤδη **Π** s.l.

καὶ τούσδε πέμψω τλημονεστέραν ἔτι,
παῖδας προσειπεῖν βούλομαι· δότ᾽, ὦ τέκνα,
δότ᾽ ἀσπάσασθαι μητρὶ δεξιὰν χέρα.                          1070
ὦ φιλτάτη χείρ, φίλτατον δέ μοι στόμα
καὶ σχῆμα καὶ πρόσωπον εὐγενὲς τέκνων.
εὐδαιμονοῖτον, ἀλλ᾽ ἐκεῖ· τὰ δ᾽ ἐνθάδε
πατὴρ ἀφείλετ᾽· ὦ γλυκεῖα προσβολή,
ὦ μαλθακὸς χρὼς πνεῦμά θ᾽ ἥδιστον τέκνων.                   1075
χωρεῖτε χωρεῖτ᾽· οὐκέτ᾽ εἰμὶ προσβλέπειν
οἷά τε πρὸς σφᾶς, ἀλλὰ νικῶμαι κακοῖς.
καὶ μανθάνω μὲν οἷα δρᾶν μέλλω κακά,
θυμὸς δὲ κρείσσων τῶν ἐμῶν βουλευμάτων,
ὅσπερ μεγίστων αἴτιος κακῶν βροτοῖς.                        1080

Χο.    πολλάκις ἤδη διὰ λεπτοτέρων
μύθων ἔμολον καὶ πρὸς ἁμίλλας
ἦλθον μείζους ἢ χρὴ γενεὰν
θῆλυν ἐρευνᾶν·
ἀλλὰ γὰρ ἔστιν μοῦσα καὶ ἡμῖν,                              1085
ἣ προσομιλεῖ σοφίας ἕνεκεν,
πάσαισι μὲν οὔ, παῦρον δὲ γένος
⟨μίαν⟩ ἐν πολλαῖς εὕροις ἂν ἴσως)
οὐκ ἀπόμουσον τὸ γυναικῶν.
καί φημι βροτῶν οἵτινές εἰσιν                               1090
πάμπαν ἄπειροι μηδ᾽ ἐφύτευσαν
παῖδας προφέρειν εἰς εὐτυχίαν
τῶν γειναμένων.
οἱ μὲν ἄτεκνοι, δι᾽ ἀπειροσύνην
εἴθ᾽ ἡδὺ βροτοῖς εἴτ᾽ ἀνιαρὸν                               1095
παῖδες τελέθουσ᾽ οὐχὶ τυχόντες,
πολλῶν μόχθων ἀπέχονται·

---

1071 στόμα **p**: κάρα **p**    1077 τε πρὸς σφᾶς Page: τε πρὸς ὑμᾶς fere **p**: τ᾽ ἐς
ὑμᾶς **p**    1078 δρᾶν μέλλω **p**, testimonia: τολμήσω **p**    1087 γένος Reiske:
δὴ γένος **p**: τι γένος **p**: τι δὴ γένος **Π** (coni. Schoemann)    1088 μίαν add.
Elmsley    1089 οὐκ **Π** (coni. Reiske): κοὐκ **o**

οἷσι δὲ τέκνων ἔστιν ἐν οἴκοις
γλυκερὸν βλάστημ', ἐσορῶ μελέτηι
κατατρυχομένους τὸν ἅπαντα χρόνον,  1100
πρῶτον μὲν ὅπως θρέψουσι καλῶς
βίοτόν θ' ὁπόθεν λείψουσι τέκνοις·
ἔτι δ' ἐκ τούτων εἴτ' ἐπὶ φλαύροις  1103
εἴτ' ἐπὶ χρηστοῖς  1103a
μοχθοῦσι, τόδ' ἐστὶν ἄδηλον.
ἒν δὲ τὸ πάντων λοίσθιον ἤδη  1105
πᾶσιν κατερῶ θνητοῖσι κακόν·
καὶ δὴ γὰρ ἅλις βίοτόν θ' ηὗρον
σῶμά τ' ἐς ἥβην ἤλυθε τέκνων
χρηστοί τ' ἐγένοντ'· εἰ δὲ κυρῆσαι
δαίμων οὕτω, φροῦδος ἐς Ἅιδου  1110
Θάνατος προφέρων σώματα τέκνων.
πῶς οὖν λύει πρὸς τοῖς ἄλλοις
τήνδ' ἔτι λύπην ἀνιαροτάτην
παίδων ἕνεκεν
θνητοῖσι θεοὺς ἐπιβάλλειν;  1115

Μη.  φίλαι, πάλαι τοι προσμένουσα τὴν τύχην
καραδοκῶ τἀκεῖθεν οἶ προβήσεται.
καὶ δὴ δέδορκα τόνδε τῶν Ἰάσονος
στείχοντ' ὀπαδῶν· πνεῦμα δ' ἠρεθισμένον
δείκνυσιν ὥς τι καινὸν ἀγγελεῖ κακόν.  1120

ΑΓΓΕΛΟΣ

[ὦ δεινὸν ἔργον παρανόμως εἰργασμένη,]
Μήδεια, φεῦγε φεῦγε, μήτε ναῖαν
λιποῦσ' ἀπήνην μήτ' ὄχον πεδοστιβῆ.

1103 φλαύροις **p**: φαύλοις **pΠ**    1106 κακόν **p**: κακῶν **p**    1107 βίοτόν θ' ηὗρον **p**: βίοτον ηὗρον **p**: βιοτὴν ηὗρον Lenting    1108 ἤλυθε **p**: ἦλθε(ν) **pΠ**    1110 οὕτω **Πp**: οὗτος **p**    Ἅιδου **Π** (coni. Earle): fere ἀίδην **o**    1119 δ' Hermann: τ' **o**    1121 om. **p**, del. Lenting

Μη. τί δ' ἄξιόν μοι τῆσδε τυγχάνει φυγῆς;
Αγ. ὄλωλεν ἡ τύραννος ἀρτίως κόρη                    1125
Κρέων θ' ὁ φύσας φαρμάκων τῶν σῶν ὕπο.
Μη. κάλλιστον εἶπας μῦθον, ἐν δ' εὐεργέταις
τὸ λοιπὸν ἤδη καὶ φίλοις ἐμοῖς ἔσῃ.
Αγ. τί φῄς; φρονεῖς μὲν ὀρθὰ κοὐ μαίνῃ, γύναι,
ἥτις, τυράννων ἑστίαν ᾐκισμένη,                    1130
χαίρεις κλύουσα κοὐ φοβῇ τὰ τοιάδε;
Μη. ἔχω τι κἀγὼ τοῖσι σοῖς ἐναντίον
λόγοισιν εἰπεῖν· ἀλλὰ μὴ σπέρχου, φίλος,
λέξον δέ· πῶς ὤλοντο; δὶς τόσον γὰρ ἂν
τέρψειας ἡμᾶς, εἰ τεθνᾶσι παγκάκως.                1135
Αγ. ἐπεὶ τέκνων σῶν ἦλθε δίπτυχος γονὴ
σὺν πατρὶ καὶ παρῆλθε νυμφικοὺς δόμους,
ἥσθημεν οἵπερ σοῖς ἐκάμνομεν κακοῖς
δμῶες· δι' ὤτων δ' εὐθὺς ἦν πολὺς λόγος
σὲ καὶ πόσιν σὸν νεῖκος ἐσπεῖσθαι τὸ πρίν.           1140
κυνεῖ δ' ὁ μέν τις χεῖρ', ὁ δὲ ξανθὸν κάρα
παίδων· ἐγὼ δὲ καὐτὸς ἡδονῆς ὕπο
στέγας γυναικῶν σὺν τέκνοις ἅμ' ἑσπόμην.
δέσποινα δ' ἣν νῦν ἀντὶ σοῦ θαυμάζομεν,
πρὶν μὲν τέκνων σῶν εἰσιδεῖν ξυνωρίδα,              1145
πρόθυμον εἶχ' ὀφθαλμὸν εἰς Ἰάσονα·
ἔπειτα μέντοι προυκαλύψατ' ὄμματα
λευκήν τ' ἀπέστρεψ' ἔμπαλιν παρηίδα,
παίδων μυσαχθεῖσ' εἰσόδους· πόσις δὲ σὸς
ὀργάς τ' ἀφῄρει καὶ χόλον νεάνιδος,                 1150
λέγων τάδ'· Οὐ μὴ δυσμενὴς ἔσῃ φίλοις,
παύσῃ δὲ θυμοῦ καὶ πάλιν στρέψεις κάρα,
φίλους νομίζουσ' οὕσπερ ἂν πόσις σέθεν,
δέξῃ δὲ δῶρα καὶ παραιτήσῃ πατρὸς
φυγὰς ἀφεῖναι παισὶ τοῖσδ' ἐμὴν χάριν;              1155
ἡ δ', ὡς ἐσεῖδε κόσμον, οὐκ ἠνέσχετο,

1130 ἑστίαν **p**: οἰκίαν **p**    ᾐκισμένη **p**: -μένην **p**    1132 τοῖσι **p**: τοῖς γε **p**

ἀλλ' ἤινεσ' ἀνδρὶ πάντα, καὶ πρὶν ἐκ δόμων
μακρὰν ἀπεῖναι πατέρα καὶ παῖδας σέθεν
λαβοῦσα πέπλους ποικίλους ἠμπέσχετο,
χρυσοῦν τε θεῖσα στέφανον ἀμφὶ βοστρύχοις          1160
λαμπρῶι κατόπτρωι σχηματίζεται κόμην,
ἄψυχον εἰκὼ προσγελῶσα σώματος.
κᾆπειτ' ἀναστᾶσ' ἐκ θρόνων διέρχεται
στέγας, ἁβρὸν βαίνουσα παλλεύκωι ποδί,
δώροις ὑπερχαίρουσα, πολλὰ πολλάκις          1165
τένοντ' ἐς ὀρθὸν ὄμμασι σκοπουμένη.
τοὐνθένδε μέντοι δεινὸν ἦν θέαμ' ἰδεῖν·
χροιὰν γὰρ ἀλλάξασα λεχρία πάλιν
χωρεῖ τρέμουσα κῶλα καὶ μόλις φθάνει
θρόνοισιν ἐμπεσοῦσα μὴ χαμαὶ πεσεῖν.          1170
καί τις γεραιὰ προσπόλων, δόξασά που
ἢ Πανὸς ὀργὰς ἤ τινος θεῶν μολεῖν,
ἀνωλόλυξε, πρίν γ' ὁρᾶι διὰ στόμα
χωροῦντα λευκὸν ἀφρόν, ὀμμάτων τ' ἄπο
κόρας στρέφουσαν, αἷμά τ' οὐκ ἐνὸν χροΐ·          1175
εἶτ' ἀντίμολπον ἧκεν ὀλολυγῆς μέγαν
κωκυτόν. εὐθὺς δ' ἡ μὲν ἐς πατρὸς δόμους
ὥρμησεν, ἡ δὲ πρὸς τὸν ἀρτίως πόσιν,
φράσουσα νύμφης συμφοράν· ἅπασα δὲ
στέγη πυκνοῖσιν ἐκτύπει δραμήμασιν.          1180
ἤδη δ' ἀνελθὼν κῶλον ἔκπλεθρον δρόμου
ταχὺς βαδιστὴς τερμόνων ἂν ἥπτετο·
ἡ δ' ἐξ ἀναύδου καὶ μύσαντος ὄμματος
δεινὸν στενάξασ' ἡ τάλαιν' ἠγείρετο.
διπλοῦν γὰρ αὐτῆι πῆμ' ἐπεστρατεύετο·          1185
χρυσοῦς μὲν ἀμφὶ κρατὶ κείμενος πλόκος
θαυμαστὸν ἵει νᾶμα παμφάγου πυρός,
πέπλοι δὲ λεπτοί, σῶν τέκνων δωρήματα,

λευκὴν ἔδαπτον σάρκα τῆς δυσδαίμονος.
φεύγει δ' ἀναστᾶσ' ἐκ θρόνων πυρουμένη,　　　　1190
σείουσα χαίτην κρᾶτά τ' ἄλλοτ' ἄλλοσε,
ῥῖψαι θέλουσα στέφανον· ἀλλ' ἀραρότως
σύνδεσμα χρυσὸς εἶχε, πῦρ δ', ἐπεὶ κόμην
ἔσεισε, μᾶλλον δὶς τόσως ἐλάμπετο.
πίτνει δ' ἐς οὖδας συμφορᾶι νικωμένη,　　　　1195
πλὴν τῶι τεκόντι κάρτα δυσμαθὴς ἰδεῖν·
οὔτ' ὀμμάτων γὰρ δῆλος ἦν κατάστασις
οὔτ' εὐφυὲς πρόσωπον, αἷμα δ' ἐξ ἄκρου
ἔσταζε κρατὸς συμπεφυρμένον πυρί,
σάρκες δ' ἀπ' ὀστέων ὥστε πεύκινον δάκρυ　　　　1200
γνάθοις ἀδήλοις φαρμάκων ἀπέρρεον,
δεινὸν θέαμα. πᾶσι δ' ἦν φόβος θιγεῖν
νεκροῦ· τύχην γὰρ εἴχομεν διδάσκαλον.
πατὴρ δ' ὁ τλήμων συμφορᾶς ἀγνωσίαι
ἄφνω παρελθὼν δῶμα προσπίτνει νεκρῶι.　　　　1205
ᾤμωξε δ' εὐθὺς καὶ περιπτύξας χέρας
κυνεῖ προσαυδῶν τοιάδ'· Ὦ δύστηνε παῖ,
τίς σ' ὧδ' ἀτίμως δαιμόνων ἀπώλεσεν;
τίς τὸν γέροντα τύμβον ὀρφανὸν σέθεν
τίθησιν; οἴμοι, συνθάνοιμί σοι, τέκνον.　　　　1210
ἐπεὶ δὲ θρήνων καὶ γόων ἐπαύσατο,
χρήιζων γεραιὸν ἐξαναστῆσαι δέμας
προσείχεθ' ὥστε κισσὸς ἔρνεσιν δάφνης
λεπτοῖσι πέπλοις, δεινὰ δ' ἦν παλαίσματα·
ὁ μὲν γὰρ ἤθελ' ἐξαναστῆσαι γόνυ,　　　　1215
ἡ δ' ἀντελάζυτ'· εἰ δὲ πρὸς βίαν ἄγοι,
σάρκας γεραιὰς ἐσπάρασσ' ἀπ' ὀστέων.
χρόνωι δ' ἀπέστη καὶ μεθῆχ' ὁ δύσμορος
ψυχήν· κακοῦ γὰρ οὐκέτ' ἦν ὑπέρτερος.

1201 γνάθοις Blaydes: fere γναθμοῖς o　　1205 παρελθὼν Nauck: προσελ-
θὼν o　　1206 χέρας p: δέμας p　　1218 ἀπέστη o: ἀπέσβη Scaliger

κεῖνται δὲ νεκροὶ παῖς τε καὶ γέρων πατὴρ                    1220
πέλας, †ποθεινὴ δακρύοισι συμφορά.†
καί μοι τὸ μὲν σὸν ἐκποδὼν ἔστω λόγου·
γνώσηι γὰρ αὐτὴ ζημίας ἐπιστροφήν.
τὰ θνητὰ δ' οὐ νῦν πρῶτον ἡγοῦμαι σκιάν,
οὐδ' ἂν τρέσας εἴποιμι τοὺς σοφοὺς βροτῶν                    1225
δοκοῦντας εἶναι καὶ μεριμνητὰς λόγων
τούτους μεγίστην μωρίαν ὀφλισκάνειν.
θνητῶν γὰρ οὐδείς ἐστιν εὐδαίμων ἀνήρ·
ὄλβου δ' ἐπιρρυέντος εὐτυχέστερος
ἄλλου γένοιτ' ἂν ἄλλος, εὐδαίμων δ' ἂν οὔ.                   1230
Χο.   ἔοιχ' ὁ δαίμων πολλὰ τῆιδ' ἐν ἡμέραι
κακὰ ξυνάπτειν ἐνδίκως Ἰάσονι.
[ὦ τλῆμον, ὥς σου συμφορὰς οἰκτίρομεν,
κόρη Κρέοντος, ἥτις εἰς Ἅιδου δόμους
οἴχηι γάμων ἕκατι τῶν Ἰάσονος.]                             1235
Μη.   φίλαι, δέδοκται τοὔργον ὡς τάχιστά μοι
παῖδας κτανούσηι τῆσδ' ἀφορμᾶσθαι χθονός,
καὶ μὴ σχολὴν ἄγουσαν ἐκδοῦναι τέκνα
ἄλληι φονεῦσαι δυσμενεστέραι χερί.
πάντως σφ' ἀνάγκη κατθανεῖν· ἐπεὶ δὲ χρή,                    1240
ἡμεῖς κτενοῦμεν οἵπερ ἐξεφύσαμεν.
ἀλλ' εἶ' ὁπλίζου, καρδία· τί μέλλομεν
τὰ δεινὰ κἀναγκαῖα μὴ ⟨οὐ⟩ πράσσειν κακά;
ἄγ', ὦ τάλαινα χεὶρ ἐμή, λαβὲ ξίφος,
λάβ', ἕρπε πρὸς βαλβῖδα λυπηρὰν βίου,                        1245
καὶ μὴ κακισθῆις μηδ' ἀναμνησθῆις τέκνων,
ὡς φίλταθ', ὡς ἔτικτες, ἀλλὰ τήνδε γε
λαθοῦ βραχεῖαν ἡμέραν παίδων σέθεν
κἄπειτα θρήνει· καὶ γὰρ εἰ κτενεῖς σφ', ὅμως
φίλοι γ' ἔφυσαν· δυστυχὴς δ' ἐγὼ γυνή.                       1250

1220–1 del. West, 1221 Reeve   1223 ἐπιστροφήν Lenting e scholio: ἀποστροφήν o   1227 μωρίαν editio Aldina: ζημίαν o   1233–5 del. Weil
1234 δόμους p: πύλας p   1240–41 del. Valck.   1243 οὐ add. Elmsley

Χο.  ἰὼ Γᾶ τε καὶ παμφαὴς                    [στρ.
      ἀκτὶς Ἁλίου, κατίδετ' ἴδετε τὰν
      ὀλομέναν γυναῖκα, πρὶν φοινίαν
      τέκνοις προσβαλεῖν χέρ' αὐτοκτόνον·
      σᾶς γὰρ χρυσέας ἀπὸ γονᾶς                1255
      ἔβλαστεν, θεοῦ δ' αἷμα ⟨χαμαὶ⟩ πίτνειν
      φόβος ὑπ' ἀνέρων.
      ἀλλά νιν, ὦ φάος διογενές, κάτειρ-
      γε κατάπαυσον, ἔξελ' οἴκων τάλαι-
      νάν φονίαν τ' Ἐρινὺν †ὑπ' ἀλαστόρων†.     1260

      μάταν μόχθος ἔρρει τέκνων,               [ἀντ.
      μάταν ἄρα γένος φίλιον ἔτεκες, ὦ
      κυανεᾶν λιποῦσα Συμπληγάδων
      πετρᾶν ἀξενωτάταν ἐσβολάν.
      δειλαία, τί σοι φρενοβαρὴς                1265
      χόλος προσπίτνει καὶ ζαμενὴς ⟨φόνου⟩
      φόνος ἀμείβεται;
      χαλεπὰ γὰρ βροτοῖς ὁμογενῆ μιά-
      σματ' †ἐπὶ γαῖαν† αὐτοφόνταις ξυνωι-
      δὰ θεόθεν πίτνοντ' ἐπὶ δόμοις ἄχη.        1270

                    ΠΑΙΣ (ἔσωθεν).

      ἰώ μοι.                                 1270a

Χο.  ἀκούεις βοὰν ἀκούεις τέκνων;             [στρ. 1273
      ἰὼ τλᾶμον, ὦ κακοτυχὲς γύναι.           1274

1252 Ἁλίου Hermann: ἀελίου o    1253 φοινίαν editio Aldina: φονίαν o
1255 χρυσέας ἀπὸ Musgrave: ἀπὸ χρυσέας o    1256 αἷμα p: αἵματι vel αἷμα
τι p    χαμαὶ add. post Hermann Diggle    1259–60 τάλαιναν φονίαν τ'
Seidler: φονίαν τάλαινάν τ' o    1262 μάταν ἄρα Musgrave: ἄρα μάταν p:
μάταν p    1265 φρενοβαρὴς Seidler: φρενῶν βαρὺς o    1266 ζαμενὴς Porson: δυσμενὴς o: δαιμενης Π s.l.    φόνου add. Wecklein    1270a ιωι μ[οι Π:
om. o    1273–4 transp. Seidler, et ante et post 1271–2 habet Π: 1273–4 post
1271–2 o

Πα.ᵅ    οἴμοι, τί δράσω; ποῖ φύγω μητρὸς χέρας;     1271

Πα.ᵝ    οὐκ οἶδ', ἀδελφὲ φίλτατ'· ὀλλύμεσθα γάρ.     1272

Χο.    παρέλθω δόμους; ἀρῆξαι φόνον     1275
      δοκεῖ μοι τέκνοις.

Πα.ᵅ    ναί, πρὸς θεῶν, ἀρήξατ'· ἐν δέοντι γάρ.

Πα.ᵝ    ὡς ἐγγὺς ἤδη γ' ἐσμὲν ἀρκύων ξίφους.

Χο.    τάλαιν', ὡς ἄρ' ἦσθα πέτρος ἢ σίδα-
      ρος, ἅτις τέκνων     1280
      ὃν ἔτεκες ἄροτον αὐτόχει-     1281
      ρι μοίραι κτενεῖς.     1281a

μίαν δὴ κλύω μίαν τῶν πάρος     [ἀντ.
      γυναῖκ' ἐν φίλοις χέρα βαλεῖν τέκνοις,
Ἰνὼ μανεῖσαν ἐκ θεῶν, ὅθ' ἡ Διὸς
δάμαρ νιν ἐξέπεμπε δωμάτων ἄλαις·     1285
πίτνει δ' ἀ τάλαιν' ἐς ἅλμαν φόνωι
      τέκνων δυσσεβεῖ,
ἀκτῆς ὑπερτείνασα ποντίας πόδα,
δυοῖν τε παίδοιν ξυνθανοῦσ' ἀπόλλυται.
τί δῆτ' οὐ γένοιτ' ἂν ἔτι δεινόν; ὦ     1290
      γυναικῶν λέχος
      πολύπονον, ὅσα βροτοῖς ἔρε-     1292
      ξας ἤδη κακά.     1292a

Ια.    γυναῖκες, αἳ τῆσδ' ἐγγὺς ἕστατε στέγης,
ἆρ' ἐν δόμοισιν ἡ τὰ δείν' εἰργασμένη
Μήδεια τοισίδ' ἢ μεθέστηκεν φυγῆι;     1295
δεῖ γάρ νιν ἤτοι γῆς γε κρυφθῆναι κάτω
ἢ πτηνὸν ἄραι σῶμ' ἐς αἰθέρος βάθος,
εἰ μὴ τυράννων δώμασιν δώσει δίκην.

---

1281 ὃν Π (coni. Seidler): ὧν o    μοίραι o: τολμαι Π (coni. Nauck)    1285 ἐξέπεμπε p: ἐξέπεμψε p    1285 ἅλαις Π: ἄληι fere o, Π s.l.: ἄλαι Π altera    1290 δῆτ' οὐ Π (coni. Hermann): δὴ ποτ' οὖν o    1292 ὅσα Seidler: ὅσ(σ)α δὴ oΠ    1295 τοισίδ' Canter: τοῖσιν pΠ: τοῖσδέ γ' p    1296 γῆς γε Π (coni. Elmsley): γῆ(ς) σφε o

πέποιθ' ἀποκτείνασα κοιράνους χθονὸς
ἀθῶιος αὐτὴ τῶνδε φεύξεσθαι δόμων;                1300
ἀλλ' οὐ γὰρ αὐτῆς φροντίδ' ὡς τέκνων ἔχω·
κείνην μὲν οὓς ἔδρασεν ἔρξουσιν κακῶς,
ἐμῶν δὲ παίδων ἦλθον ἐκσώσων βίον,
μή μοί τι δράσωσ' οἱ προσήκοντες γένει,
μητρῶιον ἐκπράσσοντες ἀνόσιον φόνον.            1305

Χο.  ὦ τλῆμον, οὐκ οἶσθ' οἷ κακῶν ἐλήλυθας,
Ἰᾶσον· οὐ γὰρ τούσδ' ἂν ἐφθέγξω λόγους.

Ια.  τί δ' ἔστιν; ἦ που κἄμ' ἀποκτεῖναι θέλει;

Χο.  παῖδες τεθνᾶσι χειρὶ μητρώιαι σέθεν.

Ια.  οἴμοι, τί λέξεις; ὥς μ' ἀπώλεσας, γύναι.       1310

Χο.  ὡς οὐκέτ' ὄντων σῶν τέκνων φρόντιζε δή.

Ια.  ποῦ γάρ νιν ἔκτειν'; ἐντὸς ἢ 'ξωθεν δόμων;

Χο.  πύλας ἀνοίξας σῶν τέκνων ὄψηι φόνον.

Ια.  χαλᾶτε κλῆιδας ὡς τάχιστα, πρόσπολοι,
ἐκλύεθ' ἁρμούς, ὡς ἴδω διπλοῦν κακόν,             1315
τοὺς μὲν θανόντας, τὴν δὲ — τείσωμαι δίκην.

Μη.  τί τάσδε κινεῖς κἀναμοχλεύεις πύλας,
νεκροὺς ἐρευνῶν κἀμὲ τὴν εἰργασμένην;
παῦσαι πόνου τοῦδ'. εἰ δ' ἐμοῦ χρείαν ἔχεις,
λέγ' εἴ τι βούληι, χειρὶ δ' οὐ ψαύσεις ποτέ·      1320
τοιόνδ' ὄχημα πατρὸς Ἥλιος πατὴρ
δίδωσιν ἡμῖν, ἔρυμα πολεμίας χερός.

Ια.  ὦ μῖσος, ὦ μέγιστον ἐχθίστη γύναι
θεοῖς τε κἀμοὶ παντί τ' ἀνθρώπων γένει,
ἥτις τέκνοισι σοῖσιν ἐμβαλεῖν ξίφος              1325
ἔτλης τεκοῦσα κἄμ' ἄπαιδ' ἀπώλεσας.
καὶ ταῦτα δράσασ' ἥλιόν τε προσβλέπεις
καὶ γαῖαν, ἔργον τλᾶσα δυσσεβέστατον;
ὄλοι'. ἐγὼ δὲ νῦν φρονῶ, τότ' οὐ φρονῶν,
ὅτ' ἐκ δόμων σε βαρβάρου τ' ἀπὸ χθονὸς           1330

1308 ἦ που fere **o**, Π s.l.: οὔ που Π (coni. Barthold)     1316 del. Schenkl
τίσωμαι δίκην **p**: τίσομαι φόνωι **p**

Ἕλλην' ἐς οἶκον ἠγόμην, κακὸν μέγα,
πατρός τε καὶ γῆς προδότιν ἥ σ' ἐθρέψατο.
τὸν σὸν δ' ἀλάστορ' εἰς ἔμ' ἔσκηψαν θεοί·
κτανοῦσα γὰρ δὴ σὸν κάσιν παρέστιον
τὸ καλλίπρωιρον εἰσέβης Ἀργοῦς σκάφος.          1335
ἦρξω μὲν ἐκ τοιῶνδε· νυμφευθεῖσα δὲ
παρ' ἀνδρὶ τῶιδε καὶ τεκοῦσά μοι τέκνα,
εὐνῆς ἕκατι καὶ λέχους σφ' ἀπώλεσας.
οὐκ ἔστιν ἥτις τοῦτ' ἂν Ἑλληνὶς γυνὴ
ἔτλη ποθ', ὧν γε πρόσθεν ἠξίουν ἐγὼ          1340
γῆμαι σέ, κῆδος ἐχθρὸν ὀλέθριόν τ' ἐμοί,
λέαιναν, οὐ γυναῖκα, τῆς Τυρσηνίδος
Σκύλλης ἔχουσαν ἀγριωτέραν φύσιν.
ἀλλ' οὐ γὰρ ἄν σε μυρίοις ὀνείδεσιν
δάκοιμι· τοιόνδ' ἐμπέφυκέ σοι θράσος·          1345
ἔρρ', αἰσχροποιὲ καὶ τέκνων μιαιφόνε.
ἐμοὶ δὲ τὸν ἐμὸν δαίμον' αἰάζειν πάρα,
ὃς οὔτε λέκτρων νεογάμων ὀνήσομαι,
οὐ παῖδας οὓς ἔφυσα κἀξεθρεψάμην
ἔξω προσειπεῖν ζῶντας ἀλλ' ἀπώλεσα.          1350
Μη.   μακρὰν ἂν ἐξέτεινα τοῖσδ' ἐναντίον
λόγοισιν, εἰ μὴ Ζεὺς πατὴρ ἠπίστατο
οἷ' ἐξ ἐμοῦ πέπονθας οἷά τ' ἠργάσω.
σὺ δ' οὐκ ἔμελλες τἀμ' ἀτιμάσας λέχη
τερπνὸν διάξειν βίοτον ἐγγελῶν ἐμοὶ          1355
οὐδ' ἡ τύραννος, οὐδ' ὅ σοι προσθεὶς γάμους
Κρέων ἀνατεὶ τῆσδέ μ' ἐκβαλεῖν χθονός.
πρὸς ταῦτα καὶ λέαιναν, εἰ βούληι, κάλει
καὶ Σκύλλαν ἢ Τυρσηνὸν ὤικησεν πέδον·
τῆς σῆς γὰρ ὡς χρῆν καρδίας ἀνθηψάμην.          1360
Ια.   καὐτή γε λυπῆι καὶ κακῶν κοινωνὸς εἶ.

1356 οὐδ'... οὐδ' Elmsley: οὔθ'... οὔθ' o     1357 ἀνατεὶ p: ἄτιμον p     1359
del. Verrall     πέδον o: σπέος Musgrave, πέτραν Elmsley     1360 χρῆν
Reiske: χρὴ o

Μη.   σάφ' ἴσθι· λύει δ' ἄλγος, ἢν σὺ μὴ 'γγελᾶις.
Ια.   ὦ τέκνα, μητρὸς ὡς κακῆς ἐκύρσατε.
Μη.   ὦ παῖδες, ὡς ὤλεσθε πατρώιαι νόσωι.
Ια.   οὗτοι νιν ἡμὴ δεξιά γ' ἀπώλεσεν.                    1365
Μη.   ἀλλ' ὕβρις οἵ τε σοὶ νεοδμῆτες γάμοι.
Ια.   λέχους σφε κἠξίωσας οὕνεκα κτανεῖν;
Μη.   σμικρὸν γυναικὶ πῆμα τοῦτ' εἶναι δοκεῖς;
Ια.   ἥτις γε σώφρων· σοὶ δὲ πάντ' ἐστὶν κακά.
Μη.   οἵδ' οὐκέτ' εἰσί· τοῦτο γάρ σε δήξεται.               1370
Ια.   οἵδ' εἰσίν, οἴμοι, σῶι κάραι μιάστορες.
Μη.   ἴσασιν ὅστις ἦρξε πημονῆς θεοί.
Ια.   ἴσασι δῆτα σήν γ' ἀπόπτυστον φρένα.
Μη.   στύγει· πικρὰν δὲ βάξιν ἐχθαίρω σέθεν.
Ια.   καὶ μὴν ἐγὼ σήν· ῥάιδιοι δ' ἀπαλλαγαί.               1375
Μη.   πῶς οὖν; τί δράσω; κάρτα γὰρ κἀγὼ θέλω.
Ια.   θάψαι νεκρούς μοι τούσδε καὶ κλαῦσαι πάρες.
Μη.   οὐ δῆτ', ἐπεί σφας τῆιδ' ἐγὼ θάψω χερί,
      φέρουσ' ἐς Ἥρας τέμενος Ἀκραίας θεοῦ,
      ὡς μή τις αὐτοὺς πολεμίων καθυβρίσηι                  1380
      τύμβους ἀνασπῶν· γῆι δὲ τῆιδε Σισύφου
      σεμνὴν ἑορτὴν καὶ τέλη προσάψομεν
      τὸ λοιπὸν ἀντὶ τοῦδε δυσσεβοῦς φόνου.
      αὐτὴ δὲ γαῖαν εἶμι τὴν Ἐρεχθέως,
      Αἰγεῖ συνοικήσουσα τῶι Πανδίονος.                     1385
      σὺ δ', ὥσπερ εἰκός, κατθανῆι κακὸς κακῶς,
      Ἀργοῦς κάρα σὸν λειψάνωι πεπληγμένος,
      πικρὰς τελευτὰς τῶν ἐμῶν γάμων ἰδών.
Ια.   ἀλλά σ' Ἐρινὺς ὀλέσειε τέκνων
      φονία τε Δίκη.                                        1390
Μη.   τίς δὲ κλύει σοῦ θεὸς ἢ δαίμων,
      τοῦ ψευδόρκου καὶ ξειναπάτου;
Ια.   φεῦ φεῦ, μυσαρὰ καὶ παιδολέτορ.

1365 οὗτοι νιν p: οὗτοι νυν fere p   γ' Hermann: σφ' o   1374 στύγει Weil:
στυγῆι o   1375 ῥάιδιοι p: ῥάδιον p   1382 προσάψομεν p: -ομαι p

Μη.  στεῖχε πρὸς οἴκους καὶ θάπτ' ἄλοχον.

Ια.  στείχω, δισσῶν γ' ἄμορος τέκνων.        1395

Μη.  οὔπω θρηνεῖς· μένε καὶ γῆρας.

Ια.  ὦ τέκνα φίλτατα. Μη. μητρί γε, σοὶ δ' οὔ.

Ια.  κἄπειτ' ἔκανες; Μη. σέ γε πημαίνουσ'.

Ια.  ὤμοι, φιλίου χρῄζω στόματος
     παίδων ὁ τάλας προσπτύξασθαι.        1400

Μη.  νῦν σφε προσαυδᾷς, νῦν ἀσπάζῃ,
     τότ' ἀπωσάμενος. Ια. δός μοι πρὸς θεῶν
     μαλακοῦ χρωτὸς ψαῦσαι τέκνων.

Μη.  οὐκ ἔστι· μάτην ἔπος ἔρριπται.

Ια.  Ζεῦ, τάδ' ἀκούεις ὡς ἀπελαυνόμεθ'        1405
     οἷά τε πάσχομεν ἐκ τῆς μυσαρᾶς
     καὶ παιδοφόνου τῆσδε λεαίνης;
     ἀλλ' ὁπόσον γοῦν πάρα καὶ δύναμαι
     τάδε καὶ θρηνῶ κἀπιθεάζω,
     μαρτυρόμενος δαίμονας ὥς μοι        1410
     τέκνα κτείνασ' ἀποκωλύεις
     ψαῦσαί τε χεροῖν θάψαι τε νεκρούς,
     οὓς μήποτ' ἐγὼ φύσας ὄφελον
     πρὸς σοῦ φθιμένους ἐπιδέσθαι.

[Χο.  πολλῶν ταμίας Ζεὺς ἐν Ὀλύμπωι,        1415
     πολλὰ δ' ἀέλπτως κραίνουσι θεοί·
     καὶ τὰ δοκηθέντ' οὐκ ἐτελέσθη,
     τῶν δ' ἀδοκήτων πόρον ηὗρε θεός.
     τοιόνδ' ἀπέβη τόδε πρᾶγμα.]

1398 ἔκανες Elmsley: ἔκτανες o    1404 ἔπος p: δ' ἔπος p: λόγος p    1409
κἀπιθεάζω Blomfield: -θοάζω o    1410 μοι p: μου p    1415–19 del.
Hartung

# COMMENTARY

### *1–130    Prologue*

The opening scenes of the play ('prologue' in the wider sense defined in *Poetics* 12, 1452b19–20, as 'the whole portion of the drama preceding the entrance-song of the chorus': SE 2) offer some sparing hints of the past history, expose the distraught and emotional state of Medea under the pressure of Jason's betrayal, and introduce the new event (the decree of exile) that motivates the action (conceived, as usual for Greek tragedy, as events completed within a single day: *Poetics* 1449b12–13). The sequence may be divided into three parts by variations in form and by entrances and exits (SE 2): 1–48 nurse alone in iambic monologue, 49–95 (entrance during 45–9) iambic dialogue of nurse and tutor (with silent boys), 96–130 (gradual departure indoors during 89–105: 89n.) anapaests, chanted by nurse outdoors and sung by Medea indoors. This third part in fact flows almost seamlessly into the parodos (SE 2), since the chorus' lyric is interspersed with more anapaests from both the nurse and Medea, the chorus being alone only for 204–13.

### *1–48    Monologue of the nurse*

Eur. routinely begins his plays with a single speaker addressing the audience more or less directly, a technique that permits the clear presentation of background details and that openly acknowledges the theatrical situation and the role of the audience as interpreters witnessing an enacted sequence of events (compare the remarks of Aristophanes' 'Euripides' in *Frogs* 946–7, 1122). When the prologue-speaker is a human being, delivery of the prologue by a major character provides that character with immediate access to the sympathy of the audience. In *Medea*, however, the speaker is a minor character, one who will not be seen again after the prologue-scenes (see 204n., 820n.): this technique distances the audience from quick emotional involvement with the protagonist(s), but arouses ominous anticipation (compare Aesch. *Ag.* and *Eum.*, and the comic counterpart of this technique in Ar. *Wasps* and *Peace*). So the nurse shows anxiety about

160

Medea's distraught state and fear about her potential for harming others; these concerns are reinforced in the conversation with the tutor and then borne out by the cries heard from within. Medea thus does not appeal directly to the audience for sympathy, and the sympathy elicited for her by her well-disposed nurse is tempered by the fears the nurse expresses. The audience must wait until line 214 to observe Medea directly, appealing to others (the chorus, Aegeus) and manipulating all who converse with her.

**1–8** By opening with a contrary-to-fact wish, the nurse immediately sets a tone of strong regret and introduces the note of heroic achievement gone sour. The two major triumphs of the Argonautic expedition are alluded to: passage of the Clashing Rocks (which implies their becoming fixed, opening the Black Sea to other seafarers) and capture of the Golden Fleece. But in despair the nurse wishes not only that the ship had never come to Colchis, but that it had never even been built (compare *Il.* 5.62–4, Phereclus built Paris' ships, which were ἀρχεκάκους, 'the origin of evils'). Unlike many other Euripidean prologue-speakers, the nurse does not dwell on the more remote details, and so the audience is given no third-party narrative against which to judge what Medea and Jason themselves later claim about their past.

**1**　**Εἴθ' ὤφελ':** ὤφελον with the infinitive is, from Homer onward, a standard alternative to expressing a contrary-to-fact wish with a particle such as εἴθε and a past tense of the indicative (or in Homer sometimes the optative): Smyth §1781; Goodwin §§734–6. The redundant addition of the particle εἴθε, found mainly in poetry, adds emphasis.

　　**Ἀργοῦς ... σκάφος:** Ἀργοῦς is gen. sing. of Ἀργώ, an o-stem of the type of πειθώ or Σαπφώ (Smyth §279). Periphrasis consisting of a noun in the gen. ('defining gen.') dependent on another noun is very common in tragedy (see LS 10.a); same phrase at 1335 and with adj. Ἀργῶιον at 477. σκάφος is literally 'hull', but in tragedy often 'ship' by synecdoche (see LS 31), with or without a defining gen. (νεὼς σκάφος *IT* 742 and elsewhere).

　　**διαπτάσθαι** is aor. middle inf. of διαπέτομαι (διεπτάμην), 'fly through', governing Συμπληγάδας. The metaphor of flight for the propulsion of a ship is traditional, esp. with πτερόν or the like used of oars or sails (see West on Hesiod, *WD* 628), but the vivid verb here may allude to the heroic effort needed to speed the Argo through the dangerous passage.

**2 Κόλχων ἐς αἶαν** 'to the Colchians' land'. Aeetes was originally lord of Aia, a mythical land on the Ocean stream at the eastern edge of the world (Lesky (1948)); in the historical period the Greeks identified this with Colchis, the territory at the eastern extreme of the Black Sea, around the mouth of the Phasis River (modern River Rioni, whose mouth is at Poti, Georgia). Gen. plural proper noun + preposition + αἶαν is a stereotyped tragic phrase, but it is possible that Euripides is punning here on the proper name Αἶα (which may be etymologically the same and could not, of course, be distinguished in ancient writing).

**κυανέας Συμπληγάδας:** the Clashing Rocks were in origin a mythical obstacle to passage from the everyday world to a distant magical realm (compare ancient conceptions of the Hyperboreans, the Pillars of Heracles with the impassable seas near them, or the Aethiopes); in archaic times they were located at the Bosporus, famous for its treacherous currents, on the assumption that the rocks no longer moved (their magic having been terminated by the Argo's successful passage: Pindar, *Pyth.* 4.210–11). For discussion, bibliography, and the relation of Symplegades to Planctae ('Wandering Rocks'), see Heubeck's note on *Od.* 12.55–72; for ancient geographers' claims about the rocks, see Tozer (1893) 198–9. The name Symplegades happens to be extant first here; 'Dark Rocks' (Κυάνεαι) is an alternative name first found in Hdt. and the tragedians.

**3 Πηλίου:** Mt Pelion in Magnesia (Thessaly) towers over the north end of the Gulf of Pagasae (modern Gulf of Volos), where Iolcus (modern Volos), Jason's family home and the starting-point of the voyage of the Argo, is situated. The ancient associations of the mountain include Centaurs, especially Chiron as educator of heroes (Achilles, Jason), and Peleus (wrestling match with Thetis, famous ash-spear, marriage attended by the gods). The story of the construction of the Argo was presumably narrated in lost epic sources: *Od.* 12.70 Ἀργὼ πασιμέλουσα, 'the Argo, in which all take an interest', alludes to the fame of the Argonautic saga in epic recitations earlier than and contemporary with the *Od.*

**4 ἐρετμῶσαι:** the word was probably coined for this passage, in a typically bold usage, 'equip with oars' with 'pine tree' as subject (the verb reappears in late epic in various senses, normally with persons as subject); for similarly innovative use of derived verbs, cf. τεκνόω in *Her.* 7, *Phoen.* 869, and see LS 31.

**5 ἀνδρῶν ἀρίστων:** the company of Argonauts was made up of select volunteers, heroes eager to show the world their mettle (Pindar, *Pyth.* 4.188 ναυτῶν ἄωτος; Ap. Rhod. 1.229 ἀριστῆας; Theocr. 13.17–18 ἀριστῆες ... πασᾶν ἐκ πολίων προλελεγμένοι ὧν ὄφελός τι). [Diggle accepts Wakefield's ἀριστέων, from ἀριστεύς, an easy corruption; but the tragic parallels do not permit any clear choice: *Phoen.* 1267, *Rhes.* 409, Soph. *Aj.* 1380, *Ant.* 197 vs *IA* 28, *Rhes.* 479, *Phil.* 997.]

**5–6 τὸ πάγχρυσον δέρος | ... μετῆλθον:** the quest is often referred to in these terms, but with epic κῶας for δέρος: Hdt. 7.193.2 ἐπὶ τὸ κῶας ἔπλεον; Ap. Rhod. 1.4 χρύσειον μετὰ κῶας; Theocr. 13.16 τὸ χρύσειον ἔπλει μετὰ κῶας.

**6 Πελίαι:** dat. of interest, 'to fetch for Pelias, to give to Pelias'. Pelias was the brother of Aeson, Jason's father, from whom he had seized the throne. In the usual fashion of such myths, he assigned a quest as a condition of Jason's recovery of the throne, in the hope that Jason would die trying to complete it. Pindar, *Pyth.* 4.156–68 tells the story of Pelias' demand; more briefly already Hes. *Theog.* 994–6.

**7 πύργους γῆς ... Ἰωλκίας** 'towers of the Iolcian land' is not a colourless periphrasis for 'city of Iolcus', for πύργος implies that Iolcus is a protecting refuge for Jason and Medea in their flight from Colchis. For the acc. of the goal of motion without a preposition see LS 12.b.

**8 ἔρωτι ... Ἰάσονος:** for the separation of the gen. from the noun it depends on, see LS 35. Later in the play Medea and Jason dispute the degree to which either of them is now motivated by sexual attraction or jealousy, but for the earlier stage of their relationship the extant sources agree in the view that Medea acted out of infatuation with the handsome hero – an infatuation attributed to the will of the gods (Pind. *Pyth.* 4.213–19; Hes. *Theog.* 992–4). See Introd. 4.

**θυμὸν ἐκπλαγεῖσ':** θυμόν may be loosely termed an acc. of respect (Smyth §§1600–1) with ἐκπλαγεῖσα (aor. pass. part. of ἐκπλήττω), but the construction has its origin in the Homeric use of acc. objects of the whole and the part (Smyth §985), the acc. of the part being retained when the person representing the whole becomes the subject of a passive verb form.

**9–10  κτανεῖν ... Πελιάδας κόρας | πατέρα:** it is not clear whether, upon Jason's return with the Golden Fleece, Pelias fulfilled his pledge to give him the throne or resisted. In the former case the murder of Pelias appears to be an aggressive extension of the familial enmity, in the latter retaliation for further injustice on Pelias' part. As far as we can tell, Medea was acting on Jason's behalf and not for a personal motive (she lists it as one of her services to Jason in 486–7, 507–8). For more details see Introd. 4.

**κατώικει:** heroic myth is full of incidents of exile, and many are explained by the need to expiate blood-guilt, whether through an agreed temporary absence (as for Theseus in Troezen for a year, *Hipp.* 37) or by permanent exile serving to remove the killer from relatives bent on revenge (Theoclymenus in *Odyssey* 15.223–78) or to free the land from pollution (Oedipus). For Jason and Medea exile from Iolcus is permanent and shared: from 552–67 it is apparent that Jason cannot divorce Medea and return to Iolcus as though the guilt attached solely to her.

**11  ἁνδάνουσα μέν** is answered by αὐτῶι τ'... ξυμφέρουσ' in 13, with τε instead of δέ perhaps indicating the similarity of the two actions, which involve the familiar Greek pairing of *polis* and *oikos* as contrasting but also parallel arenas of social interaction. The fact that Medea has a relationship with the citizens of Corinth is one of the marks of her assimilation of male norms and privileges (Introd. 2(*b*)). The nurse's testimony to these amicable relations prepares for the chorus' declaration of friendship (138) and Medea's remarks about the circumspect behaviour required of an outsider (222–4). The scholiasts offer as one explanation of acceptance of Medea the fact that she cured a famine by her spells; this could be *ad hoc* invention, but if it is a tradition older than Eur., he seems to have suppressed the exact details in order to downplay Medea's magical powers, but mentioned favourable reception to enhance her status.

**12 φυγὰς πολίταις** 'pleasing ⟨in her behaviour⟩ as an exile to the citizens to whose land she had come'. This reading combines Pierson's emendation φυγάς for φυγῆι with the dative πολίταις derived from the scholiasts' attempt to explain the unsatisfactory πολιτῶν. This is the simplest correction that makes good sense, but a deeper corruption may be present. Diggle (1994) 273–5 shows the problems with various interpretations of the transmitted text and justifies πολίταις, and Harrison (1986) supports φυγάς.

**13 αὐτῶι** intensifies Ἰάσονι in antithesis to 'the citizens'; unless a deeper corruption is present in 11–12, transmitted αὐτή has no point, since Medea 'herself' is also the agent responsible for 'pleasing the citizens'.

**πάντα ξυμφέρουσ':** possible connotations are 'assisting in all matters' (as in Soph. *Phil.* 627), 'yielding to, following the lead of, in all matters' (as in Soph. *El.* 1465), and perhaps even 'agreeing with in all matters' (like middle συμφέρεσθαι). The ambiguity matches the divergent interpretations of Medea and Jason themselves: is she a valuable agent to be treated as an equal, or is she a mere tool to be assumed to be subordinate?

**14 ἥπερ** is fem. by attraction of gender to the predicate noun (before attraction it would be ὅπερ, 'which very thing', since the neuter pronoun is used when the antecedent is a previous proposition or action – here τὸ συμφέρειν): Smyth, §§2501a, 2502d.

**γίγνεται** 'proves to be' or 'shows itself to be' or the like is frequently the best English equivalent for γίγνομαι followed by a predicate noun or adj.

**15 διχοστατῆι:** διχοστατεῖν and διχοστασία belong to the language of civil strife, so that the verb here again points to the analogy between the city and the family. By making the wife the subject of the verb, the nurse adopts the culturally approved hierarchy familiar in other maxims about the subordination of women to men, as if obedience from the subjected side is the only desideratum. But the political metaphor may suggest that just as civic concord depends on *isonomia* and the checks and balances of constitutional procedures, so a harmonious marriage is more likely if there is a two-sided relationship of respect, consultation, and compromise. The praise of harmonious marriage is more balanced in Odysseus' famous words to Nausicaa (*Od.* 6.182–4): 'there is nothing better and finer than this, when a husband and wife as a pair keep a household, sharing one mind (ὁμοφρονέοντε)'.

**16** νῦν δ' 'but as things are now'; this answers the rosy picture painted in the participial continuation of the sentence 9–13, with its appended maxim in 14–15. In the glide from the regretful 'nor would she have killed Pelias and now be dwelling here in exile' to the positive evaluation of Medea's previous success as a resident of Corinth, we find a rhetorical compression that is easy enough to follow (Kovacs' assumption of a lacuna to make room for an explicit transition is not needed).

ἐχθρὰ πάντα καὶ νοσεῖ τὰ φίλτατα 'now all ⟨between them⟩ is full of hatred, and ⟨what was⟩ the closest tie of affection is diseased'. Elsewhere τὰ φίλτατα is a tragic idiom referring to a person one holds dear (husband, daughter, son) or to one's own life (*Alc.* 340, *Hipp.* 965); but neuter adjectives can be used as substantives with great variety and freedom, and the particular sense here is created contextually by the polar contrast with ἐχθρά.

**17** προδούς is a strong condemnation by a third party, later matched by the judgment of the chorus (578) (Aegeus is also strongly disapproving at 695, 699, but does not use the term 'betrayal'). Medea herself uses the term four times of Jason (489, 606, 778, and 206 – quoted by chorus), but also notes that she herself is a betrayer of her father and house, for Jason's sake (483, 503; so too the nurse at 32 and Jason at 1332). Similarly, the nurse and chorus agree with Medea that she is a victim of injustice on Jason's part: 26, 157, 165, 207, 267, 578. The opinion of such humble, nameless figures as the nurse and the chorus is often in tragedy a useful pointer to the viewpoint the drama is designed to shape and elicit in the audience.

αὐτοῦ τέκνα: the nurse agrees with Medea's view that Jason wrongs his children as well as her; for Jason's claim that his actions will help his children, see 559–67 with 565n.

**19**  γήμας is aor. act. part. of γαμέω, 'marry' (cf. 42 γήμαντα). In poetry γάμος and γαμέω can refer to rape and illicit sexual union as well as the sanctioned bond of 'marriage', but the belief of Medea and her supporters that she is truly a wife to Jason can be taken seriously because the play operates in the heroic world and does not reflect precisely the legal conditions of contemporary Athens. In the world of the play, it is not proper to excuse Jason on the grounds that Medea was not given by her father or that she is a foreigner (Athenians were discouraged from marrying non-Athenians by the citizenship law of Pericles passed in 451).

**αἰσυμνᾶι:**  only here in tragedy (later in poetry only Call. *Iamb.* 2, fr. 192.6), used by Eur. as a recondite synonym for βασιλεύει or ἄρχει, which is possible since the word is foreign to everyday Attic (though probably a prosaic word in places where the office of *aisymnētēs* was known: see *OCD* s.v. *aisymnētēs*).

**20**  ἠτιμασμένη:  a significant part of Medea's assimilation of heroic and male traits is her attitude toward honour and dishonour and her competitive insistence that others regard her with respect or fear. For the τιμ- root, see ἀτιμάζω here and 33, 1354, ἄτιμος in 438, 696, μὴ τιμᾶν in 660. For related terms, see 383n. (avoidance of mockery), Introd. 2(*b*).

**21–2**  Medea has a claim upon decent treatment from Jason on the basis of being his wife and mother of his children, but she and others frequently cite additional claims based on her unusual autonomy and power within the heroic enterprises of Jason's life. At a normal Greek wedding, both the bride's father or legal guardian, as giver, and the groom, as receiver, made formal statements that accomplish the union ('performative utterances'), but the woman's voice had no role in the ceremony. Medea's connection to Jason, however, is represented as an exchange between the spouses-to-be, sanctified by solemn invocation of the gods. Likewise, the physical linking of hands in a Greek wedding is a gesture of equals between father of bride and groom (Oakley and Sinos (1993) 2, and fig. 1), but hierarchical between the newlyweds themselves, as the groom takes the bride's arm (at the wrist: Oakley and Sinos (1993) 32, and figs. 84, 85, etc.; Verilhac and Vial (1998) 317) and guides her toward his own dwelling, into his own power (gestures alluded to in the final scene of

*Alcestis*). But Medea has exchanged with Jason the hand-clasp of equals, of male *philoi*, 'a mighty pledge'. See Introd. 2(*c*) and (*d*).

**21  βοᾶι μὲν ὅρκους:** 'shouts in protest about their oaths' is an adequate English paraphrase; the internal object ὅρκους actually represents a 'quotation' of the cry of protest ὦ ὅρκοι (so too in 31, 168–9; see Mastronarde on *Phoen.* 1154–5). On the tricolon crescendo that begins with this short phrase see LS 32.

**23  οἵας ἀμοιβῆς** 'what a shabby return'; it is characteristic of Greek idiom to use vague demonstrative, interrogative, and relative pronouns or adjs. and leave their specific nuance to be inferred from the context (and tone of voice?), but English idiom generally prefers more concreteness and specificity.

**24  κεῖται δ' ἄσιτος:** loss of appetite and inactivity, such as staying in bed, are signs of severe psychic turmoil (from grief or love); see the fasting of Achilles in *Iliad* 18–24, Penelope worrying over Telemachus (*Od.* 4.788 κεῖτ' ἄρ' ἄσιτος), Ajax after realizing his situation (*Ajax* 323–5), Phaedra at the beginning of *Hipp.*, Simaetha in Theocr. 2.85–90 (also Orestes in *Or.* 39–42, from a combination of madness and remorse).

**ὑφεῖσ' ἀλγηδόσιν:** an unusual use of ὑφίημι, apparently implying 'passively allowing to be subject to', the same connotation as in *Alc.* 524 κατθανεῖν ὑφειμένην, 'freely submitting to die'.

**25  τὸν πάντα συντήκουσα δακρύοις χρόνον:** 'consuming all the time dissolved in tears' catches the sense, but this is an odd usage, conflating the consumption of time (normally διάγειν or ἀναλίσκω) with the wasting away of the person crying (συντήκεσθαι). τήκει βιοτήν is easier (141n.), and the inverse construction in *IA* 398 (ἐμὲ δὲ συντήξουσι νύκτες ἡμέραι τε δακρύοις) is more natural. Since phrases like τὸν πάντα ... χρόνον are often found as acc. of time, there is some temptation simply to hear συντήκουσα as intransitive, but there is no parallel for that in the usage of τήκω and compounds.

**26  πρὸς ἀνδρός:** in poetry (and occasionally in prose) πρός + gen. may express personal agent with a passive verb (ἠδικημένη).

**27–8  οὔτ' ὄμμ' ... | πρόσωπον:** downcast eyes are a means of avoiding or withdrawing from interpersonal contact, and the gesture fits many situations or emotions, including modesty, shame, dejection, and grief. Here it fits Medea's self-absorption in her distress and refusal of admonition or comfort from others. For the fullness of expression and structure of this phrase, see LS 32.

**28–9  πέτρος ἢ θαλάσσιος | κλύδων:**   from Homer (e.g. *Il.* 16.34–5 (Patroclus to Achilles) γλαυκὴ δέ σε τίκτε θάλασσα πέτραι τ' ἠλίβατοι, ὅτι τοι νόος ἐστὶν ἀπηνής, *Od.* 23.103) onwards, rock and sea (and iron: 1279 below) are emblems of what is harsh, cruel, inflexible, or insensitive. For failure to respond, cf. in particular *Prom.* 1001, *Hipp.* 304–5, *Andr.* 537–8 τί με προσπίτνεις, ἁλίαν πέτραν ἢ κῦμα λιταῖς ὡς ἱκετεύων;

**29  φίλων** goes with ἀκούει, though by its position it also suggests 'when admonished ⟨by her friends⟩'.

**30  ἢν μή ποτε:**   the exception, 'unless she ever . . .', 'except when . . .' follows upon the understood thought 'with no response at all' implied by 'listens like a rock'.

**στρέψασα πάλλευκον δέρην:**   whether or not she makes any eye-contact with those trying to console her, Medea turns away before speaking even to herself, to avoid any semblance of contact (923n.). πάλλευκον here is probably not emphatic, but simply a metrical variation on λευκός, a standard epithet in reference to parts of the female body (e.g. neck or cheek at 923, 1148, *Hipp.* 1171, *El.* 1023, *IA* 875), since respectable females were expected to spend almost all their time indoors or well veiled.

**33  σφε**   'her'; for this pronoun, see LS 6.e.

**ἀτιμάσας ἔχει**   'has dishonoured'; 'has put in a state of dishonour' would convey the force of the periphrasis: see LS 22.

**34  συμφορᾶς ὕπο:**   ὑπό + gen. of abstract nouns (esp. emotions) expresses cause or agency or attendant circumstances; even with an active verb there is often a connotation of passivity ('under the compulsion of'; here, 'taught by'). For anastrophe of the preposition, see LS 24.

**35  οἶον**   'what a valuable thing' (23n.); ἐστί is understood and its subject is inf. μὴ ἀπολείπεσθαι (μὴ ἀ- forms one syllable by crasis: PM 11).

**36**  Mention of Medea's attitude toward her children is brief and undeveloped here, after long sections on her attitude toward Jason's betrayal (20–8) and her regret about her betrayed homeland (28–35). Barthold deleted the line, and there are certainly difficulties in the following lines (see next note). But the brevity is probably purposeful: it prepares for the important theme of the children, but does not anticipate the fuller revelation of the nurse's anxiety in the next scene.

**37–45**  The passage has long been subject to the suspicion that it has been padded by interpolation, that is, by the deliberate or accidental insertion of verses that do not belong. Deliberate interpolations may be due either to actors who altered a repertory text in later productions or to readers who supplemented a passage they found elliptical or obscure. Accidental interpolation results when a parallel passage or an explanation written in the margin is inserted into a text by a later scribe who mistakes its nature. The main reasons for suspicion here are (1) the appearance at 379–80 of lines almost identical to 40–1 (only ὥσῃι/ὥσω is adjusted to each context); (2) clumsy repetitions (of γάρ-connection and fear-words) and obscurities in the lines; (3) the anticipation (viewed as premature by many) of Medea's scheme. For general remarks on repeated lines and interpolation, see Mastronarde on *Phoen.* 143, with refs.

Three solutions deserve the most consideration. (1) The deletion of 38–43 (Diggle following Dindorf and many others) eliminates all the obscurities, and may be correct, but it leaves the sequence of 37 to 44 rather bald. It may be preferable to delete only 38–42 (with Barthold). The nurse vaguely hints that Medea will plot something and thereby bring even more trouble upon herself. 43 is an after-effect of the positive action of 37, and thus δεινὴ γάρ explains 37. (2) The deletion of 41 alone (Musgrave) has been defended in detail by Willink (1988). On Willink's view, line 40 means 'lest she thrust a sharpened sword through her own liver', a reference to the possibility that Medea may commit suicide (cf. Medea's own wishes in 97, 114, 144–7). Then ἢ καί in 42 introduces a true alternative, killing her foes instead of herself (with Hermann's τυράννους = 'the king and the princess', all three are implied in one line), which would lead to retribution (43), including (an audience might think) retaliation by the

Corinthians against her own children. But a sword-thrust to the liver
is familiar in reference both to suicide (*Trach.* 931, *Ant.* 1315, *Her.* 1149,
*El.* 688, *Hel.* 983, *Or.* 1063: in all these passages a pronoun or possessive or the preceding context makes reference to suicide clear) and
to the killing of others (often in combat in Homer, and in combat or
murder in Eur. *Her.* 979, *Phoen.* 1421, frs. 495.29, 979.2). Since 40 by
itself is not at all clear about whose liver is meant, and since the lead-
up to 40 suggests that Medea may harm others, as she has in the past,
a reference to suicide is unlikely. If murder is intended, whose liver is
to be stabbed? If it is the princess', this becomes somewhat clear only
retrospectively, if 41 is retained or if 42 (with τύραννον) eliminates
Creon and Jason as potential victims in 40. One scholiast suggests
that the liver is the children's, but that too is an unclear reference
and would make 42–3 anticlimactic. (3) For those who can tolerate
the repetitions, the deletion of 42 alone may be attractive: the reference of 40–1 then is to murder of the princess.

**37**  δέδοικα δ' αὐτὴν μή:  the pronoun is a 'proleptic' object, anticipating the subject of the dependent clause (Smyth §2182; cf. bib-
lical 'I know thee who thou art'); here this is not merely a rhetorical
figure, but provides a pointed emphasis.

νέον:  as often, the adj. connotes an unpleasant or dangerous
novelty (LSJ s.v. II.2).

**38**  ἀνέξεται:  future middle of ἀνέχω, 'will put up with, will endure', with supplementary participle (Smyth §2098).

**39**  ἐγᾦδα τήνδε seems to have little point, and the expedient of
setting it off as a parenthesis, with Willink, does not remove the objection. ἐγᾦδα = ἐγὼ οἶδα (crasis: PM 11).

δειμαίνω τέ νιν after δέδοικα δ' αὐτήν two lines earlier seems an
unusually weak repetition. For pronoun νιν see LS 6.e.

**40**  ὤσηι:  aor. subj. of ὠθέω, 'push, thrust'. On the liver as site of
fatal wounds, see 37–45n.

**41**  σιγῆι is a clue (for many who retain this line: 37–45n.) that Medea is to make a stealthy entry into the royal palace to attack the new
bride. For those who refer 40 to suicide, this word alludes to Medea's
need not to be prevented by her servants from committing suicide,

and Medea's seeking of her marriage-bed would be a conventional motif (seen in the suicide of Deianeira in *Trach.*).

**ἵν':** ἵνα is often used with the indicative in poetry (but very rarely in Attic prose) in the sense 'where' (so too in 200).

**ἔστρωται** is perfect mid.-pass. of στρώννυμι, 'spread'.

**42 ἢ καὶ τύραννον τόν τε γήμαντα:** καί is not coordinated with τε, but goes closely with ἤ, marking addition or climax. If the preceding lines refer to an attack on the princess, then τύραννον will be her father and 'him who married ⟨her⟩' will be readily understandable as Jason. But for those who remove the reference to the princess by deletion or interpretation, two difficulties arise: Creon (the most obvious referent of τύραννον) would be mentioned instead of the princess, and τὸν γήμαντα would be less clear with no recent reference to the princess to suggest its object. Some solve these difficulties by understanding τύραννον to be fem. (see 877n.; Kayser emends καὶ to τὴν) or by emending to τυράννους (Hermann).

**43 κἄπειτα μείζω … τινά:** κἄπειτα = καὶ ἔπειτα (crasis); μείζω is alternative acc. sing. masc./fem. form for μείζονα (LS 5.c). The indefinite τινά helps express a reluctance to be more specific.

**44 οὔτοι:** τοι here simply adds strength to the negation.

**44–5 συμβαλὼν | ἔχθραν … αὐτῆι** 'engaging in enmity with her' or 'clashing in enmity with her'; similar idiom in 521 φίλοι φίλοισι συμβάλωσ' ἔριν. The accentuation shows that this is the noun ἔχθρα (also 897), not the adj. ἐχθρός (16, 95, *passim*).

**45 καλλίνικον ἄισεται:** ἄισεται is future of ἄιδω, the contracted (ordinary Attic) form of ἀείδω. With καλλίνικον understand ἄισμα or μέλος from the verb, 'the song of fair victory', an allusion to the practice of hailing Heracles (prototype of the athletic victor) with the cry τήνελλα καλλίνικε. With οἴσεται (MSS), 'will win for himself as prize', an article would be needed for καλλίνικος to be understood as a substantive. See Stinton (1990) 291.

**46 *Action*:** the nurse calls attention to the group of the tutor and the two young children of Medea, who are entering from the side that is imagined to lead to the city-centre (marketplace, fountain (69n.), and palace): Introd. 3.

**46** ἐκ τρόχων πεπαυμένοι 'having finished their running'; that is, the tutor had taken the boys to an open area or *gymnasion* to get exercise; the same phrase in fr. 105 refers to a group of adults who have completed their exercises, and Aristophanes fr. 645 K–A expresses a similar meaning with ἐξ ἀποτρόχων. Tryphon, a scholar of the first century BCE cited in Ammonius, *de voc. diff.* 478 Nickau, may have interpreted ΤΡΟΧΩΝ as τροχῶν from τροχός, 'wheel, hoop', as if the boys have finished playing with hoops (which would then be a prop brought back to the house). Hoops are seen as toys or exercise-equipment for youths on many Attic vases, esp. in scenes of Ganymede (*LIMC* s.v. Ganymedes, nos. 12, 19, 25, 27, 31, etc.), and Roux (1972) 44–6 makes an eloquent case for the suitability of such a toy for the young children here, visually evoking their childish innocence. But the two parallels cited favour 'running'.

**48** νέα ... φροντίς 'a young mind', 'a child's mind'; this sense of φροντίς (normally 'concern', 'anxiety') is found elsewhere only a few times in Soph. (LSJ s.v. II).

### 49–95 *Dialogue of nurse and tutor*

**49** οἴκων κτῆμα: gen. and noun form one concept, 'household possession', and the possessive gen. δεσποίνης is then applied to the whole.

**50** τήνδ᾽ ἄγουσ᾽ ἐρημίαν 'being alone like this'; this unique juncture is based on idioms like ἡσυχίαν ἄγειν, σχολὴν ἄγειν (LSJ s.v. ἄγω A.IV.3).

**51** θρεομένη ... κακά: the tutor is understood to have overheard some of the nurse's remarks while entering, since he can identify the content as κακά. θρέομαι is a poetic verb found only a few times in Aeschylus and Eur., used of women crying out loudly or, as here, speaking with special anguish (it is the shocking content, not volume of voice, that makes the chorus use θρεομένας of Phaedra's revelation in *Hipp.* 363).

**52** σοῦ μόνη 'alone without you', with gen. of separation, as also in Soph. *Ajax* 511, *OC* 1250; the gen. here is also felt with λείπεσθαι.

**53** ὁπαδέ: for the form with 'Doric alpha' in dialogue see LS 3.

**54** χρηστοῖσι δούλοις: for the concept of the 'good slave', defined by loyalty to the master's interests and espoused by slaves themselves, compare *Andr.* 56–9, 87–90, *Ion* 850–8, *Hel.* 726–33, 1641, frr. 85, 93, 529. The loyal slave has literary precedent in Eumaeus, Philoetius, and Eurycleia in *Od.*, while the disloyal slave, first exemplified in Melanthius and Melantho in *Od.*, is not portrayed in tragedy (but lies behind the tricky slave of the comic tradition). The concept is largely a projection of what slave-owners would like to believe, and in literature often reflects on the worthiness of the master to whom the slave is loyal, but it may also be correlated to a behaviour that could be adopted by some privileged slaves (esp. nurses and tutors, those entrusted with the care of the master's children) as the best available mechanism for coping with their status. Claims of 'virtue' by slave-characters in tragedy, however, fit with the questioning or destabilization of categories that is characteristic of the genre. On slaves in general see Garlan (1988), esp. 146, 192, and for slaves in tragedy and in Eur., Vogt (1965) 14–15, Synodinou (1977), esp. 61–76, and Hall (1997) 113–18, 123–4.

**55** κακῶς πίτνοντα 'when they turn out bad', 'when they suffer reversals'; the metaphor is from games involving dice or knuckle-bones.

**56** ἐς τοῦτ᾽ ἐκβέβηκ᾽ ἀλγηδόνος 'I have reached such an extreme degree of anguish' ('extreme' translates the force of ἐκ-); this is a Euripidean variant on a prosaic idiom in which a verb of motion is used with ἐς τόδε/τοῦτο/τοσοῦτο + gen. of abstract noun, followed by a result clause (see Mastronarde on *Phoen.* 963).

**57–8** It is a dramatic convention that the characters of Greek tragedy hold their conversations and even their monologues outdoors, and insertion of realistic motivations is optional and inconsistent (like many gestures toward realism on the tragic stage). Here the interest of the narrative and the nurse's evident anguish have been enough to engage the audience's full attention, and the motivation is supplied only retrospectively in answer to the tutor's challenge. The desire to share one's strong emotions with the external elements may have some basis in the Greek way of life, where so much activity took place out of doors (Barrett on *Hipp.* 601).

**μ' ὑπῆλθε ..|. μολούσηι:** μ' is elided με, not μοι (μοι is not elided in tragedy). The dat. participle referring to the nurse results from a phenomenon that is not uncommon in Greek when an infinitive depends on an impersonal verb or similar expression: both dat. and acc. are often permissible with such verbs, and modifiers of the subject of the inf. (esp. participles) may shift freely between the acc. (default case for subject of an inf.) and the dat. (by attraction to the dative of the person that is frequent with impersonal expressions and thus mentally available even in a passage where the acc. has just been used instead); compare 1236–7 below and see K–G II.111–13.

**κοὐρανῶι:** καὶ οὐρανῶι (crasis).

**λέξαι:** the inf. may be regarded either as in apposition to ἵμερος or as complementary with the whole verbal phrase, which is equivalent to 'I became eager' (Smyth §§1987, 2001).

**59 γάρ** is used in a variety of ways in dialogue to connect one speaker's utterance to the previous statement (LS 27). Here, it expresses the tutor's inference from the nurse's emphasis on her mistress' misfortune: 'So then, the unhappy woman does not yet give up her lamentations?'

**60 ζηλῶ σ':** ironic, 'I envy you' (sc. for your simplicity, that you can believe she might be close to ceasing her sorrows).

**ἐν ἀρχῆι ... μεσοῖ:** the terminology of beginning and middle is probably medical, while πῆμα is a poetic variation on the physicians' terms πάθος/πάθημα; cf. Aesch. *Pers.* 435 μηδέπω μεσοῦν κακόν. Greek physicians recorded the course of a disease, from onset to middle phase to crisis and resolution (e.g. μεσοῦντος δὲ τοῦ χρόνου in Hippocr. *Epidem.* 7.50, 51 = v.418 Littré; [Hippocrates] *Epist.* 18 'The physician ought to examine the patterns as much as possible, and consider whether the illness is beginning or in the middle or ending' (πότερον ἄρχοιτο τὸ πάθος ἢ μεσάζοι ἢ λήγοι)).

**61 μῶρος:** fem., referring to Medea (LS 5.d). To judge from other instances (Soph. *El.* 1326, *OC* 592) and from the following 'apology', the tone of this exclamation must be very strong, expressing impatience that Medea has not by now come to grips with the troubles she already knows of. ὢ μῶρος is nominative of exclamation (Smyth §1288), a use derived from predication to an understood verb ('oh, [she is] foolish!'): so too 96 δύστανος ἐγώ.

**εἰ χρή** 'if it is proper', 'if it is permitted', a softened sense occasionally found in tragedy (Soph. *OT* 1110, Eur. *El.* 300, *Her.* 141, *IT* 1288, *Antiope* v.17 *TGFS*).

**δεσπότας εἰπεῖν τόδε** 'use this word of one's masters', with τόδε internal acc. referring to the word 'fool'. Compare the construction of the idiom κακὰ λέγειν τινά.

**62 ὡς:** better taken as exclamatory than as causal: 'how ignorant she is of the more recent trouble'.

**64** Carriers of bad news are often reluctant to reveal it: this increases suspense for the recipients and the audience and underlines the gravity of the news. Examples include Teiresias in *OT* and *Phoen.*, messengers in *Ag.* and *Phoen.*, and Cadmus and Amphitryon dealing with Agave and Heracles in *Bacch.* and *Her.*

**μετέγνων καὶ τὰ πρόσθ' εἰρημένα:** καί responds to the refusal of explanation conveyed in οὐδέν, '⟨I'll say no more:⟩ I regret ⟨saying⟩ even what I said just now.' The aor. μετέγνων represents the action as already complete, perhaps in an attempt to portray the change of mind as irrevocable (LS 13).

**65 πρὸς γενείου:** standard phrases with πρός + gen. are used both with expressed verbs of supplication or request and with ellipsis of the verb, as here. Translate 'I appeal to you by your chin'. This is a stereotyped, weakened sort of supplication, not the strong form in which the suppliant clings insistently to the supplicated (see 324–5 n.). In staging, it is probably sufficient for the nurse to reach her hand briefly toward the tutor's face.

**σέθεν:** for this gen. pronoun, see LS 6.c.

**66 σιγὴν ... θήσομαι:** equivalent to σιγήσομαι, since in poetry the middle of τίθημι is often used with a verbal noun as a periphrasis for a simple verb (in prose the equivalent idiom uses the middle of ποιέω with verbal noun, as at 909 below).

**πέρι:** anastrophe (LS 24).

**67 ἤκουσά του ... κλύειν:** the two different verbs are used merely for rhetorical variation here, although there are some contexts in which a distinction between 'hear' and 'pay attention to' is clearly present. του is the alternative gen. form of indefinite τινος.

**68** πεσσούς 'the place where draughts are played', presumably a section of some public space equipped with benches. Cratinus fr. 7 K–A also mentions a place called πεσσοί. For this habit of naming an area from the activity that occurs there, compare τὸ μύρον for the perfume market, τὸ ὄψον for fishmarket (more exx. in K–G 1.12). For a discussion of games using πεσσοί see Kurke (1999) 247–98, with an illustration of game pieces in her fig. 9, p. 274. For a gathering of elders to play games in a public space one may compare the modern chess and checker players and contestants in *boules* or *bocce* who may be seen in the piazza of a Mediterranean town, in the parks of Manhattan, or on the beaches of Florida.

**69** σεμνὸν ἀμφὶ Πειρήνης ὕδωρ: Peirene is the most famous spring of Corinth, the one associated with important ritual functions, such as supplying water for pre-wedding baths or funerals (hence σεμνόν). In classical times the name probably applied only to the spring right by the city-centre described by Pausanias 2.3.2–3: see Hill (1964). In the Roman period, there was also an upper spring Peirene on Acrocorinth: see Stillwell (1930) 31–60.

**70** γῆς ἐλᾶν: the gen. of separation depends directly on the verb: LS 10.d.

**72** εἰ σαφής: for the postponed conjunction, see LS 35; for the omission of ἐστί even in a subordinate clause see LS 30. Note that σαφής often connotes reliability, accuracy, and truthfulness rather than simple clarity.

**73** οὐκ εἶναι: after βούλομαι, one expects μή with an inf., but οὐκ fits the metre and μή does not; possible explanations of the licence are that Eur. assimilates the phrase to οὐκ ἂν βουλοίμην or that he treats οὐκ εἶναι as a unitary concept, 'be false'. Ar. *Frogs* 866 presents a similar licence.

**74–5** παῖδας ἐξανέξεται | πάσχοντας: supplementary participle (38n.) agreeing with the object noun, 'will he put up with his sons suffering this?' or 'will he allow his sons to suffer this?'.

**75** εἰ καί: this combination often introduces as a condition what is an admitted fact, 'even though' ('even if it is also/indeed true that').

**76 παλαιὰ καινῶν λείπεται:** note the expressive juxtaposition of the antonyms 'old' and 'new' (LS 35); so again in 79. Understand κηδεύματα with παλαιά. The gen. is one of exchange (or price and value: Smyth §1372), as found more commonly with ἀλλάσσω and compounds: 'is abandoned in favour of'.

**77 κοὐκ:** καί οὐκ (crasis).

**78 ἀπωλόμεσθ᾽ ἄρ᾽:** ἄρα often expresses a lively realization; the combination with ἀπωλόμην or -μεθα is also found in *Alc.* 386, *Andr.* 74, *Or.* 1271, and Ar. *Birds* 338 (deleted by Dunbar). This idiomatic aorist expresses an event which is viewed as inevitable and thus virtually complete, although it actually refers to the future and may be combined with a future indicative in a condition (or in an explanation in asyndeton). See Smyth §1934, Schwyzer II.282.

**προσοίσομεν** is future indicative of προσφέρω, 'add (to)'.

**79 ἐξηντληκέναι:** perf. act. inf. of ἐξαντλέω; the metaphorical use of ἀντλέω and ἐξαντλέω is a Euripidean mannerism (elsewhere only Aesch. *Cho.* 748, *Prom.* 375). From 'bale out the bilge-water' it comes to mean 'drain to the dregs', 'suffer to the bitter end', or just 'suffer'.

**80 ἀτάρ:** this strong adversative (like ἀλλά) is a carry-over into tragedy of a traditional poetic conjunction (also colloquial, in comedy and Plato, but not used in formal Attic prose).

**γάρ** here has its anticipatory use, that is, its clause explains what follows, intervening parenthetically between the subject and the verbs that carry the meat of the sentence. Compare 89. See Denniston 68–9.

**82 οἷος εἰς ὑμᾶς πατήρ** 'how badly your father behaves toward you' (23n.).

**83 ὄλοιτο μὲν μή:** the effect of the word-order and of μέν may be expressed in a paraphrase like 'I don't go so far as to curse him, for he is my master, but ...' The postponement of the negative lets the temptation to utter a curse be seen, but the phrase as a whole is a suppression of a curse, set in contrast (μέν) to the judgment she will go on to declare.

**84** ὧν ... ἁλίσκεται: supplementary participle with ἁλίσκομαι, 'to be caught or detected' doing something bad (LSJ II.1).

**85** τίς δ' οὐχὶ θνητῶν; 'What mortal does *not* [sc. get caught treating his friends badly]?' As more commonly in stichomythia (SE 3b; LS 29), the tutor's utterance assumes syntactic elements from the previous speaker's line.

**86** πᾶς τις: stronger than πᾶς alone, 'every single one' or 'everyone, no matter who'.

τοῦ πέλας: gen. of comparison with μᾶλλον. ὁ πέλας and the more common οἱ πέλας are used in poetry and prose, esp. in ethical contexts, to refer to 'other people' or 'one's fellow men' (cf. 'Love thy neighbour').

**[87]** This line weakens the rhetorically necessary universal force of 86 and obscures the connection between 86 and 88; the scholion shows that ancient scholars already objected to the line as intrusive. It apparently intruded from a marginal quotation where a line similar to 86 may have been followed by 87, both drawn from a context that admitted such a distinction in motivation.

**88** εἰ ... γ' ... οὐ: γε here marks the condition as virtually causal (Denniston 142), and the causal, factual nature of the proposition explains why οὐ is used instead of μή (Smyth §2698b, d).

εὐνῆς οὕνεκ': the tutor assumes, like Medea, that there is a sexual element in Jason's decision to take a new bride (Introd. 2(*b*)). The use of οὕνεκα (originally a conjunction, οὗ ἕνεκα) as a preposition is common in both tragedy and comedy.

**89** ἴτ': the movement of the children and tutor in response to this command is clearly gradual, as they do not disappear indoors until shortly after 105, the third command after 89 and 100. The slowness is first occasioned by the nurse's continuation in 90–5 with instructions and then by Medea's cry. The children may mime fear and reluctance during 96–105. See Mastronarde (1979) 109.

εὖ γὰρ ἔσται: this insistently parenthetic (80n.) reassurance that 'things will be all right' seems to be an attempt to soften the truth for the children, since the nurse is in fact afraid for them (36, 90–5).

**90 ὡς μάλιστα:** superlative with ὡς (δύναται or the like understood), 'as much as possible' (Smyth §1086).

**ἐρημώσας ἔχε** 'keep them in isolation'; for the perfective force of this periphrasis see LS 22.

**92 ὄμμα ... ταυρουμένην:** the sense is clear, although one cannot be sure whether the participle is middle, 'making her own gaze bull-fierce', or passive, 'being (made) bull-like in respect to her gaze'. For the glance of the bull as emblematic of ferocious anger, see 188 below and Ar. *Frogs* 804 (of angry Aeschylus) ἔβλεψε γοῦν ταυρηδὸν ἐγκύψας κάτω; also related are the rolling eyes and askance gaze of the agitated, resisting bull in *Hel.* 1557–8 or of the maddened Heracles likened to a bull in *Her.* 868–9, and the playful use in Plato *Phaedo* 117b (Socrates) ὥσπερ εἰώθει ταυρηδὸν ὑποβλέψας.

**93 τοῖσδ':** this may be translated 'at them', 'toward them', giving the direction of the gaze, but is actually a dative of disadvantage (Smyth §§1485, 1532). For the enjambment and pause after first syllable, which is not necessarily emphatic, see 793n.

**δρασείουσαν** 'being eager to do', 'be on the verge of doing'; the suffix -σείω (used once in Homer, occasionally in drama and Thucydides among Attic authors) creates a desiderative verb (Smyth §868).

**94 κατασκῆψαί τινι:** in prose the unexpressed subject of such an inf. would normally be the same as the subject of the main clause, but in poetry it may be supplied from another noun of the previous clause, so χόλον is to be understood here. κατασκήπτω carries the image of a lightning-strike (cf. 106–8), but it frequently has wrath, disease, or demonic visitation as its subject: e.g. μῆνις in Hdt. 7.134, 137, ὀργαί in *Hipp.* 1418. The verb is elsewhere absolute or followed by εἰς + acc. or rarely the dat. (Hdt. 7.134; possibly Anaxippus fr. 3.6 K–A (corrupt)).

**95 γε μέντοι:** the combination is strongly adversative, as again in 534 below (Denniston 412).

### 96–130 Anapaests of Medea and the nurse

**Metre:** an anapaestic scene serves as a transition between the dialogue of the second prologue-scene and the entrance of the chorus (SE 1). Medea's cries intensify the nurse's anxiety, so that she matches

Medea's anapaestic rhythm, but there is still a contrast between the unrestrained emotion of Medea in her sung anapaests 96–7 and 111–14 and the more controlled chanted anapaests of the nurse (98–110 and 115–30). Period-end is marked by the paroemiacs at 110, 114, and 130, but there is presumably also period-end at full metron 97 in the sung anapaests (for the possibility of period-end at full metra 104 and 118, see 184–204n.). See PM 21–3.

**96** (ἔσωθεν): cries from inside the *skēnē* are found in many plays, esp. at a moment of murder (1272–8 below; Aesch. *Ag.* 1343–6, *Cho.* 869 are the earliest examples) or discovery of a suicide (e.g. *Hipp.*): see Hamilton (1987) (with refs.) and 1270a n. This instance is unusual because Medea sings four passages of anapaests spread over the conclusion of this scene and the first half of the parodos. Her cries of distress confirm what the nurse has been saying about her and develop suspenseful expectation of her eventual appearance to the audience. Compare Soph. *Ajax* 333–43 (Ajax in his tent, three separate exclamations, then a couplet in trimeters), Eur. *Bacch.* 576–95 (Dionysus in the palace, four short lyric utterances, mainly pherecratean and dactylic). It will have required considerable skill on the part of the actor to make his lines clear to the large outdoor audience when singing from within, although this would be easier with the temporary wooden *skēnē* (perhaps with panels of fabric rather than solid wall construction) used in the fifth century.

**96a** ἰώ is *extra metrum*, that is, outside of the metrical scheme of Medea's sung anapaests. Exclamations are often (but not always) so treated in Greek drama: so too 111a and 144a αἰαῖ, and 1270a ἰώ μοι, and in dialogue 292a φεῦ φεῦ, 386a εἶέν, 1056a ἆ ἆ.

**96b** δύστανος: note the Doric alpha (Ionic-Attic δύστηνος), a marker of a fully lyric voice and of the greater emotional excitement of Medea. See LS 2, PM 23.

πόνων is gen. of source or cause, as commonly with exclaimed adjs. meaning 'wretched' and the like (LS 10.c).

**97** πῶς ἂν ὀλοίμαν: a potential opt. question introduced by πῶς is often in tragedy an equivalent of a wish (Smyth §1832), sometimes more anguished than the opt. of wish, as here, and sometimes more restrained (as in 173–4 below).

**98** τόδ᾽ ἐκεῖνο 'this is just what I feared' or 'this is just what I was saying'; for the former connotation see Soph. *El.* 1115 (cf. Eur. *Tro.* 624), for the latter compare the 'I told you so!' use seen in Ar. *Ach.* 41 and *Lysistrata* 240, τοῦτ᾽ ἐκεῖν᾽ οὑγὼ ᾽λεγον. τόδ᾽ ἐκεῖνο is a variation (for metrical reasons) on the colloquial expression τοῦτ᾽ ἐκεῖνο, which conveys a simple recognition (Arist., *Rhet.* 1371b9, 1410b19), but often with various lively connotations ('This is it!' Ar. *Birds* 354; 'That's the way!' *Peace* 516; 'Here we go again!' *Ach.* 820; 'There's your answer, then!' *Ion* 554).

**99** κινεῖ ... κινεῖ: for the anaphora, see LS 36.

κραδίαν: following Homer and the lyric poets, the tragedians sometimes use the form κραδία (instead of καρδία) in lyric passages where it suits double-short rhythm. So too in 433 below. The two forms derive from alternative vocalizations of syllabic r (Schwyzer 1.341–2).

**100** θᾶσσον: this comparative adverb (from ταχύς) is frequently to be translated into English with the positive form 'quickly', although it is clear that originally it had an intensive meaning in contexts of impatience or urgency (K–G 11.306).

**103–4** ἄγριον ἦθος ... | φρενὸς αὐθάδους: both ἄγριος and αὐθάδης are the sorts of words characteristically used of the so-called 'Sophoclean hero' in his or her ferocious temper and stubborn self-will (see Knox (1964) 23, 42–3). For ἄγριος see Soph. *OT* 344, *Phil.* 1321. For the root αὐθαδ- see esp. *Prom.* (7 times), Soph. *Ant.* 1028, *OT* 549. Although Medea takes pains to dissociate herself from the αὐθάδης in 223, Jason uses the term αὐθαδία against her in 621 and Medea herself laments her own αὐθαδία in 1028.

**105** ἴτε νυν: the enclitic νυν is constantly used with imperatives to convey emphasis ('please') or mild logical connection ('then, so then'). In this line the combination lends emphasis to the following imperative (like plain ἴτε or like ἴθι νυν in comedy and prose), 'come on then, go in'. Cf. *Antiope* fr. v.109 *TGFS* ἴτε νυν, κρατύνετ᾽ ἀντ᾽ ἐμοῦ τῆσδε χθονός.

ὡς τάχος 'as quickly as possible' (lit. 'as ⟨there is⟩ swiftness', with ἐστι understood), an idiom esp. common in tragedy, usually with commands; compare 950 ὅσον τάχος.

**106–8** δῆλον δ' ἀρχῆς κτλ. 'it is clear that soon with greater passion she will kindle the cloud of lamentation that is now rising from its birth' (Page). Understand ἐστί with δῆλον and observe that ὡς is a postponed conjunction (LS 35), actually introducing the clause that begins with ἀρχῆς. The prominent position of the object phrase ἀρχῆς ἐξαιρόμενον νέφος οἰμωγῆς serves to build up a picture, the towering and darkening growth of a thunderhead cloud as it approaches; then the verb phrase brings a climax, with the flash of lightning in the dark cloud. The cloud is the ominous cries and laments heard by the nurse before the play began and just heard by the audience; the lightning is the violent action that the nurse fears will soon come from Medea (cf. 94). Diggle (1994) 276–7 objects to the unqualified use of plain ἀρχῆς here and proposes δῆλον ἀπ' ἀρχῆς, which he takes as 'it is clear from the beginning, as it arises'; this seems too prosaic a sense in a passage of such intensity (marked by imagery, word order, and the weighty pair of epithets in 109).

**107** νέφος οἰμωγῆς: for this metaphor (a 'synaesthetic' one, combining sight and sound) see Bond on *Her.* 1140 and Mastronarde on *Phoen.* 1308, 1311.

ἀνάψει 'will kindle, make flash with lightning' (so too, probably, *Phoen.* 250–1 νέφος ... φλέγει suggests flashing lightning). Diggle (1994) 278 argues that Eur. here intends not the lightning, but the thunder that, by the theory of some Greek philosopher/scientists, is caused by the effect of fire on a cloud. But it seems doubtful that Eur. alludes to such a specific theory, and what concerns the nurse is not just the climactic boom but also the destructive flash – Medea is going to hurt someone else.

**109** μεγαλόσπλαγχνος δυσκατάπαυστος: a weighty juxtaposition of rare, long compound adjs., restating Medea's intransigent 'heroic' character (103–4n.). The first adj. is virtually a poetic coinage (variation on μεγάθυμος, μεγαλήτωρ, μεγαλόφρων) since it is otherwise a technical term of medicine in a literal sense; the second is shared in extant fifth-century texts only with Aesch. *Cho.* 470 ('hard to check' is the sense in both places; LSJ errs). See LS 31.

**110** ψυχή: the 'spirit' or 'heart' is here virtually identified with the whole person or personality, as is clear from its being subject of 'whatever will she/it do? (ἐργάσεται). Cf. 247 πρὸς μίαν ψυχὴν βλέπειν with n. and cf. Soph. *Phil.* 712–13 ὦ μελέα ψυχή, ὃς κτλ.

**δηχθεῖσα:**   aor. pass. part. of δάκνω, 'to bite, sting'.

**111   ἔπαθον ... ἔπαθον:**   the repetition is structurally similar to those in 99 and 131, but in this case there is a true syntactic redundancy that is characteristic of emotional 'doubling' in lyric (anadiplosis, Smyth §3009, or epanalepsis) – a stylistic trait more frequent in later Eur. (e.g. in the monody of the Phrygian slave in *Or.* 1369–1502) and readily mocked by Aristophanes (*Frogs* 1336, 1352–5, with Dover on *Frogs* 1329–63 (p. 358)). See also 976–9n.

**112   ἄξι:**   ἄξια, 'things (woes) worthy of extreme lamentation'.

**112–14**   Medea's passionate cursing address to her own sons is striking, and her imprecation is fulfilled in an ironic way by Medea herself, as Medea separates herself from the 'house of Jason' and becomes the destructive agent that undoes it (608, 1333).

**113   στυγερᾶς ματρός:**   (with παῖδες) 'of a hateful mother' (strongly expressing Medea's self-loathing and suicidal mood); a milder meaning of the adj., 'wretched' (LSJ s.v. 1.2) is not firmly established (Soph. *Trach.* 1017 is textually uncertain, but probably includes 'hateful life' because Heracles desires death; Ar. *Ach.* 1207 στυγερὸς ἐγώ could imply 'I am hated by the gods').

**116   δέ:**   the conjunction is used to link the question to Medea's curse; for the postponement of the connection caused by an exclamation or vocative see Denniston 174, 189.

   **σοι**   'in your eyes', 'in your judgment', dat. of reference (Smyth §1496).

**117   τούσδ':**   neither this demonstrative nor the vocative τέκνα in the next line need imply that the children are still visible to the audience; indeed, the content of Medea's curse would suggest that she has seen the children back in the house, despite the nurse's wish that they be kept from her sight.

**118   πάθηθ':**   πάθητε elided (subj. in μή-clause depending on ὑπεραλγῶ treated as verb of fearing).

ὡς ὑπεραλγῶ: ὡς is exclamatory, 'how much I feel painful anxiety for ⟨you⟩ (ὑπερ-)' or possibly 'how exceedingly (ὑπερ-) I suffer painful anxiety'. There are parallels for both meanings of the verb, but in the latter sense classical authors tend to use it of grieving 'too much' or beyond a norm, a connotation that does not suit here.

**119–30** The nurse ends the scene with a generalizing reflection that emphasizes the distance in behaviour and perspective between the heroic elite individuals and humble anonymous persons like herself, the tutor, and the chorus. This dichotomy parallels the contrast between the aristocratic values of the heroic world and the prevailing civic ideology of the Athenian citizen; but an audience will have felt attraction to both sets of values (cf. Introd. 2(b)). It is typical of Euripides to extend even to slave- and women-characters the ability to analyse, criticize, and generalize about human life and to speak for an ethical point of view that may represent the view of the 'ordinary person'.

**119** δεινὰ ... λήματα: understand ἐστί (LS 30).

τυράννων: in many passages in tragedy, τύραννος and its derivatives are clearly synonymous with βασιλεύς and its derivatives and they carry no negative connotation for the speaker within the play or for the audience member who is used to distinguishing between the cultural tradition of high poetry (and myth) and the political discourse of the contemporary city. Yet in that political discourse, τύραννος was clearly a term fraught with negative associations, and even βασιλεύς may have been an odious term to Athenians, at least when applied to contemporary humans other than the ἄρχων βασιλεύς. In the proper context in tragedy, therefore, the poet may be exploiting the resonance of these terms. Here the criticism of kingly wilfulness is traditional (going back to *Il.* 1.78–83), but the critical stance of the nurse as commoner may be slightly strengthened by the use of τυράννων. On the problem of the connotations of τύραννος, see O'Neal (1986); Hall (1989) 155 n. 184.

καί πως: the particle πως here makes the whole statement a little less forceful: 'and somehow it comes about that kings ...' Compare Soph. *Phil.* 448–9 καί πως τὰ μὲν πανοῦργα καὶ παλιντριβῆ | χαίρουσ᾽ ἀναστρέφοντες ἐξ Ἅιδου κτλ.

**120** ὀλίγ᾽ ἀρχόμενοι, πολλὰ κρατοῦντες 'because they are ruled in few matters, but hold full sway in many' (internal accs.). This imbalance is in contrast to a widespread Greek view in the classical city-states that the good citizen should be capable equally of ruling and being ruled, ἄρχειν καὶ ἄρχεσθαι (Arist. *Pol.* 1277a25–b32).

**121** χαλεπῶς ὀργὰς μεταβάλλουσιν 'with difficulty do they alter (overcome, control) their passionate anger'. Compare *Il.* 1.80–1, where Calchas is complaining to Achilles that if king Agamemnon is annoyed by Calchas, the king will retain his wrath and eventually get his revenge. Eustathius, who links these two passages, notes that the mighty, once angered, are δυσκατάλλακτοι, 'hard to bring to peaceful reconciliation' (cf. 109, 103–4 with n.). Others understand the present phrase as 'change their purpose/will with difficulty' or 'change their mood roughly, harshly' (taking ὀργάς in a neutral sense).

**122** γάρ: the connection is imprecise; what is implied is 'kings behave in this undesirable way because they lack a proper sense of limits, and it is better . . .' See Denniston 61; LS 27.

  εἰθίσθαι: perfect mid.-pass. inf. of ἐθίζω, 'to habituate, accustom'.

  ἐπ᾽ ἴσοισιν 'on equal terms' or 'in conditions of equality' (LSJ s.v. ἐπί в.III.3).

**123–4** ἐμοὶ γοῦν . .|. εἴη 'may it be granted to me, in any case', with inf. καταγηράσκειν as grammatical subject (this is the optative version of ἔστι + inf., 'it is possible'). γοῦν here is limitative, slightly stronger than γε, implying 'even if others may not be content with moderation, *I* think it is better and so I wish etc.'

**123** ἐπὶ μὴ μεγάλοις 'in moderate circumstances', 'in conditions of no greatness or excess'; same use of ἐπί as in ἐπ᾽ ἴσοισιν. Because the phrase is within a wish, the negative μή is used with the adj., even though the adj. is used factually ('circumstances that are in fact not great'): Smyth §§2735, 2737. For rejection of great power or wealth, compare Archilochus 19 West οὔ μοι τὰ Γύγεω τοῦ πολυχρύσου μέλει κτλ.; and other rejections of tyranny (Mastronarde on *Phoen.* 549), and Hdt. 1.30–2 (Solon and Croesus). This text is Barthold's necessary correction of εἰ μὴ μεγάλως. The MSS text would apparently mean 'if I cannot live in greatness, may I at least grow old securely', but it completely spoils the argument of 119–30 if the humble nurse admits to any longing for greatness.

**124** ὀχυρῶς γ': γε is emphatic, marking the adverb as the essential point: the great may seem to have things their way, but their prosperity and power is not *secure*. This is a fundamental feature of the archaic and classical world-view, whether the danger to the great is regarded as an amoral force of limitation on mortals (the *phthonos* of the gods) or the precariousness of prosperity is moralized by the assumption that the prosperous inevitably overstep and bring destruction on themselves.

**125–7** 'For first of all the mere name of what is the moderate wins first prize in the speaking of it, and (secondly) in action moderation is by far the best thing for mortals.' The infinitives εἰπεῖν and χρῆσθαι are thus taken as epexegetic, and τὰ μέτρια is understood from τῶν μετρίων as subject of λῶιστα (ἐστί). But one cannot rule out a different analysis of the syntax, with essentially similar meaning: with the infinitives as subjects, 'For first of all simply speaking the name of what is the moderate wins first prize, and (secondly) to act with moderation is by far the best thing for mortals'; in this analysis, τοῖς μετρίοις is understood from τῶν μετρίων and the neut. pl. appears as predicate of an infinitive subject (384–5n.). For μέν balanced by τε compare 11–13. The word/deed polarity emphasizes the completeness of the superiority of moderation. Compare the proverb μέτρον ἄριστον ascribed to Cleobulus of Lindos (one of the Seven Wise Men), the Delphic μηδὲν ἄγαν, and Aesch. *Eum.* 530 παντὶ μέσωι τὸ κράτος θεὸς ὤπασεν; for the contrast of the lot of kings with the middling life of an average citizen, see Pindar, *Pyth.* 11.52–3 τῶν γὰρ ἀνὰ πόλιν εὑρίσκων τὰ μέσα μακροτέρωι | ὄλβωι τεθαλότα, μέμφομ' αἶσαν τυραννίδων. For praise of the name as a prelude to praise of the concrete effects compare the argument for *isonomia* in Hdt. 3.80, πλῆθος δὲ ἄρχον πρῶτα μὲν οὔνομα πάντων κάλλιστον ἔχει, ἰσονομίην, δεύτερα δὲ κτλ.; Cicero *Phil.* 2.113 *et nomen pacis dulce est et res ipsa salutaris*; and conversely *Hec.* 357–9 (Polyxena) 'but now I am a slave: firstly, the name itself, being unaccustomed to me, makes me long to die; secondly, etc.'

**126** τοὔνομα: τὸ ὄνομα (crasis).

**127 λῶιστα:** superlative of the archaic comparative λωῖων/ λώιων, 'better' (no positive form from this root); both words are mainly poetic.

**128 οὐδένα καιρὸν δύναται:** a bold and difficult expression; the general sense is clear (excessive power or prosperity is not really good for mortals), but the precise syntax is uncertain. Possible interpretations, in descending order of preference, include: (1) 'holds sway with no proper measure' (treating καιρόν as an internal acc., 'has a power that is no due measure'); (2) 'is not able to create (or provide) any due measure' (καιρόν a direct object, with a brachylogy or pregnant use of δύναμαι, possibly supported by one usage in Plato, *Phlb*. 23d9–10 διάκρισιν δυναμένου ('a thing able to provide a separation'), for which Bury ad loc. and Ast, *Lex. Plat.* s.v. δύναμαι cite as parallels only instances with neut. pronoun objects, which are more easily understood as internal objects; (3) 'means no due measure' or 'means no profit/ advantage' (but this sense of δύναμαι is highly prosaic and technical, and in this context καιρός is far more likely to be 'due measure' than 'profit', although the latter sense is correctly seen in *Andr.* 131 and Soph. *Phil.* 151). In archaic and poetic usage καιρός frequently refers to 'due measure' or 'right degree' with no connotation of time (see Barrett on *Hipp.* 386–7; Race (1981)).

**129 μείζους:** alternative acc. pl. masc./fem. (μείζονας): LS 5.c.

**ὀργισθῆι:** aor. pass. subj. of ὀργίζομαι, with inceptive sense, 'becomes angry'. The anger of divine power against the house probably implies that the prosperous mortal has misbehaved, and this was presumably also intended in οὐδένα καιρόν in the previous line.

**130 ἀπέδωκεν** 'gives in return' or 'brings in return', with the connotation that it is an owed or just reversal; this is a gnomic aorist (LS 15).

### *131–213  Parodos*

The parodos (SE 2) of *Medea* is closely integrated into the structure of the preceding scene: the nurse remains present and interacts with the chorus in a lyric/anapaestic dialogue; the imprecations of Medea heard from indoors in the previous scene are heard again during the parodos, and the earlier cries are cited as the cause for the arrival of the Corinthian women, who come to ascertain Medea's current state and to offer sympathy. Inquiry and sympathy are standard elements of many choral entries, and likewise the admonition to restrain grief and despair is a typical motif of the tragic chorus, as the moderation of the anonymous collective is shown in counterpoint to the heroic individuals with their strong passions.

Medea's lines sung from inside turn the parodos into a three-way exchange. Medea is absorbed in her own emotions and has no awareness of her listeners and their comments as she continues to sing in anapaests. The chorus' part begins with an astrophic section that is comparable to the chanted anapaests that are found before the strophic lyrics in some parodoi, but here the chorus is quite agitated from the start, and the long-alpha vowels and the quick transition to other rhythms indicate that these entry-anapaests are sung. The nurse, who is more reflective and more knowledgeable, continues with her relatively calmer chanted anapaests.

### Metre

Metrical analysis: the astrophic opening (131–8) consists of a period of 6 sung anapaests (PM 23), containing within it a phrase (Κολχίδος οὐδέπω ἤπιος) that anticipates the shift to pure dactylic rhythm in the next period. The clausula, in the text accepted here, is an aeolic colon, a foretaste of the rhythm of the strophic pair. (With a different text, the clausula is iambic.) The stanza is often analysed differently; for this analysis and the reasons for it, see Diggle (1994) 278–83. There is epic correption (PM 7) in 132–3 οὐδέπω ἤπιος and twice in 136–7 συνήδομαι, ὦ γύναι, ἄλγεσι. In 133 γεραιά is scanned ∪∪ – with internal correption (PM 6).

The chorus' strophic pair (148–58 = 173–83) is surrounded by runs of anapaests: nurse (chanted) 139–43 (paroemiac 143), Medea (sung) 144–7 (paroemiac 147), strophe (SE 1), Medea (sung) 160–7 (probably period-end without catalexis at change of speaker 167), nurse (chanted) 168–72 (paroemiacs 170 and 172), antistrophe (SE 1), nurse (chanted) 184–204 (paroemiac 204; see below 184–204n. for the possibility of period-end without catalexis). Like the preceding astrophic stanza, the strophic stanza starts off with anapaests (5 metra, without catalexis, but ending with three fully spondaic metra), but here the remainder of the stanza is in aeolic rhythm (PM 26), with the hagesichorean used repeatedly and the reizianum as clausula at 154/179 (confirmed by hiatus). There are at least three periods in the stanza, but the two sequences of hagesichoreans create uncertainty. A colon with the dragged close ∪ − − is usually clausular, but in a sequence such as 151–4 the hagesichorean seems to be non-clausular (but Dale, *MATC* iii.279 treats 151–4 as four periods); in 155–7 a similar sequence is probably repeated with a different clausula, although the rhetorical phrasing might perhaps support recognition of a separate period for each colon.

After the nurse goes in to fetch Medea, the chorus sings another astrophic stanza (204–12), which may be felt as an epode (SE 1) to the preceding pair, though this relationship is obscured by the long intervention of the nurse. The opening seems to carry on the aeolic strain of the strophic pair, but via an ambiguous transition the single-short and double-short elements are then articulated somewhat differently, in cola that are classed as 'dactylo-epitrite' (PM 27), the type of rhythm that is featured in most of the remaining songs of this chorus. In this stanza, the affinity to aeolic is revived at the end by the clausula of pherecratean shape. In the following scheme, 207 could also be interpreted as a modified hagesichorean (one with extended kernel and with anaclasis or reversal of relative positions of elements: symbol ¨hag^d). In 205 ἄϊον is treated as lacking temporal augment (as in *Hipp.* 362); if ἰαχάν is read here, the colon may be viewed as diomedean + cr (Itsumi (1991–93)).

∪ ∪ − − − | ∪ ∪ − ∪ ∪ − |
ἔκλυον φωνάν, ἔκλυον δὲ βοὰν     131 2 anap

− − − − |− ∪ ∪ − ∪ ∪ |
τᾶς δυστάνου Κολχίδος· οὐδέπω     132 2 anap

− ∪ ∪ − − |∪ ∪ − − − ‖^b
ἤπιος; ἀλλ' ὦ γεραιά, λέξον.     133 2 anap

− ∪ ∪ − ∪ ∪ − ∪ ∪ − ∪ ∪ |
ἀμφιπύλου γὰρ ἔσω μελάθρου γόον     134–5 4 da

− ∪ ∪ − ∪ ∪ −∪ ∪ − ∪ ∪ |
ἔκλυον· οὐδὲ συνήδομαι, ὦ γύναι,     136 4 da

− ∪ ∪− ∪ ∪ |
ἄλγεσι δώματος,     137 2 da

∪ – – ∪∪ –∪ – – ‖

ἐπεί μοι φιλία κέκραται.                    138 hipponactean

– – – – – – – – –

– ∪ ∪ – – | – – ‾∪‾ – |

ἄιες, ὦ Ζεῦ καὶ Γᾶ καὶ φῶς,                148 2 anap
πῶς ἂν ἐς ὄψιν τὰν ἀμετέραν                173

– – – – | – – – – |

ἀχὰν οἷαν ἁ δύστανος                       149 2 anap
ἔλθοι μύθων τ' αὐδαθέντων                  174

– – – – ‖ʔ

μέλπει νύμφα;                              150 anap
δέξαιτ' ὀμφάν,                             175

– – ∪ ∪ –∪ – – |

τίς σοί ποτε τᾶς ἀπλάτου                   151 hagesichorean
εἴ πως βαρύθυμον ὀργὰν                     176

– – ∪ ∪ – ∪ – – |

κοίτας ἔρος, ὦ ματαία;                     152 hagesichorean
καὶ λῆμα φρενῶν μεθείη;                    177

– – ∪ ∪ – ∪ – – |

σπεύσεις θανάτου τελευτάν;                 153 hagesichorean
μήτοι τό γ' ἐμὸν πρόθυμον                  178

‾∪‾ – ∪ ∪ – – ‖ʰ

μηδὲν τόδε λίσσου.                         154 reizianum
φίλοισιν ἀπέστω.                           179

– ∪ – ∪ – – ∪ ∪ – ∪– – |

εἰ δὲ σὸς πόσις καινὰ λέχη σεβίζει,        155 (cr, hipponactean)
ἀλλὰ βᾶσά νιν δεῦρο πόρευσον οἴκων         180

– – ∪ ∪ – ∪ – – |

κείνωι τόδε μὴ χαράσσου·                   156 hagesichorean
ἔξω· φίλα καὶ τάδ' αὔδα,                   181

– – ∪∪ – ∪ – – |

Ζεύς σοι τάδε συνδικήσει.                  157 hagesichorean
σπεύσασά τι πρὶν κακῶσαι                   182

– ∪ – – – – ∪ ∪ –∪ – ∪– – – ‖

μὴ λίαν τάκου δυρομένα σὸν εὐνάταν.        158–9 (cr, glyconic, sp)
τοὺς ἔσω· πένθος γὰρ μεγάλως τόδ'          183
  ὁρμᾶται.

– – – – – – – – –

$- \; - \cup \cup \; - \cup - \cup \; - \cup - \; |$
ἀχὰν ἄιον πολύστονον γόων,                    204 11-syllable
                                              aeolic (telesillean, ia)

$\cup \; \widehat{\cup \cup} \; \cup \widehat{\cup} \cup \; \widehat{\cup} \cup \cup \; - |$
λιγυρὰ δ' ἄχεα μογερὰ βοᾷ                     205 2 ia (∪E)

$\cup \; - \cup - \cup \cup \; - \; \cup \cup \; - - \; ||^{?}$
τὸν ἐν λέχει προδόταν κακόνυμφον·             206 11-syllable
                                              aeolic (ᴧe∪D−)

$\widehat{\cup} \cup \; \cup \; - \; \cup \widehat{\cup} \; \cup \; - \cup |$
θεοκλυτεῖ δ' ἄδικα παθοῦσα                    207 2 tro (E∪)

$- \; - \cup - \cup \; - \; \cup \cup \; - \cup \cup \; - \cup \; |$
τὰν Ζηνὸς ὁρκίαν Θέμιν, ἅ νιν ἔβασεν          208–9 iambelegus
                                              +∪ (−e∪D∪)

$- \cup \cup \; - \cup \cup \; - |$
Ἑλλάδ' ἐς ἀντίπορον                           210 hemiepes (D)

$\cup \; \widehat{\cup} \cup \; \widehat{\cup} \cup \cup \; - \; \cup - |$
δι' ἅλα νύχιον ἐφ' ἁλμυρὰν                     211–12 2 ia (∪E)

$- - \; - \; \cup \cup \; - - \; |||$
Πόντου κλῇδ' ἀπεράντου.                        213 pherecratean
                                              (eᴧ d−)

**131** **ἔκλυον φωνάν, ἔκλυον δὲ βοάν:** anaphora of the verb, parallel syntax of the two metra, and 'rhyming' ending of the almost
synonymous nouns all mark the emotional engagement with Medea's
plight declared by the chorus in its opening stanza. The initial entry
of a Euripidean chorus is often motivated by a sense of sympathy
and concern, sometimes explained by the chorus' having heard of the
distraught or threatened condition of a major character (*Alc.*, *Hipp.*,
*Andr.*, *Or.*, etc.; cf. Soph. *Trach.*); and in other cases a chorus is summoned to share in lamentation (*Troades*, *IT*, *Hel.*). This instance is
unusual in that the chorus responds to the same cries the audience
has just heard, but Medea is not in a condition deliberately to sum-
mon the chorus. Nevertheless, she subsequently manipulates the
chorus' sympathy more effectively than characters generally do in
other plays.

**ἔκλυον:** the sing. verb is not evidence for the number of speakers of an anapaestic or lyric choral part; rather, since the chorus is by
convention a collective group, there is usually indifferent variation
between sing. and pl. verbs and pronouns in such utterances of the

chorus (note, e.g., 173 ἀμετέραν followed by 178 ἐμόν; 654 εἴδομεν followed by 655 ἔχω). Conversely, actors may shift between sing. and pl. in addressing the group (e.g. 214, 252, 253, 259). See in general Kaimio (1970).

**132 Κολχίδος:** the chorus' first reference to Medea is by the ethnic adj. that emphasizes her exotic origin; and since the Athenians associated songs of lamentation with foreign origin (Garvie on Aesch. *Cho.* 423–4; Hall (1989) 128–33), the ethnic may have additional force here. But any interpretation that lays emphasis on Medea's foreignness must also acknowledge the features of the drama that downplay its importance or that undercut any sense of the superiority of Greeks. See Introd. 2(*c*).

**133 ἤπιος:** for treatment of the adj. as of two terminations see LS 5.d. When used of persons, ἤπιος normally denotes a settled disposition of mildness, gentleness, kindness. The sense here is instead 'calm', 'soothed', almost 'recovered from her passionate distraction', and this is probably a medical use of the word: cf. LSJ s.v. 1.3; Thuc. 2.59 ἐβούλετο θαρσῦναί τε καὶ ἀπαγαγὼν τὸ ὀργιζόμενον τῆς γνώμης πρὸς τὸ ἠπιώτερον καὶ ἀδεέστερον καταστῆσαι; Hippocrates, *Epid.* 5.20 ἠπίωσε τῶι σώματι. See 6on. οὐδέπω ἤπιος must be treated as a question; otherwise the request λέξον makes no sense.

**135–6 ἀμφιπύλου γὰρ ἔσω μελάθρου γόον | ἔκλυον** 'for I heard her lamentation inside the two-gated structure'; it seems best to understand that the structure is Medea's house and that ἔσω μελάθρου is thus an attributive modifier of γόον; some interpreters instead take the phrase as adverbial with ἔκλυον, referring to the women's own houses. ἀμφίπυλος (extant only here and in the scholia on this line) is, like ἀμφίθυρος in Lysias 12.15, an adj. referring to the fact that a Greek house might have two doors, not only the main front door between the street/plaza and the internal courtyard, but also a small rear door. The point of referring to the existence of the second door is to suggest that the sound of Medea's cries reached her neighbours through the back alley and they have as a result gathered before her house to make inquiries. The MSS transmit ἐπ' ἀμφιπύλου ... ἔσω μελάθρου, and Σ gives the unlikely rendering 'I, being nearby the vestibule, heard her cry inside her house' (whose vestibule? Σ seems to intend Medea's, Wecklein understands the women's). The elimination of ἐπ' both clarifies the syntax and makes the metrical structure smoother. γόον, Elmsley's emendation, is needed for the metre (βοάν could easily have intruded from 131). For discussion of the text and meaning see Diggle (1994) 278–83.

**138 φιλία κέκραται** 'a tie of friendship has been blended', with κέκραται, perf. pass. of κεράννυμι, 'mix, blend'. φιλία is Porson's emendation; he cited passages with φιλία as object of ἀνα- or συγκεράννυμι (*Hipp.* 253–4, Hdt. 4.152.5, 7.151; he also cited Aesch. *Cho.* 344 νεοκρᾶτα φίλον, which probably has a different explanation: see Garvie). The idea of mixing is perhaps borrowed from the mixing of wine for libations ratifying peace or alliance or for the 'cup of friendship' (LSJ s.v. φιλοτήσιος II). (The MSS have φίλον κέκρα(ν)ται, which would be 'the house (δῶμα) has been accomplished (or ordained?) as dear to me' (with an inappropriate use of κραίνω and dubious predicate adj. construction) or 'the house has been blended as dear to me').

**139–43** The nurse recapitulates for the chorus some key points of the prologue: 139 ≈ 16, 140 ≈ 18, 141 ≈ 24–6, 142–3 ≈ 28–9; so too 171–2 ≈ 37 + 44–5.

**139 οὐκ εἰσὶ δόμοι** 'the house is undone' or 'the house is no more', as in *IT* 153 οὐκ εἴσ' οἶκοι πατρῷοι; compare, with the more explicit οὐκέτι, *Hipp.* 357 οὐκέτ' εἴμ' ἐγώ; *Hec.* 683 οὐκέτ' εἰμὶ δή.
   **τάδ'** 'what we had here'.

**140 λέκτρα τυράννων:** better taken as 'marriage with the royal family' than as 'the bed of the princess' (with poetic pl. for sing.).

**141 τήκει βιοτήν** 'wastes away her life-force'; cf. *Hcld.* 645 ψυχὴν ἐτήκου, *Od.* 19.264 μὴ θυμὸν τῆκε. See 25n.

**142–3 φίλων οὐδενὸς ..|. μύθοις:** the word-order is almost concentric, with οὐδενός depending on μύθοις. For φρένα see 8n.

**144 φλὸξ οὐρανία:** a tragic periphrasis for 'lightning bolt from Zeus'; for such a suicidal wish, cf. *Prom.* 582 (Io to Zeus) πυρί με φλέξον, Eur. *Supp.* 831 πυρός τε φλογμὸς ὁ Διὸς ἐν κάραι πέσοι, *Andr.* 847.

**145** βαίη is aor. opt. of βαίνω in a wish.

τί δέ μοι ζῆν ἔτι κέρδος 'What profit is there for me any longer in living?' (Syntactically, ζῆν is subject of understood ἐστι, and τί κέρδος is predicate.) Tragic characters in desperate straits commonly question why they should live on. For κέρδος in such contexts, see *Prom.* 745, *Alc.* 960, *Her.* 1301 (the motif is also seen in [798–9]: see n.).

**146** καταλυσαίμαν: intransitive or absolute in sense, 'may I take my rest' like a weary traveller at an inn (from the notion of undoing one's baggage or unyoking one's team).

**148** ὦ Ζεῦ καὶ Γᾶ καὶ φῶς: the final two elements of the triplet suggest the universalizing polar opposites earth and sky, so that Zeus as a person and the whole natural world are invoked; for similar invocations see Mastronarde on *Phoen.* 1290. Although it cannot be ruled out that ἄιες is addressed to Zeus, it is more likely that the question is self-addressed (the vocatives being an emotional exclamation). Choruses often call attention to a sight or sound by such a question or imperative, and the second person sing. and pl. are used indifferently: see Kaimio (1970) 137–43.

**149** ἀχάν was restored here by Elmsley for ἰαχάν: fully spondaic metra are characteristic of strongly emotional lyric anapaests, the syllables ια- in ἰαχή are not certainly double short in any passage in tragedy (although double short is found sometimes in verb ἰάχω and noun ἰάχημα), and ἰαχά is a frequent corruption of ἀχά (see Mastronarde on *Phoen.* 1040). The same correction is needed in 204 below, where a single syllable before the choriamb of the aeolic colon is somewhat more likely.

**150** νύμφα: this term alludes to the nubile or sexually attractive status of a girl or woman (mostly used of young women just before and after marriage, but also of, e.g., Andromache in *Andr.* 140 and Helen in *Tro.* 250), and elsewhere in this play always refers to the princess, so there is some pathos when the chorus uses the term of Medea here.

**151–2** τᾶς ἀπλάτου | κοίτας 'the terrible bed of rest', that is, death; the chorus is shocked by Medea's death-wish, and extends the metaphor she used in 146 καταλυσαίμαν. Elmsley restored the sense required by the context by recognizing that transmitted ἀπλάστου/ ἀπλήστου, taken as 'insatiable' by the scholiasts, is the very common corruption of ἄπλητος/ἄπλατος, literally 'unapproachable' (cf. πέλας, πλησίον). Although excessive *erōs* is one of the strands of motivation thematized in the play (Introd. 2(*b*)), this does not justify the defence of 'insatiable bed' by Gentili (1972), following Wilamowitz.

ὦ **ματαία:** literally 'foolish woman', but like some other admonitory addresses, ματαία 'combines pity and reproach in varied proportions' (Gow on Theocr. 15.4): here the chorus is urging moderation, suggesting that no sensible person would wish for death; at 333 Creon addresses the same vocative to Medea to suggest she is wasting her time, and Jason uses it in 959 to imply Medea's lack of logical calculation of the relative resources of herself and the princess.

**153** σπεύσεις θανάτου τελευτάν 'will you hasten the end that is death?' A second-person question is best here, since the point must be that death will come soon enough for a mortal, so one should not seek it out. Blaydes' σπεύσεις, a small change of the variant σπεύσει, is needed; adjusting σπεύσει to unambiguous second person σπεύσηι is less attractive because the middle is unlikely (the active appears over 70 times in tragedy, the middle once in Aeschylus). Some follow Weil in altering to τελευτά and keeping σπεύσει as third person (Kovacs: 'death will come all too quickly'), but this is less attractive because σπεύδω normally has an animate subject and emphasizes intentional speed. Least likely is the interpretation of the scholiasts, who treat the verb as third person with ἔρος as the subject.

**156** κείνωι τόδε μὴ χαράσσου 'do not be sharpened in anger at him on this account'; a rare usage (elsewhere in classical authors only Hdt. 7.1, Δαρεῖον ... μεγάλως κεχαραγμένον τοῖσι Ἀθηναίοισι; cf. the active 'arouse, torment' in Eur. fr. 431.3 (Ἔρως) καὶ θεῶν ἄνω ψυχὰς χαράσσει); θήγω and ὀξύνω have a similar metaphorical use. τόδε is internal acc., to be translated adverbially.

**157** Ζεύς ... συνδικήσει: independently of Medea's own claim on the gods' support (22), the Corinthian women assume that Zeus is on Medea's side. The asyndeton is explanatory (LS 28). συνδικεῖν is a technical legal term for the action of a third party who assists in a court case by delivering a supporting speech (so Apollo comes both to be witness and ξυνδικήσων in Aesch. *Eum.* 579). Thus Medea will be in an exceptionally strong position if Zeus, who is also the ultimate judge/juror, plays the role of σύνδικος as well.

**159  εὐνάταν**, the minority reading, is a form of the noun recorded in Hesychius and found as a variant in *Or.* 1392. This form responds more exactly to 183 ὁρμᾶται, and there is some doubt whether the penultimate syllable in an aeolic verse of this type can be anceps (Itsumi (1984) 78–80), as it would be with the majority reading εὐνέταν. It is typical of the richness of poetic vocabulary that tragedy also uses εὐνάτωρ and εὐνητήρ.

**160  Θέμι ... Ἄρτεμι:** Themis is a personification of established law and custom (same root as τίθημι) and so symbolic of the gods' concern for the moral behaviour of mortals (including oath-breaking). Artemis has no particular connection to oaths, but has close connections with the life of women (childhood, marriage, childbirth) and so may be invoked here as a protector of female rights. Artemis is also sometimes identified with Hecate, with whom Medea has a special connection, as she herself later declares (397).

**162  ἐνδησαμένα:** the metaphor of binding by oaths, familiar in English, does not appear to be common in Greek (elsewhere Hdt. 3.19 ὁρκίοισί ... μεγάλοισι ἐνδεδέσθαι).

**164  αὐτοῖς μελάθροις** 'together with their house', 'house and all'; for this idiomatic use of the dat. of a noun accompanied by intensifying αὐτός, see Smyth §1525, LSJ s.v. 1.5.

  **διακναιομένους** 'violently destroyed', with the connotation of laceration and torment, but perhaps not a strongly imagistic word (the verb is used to allude to Alcestis' death in *Alc.* 109 τῶν ἀγαθῶν διακναιομένων).

**165  οἷ' ... ἀδικεῖν** 'what sort of injustice they dare to commit against me'; οἷα is internal acc. with ἀδικεῖν, and the clause, exclamatory in origin, may be translated in English with causal force, 'because they dare to commit such injustice' (Barrett on *Hipp.* 877–80). Kaibel's emendation οἷ' ἐμέ, reported in Bierl, Calder, and Fowler

(1991) 38, gives a more forceful sense than οἵ γ᾽ ἐμέ: relative with γε would appropriately connote cause, but the combination is rather prosaic, otherwise found in trimeters only.

**πρόσθεν:** in Greek thinking, causing harm first, without provocation, is almost definitive of injustice, whereas causing harm second, in retaliation, is widely sanctioned as legitimate revenge. See Burnett (1998) xv–xvi; Dover (1974) 180–2.

**166–7** This couplet echoes the nurse's report in 31–5 and prepares for the subsequent references to Medea's lack of safe anchorage from her woes (255–8, 441–3).

**166** ὧν ἀπενάσθην: the separative gen. depends on the preposition in the compound. The connotation of relocation in the verb (which is aor. pass. of ἀποναίω) is important thematically: 'which I left ⟨for a new home⟩', 'from which I have been parted'.

**167** αἰσχρῶς is probably best taken with ἀπενάσθην, and then the following participial phrase explains the adverb. Others attach 'shamefully' to κτείνασα so that it alludes to the manner of the killing, but how Medea killed her brother may not have been clear to Eur.'s audience.

**κτείνασα κάσιν:** the death of Medea's brother (Apsyrtus in most sources) is alluded to only here (vaguely) and in 1334, where a particular version is implied (see Introd. 4). Medea's utterance ends in a full anapaestic dimeter, and some critics believe some words have been lost that would restore a paroemiac, as at 114 and 147 (another way to obtain a paroemiac is by transposition, but Heimsoeth's proposal ὧν κάσιν αἰσχρῶς | τὸν ἐμὸν κτείνασ᾽ ἀπενάσθην produces an inferior word-order). But 97 is also a full dimeter at the end of an utterance by Medea. It is impossible to say whether there is period-end at 97 and/or 167 (see 184–204n.).

**168–9** κἀπιβοᾶται | Θέμιν εὐκταίαν 'she shouts an invocation of Themis' (21n.); καὶ ἐπιβοᾶται (crasis), and εὐκταίαν predicative in sense, 'so that she is invoked in her present utterance' (cf. *Or.* 213–14 Λήθη κακῶν ... τοῖσι δυστυχοῦσιν εὐκταία θεός). Others interpret εὐκταίαν less probably as either 'invoked in the εὐχαί that once accompanied the oaths' or 'guardian of oaths'.

**169  Ζῆνα:** in epic and high-style poetry, including tragedy, the declension Ζεύς, Ζηνός, Ζηνί, Ζῆνα provides convenient alternative forms for Ζεύς, Διός, etc. It was a ζήτημα (interpretive puzzle for ancient scholars) to explicate why the nurse refers to an invocation of Themis and Zeus when Medea has just called on Themis and Artemis. Various far-fetched answers are given in the scholia, and Nauck proposed Ζηνὸς ὃς for Ζῆνά θ᾽ ὃς (cf. 209). The likely explanation is that the mention of the oaths violated by Jason may be taken to call upon the attention of Ζεὺς ὅρκιος, whose role is paraphrased in the relative clause ὃς ... ταμίας νενόμισται (cf. 209 τὰν Ζηνὸς ὁρκίαν Θέμιν with n.).

**171  οὐκ ἔστιν ὅπως:** an emphatic periphrastic negation, more forceful than οὐδαμῶς, 'there is no way how'. Similar periphrases may be formed with other indefinite relatives, and οὐκ ἔστιν ὅστις (more forceful than οὐδείς) is the most common (Smyth §§2515, 2557). Compare 1339 οὐκ ἔστιν ἥτις, 793 οὔτις ἔστιν ὅστις.

ἔν τινι μικρῷ 'in some small deed' or 'in some trivial gesture'.

**173–4  πῶς ἂν ... | ἔλθοι:** equivalent to 'I wish she would come' (97n.).

**174–5  μύθων τ᾽ αὐδαθέντων | δέξαιτ᾽ ὀμφάν** 'would accept [i.e. not ignore, as up to this time, 29, 142–3] the sound of spoken words'. For the defining gen. phrase see LS 10.a.

**176–7  εἴ πως ..|. μεθείη:** '⟨so that we may see⟩ if somehow she might let go ...' εἴ πως here may be taken to introduce a prospective indirect question, as if 'to find out' or 'to show' were understood (the idiom is equivalent to English 'in case'). See K–G ii.534 Anm. 16. μεθείη is third sing. aor. act. optative of μεθίημι (μετα + ἵημι), 'let go, slacken'.

λῆμα φρενῶν 'the strong passion of her mind', that is, her wish for suicide and wish to do harm to her enemies.

**178  τό γ᾽ ἐμὸν πρόθυμον** 'my eager good will', equivalent to ἡ ἐμὴ προθυμία, since in a variety of styles and genres in Greek the neut. adj. may be used as an abstract substantive (Smyth §1023).

**179  ἀπέστω:** third sing. imperative of ἄπειμι, 'be absent'. The dat. is one of interest/disinterest.

**181** φίλα καὶ τάδ' αὔδα 'tell her that *our* attitude too is support-ive', with τάδε meaning 'the situation here', hence 'our presence' or 'our attitude' and καί implying 'in addition to' the supportive stance of the nurse and others in the household.

**182** σπεύσασά τι πρὶν κακῶσαι: in accordance with a tendency of enclitic position in Greek (and related languages), τι is drawn to the second position in the participial phrase, even though it belongs with the subordinated πρίν-phrase as internal object of κακῶσαι.

**183** τοὺς ἔσω: that is, the children; the audience may assume that the chorus heard Medea call her sons 'accursed' and wish for their destruction (112–13), or may view this as a natural fear either because of the mythological parallel of Procne and Itys or because such be-haviour was known in everyday life (as it is in modern society). In any case, Eur. clearly prefers to anticipate the eventual turn of the plot rather than make it a complete surprise (if it was an innovation: see Introd. 4).

**184–204** This passage contains 37 anapaestic metra before the fi-nal paroemiac, an unusually large number of full metra delivered by one voice, esp. since this seems a relatively calm recitative. Compare the nurse's earlier generalizing passage at 115–30, with 30 metra before paroemiac. Through these two speeches, Eur. maintains the more intense emotional register of the sequence 96–213 while mak-ing the nurse a spokesperson for generalizations important to the themes of the play. Other long runs are less reflective and often por-tray some vehemence or defiance or breathless accumulation of add-on items: Soph. *Phil.* 1452–68 (32), Soph. *Ajax* 1402–16 (27); and with changes of speaker, *Hipp.* 208–38, *El.* 1308–31 and 1334–56. The changes of speaker in the latter passages raise the possibility of (un-detectable) period-end without catalexis. In passages of anapaestic dialogue there are a few cases of elision (as in 1398 below) or cor-reption (as in *El.* 1331) across change of speaker, proving synapheia; but there are also a few cases of hiatus and *brevis in longo* at change of speaker, proving period-end without catalexis (so 1396 below). Thus the extent of the nurse's two runs could be reduced by positing a pause at 189 before the long criticism of poetry, or at 118 before the generalization about the kings (and within 98–110 at 104).

**184 φόβος εἰ πείσω:** an unusual construction with indirect question (Smyth §2234) equivalent to the fear-clause μὴ οὐ πείσω: 'I fear I will not persuade her', 'I strongly doubt whether I'll persuade her'; similarly *Hcld.* 791 φόβος γὰρ εἴ μοι ζῶσιν οὓς ἐγὼ θέλω. For Medea's resistance to suasion or to any conversation at all, see 27–31, 142–3.

**186 ἐπιδώσω** 'give in addition ⟨to my previous toils⟩'; perhaps there is a connotation also of 'give freely' (LSJ s.v. ἐπιδίδωμι 1.3).

**187–8 τοκάδος δέργμα λεαίνης | ἀποταυροῦται** 'she glares with savage ferocity, like a lioness with newborn cubs', or more literally, 'she makes herself bull-like with respect to her gaze, so that it is the gaze of a lioness with newborn cubs' (middle-passive verb in reflexive sense, with accusative of respect and proleptic modifying genitive; or possibly middle verb with acc. object and proleptic modifier). This mixed image is an intensification of the proverbial bull-like glance (92n.). Lions are fierce opponents in Homeric similes and 'strongest and boldest' among animals in Hdt 3.108, and the lioness is the emblem of a savage woman in Aesch. *Ag.* 1258 (Cassandra speaking of Clytemnestra); Jason will throw this accusation at Medea at the end of the play (1342, 1407). τοκάδος reflects the knowledge that wild animals protecting their young are most dangerous to humans; and lions were particularly believed to be protective of their young (*Il.* 17.133–6, 18.318–22, Callimachus, *Hymn Dem.* 51–2 ὑποβλέπει ... λέαινα ὠμοτόκος, τᾶς φαντὶ πέλειν βλοσυρώτατον ὄμμα). It is ironic that Medea will display the ferocity of a lioness (1342 λέαιναν οὐ γυναῖκα), but direct it toward her own children. On animal imagery in the play see Introd. 2(*f*).

**190–204** Here is another extended reflection by the nurse (see 119–30n.). This one features a rhetorical gesture typical of Euripidean characters, finding fault with the disposition of the world, whether viewed as the arrangement created by the gods or as a usage sanctioned by human custom (see Leo (1912) 113–17). To cite examples only from *Medea* and the nearly contemporary *Hipp.*, compare 516–19 (same pattern as here: why is there a test for false coins, but not for false human character?), 573–5, *Hipp.* 191–7, 616–24, 916–20, 925–31. The observation here has a metatheatrical or metapoetic thrust, since it is a given of Greek poetics from the earliest times that song is a delight to mortals, even songs of destruction and misery so long as the audience is at a remove from the events depicted. Tragedy itself is a musical performance conducted amidst festivities, and audience enjoyment is one of its effects and goals. The nurse is too directly involved in the event to derive solace or pleasure from music, and her attack is matched by the chorus' claim in the first stasimon (see 410–45n.). For the sake of her argument, she alleges that no songs have been invented to stop grief, but the epic tradition assumed otherwise (Hes. *Theog.* 98–103; Achilles' singing in *Il.* 9.186–9 may be viewed as a distraction from his vexation, and Demodocus' song in *Od.* 8 contributes to defusing a situation of strife). Moreover, the Greeks did have cathartic music (for a literary representation of which, see *Helen* 1301–52).

**190  σκαιούς** 'unintelligent, misdirected', an extension of the widespread cultural stereotype of lefthandedness as clumsy or 'sinister' in antithesis to the 'dexterity' of the right hand: Lloyd (1962), Lloyd (1966) 37–42. For σκαιός/σοφός in antithesis, see also 298 below, *Hcld.* 458–9, *El.* 972, *Her.* 299–300, frr. 290, 657.2.

**190–1  λέγων .|.. ἁμάρτοις:** just as in English maxims like 'you can't win them all' or 'you can't take it with you', in Greek the second sing. may provide a generic, imagined addressee (with masc. as universalizing gender, as usual), an alternative to generalization using a third-person verb with τις; so too in 298–301. The participle λέγων is supplementary with ἁμάρτοις ('you would not err in saying'), but may also be translated as conditional ('if you should say').

**κοὐδέν:** καὶ οὐδέν (crasis).

**192  οἵτινες:** a relative clause may be causal in sense ('because they ...') (Smyth §2555); compare ἥτις in 589, 1130, 1234.

**ἐπὶ μὲν θαλίαις:** μέν is balanced by the δέ of 195; one expects something like 'but in times of unhappiness', but the construction shifts from relative clause to new main clause (a common shift in Greek idiom: Smyth §§2517–18), the subject changes, and ηὕροντο and ηὕρετο have different constructions.

**194  ηὕροντο βίωι τερπνὰς ἀκοάς** 'invented for our life as delightful things to hear'; βίωι is Page's emendation of βίου, which would give the sense 'invented as life's delightful aural entertainment', in which the loose gen. ('belonging to life') is odd, but perhaps possible.

**195  βροτῶν:** it is uncertain whether this is to be taken with οὐδείς (a very common combination) or with στυγίους … λύπας (where it has greater point).

**199  κέρδος:** understand ἐστί, 'it is a profit' or 'it is a benefit', with the acc. and inf. phrase 'that mortals cure these banes with their songs' as true subject.

**200–1  ἵνα δ' εὔδειπνοι | δαῖτες:** εἰσί is to be understood (LS 30; for ἵνα 41n.), and the similarity of meaning in the noun and in the root of the accompanying adj. is typical of tragic style (fullness, LS 32).

**201  τείνουσι βοήν** 'make taut', so 'make shrill their loud voice', 'modulate their voices in loud song' (not 'extend ⟨in time⟩, draw out long', as suggested in LSJ).

**202–3  τὸ παρὸν … | δαιτὸς πλήρωμα** 'the ready-to-hand fullness of the feast'.

**204–13**  The chorus' epode-like stanza provides a conventional cover for the time during which the nurse goes in, finds Medea, and delivers her message, and Medea makes her way to the door. The content of the lyric is mainly recapitulation of previous details.

**204  ἀχάν:** see 149n. For the fullness of expression in ἀχάν … πολύστονον γόων, see LS 32.

**205–6  λιγυρὰ δ' ἄχεα μογερὰ βοᾶι | τὸν ἐν λέχει προδόταν κακό-νυμφον** 'she shouts out shrill grievous cries of woe about the evilly married one who is betrayer of her bed'. ἄχεα is the internal object of βοᾶι, and τὸν κτλ. may be considered either the external object of the whole previous phrase (342–3n.) or the content of the cry (21n.), since the article τόν indicates that the chorus is citing Medea's words. ἐν λέχει is literally 'in respect to the marriage-bed' (LSJ s.v. ἐν I.7). The article and word order imply that κακόνυμφος is a substantive here, and προδόταν is used adjectivally or in apposition. Note the difference in meaning (contextually determined) between κακόνυμφος here ('ill-married ⟨because harming Medea⟩') and in 990 ('ill-

married ⟨because of the harm he is bringing upon himself, his children, and new bride⟩'). Such variation is typical of tragic style.

**208–9 τὰν Ζηνὸς ὁρκίαν Θέμιν:** both this passage and Aesch.
*Supp.* 360 seem to make Themis the daughter of Zeus, on the alle-
gorical basis that Zeus is the sponsor of law and order (see Lloyd-
Jones (1983)). The more usual genealogy makes Themis a Titan
(daughter of Gaea) and one of the early 'wives' of Zeus (Hes. *Theog.*
901–6). Another possibility is that 'Zeus' Themis' means merely that
she is agent or helper of Zeus. Friis Johansen and Whittle on Aesch.
*Supp.* 360 prefer this interpretation, judging that the plain genitive
(without a word for 'daughter' or 'offspring') does not 'suffice to
convey this novel relationship'.

**ἅ νιν ἔβασεν** 'who made her travel', that is, it was the solemn
oath of Jason that induced Medea to leave her homeland. ἔβησα is
transitive weak aor. of βαίνω with a causative meaning, an inheri-
tance from epic, absent from Attic prose.

**210 ἀντίπορον:** either 'on the other side of the sea crossing' or
'that lies across the strait' (referring specifically, as elsewhere, to the
narrow divide between Asia and Europe at the Hellespont and
Bosporus).

**211 νύχιον** implies flight by night, a time when most Greek ships
did not travel.

**212–13 ἐφ' ἁλμυρὰν | Πόντου κλῆιδ' ἀπεράντου:** probably an
elaborate periphrasis for the Bosporus, 'toward the salt-water closure
of the impenetrable(?) Pontus', alluding (as elsewhere: 1263–4n.) to
the crucial boundary between different worlds and different cultures
that Medea has crossed. The text and meaning have been much disputed. ἀπεράντου (the poet Milton's emendation) is stylish, giving
one epithet to each noun in the phrase. Since there may have been
some conflation of different senses in words featuring πε(ι)ρ- and
περα(ι)ν- (see Fraenkel on Aesch. *Ag.* 1382 ἄπειρον, Griffith on *Prom.*
1078–9), it seems best to interpret ἀπεράντου as 'not to be traversed
or penetrated', hence 'not to be travelled', alluding to the notion that
the Pontus is inhospitable to travellers (ἄξεινος, whence by euphemism εὔξεινος). The usual sense is 'limitless, immense', which is not
entirely apposite here (though some have seen an allusion to *Il.*

24.545 Ἑλλήσποντος ἀπείρων). The MSS present ἀπέραντον agreeing with κλῆιδ᾽, which makes no sense if the meaning is 'immense' but
is perhaps possible with the meaning 'impenetrable' (but the barrier
was no longer impenetrable after the outward voyage of the Argo).
ἀπέραντον and ἀπέρατον are often confused in MSS (Griffith on
*Prom.* 154), so it is a small step to accept Blaydes' ἀπέρατον, as
Kovacs does, translating 'a gateway few traverse'.

**κλῆιδ᾽:** note the general sense of κλῆις, 'closure, barrier' rather
than specifically 'bar' or 'key': see also 661 and compare the tragic
use of κλῆιθρον (Barrett on *Hipp.* 577–81).

*214–409    First episode*

The opening of the play emphasized Medea's emotional and intransigent nature and contrasted the excesses of her status and moods
with the moderation of the ordinary citizen. But the expectations
created by this build-up are sharply challenged by her actual appearance in the first episode (SE 2). She emerges under her own
power (unlike Phaedra in *Hipp.*) and launches a lengthy, closely rea-
soned iambic speech to solidify the favour of the women of the chorus. And when Creon arrives to inform her of her exile (news concealed from her by her servants for fear of her reaction), she controls
her response and applies her verbal skill again to winning a temporary reprieve.

Some questions of staging affect the impact of this and following
scenes. On Medea's costume, see Introd. 3. On the presence and
number of her silent attendants (probably two), see Introd. 3, where
it is also argued that they are nameless figures distinct from the
nurse, against the belief of many that the nurse is addressed in 820
and thus must return to stage with Medea at this point.

**214 Κορίνθιαι γυναῖκες:** this is more formal than simply to address the chorus as γυναῖκες or φίλαι, and it both shows (a calculated)
respect and prepares for Medea's careful deployment of her status
as a non-Corinthian. Compare Phaedra's formal address Τροζήνιαι
γυναῖκες (*Hipp.* 373) when she begins her great rhesis (SE 3a) to the
chorus, attempting to take control of her situation after rising from
her sick-bed.

**215–24**  Medea uses a heavy concentration of generalizations, at once displaying to the chorus her command of the dynamics of social life and deflecting many possible sources of distrust without directly ascribing them to the women present. She concedes that there are people who deserve reproach before she expands on one kind of un-deserved reproach (not the kind that applies in her case), and the unfairness of hasty judgment in such cases is preparatory foil for the duties of the proper *xenos* – the point at which she homes in specifi-cally on her own situation.

**216  σεμνούς:**  the use of σεμνός with negative connotations ('haughty, pompous', of human beings or their attributes) seems to be a reflection of the egalitarian ethos of Athenian democracy, as this sense emerges in Soph. *Ajax* 1107 (τὰ σέμν' ἔπη, Teucer to Mene-laus), Eur., and comedy (note esp. the play on positive vs negative sense in *Hipp.* 88–99).

**γεγῶτας:**  contracted form of γεγαώς (the epic perf. part. of γίγνομαι), a poetic alternative to prosaic γεγονώς. The participle sometimes is equivalent to πεφυκώς, to express an innate quality (Barrett on *Hipp.* 995), but may also, as here, bear the sense 'having shown oneself to be' or 'having proved to be' (so also 467, *Alc.* 860, *Hel.* 1030, etc.). With the following division of circumstances, this seems to make better sense than 'are by nature', 'are really'.

**ὀμμάτων ἄπο**  'out of sight', 'out of the public gaze', a sense that is more common with verbs of motion and with ἐξ (*Alc.* 1064, *IA* 743, etc.; but *Tro.* 1093 κομίζουσι ... σέθεν ἀπ' ὀμμάτων), but clear here from the contrast with ἐν θυραίοις, 'among people out in public'. Medea will not offend either by keeping herself inaccessible or by acting haughtily toward the women assembled before her.

**217  οἱ δ'**  'others' (besides those who are haughty).

**ἀφ' ἡσύχου ποδός**  'by behaving quietly', 'by lack of visible pub-lic activity'. For πούς in metaphorical phrases, compare Soph. *Phil.* 91 ἐξ ἑνὸς ποδός, 'acting all alone'; *Hipp.* 661 σὺν πατρὸς μολὼν ποδί, 'coming when my father arrives'. ἡσυχία and the related adjectives refer to values that were contested in fifth-century Greece. For aris-tocratic, oligarchic, and conservative states or persons, they refer to tranquillity, to peaceful acceptance of the hierarchical status quo, to non-interference with the traditional prerogatives of others. The opposite is πολυπραγμοσύνη, a dangerous meddling in the affairs and privileges of others. From the democratic viewpoint, however, πολλὰ πράττειν is no cause for shame, but rather ἡσυχία is scorned as lazy or hostile inactivity, the ἀπράγμων is disparaged for failure to participate in the communal functions of the democracy and the Athenian empire. See Collard on *Supp.* 324–5, Bond on *Her.* 266, Ehrenberg (1947), and Carter (1986).

**218  δύσκλειαν ... καὶ ῥαιθυμίαν** 'a bad reputation and ⟨a reputation for⟩ sloth' = 'a bad reputation for sloth', hendiadys (see Sansone (1984)).

**220  ὅστις:** a sing. indefinite relative sometimes follows an antecedent that is collective (as βροτῶν here): *Hec.* 360, *El.* 934, *Phaethon* 226; Smyth §2502c.

**σπλάγχνον** 'inmost organ/heart/soul', that is, one's true nature that may (in some cases) be concealed by surface appearances (or verbal camouflage). For the traditional anxiety about determining the real character or intentions of those one associates with, compare 516–19 and 659–61 below, *Hipp.* 925–31, the Attic skolion PMG 889 (quoted on 661), Theognis 87–96, 119–24, *Il.* 9.312–13 (see Leo (1912) 114–15).

**221  δεδορκώς:** perfect of the poetic verb δέρκομαι; this perfect is normally equivalent to a present, allowing it to be used as a variation of ὁράω, as in 1118 καὶ δὴ δέδορκα τόνδε . . | στείχοντ'. Note the emphasis lent by the rhetorical ring-structure in which δεδορκώς picks up ὀφθαλμοῖς and οὐδὲν ἠδικημένος expands δίκη ... οὐκ ἔνεστ'.

**222  ξένον μέν** is phrased as if ἀστὸν δέ ('a citizen should be pleasant to his fellow citizens') were to follow, but the shift in construction allows Medea to assert her own solidarity with the community's values.

**προσχωρεῖν πόλει** 'make himself agreeable to the city' by complying with its customs and demands; the verb connotes taking sides with someone in a dispute, following a lead and not asserting an independent stance. For recognition of the circumspection expected of metics or *xenoi*, compare *Supp.* 892–5 (esp. λυπηρὸς οὐκ ἦν οὐδ' ἐπίφθονος πόλει), Aesch. *Supp.* 195–203 (esp. μέμνησο δ' εἴκειν), Soph. *OC* 171–2 ἀστοῖς ἴσα χρὴ μελετᾶν, εἴκοντας ἃ δεῖ κἀκούοντας.

**223** ἤινεσ᾽:  probably to be classed as a 'dramatic' aorist (LS 13), as in *Her.* 222 οὐδ᾽ Ἑλλάδ᾽ ἤινεσ᾽; Lloyd (1999) 41 explains this instance as polite and tentative and that in *Her.* as moderating, but both seem quite emphatic – the speaker turns with emphasis to a new point and speaks *as though* the sense of disapproval has just come over her or him (Stevens on *Andr.* 785 offers a somewhat different analysis). Without a negative, the 'dramatic' aor. ἤινεσα is often used by Eur. in stichomythia (*Ion* 1614, *IT* 1023, etc.).

**224** ἀμαθίας ὕπο:  for anastrophe and the sense of the prep., see 34n. ἀμαθία often combines simple ignorance with morally culpable neglect of norms accepted by better people (see Denniston on *El.* 294–6). So here the citizen who is by nature self-willed earns reproach because he is not sensitive enough to adjust to the demands of social interaction in an egalitarian society.

**225** ἐμοὶ δ᾽:  Medea finally turns to her own case: having distinguished herself from various types who attract the resentment of their neighbours, she now explains how she has found herself in a position to attract so much attention and concern.

ἄελπτον is perhaps better taken as predicative than as attributive: 'this situation, having befallen me unexpectedly' (similar construction in fr. 964.6 νεῶρες προσπεσόν, 'having befallen as something fresh and unanticipated').

**226** οἴχομαι:  as with βέβηκα (439n.), this verb develops from Homeric usage into tragic style so that it can be used absolutely to mean 'be dead' or 'be as good as dead', 'be undone'; compare the more explicit idiom οἴχεται/οἴχομαι θανών, as in *Tro.* 395, Soph. *Phil.* 414, etc.

**228** ἐν ὧι:  the relative clause is 'prepended', as often in Greek, the antecedent being 'my husband' in 229; translate 'the one in whom all my hopes rested' or 'the one on whom I totally depended'.

γιγνώσκω καλῶς:  like parenthetic σάφ᾽ οἶδα, this phrase emphasizes the preceding words (so at 935 below and *Hcld.* 982). γιγνώσκω is Canter's emendation of γιγνώσκειν, which yields no suitable sense and was already recognized as defective in ancient times (whether or not the ancient commentators were right to ascribe

the fault to actors). One might have expected the emphasis on realization to go with 'has turned out to be the worst of men'; but Medea
is presenting herself as fully aware of the importance of the man in
marriage, in agreement with the nurse's comment in 13–15 and in
preparation for her own in 241–7. Page preferred the smaller change
γιγνώσκει (subject Jason; Medea asserts that he is not acting in
ignorance), but the parenthesis is then less idiomatic and gives too
much prominence to an *ad hominem* point in a context in which Medea concentrates on self-presentation and generalization to the fate
of all women.

**229 ἐκβέβηχ' οὑμός:** that is, ἐκβέβηκε ὁ ἐμός (elision and crasis).
For ἐκβαίνω = 'turn out' with a predicate adj., cf. 592, *Phoen.* 1479.

**230–51** This section of the speech provides a general demonstration of the unfair inferior status of women. For Medea's purpose it
is rhetorically effective in appealing to the ordinary women of the
chorus, proving her emotional and intellectual solidarity with them
(note the first-person pl. forms in 231, 241, 247–9), even though some
of the details do not apply to her own case. Yet this exposition en-
courages a listener (not just the chorus) to classify Jason's mistreatment of Medea as a further instance of an unfair social structure,
and for the audience it also shows Medea to be an acute observer
with independent judgment.

**230–1** For the generalization compare *Il.* 17.446–7 (Zeus speaking):
'there is certainly nothing more wretched than a man, of all things
that breathe and move upon the earth'. Medea challenges traditional
wisdom by claiming the superlative state of wretchedness for women
in particular; compare the challenge in 248–51 below.

**230 γνώμην ἔχει** 'have an intellectual faculty' is a crucial addition, since women are not dumb beasts (who are also ἔμψυχα) but are
fully aware of their mistreatment.

**231 φυτόν:** the sense 'creature' is rare and normally disparaging
or contemptuous, as in *Hipp.* 630 ἀτηρὸν ... φυτόν (of a bride taken
into one's home), Alexis fr. 145.1 K–A εἶτ' οὐ περίεργόν ἐστιν ἄνθρωπος φυτόν ...; , [Men.] *Sent.* 304 (women an evil), Theodectas *TrGF*
72 F 1a (imitation of this passage).

**232 χρημάτων ὑπερβολῆι:** in the heroic world, a bride's family is won over or compensated by gifts from the successful suitor (ἕεδνα), but it is a normal 'anachronism' of tragedy to view the heroic world through the lens of the contemporary custom of dowry (property from her family that accompanies the bride into the marriage) – although there are also signs of dowry in Homer. From the opposite point of view, Hippolytus refers to this custom as a proof of the worthlessness of women (*Hipp.* 627–9). For a general discussion of aspects of anachronism in Greek tragedy, see Easterling (1985).

**233 πρίασθαι:** aor. inf. of the defective verb ἐπριάμην (listed under *πρίαμαι in LSJ), 'buy'. Compare, in another woman's complaint about the harshness of the experience of marriage, Soph. fr. 583.7 ὠθούμεθ᾽ ἔξω καὶ διεμπολώμεθα.

**234** 'For ⟨I add the notion of getting a master of our bodies because⟩ this is a second evil even more painful than the first (paying to get a husband).' The γάρ-clause here gives the reason for uttering the previous phrase; the same use is seen in 465, 663, and 1370: Denniston 60.

**235–6 κἀν τῶιδ᾽:** καὶ ἐν (crasis) 'and in this act', that is, acquiring a husband.

ἀγὼν μέγιστος 'the stakes of the contest are of supreme importance'; for this and related phrases see Mastronarde on *Phoen.* 860. As elsewhere, ἀγών is defined by the inf. in apposition (here, with 'either … or', equivalent to an indirect question).

κακὸν ..|. χρηστόν: πόσιν is understood.

**236 οὐ ... εὐκλεεῖς ἀπαλλαγαί:** a woman caught in adultery could be sent back to her father's house by the wronged husband. A wife could also choose to return to her father's house because of objectionable behaviour of her husband, or in unusual circumstances a father might apply pressure for her to do so (as in Menander's *Epitrepontes* and the comic fragment of the Didot Papyrus, adesp. fr. 1000 K–A, also printed on pp. 328–30 of Sandbach's OCT of Menander). But the divorcing wife might not be welcomed by her old family (for economic or social/political reasons) and would be subject to defaming rumour abetted by the sexual double standard prevalent in

Greek as in other societies. Anaxandrides fr. 57 K–A are the words of a father telling his daughter that the path back to a father's house is very difficult, 'for the return-leg ⟨from husband to father⟩ is one that carries shame'. On divorce, see Harrison (1968) 38–45, Garland (1990) 236–7, Cohn-Haft (1995).

**237**  οἶόν τ': for οἶόν τε (ἐστι) = 'it is possible' see LSJ s.v. οἶος III.2 (τε in this idiom is a survival into ordinary Attic of 'epic τε': Denniston 520–8).

ἀνήνασθαι πόσιν: the sense is probably 'refuse a husband', that is, refuse him his 'marital rights' to sexual intercourse, which makes a separate point following up on δεσπότην σώματος. The notion that a husband has rights to intercourse regardless of his wife's wishes is prevalent in many cultures, ancient and modern, and the legal concept of 'spousal rape' was established with difficulty only in the recent past. This interpretation best fits the aorist aspect (usually 'say no to a specific request or order addressed to one'), and the meaning is paralleled in later Greek: Philip, *Anth. Gr.* 9.307.1 Φοῖβον ἀνηναμένη Δάφνη; Oppian, *Cyneg.* 3.375 ἀνηναμένη φεύγηι φιλοτήσιον εὐνήν (cf. 3.525); epigram in the *vita Homeri Herodotea*, 417–18 Allen, δὸς δὲ γυναῖκα | τήνδε νέων μὲν ἀνήνασθαι φιλότητα καὶ εὐνήν; Harpocration s.v. ἀναίνεσθαι· κοινῶς μὲν τὸ ἀρνεῖσθαι, ἰδίως δὲ ἐπὶ τῶν κατὰ τοὺς γάμους καὶ τὰ ἀφροδίσια λέγεται; compare the present ('continuously shun') in *Hipp.* 14 ἀναίνεται δὲ λέκτρα κού ψαύει γάμων. Kovacs translates 'refuse wedlock' in the sense 'not marry in the first place', but Medea does not seem even to contemplate that possibility here, and one would perhaps expect 'marriage' or 'suitor' as object rather than 'husband'. Wecklein understands the phrase as referring to divorce, in a restatement of the previous clause.

**239**  μὴ μαθοῦσαν οἴκοθεν  'without having learned ⟨the necessary skills⟩ at home' (μή with the factual participle because it depends on an inf. phrase: Smyth §§2728, 2737). For the strong contrast between the carefree (ignorant) life of the unmarried girl in her father's home and her new life in marriage, compare Soph. *Trach.* 141–52, Soph. fr. 583 = *Tereus* ii *TGFS*. Greek girls sometimes married shortly after menarche: see Garland (1990) 26. For the desirability to some Greek men of an unformed, inexperienced girl as bride, see Xenophon, *Oeconomicus*, ch. 7.

**240** οἵωι μάλιστα χρήσεται ξυνευνέτηι 'with what manner of man in particular [sc. of all the possible types] she will have to deal as a husband'. The bride must figure out for herself the best way to live with the stranger who is now her husband. χρήσεται is here 'deal with, cope with'. The transmitted text ὅτωι μάλιστα is unacceptable; Musgrave proposed οἵωι, and Meineke ὅπως, and in either case μάλιστα will have to have the sense 'precisely, in particular' that it sometimes has (esp. in dialogue) with relative, demonstrative, or interrogative (Soph. *OT* 1005, *OC* 652, 901, *Ichneutae* 257; Ar. *Birds* 1072, *Wealth* 966), and the adverb seems to follow up on the bewilderment implied in δεῖ μάντιν εἶναι. A more obvious expression with ὅπως would be ὅπως ἄριστα (Barthold), adopted by Kovacs; but Medea is perhaps referring to the initial stage of adjustment of married life, not to the long haul of living with a husband.

**241** κἄν = καὶ ἄν (ἐάν). In the balancing condition in 243, where the verb is omitted, it is normal to have εἰ δὲ μή instead of ἐὰν δὲ μή (Smyth §2346d; Goodwin §478).

ἐκπονουμέναισιν: the middle of this verb is rare; here it implies that women must work hard at these tasks 'for their own good'.

**242** μὴ βίαι 'without compulsion (being applied to him)', that is, tamely and voluntarily; βίαι can express either the cause that compels one to do something (here, 335, *Alc.* 829, etc.) or the violent manner in which one does something (*Alc.* 69, *Hcld.* 234, etc.).

**244** τοῖς ἔνδον: τοῖς is masc. for common personal gender, pl. for generalization, though 'the people in the house' refers primarily to the wife.

**245** ἔπαυσε καρδίαν ἄσης: Eur. probably expected his audience to hear the medical connotations of the last word, which is extremely rare in literature: 'nausea' often in the Hippocratic corpus, ἄση περὶ τὴν καρδίαν in *Epid.* 7.10. See Page (1955) 6. ἄσης is gen. of separation with ἔπαυσε, and the verb is an instance of gnomic aorist (LS 15).

**[246]** The transmitted reading ἥλικα τραπείς involves metrical lengthening of final vowel (short alpha) before mute and liquid (τρ) in a separate word, a phenomenon that scholars agree is impossible in the spoken verse of tragedy and that is extremely rare in tragic lyric (some editors emend all of the few lyric examples). This fault could be repaired by Porson's ἥλικας (now found in a late MS of no great authority), but the rhetorical contrast of τοῖς ἔνδον in 244 and ἔξω μολών in 245 does not require this elaboration. Wilamowitz thought that ἔξω μολών meant 'go out to have sex with a prostitute or courtesan' and that 246 was added by a schoolmaster to eliminate such indelicacy; but Medea's language is deliberately vague.

**247 πρὸς μίαν ψυχὴν βλέπειν:** ψυχή suggests not just 'one person' but also 'one fixed personality'. For βλέπω πρός with the connotation 'depend on' see *Her.* 81; more common in this sense is βλέπω εἰς, *IT* 1056, Soph. *Ajax* 514, *Ant.* 923.

**248–51 λέγουσι δ' ἡμᾶς:** a mild form of hypophora, the posing of a counter argument that might be expected from an opponent, followed by its rebuttal. For the modern reader of Attic tragedy (and probably for the ancient audience as well, depending on how often and how early Aeschylus' *Oresteia* was reperformed), the intertextual allusion of this passage is to that famous trilogy, where the contrast between 'stay-at-home' women (and womanized Aegisthus: *Ag.* 1625–7) and warriors toiling abroad is repeatedly developed: see in particular *Cho.* 919 μὴ ἔλεγχε τὸν πονοῦντ' ἔσω καθημένη, 921 τρέφει δέ γ' ἀνδρὸς μόχθος ἡμένας ἔσω. The traditional misogynistic view associates men with the toil and risk of war, athletics, politics, and agriculture and belittles women as idle consumers sitting safe at home. Medea cleverly focuses the contrast on a parallelism promoted by public ideology: serving as a soldier is the fulfilment of a man's life in the polis, and bearing a child is the fulfilment of a woman's, and death in childbirth was creditable just as death in battle was (Garland (1990) 65–6).

**248 ἡμᾶς:** proleptic object (37n.).

**ἀκίνδυνον:** Medea's rebuttal probably refers quite broadly to the pain and toil of childbirth and not exclusively to the risk of death in childbirth, though this risk was substantial (Garland (1990) 65; Demand (1994) 71–86).

**250 κακῶς φρονοῦντες:** κακῶς φρονεῖν (and its opposite εὖ φρονεῖν) can apply either to intellectual quality, 'have bad (good) sense', 'think imprudently (wisely)', or to disposition (with dat. or εἰς), 'be ill(well)-disposed toward'. The former is the sense here and in 1014 and (e.g.) *Alc.* 303; for the latter, see 464, 823, 892.

**ὡς** 'for, because'.

**250–1 τρὶς ἄν . . | . θέλοιμ᾽ ἄν:** the two separate tendencies for the modal particle to gravitate, as a postpositive, to an early position in the sentence (here after the emphatically placed adverb) and to attach itself closely to the verb form it modifies often lead to a redundant repetition of ἄν in a sentence (Barrett on *Hipp.* 270): see also 616.

**παρ᾽ ἀσπίδα στῆναι** 'stand in the line of battle', a locution based on the close formation of Greek hoplites, who form a continuous barrier with shield side by side with shield; in the ephebic oath one swore οὐδὲ λείψω τὸν παραστάτην (see Mastronarde on *Phoen.* 1073–4).

**252 ἀλλ᾽ οὐ γάρ:** this combination of particles probably arose from an ellipsis and often has the effect of dismissing a previous topic and moving on to a more decisive point (Denniston 100–3; LS 27; 1301n.): 'but what I have just discussed is beside the point, for'. Medea devotes 252–8 to the special liabilities of her isolation as a foreigner: divorce may be difficult for a normal woman, but within her own community such a woman will still have some social connections that could provide refuge or leverage.

**αὐτὸς . . . κἄμ᾽:** crasis, ὁ αὐτός and καὶ ἔμ᾽ (ἐμέ).

**254 βίου τ᾽ ὄνησις:** recalls Medea's opposite condition, 226–7 βίου χάριν μεθεῖσα.

**255 ἔρημος ἄπολις:** the asyndeton expresses vehemence or pathos (LS 28), although this instance is a little unusual: more typical is a triplet like *Hec.* 811 ἄπολις ἔρημος ἀθλιωτάτη βροτῶν or an alpha-privative pair like *Hipp.* [1029] ἄπολις ἄοικος. Medea uses ἔρημος of herself repeatedly (also 513, 604, 712). ἔρημος varies between two-ending and three-ending declension (LS 5.d) even in prose.

**ὑβρίζομαι:** the passive of this verb suggests a violation of status, being treated as insignificant by someone who overestimates his strength or the privileges of his status; thus it reflects Medea's sense of being denied the honour due her (20n.) and her sensitivity to the superior attitude of her enemies (383n.). At 603 Medea tells Jason ὕβριζ, 'go ahead and enjoy your advantage' or 'insult me with impunity', and at 1366 she insists that Jason's ὕβρις led to the death of their sons. The need to prevent her enemies from killing her sons (1061 καθυβρίσαι) or defiling their grave (1380 καθυβρίσηι) is closely related to Medea's insistence that her enemies not be able to laugh at her (383n.). On *hybris* in general see Fisher (1992).

**257** The line features a rising tricolon structure (LS 32), with anaphora of οὐ (Fehling (1969) 210).

**258** μεθορμίσασθαι τῆσδ'... συμφορᾶς: epexegetic inf. and separative gen., 'having no mother, no brother, no kinsman, to whom I could shift my anchorage, away from this misfortune'; this phrase is echoed by the chorus in 441–3. On storm- and sea-imagery see Introd. 2(*f*).

**259** τοσοῦτον οὖν: the logical connection implied is 'since our situations are different and I must act on my own (as you would not have to)', but there may be a subtle suggestion of 'since I am so alone, I deserve some help from you'. As often, τοσοῦτον means 'just this much and no more', 'just this little thing'.

βουλήσομαι: the future makes the request more contingent (as if expression of the desire depends on the listeners' permission) and thus more gracious than the present (Lloyd (1999) 34): compare Soph. *OC* 1289–90 καὶ ταῦτ' ἀφ' ὑμῶν, ὦ ξένοι, βουλήσομαι | καὶ ταῖνδ' ἀδελφαῖν καὶ πατρὸς κυρεῖν ἐμοί, Antiphon *de chor.* 8 ἔπειτα περὶ τῶν ἄλλων ὧν οὗτοι κατηγοροῦσιν, ἐὰν ὑμῖν ἡδομένοις, βουλήσομαι ἀπολογήσασθαι). For a somewhat different use of this future see 726n.

**261** πόσιν δίκην ... ἀντιτείσασθαι 'exact a penalty for these wrongs from my husband'; double acc., external object of the person and internal object of the penalty (various other constructions are also possible with τίνω/τίνομαι).

**[262]** Although Medea has been heard by the chorus cursing the princess as well as Jason (and her anger against the royal family is publicly known, as Creon soon declares), her argument in the speech has concentrated on the imbalance between husbands and wives and the particular offences of her husband Jason. Thus, the most logical (and manipulative) conclusion to her persuasion would be to mention vengeance against Jason alone. Since the transmitted text is also un-idiomatic (see below), it is best to regard this line as an interpolation, of the same officious nature as that in 38–42, anticipating the content of 288 τὸν δόντα καὶ γήμαντα καὶ γαμουμένην. On the other hand, one should not ascribe much weight to the realistic concern that the chorus might not go along with vengeance against their own king, as they make no objection to this subsequently and attempt dissuasion of Medea only in regard to the plan to kill the children.

**ἥν τ᾽ ἐγήματο** would have to be 'and the woman that he (my hus-band) married', but this is contrary to Greek idiom (a man 'takes a wife' (γαμεῖ), the woman 'gives herself in marriage to' (γαμεῖται)); it is not likely that the meaning should be 'and the woman that he (Creon) gave in marriage', since this is unparalleled (γαμέσσεται is not likely to be correct in *Il.* 9.394, but even it would refer to the groom's father picking a bride for his son). Porson's ἥ τ᾽ ἐγήματο, 'and the woman who married (Jason)', corrects the idiom; but it is better to delete the line.

**263 σιγᾶν:** since Greek tragedy by convention takes place out-doors and since the chorus is normally present continuously from its entrance to the end of the play, it is often a dramatic necessity for the actors to request the silence of the chorus (see Barrett on *Hipp.* 710–12 for a survey of examples). At times the chorus' complicity is well motivated by the development of a strong rapport between a char-acter and the chorus (as in *Hipp.* or *IT* or Aesch. *Cho.*), at other times the agreement is treated in a more perfunctory way (*IA*). While ini-tially the silence of the Corinthian women is well justified by their sympathy for Medea and by her persuasive appeal, there is some strain, if we judge in naturalistic and psychological terms, when the silence continues after the scope of Medea's revenge becomes wider (unlike the chorus in *Hipp.*, they are not under oath). The tragic chorus is not, however, solely or consistently a 'character' within the dramatic world with full psychological motivation (Mastronarde (1998) and (1999)), and the other functions of the chorus were im-portant enough to outweigh for the tragedians and their audience any pull toward complete naturalism.

**γυνὴ γάρ κτλ.:** Medea's concluding generalization, offered as a justification for expecting the chorus' accession to her request for complicit silence, raises the problem of misogynistic statements put in the mouths of female characters in tragedy. Are they due to un-reflective insertion of the dominant group's stereotype (or widely accepted 'gnomic wisdom') into the represented female, are they an imitation of real women who have accepted the status quo and speak out to preserve it, or are they spoken with awareness of the incongruity, on the part of either the audience or the speaker? A further possibility here is that in her effort to establish and maintain her heroic status Medea may be envisioning 'all that is female as despicable' (Foley (2001) 264–5). Another complication here is that Medea is striving to evoke and strengthen solidarity between herself and the chorus, and so rhetorically tailors the maxim to her audience, over-simplifying her own situation: she is different, she has already acted bravely and murderously before being wronged by Jason, and the wrong she complains of may be viewed as more than sexual in nature (Introd. 2(b)).

**τἄλλα μέν** 'in ⟨all⟩ other matters'; acc. of respect (crasis, τὰ ἄλλα).

**πλέα:** fem. of Attic πλέως, 'full of'.

**264 κακή τ' ἐς ἀλκὴν καὶ σίδηρον εἰσορᾶν:** probably 'cowardly in regard to battle and unable to look upon weaponry of iron' (that is ἐς ἀλκήν and σίδηρον εἰσορᾶν are separate complements of κακή) rather than 'bad at looking upon battle and cold steel', since εἰσορᾶν almost never takes a preposition (never in tragedy). For εἰσορᾶν in the sense 'look upon steadily, without fear, without flinching' see Aesch. *Pers.* 111 ἐσορᾶν πόντιον ἄλσος, and compare the use of ὁρῶν in Tyrtaeus 12.11 and βλέπει τε κἀντιδέρκεται in *Her.* 163.

**265 ἠδικημένη κυρῆι:** κυρέω is a poetic verb, synonymous with τυγχάνω in its various senses and constructions. The periphrasis is more emphatic than simple ἀδικῆται: 'when she has in fact been wronged' or 'when she finds herself to have been wronged'.

**267 ἐνδίκως:** the chorus had already accepted the injustice of Jason's position in 157 and 208. Now they indicate their approval of 'bloody murder' in retaliation, for Medea's appeal has ended with the striking and emphatic μιαιφονωτέρα.

**268** πενθεῖν δ' οὔ σε θαυμάζω τύχας: indirect discourse acc. and inf. after θαυμάζω is a rare, poetic construction (K–G 11.73–4); compare *Alc.* 1130 ἀπιστεῖν δ' οὔ σε θαυμάζω τύχῃ.

**269** *Action*: Creon enters from city-side, recognizable at least by the splendour of his costume (the actor could also carry a sceptre, and there might be a crown on the white hair of the wig attached to the mask) and by his being attended by silent extras (Introd. 3). We cannot be sure how many attendants are present: the minimum is probably two, but a king coming to enforce a decree might make a larger show of force. See Stanley-Porter (1973).

καί marks the sight of Creon as a new point to attend to, but is barely translatable into English ('but, look here, I see Creon' is a bit too strong).

**270** καινῶν ἄγγελον βουλευμάτων: the audience already knows why Creon has come, having heard the tutor's report in 67–73; the chorus-leader correctly infers from Creon's official appearance with attendants that he has come to announce some decision.

**271** σὲ τὴν σκυθρωπόν: 'a peremptory and belligerent mode of address, in sharp contrast to the customary civilities of tragic dialogue' (Griffith on *Prom.* 944–6, with further exx.; see also Barrett on *Hipp.* 1283–4). The acc. phrase is governed by ἀνεῖπον.

σκυθρωπόν 'grim-faced' or 'sullen'; Medea's unchanging mask is presumably of sad and wasted appearance, but a good actor can also intensify an appearance of hostility by posture and subtle tilting of the head.

**272** Μήδει', ἀνεῖπον: this is a redivision of what the MSS present as Μήδειαν εἶπον; such division has no ultimate authority because the texts were without division between words for over a millennium and without lectional signs for about two centuries (in any given case, in fact, the breathings and accents may have been absent until the ninth century CE). The vocative is idiomatically necessary after σὲ τὴν κτλ. and ἀνεῖπον (pres. ἀναγορεύω) is the precise term for proclamation of an order. ἀνεῖπον is here a performative 'dramatic' aor. (LS 13): if Lloyd (1999) is right about the relative politeness of such aors., then Creon shows a 'combination of superficial brusqueness with polite diffidence'.

**274–5** βραβεὺς λόγου | τοῦδ' 'enforcer of this order'; the noun may have referred originally to the umpire of an athletic contest, but in tragedy and fourth-century prose extended uses are found for this noun and derived words.

**278** ἐξιᾶσι πάντα δὴ κάλων: κάλως is a brail (the noun is to be distinguished from adjective καλός, 'beautiful', by its accentuation). Brails 'were a series of lines made fast at fixed intervals along the foot [bottom of the sail], whence they traveled up the front surface of the sail guided by fairleads [loops or rings], over the yard, and then down to the deck aft. Sails could be taken in quickly and efficiently merely by hauling on the brails, which bunched the sail toward the yard much in the manner of a venetian blind' (Casson (1971) 70; also 229–31 and figs. 89–91, 144). To let out every brailing-rope is to expose the entire sail to the wind, to push for maximum speed, and thus metaphorically to make the fullest effort (also Ar. *Knights* 756 νῦν δή σε πάντα δεῖ κάλων ἐξιέναι σεαυτοῦ; further exx. in Page). See 524n.

**279** εὐπρόσοιστος ἔκβασις maintains the nautical imagery, since ἐκβαίνειν is often 'disembark' and ἔκβασις 'landing-place', and εὐ-πρόσοιστος, 'easily accessible', may call to mind, among the many meanings of προσφέρειν and προσφέρεσθαι, 'put into harbour' (Xen. *Cyr.* 5.4.6). There may possibly be a suggestion, in view of ἄτης, of 'easily applied', from προσφέρειν 'to apply a remedy'. The adj. is extant only here, but ἀπρόσοιστος in Aesch. *Pers.* 91 and δυσ-πρόσοιστος in Soph. *OC* 1277 are also unique.

**280** καὶ κακῶς πάσχουσ' ὅμως: ὅμως, 'nevertheless', will be at-tached in English translation to the main verb, but in Greek phrasing is sometimes placed with the participle phrase, as here: see LSJ s.v. II.2, Smyth §2082.

**281** ἕκατι: not a native Attic word, absent from prose; tragedians and Aristophanes use the form with long alpha from the lyric tradi-tion (LS 3), not the epic form ἕκητι.

**282** παραμπίσχειν λόγους 'deceptively (παρ-) cloak my meaning'. For the connotation 'aside (for the true path), astray, amiss' of παρά in compounds, compare, e.g., παράγω, παρακούω, παρακόπτω.

**284** συμβάλλεται δὲ πολλὰ τοῦδε δείγματα   'many points of evidence for this fear come together'. (LSJ's definition of δεῖγμα is misleading; the primary sense should be 'proof, evidence, demonstration', with 'example' as a secondary sense.) The MSS have τοῦδε δείματος, which some have wanted to interpret as 'many things contribute to this fear of mine', which makes fine sense in the context; but it is not at all likely that Eur. would have chosen to use such an odd construction when the idiomatic πολλὰ τῶιδε δείματι is metrically identical. Schöne emended to τῶιδε δείματι, but Wieseler's emendation more convincingly explains how the corrupt reading arose (assimilation of case and psychological error from δέδοικα).

**285** κακῶν   'means of harm', 'harmful devices', alluding rather vaguely to her magic powers, which Eur. downplays to the extent possible (Introd. 2(c)).

**286** ἐστερημένη:   perf. part. of στερέω, 'deprived'.

**287** κλύω ... ἀπαγγέλλουσί μοι:   this refers to events before the play began, but fits fairly closely with the audience's own knowledge, even if the allusions to harming Creon in 42 and 262 are inauthentic (37–45n., 262n.): see 44–5 and esp. 163–4 (against Jason and the princess, 'house and all').

**288** γήμαντα καὶ γαμουμένην:   for the usage of active and middle, see 262n.

**290** ἀπεχθέσθαι:   aor. mid. inf. of ἀπεχθάνομαι, 'incur enmity'.

**291** μαλθακισθένθ':   doing harm to others was viewed as legitimate when it was in response to the prior harm done by them (165n.), but the Greeks were more ambivalent about the morality of the 'preemptive strike' (289 πρὶν παθεῖν φυλάξομαι), and so Creon tries to buttress his position in his own eyes by putting his action in terms of manliness vs cowardice. This attempt may form a pattern with the pugnacity of his opening address to Medea (which, to Page, 'reveals his inward disquietude') and the self-deception of his parting speech (355–6n.).

ὕστερον μεταστένειν   'afterwards groan in regret' (μετα- implying changed attitude), not simply 'groan afterwards' with redundant μετα-, although redundancy can be idiomatic (Diggle (1994) 210–11, referring to Renehan (1976) 61–2). In the variant μέγα στένειν, μέγα would follow up on 283 ἀνήκεστον κακόν.

**292a  φεῦ φεῦ:** an *extra metrum* exclamation (91a n.).

**292  οὐ νῦν με πρῶτον:** Medea cleverly refrains from a direct attack on Creon's reasoning and instead adopts a tone of more general regret and works slowly toward reassurance and false flattery before asking that the decree of exile be rescinded.

**293  μεγάλα τ' εἴργασται κακά:** the verb is middle in sense, with δόξα as subject and με and κακά as the two objects, ἐργάζομαι being used in the same way as ποιέω or δράω.

**294  χρὴ δ' οὔποθ':** even though the negative logically belongs with the inf. ἐκδιδάσκεσθαι, the negative with χρή is often οὐ instead of μή because of conflation with constructions where the negative truly belongs to χρή (Smyth §2714).

**295  παῖδας ... ἐκδιδάσκεσθαι σοφούς** 'have his sons taught to be exceptionally clever' (σοφούς predicate adj.). For use of the middle voice of a verb such as διδάσκω and παιδεύω in a causative sense, see Smyth §1725; K–G i.108.

**296  χωρὶς ... ἄλλης ἧς ἔχουσιν ἀργίας** 'apart from the other disadvantage, namely, idleness', not 'apart from other idleness' in the sense that φθόνος is a type of idleness. This is an idiomatic appositional use of ἄλλος, here reinforcing χωρίς (cf. 444n.). ἧς is gen. by attraction (from ἥν): Smyth §2522. The association of idleness with intellectual pursuits is clear in Aristophanes' treatment of intellectuals in his comedies, and the same theme was developed in the debate between Zethos and Amphion in Eur.'s late play *Antiope* (see frr. 187–8 N = i–ii *TGFS*). The beginnings of this attitude may go back to an earlier period, but it would have been intensified greatly in the Athenian context both by egalitarian ideology and by the official attitude toward service to the polis. See Carter (1986) chs. 6–7, esp. 146–7.

**297  ἀλφάνουσι** 'earn, bring in'; the aor. of this verb is found in literary texts exclusively in Homer (four times) until late Greek, and the present is extant in very few places (in Eur. also fr. 326); two comic uses (Ar. fr. 339 K–A, Eupolis fr. 273 K–A) refer to auctions and *IG* i³ 84.15 has ὁπόσην ἂν ἄλφηι μίσθωσιν τὸ τέμενος, so ἀλφάνω was not poetic, but perhaps rather a term of commercial language (an archaic survival?) that Eur. (alone?) admitted into tragic trimeters.

**298–301** The dual charges that were said in 296–7 to come generally 'from one's fellow-citizens' are now analysed in terms of separate subgroups, the uneducated and the clever. For the second-person verbs see 190–1n.

**299** κοὐ: crasis, καὶ οὐ.

**300** δ' αὖ is a somewhat stronger complement to μέν than plain δέ, although at times it is used instead of δέ simply for metrical convenience.

**301** κρείσσων νομισθεὶς ἐν πόλει λυπρὸς φανῆι 'if you are considered in the city (or, by the citizens) superior to those who seem to have some special knowledge, you will seem annoying ⟨to them⟩'; the dative of reference needed to balance σκαιοῖσι (δόξεις) is to be supplied from τῶν ... δοκούντων.

**302** καὐτή: crasis, καὶ αὐτή.

**303–15** In this section, when Medea argues 'I am not so wise and I am not a danger', her sentences and clauses become much shorter and often feature strong punctuation in mid-line and enjambment. After the composition by well-rounded couplets in 292–301, this gives a semblance of simplicity and artlessness.

**303 + 305** have the rhetorical structure called κύκλος, starting and ending with the same word. This structure reinforces Medea's argument, as she admits to being σοφή but suggests that the major problem with this quality arises from unfair judgments by the outside world, not from an inherent danger, and then concludes that she is 'not really so very clever'. The μέν-δέ contrast in the heart of this period resumes the contrast made in 298–302, in chiastic order: 'to the one group (the other clever people) I am an object of envy, to the rest (the uneducated masses) I am irksome'. Since it is clear that ἐπί-φθονος must apply to the clever rivals, a listener has no trouble interpreting προσάντης as a vaguer term describing the average citizen's disapproval of the idleness and uselessness of the intellectual.

**[304]**   This line (very similar to 808) could have been added by someone who wanted a more explicit resumption of ἀργία and ἀχρεῖος than προσάντης gives. τοῖς δ' ἡσυχαία gives that explicitness, but the second half of the line makes no sense in this context and τοῖς δ' αὖ προσάντης is deprived of its point.

**305   προσάντης:**   not 'hostile' (as LSJ) or 'adverse' in an active sense, but rather in a passive sense, 'irksome', like the senses 'in the way', 'serving as a hindrance', 'objectionable' seen in 381, *IT* 1012, *Or.* 790.

**306   σὺ δ' οὖν:**   the particles indicate that Medea is breaking off from the generalizing section and concentrating on Creon as the one whose opinion is essential: Denniston 462.

**307   οὐχ ὧδ' ἔχει μοι:**   ambiguous, since it could mean 'I am not in a condition to do wrong against a king' (admitting weakness, but not denying the desire to do wrong), or 'the situation is not such in my judgment that I would do wrong against a king' (implying that Creon is not to blame and she has no desire to hurt him). The latter is the sense Medea intends Creon to understand, as 309–11 explain. She does not go so far as to deny that she has been wronged or that she hates Jason, but tries to distinguish Creon from Jason and to show that she has finally learned her lesson.

**308   τυράννους ἄνδρας:**   generalizing poetic pl. (LS 33).

**309   σὺ γὰρ τί:**   most of the MSS have τί γὰρ σύ, which is a typical error of transmission – substitution of the simpler word order for the expressive fronting of the pronoun and postponement of the interrogative (LS 35).
   **ἐξέδου:**   second sing. aor. mid. ind. of ἐκδίδωμι; the active of this verb is commoner in the sense 'give in marriage', but the mid. is not only metrically convenient here, it also suits Medea's rhetoric 'you gave out *your own* daughter *in your own interest*'.

**313   νυμφεύετ':**   after σόν in 312, the plural is vague, 'you and yours'; and 'have your marriage' may be literal (Medea giving her

consent to what has already taken place) or used in an extended sense
('keep on enjoying and celebrating the newly consecrated tie').

**314–15** ἠδικημένοι | ... νικώμενοι: in tragedy, when a female
uses a first-person pl. verb as equivalent to sing., any nom. modifiers
may be either in the generalizing masc. pl. or in the fem. sing.:
Smyth §1009.

**315** σιγησόμεσθα, κρεισσόνων νικώμενοι: with this weighty concluding line consisting of only three long words, Medea seems to
agree to abandon the loud complaints and threats that have worried
her friends and alarmed her enemies, and 'being subdued by those
who are more powerful' seems to acknowledge defeat and accept the
conventional hierarchical relationship in which women are inferior
to men (Introd. 2(c)).

**316** ἀκοῦσαι μαλθάκ' 'words that are mild (or soothing) to hear'
(epexegetic inf.), but perhaps an undertone of 'cowardly, unag-
gressive, non-belligerent' is present and the word contributes to the
pattern of language highlighting Medea's appropriation of male
prerogatives.

ἔσω φρενῶν 'within your heart'; that is, the phrase is part of
the μή-clause, moved forward in the sentence for greater force;
this interpretation gives a sharper antithesis and one more relevant to
the ethical concerns of the play. Others interpret as 'within my
heart', but the antithesis 'your words soothe my ears, but in my heart
I am very afraid' (cf. Soph. *Ant.* 317–19) is weaker and somewhat
frigid.

**317** ὀρρωδία: Eur. is the only poet who uses this rare term for extreme fear (see Mastronarde on *Phoen.* 1388–9).

βουλεύῃς 'may be currently planning', pres. subj., with present-
stem aspect (Elmsley's emendation). Transmitted aor. subj. βου-
λεύσῃς would be 'may form a plan'. The pres. is clearly more apposite since Creon suspects Medea is concealing evil intentions behind
soothing words.

**319** ὡς δ' αὔτως ἀνήρ: after Homer ὥς and αὔτως coalesced into
one word, ὡσαύτως, but the form divided by δέ continued as an alternative choice in a minority of instances in poetry and prose. Eur.

has the divided form at *Andr.* 673 (the same half line as here), but ὡσαύτως at *IT* 833.

**320 ἢ σιωπηλὸς σοφός** 'than a clever person who keeps silent (about his or her angry intentions)'; under the influence of the parenthetic addition 'and likewise a man (who is quick to visible anger)', the comparandum is generalized or attracted to the masc. Diggle emends to σιωπηλὸς σοφή (with the rare adj. treated as of two terminations: LS 5.d), which maintains agreement with γυνή, Creon's major focus, and would very easily have been corrupted to σοφός. This may be right.

**321 μὴ λόγους λέγε:** 'do not keep on speaking futile words', with a deprecatory sense of λόγοι (see Diggle on *Phaethon* 59, Bond on *Her.* 76–7).

**322 ἄραρε:** intransitive perf. of ἀραρίσκω, 'be firmly fixed and secure'; cf. 413, 745.

**κοὐκ ἔχεις τέχνην ὅπως** 'and you have no device (or, trick) by which'; the ὅπως-clause here may be classed with the normal object clauses with verbs of effort and striving (Smyth §§2209–11).

### *324–51  Supplication of Creon*

There are at least two ways to stage this passage, depending on whether the first words of supplication in 324 are accompanied by full supplicatory action or not. (1) At 324 Medea kneels at Creon's feet and touches or grasps at least his knees at this point. She then remains kneeling, and Creon makes no move to get away from her, during nine lines of stichomythia (SE 3b) in which Medea in fact breaks off direct dialogue contact (328n.). Creon shows impatience in 333–5, but then Medea strengthens her supplication by clinging to his hand (336–9). (2) At 324 Medea merely steps closer to Creon and extends her arm toward his knees, in what Gould calls a figurative supplication (see Gould (1973) 77, and 85–6 on this passage). Creon says 'you are wasting your words' because only words have so far been used. Only at 336 does Medea fall at Creon's feet and grasp his hand. The latter seems preferable. In either case, it is uncertain when Medea releases Creon and stands up again, but this probably happens at 351, since the ritual seems to require her to maintain contact until Creon consents in 351. See Gould (1973); Kaimio (1988) 49–61, esp. 51.

**324  μή, πρός σε γονάτων:**  doubly elliptical, lacking the verb with μή (e.g. τοῦτο δράσῃς) and the verb governing σε (ἱκετεύω); the latter omission is common when πρός is used with the gen. in strong appeals in the sense 'by your knees (chin, hand, etc.)'. The earnestness of the appeal is perhaps also marked by the double resolution in the line (PM 19). The intrusion of the enclitic σε between the preposition and the noun governed by it is an example of the tendency of enclitic words in Greek (as in some other Indo-European languages) to attach themselves to the first word of the clause, regardless of syntactic or semantic affinity (see Barrett on *Hipp.* 10 ὁ γάρ με Θησέως παῖς; also 250–1n.).

**τῆς τε νεογάμου κόρης:**  in addition to supplicating by knee or chin or hand, one may supplicate in the name of someone especially dear to the person who is supplicated.

**326  αἰδέσῃι λιτάς:**  for αἰδώς as the proper attitude of the supplicated toward suppliants, compare *Hipp.* 335 σέβας γὰρ χειρὸς αἰδοῦμαι τὸ σόν (with Barrett's note), and (for anyone confronted with a suppliant to the gods) *Hcld.* 101 εἰκὸς θεῶν ἱκτῆρας αἰδεῖσθαι. See also 348–9n. and Cairns (1993) 277–8.

**327  φιλῶ γὰρ οὐ σέ κτλ.**  'Yes, because my affection goes not to *you* more than to my *family*'. οὐ γὰρ φιλῶ σέ would also have fit the metre, but the word order chosen here highlights 'loving' as the topic and puts 'you' in stronger contrast with the 'house'.

**328  ὦ πατρίς:**  the apostrophe here and in 332 and the exclamation in 330 are all signs that Medea is withdrawing from dialogue contact with Creon, temporarily abandoning her plea (this makes more sense if she is still standing than if she is at Creon's knees: 324–51n.). Creon nevertheless makes capping remarks to the first two lines and reacts to the threatening third one with a direct order.

**329  γάρ:**  as often in stichomythia, a speaker assents to the statement just made by the other speaker by giving a reason for agreement: Denniston 73–4.

**φίλτατον πολύ:**   the notion that one's own homeland is dear or beloved is a commonplace: *Phoen.* 359, 388, 406–7, *Hcld.* 506–7, fr. 360.53–4; for rating this love before or after that of children (or parents) see also *Erechtheus* fr. 1 *TGFS*.

**331  ὅπως ἄν, οἶμαι, καὶ παραστῶσιν τύχαι**   '⟨no, the nature of love varies⟩, I suppose, in whatever way events in fact attend one.' Compare 627–44 (the chorus contrasts excessive love with a moderate and safe experience of Aphrodite), and the motif of the bittersweet nature of love, e.g. Sappho 130 L–P Ἔρος ... γλυκύπικρον ἀμάχανον ὄρπετον; *Hipp.* 347–8 (ΦΑ) τί τοῦθ᾽ ὃ δὴ λέγουσιν ἀνθρώπους ἐρᾶν; | (ΤΡ) ἥδιστον, ὦ παῖ, ταὐτὸν ἀλγεινόν θ᾽ ἅμα.

**332  ὃς αἴτιος:**   ἐστί is understood, and the clause introduced by the simple relative is equivalent to an indirect question (although it can also be analysed as a relative clause with the antecedent 'the one' implied): Smyth §2668.

**333  ὦ ματαία:**   151–2n.

**334  πονοῦμεν ἡμεῖς κτλ.:**   Medea reacts sharply to Creon's complaint about his 'toils', emphatically spitting the word back at him: the sense is either 'Toils are what I have, and I have no shortage of them!' or (Elmsley's idea, with a bitter jest) 'Toils are what I have, and I have no need of more (from your supply)!' κεχρήμεθα in the sense 'be in want of' governs the gen. while κεχρημένους (347), 'experience', governs the dat.

**335  τάχ᾽**   frequently introduces in tragedy threats of physical violence that are not in fact carried out, but forestalled by argument or intervention (Aesch. *Supp.* 906, *Ag.* 1649, Soph. *OC* 834, Eur. *Hel.* 452, *IA* 311, *Cycl.* 210).

**ἐξ ὀπαδῶν χειρός**   'by my attendants' hands'; the addition of χειρός reinforces βίαι, since χείρ itself may connote the use of force (LSJ s.v. II.5.d–e, II.6.e).

**ὠσθήσηι:**   future passive of ὠθέω, 'push, thrust'.

**336  μὴ δῆτα τοῦτό γ᾽:**   δράσηις or κελεύσηις is understood; the ellipsis in passionate denial is perhaps somewhat colloquial (*Hel.* 939, *Phoen.* 735, Soph. *Phil.* 762, 1367, five times in Aristophanes).

ἄντομαι:   this is Wecklein's correction for αἰτοῦμαι, which lacks the needed object of the thing asked for (see Diggle (1994) 283–4). On the action accompanying this line, see 324–51n.

**337**  ὄχλον παρέξεις  'you're going to make yourself a nuisance', a colloquial expression (Stevens (1976) 56).

**338**  τοῦθ'... σου τυχεῖν  'to obtain (receive) this from you' (LSJ s.v. τυγχάνω B.II.2.b–c). τοῦτο replaces μὴ φεύγειν, the neuter demonstrative's meaning being inferred from the context.

**339**  τί δ' αὖ:   if this reading is correct, then αὖ may be taken as 'in turn', 'on the other hand', with the particles conveying exasperation, 'if you are not appealing your exile, then what in turn is it that makes you continue to apply compulsion and refuse to let go of my hand?' Less likely, αὖ may mean 'again' (if Medea grasped Creon's hand at 324–6 and let it go (at 328?) and then grasped it again at 336), but if the first supplication is physical instead of figurative (324–51n.), it would be rather half-hearted. Several editors accept Housman's τί δαί (1012n.), but δαί is a colloquial and informal particle. That might be suitable if Creon showed signs of relaxing and said simply 'what then is it you want?', but the use of βιάζηι and the elaborate κοὐκ ἀπαλλάσσηι χερός suggest continued tension and a serious tone.

βιάζηι:   for the compulsive force of supplication, compare *Hipp.* 325 τί δρᾶις; βιάζηι, χειρὸς ἐξαρτωμένη; As long as there is no physical contact, it is much easier for the supplicated to turn away and dismiss the suppliant's appeal. But once physical restraint is present, it requires a more concrete shunning by the supplicated (or voluntary withdrawal by the suppliant) to end the appeal, and thus the supplicated whose hand is held may feel more in jeopardy of attracting the resentment of the gods. See Cairns (1993) 277–8.

χερός:   a few recent editors retain χθονός (MSS), but the emendation χερός is necessary. As in *Hipp.* 325, reference to clinging to the hand is needed to clarify the specific sense of βιάζηι. With χθονός, if Creon asks 'why don't you leave the land?' after just acknowledging that Medea wants to ask for something other than remaining in Corinth, he would appear to be rather dense.

**340–7**  contain a perceptible alliteration of m and p, perhaps expressive of Medea's earnest tone.

**341** ξυμπερᾶναι: the compound here means 'bring to full completion' (συν- as prefix of completion), but in 887 'assist in accomplishing' (συν- of association).

ἧι φευξούμεθα: ambiguous between 'by what road we shall go into exile', 'in what manner we shall go into exile', and 'in what manner we shall live in exile'; Creon is to understand the first or third, the audience may also hear the second. Kovacs' 'my plans for exile' catches the ambiguity in English.

**342–3** παισίν τ᾽ ἀφορμὴν κτλ.: best taken as object of the phrase ξυμπερᾶναι φροντίδα in (unbalanced) pairing with the clause ἧι φευξούμεθα: 'complete my planning for resources for my sons'; for a verb-and-object phrase treated as a verb governing another noun as object, see Smyth §1612 and Diggle (1981) 58. Some instead take ἀφορμήν as object of ξυμπερᾶναι, 'complete', in parallel with φροντίδα. Others have preferred to punctuate after προτιμᾶι and thus make μηχανήσασθαι govern ἀφορμήν, but this requires emendation of τέκνοις (Earle's τινα is adopted by Kovacs, but the separation of τινα from its noun is then unusually large).

οὐδὲν προτιμᾶι μηχανήσασθαι 'does not care to contrive any aid at all' or perhaps, with οὐδέν doing double duty, 'does not care at all to contrive any aid'. προτιμάω implies ranking and preference, so the word suggests that Jason does not set a high enough value on his children. In the next episode, Jason does in fact come spontaneously to offer financial assistance to the exiles (460–4, 610–15).

**344** καὶ σύ τοι: τοι here probably marks a soothing and persuasive tone (Denniston 540–1).

**345** εἰκός δέ σφιν: understand ἐστί: 'it's only reasonable that you should bear good will toward them'. δέ σφιν is Vitelli's emendation. The MSS have εἰκὸς δ᾽ ἐστὶν or εἰκός ἐστιν, but Eur. frequently uses εἰκός without ἐστί, and the specification 'toward them' (as opposed to me) is very much needed here.

**346** τοὐμοῦ: crasis, τοῦ ἐμοῦ; gen. of neut. τὸ ἐμόν, in tragic style an approximate synonym of 'me', but more weighty and always widening the reference in some way; here 'my own situation'. See Mastronarde on *Phoen.* 774–7.

**348–9** τυραννικόν, | αἰδούμενος: kings and tyrants are assumed to be self-willed and unaccustomed to taking into consideration the interests and feelings of others. αἰδώς is essentially a quality of social tact, in that one shows αἰδώς in acknowledging the status of others by limiting one's own behaviour, as in a woman's modesty in the presence of males or a youth's silence and physical deference in the presence of elders; see in general Cairns (1993). Absolute rulers are in a grossly unequal (superior) social position in which αἰδώς potentially plays no part. But Creon has been manipulated by Medea into allowing his sense of αἰδώς to come to the fore.

**349** πολλὰ δὴ διέφθορα 'I have often managed matters ruinously.'

**352** ἡ 'πιοῦσα λαμπὰς ... θεοῦ 'the coming [ἐπιοῦσα, prodelision: PM 10] torch of the god', 'tomorrow's sun'; for θεός of the sun, see Diggle (1994) 405–6. The periphrasis adds solemnity to the warning.

**354** λέλεκται μῦθος ἀψευδὴς ὅδε: phrases like εἴρηται λόγος are formulas of conclusion and are sometimes the last words of speech (see Mastronarde on *Phoen.* 1012). The variation we see here is, however, not a simple 'I've no more to say,' but a declaration of the certainty of the threat just made.

**355–6** Nauck deleted this couplet because he found Creon's reasoning absurd and he took 354 to be a formula of closure; Diggle has followed him. What we have here, however, is a forced claim of confidence, self-deceiving and tragically ironic, that fits well with the bluster and vacillation that Creon has shown.

**356** τι ... ὧν φόβος μ' ἔχει: 'any of the terrible things that I fear', lit., 'anything [of those things] fear of which possesses me'.

**358–63** Instead of a couplet from the chorus-leader to articulate the episode at the departure of Creon, the chorus chants a brief passage of anapaests (if 357 is kept and 361 deleted, 9 metra and a concluding paroemiac): see SE 1, PM 22. This kind of minor interlude within an episode is not very common, but Eur. uses it twice in this play (see 759–63n.). In both cases there is sharp contrast between the chorus' naive understanding of the situation they have just observed and Medea's true intention, revealed just after the anapaestic passage. Thus Medea's difference from the norm and her manipulative power are underlined.

**358–7**   The transposition puts φεῦ φεῦ in its normal position for Eur., who otherwise has this exclamation at the opening of a speech or sentence (there are a few cases of parenthetic φεῦ φεῦ in lyric passages of Aesch. and Soph.: *Sept.* 135, *Ag.* 1483, *Cho.* 396, *Aj.* 958). The words δύστανε γύναι (δύστηνε Diggle, because these are normal chanted anapaests) are missing in part of the MS tradition; after accidental omission, the words were presumably restored in the wrong position: Diggle (1994) 266–8.

**358**   μελέα ... ἀχέων:   96n.

**359–60**   τίνα πρὸς ξενίαν | ... ἢ χθόνα:   with the deletion of 361 (see n.), the chorus follows up ποῖ τρέψηι with more specific questions with the same verb understood: 'to what relationship of guest-friendship or to what house or land ... ?'

**360**   χθόνα σωτῆρα κακῶν   'land providing rescue from your troubles'; the appositive noun σωτῆρα is treated as an adjectival modifier of χθόνα: for other examples see Mastronarde on *Phoen.* 1569 (μαστὸν ... ἱκέτιν).

**361**   [ἐξευρήσεις]:   the verb is most likely an addition made by a reader or actor who did not understand the adjectival use of σωτῆρα in 360 and so added a verb that could govern it as a predicate noun (the interpolator may also have failed to take τίνα πρὸς with all three nouns, understanding 'what house or land for guest-friendship ...'). For this type of syntactic addition, compare the addition of ἴδω in some ancient copies at *Phoen.* 167. Kovacs keeps the verb and accepts the minority reading προξενίαν, but this noun (found in Pindar) is not attested in tragedy or comedy, perhaps because it was too closely associated in the Attic context with the official diplomatic language of the city.

**362–3**   κλύδωνα .|.. κακῶν:   the metaphor of a 'sea of troubles' is common in tragedy: with κλύδων also *Tro.* 696, Soph. *OT* 1527,

Aesch. *Pers.* 599 (and seven passages with πέλαγος). See Introd. 2(*f*). By an artful interlacing, the two words referring to Medea are enclosed in the phrase 'inextricable sea-swells of woes'.

**364 κακῶς πέπρακται** 'the situation is bad', 'the fortune that has been experienced is bad', with an impersonal passive use of πράσσω. Cf. *Rhesus* 756; Aesch. *Ag.* 551 has εὖ γὰρ πέπρακται. For the impersonal passive in Greek see K–G 1.125 Anm. 2, Schwyzer 11.239–40 (Smyth §1746 is somewhat misleading).

**ἀντερεῖ:** suppletive future of ἀντιλέγω, more common than ἀντιλέξω.

**365 οὔτι ταύτηι ταῦτα, μὴ δοκεῖτέ πω** 'by no means will these things go along in this path ⟨that you expect⟩, don't assume that yet'. A verb like γενήσεται or εἶσι is understood. The brief elliptical and alliterative phrase is an effective token of Medea's hidden strength, answering (bitingly?) to the more regretful alliteration in 364.

**367 τοῖσι κηδεύσασιν:** presumably poetic pl., 'him who made the marriage-tie' (Creon), since Jason is included in 366 νυμφίοις, 'newlyweds'. κηδεύω has a very general sense 'form a (marriage-)tie' and can have bridegroom or father of the bride as subject.

**σμικροί:** this form is archaic and poetic, also used frequently by Plato, while the Attic orators generally avoid it in favour of μικρός. In tragedy it is probable that forms without initial sigma are used only when metrically required (Diggle (1994) 146).

**368 δοκεῖς γὰρ ἄν με:** postpositive ἄν is attached to δοκεῖς as the first word of the sentence (note the order of precedence of the three postpositives), but syntactically it goes with θωπεῦσαι, the indirect form of ἐθώπευσα ἄν (contrary-to-fact condition, with the condition in participial form). Cf. 250–1n.

**369 εἰ μή τι κερδαίνουσαν:** because of its use in many elliptical expressions in which it can often be translated as 'except', εἰ μή becomes frozen as a unit, and so is used here with the conditional participle instead of plain μή (as a clause it would be εἰ μή τι ἐκέρδαινον).

**370 οὐδ' ... οὐδ'** 'I would not *even* have spoken to him, *nor yet* would I have touched him with my hands' (not the same as οὔτε ... οὔτε ...).

**χεροῖν:** dat. (dual) 'with my hands' rather than gen. '(touch) his hands', since this dat. is very common in tragic style with verbs of grasping, holding, and touching (compare already the supplication in *Il.* 20.468 ἥπτετο χείρεσι γούνων, 10.454–5), and the supplicant uses both hands but need grasp only one hand of the supplicated person.

**371   ἐς τοσοῦτον μωρίας ἀφίκετο:**   see 56n.

**372   ἐξὸν ... ἐλεῖν:**   acc. abs. part. of an impersonal verb (Smyth §2076), 'although it was possible for him to disarm my plotting'. For the sense of ἐλεῖν, compare the meanings 'seize, catch' and 'capture, overcome'; for βουλεύματα as object of such a verb cf. Hdt. 9.2.2 ἕξεις ἀπόνως ἅπαντα τὰ ἐκείνων βουλεύματα. τἄμ᾽ is from τὰ ἐμά (crasis).

**373   ἐκβαλόντι:**   the object με is understood from τἄμ᾽ in 372.

**ἐφῆκεν:**   for the sense 'permit, allow' see LSJ s.v. ἐφίημι II.1.c, Soph. *El.* 631 ἐπειδὴ σοί γ᾽ ἐφῆκα πᾶν λέγειν. The MSS read ἀφῆκεν: although ἀφίημι can take an epexegetic inf. such that the meaning is almost 'permit' (LSJ s.v. IV.1), this applies only in contexts where the sense of dismissal and sending away from oneself is present, as it is not here. (See Diggle (1994) 284–5, who also gives exx. of ἐφῆκ-/ ἀφῆκ-confusion in MSS; also 633–5n.)

**374   τρεῖς ... νεκρούς:**   νεκρούς is predicate acc.: 'make three of my enemies into corpses'. If line 262 is deleted (as argued above), this is the first open statement by Medea that she intends to kill all three of her enemies, but Creon said in 287–9 that he had heard of her threats against all three (the nurse also mentioned the danger of Medea's vengeance, but the specific reference to Creon and his daughter is widely regarded as not genuine: 37–45n.). Medea's enumeration maintains in the audience's mind the false expectation that Jason will be a victim of his angry wife, like Agamemnon. Eur. puts no objection or comment on the wider plan in the chorus' mouth at this point or in the next stasimon.

**379–80** are almost identical to 40–1; see 37–45n. for the argument that 40–1 are spurious. Both lines are integral here: the reference to 'many ways' in 376 and the *aporia* ὁποίαι πρῶτον in 377 are clearly rhetorical preparation for the consideration of more than one alternative; the standard pair of fire and sword (see Mastronarde on *Phoen.* 1557–8) are contemplated as separate possibilities, then an objection is raised, so that Medea must turn in climactic fashion to poison as means. Deletion of 380 (Willink (1988)) spoils the rhetorical development and removes the preparation for 393–4.

Although Medea has just mentioned three victims, the idea of sneaking into the bridal bedchamber and using a sword apparently accounts for two victims, Jason and his bride. In hearing so briefly of this rejected plan, an audience has neither the time nor the pedantry to ask how Medea would then kill Creon.

**381  ἕν τι:**  εἷς τις is often indefinite, 'some (unspecified) one', 'any one at all', but sometimes, as here, more definite or emphatic, 'a certain single thing' or 'just one thing': compare *Her.* 207 ἕν τί σ' ἡγοῦμαι σοφόν (*IT* 999, if sound), Lysias 31.1 ἐπειδὴ δὲ οὐχ ἕν τι μόνον ἀλλὰ πολλὰ τολμηρός ἐστιν, Xen. *Oecon.* 2.10 ὁρῶ γάρ σε … ἕν τι πλουτηρὸν ἔργον ἐπιστάμενον περιουσίαν ποιεῖν.

**πρόσαντες**  '(serving as) a hindrance' (305n.).

**382  δόμους ὑπερβαίνουσα**  'entering the house', with the prefix ὑπερ- implying crossing over the threshold (see Barrett on *Hipp.* 782–3).

**383  θήσω τοῖς ἐμοῖς ἐχθροῖς γέλων**  'I'll afford my enemies an opportunity for mockery.' It is usually male heroes, engaged in a contest for recognition and supremacy, who are extremely sensitive to the possibility that their enemies may have a laugh at their expense (see esp. Soph. *Ajax* 79, 303, 367, *et passim*, *Ant.* 483, 647). The theme of escaping mockery, repeated from here to the end of the play, is thus a part of Medea's engagement in male categories of value and social standing: Introd. 2(*b*). (See Knox (1964) 30–1.)

**γέλων:**  for this alternative acc. form see LS 5.c.

**384–5  κράτιστα ..|. ἑλεῖν:**  understand ἐστί, 'it is best … to destroy them by poison drugs'; the neut. pl. predicate adj. with inf. as subject seems to be an archaic construction, retained esp. in poetry and Thucydides (Smyth §1052; K–G 1.66–8).

**τὴν εὐθεῖαν:**  adverbial acc., 'along the straight path', 'by direct means', used as if a fem. participle meaning 'proceeding' and referring to Medea were present. Compare Aesch. fr. 195.1 εὐθεῖαν ἕρπε τήνδε (sc. ὁδόν).

ἧι ... | σοφοὶ μάλιστα: the relative clause anticipates φαρμάκοις rather than defining τὴν εὐθεῖαν; both adverbial elements are vague and create rhetorical 'suspense' that is resolved by φαρμάκοις: 'using the means in which I am most skilled, kill them with poison'. With the emendation σοφοί, Medea is speaking only of herself (for masc. pl. of Medea alone, see 314–15n.): she is by nature skilled in magic drugs because of her descent from Helios and kinship with an exotic family (Circe is her aunt). The MSS have σοφαί, which gives 'in which we women (in general) are by nature skilled', but this is neither true nor as pointed, although the use of drugs and poison, as a learned skill, was associated with females rather than males in male-dominated Greek thought.

**386** καὶ δὴ τεθνᾶσι 'granted then, they are dead'; for this force of καὶ δή compare *Hipp.* 1007 καὶ δὴ τὸ σῶφρον τοὐμὸν οὐ πείθει σ᾿ ἴτω, *Hel.* 1059 καὶ δὴ παρεῖκεν· εἶτα πῶς ἄνευ νεὼς κτλ.; see Denniston 253 (imaginary realization).

**387–8** γῆν ἄσυλον .. |. παρασχών 'by granting ⟨to me⟩ a land that allows no seizure and a home reliably secure'; LSJ s.v. ἄσυλος II is somewhat misleading. The general assumption in many Greek mythic narratives (and to a great extent in real life in the separate poleis) is that a foreigner has no rights except through a personal local representative or by consent of the local authorities. Thus a criminal or an enemy could be pursued and seized in foreign territory unless the locals objected. This need for protective refuge is answered for Medea by the opportune arrival and ready consent of Aegeus (663–823n.).

**388** ῥύσεται τοὐμὸν δέμας 'will protect my person'; the verb is future of ἐρύομαι/ῥύομαι (LSJ ἐρύω (B); cf. ἔρυμα 597, 1322); tragedy often uses δέμας in dignified periphrases, among which are ἐμὸν δέμας and σὸν δέμας. τοὐμόν is from τὸ ἐμόν (crasis).

**391** On the interlaced word order see LS 35.

**392–4** Medea reverts to the plan of direct violence, ignoring the obstacle pointed out in 381–3. Such an inconsistency is better understood in terms of narrative or dramatic goals of the text than in terms of psychology or elaborate inferences about a character's unexpressed reasoning. Here the audience is left with the impression that Medea's use of drugs is not yet completely planned out, and suspense is maintained about what exactly is going to happen.

**394** τόλμης δ' εἶμι πρὸς τὸ καρτερόν 'I'll go forth to bold violence', literally, 'I'll advance to the forceful part of daring', probably a metaphor from moving forward toward the enemy in battle. καρτερόν implies brute force, and is contrasted with δόλος also in *Prom.* 212–13 ὡς οὐ κατ' ἰσχὺν οὐδὲ πρὸς τὸ καρτερὸν | χρείη, δόλωι δέ, τοὺς ὑπερσχόντας κρατεῖν, Hdt. 1.212.

**397** Ἑκάτην: Hecate is a minor goddess who is associated with doors and pathways, especially crossroads, and has connections with the underworld, ghostly epiphanies, the night, and the moon. On account of the latter aspects she is also a patron of witchcraft. This is the only allusion to the goddess of magic in the play, a sign of Eur.'s restraint in showing the sorceress aspect of Medea: Introd. 2(*c*); contrast the treatment of magic in Seneca's *Medea*, where Hecate is named four times. In Greek cult Hecate was worshipped outdoors, in streets, and at crossroads, so Medea's statement that the goddess dwells within her house, virtually in displacement of Hestia, conveys both an exotic transgression of the norm and a special personal intimacy.

μυχοῖς ναίουσαν: locative dat. without preposition (LS 11.a).

**398** χαίρων: οὐ χαίρων with a future indicative verb is a widely used idiom for 'you won't get away with doing X' or 'he'll be sorry for doing X' or the like (LSJ s.v. χαίρω iv.2). Medea's resolve and vehemence is conveyed rhetorically by the long oath separating οὐ in 395 and χαίρων here.

**399–400** πικροὺς ... γάμους, | πικρὸν δὲ κῆδος: the emphatically placed predicate adj. πικρός, strengthened further here by anaphora, is found in other threatening expressions (again of the 'you'll be sorry!' type); compare 1388 πικρὰς τελευτὰς τῶν ἐμῶν γάμων ἰδών. For other exx. see Mastronarde on *Phoen.* 949–50.

**400** φυγὰς ἐμὰς χθονός 'my exile from this land' (πικράς is understood).

**401–7**  Medea addresses herself, strengthening her own resolve. At this point in the play, there is no hint that Medea is reluctant and that such self-exhortation is needed to overcome hesitation. But this rhetorical stance shows a woman capable of stepping back to observe herself and thus prepares for the more emotionally fraught instances of self-address in 1056–8 and 1242–50.

**401**  ἀλλ' εἶα often marks a shift from comment to command or exhortation. LSJ gives εἶα with smooth breathing, but the rough breathing is established by ancient papyri of Sophocles (Mastronarde on *Phoen.* 970).

φείδου μηδέν:  also in *Hec.* 1044, *Her.* 1400, Soph. *Aj.* 115, Ar. *Birds* 987.

μηδὲν ὧν ἐπίστασαι:  attraction of the relative, 'none of the things that you know'.

**402**  βουλεύουσα καὶ τεχνωμένη:  this first participle recalls βου-λεύματα in 372, and the other is the third appearance of the form in 34 lines (371, 382). Following the name Medea, they allude to the apparent etymological meaning of her name: cf. μήδομαι, μήδεα. Greek poets are fond of alluding to the suitability of the (actual or forced) etymology of a proper name: see Dodds on *Bacch.* 367 and Griffith (1978) 84 n.5.

**403**  ἕρπ' ἐς τὸ δεινόν· νῦν ἀγὼν εὐψυχίας:  the latter half of the line certainly evokes miltiary action and the bravery to which men are exhorted before battle (e.g. Tyrtaeus fr. 10.13–18, 11.3–6 West), and the first half too perhaps alludes to advancing toward dreadful battle (Kovacs: 'Into the fray!'), although a more general sense seems present in Soph. fr. 351 ὅστις δὲ τόλμηι πρὸς τὸ δεινὸν ἔρχεται, | ὀρθὴ μὲν ἡ γλῶσσ' ἐστίν, ἀσφαλὴς δ' ὁ νοῦς.

**404**  γέλωτα ... ὀφλεῖν:  for Medea's concern with being mocked by enemies, see Introd. 2(b); ὀφλισκάνω (aor. ὦφλον), 'incur', has a technical legal meaning (581n.), but is often used metaphorically with undesirable objects like γέλως (LSJ s.v. ii); see also 1227n. for an extended use of this idiom.

**405**  Σισυφείοις:  a contemptuous synonym for 'Corinthian', since Sisyphus was once king of Corinth; he was a notorious trickster, clever with deceptive oaths, so perhaps there is some implication of Jason's faithlessness. The adj. is also contemptuous in *IA* 524, but there it alludes to the nasty story that Laertes was a cuckold and that Odysseus was begotten by Sisyphus (as also Soph. *Aj.* 190, *Phil.* 417, 1311).

γάμοις is dat. of cause (a subclass of instrumental dat.), Smyth §1517.

**406  ἄπο:**   anastrophe (LS 24).

**407  ἐπίστασαι δέ** 'and you do know how' (sc. to plan and devise wiles). This adds nothing significant, merely sets the stage for the addition that follows. The rhetorical force is similar to 'and apart from your knowledge, there is also the fact that . . .'

πρός:   here adverbial, 'in addition'.

**407–8  πεφύκαμεν γυναῖκες** 'we have been born (and endowed with the nature of) women'; in favour of the interpretation of γυναῖκες as predicate (with Elmsley and Paley) are parallels like *IT* 1061–2 γυναῖκές ἐσμεν, φιλόφρον ἀλλήλαις γένος, σώιζειν τε κοινὰ πράγματ' ἀσφαλέσταται, fr. 276 γυναῖκές ἐσμεν· τὰ μὲν ὄκνωι νικώμεθα, τὰ δ' οὐκ ἂν ἡμῶν θράσος ὑπερβάλοιτό τις (cf. below 823, 890). Some editors print no comma after γυναῖκες and some interpreters take the noun as subject ('we women are by nature . . .'), as is true of γυναῖκές ἐσμεν in 231 above and *Andr.* 353.

**408–9  ἐς μὲν ἔσθλ' ἀμηχανώταται, | κακῶν δὲ πάντων τέκτονες σοφώταται** 'completely without resources for noble actions, but the most skilled contrivers of every form of harm'. With ἐσθλά Medea refers bitterly to the displays of valour on which men pride themselves (248–52), from which women are excluded by the restrictive conditions of their lives, leaving them only with the arena of κακά (underhanded and ignoble actions) in which to compete (see von Fritz (1959) 59–62 = (1962) 361–4). This final generalization is a kind of defiant appropriation of a misogynistic stereotype (263–6n.), and the notions of competition between genders and the unfair position of women prepare for the themes of the following stasimon. The similar endings of 407 and 408 (homoioteleuton) are reinforced by the further contrast of ἔσθλ' and κακῶν (Fehling (1969) 314).

## *410–45*   First stasimon

Choral songs often step back from the action and speeches just witnessed through the use of opening devices such as gnomic statements, myth, and apostrophe. In addition, a stasimon (SE 2) may hark back to the opening of the previous episode rather than take off from its end (cf. the first stasimon of Soph. *OT*). Here the chorus and audience have just been made privy to Medea's plans for violent revenge, but the Corinthian women at this point show no response to the revelation. Instead their subject is the moral crisis caused by Jason's betrayal of his oath to Medea and the change in gender-relations that this implies for the whole Greek world. The women thus not only reinforce the passionate cries about justice and oaths that they heard from Medea in the parodos but also accept and extend Medea's assertion, offered in her first speech on-stage, that the relative positions of men and women are unfair. Ironically, caught up as they are in the mythical moment of their drama, they proclaim the arrival of a new discourse about women and men, while with its wider perspective the audience understands that this anticipation of female fame is doomed to frustration. In accord with a structure common in many choral odes, the second pair of stanzas shifts more particularly to Medea with initial σὺ δ'. Even in this part, however, they continue to echo complaints made by Medea in the first half of the previous episode and to elide the plotting of violence that ended it. Thus the song functions on several levels: the theme of Jason's treachery is given great prominence (it is not merely a personal offence against Medea but a more general one against the gods and a Greek cultural institution); dramatic tension over the revenge-plot is deferred so that the attention may be focused for the moment on the themes to be explored in the following *agōn*; the chorus' skewed response attests to the manipulative power of Medea, and may reflect what might be called a moral disconnection of the chorus from the actions before them.

In the opening stanza the trickery and faithlessness of men are regarded as a symptom of a world turned upside down, a world in which the traditional misogynistic discourse will be reversed. The second stanza particularizes the source as specifically the authoritative poems of the male-dominated tradition, and the singing women (who are in fact, by Greek theatrical convention, men dressed as women) paradoxically present their own sex as deprived of the skill for poetry, but assertively point out that women poets would be able to construct an equivalent anti-male discourse (424n.). The third stanza then addresses Medea to rehearse her disadvantages, but the moral complaint of the first stanza returns insistently in the first two lines of the final stanza, with its Hesiodic echo of justice abandoning a corrupt world. The final stanza thus reiterates in miniature the structure of the first three stanzas.

*Metre*

The first pair of stanzas is written in dactylo-epitrite (PM 27) and appears to consist of six periods in seven lines, perhaps a slow and dignified movement, with pauses closely matching the largely asyndetic sentence-structure. The dactylic element is probably meant to recall epic (and perhaps narrative choral lyric such as the work of Stesichorus), since one theme of these stanzas is the representation of women in the authoritative poetry of the past (note also the epic tags in 410 and 425, other epicizing features in 423). The second pair also features cola with mixed single-short and double-short rhythm, but their character is aeolic (PM 26), and the stanza is built of only two or three periods, with the extended length of the final period perhaps expressive of greater emotion. The final period is analysed by some without word overlap, giving the sequence telesillean, 3 hagesichoreans, reizianum; such a sequence of hagesichoreans would be comparable to sequences in the parodos (131–213n.), but because this would involve triply repeated period-end without rhetorical pause, it seems slightly less attractive than the division shown here (see Stinton (1990) 331–2).

$\underset{\smile}{} - \smile \ \smile - \smile \smile - \ - \ - \smile \ - \ - \ \|^?$

| | |
|---|---|
| ἄνω ποταμῶν ἱερῶν χωροῦσι παγαί, | 410–11 ×D − e − |
| μοῦσαι δὲ παλαιγενέων λήξουσ᾽ ἀοιδῶν | 421–2 |

$- \smile - \ - - \smile \smile - \ \smile \smile - \ \|^h$

| | |
|---|---|
| καὶ δίκα καὶ πάντα πάλιν στρέφεται· | 412 e − D |
| τὰν ἐμὰν ὑμνεῦσαι ἀπιστοσύναν. | 423 |

$- \ \smile \smile - \ \smile \smile - - \ - \smile -$

| | |
|---|---|
| ἀνδράσι μὲν δόλιαι βουλαί, θεῶν δ᾽ | 413 D − e |
| οὐ γὰρ ἐν ἁμετέραι γνώμαι λύρας | 424 |

‒ ∪ ∪ ‒ ∪ ∪ ‒ ‒ ‖

οὐκέτι πίστις ἄραρεν·                                   414 D ‒

ὤπασε θέσπιν ἀοιδὰν                                    425

‒ ∪ ‒ ‒ ‒ ∪ ∪ ‒ ∪ ∪ ‒ ‒ ‒ ∪ ‒ ‒ ‖ʰᵇ

τὰν δ' ἐμὰν εὔκλειαν ἔχειν βιοτὰν          415‒16 e ‒ D ‒ e ‒

στρέψουσι φᾶμαι·

Φοῖβος ἀγήτωρ μελέων· ἐπεὶ ἀντάχησ'      426‒7

ἂν ὕμνον

‒ ∪ ‒ ‒ ‒ ∪ ‒ ‒ ‒ ∪ ‒ ‖ʰ

ἔρχεται τιμὰ γυναικείωι γένει·               417‒18 E ‒ e

ἀρσένων γένναι. μακρὸς δ' αἰὼν ἔχει       428‒9

‒ ∪ ∪ ‒ ∪ ∪ ‒ ‒ ‒ ∪ ‒ ∪ ‒ ‒ ‖

οὐκέτι δυσκέλαδος φάμα γυναῖκας ἕξει.    419‒20 D ‒ e, ba

πολλὰ μὲν ἁμετέραν ἀνδρῶν τε μοῖραν      430‒1

εἰπεῖν.

‒ ‒ ‒ ‒ ‒ ‒ ‒ ‒ ‒ ‒

∪ ‒ ∪‒ ‒ ∪ ∪ ‒ ∪ ‒ ‒ ‖ᵖ

σὺ δ' ἐκ μὲν οἴκων πατρίων ἔπλευσας       432 ia, aristophanean

βέβακε δ' ὅρκων χάρις, οὐδ' ἔτ' αἰδὼς      439

‒ ∪ ∪ ‒ ∪∪ ‒ ∪∪ ‒ ∪ ‒ ∪ ‒ ‒ ‖ᵖ

μαινομέναι κραδίαι, διδύμους ὁρίσασα       433‒4 aristophanean

Πόντου                                                  with triple dactylic
                                                         extension (ar³ᵈ)

Ἑλλάδι τᾷ μεγάλαι μένει, αἰθερία δ'         440‒1

ἀνέπτα.

‒ ‒ ∪ ∪ ‒ ∪ ‒ |

πέτρας· ἐπὶ δὲ ξέναι                               435 telesillean

σοὶ δ' οὔτε πατρὸς δόμοι,                       442

‒ ‒ ∪ ∪ ‒ ∪ ‒

ναίεις χθονί, τᾶς ἀνάν‒                           436 telesillean

δύστανε, μεθορμίσα‒                              443

‒ ‒ ∪ ∪ ‒ ∪ ‒

δρου κοίτας ὀλέσασα λέκ‒                        437 glyconic

σθαι μόχθων πάρα, σῶν τε λέκ‒              444

‒ ∪̮ ‒ ∪ ∪ ‒ ∪ ‒

τρον, τάλαινα, φυγὰς δὲ χώ‒                    438a glyconic

τρων ἄλλα βασίλεια κρείσ‒                       445a

```
     – ◡– ◡ ◡ – – |||
```
ρας ἄτιμος ἐλαύνηι.                          438b pherecratean
σων δόμοισιν ἐπέστα.                         445b

**410–11  ἄνω … χωροῦσι:** the imagining of a violation of the
natural order to express surprise, shock, or outrage is a common
figure of Greek poetry (the so-called *adynaton*, cf. in general Canter
(1930), Dutoit (1936); on this passage Dutoit 16–18). The notion of
the reversal of the natural flow of water is taken up in many later
examples in Latin poetry: see Sentieri (1919) 180–1. The phrase ἄνω
ποταμῶν was proverbial for reversals (cf. Radt on Aesch. fr. 335), but
it is unclear whether the proverb was a shortened version of a phrase
structured like Eur.'s phrase here (ποταμῶν dependent on a noun) or
was self-standing (ποταμῶν depending on ἄνω); if the latter, then
Eur. playfully quotes the proverb and immediately creates his own
syntactic variation.

   **ποταμῶν ἱερῶν:** the epithet is traditional (*Od.* 10.351, Hes. *Theog.*
788), but has specific relevance in 846 and probably here as well,
since allusion to the divine power in the rivers suggests the cosmic
significance of their change of course.

**413  ἀνδράσι μέν:** this μέν is balanced by δ' in 414 τὰν δ' ἐμὰν κτλ.
('my' implies 'of us women' in contrast to 'men'), not by θεῶν δ'.
There is no contrast between 'men' and 'gods' here (see next note);
rather, 412–15 follow 410–11 in explanatory asyndeton (LS 28), specifying the change in human affairs that causes the chorus to posit
cosmic reversal. Thus a colon is preferable at the end of 414, and
Elmsley's θεῶν τ' has some attraction. ἀνδράσι is dat. of possession, 'men have deceptive counsels'. Since deception is associated
with women (408–9n., 419–20n.), the present claim reverses a
stereotype.

**413–14  θεῶν .|.. πίστις** '⟨men's⟩ pledges made in the name of
the gods', with the gen. as in θεῶν ὅρκος (*Hipp.* 657, 1037 ὅρκους πα-
ρασχών, πίστιν οὐ σμικράν, θεῶν; Soph. *OT* 647). This clause is a
restatement in negative form of the same thought as the preceding
clause.

**414  ἄραρεν:** 322n.

**415–16** τὰν ... | φᾶμαι 'Common report will turn my life about, so that it has good fame.' ἔχειν is epexegetic. The interlaced word order is typical of high-style lyric. The future is Elmsley's emendation of transmitted στρέφουσι: responsion of short to long in this anceps position would be acceptable, but the future goes better with the following ἔξει and λήξουσ', and the present might be a little too confident. It is also possible to take στρέψουσι as intransitive (LSJ s.v. D), yielding 'common report will turn about, so that my life has good fame (or so that good fame holds my life)', but it would be unusual for such a long result-infinitive phrase to precede the governing verb.

**417–18** γένει: dat. of advantage shading into dat. of goal of motion (LS II.b).

**419–20** δυσκέλαδος φάμα: the 'ill-sounding repute' alludes to the misogynistic tradition in Greek poetry, including the treatment of Clytemnestra in the *Odyssey*, Hesiod on Pandora (*Theog.* 570–89, *WD* 60–95) and women in general (*Theog.* 590–612, *WD* 373–5, 698–705), Semonides (fr. 7 West) on the types of women, Alcaeus 42 L–P on blameworthy Helen, the myths of the first stasimon of Aesch. *Cho.* (585–651). In Greek thought woman herself is a *dolos*, and cunning and deception are in many contexts marked by association with the female rather than the male: see Detienne and Vernant (1978); Zeitlin (1996), chs. 2 and 3.

**423** ὑμνεῦσαι: fem. nom. pl. present active participle of ὑμνέω, supplementary participle with λήγω, a synonym of παύω. For the contraction see LS I.e and Barrett on *Hipp.* 167, who notes that in other cases the unusual contraction occurs in poetic verbs not native to Attic. That explanation does not apply here, where the form is chosen for epic colouring to suit the subject-matter of these lines.

ἀπιστοσύναν: extant only here in literature, coined as a metrically convenient and weightier alternative to ἀπιστία.

**424** γάρ: as in 122, the connection is imprecise: 'they will cease what they always did in the past, and they were able to do what they did before because Apollo gave poetic skill to men, but not to women'. As with the nurse's complaints about music (190–204n.), the chorus' claim does not accurately fit the poetic tradition known to the audience, in which there were at least a few female poets (Snyder (1989)). Sappho, Praxilla, and Telesilla wrote earlier than *Medea*, and possibly Corinna as well (her date is disputed: West (1990), Stewart (1998) 278–81). Of Sappho enough survives for us to detect at times a distinctly female, or anti-male, point of view; for the others any such judgment must remain highly speculative (McClure (1999a) 36–7 with refs.).

**424–5** λύρας |... θέσπιν ἀοιδάν 'god-inspired song accompanied by the lyre', with a loose gen. of connection; θέσπιν ἀοιδάν is a verbatim imitation of the Homeric line-ending applied to Phemius and Demodocus in *Od.* 1.328, 8.498.

**426–7** Φοῖβος ἀγήτωρ μελέων: for this concept compare the epithet Μουσηγέτης and the splendid description of Phoebus leading the Muses in *Hom. Hymn Ap.* 182–206. ἡγήτωρ is a specifically epic word, used only here in extant tragedy – another bit of deliberate epic colouring.

ἐπεί 'since ⟨if the gods had granted poetic skill to us women⟩'.

ἀντάχησ' ἄν 'I would have sung in opposition' (aor. of ἀντηχέω with Doric alpha).

**430–1** πολλὰ μὲν ἀμετέραν ἀνδρῶν τε μοῖραν εἰπεῖν: the construction is unbalanced, starting as if the contrast were to be πολλὰ μὲν ἀμετέραν (μοῖραν), πολλὰ δὲ ἀνδρῶν μοῖραν, but using τε instead as if the phrase were πολλὰ ἀμετέραν τε ἀνδρῶν τε μοῖραν. πολλά is the object of ἔχει, and εἰπεῖν is epexegetic (with acc. object in sense 'say about').

**432** σὺ δ': this narrowing of focus to the particular individual (often, as here, the actor present on stage) is a typical strategy of choral odes, whether the preceding lines are generalizations or first-person statements of the chorus (intended as ethically exemplary) or other comments on the situation: see 656, 848, 990, *Andr.* 302, 790, Soph. *Trach.* 126, *El.* 1084, etc.

**433** μαινομέναι κραδίαι: dative of manner, 'with heart crazed with love'; the same phrase occurs in *Hipp.* 1274, also of one stricken by love, and was earlier applied (without ref. to love) to Oedipus in Aesch. *Sept.* 781; compare μαινόλαι θύμωι in Sappho 1.18 L–P, φρεσὶ μαινομένηισιν in *Il.* 24.114, 135 (Achilles) and μαινομέναις φρασίν in Pind. *Pyth.* 2.26 (Ixion).

**434–5 διδύμους ὁρίσασα Πόντου | πέτρας:** the 'twin rocks' are the craggy shores of the Bosporus. ὁρίσασα, 'marking the boundary between', is used with a pregnant force typical of tragic style (esp. in lyric: LS 31) to imply 'travelling between' (LSJ misleads by turning this implication into a separate rubric). Compare Aesch. *Supp.* 544–6, where Friis Johansen and Whittle explain ἀντίπορον γαῖαν … ὁρίζει (of Io) as 'mark out the boundary of Asia by giving her name to the Bosporus'. The aorist participle is here 'coincident' with the action in ἔπλευσας (LS 14). For δίδυμος treated as an adj. with two endings see LS 5.d.

**436–7 τᾶς ἀνάν | δρου κοίτας ὀλέσασα λέκτρον:** lit., 'having lost the bed of your husbandless marriage-tie', with the modifier used in a proleptic sense, hence, 'having lost your marriage-bed, which is now abandoned by your husband'. κοίτας λέκτρον could be a case of tragic fullness (synonymous defining gen., as *Alc.* 925 λέκτρων κοίτας), or κοίτας may add (or clarify) the implication of sexual union. For proleptic adj. in attributive position with article, see Soph. *OC* 1200 τῶν σῶν ἀδέρκτων ὀμμάτων τητώμενος, 'being deprived of your eyes, which are now sightless'.

**438 ἄτιμος:** the adj. may carry a connotation from its use in contemporary civic/legal discourse ('without citizen rights', 'punished with diminution of civic rights'), in which case it contributes to Medea's assimilation of male prerogatives (since 'civic rights' belong to and are lost by Athenian men, not women), but its primary force is to pick up ἀνάνδρου and refer to Medea's abandonment, a dishonouring of the role of wedded wife (20n.).

**439–40** This couplet clearly recalls Hes. *WD* 180–201, the description of the future deterioration of the Iron Age that will bring destruction from Zeus: esp. 190–1 οὐδέ τις εὐόρκου χάρις ἔσσεται οὐδὲ δικαίου | οὐδ' ἀγαθοῦ, 192–4 δίκη δ' ἐν χερσί· καὶ αἰδὼς | οὐκ ἔσται, βλάψει δ' ὁ κακὸς τὸν ἀρείονα φῶτα | μύθοισι σκολιοῖς ἐνέπων, ἐπὶ δ' ὅρκον ὀμεῖται, 197–200 καὶ τότε δὴ πρὸς Ὄλυμπον … ἴτον προλιπόντ' ἀνθρώπους | Αἰδὼς καὶ Νέμεσις.

**439** βέβακε:   the absolute use of perfect βέβηκα to mean 'has dis-appeared', 'is gone', sometimes even 'is dead and gone', is a man-nerism of tragic style (cf. tragic use of οἴχομαι, 226n.).

χάρις suggests both 'charm, enchanting force' and 'amiable re-ciprocal connection/attitude'.

**440** Ἑλλάδι τᾶι μεγάλαι   'in the ⟨whole⟩ wide expanse of Greece' (locative dative without preposition, LS 11.a); Eur. uses the same phrase in *Tro.* 1115 and has in *IA* 1378 Ἑλλὰς ἡ μεγίστη πᾶσα. The prosaic use of this phrase for Greek Italy (Magna Graecia) is first extant in Polybius, but he describes it as a name used at the time of the Pythagoreans (late sixth and early fifth centuries).

**441** αἰθερία δ' ἀνέπτα:   the adj. has predicative force, and like many Greek adjs. of time and position is equivalent to an adverbial phrase (εἰς τὸν αἰθέρα). ἀνέπτα is third-person sing. aor. act. of ἀνα-πέτομαι (cf. 1 διαπτάσθαι).

**442–4** οὔτε ... τε:   for this unbalanced combination (mainly a poetic construction), see LSJ s.v. οὔτε 11.4.

**443–4** μεθορμίσα|σθαι μόχθων:   epexegetic inf., 'you do not have available your father's house, to shift to a new anchorage there, clear of your toils'. See 258n.

πάρα:   because of the separation of this word from both σοί and δόμοι, it cannot be determined whether it stands for πάρεισι (with plain separative gen. as in 258 or as with μεθορμιεῖ in *Alc.* 797–8) or is the preposition in anastrophe with μόχθων (εἰσί being easily under-stood with σοὶ ... δόμοι).

**444–5** 'And another woman, a royal princess, superior to your wedding-bed (or marriage), has taken control of your house.' ἄλλος with noun in apposition is used idiomatically (296n.): not 'another queen' (like you), since the chorus, unlike the nurse, does not dwell on Medea's royal parentage and treats Medea like an ordinary woman. With σοὶ δ' at the head of the sentence, τῶν τε (Elmsley for transmitted τῶνδε) λέκτρων can be taken as 'your bed', gen. of com-parison, with the most common meaning of κρείσσων. Some have interpreted κρείσσων rather as 'mistress of' or 'ruling over', as if synonymous with κρατοῦσα (the gen. is then virtually objective), and have translated '*your* marriage' (although 'Jason's marriage-bed' might also be understood). But this construction is not securely established (1079n. and Appendix). Porson's σῶν τε (preferred by Diggle and Kovacs) would make the standard construction as gen. of comparison almost unmistakable and would add emphasis to Medea's ownership of what the princess is usurping. ἐπέστα is strong (intransitive) aor. of ἐφίστημι, with Doric alpha; for the sense see LSJ s.v. B.II.

### 446–626    Second episode

This episode is dominated by the *agōn logōn*, a standard dramatic form in Sophocles and Euripides (SE 3a; see further Duchemin (1945), Lloyd (1992)). The *agōn* commonly presents antithetic views of a major conflict. The form has analogues in the serious business of the Athenian assembly and courts, but also in the practice of the contemporary higher education in argumentation and speech-making offered by the sophists, in which high value was placed on the ability to argue skilfully on both sides of a question, to argue for a paradoxical thesis, or to put forward the best possible arguments for a position rejected by conventional mores. Euripides' *agōn* speeches show a great degree of self-conscious rhetorical structuring and do indeed appeal to the taste for display and iconoclastic argumentation associated with the sophists. But in the best examples, as here, there is also a serious depiction of contrasting modes of life and values (see Scodel (2000)). The debate is not designed to depict one party swaying the other through argument, but to show how the speakers on the two sides lack the basis for mutual understanding and talk right past each other. Many debates exacerbate tensions, a result that may be evident formally in the argumentative shorter dialogue (sometimes stichomythic or distichomythic: SE 3b) that follows.

**446** *Action*:  Jason enters unannounced and launches into his criticism of Medea without addressing her directly – a brusqueness typical of the superior attitude he adopts throughout the scene. The lack of announcement from Medea is unsurprising, since an actor already on-stage announces a newcomer mainly when some special eagerness is portrayed. The chorus' failure to note the new arrival emphasizes their concentration on Medea's plight and close identification with her position. Even before Jason names himself indirectly in the seventh line of his speech, his identity will probably be obvious to the audience from his rich costume, his age (as indicated by his mask and hair), and his arrival from the direction of Creon's palace. It is uncertain whether Jason is attended by silent extras: see Introd. 3.

**446–7** A general observation as prelude to a specific application (to Medea, 448 σοὶ γάρ) is a rhetorical strategy very common in speech in many genres (so e.g. above 215–25, 231–52, 294–302) and is sometimes used as here in contemptuous criticism of an opponent (e.g. 579–84, *Hipp.* 616–51, *Andr.* 184–6, 319–24, 693–703).

**447** τραχεῖαν ὀργήν: proleptic object (37n.); so again 'Ἰάσον' in 452.

**448** παρόν: acc. absolute (372n.), 'although it was open to you to keep dwelling in . . .'

**449** κούφως φερούσηι κρεισσόνων βουλεύματα: the metaphor in 'bear lightly' is of compliant animals under the yoke (242n.), and this form of imagery is characteristic of tyrants and overbearing rulers in tragedy (e.g. Aegisthus in *Ag.* 1624, 1639–42, Creon in *Ant.* 291–2, 477–8). In using κρεισσόνων Jason presupposes a strongly hierarchical relationship, whereas Medea has been emphasizing the relationship between peers sanctified by pledges and oaths (Introd. 2(*a*) and (*b*)). βουλεύματα, finally, is the first hint of Jason's facile assumption that he has deliberated and planned extremely well while Medea, a woman and prey to her emotions, seems to him incapable of such action.

**450** λόγων ματαίων: Jason insists on regarding Medea's resentment as foolish: 457 μωρίας, 600 οἶσθ' ὡς μετεύξηι καὶ σοφωτέρα φανῆι, 614 μωρανεῖς. Cf. 151–2n. on μάταιος and 866–975n. on Medea's deception of Jason by a pretended admission of her folly.

ἐκπεσῆι: ἐκπίπτω serves as the passive of ἐκβάλλω, 'to be cast into exile'.

**451** οὐδὲν πρᾶγμα 'a matter of no consequence', 'no big deal'; probably colloquial, since the phrase occurs also in Ar. *Thesm.* 244 and several times in Plato (Stevens (1976) 55).

**453** ἃ δ' ἐς τυράννους ἐστί σοι λελεγμένα: 'as far as concerns the statements you have made against the king'; the relative clause at the head of the sentence with unexpressed neuter antecedent may be treated as a kind of acc. of respect announcing a topic vital to the sense of the main clause. Cf. 547 below, *Hel.* 1009 ἃ δ' ἀμφὶ τύμβωι τῶιδ' ὀνειδίζεις πατρός, | ἡμῖν ὅδ' αὐτὸς μῦθος, and Soph. *OT* 216 ἃ δ' αἰτεῖς κτλ.

**σοι:** dat. of agent with the perfect passive verb (Smyth §1488).

**454** πᾶν κέρδος ἡγοῦ ζημιουμένη φυγῆι 'consider it entirely a profit that you are being punished ⟨merely, with no more than⟩ exile'.

**455** βασιλέων: poetic plural for Creon alone, as again in 458 τυράννους.

**456** ἀφήιρουν 'kept trying to assuage, diminish'. The audience has only Jason's word for this claim (Creon made no mention of Jason's role in his decision), but in tragedy an audience may be induced to doubt such a claim either directly by an explicit contradiction by another character or indirectly (and so more uncertainly) by the speaker's flagrant display of unattractive behaviour. The latter perhaps applies in Jason's case.

**457** ἀνίεις: imperfect of ἀνίημι, in the intransitive sense 'let up on', 'cease from' with separative gen. (LSJ s.v. ii.8.c).

**458** ἐκπεσῆι χθονός: there is probably something smug in the repetition of these words from 450, with τοιγάρ underlining the conclusion of the neatly antithetic demonstration in 451–8.

**459** κἀκ τῶνδ' 'even in these circumstances' (literally, 'even as a consequence of these things'). κἀκ crasis, καὶ ἐκ.

ἀπειρηκώς: perf. act. participle of defective verb ἀπεῖπον/ ἀπείρηκα, in the special intransitive sense 'fail, tire, give up from exhaustion' (LSJ s.v. iv.3), here with dat. of interest, 'having given up on my loved ones' or 'failing my loved ones'.

**460** τὸ σὸν δὲ προσκοπούμενος 'looking out for your interest'; compare *Andr.* 257 κοὐ τὸ σὸν προσκέψομαι, *Phoen.* 473–4 with Mastronarde's note.

**464 κακῶς φρονεῖν:** 250n.

**465–519** Medea's speech is a small masterpiece of rhetorical invective, combining clear structure and self-consciousness with a justified and controlled display of emotion. The proem in 465–74 features the strongly emotive terms παγκάκιστε, ἀνανδρίαν, ἀναίδει᾽ and vehement anaphora (467n.) but also evinces the analytic in the two γάρ-clauses and in the insistence on distinction between terms in 469–72. The second section of the speech (475–87) forms a kind of narration (Medea's services to Jason), but incorporates argumentative details (citation of witnesses against Jason in 476–7, comment on her misplaced good will in 485). In the third, directly argumentative section, 488–515, Medea exposes the injustice of Jason's return for her favours, with lively variety (direct address, apostrophe to her own hand, ironical suppositions, sarcastic use of positive terms like μακαρίαν, θαυμαστόν, πιστόν, καλόν), ending with an echo of the opening of the narration (515n.). Finally, there is a typical concluding generalization in the form of an address to Zeus involving a critique of the ways of the world 516–19n.). On this speech see Lloyd (1992) 41–3 (but he unnecessarily judges that the emotional qualities of Medea's speech are in conflict with her rhetorical control); McClure (1999b).

**465 παγκάκιστε:** this vehement vocative is found twice in Sophocles and seven times in Eur. (who also uses nom. ὁ παγκάκιστος once); the adj. does not reappear until the Roman period (where many of the uses imitate or allude to tragic style).

**465–6 τοῦτο γὰρ ..|. κακόν** 'for this is the worst abuse which my tongue can speak against your unmanliness'. γάρ is used because the parenthetic clause (the vocative leads to the incredulous question in 467) explains why Medea has blurted out the strong epithet (234n.). σε is the overall object of her insulting address (εἰπεῖν κακόν + acc. of person), and εἰς specifies the particular area of criticism. For ἔχω + inf., 'be able to', see LSJ s.v. A.III.1.a. γλώσσηι is added somewhat redundantly to suggest the contrast word vs deed, as if Medea were to add 'since I, a woman, can't punish your betrayal by physical force'.

**467 ἦλθες ... ἦλθες:** for the emotional force of this structure see LS 36; cf. Fehling (1969) 177. For γεγώς see 216n.

**468** is identical to 1324, and such repetition within a single play is usually suspect (37–45n.). In the latter passage the extension of the hatred earned by the malefactor (Medea) to gods and the whole race of men is a due reaction to the killing of the children. Here such extension intrudes on Medea's sense of personal grievance and needlessly anticipates the citation of the gods in 492–5. The line could have been added for melodramatic effect by actors, or added in the margin by a reader.

**469** θράσος: in prose and in a majority of poetic usages θράσος is opposed to θάρσος/θάρρος as rashness and over-confidence to courage and confidence, but for metrical convenience poets sometimes use θράσος in the 'good' sense, as here.

**470** δράσαντ᾽ ἐναντίον βλέπειν: the inf. phrase is in apposition to τόδ᾽; δράσαντα agrees with the unexpressed subject, and ἐναντίον is adverbial acc. For the 'mid-line caesura' with elision, see PM 17 (with footnote).

**473–4** ἐγώ τε γὰρ λέξασα .. |. κλύων: the interlaced word-order in the first limb (ABba) lends emphasis to the participle and verb, which are answered chiastically in λυπήσηι κλύων. κουφισθήσομαι has a medical connotation, reinforced by its pairing with λυπήσηι. λυπήσηι is passive in sense, a normal use of the so-called 'future middle' form (Smyth §§802, 807–9; Schwyzer 1.756).

λυπήσηι κλύων 'you will feel pain as you listen to it'; West (1984) 174 argues for aor. κλυών here on the ground of parallelism with the preceding aor. λέξασα, but the present aspect is better in accompaniment with the feeling provoked by hearing (cf. West (1984) 176). See 678n.

**475** ἐκ τῶν δὲ πρώτων πρῶτον: it is common for Euripidean speakers engaged in lengthy argumentation to call attention self-consciously to the rhetorical structure of the rhesis, esp. in its opening phases, emphasizing their control of themselves at a moment of great tension and implying the efficiency and completeness of their argument (Lloyd (1992) 19–36, esp. 34–5; Scodel (2000), esp. 134, 138–9). In the narration (διήγησις) of a forensic speech a litigant will often claim to tell the whole story from the beginning (e.g. Lysias 1.5,

12.3, Dem. 21.12). So Medea begins with τὰ πρῶτα, 'our first inter-actions'. For the juxtaposition πρώτων πρῶτον see 513n.

**476** This line was parodied as an example of Eur.'s excessive ac-cumulation of sigmas in a short space by Plato Com. fr. 29 K–A, Eubulus fr. 26 K–A. Both here and in *Ion* 386 (Creusa reproaching Apollo, ὅς γ' οὔτ' ἔσωσας τὸν σὸν ὃν σῶσαί σ' ἐχρῆν) the alliteration seems to reflect vehemence or exasperation. For statistics on 'sigma-tism' in Greek poetry and evidence for its avoidance, see Clayman (1987).

ἔσωσα: for the mythic event alluded to, see Introd. 4. The lan-guage of salvation recurs in 482 and 515, and then in Jason's attempt at refutation, 528, 531, 534.

**477** ταὐτόν: crasis, τὸ αὐτό, with optional nu for metrical conve-nience (though ταὐτόν is also found in Attic prose, esp. Isocrates and Plato).

**478–9** πεμφθέντα … ἐπιστάτην | … σπεροῦντα: the predicate noun ἐπιστάτην is equivalent to 'to be the supervisor/controller' and is thus easily paired with σπεροῦντα, the future participle which is used idiomatically with a personal object of πέμπειν to express the purpose of the mission (Smyth §2065). The dependent nouns are probably to be construed as adnominal dat. ζεύγλαισι governed by ἐπιστάτην (by analogy to the normal construction of ἐπιστατέω: LS II.c) and gen. ταύρων modifying ζεύγλαισι: 'sent to control the yoke-loops (or by synecdoche, yoke) of the fire-breathing bulls'. If ταύρων depends directly on ἐπιστάτην, which is normally used with an ob-jective gen., then ζεύγλαισι would be an adnominal instrumental dat., a harsher but not impossible construction (Smyth §1510; Schwyzer II.166).

θανάσιμον γύην 'the deadly field', that is, 'sow the field with a deadly crop' (the armed men who sprang from the sown teeth).

**482** κτείνασ': on the various traditions about the killing of the guardian serpent see Introd. 4. Unless 'having killed' is meant as shorthand for 'gave you the means to kill', this detail may magnify Medea's service to Jason.

ἀνέσχον σοι φάος σωτήριον: light is a familiar symbol of salva-tion from danger and death (e.g. *Iliad* 18.102, Aesch. *Cho.* 961 πάρα τὸ φῶς ἰδεῖν, Eur. *Her.* 531 ὦ φάος μολὼν πατρί). ἀνέχω is frequently used of holding aloft a torch, so the metaphor that Medea uses may remind an Athenian audience of Eleusinian initiation, at which torches provided light in the great dark hall of the Telesterion and a sudden blazing light in the darkness was a climactic moment in the path toward ritual salvation.

**483   αὐτή** 'by myself', 'by my own choice', 'of my own accord' (LSJ s.v. αὐτός 1.2). Pindar too emphasizes Medea's power to decide her own course, *Pyth.* 4.250 κλέψεν τε Μήδειαν σὺν αὐτᾶι.

**προδοῦσ':** see 17n.

**485   πρόθυμος μᾶλλον ἢ σοφωτέρα** 'acting with friendly zeal rather than wisdom'; it is Greek idiom to use the comparative in the second limb of such a comparison (Smyth §1080).

**486   ὥσπερ ἄλγιστον θανεῖν:** the inf. is epexegetic, and ὥσπερ goes only with adverb ἄλγιστον, a more emphatic variation on ὡς ἄλγιστον, 'in the most grievous manner possible'.

**487   πάντα τ' ἐξεῖλον δόμον:** Medea's method goes beyond eliminating the particular wrongdoer Pelias: his daughters are made the agents of his death and (instead of tending his body in ritual mourning) are responsible for its mutilation. In Eur.'s *Peliades*, unlike earlier sources, Pelias apparently had no male offspring (cf. *masculaeque prolis defectu* in the summary of Moses Chorenensis, quoted in Nauck). Thus, 'destroyed the entire house' is a justified boast, and the fullness of the revenge will be matched by how she deals with Creon and Jason. The variant φόβον ('I removed the entire source of your fear', but 'from you' should have been expressed), if not an accidental substitution, perhaps originated in a pedantic concern about the literal accuracy of πάντα ... δόμον.

**489   προύδωκας:** προέδωκας with crasis (editorial conventions vary; sometimes προὔδωκας is printed, with the coronis). See 17n.

**490   παίδων γεγώτων:** since the culturally sanctioned purpose of marriage was the begetting of legitimate (male) children to carry on the family, lack of offspring (assumed, as in many cultures, to be the woman's fault) was an accepted cause for dismissal of a wife and remarriage. Conversely, the provision of an heir normally solidified the position of the wife and represented a pledge of a lasting marital bond (see Mastronarde on *Phoen.* 16).

**491** συγγνώστ': for the neuter pl. predicate adj. with inf. subject see 384–5n.

**492** ὅρκων δὲ φρούδη πίστις recalls 412–13 and 439 in the previous stasimon, which prepared for Medea's indictment of Jason. 476–91 made the point that Jason has failed the test of human χάρις by returning treachery for benefactions. 492–5 turn to the oaths and Jason's offence against the gods who oversee them.

**493** θεοὺς ... τοὺς τότ' 'the gods who were in power then ⟨when we exchanged our oaths⟩'.

**494** καινὰ κεῖσθαι θέσμι': θέσμιον/θέσμια is a rare and solemn poetic synonym of νόμος, etymologically suggesting fixity, so that καινά may be somewhat paradoxical. The phrase is thus a version of the common νόμος κεῖται (LSJ s.v. κεῖμαι IV.3), in which the verb stands in for the perfect passive of τίθημι. For the notion of a change in the rules of human life established by the gods (treated as an impossibility), compare *Hipp.* 459–61, *Her.* 655–6.

τὰ νῦν: better taken as independent adverb (*Hel.* 631, *Or.* 436, 660, etc.; also τὰ νῦν τάδε, *Hcld.* 641, *Her.* 246) than as attributive with θέσμι'.

**495** σύνοισθα: συν- may here be intensive, 'you know full well', or, if the dat. reflexive pronoun is understood, may suggest guilty knowledge (cf. Latin *con-scientia*) and imply that Jason could bear witness against himself. The same possibilities exist in the famous line *Or.* 396 ἡ σύνεσις, ὅτι σύνοιδα δείν' εἰργασμένος (in answer to τί χρῆμα πάσχεις; τίς σ' ἀπόλλυσιν νόσος;).

**497** καὶ τῶνδε γονάτων: this is added in coordination with ἧς as another object of ἐλαμβάνου, 'as you also did my knees'; compare οὓς ... καὶ πάτραν in 503. There is no parallel for taking it with φεῦ: exclamatory gen. and exclamatory voc./nom. are alternatives never combined elsewhere.

κεχρώισμεθα: LSJ misleadingly places this under the rubric 'taint, defile' (s.v. χρώιζω 3), whereas it is simply 'we have been touched (in supplication)', as in *Phoen.* 1625 γόνατα μὴ χρώιζειν ἐμά (cf. *Hel.* 831 οὐκ ἄχρωστα γόνατ'). The negative connotations of the whole phrase derive from μάτην and κακοῦ πρὸς ἀνδρός.

**498 πρός:** 26n.

**499 ἄγ'** demands Jason's attention again after the brief partial withdrawal of the self-address in 496–8. γάρ then explains why she has turned back to Jason.

**ὡς φίλωι ... κοινώσομαι:** it is a duty of friendship to offer advice when a friend faced with a problem seeks counsel: so Aegeus is on his way to his friend Pittheus (685–7); on a more humorous note, Sostratos consults Chaireas in the first scene of Men. *Dysc.*

**500 δοκοῦσα μὲν τί:** the rhetorical question is spoken in a disbelieving tone, and is thus equivalent to a negative statement, 'not that I am expecting that I'll get any benefit from *you*!' The emphasis on δοκοῦσα leads to the postponement of the interrogative (LS 35).

**501 ὅμως δ':** understand κοινώσομαι or λέξω.

**φανῆι:** second sing. fut. mid. of φαίνω, 'you'll be clearly shown to be' (understand ὤν with αἰσχίων).

**504 καλῶς γ' ἂν οὖν:** the two particles mark καλῶς as ironic: 'Oh, they'd receive me *really* well'; see Denniston 449, and compare 588 below, where καλῶς γ' accompanied by οἶμαι has a similar tone, and 514 καλόν γ'.

**507 καθέστηχ':** καθέστηκα, 'I have become'.

**508 δρᾶν, σοί** features an uncommon position for punctuation (793n.), which here contributes to the emphasis on σοί (δρᾶν is not particularly emphatic, since it can easily be anticipated).

**509 πολλαῖς:** dat. of reference, 'in the eyes of many', 'in the judgment of many'.

**μακαρίαν:** the epithet alludes bitterly to the portion of the wedding in which the bride was pronounced blessed by her kin and their guests (*makarismos*): Garland (1990) 221. Cf. 957 μακαρίαι νύμφηι.

**510 ἀντὶ τῶνδε** 'in return for these favours' (performed in Colchis and Iolcus, 503–8).

**512 εἰ φεύξομαί γε:** the particle makes the condition virtually causal and implies that this is the only fact that really matters (Denniston 142).

**513 μόνη μόνοις:** this rhetorical strengthening by juxtaposition of different forms of the same word is called polyptoton or paregmenon (for similar exx. see Fehling (1969) 182).

**514 καλόν γ':** ironic (504n.).

**515 ἤ τ' ἔσωσά σε:** short for ἐμέ τε ἤ σ' ἔσωσα. Medea ends the argument with Jason on the note with which she began the exposition in 476, with ἔσωσά σ' (ring composition). What follows is a generalization, a typical feature of closure of tragic rheseis, esp. *agōn* speeches: see Friis Johansen (1959).

**516–19** contain a suggestion for better arrangement of the world that is typical of Euripidean characters (190–204n.). With the direct address to Zeus, this case is one of those in which the gods are criticized most explicitly as responsible for the imperfections of the world: cf. *Hipp.* 616–24, and for the poetic tradition of prayers to Zeus that are critical or even insulting, such as *Il.* 13.631–9, Theognis 373–80, 731–52, see Labarbe (1980) and Pulleyn (1997) 196–216. Since the Hesiodic view of woman is that she is the quintessential fair surface concealing a false interior, what Hippolytus calls κίβδηλον ... κακόν in *Hipp.* 616, Medea's use of this imagery in complaining about Jason is an aspect of the overturn of tradition heralded by the chorus in the previous stasimon. For comparable passages, see 220n. Most similar is Theseus' complaint in *Hipp.* 925–7 φεῦ, χρῆν βροτοῖσι τῶν φίλων τεκμήριον | σαφές τι κεῖσθαι καὶ διάγνωσιν φρενῶν, | ὅστις τ' ἀληθής ἐστιν ὅς τε μὴ φίλος.

**516 χρυσοῦ:** tragedy uses metaphorical language from coinage, but avoids direct allusion to coins, maintaining the distance of the heroic age by referring to uncoined metal and especially to gold as a medium of exchange (classical Athens issued no gold coins, only silver, and temporarily at the end of the Peloponnesian War silver-coated bronze). See Easterling (1985) 6–7; Seaford (1998).

**ὅς κίβδηλος ἦι:** in tragedy a general relative clause may sometimes have the subjunctive without ἄν, a construction inherited from

Homer (Smyth §2567b; Bers (1984) 142–64). κίβδηλος properly describes adulterated metal, and in Greece the adulteration usually took the form of concealing a base-metal interior within a noble-metal shell. The analogy between deceptive coinage and deceptive human speech, behaviour, or character was widespread (as early as the sixth century if certain passages of 'Theognis' are that old, and found in Herodotus and Democritus closer to the time of *Medea*). See Kurke (1999) 53–8.

**517** τεκμήρι' ... σαφῆ:  Eur. uses this combination also in *Hipp.* 925 and fr. 382.2, and Xenophon has it thrice. The tests used in classical Greece for purity of gold and silver included the more elaborate process of melting and heating and more widespread, accessible tests such as visual inspection, 'ringing' for aural clues (κωδωνίζειν), use of a touchtone (βάσανος), and precise weighing in a balance. The primary reference here is probably to the touchstone, a rock on which the tester scratches both the coin/metal to be tested and a known sample in order to compare the colour of the traces: see Lord (1936–37); Bogaert (1976).

**518** ἀνδρῶν may be taken with both τὸν κακόν (partitive) and σώματι (possessive).

  **διειδέναι:**  see the passages cited in 220n.

**519** χαρακτήρ (< χαράσσω) is the design stamped on a coin to identify it as the official issue of a polis, thus certified to be of the proper purity and weight; but it was in fact possible to counterfeit the stamp, as is proved by an Athenian law of 375/4 (Stroud (1974)). Metaphorical uses of this term begin in tragedy and fifth-century prose.

**520–1** Major rheseis in tragedy are usually followed by a couplet spoken by the chorus-leader, allowing the performance to 'sink in' before it is answered by an opponent or followed up with further questions. In *agōn*-scenes, the leader's contributions often are rather bland or comment on the vehement spirit of the argument rather than on the facts of the case, pointing up the contrast between the intensely involved heroic characters and the remotely involved observers. This couplet is more relevant to a long-term perspective on the situation than to the details of Medea's speech.

**520  δεινή τις:**  the addition of τις to the adj. here makes it more emphatic, 'quite terrible'.

**521  συμβάλωσ' ἔριν:**  see 44–5n.

**522–75**  Jason's speech answers Medea's in many details, as is often the case with debates in tragedy. 522–5 are a self-conscious opening that carries invective against Medea's vehemence (seen esp. in her opening lines 465–72). Medea began with her role as saviour (475–6), so Jason in 526–33 first diminishes this role, by attributing sole credit to Aphrodite and assigning Medea's action to compulsion rather than voluntary choice (cf. 483, 488). To Medea's claim of benefactions Jason next opposes in 534–44 the benefits she has herself received from him: this is the most telling passage for the wide gulf between his understanding of the world and hers and for the challenge of the play to conventional thinking, as Jason takes for granted points that have already been convincingly denied by Medea and the chorus (superiority of Greece and its laws and justice, importance of being recognized as σοφή, paramount value of δόξα). 545–6 provide a self-conscious transition, and then 547–67 give an extended reply to 489–91, arguing that his remarriage demonstrates multiple virtues. Finally, he reduces Medea's motivation to sexual jealousy alone (568–75), ending in a complaint about the arrangement of the world that answers her conclusion by its restatement of the Hesiodic calumny. The language of profit, economics, and commerce (Introd. 2(ƒ)) is used insistently by Jason: 527 ναυκληρίας, 532 ἀκριβῶς θήσομαι, 533 ὤνησας, 535 εἴληφας, δέδωκας, perhaps 533 εὕρημα ηὗρον, 560 σπανιζοίμεσθα, 561 πένητα, 565 εὐδαιμονοίην, 566 λύει, 567 ὀνῆσαι. This is in sharp contrast to Medea's concentration on salvation and on traditional values such as loyalty, *philia*, and adherence to oaths. Similar contesting world-views espoused by exemplary characters may be seen in Sophocles in the contrasts between Ajax and Odysseus, Philoctetes and Odysseus, and Antigone and Creon.

**522  μὴ κακὸν φῦναι λέγειν:**  φῦναι, a poetic synonym of γενέσθαι, here 'prove myself, show myself', is inf. with δεῖ; μὴ κακόν is litotes for ἀγαθόν, so this is an alternative phrasing of δεινὸς λέγειν, 'skilled at speaking'.

**523  ναός** is gen. sing. of ναῦς with Doric vocalism (see LS 1.c).

**οἰακοστρόφον:** given its numerous islands and lengthy coastline, it is no surprise that in ancient Greece similes and metaphors from seafaring were common (cf. Introd. 2(ƒ)), and directing the course of a ship was a skilled job, often metaphorical for political leadership. Greek ships of the classical period were steered with dual steering-oars (πηδάλια) fixed on either side at the back of the ship, each controlled by a tiller bar called οἴαξ, but the latter term was also applied to the whole assemblage. See Casson (1971) 224–8 and figs. 146, 147, 179. The man in control of the helm is termed κυβερνήτης, or (in poetry) πρυμνήτης, οἰακοστρόφος or οἰακονόμος.

**524** **ἄκροισι λαίφους κρασπέδοις** 'by using just the very fringes of the sail'; that is, the sail is rolled up (using brails: 278n.) almost completely on its yard, leaving only a small surface exposed to a strong wind; this is the prudent sailor's practice, referred to with the verbs συστέλλειν and ὑφίεσθαι, while an imprudent sailor, eager to sail faster, leaves too much sail exposed, risking capsizing or damage to sail and mast.

**525** **τὴν σὴν στόμαργον ... γλωσσαλγίαν:** the etymological play and reinforcing redundancy is mocking in tone, 'your uncontrolled incessant tongue-blather'. The suffix -αργος in στόμαργος apparently derives from the form γλώσσαργος (extant in a Pindaric fragment and *TrGF* adesp. 562), which is formed by dissimilation from γλώσσαλγος. Apart from the Pindaric use, both roots are found only a few times in the tragic texts and then in much later Greek.

**526** **καί:** the particle could simply add emphasis to λίαν or λίαν πυργοῖς, but it may be what Denniston 297 calls responsive καί in inversion, 'I *for my part*, since you also on your side build up ...'.

**527** **Κύπριν:** because the name Ἀφροδίτη has a metrical shape that is difficult to fit into strict iambic verse (∪∪ − −), it is confined to lyric passages until the later plays of Euripides, and instead Κύπρις, 'the goddess from Cyprus', is the name more commonly used in tragedy.

**ναυκληρίας:** Jason means by this simply 'voyage', in the extended meaning of the root ναυκληρ- found elsewhere in tragedy; but its etymological and everyday meaning refers to shipowning and trading by ship, so within Jason's speech an undertone of commercial, unheroic activity may possibly be heard.

**528 σώτειραν:** on the repetition of this motif in the two speeches see 476n.

**θεῶν τε κἀνθρώπων μόνην:** this is an extreme claim by Jason, typical of eristic rhetoric, for in traditional versions Jason had the important support of Athena and Hera; moreover, for the Greeks, acknowledging the favour and support of the gods did not exclude a simultaneous recognition of the importance of any special human achievement (e.g. *El.* 890–2 θεοὺς μὲν ἡγοῦ πρῶτον, Ἠλέκτρα, τύχης | ἀρχηγέτας τῆσδ', εἶτα κἄμ' ἐπαίνεσον | τὸν τῶν θεῶν τε τῆς τύχης θ' ὑπηρέτην).

**529 σοὶ δ' ἔστι μὲν νοῦς λεπτός:** the μέν-clause, as often, has concessive force: 'as for you, you do have, to be sure, a subtle mind; but . . .'. In Homer λεπτή as an epithet of μῆτις means 'scant, weak' (*Il.* 10.226, 23.590), but in the fifth century the adj. denotes an intellectual quality admired by some, probably under the influence of 'Sophistic' notions of mental agility, and denigrated by others. The adj. occurs a few times in Eur. and, along with λεπτότης and λεπτολογεῖν, is mockingly associated with Euripides and Socrates in Aristophanes' *Clouds* and *Frogs*. Subsequently λεπτός/λεπταλέος became a catchword for the refined and subtle style of Alexandrian poets: see Cameron (1995) 323 with n. 104.

**529 ἐπίφθονος λόγος διελθεῖν ὡς** 'it is a story invidious to go through in detail ⟨to tell⟩ how'; the inf. is epexegetic.

**531 τόξοις ἀφύκτοις:** for Eros' inescapable arrows see 633–5n., 635n. Strengthening ἠνάγκασεν, this phrase clearly reinforces Jason's point better than the variant πόνων ἀφύκτων (going with ἐκσῶσαι).

**532 ἀκριβῶς αὐτὸ θήσομαι:** probably a term of accounting: 'I shall not make too exact an entry of the item' (implying that an exact entry would give all credit to Aphrodite and none to Medea).

**533 γὰρ οὖν** emphasizes the essential point, 'where you *really did* help me' (Denniston 446), but the context implies that this was not so much, so the compliment is backhanded.

**ὤνησας:** aor. of ὀνίνημι, 'benefit, help'; cf. aor. act. inf. ὀνῆσαι in 567; for the middle intransitive use see 1025, 1348.

**534 γε μέντοι:** 95n.

**τῆς ἐμῆς σωτηρίας:** gen. of exchange (76n.), 'in return for my being saved'.

**535 ὡς ἐγὼ φράσω:** note the self-conscious reference to the performance of the argument, and compare 522–5, 548–50; see 475n.

**536–8** Jason smugly refers to the superiority of Greece and its laws to barbarian lands and their lack of justice. Although this reflects a xenophobia or sense of ethnic superiority that can be paralleled in other contemporary texts, it would be wrong to see this as proof of tragedy simply reinforcing the dominant ideology of the culture in which it is written, for the claim is certainly undercut here by the fact that Jason's betrayal of his oaths has been described in terms of total moral decline in Greece (439–40) and that Medea has no legal recourse for bringing him to justice (see also Introd. 2(c)). The denial of 'justice' to barbarian lands results from two types of opposition between the Greek polis and non-Greek communities: on the one hand, there are tribes and nomads who lack polis-culture and may lack written laws as well; on the other hand, there are the eastern kingdoms and empires with highly organized societies in which the Greeks notice most of all the absolute power of one ruler, which is antithetic to the ideology of the classical polis. See in general Hall (1989).

**538 μὴ πρὸς ἰσχύος χάριν** 'in a way that does not give free reign to force' (literally, 'not with a view toward gratification of force'). Cf. Hesiod's fable of the hawk and the nightingale in *WD* 202–12 (also 192 δίκη δ' ἐν χερσί) and Odysseus' question about those he encounters (e.g. *Od.* 6.120–2 ἦ ῥ' οἵ γ' ὑβρισταί τε καὶ ἄγριοι οὐδὲ δίκαιοι, | ἦε φιλόξεινοι καί σφιν νόος ἐστὶ θεουδής;).

**539–40 ἤισθοντ' ... σοφὴν καὶ δόξαν ἔσχες:** this is another detail that is particularly ill-suited to the addressee of the argument, since Medea explained earlier (292–305) the disadvantages of reputation and of being brought up to be, or being believed to be, wise/

clever. For the high value ascribed to fame, see next note and compare Cassandra's paradoxical consolation of Hecuba in *Tro.* 394–402.

**542–4**  Jason reveals his primary commitment to fame, honour, or glory by putting it ahead of other possible goods in life. Medea correctly taunts him on this in 591–2. The goods mentioned in this passage suggest the tripartite scheme of human values and pleasures that is familiar in Plato and Aristotle, but is already implied in an anecdote about Pythagoras related in Diogenes Laertius 8.8 ('he said that life is like a festival gathering: just as some come to this to compete, others for commerce, and the best people as spectators, so in life some are slavish pursuers of fame or of great wealth, but those who love wisdom are pursuers of truth') and is identified in Pericles' oration in Thuc. 2.40.1 by Rusten ad loc. Here gold stands for the life of wealth and bodily pleasure; poetic skill as a subspecies stands for the life of the intellect; and Jason's choice is clearly the life of honour.

**542**  εἴη:  for a prayer of this type, see 123–4 with note; here a noun subject is coordinated with inf. subject, ὑμνῆσαι, 'the ability to sing'.

**543**  Ὀρφέως κάλλιον:  either 'more beautifully than Orpheus' with adverbial κάλλιον, or 'sing poetry more beautiful than ⟨that of⟩ Orpheus' with adjective and compendious comparison (Smyth §1076, K–G ii.310–11). There is some irony in Jason's referring to Orpheus, famed for his loyalty to his wife Eurydice; see Mezzabotta (1994).

**544**  εἰ μὴ 'πίσημος ἡ τύχη γένοιτό μοι  'if my lot in life should not turn out to be conspicuous'; note the prodelision in μὴ ἐπίσημος (PM 10).

**546**  ἅμιλλαν ... λόγων:  this quasi-metatheatrical acknowledgment by the character of the nature of the debate scene is found in other Euripidean *agōn*-scenes as well: *Held.* 116 πρὸς τοῦτον ἀγὼν ἆρα τοῦδε τοῦ λόγου, *Hipp.* 971 τί ταῦτα σοῖς ἁμιλλῶμαι λόγοις ...;, *Supp.* 427–8 ἐπεὶ δ' ἀγῶνα καὶ σὺ τόνδ' ἠγωνίσω, | ἄκου· ἅμιλλαν γὰρ σὺ προύθηκας λόγων, *Andr.* 234, *Her.* 1255.

**547**  ἃ δ' ... ὠνείδισας:  'in respect to the reproaches you made'; for the construction see 453n.; here the introductory idea is picked up by ἐν τῷδε.

**548** δείξω ... γεγώς: 'I'll demonstrate that in this matter I have been first of all wise, etc.' For the nom. supplementary participle construction see Smyth §2106. δείξω probably evokes the common use of ἀποδείξω, ἐπιδείξω, and δείξω in oratory, where it reflects the speaker's self-consciousness of his argumentative task. Jason's demonstration is mostly about his prudence in arranging a more secure future; this is what he is most proud of and this is the point he concludes with in 567 μῶν βεβούλευμαι κακῶς. The proof of being σώφρων lies only in his claim not to have acted from desire for a new, young sexual partner. His 'friendship' is closely based on his unilateral and self-centred planning for the future.

**550** ἀλλ᾽ ἔχ᾽ ἥσυχος: predicate adj. with intransitive ἔχε, like English 'stay calm' or 'keep calm'. The same phrase occurs in *Hipp.* 1313, *IA* 1133, Ar. *Clouds* 1244, *Wealth* 127; compare *Or.* 1273 ἄφοβος ἔχε and the phrase ἔχ᾽ ἀτρέμα(ς). Medea has reacted physically to the outrageous μέγας φίλος, as if about to break in on Jason's speech. It is impossible to judge how busy or how statuesque the movements and gestures of the bystanders (actors and chorus) were when another actor was performing a long rhesis; but they may have been in general less frequent, less mimetic, and less distracting than might suit the taste of many modern directors, actors, and audiences. Occasionally, when a gesture is highly significant, it is referred to in the words of the speaker, as here. The gestural style of the speaking actor himself was varied and probably became more lively in the late fifth century and fourth century: see Aristotle *Poetics* 1461b34–62a1, Pickard-Cambridge (1968) 171–6.

**553** τοῦδ᾽... εὕρημ᾽: εὕρημ᾽ here has a pregnant sense, not simply 'plan or idea (discovered)', but 'plan to remedy ⟨my distress⟩', as in *Hipp.* 716 εὕρημα δή τι τῆσδε συμφορᾶς ἔχω. Although τοῦδ᾽ might refer to the whole content of 552 and be objective gen., it is more likely gen. of comparison, preparing for ἢ γῆμαι (same sequence of τοῦδε and ἤ with inf. in *Hcld.* 297, *Supp.* 1120, cf. Lys. 10.28, Plato, *Crito* 45c).

**555–65** This whole passage runs on from the nom. subject of γῆμαι in 554, first with negated causal participles, then after ἀλλά with the balancing purpose clauses. In English one may simply supply 'I did this' to introduce 555.

**555** οὐχ, ἧι σὺ κνίζηι, σὸν μὲν ἐχθαίρων λέχος 'not – the point by which you are nettled – because I loathed your bed'; the prepended clause is in apposition to the idea of the following participle phrase (compare 384). The quick reference to Medea's sexual jealousy prepares for 568–72.

**557** εἰς ἄμιλλαν πολύτεκνον σπουδὴν ἔχων 'setting my heart on a competition [sc. with other men] to beget a multitude of children'.

**561** πένητα φεύγει πᾶς τις ἐκποδὼν φίλον: for the idea that bad fortune and poverty lead to abandonment by friends, see *Phoen.* 403 τὰ φίλων δ' οὐδέν, ἤν τις δυστυχῆι, *Her.* 55–9 (with Bond's note on 55–7), Theognis 209–10 οὐδείς τοι φεύγοντι φίλος καὶ πιστὸς ἑταῖρος· | τῆς δὲ φυγῆς ἐστιν τοῦτ' ἀνιηρότερον; for the effect of poverty see also *El.* 1131 πένητας οὐδεὶς βούλεται κτᾶσθαι φίλους. This last line is the inspiration for Driver's emendation φίλον, which gives a sharper point and more elegant wording than the MSS' φίλος (and in any case if the friend is to be the subject, then πᾶς τις φίλων would be the more idiomatic expression).

**563–4** τοῖσιν ἐκ σέθεν τέκνοις | ἐς ταὐτὸ θείην 'I might hold them in the same esteem as my sons by you'; τέκνοις is best taken as dat. with ταὐτό (Smyth §1500), though it cannot be excluded that it is also felt to be a dat. of interest with σπείρας.

**565** εὐδαιμονοίην: the sing. may strike us as very self-centred, but it is fully consonant with Jason's attitude in the speech, and this feature should not be softened by emendation (εὐδαιμονοῖμεν Elmsley). There is also a naiveté in this claim, similar to that in Jason's praise of Greek justice and law (536–8n.). The audience will have been aware of myths in which murder and strife afflict children born of different mothers (for instance, the murder of Phocus by Peleus and Telamon) or second wives persecute the children of the first wife (for instance, Ino and the first children of Athamas, Idaea and the first children of Phineus; apparently Medea herself in Eur. *Aigeus*, fr. 4, 'a wife married second is somehow hostile to previous children'). Moreover, there were presumably in Greek culture real tensions in blended families (Garland (1990) 259–61).

παίδων: Jason apparently means 'additional children', corresponding to what he says of himself in the next line; but the line, so baldly expressed, can also be heard ominously as 'what need have you of (our present) children?', as though they are more dispensable to her than to him.

τί is postponed because of the contrastive force of σοί τε ... ἐμοί τε (LS 35).

**566  λύει:** idiomatic impersonal use (LSJ s.v. v.2), 'it is profitable', 'it is worthwhile', a shortened form of τέλη λύει, 'it discharges a debt or assessment', the origin of the prosaic λυσιτελέω and λυσιτελής.

**τέκνοις:** persons may be used in the dat. of means, as here, when they are regarded as instruments. But it is indicative of Jason's cold and calculating approach to human relationships that he uses this construction.

**567  τὰ ζῶντ'** 'living' in contrast to 'those who will be born' (instead of in contrast to 'the dead') is an unusual usage, perhaps again chosen by Eur. for an ironic effect at Jason's expense, who has no idea at all that the boys could be in danger (though the nurse was able to sense this).

**ὀνῆσαι:** 533n.

**μῶν βεβούλευμαι κακῶς:** μῶν (a contraction of μὴ οὖν) here expresses incredulity at the thought of a positive answer: 'surely, I have not laid my plans badly, have I?' (On the use of μῶν in general see Barrett on *Hipp.* 794.) The verb used here is significant, for Medea will throw it back at Jason in her deception (874, 882, 886, 893); moreover, the root βουλευ- has been and will be instrumental in Medea's own course toward revenge and child-killing (37, 317, 372, 402, 769, 772, 1044, 1048, 1079; see Introd. 2(a)).

**569  ἐς τοσοῦτον ἥκεθ'** 'you women have arrived at such a point' (that is, of overvaluation of the sexual tie); compare English 'you go so far'. Further exx. of this idiom in Mastronarde on *Phoen.* 1328. See also 56n.

**570  πάντ' ἔχειν** 'to be fully satisfied', 'to have all one needs or could desire', compare 732 below, *Ion* 1018, *Rhesus* 605, Soph. *Ant.* 498.

**573  τίθεσθε** 'consider, regard' (LSJ s.v. II.1).

**χρῆν** 'it ought to be the case' (but is not) – imperfect of unfulfilled obligation, Smyth §§1774–8. Compare the uses in similar complaints about the arrangement of the world (190–204n.) by Hippolytus and Theseus, *Hipp.* 619, 925. Hippolytus has a more detailed version of Jason's fantasy of reproduction without women, *Hipp.* 618–24.

**γάρ:** the implied connection seems to be 'I criticize women so vehemently because I can imagine a better arrangement without them, but as things are they make life miserable.' Cf. 122n.

**575 χοὔτως:** crasis, καὶ οὕτως.

**576–8** The chorus-leader recognizes the split between the rhetorical skill of the speech (εὖ ... ἐκόσμησας) and the morality of its claims; this was a major concern in late fifth-century attitudes toward the professional rhetorical training offered by the sophists. Compare the famous choral couplet that follows Eteocles' praise of tyranny/kingship, *Phoen.* 526–7 οὐκ εὖ λέγειν χρὴ μὴ 'πὶ τοῖς ἔργοις καλοῖς· | οὐ γὰρ καλὸν τοῦτ', ἀλλὰ τῆι δίκηι πικρόν (see Mastronarde ad loc.).

**577 κεἰ παρὰ γνώμην ἐρῶ** 'even if what I shall say is contrary to your judgment', 'even if I offend you'; that is, the leader will be forthright in criticizing the male hero, unlike the many choral comments that are deferential to the powerful. Aesch. *Ag.* 931 τόδ' εἰπὲ μὴ παρὰ γνώμην ἐμοί, 'tell me this without concealing what you really believe', suggests that if γνώμη were that of the chorus leader instead of Jason, the meaning would be 'speak contrary to what I really think' (unsuitable here), not, as Verrall claimed, 'contrary to my better judgment', 'indiscreetly', which seems quite inapposite to the stance of the chorus.

**578 προδοὺς ... οὐ δίκαια:** for judgment of Jason as betrayer and unjust, see 17n.

**579 πολλὰ πολλοῖς:** expressive polyptoton (513n.); πολλά is acc. of respect, 'in many respects', 'in many judgments'. See 1165n., Fehling (1969) 182.

**580 ἐμοί** 'in my judgment', 'to my mind' (dat. of reference).

**σοφὸς λέγειν** is a variation on δεινὸς λέγειν, found also in fr. 189.2; cf. *Rhesus* 625 νοεῖν σοφός, Soph. fr. 524.7 εὖ φρονεῖν σοφώτερος.

**581 ζημίαν ὀφλισκάνει:** both words have technical legal meanings, 'incurs a penalty' assessed as a fine on conviction of a charge in court.

**582 αὐχῶν:** not 'boasting loudly' or 'saying brazenly', but 'believing (over)confidently' or 'feeling (unjustifiably or foolishly) confident', as *Alc.* 95, 675, *Hcld.* 333, *Tro.* 770, *Bacch.* 310 (see Barrett on *Hipp.* 952–5).

**583 ἔστι δ' οὐκ ἄγαν σοφός:** relying on the unstated premise that wrongdoers cannot be totally and permanently successful, Medea implies that the over-confident villain will in fact be confuted on some point and thus lose the protection of his glib rhetoric. This half-line is reminiscent of Medea's εἰμὶ δ' οὐκ ἄγαν σοφή (305), and in a play in which the roots σοφ-, βουλευ-, and the like are so important the repetition is unlikely to be accidental: it apparently points to the fact that Medea will share with Jason the fate of being damaged by the results of her own cleverness.

**584 ὡς καὶ σύ· μή νυν:** many editors have accepted this as a continuous clause, as in the other tragic instances of ὡς καὶ σύ (*Hipp.* 651, *Andr.* 703, Soph. *El.* 1086), but those passages contain indicative verbs illustrating the claim made before ὡς. Here the prohibition and the presence of μή νυν (elsewhere always first in its clause) make a difference, so an ellipsis should be assumed: 'as your case too illustrates'.

**εὐσχήμων γένηι** 'put on a seemly façade'.

**585 ἐκτενεῖ:** fut. of ἐκτείνω, 'lay out flat', apparently a metaphor from wrestling (or boxing?), though this verb is not elsewhere so used. Cf. ἐκπετάσουσι in *Her.* 887 of Heracles brought down by Furies. No proof is available that either verb was a technical term, as Wilamowitz on *Her.* 890 declared.

**586 χρῆν:** 573n.

**587 γαμεῖν γάμον:** for this idiomatic internal acc. construction see 626, 777–8, LSJ s.v. γαμέω I.1, and compare 594n.

**σιγῆι φίλων** 'in secrecy from your dear ones', on the analogy of the more common λάθραι + gen.; compare Hdt. 2.140.1 σιγῆι τοῦ Αἰθίοπος. Medea assumes that her relationship with Jason was one of equals, the sort of φίλοι who share their plans and consult each other (499n.).

**588** **καλῶς γ᾽ ... οἶμαι:** for the ironic force of καλῶς γ᾽, see 504n.; for ironic οἶμαι, see *Hcld.* 511, 968.

**589** **ἥτις:** the indefinite relative is used with a specific antecedent because the clause conveys a characteristic of the antecedent (Smyth §2496), which may also be regarded as causal ('since not even now you . . .'); compare 1130, 1234, 1280.

**591** **οὐ τοῦτό σ᾽ εἶχεν** 'this is not what was on your mind', τοῦτο meaning 'your concern about how angrily I might react if you told me'. Another possible translation is 'this is not what was restraining you (from seeking my consent)'; but the sense 'check, restrain' is normally conveyed by ἔσχον, not εἶχον.

**592** **πρὸς γῆρας** 'with the approach of old age', virtually 'in old age' (so too Pindar, *Nem.* 9.44; but 'up into old age', 'until old age' in *Supp.* 917, Plato, *Laws* 888c).

**οὐκ εὔδοξον ἐξέβαινέ σοι** 'was going to turn out (229n.), as you saw it, of insufficient status'; the imperfect here is equivalent in sense to ἔμελλε ἐκβήσεσθαι (a conative use: Smyth §1895a). Jason's keen interest in high position in the community is evident in 544, 552–4, 562–5.

**593** **μὴ γυναικὸς οὕνεκα:** note the disjunction between Medea's and Jason's perceptions of the situation: Medea was accusing Jason of social climbing, but in rebuttal Jason focuses on her use of λέχος and denies only a sexual cause, in fact confirming Medea's diagnosis by the phrase φῦσαι τυράννους παῖδας (597) even as he claims he wanted to keep her safe. The negative of the indirect statement is μή because it is a strong, emotional asseveration (Smyth §2725).

**594** **γῆμαί με λέκτρα βασιλέων:** for the inf. of indirect discourse after οἶδα (much less common than participial construction or ὅτι-clause), see LSJ s.v. εἴδω B.4 and Smyth §2139 (but the construction is assisted here by τόδ᾽, since the inf. can be felt to be in apposition to the pronoun). λέκτρα is internal acc., used as a synonym of γάμον: 'I made a marriage with the royal family'; cf. 140 λέκτρα τυράννων with n., and 587n.

**595** θέλων: nom. by attraction to the subject of nearby εἶπον, even though logically it goes with με to balance μὴ γυναικὸς οὕνεκα.

σῶσαι carries an extraordinary claim, as though Medea was in danger *before* Jason sought marriage with the princess (the aor. is 'rescue from danger', while the present would be 'keep secure' or 'maintain in safety'). There is no indication of such danger in Eur.'s version, although some ancient versions (Introd. 4) and many modern adaptations exploit the notion that Medea is distrusted and disliked by the Corinthians or threatened with surrender to Pelias' kin. This seems to be a shameless exaggeration on Jason's part: not only did Medea not save him, he has worked to save her.

**596** σέ: the enjambment and minor punctuation after the first syllable of the line here seem to reinforce the exasperated tone (793n.).

**597** ἔρυμα δώμασιν: the adnominal dat. of interest (LS 11.c) is used instead of the objective gen. seen in 1322 ἔρυμα πολεμίας χερός.

**598** μή μοι γένοιτο λυπρὸς εὐδαίμων βίος 'may I never get a prosperous life that is painful (to my spirit)'; for the need to understand ὤν with one of the adjs. in brachylogic sentences like this, see Mastronarde on *Phoen.* 442 πένης γὰρ οὐδὲν εὐγενὴς ἀνήρ.

**599** κνίζοι: third appearance of this word within 50 lines (555, 568); the verb of the relative clause is optative by attraction to the optative of wish of the main clause (Smyth §2186a).

**600** οἶσθ᾽ ὡς μετεύξῃ: μετεύχομαι, 'change one's prayer', is extant only here (and in the scholia here). Diggle accepts Elmsley's emendation to aor. imperative μέτευξαι, which was proposed for conformity with the idiom οἶσθ᾽ οὖν ὃ δρᾶσον and some similar phrases, found about a dozen times in Euripides and comedy. In this idiom an originally interrogative οἶσθ᾽ ὡς or οἶσθ᾽ ὅ has become frozen as a lively lead-in to δρᾶσον or other imperatives meaning 'do' (ποιείτω in Ar. *Ach.* 1064, ποίησον in Men. fr. 649 K–A, σύμπραξον in *Hcld.* 451). But it is not certain that the idiom should be carried over to a verb like μετεύχομαι. Eur. has other variations, but with forms of δρᾶν: *IT* 759 οἶσθ᾽ ὃ δράσω, *Supp.* 932 οἶσθ᾽ ὃ δρᾶν σε βούλομαι.

**601–2** φαίνεσθαι ... δοκεῖν: the infs. depend on 'pray' understood from μετεύξῃ: 'pray that what is good never appears to you to be painful, and that you do not believe you are unfortunate when you have good fortune'. The admonition is weakened somewhat if Jason himself utters the imperatives (MSS have φαινέσθω and δόκει) as direct discourse.

**604 φευξοῦμαι:** the contracted future is not found in Aeschylus or Sophocles, but Eur., like Aristophanes, uses φευξοῦμαι and φευξούμεθα as well as uncontracted φεύξομαι and φευξόμεσθα. Normally the choice conforms to metrical necessity (see 341, 346, 512), but here and in Ar. *Ach.* 203 we find φευξοῦμαι where φεύξομαι would also scan, and in *Hipp.* 1093 we find φευξούμεσθα where φευξόμεσθα would scan (but there is MS variation in all three places).

**605 αἰτιῶ:** second sing. present middle-passive imp. of αἰτιάομαι, 'blame'.

**606–7** No main verb is used in these lines, as the participles all depend on the subject of εἵλου in 605, a typical method of continuing and sharing syntactic structure in stichomythia (LS 29).

**606 μῶν γαμοῦσα:** the sarcastic tone is strengthened by the implication of disbelief in μῶν and by Medea's adoption of the active voice of γαμέω (suited for the male: 262n.) as she alludes to Jason's own misdeeds: 'you mean by my taking a wife and betraying you?'

**608 καὶ σοῖς ἀραία γ':** the particles provide separate emphases, καί implying 'your house too (as well as the royal family)' and γε ('yes, ...') marking the adj. as a riposte to ἀρωμένη. Note that 'Jason's house' implies his offspring: although Jason himself shows no awareness at all of danger to his children, the audience can certainly hear the bad omen in these words, whether it suspects that Medea has already hatched a plan or (later) assumes that she thinks of killing the children only after Aegeus' visit (Introd. 2(*b*)).

οὖσα τυγχάνω is here just a rhetorically more weighty synonym for εἰμί: see *IT* 607 and LSJ s.v τυγχάνω A.II.1.

**609 ὡς** here, at the opening of a speech, introduces a strong asseveration, and one may assume an ellipsis of εὖ ἴσθι, 'know well', or the like (Diggle (1981) 88). Contrast ὡς = 'because', 'for' in 612.

κρινοῦμαι ... τὰ πλείονα: the middle-passive κρινοῦμαι means 'dispute', but with the implication 'allow myself to be judged in a contest with you'. Jason is simply cutting off further debate, so τὰ πλείονα is perhaps simply a metrically convenient alternative to plain πλείονα (compare Eur. fr. 417.4, *Rhes.* 78); Page, however, suggests that the implication is 'the more that might follow'.

**611 προσωφέλημα χρημάτων ἐμῶν:** προσωφέλημα is extant nowhere else; χρημάτων may be taken with λαβεῖν as gen. of source ('from my wealth') or partitive ('some of my wealth'), or less likely as a defining gen. with the noun, 'assistance afforded by my wealth'. Notice that Jason again falls into a concentration of quasi-financial terms: χρημάτων, ἀφθόνωι, κερδανεῖς.

**612 λέγ':** the single syllable at line-beginning with following punctuation is rhythmically unusual and in this case probably emphatic (793n.).

ἕτοιμος: εἰμί is understood with this adj. here and elsewhere (see LS 30, and Mastronarde on *Phoen.* 968–9).

**613 σύμβολ':** *symbola* are formed from any physical token divided in two and kept separately by the parties to an agreement or transaction; the two pieces could later be rejoined to verify their fit and so authenticate the origin of a message. Knucklebones and other small items could serve this purpose.

οἳ δράσουσι: the fut. indicative in a relative clause may convey purpose (Smyth §2554).

**616 οὔτ' ἄν ... χρησαίμεθ' ἄν:** for double ἄν see 250–1n.

**617 δίδου:** the present-stem aspect of this imperative conveys 'don't even offer me anything' or 'don't try to give me anything'.

**618** Medea's generalization is similar to Soph. *Aj.* 665 ἐχθρῶν ἄδωρα δῶρα κοὐκ ὀνήσιμα, which reflects the mythic motif of apparent gifts from enemies that produce disaster (e.g. Hector's sword given to Ajax, the Trojan Horse, the gift of Nessus to Deianeira). But Medea speaks not of enemies, but of 'a base man' and thus her complaint recalls aristocratic Theognidean complaints about the unsuitability of κακοί as friends and companions (Theognis 31–8, 101–12, 305–8, 1165–8).

**619** ἀλλ' οὖν:  after Medea's rejection of his offer, these particles mark a breaking off and turning to a fallback position in which Medea's consent is no longer needed (compare Denniston 442–3).

δαίμονας μαρτύρομαι:  invocation of the gods as witnesses is a common rhetorical and social device to emphasize that one has done all in one's power to satisfy claims against one and to address the issues of a dispute, but that the other party has not been flexible and must be held accountable for future violence and suffering (cf. e.g. Thuc. 1.78.4, 2.74.2).

**621** αὐθαδίαι:  see 103–4n.

**622** ἀλγυνῆι:  second sing. future middle (as the accent shows) in passive sense, 'you will be pained'.

**623** χώρει:  Jason has probably begun his movement on his own accord, and Medea adds mocking encouragement and then a threat spoken behind his back: compare Electra speaking behind Cly-temnestra's back in *El.* 1139–46, or Amphitryon behind Lycus' in *Her.* 726–33 (see Taplin (1977) 221–2).

νεοδμήτου:  coined as a variation on νεόδμης (1366, *Hom. Hymn Aphr.* 231) and imitated a few times in later poetry; there is perhaps a mocking hint of the docility of the young bride in contrast to the fierce independence of the mature Medea.

**624** ἐξώπιος:  a Euripidean coinage, literally 'out of the sight of' (*Alc.* 546), but serving as a convenient variation on ἔξω here and *Supp.* 1038, a usage recognized as peculiarly Euripidean by Ar., *Thesm.* 881, 884.

**625** σὺν θεῶι δ' εἰρήσεται:  εἰρήσεται is future perfect mid.-pass. indicative from εἴρηκα, εἴρημαι. This phrase (also in Ar. *Wealth* 114) seems to be a more confident form of a pious expression meaning 'may it be said with the gods' favour': compare parenthetic epex-egetic inf. σὺν θεῶι εἰπεῖν in Soph. fr. 479.1–2, Plato, *Theaet.* 151b4, *Protag.* 317b7, *Laws* 858b2; also Hdt. 1.86 ὡς οἱ εἴη σὺν θεῶι εἰρημένον. The piety of the expression is a foretaste of the collusion of the gods in Medea's violence, and the confidence of the future tense (in place of an optative of wish) is a hint of Medea's almost prophetic power.

**626** γαμεῖς ... γάμον: 587n. γαμεῖς may be present or future; if future, it perhaps has the pregnant meaning 'you will find that you are making a marriage ...'

**τοιοῦτον ὥστε θρηνεῖσθαι γάμον** 'such a marriage as will make you lament' (instead of celebrate, as is normal), with rare middle θρηνεῖσθαι as in *Prom.* 43, Soph. *Aj.* 852. This is Dodds' emendation for transmitted ὥστε σ' ἀρνεῖσθαι γάμον, which is taken to mean 'such a marriage that you would renounce it' (but in what sense would Jason be disavowing the marriage?) or 'such a marriage that you would deny it is a marriage' (because it has turned into a funeral?) – a rather weak scene-ending.

## *627–62   Second stasimon*

As in the first stasimon the chorus here remains fixed in its stance of sympathy for Medea and disapproval of the treachery of Jason. This song provides a suitable closure to the intervening *agōn* between Jason and Medea and again avoids any forward reference to planned or feared actions. Here too the opening shows a deliberate distancing from the preceding lines, as the chorus begins with a gnomic claim about love and continues with first-person wishes that take an apotropaic form. Apotropaic prayer or wish is a common device in choral odes of all three tragedians, underlining the contrast between the extremes experienced or embraced by the heroic individuals and the relative safety and quietism of the humble collective. The wish for safe marriage and moderate love is clearly conceived in contrast to Medea's situation, but the chorus does not specify this connection. Rather, they turn in the second pair of stanzas to the theme of an exile's helplessness, again wishing never to experience such a disadvantage, and this is the theme that is explicitly tied to Medea in the final stanza. It re-emphasizes the pressure put upon Medea by Creon's decree and by her refusal of Jason's aid and recalls Medea's need for a safe haven just before that need is to be obviated by Aegeus.

The themes are the same as in the first stasimon, but in a different balance. There, the main theme was faithlessness and broken oaths, with a brief allusion to the erotic tie and more attention to the theme of separation from family and fatherland. Here erotic passion and erotic rivalry loom larger, the theme of exile is as prominent as

before, and the disapproval of false friendship forms the brief coda.
The two stasimons thus provide alternating support for the two ways
of looking at the conflict between Medea and Jason (Introd. 2(*b*)).
The final curse echoes Medea's own complaint about counterfeit
friends (516–19) and thus has a backward reference to Jason. But
there is a forward reference that the chorus cannot be aware of:
Aegeus enters as a friend and open-heartedly shows himself to be a
friend in need, grateful for a promised favour – thus the opposite of
Jason; on the other hand, Medea, whom the chorus considers a
friend, deals with Aegeus with concealment and trickery, proving
herself as counterfeit as Jason.

*Metre*

As in the first stasimon, we find here a first pair written in dactylo-
epitrite (3 periods, or 4 if there is also period-end after the first colon)
and a second pair consisting of aeolic and enoplian cola (2–4 shorter
periods and a final longer one): see PM 26–7. The ethos of the
dactylo-epitrite pair is perhaps more stately, that of the aeolic pair
more agitated or emotionally expressive, as there is a shift from the
regularity of the D elements ($-\cup\cup-\cup\cup-$) to the many variations in
the aeolic lines – the double choriamb that opens the stanza, the
kindred opening of the diomedean (a headless D), and the changing
position of the choriambic kernel in other lines.

647–8 and 650 are compound cola of a type discussed by Itsumi
(1991–93). One would expect period-end at 648, and it is possible to
obtain it there by changing αἰῶν' to αἰῶ (Wilamowitz (1921) 540 n. 1),
an alternative acc. form found in Aesch. *Cho.* 350 (1162n.). With a
different choice of reading 649 = 658 could fit well as hemiepes
(649n.); the dodrans shown here is the reversed form ($-\cup-\cup\cup-$
for $-\cup\cup-\cup-$ by anaclasis). The final period 651–3 = 660–2 is divided by some as 10-syllable aeolic + glyconic + aristophanean (an
approximate echo of the first period of the stanza), but the division
here reflects an alternative offered by Dale, *MATC* 1.53 that keeps
662 ἐμοὶ μέν in the same colon.

$\underline{\cup}\ -\cup\ \cup\ -\cup\cup\ -\ -\ -\cup\ -\ -\ -\cup\ -\ |$

| | |
|---|---|
| ἔρωτες ὑπὲρ μὲν ἄγαν ἐλθόντες οὐκ εὐδοξίαν | 627–28 ×D−E |
| στέργοι δέ με σωφροσύνα, δώρημα | 636–7 |
| κάλλιστον θεῶν· | |

– ⏑⏑ – ⏑ ⏑ – ⏟ – ⏑ ⏑ – ⏑ ⏑ – – ‖²
οὐδ' ἀρετὰν παρέδωκαν ἀνδράσιν· εἰ δ' ἅλις     629–30 D×D –
ἔλθοι

μηδέ ποτ' ἀμφιλόγους ὀργὰς ἀκόρεστά τε     638–9
νείκη

–⏑ – – – ⏑ ⏑ – ⏑ ⏑ – –‖²
Κύπρις, οὐκ ἄλλα θεὸς εὔχαρις οὕτω.     631–2 e – D –
θυμὸν ἐκπλήξασ' ἑτέροις ἐπὶ λέκτροις     640–1

– ⏑ – – – ⏑⏑ – ⏑⏑ – – –⏑ – –
μήποτ', ὦ δέσποιν', ἐπ' ἐμοὶ χρυσέων τόξων     633–4 e – D – e –
ἀφείης

προσβάλοι δεινὰ Κύπρις, ἀπτολέμους δ'     642–3
εὐνὰς σεβίζουσ'

– ⏑ – – – ⏑ – ⏑ – – ⫶⫶⫶
ἱμέρωι χρίσασ' ἄφυκτον οἰστόν.     635 E, ba
ὀξύφρων κρίνοι λέχη γυναικῶν.     644

— — — — — — — — — —

–⏑ ⏑ – – ⏑ ⏑ – |
ὦ πατρίς, ὦ δώματα, μὴ     645 2 choriambs
εἴδομεν, οὐκ ἐξ ἑτέρων     654

– ⏑⏑ – ⏑ – – ‖
δῆτ' ἄπολις γενοίμαν     646 aristophanean
μῦθον ἔχω φράσασθαι·     655

⏑ ⏑ – ⏑ – ⏑ – ⏑ – ⏑ – –
τὸν ἀμηχανίας ἔχουσα δυσπέρατον αἰῶν',     647–8 diomedean +
    ithyphallic

σὲ γὰρ οὐ πόλις, οὐ φίλων τις οἰκτιρεῖ     656–57
παθοῦσαν

– ⏑ ⏜ ⏑⏑ – ‖²
οἰκτρότατον ἀχέων.     649 dodrans
δεινότατα παθέων.     658

⏑ ⏑ – ⏑ ⏑ – ⏑ – ⏑ – –‖²
θανάτωι θανάτωι πάρος δαμείην     650 diomedean + sp
ἀχάριστος ὄλοιθ' ὅτωι πάρεστιν     659

– ⏑ – – – ⏑⏑–
ἀμέραν τάνδ' ἐξανύσα-     651 wilamowitzian
μὴ φίλους τιμᾶν καθαρᾶν     660

ᴗ – –ᴗ̱ – ᴗ ᴗ –
σα· μόχθων δ' οὐκ ἄλλος ὕπερ-      652 wilamowitzian
ἀνοίξαντα κλῇδα φρενῶν·              661

ᴗ – – ᴗ ᴗ – ᴗ – – |||
θεν ἢ γᾶς πατρίας στέρεσθαι.        653 hipponactean
ἐμοὶ μὲν φίλος οὔποτ' ἔσται.       662

**627–44** The compulsive, violent, and destructive force of Eros and Aphrodite is featured impressively in other tragic choral odes: Soph. *Trach.* 497–530, *Ant.* 781–800, *Hipp.* 525–64, 1268–82, *IA* 543–89.

**627 ἔρωτες ὑπὲρ μὲν ἄγαν ἐλθόντες** 'loves that come in very great excess'. ὑπέρ is probably to be heard as in tmesis (Smyth §1650–1) rather than as an adverb, since the few other possibly adverbial uses may also be explained as instances of tmesis: Aesch. *Pers.* 113, Soph. *Ant.* 518 (but cf. *Aj.* 1231). ὑπερελθόντων is used in the sense 'excel' in Pindar, *Ol.* 13.15; in drama a number of compounds in ὑπερ- are reinforced by ἄγαν (*Held.* 388 τῶν ἄγαν ὑπερφρόνων; Aesch. *Pers.* 794, 827, *Sept.* 238, *Eum.* 824, Soph. *Aj.* 951, Ar. *Wealth* 354; cf. adverb ὑπεράγαν, common in the Roman period but not extant earlier). ἔρωτες is positioned first as the topic of the whole contrast, but the contrast is artfully unbalanced, with participle answered by εἰ-clause and ἔρωτες resumed by Κύπρις.

**629 παρέδωκαν:** 'bestow', gnomic aor.

ἀνδράσιν 'mortals', 'human beings' generically, as often in poetry, whereas in the first stasimon (413, 431) the chorus used ἄνδρες of 'males' in opposition to women.

**630–1 εἰ δ' ἅλις ἔλθοι | Κύπρις:** compare *IA* 554–7 εἴη δέ μοι μετρία μὲν χάρις, πόθοι δ' ὅσιοι, καὶ μετέχοιμι τᾶς Ἀφροδίτας, πολλὰν δ' ἀποθείμαν, the conclusion of a stanza that may be compared as a whole for its contrasting of moderate experience of love with destructive excess.

**633–5 μήποτ' ..|. οἰστόν** 'may you never, lady goddess, shoot against me from your golden bow an inescapable arrow, having anointed it with desire'. The arrow of love represents involuntary imposition of compulsive desire, not a moderate experience of Aphrodite. Elsewhere, arrows are the weapon of Eros, the son and agent of Aphrodite: first explicitly in literature in Eur. (530–1 above, *IA* 548, and esp. *Hipp.* 530–2 οὔτε γὰρ πυρὸς οὔτ' ἄστρων ὑπέρτερον βέλος οἷον τὸ τᾶς Ἀφροδίτας ἵησιν ἐκ χερῶν Ἔρως ὁ Διὸς παῖς), although metaphors of missiles and archery are applied to desire in Aesch. *Supp.* 1004–5 and *Prom.* 649–50; in artworks Eros the archer appears first in a lekythos of *c.* 490 (*LIMC* s.v. Eros, no. 332), although the motif is rare until the fourth century. Here either the weapon is transferred to Aphrodite, or we are to assume Eros' agency, ἀφείης being more or less causative in sense. For the wish, compare *Hipp.* 528–9 (addressed to Eros) μή μοί ποτε σὺν κακῷ φανείης μηδ' ἄρρυθμος ἔλθοις.

**ἀφείης** is an emendation of MSS' ἐφείης (for the interchange of these prefixes see 373n.), preferred because the separative gen. τόξων is more readily understandable and the variation in ἐφ' ἡμῖν ... ἀφείης is more elegant; but ἐφείης is not impossible.

**635** **ἄφυκτον οἰστόν:** the chorus' phrase actually echoes Jason's words in 531 τόξοις ἀφύκτοις. Unerring arrows are also ascribed to Artemis (*Hipp.* 1422 τόξοις ἀφύκτοις) and Heracles (Soph. *Phil.* 105).

**636** **στέργοι δέ με σωφροσύνα:** this is an unusual reversal of construction, since normally a person as subject 'accepts gladly' some abstract noun as object. The effect of the reversal is, first, to suggest almost a personification of moderation/self-control, since the verb is sometimes used of divine favour (Aesch. *Eum.* 911, Ar. *Frogs* 229), and, second, to acknowledge the gods' potential control of a person's mindset, a pious stance seen in other apotropaic prayers (e.g. *Hipp.* 1111–19, Soph. *OT* 863–5).

**638–44** 'And may the dread Cyprian goddess never impose ⟨upon me⟩ quarrelsome anger and insatiable strife, stunning my heart with desire for another bed; may she rather, showing respect for marriage-beds free of conflict, determine with keen intelligence the liaisons of women.' The chorus continues to use what may be called the 'ethical' first person to espouse moral positions that are meant to be exemplary of what is to be expected of all decent persons. There is, however, a curious dislocation in the relation of the chorus' wish to the situation of Medea and Jason. Medea got herself into her predicament partly because of her passion for Jason, and now feels so strongly about abandonment partly because of her passion. But the anger and strife the audience has just witnessed are caused by Jason's straying to 'another bed', and this is in fact the 'normal' social pattern: a woman who pursues a lover outside of marriage does not simply have strife with her husband, she is divorced from him (or in myth some other disaster follows, such as death of the husband or doom for the unfaithful wife). Strife within the marriage is caused rather by the husband's infidelity, a motif as old as *Od.* 1.429–33, where Laertes avoids his wife's anger by never sleeping with Eurycleia, and used by Eur. in *Hipp.* 151–4 (the chorus speculates whether Phaedra is sick because Theseus has an extramarital affair) and *Andr.* (esp. 464–70). This blurring of the positions of the two genders may result partly from the role of the chorus as conveyer of gnomic wisdom and be an effect of the chorus' wish to dissociate itself apotropaically from the excesses of both Medea and Jason. But it perhaps also reflects the sense of reversal about which the women sang in the previous stasimon, and resonates with Medea's assumption of male terms and values.

**640–1 θυμὸν ἐκπλήξασ᾽:** this verb is used of various strong emotional upsets, especially fear, shock, and surprise, but for the erotic sense compare 8 above and *Hipp.* 38. λέκτροις here provides the specification that in the other two instances is given by ἔρωτι and κέντροις ἔρωτος.

**ἑτέροις ἐπὶ λέκτροις** 'because of another bed (sexual union)', other than my husband's, with ἐπί of cause or occasion (LSJ s.v. B.III.1). Compare Pindar, *Pyth.* 11.24 ἑτέρωι λέχεϊ δαμαζομέναν of Clytemnestra, 'made subject to another bed' (Aegisthus'); *Andr.* 487 ἑτέρωι λέχει, 'her husband's other sexual union', 'her rival' (Andromache). Some have wished to make the chorus' wish directly parallel to Medea's situation (638–44n.) by understanding 'because of ⟨my husband's⟩ other bed' (see Meridor (1986)); but the proper antithesis of the speaker's *sophrosyne* is her own inappropriate erotic infatuation (θυμὸν ἐκπλήξασ᾽).

**642–3 δεινὰ Κύπρις:** the same epithet is used of Cypris in *Hipp.* 563 (in the same ode from which other parallels for this song have been cited); in both cases it can be translated adverbially, 'with dreadful power'.

**ἀπτολέμους:** for this form of ἀπόλεμος see LS 4; this is the only occurrence of πτολεμ- in extant drama.

**644 ὀξύφρων:** extant here alone until late Greek; the adj. is predicative, equivalent to an adverb, 'using keen intelligence'.

**κρίνοι λέχη γυναικῶν:** this 'judgment' of Aphrodite is to be understood as her general disposition for mortals of their fortune and experience of sexuality. The chorus is asking that the goddess recognize (as the chorus themselves do) the superior value of peaceful unions and determine her apportionment of sexual experience intelligently, in accordance with that recognition. Once again, as at 516–19, we have an implied criticism of how the gods run the world: the influence of Aphrodite on human life suggests that she has no compunction about causing human misery and does not respect peaceful marriages. This final clause is thus a rephrasing of 630 ἅλις ἔλθοι, a wish that the goddess 'come in sufficiency' and not in excess and transgression. Page is mistaken in seeking a narrow relevance to Medea's experience and concluding that the wish should refer to the period after marriage: 'showing respect for marriages that ⟨she observes⟩ are ⟨already⟩ peaceful, may she shrewdly judge women's unions', that is, may she judge between different married women and not 'choose the victims of her malice among the peaceful' – this would make the chorus accept the goddess' persecution of women who are already unhappy in marriage.

**647–8 τὸν ἀμηχανίας ... δυσπέρατον αἰῶν'** 'having the life of helplessness, hard to live through (or, hard to escape from)'; the article here has the force 'the one that exile entails'; since περάω may refer to motion across an expanse or motion across a limit and thus out of an expanse, it cannot be determined which sense is foremost here in δυσπέρατος.

**649 οἰκτρότατον ἀχέων:** the MSS transmit οἰκτροτάτων ἀχέων, which does not correspond metrically to 658 δεινότατα παθέων. Triclinius (a Byzantine scholar of the first quarter of the fourteenth century who understood strophic response and emended many dramatic texts on the basis of this rare knowledge) made 658 conform to 649 by changing to δεινότατον παθέων (the line is then a hemiepes, perfectly suitable in this context). But οἰκτροτάτων ἀχέων gives somewhat feeble rhetoric, as a descriptive genitive that adds little to the striking phrasing of 648. Musgrave's change of οἰκτροτάτων to οἰκτρότατον produces much better sense (apposition to αἰῶν' or (better) to the whole verbal phrase τὸν ... ἔχουσα ... αἰῶν' (LS 12.a)) and requires no change in 658. The line is then a dodrans with resolved long, in the analysis given above; some consider it rather a continuation of the rhythm of the ithyphallic ending of 647–8, treating ἀχέων and παθέων as disyllabic by synizesis, but an isolated 'pentapody' (– ∪◡∪ –) is hard to accept (this pattern is either associated with dochmiacs as the hypodochmiac or repeated in a syncopated iambo-trochaic context as a short colon).

**650** θανάτωι θανάτωι:　anadiplosis for emotional effect (LS 36).

**651** ἀμέραν τάνδ' ἐξανύσασα　'bringing my life's daylight to an end' (Kovacs); the participle is in the 'coincident aorist' (LS 14); for ἡμέρα in metonymy for 'life' cf. LS 31, LSJ s.v. 1.2.

**652–3** οὐκ ἄλλος ὕπερ | θεν:　understand μόχθος with ἄλλος (from partitive μόχθων) and ἐστί; ὕπερθεν is equivalent to predicate adj. ὑπέρτερος. For the sentiment see 329n.

**654** οὐκ ἐξ ἑτέρων:　for this way of emphasizing direct experience and knowledge, cf. Aesch. *Pers.* 266–7 καὶ μὴν παρών γε κοὐ λόγους ἄλλων κλυών, Πέρσαι, φράσαιμ' ἄν; Soph. *OT* 6–7 δικαιῶν μὴ παρ' ἀγγέλων, τέκνα, | ἄλλων ἀκούειν αὐτὸς ὧδ' ἐλήλυθα; Eur. *Supp.* 684, *Tro.* 481–3, *IT* 901; Diggle (1994) 81 n. 60.

**655** ἔχω φράσασθαι:　probably a mere variation (for metrical convenience) on the very common ἔχω φράσαι, 'I am able to tell', esp. since φράζειν often takes λόγον, μῦθον, or the like as object. Eur. has no other middle-passive form of φράζω except *Hec.* 546 ἐφράσθη, 'she perceived', and the middle is absent from comedy (except for mock-oracles) and from Attic prose. The middle is thus a feature of older poetic styles, and Aeschylus and Sophocles have half a dozen instances with meanings like 'beware', 'perceive', 'plan', 'reflect'. Page thinks that this middle too must have the standard poetic meaning and translates 'reflect upon'.

**656–7** γάρ is used to introduce the content of the statement (μῦ-θον): see Denniston 59.

οἰκτιρεῖ: the MSS have the imperfect, which does not fit the metre. Emendation to the future is best since the chorus is thinking forward to Medea's future fate (and thus preparing for Aegeus' entrance); Musgrave changed instead to aor. ὥικτισεν, but the statement is not then strictly true (the chorus has been a 'friend' and expressed pity; no city has yet been asked to show pity for Medea).

**658** δεινότατα: for uncertainty about the metre and text here, see 649n.

**659** ἀχάριστος ὄλοιθ' ὅτωι κτλ. 'May he be destroyed, any ungrateful man who has it in his heart not to open up the doors of a pure mind and show honour to his friends. Such a man will never be a friend to *me*.' Understand ὤν with ἀχάριστος, just as is done with κακός in phrases like 1386 κατθανῆι κακὸς κακῶς (see 805–6n., and LSJ s.v. κακός D.2). This adj. is predominantly active in sense in classical authors and is unlikely to mean here 'unloved' (Kovacs, in a predicative use). For the use of impersonal πάρεστι here of character trait or disposition (instead of opportunity or ability), compare Soph. *Aj.* 1010–11 (of Telamon's severity) ὅτωι πάρα μηδ' εὐτυχοῦντι μηδὲν ἥδιον γελᾶν.

**661** ἀνοίξαντα κλῆιδα φρενῶν: for the participle in the acc. instead of dat. in agreement with ὅτωι, see 57–8n. For the image of opening up the heart or mind and the general thought of this sentence, compare the Attic skolion *PMG* 889 εἴθ' ἐξῆν ὁποῖός τις ἦν ἕκαστος | τὸ στῆθος διελόντ', ἔπειτα τὸν νοῦν | ἐσιδόντα, κλείσαντα πάλιν, | ἄνδρα φίλον νομίζειν ἀδόλωι φρενί, Soph. fr. 393 ψυχῆς ἀνοῖξαι τὴν κεκλημένην πύλην, and see 220n., 516–19n. For κλῆις as 'closure, door' see 212–13n.

**662** ἐμοὶ μέν: μέν *solitarium* with the personal pronoun (Denniston 381–2), implying 'whatever others may judge, in *my* case'.

*663–823   Third episode*

Traditional criticism of this episode has been preoccupied with the judgment of Aristotle in *Poetics* 1461b19–21: 'censure directed at both

improbability (ἀλογίαι) and depravity of character (μοχθηρίαι) is
correct whenever, despite a total lack of necessity to do so, a poet
uses the irrational (τῶι ἀλόγωι), as Euripides uses Aegeus, or bad
character (τῆι πονηρίαι), as that of Menelaus in ⟨Euripides'⟩
*Orestes*'. Aristotle's preference is for the connection of scenes and
events by 'probability or necessity', and thus many plot-devices or
patterns in Eur. that depend on surprise or on parataxis of parallel
or contrasting scenes are frowned on by critics of an Aristotelian
bent, but more appreciated by critics who recognize the legitimacy of
a variety of dramatic forms (see, e.g., Pfister (1988) on 'open' forms
of drama). We cannot be sure exactly what Aristotle had in mind in
this example (it is even possible that he was referring not to *Medea* but
to Eur.'s *Aegeus*). If he meant that Aegeus' entrance is unnecessary
because Medea's escape is later assured by other means, the criticism
is ill founded, since the audience has no notion at this point that
Helios will provide a flying chariot and Eur. is in general down-
playing the special powers of Medea. More likely, Aristotle had in
mind the fact that not only is there no preparation whatever for the
entrance of Aegeus in particular, but Aegeus' journey is not intrinsically related either to Corinth or to Medea (it is only at her prompting that he shares with her his uncertainty about the oracle) and he
departs with his ignorance uncured (although with more hope about
a cure for his childlessness). Since the plot of *Medea* is otherwise concentrated and single, Aegeus' arrival stands out sharply (contrast the
situation in plays of looser construction, for instance with the arrival
of Orestes in *Andr.*, the appearance of Evadne in *Suppl.*, or the arrival
of Pylades in *Or.*). Nevertheless, it was open to the original audience
to regard Aegeus' arrival not as a matter of blind luck, but as a con-
trivance of the gods in answer to Medea's pressing needs (see Introd.
2(*e*)) – a view that Aristotle would have been loath to countenance.
Both here in *Medea* and in the equally convenient and unprepared
arrival of the Corinthian messenger in Soph. *OT*, either one can see
the god-like manipulation of time and event by the poet to produce a
tragic plot, or one can see the divine intervention that makes the
world of the play more organized and transparent than the world
of everyday life. The preference for viewing *Medea* as a case of the
former and *OT* as a case of the latter reflects a bias toward an orga-

nized and somehow 'just' world-view and against a chaotic and amoral one – a bias that not everyone need share.

In any case, the dramatic advantages of the scene are clear. (1) Aegeus supplies an independent voice of judgment about the injustice of Jason's behaviour. (2) The interaction confirms Medea's view of her status among the elite: Aegeus recognizes her *sophia* in a positive way, he regards her as a *philos*, and he exchanges an oath with her as with an equal, establishing a tie of *xenia*. (3) His arrival solves the problem that Medea had described as a temporary obstacle to her plan (386–94), thus resolving a plot-tension. (4) Aegeus' deep concern for his childlessness either suggests to Medea the idea of hurting Jason through destruction of his present and future progeny or solidifies an idea that has already been developing in her mind. (5) Medea continues to demonstrate her verbal and strategic dominance over the male characters she encounters. (6) Aegeus provides a model of an upright oath-taker, in contrast to the Jason of the past, but at the same time Medea (now taking on Jason's qualities) is engaged in a deceptive manipulation of oaths and *philia*, keeping her own intentions secret from her partner in the way criticized at the end of the preceding stasimon. (7) Aegeus provides a connection of the story to Athens and to what is familiar to the theatre audience. For discussion of the Aegeus scene see Buttrey (1958), Dunkle (1969), Kovacs (1993) 58–9.

The scene clearly relies on the audience's familiarity with portions of the life of Theseus, in particular the circumstances of his birth and the attempt of Medea, when married to Aegeus, to bring about Theseus' death; but Eur. leaves it up to the audience to make what assumptions they will about this distant future (Introd. 4).

**663** *action*: Aegeus enters, attended by silent extras dressed as guards/servants, both a mark of his status and a necessary feature of his travels.

**663–4 Μήδεια . .|. φίλους:** Aegeus' greeting is striking in at least two ways. First, it is unusually brief and uninformative about the reason for his arrival: there has been no summons or anticipation of his arrival, there is no announcement by Medea or the chorus-leader, and Aegeus himself incorporates no details in his first speech, unlike

many other entering characters. Second, the greeting implies that
Aegeus already knows Medea, even knows where in Corinth she
dwells, and considers her a friend.

**663 προοίμιον** 'opening', a term that originated in reference to
musical and poetic preludes or forepieces, is used more widely in
tragedy of first statements and introductions, and eventually became
a technical term of rhetoric (our 'proem'). The noun is here internal
acc. with προσφωνεῖν ('make a fairer opening than this in addressing
friends').

**665 ὦ χαῖρε καὶ σύ:** Medea shows self-possession in suppressing
her own troubles and immediately eliciting information from Aegeus.
A character absorbed in her own grief might have reacted to the
greeting with a comment on the impossibility of her 'rejoicing',
with a play on χαίρειν such as is seen in *Hec.* 427 (Hecuba) χαίρουσιν
ἄλλοι, μητρὶ δ' οὐκ ἔστιν τόδε, *Phoen.* 618 (Jocasta) χαρτὰ γοῦν
πάσχω.

**σοφοῦ Πανδίονος:** Pandion has no known mythology of his
own, but is referred to mainly as the parent of figures who do have
stories attached to them (Procne and Philomela; Aegeus, Nisus, and
Pallas). On the level of character, Medea's calling him 'wise' seems
to be a bit of indirect flattery of Aegeus, a prelude to further manipulation; on the level of the poet's voice, it is the sort of detail that
ancient critics might have regarded as 'flattery of the Athenian audience', but note the irony of the contrast that emerges in this scene
between the wisdom of the oracle (675), Pittheus (686), and Medea
herself (741) and the gullibility of Aegeus.

**668 ὀμφαλὸν γῆς θεσπιωιδὸν ἐστάλης:** Delphi was deemed to be
the centre of the earth. According to a myth told by Pindar, Zeus
located the spot by releasing two eagles, one from the east and one
from the west, and noting where they met as they flew toward each
other (Strabo 9.3.6). The place was memorialized by the *omphalos*-
stone in the temple of Apollo (for illustration, see *LIMC* s.v. Erinys
nos. 46, 51, 58, Orestes at Delphi). θεσπιωιδός, a tragic coinage, is
elsewhere used of persons, but in tragic style compound adjectives
are always subject to contextual reinterpretation: so here 'where
oracles are sung'. ἐστάλης is intransitive aor. pass. of στέλλω, with

the meaning 'travel', and here governs the acc. of goal of motion (LS 12.b).

**669 ἐρευνῶν ... ὅπως γένοιτο:** the subordinate clause may be classified as a purpose clause, an indirect prospective question, or a ὅπως-clause with a verb of effort, but it makes little difference to the sense.

**670 πρὸς θεῶν, ἄπαις γάρ:** γάρ connects Medea's question to the previous line ('because you are still childless?' or 'are you still childless?'), but the interjection πρὸς θεῶν is allowed to intervene before the γάρ-clause (compare τί δ' in *Alc.* 1089 and φεῦ in *El.* 969; Denniston 80).

**δεῦρ' ἀεί:** in this tragic locution δεῦρο is temporal, '(continuously) right up to this point in time' (see Mastronarde on *Phoen.* 1209).

**671 δαίμονός τινος τύχηι:** in phrases of this kind, τύχη refers to an experience over which the human subject has no control, but which is rather a gift or intervention or disposition of fortune determined by an unseen power.

**673 εὐνῆς ἄζυγες γαμηλίου:** for the gen. of separation with the alpha-privative adjective see LS 10.b. The metaphor of yoking is often applied in tragedy to marriage (LSJ s.v. ζεύγνυμι II.1), and ἄζυξ alone can mean 'unwed' (e.g. of Athena or young girls). For application to males, see *IA* 805 ὄντες ἄζυγες γάμων, *Cresphontes* fr. 1.11 *TGFS* ἄπαιδά γ' ὄντα καὶ γυναικὸς ἄζυγα. Apollodorus 3.16.5 names Meta daughter of Hoples and Chalciope daughter of Rhexenor as wives of Aegeus from whom no children were born.

**674** For a vase-painting of Aegeus standing before the Delphic priestess (named Themis), see Fontenrose (1978) 205 = *LIMC* s.v. Aigeus no. 1.

**675 σοφώτερ' ἢ κατ' ἄνδρα συμβαλεῖν ἔπη** ⟨he spoke⟩ words too clever/wise for a mere human to understand'. κατ' ἄνδρα (and elsewhere also κατ' ἄνθρωπον) means 'after the fashion of a human being', that is, 'commensurate with the nature of a human being' (in contexts where the limitations of the human condition are an issue): cf. LSJ s.v. κατά B.IV.3. For the use after a comparative see Plato *Ap.*

20d9–e1 οὗτοι δὲ τάχ' ἂν ... μείζω τινὰ ἢ κατ' ἄνθρωπον σοφίαν σοφοὶ εἶεν. συμβαλεῖν is here an epexegetic infinitive (LS 18); for the sense see LSJ s.v. III.3.

**676 θέμις μέν:** the particle marks the question as preliminary to any further discussion (as if the contrast 'if not, there's no more to say about' were in the air): Denniston 367. For this polite way of inviting someone to share information (often oracular) while acknowledging that they may be entitled to refuse, see *IT* 938 (oracle), *Hyps.* 141 *TGFS* (fr. 1.iv.39 Bond), Aesch. *Ag.* 97–8, 263, *Prom.* 765 (virtually an oracle), Soph. *OT* 993 (oracle), Men. *Perik.* 799.

**677 ἐπεί τοι καί:** τοι adds emphasis, mutually reinforced by the following καί (Denniston 546).

**σοφῆς ... φρενός:** Medea's reputation for intelligence (292–305) is taken for granted by Aegeus, who himself has no pretensions to acumen.

**678 κλυεῖν** is equivalent in sense to μαθεῖν, hence the accentuation as an aor. infinitive is appropriate: West (1984) 172–80, esp. 178.

**679** As in many other literary/legendary oracles, the advice is given by the god in a riddling metaphorical form that requires careful interpretation (Fontenrose (1978) ch. 1 *passim*). Here the full response would have been something like 'You ask for a child. I'll give you offspring. Do not loosen/discharge the projecting foot of the skin-bag/wine-skin before you return to your own hearth.' The meaning not understood by Aegeus is that the skin-bag is the belly (so too ἀσκός in Archilochus 119 West) and its projecting foot the penis: the god is guaranteeing that the next time Aegeus has intercourse with a woman, she will conceive a son. The story is told in Plutarch, *Theseus* 3, where a hexameter version of the oracle is given (ἀσκοῦ τὸν προὔχοντα πόδα, μέγα φέρτατε λαῶν, | μὴ λύσῃς πρὶν δῆμον Ἀθηνέων εἰσαφικέσθαι; cf. Apollodorus 3.15.6), presumed to be older than Euripides' version by Parke and Wormell (1956) II.48, no. 110 (see also I.300–1). For πούς of the neck or 'spigot' of an ἀσκός, compare ποδεών in Hdt. 2.122.δ1 ἐπισπάσαντα τῶν ἀσκῶν δύο ἢ τρεῖς ποδεῶνας αὐτὸν λύειν.

**προύχοντα:** crasis, προέχοντα.

μὴ λῦσαι is an indirect command, depending on ἔχρησε, understood from Medea's question.

**680** cooperatively continues the syntax of the line that Medea interrupts, a typical feature of stichomythia (LS 29; Mastronarde (1979) 57). For πρὶν ἄν with the subj. in a temporal clause referring to the future, see Smyth §§2443–4.

ἐξίκηι: second person sing. aor. middle of ἐξικνέομαι, 'reach, arrive at'.

**682** ὡς τί χρήιζων: ὡς here goes with the participle and marks, as often, the reason or motive of the subject. For postponement of the interrogative, see 309n. and LS 35.

ναυστολεῖς: the easiest route from Delphi to points in the eastern Peloponnese is by ship from Itea (the port serving Delphi) to Lechaion, the western harbour of Corinth on the Corinthian Gulf.

**683** Πιτθεύς τις ἔστι: Aegeus' reply is given by the combination of 683 and 685, with the introduction of Pittheus as starting point in 683 and the conclusion linked by the demonstrative τούτωι in 685 (for such a gradual answer, see Mastronarde (1979) 43). Pittheus is known only through his genealogical connection to Theseus and has no separate mythology that is extant today (but Pausanias 2.31.3 mentions that Troezenian sources say Pittheus taught λόγων τέχνη). Both here (εὐσεβέστατος) and in *Hipp.* 11 (ἁγνοῦ) he is credited with piety; yet in some versions he deceived Aegeus into impregnating his daughter Aethra (an embarrassment to Plutarch, *Thes.* 3 ἄδηλον οὖν ὅ τι νοήσας ὁ Πιτθεὺς ἔπεισεν αὐτὸν ἢ διηπάτησε τῆι Αἴθραι συγγενέσθαι).

**686** ἀνήρ: crasis, ὁ ἀνήρ.

τρίβων 'skilled in, experienced in', used either with gen. or with acc. of specification, as here; the short iota differentiates it from present participle of τρίβω. This adj. is perhaps from a relatively low register of language, as Eur. alone among the tragedians uses it and in classical Greek it is otherwise extant in Hdt. 4.74 and Ar., *Wasps* 1249, *Clouds* 869–70.

**687** κἀμοί: crasis, καὶ ἐμοί.

**688  ἀλλ' εὐτυχοίης:**  there is perhaps some concluding force in these words, since ἀλλά often has break-off force (Denniston 14–16) and this phrase is elsewhere in Eur. a parting blessing. But something in Medea's tone of voice or in the gesture or tilt of head that she adopts attracts Aegeus' notice and prompts him now to ask about her situation.

**689  τί γάρ:**  the question explains Aegeus' sudden realization that all is not right with Medea, conflating the observation and the request for its reason (cf. Denniston 78); Aegeus' new awareness may also be marked by a gesture, including pointing (ὅδε).

**συντέτηχ':**  συντέτηκε, intrans. perf. of συντήκω, 'has wasted away' (25n.).

**691  φράσον:**  the aor. refers to the simple action 'explain', while Aegeus follows up with the present φράζε in 693, 'go on explaining, keep explaining'. For a similar sequence compare Ar. *Frogs* 109–19: initial request 109–12 ἵνα φράσειας ... φράσον, 117 insistence on an answer φράζε, 119 rejection of certain specific advice (μὴ) φράσῃς.

**692  οὐδὲν ἐξ ἐμοῦ παθών:**  see 165n.

**693  τί χρῆμα δράσας:**  τί χρῆμα with a form of δρᾶν is a common formula (colloquial: Stevens (1976) 21–2) for follow-up in stichomythia (cf. 748 below).

**695  οὔ που:**  this combination introduces incredulous questions, referring to what the speaker cannot believe or would prefer not to believe (Denniston 492). Transmitted ἤ που conveys the wrong tone (Denniston 286); for the error see 1308n.

**696  πρὸ τοῦ**  'previously', 'before this', a frozen phrase in which the old demonstrative force of ὁ survives even in Attic prose (LS 23).

**698  μέγαν γ' ἔρωτα:**  γε is commonly used in answers in which the reply merely adds an element to the previous speaker's syntax (LS 29). Here ἔρωτα is internal acc. with ἐρασθείς; for a cognate word added in such a reply, compare *Hel.* 1633 ἦ με προύδωκεν – καλήν γε προδοσίαν, δίκαια δρᾶν; *Bacch.* 960–70 τρυφᾶν μ' ἀναγκάσεις – τρυφᾶς γε τοιάσδ'. The asyndeton that follows this phrase is similar to explanatory asyndeton (LS 28): '⟨so great that⟩ he was not a faithful friend to his dear ones'.

**699–700** Aegeus' dismissive ἴτω νυν (798–9n.) and his reference back to Medea's first claim (κάκιστος 690) give the impression that he is concluding his inquiries, but Medea ignores the suggestion of closure and gives a more precise description of Jason's 'love', prompting further questions from Aegeus.

**701** δίδωσι ... τίς: the postponement of the interrogative (LS 35) is the result of contrastive emphasis; here Aegeus' δίδωσι follows directly on Medea's λαβεῖν to inquire about the other side of the transaction.

**703** μέντἄρ' ἦν: crasis, μέντοι ἄρα; the first particle adds strength to the declaration ('truly') and the second marks the force of inference or conclusion. The imperfect ἦν with ἄρα denotes the realization that something was true all along: 'I see that it is understandable (and was understandable from the beginning, if I had had the facts) that you feel aggrieved.' See 1279n., Smyth §1902, Goodwin §39. For the neuter pl. predicate with the inf. phrase as subject, see 384–5n.

**704** καὶ πρός γ': πρός is here adverbial (as in 407), and the whole phrase, meaning 'and what is more', appears several times in Eur. (colloquial: Stevens (1976) 57).

**705** πρὸς τοῦ 'by whom?' (τοῦ is the alternative form of interrogative τίνος).

ἄλλο καινὸν αὖ: ἄλλο αὖ is an intensifying pleonasm (see Mastronarde on *Phoen.* 417), here reinforcing καινόν.

**707** οὐδέ is adverbial, 'this too I do not approve' (in addition to what he condemned in 695–9).

ἐπήινεσα: see 223n. and LS 13.

**708** λόγωι μὲν οὐχί, καρτερεῖν δὲ βούλεται 'In words he does not permit it (argues against it), but ⟨in reality⟩ he is eager to "endure" it.' καρτερεῖν is spoken in a contemptuous, ironic tone, as Medea wishes to indicate that Jason wants her out of the way and that any reluctance is only feigned.

**709–10** ἄντομαι ..|. ἱκεσία τε γίγνομαι:   for the second time in
the play, Medea uses supplication (see 324–51n.). If it is actual supplication, then she must kneel to touch Aegeus' knees at this point.
But in that case, when does she rise again? More likely, this is figurative supplication, and Medea merely gestures to Aegeus' chin and
knees. In that case, her erect posture fits the way she controls the rest
of the scene, extracting Aegeus' oath and quickly sending him on his
way thereafter. On the double resolution in 710, see PM 19.

**711** οἴκτιρον οἴκτιρον:   emotional repetition (LS 36).

**712** ἔρημον ἐκπεσοῦσαν   'cast into exile in a desolate state'; the
adj. is predicative (cf. 513, 604); for the verb see 450n.

**713** ἐφέστιον:   the sense of this adj., when applied to persons,
varies from 'guest of one's hearth' to 'protected suppliant', from the
ordinary obligation of a host to a guest to the more specialized obligation of a protector of a suppliant. Aegeus seems to realize that
Medea will be more than a casual guest, since he is careful about not
taking her with him and anticipates that she may be sought by enemies, but he cannot foresee that she will arrive with new blood on her
hands.

**714** οὕτως   'so', that is, 'if you grant my request' (LSJ s.v. 1.3).

**715** παίδων goes with ἔρως; on the word-order see LS 35.
      καὐτός:   crasis, καὶ αὐτός.
      ὄλβιος θάνοις:   that is, 'may your prosperity and good fortune
continue all the way to the moment of your death'; the wish alludes
to the Greek maxim that one should not count any mortal happy
until one has seen his final day and ascertained that his good fortune continued to that day (*Andr.* 100–2, Aesch. *Ag.* 928–9, Soph.
*Trach.* 1–3, *OT* 1528–30, Hdt. 1.32.5, Simonides 521 *PMG*) as well as
to the notion that leaving behind male offspring to continue the
family is an essential element of a good life (Hdt. 1.30.4, on Tellus of
Athens).

**717** παύσω γε:   the clause in asyndeton explains τόδε (412n.), and
γε here lends emphasis to the causal force (Denniston 144–5). γε is an
emendation of transmitted δέ, which would have to be an instance of
δέ used with the force of γάρ (so taken by Denniston 169), but that

is not idiomatic after τόδε. The asyndeton in the next line is also explanatory.

**720    πρῶτα μὲν θεῶν:**  the gods are sponsors of the institution of supplication, and ignoring the pleas of a suppliant risks offence; but Aegeus may also feel that the gods are implicated in Medea's situation both in that she has been treated unjustly and in that pity for the unfortunate shows a due respect for the nature of human fortune.

**722    ἐς τοῦτο γὰρ δὴ φροῦδος:**  demonstrative τοῦτο vaguely refers to 'getting children' or 'my longing for children'; δή adds emphasis to γάρ (Denniston 243); the use of φροῦδος in the sense 'ruined', 'utterly undone' is rare (cf. in Eur. also σῶμα φροῦδον in *Hcld.* 703, *Or.* 390), but is comparable to tragic uses of οἴχομαι and βέβηκα (226n., 439n.).

**725–30**  As ordered in the medieval manuscripts, these lines contain some repetition that most critics have rightly found feeble and suspect. It appears that some kind of doublet or alternative version has been incorporated into the text. The text printed here (following Diggle), with 725–6 bracketed as spurious and 729 placed before 727–8, is found in a papyrus of the third century CE. A possible explanation for the trouble is that a reader or actor thought that the μέν-limb in 723 needed the clear contrast of a first-person statement to balance the σοῦ and so 725–6 were added to replace 729 (the line may then have been restored in the margin in some copies and later transmitted after 728 in our MSS); Günther (1996) 21–2 explains 725–6 instead as intended to replace 723–4 and 729. But the contrast need not be solely with the word that precedes μέν: it is rather a contrast between the whole sentences, between what Aegeus will do (once Medea gets to Athens) and what Medea must do for herself (get out of Corinth and to Athens). 729 after 723–4 expresses this contrast. The repetition of αὐτή in 727 after 729 will have to be translated as follows: 'but make your way out of this land yourself; if *all by yourself, without my aid*, you come to my house ...' Yet the repetition of αὐτή is still odd, and this solution is not certain. In defending the retention of the whole in the order of the MSS, Page argued that the repetition serves to highlight the important new point that Medea must find her own way out of Corinth and to Athens, raising suspense that is

answered only when she appears on the winged chariot at the end.
Other critics have deleted various parts of the passage (Kirchhoff
725–8; Hirzel 723–4; Kvicala 723–4 and 729–30; Prinz 723–4 and
729, with 730 placed after 726).

**[725]** seems somewhat bombastic, less suitable to Aegeus than the
vaguer and more polite οὕτω δ᾽ ἔχει μοι in 723.

**[726]** βουλήσομαι: the future here may be a colloquial substitute
for the present under the influence of the futurity of the action contemplated (compare Ar. *Wealth* 290, 319); see 259n.

**729** ἀπαλλάσσου πόδα: ἀπαλλάσσομαι by itself often means
'depart from', and the addition (here only) of πόδα as acc. of respect
(or acc. of the part retained with passive verb) is possible as a Euripidean mannerism, comparable to his use of βαίνειν πόδα and similar phrases (Diggle (1981) 37; Mastronarde on *Phoen.* 1536–8); thus it
is not certain that the unique usage can be regarded as a sign of interpolation, as some critics have felt it to be.

**728** κοὖ ... μὴ μεθῶ: οὐ μή with the aor. subjunctive expresses a
very strong denial (Smyth §§2754–5).

**730** ἀναίτιος ... καὶ ξένοις: the (aristocratic) 'guest-friends'
whom Aegeus does not want to offend are evidently Jason and Creon,
particularly the latter: if Aegeus were to take Medea under his protection within Corinth itself and escort her out of the city, it would
announce publicly his disagreement with the treatment of Medea
and threaten his aristocratic peers with loss of face. If ξένοις also includes the kin of Pelias, then again the positive action of escorting
Medea to safety might be regarded as more offensive than the more
passive role of accepting a suppliant at one's own hearth.

**731** ἔσται τάδ᾽: a formula expressing agreement with a request,
common in Euripides.

**733** μῶν οὐ πέποιθας 'surely you don't doubt my word?'; on the
reluctance or incredulity implied by μῶν see 567n.

**735–6** τούτοις δ᾽ ὁρκίοισι μὲν ζυγεὶς κτλ. 'to these enemies, if
you are constrained by oaths, you would not surrender me if they
were trying to take me from your land'. As the position of μέν in-

dicates, τούτοις and ὁρκίοισι do not go together. μεθίεμαι (μεθεῖο is
second sing. aor. mid. opt.) in the sense 'let go of' normally takes the
gen. (whereas active μεθίημι takes the acc.), so one might argue that
ἐμέ is the object only of participle ἄγουσιν and from it ἐμοῦ is understood with μεθεῖο; but this may be too artificial (note the use of
active μεθήσειν in a phrase of identical meaning at 751; see further
Mastronarde on *Phoen.* 519–20).

**737–9 λόγοις δὲ συμβὰς ... | τάχ' ἂν πίθοιο** 'but having given
agreement in words only and not being under an oath made in the
name of the gods, you might show yourself their friend and you
would perhaps heed their heralded demands'. τούτοις continues to
be felt with the δέ-limb of the contrast, providing a dative complement for φίλος and allowing the enemies to be understood as the authors of the ἐπικηρυκεύματα. The MSS present ἐνώμοτος as a variant
and read κἀπικηρυκεύματα | οὐκ ἂν πίθοιο, but the scholia show that
an alternative reading was extant in antiquity, and the required sense
is best served by the text adopted here, with emendation τάχ' ἂν (see
further in Page's comm.).

**741 ἔδειξας:** the MSS read ἔλεξας, but 'speak forethought' is un-
idiomatic, and the variants ἐν λόγοις and ὦ γύναι are best explained
if the former is the original, displaced as too clumsy after ἔδειξας was
corrupted to ἔλεξας.

**742 δρᾶν τάδ' οὐκ ἀφίσταμαι:** the complementary inf. with this
verb in the sense 'shrink from', 'refuse' is a rare poetic construction,
seen also in *Hel.* 536 ἀπέστην τοῦτ' ἐρωτῆσαι σαφῶς.

**744 ἔχοντα** agrees with με as understood subject of inf. δεικνύναι
and is supplementary participle (direct form ἔχων δείξω): 'for me
to show your enemies that I have some legitimate excuse ⟨for not
surrendering you⟩'. For shift from dat. ἐμοί to acc. see 57–8n.

**745 ἄραρε:** 322n.
**ἐξηγοῦ θεούς** 'dictate the gods ⟨by whom I should swear⟩'
(second sing. present mid.-pass. imperative of ἐξηγέομαι, 'lead the
way').

**746** For the pairing of Earth and Sun, compare the chorus' appeal
to Earth and Sky in 148 (n.).

**747** θεῶν τε συντιθεὶς ἅπαν γένος 'and the whole race of gods, including them in one group', 'counting them all together' (γένος is object of both ὄμνυ and συντιθείς); in ritual contexts the Greeks often add such a generalizing formula to be sure that no relevant power has been omitted from the prayer.

**748** τί χρῆμα δράσειν: 693n. The inf. depends on deliberative 'am I to swear?' understood from Medea's imperative in 747 (LS 29).

**749** ἐκβαλεῖν is not aorist, but future, as is normal in an oath.

**750** ἄλλος ἤν τις τῶν ἐμῶν ἐχθρῶν: take ἄλλος in apposition: 'if someone else, one of my enemies, wants to . . .', not 'if some other of my enemies' (445–6n.).

**751** ζῶν is not strictly logical but adds intensity to the oath, as in the English promise-phrase 'as long as I shall live'; ἑκουσίωι τρόπωι is likewise a rhetorically more weighty substitute for ἑκών or ἑκούσιος.

**752** φῶς τε λαμπρὸν Ἡλίου: the sense is certain, but the reading is not. MSS present readings based on λαμπρὸν ἡλίου τε φῶς, which is metrical but involves a postponed τε that is very doubtful (since there is no particular cohesiveness between adjective and genitive). This transposition is Page's suggestion, but an alternative reading found at 746 (where it does not fit) may perhaps belong here, in which case the line should end Ἡλίου θ' ἁγνὸν σέβας (Diggle (1994) 270–1).

**753** ἐμμενεῖν ἅ σου κλύω 'that I will abide by the provisions I hear from you'; the dat. object of ἐμμενεῖν that is the antecedent of ἅ is not expressed, and the relative is not attracted into the dat. (attraction is not mandatory: Smyth §2524).

**754** μὴ 'μμένων: prodelision, from μὴ ἐμμένων (PM 10).
πάθοις is optative of wish, exceptionally in a question, because of the artificiality of stichomythia: the standard oath is something like 'if I fail to keep my promise, may I be destroyed', and here we have 'if I fail . . . , may I suffer what?'.

**758** τυχοῦσ' ἃ βούλομαι 'attaining what I desire'; possibly like 753 (gen. antecedent omitted, no attraction), but for acc. of neut. pronouns after τυγχάνω see LSJ s.v. B.II.2.b, and compare the similar phrases in *Phoen.* 512, 992.

**759–63** *Metre:* seven metra of chanted anapaests closed by a paroemiac. The use of anapaests for an envoi is similar to their use for announcing entrances (SE 1), and so this short anapaestic interlude is not quite parallel to the one that follows Creon's exit at 356. See 358–63n. on the naive reaction of the chorus in contrast to Medea's understanding of what she has accomplished.

**759** ὁ Μαίας πομπαῖος ἄναξ 'Maia's son (Hermes), the lord who gives escort'; in addition to his roles as conductor of the souls of the dead and as messenger of the gods, Hermes guides and protects both heralds and other human wayfarers.

**760–1** ὧν τ' ἐπίνοιαν σπεύδεις κατέχων πράξειας 'may you accomplish those things toward which you eagerly direct your purpose'; σπεύδεις is intransitive and absolute and κατέχων ('hold fast', an intensified ἔχων: see Mastronarde on *Phoen.* 330) governs ἐπίνοιαν.

**763** δεδόκησαι: this perf. mid.-pass. of δοκέω is poetic (epic) and Ionic and is extant in drama only here and in Ar. *Wasps* 726 (also in anapaestic metre). But *δέδοξαι happens not to be extant at all. See 1417n.

**764** The invocation of Zeus and Justice recalls Medea's cries mentioned or heard in the prologue and parodos (21–2, 148, 160, 168–9, 208–9) and may suggest to the audience that Medea's progress toward vengeance has had divine support. Helios is a general witness of oaths (as in 746, 752), but his inclusion here also suggests that he may be helping Medea, and thus this invocation is a form of preparation for the loan of his chariot at the end.

**765–7** νῦν ... νῦν: for the combination of anaphora and asyndeton cf. 1401 νῦν σφε προσαυδᾶις, νῦν ἀσπάζηι, and (with a similar anticipation of 'fair victory') *Phoen.* 1252–3 νῦν πόλεως ὑπερμαχεῖς, | νῦν καλλίνικος γενόμενος σκήπτρων κρατεῖς.

**766** κὰς ὁδὸν βεβήκαμεν 'I have entered upon the ⟨required⟩ path.' The force of the perfect tense is almost 'My foot is firmly placed upon the ⟨required⟩ path.' κὰς is crasis, καὶ ἐς.

**768 ἀνήρ:** crasis, ὁ ἀνήρ.

**ἧι:** relative adverb, 'where', 'in the point where'.

**769–70 λιμὴν ..|. πρυμνήτην κάλων:** another instance of the nautical metaphor used earlier by the chorus (442–3) and Medea herself (258), mooring oneself in a harbour that shields one from dangerous waters (Introd. 2(ƒ)). κάλως here is not used in the specific sense as in 278, but in the general sense 'rope', with the modifier πρυμνήτην to produce the sense 'stern-cable' (for tying the ship up sternmost to the shore).

**769 λιμὴν ... τῶν ἐμῶν βουλευμάτων:** this metaphor is common in tragedy, and the attached gen. may have various constructions: the bad thing from which the harbour protects one (Aesch. *Supp.* 471 κακῶν; *Andr.* 891 χείματος), the valued thing that the harbour protects (as here and [Men.] *Sent.* 444 λιμὴν νεὼς ὅρμος, βίου δ᾽ ἀλυπία), or the thing that provides the shelter (Soph. *Ajax* 683 ἑται-ρείας λιμήν, *Or.* 1077 μέγας πλούτου λιμήν).

**771 ἄστυ καὶ πόλισμα Παλλάδος:** this is a high-style periphrasis for Athens, featuring hendiadys (there is no semantic distinction between the two nouns) and the poetic use of πόλισμα as a variation on πόλις; compare *IT* 1014 πόλισμ᾽ ἐς Παλλάδος, *Her.* 1323, Men. *Samia* 325 (quoting Eur. *Oedipus*) ὦ πόλισμα Κεκροπίας χθονός. For the acc. see LS 12.b.

**772 τἀμά:** crasis, τὰ ἐμά.

**773 μὴ πρὸς ἡδονήν** 'with no pleasure', '⟨spoken, revealed⟩ not in a direction aimed at pleasure'. For this use of πρός see 538n. on μὴ πρὸς ἰσχύος χάριν and compare Soph. *El.* 921 οὐ πρὸς ἡδονὴν λέγω, fr. 63.1 πᾶν πρὸς ἡδονὴν λέγει.

**774 ἐμῶν τιν᾽ οἰκετῶν:** for the identity of the silent extra sent to Jason, see Introd. 3.

**776 μαλθακοὺς ... λόγους** is reminiscent of Creon's phrase at 316, λέγεις ἀκοῦσαι μαλθάκ᾽.

**777–9** '... saying both that I agree with him and that it is well that he makes the marriage with the royal family which he now has, having betrayed us, and saying that what he has done is advantageous and well decided'. The repetitiousness shows a mocking pretence of subservience (similar to what Medea will feign in the next scene), although the relative clause in 778 is Medea 'editorializing' for the chorus, not part of what she will say to Jason's face. The text is uncertain; what is printed here involves Barnes' reinterpretation of transmitted ταῦτα as ταὐτά (trivial: the transmitted diacritics have no authority), Bolkestein's γαμεῖ for MSS' ἔχει (the corruption could have occurred easily by confusion with the next line and perhaps also by unconscious reminiscence of the idiom καλῶς ἔχει), and the acceptance of a shift of construction from ὡς-clause in 777–8 to inf. of indirect discourse in 779, with vague unexpressed subject inferred from the context (for the shift of construction, eased by the intervention of the relative clause, there are some parallels in Thucydides: see Page's commentary and Bolkestein (1949)). This solution seems better than Page's ὡς ... δοκεῖν μοι ταῦτα ... ἔχειν (unlikely use of ὡς = οὕτως, otherwise in Eur. only with optative or imperative, or as correlative in an epicism, as *Bacch.* 1066–8). But there may be a deeper corruption or an interpolation (Porson bracketed 778–9, Reiske 778 alone, Page considered but rejected cutting 779 alone).

**777** ταὐτά:   the comparative phrase 'as he does' to go with 'the same' is easily understood after 776.

**777–8** γαμεῖ | γάμους:   587n.

γάμους τυράννων:   cf. 140 λέκτρα τυράννων, 594 λέκτρα βασιλέων.

**781** λιποῦσ' ἄν:   the participial form corresponding to a potential opt.: 'not as if I would leave them in the land of my enemies'. With 782 deleted, one might supply 'really' with 'leave' in this translation to reflect the antithetic force of δόλοισι in the pairing of οὐχ ὡς ... ἀλλ' ὡς.

**[782]**   Brunck deleted this line. It is similar to 1060–1 ὅπως ἐχθροῖς ἐγὼ | παῖδας παρήσω τοὺς ἐμοὺς καθυβρίσαι and contains an unnecessary repetition of παῖδας τοὺς ἐμούς (also without variation in the noun); it anticipates a later concern (the chorus and audience can understand καθυβρίσαι only after Medea reveals her plan); and it

weakens the direct contrast of 781 and 783. If the line is kept, καθυβρίσαι would be epexegetic inf., with the dat. of interest ἐχθροῖς
providing its subject ('for my enemies to outrage').

**[785]** This line may have originated because someone wanted
Jason's bride to be mentioned explicitly as recipient of the gifts, although that is actually clear enough from the mention of her in 783
and from the description of the gifts in 786, so that λαβοῦσα in 787 is
easily understood to refer to her. What is odd about this line is the
addition of φέροντας in asyndeton after ἔχοντας, with both governing
δῶρα, and the epexegetic inf. phrase that requires a pregnant sense
for δῶρα ('gifts meant to persuade') or for φέροντας ('offering gifts to
win in return the concession'). Idiomatically, if one were trying to
express purpose after πέμψω, one would expect a future participle
(thus emending the opening to e.g. αἰτουμένους τε is no help).

**786** The line recurs *verbatim* at 949, which makes it likely, though
not certain, that it is not genuine in one of the two passages (see 37–
45n.). Here it is indispensable to specify what the gifts are so that
κόσμον ἀμφιθῆι in the next line may be understood. See 947–50n.

**πλόκον χρυσήλατον:** here a 'plaited wreath' (cf. πλέκω) of in-
tricate goldwork, elsewhere πλόκος is a crown of greenery or flowers,
as in 841 below (wild celery in Pind. *Ol.* 13.33, myrtle in *El.* 778). For
examples of golden diadems (some with vegetal motifs or leaves) see
Marshall (1911) 170–6 with plates XXVII–XXIX; Andronikos (1984)
172–3, 193, 196 (from the royal tombs at Vergina, Macedonia). A
crown is a standard element of adornment of the bride and is often
shown in vase-painting (e.g. Oakley and Sinos (1993) figs. 28, 82).

**787 κἄνπερ ... ἀμφιθῆι:** crasis, καὶ ἄνπερ/ἐάνπερ; the verb is
aor. act. subj. of ἀμφιτίθημι.

**χροῒ:** alternative dat. sing. of χρώς (Smyth §257D): see LS 5.c
and cf. 1162 εἰκώ.

**788 ὀλεῖται:** fut. middle (in passive sense) of ὄλλυμι; the verb is
understood again with πᾶς.

**789 τοιοῖσδε χρίσω φαρμάκοις δωρήματα:** it seems that through
carelessness or indifference Eur. did not give Medea a chance to
perform this essential step. The fatal gifts are brought out between

950 and 955 by a silent extra who is ordered to fetch them quickly, and they are placed in the children's hands, and they do prove to be fatally poisoned. There are at least three ways to avoid this anomaly, but none is likely. (1) Make Medea silently whisper instructions to a mute attendant and direct her into the house to do the job for her (when? either immediately after this line, or at the end of the scene). But this would weaken the premise that Medea is the one uniquely knowledgeable in magic drugs, and it is anyway unlike the dramatic technique of Greek tragedy for such an action to be done without words (esp. in a context where Medea instructs a servant in the less crucial task, fetching Jason). (2) Have Medea go indoors for part or all of the choral ode in order to do the job herself. See 823n. (3) Have Medea perform some quick and surreptitious anointing during the handing over of the gifts to the children at 956–8 (956n.). There is insufficient time for this (and where would the poison suddenly come from?), and such an action would be totally uncharacteristic of Greek stage-technique.

**790** τόνδ' ἀπαλλάσσω λόγον  'I dismiss this topic' with an unusual use of this highly flexible verb; cf. LSJ s.v. A.1.3 (but 'bring to an end' is a slight over-translation).

**791** ὤιμωξα 'dramatic' aorist (LS 13), emotionally more controlled than letting out the cry οἴμοι (contrast 899): Lloyd (1999) 28.

**792** τοὐντεῦθεν:  crasis, τὸ ἐντεῦθεν, adverbial acc., 'thereafter'.

**793** τἄμ':  the enjambment perhaps adds emphasis to the possessive adj. (crasis, τὰ ἐμά), and in any case the unusual punctuation of the line after the first syllable after carryover from the previous line suggests that the rhythm reflects some agitation in Medea. For the rarity of punctuation at this point in the trimeter, see Denniston (1936). Compare 612 (less striking because there is a comma at the end of 611) and the weaker pauses in 93, 508, 596.

ἐξαιρήσεται  'will take them from my hands' or 'will rescue them'.

**794** δόμον τε πάντα συγχέασ':  the phrase recalls 487 πάντα τ' ἐξεῖλον δόμον and points up the similarity of Medea's revenge upon Jason to the way she previously treated his enemy on his behalf. τε

joins this clause to τέκνα ... κατακτενῶ, across the parenthetic asseveration. συγχέασ' is fem. sing. nom. aor. act. participle of συγχέω,
'throw into confusion', hence 'obliterate'.

**795–6   φόνον | φεύγουσα**   'fleeing ⟨the consequences of⟩ the
murder', similar to *Supp.* 148 αἷμα συγγενὲς φεύγων χθονός, 'fleeing
his country in consequence of the pollution of kin-murder' and
Soph. *OT* 355 ποῦ τοῦτο φεύξεσθαι δοκεῖς; 'where do you imagine
you will escape the consequences of this outrage?'; not the same as
prosaic φόνου δίκην φεύγειν 'to be prosecuted for murder', 'to be
tried on a charge of murder'.

**797   οὐ γὰρ γελᾶσθαι τλητόν:**   on this motif of being laughed at
by enemies, see 383n.

**[798–9]**   It is probably best to follow Leo (and Diggle) in bracketing this couplet as an interpolation. While the latter part of this
couplet could apply to Medea, both the imperative ἴτω and the
question τί μοι ζῆν κέρδος; are difficult to construe rhetorically. The
implied subject of ἴτω and its tone are unclear. This bare imperative
may be defiant ('let it come', 'let it happen', 'so be it, I don't care') or
dismissive and acquiescent ('let it go', 'never mind that'; what Dodds
on *Bacch.* 363–5 calls 'the Greek for a shrug of the shoulders'). For
the former see 819 below, Soph. *Phil.* 120; for the latter see 699
above, *Or.* 793, *Bacch.* 365, *Hcld.* 455, *Hipp.* 1007. Here it is unclear
whether the meaning is 'let it [my killing of my children] happen
anyway!' or 'Never mind [the horror of my planned deed]!' The
question τί μοι ζῆν κέρδος; is normal in contexts where despair leads
to thoughts of suicide (or cessation of resistance to murderous enemies), but such despair is odd after the rejection of submission to
enemies implied by 797, and it is hard to see how it fits into Medea's
overall self-image of one who triumphs over her enemies. Here the
meaning would apparently have to be 'with or without my children,
what profit can I get in living?' If the lines are borrowed from elsewhere, that context presumably was one in which suicide was being
argued for.

**[799]   ἀποστροφὴ κακῶν:**   if the lines are genuine, then in the
context of this play, in which the audience has heard 31–5, 253–8,
441–3, 502–3, 603–4, 645–9, it seems inevitable that following 'I

have neither fatherland nor home' these words will be heard in the sense 'refuge from my (pre-existing) woes', which again suits a context where suicide is contemplated, but not one in which a refuge has been provided by Aegeus. In another context ἀποστροφή κακῶν might be 'means to turn aside (my impending) misfortune' (cf. *Hipp.* 1036 αἰτίας ἀποστροφήν, *Prom.* 769 τῆσδ᾽ ἀποστροφὴ τύχης). Kovacs adopts this sense in retaining the lines as genuine; Page prefers 'refuge from', but he too refers κακῶν to the misfortunes following upon the children's death.

**800  ἐξελίμπανον:** λιμπάνω is an alternative present-stem formation for λείπω (compare φυγγάνω and φεύγω and the standard formations μανθάνω, λαμβάνω, πυνθάνομαι, etc.), rare in classical Greek and rarer in Attic; on the extant evidence we cannot say whether it will have seemed colloquial or recherché.

**801  Ἕλληνος:** reversing the stereotype of the Greek as superior to the barbarian, Eur. allows Medea as foreigner to voice contempt for Jason as a Greek, as someone who should not have been trusted because he was from a different nation than she was, and perhaps also reflecting the notion of the clever and untrustworthy Greek (Aesch. *Pers.* 361–2 δόλον Ἕλληνος ἀνδρός, *IT* 1205 πιστὸν Ἑλλὰς οἶδεν οὐδέν; cf. Hdt. 1.153, Cyrus' perception of the Greek agora as an institutional locus of perjury and deceit). See Hall (1989) 80, 122–3 on the contrast between the cunning intelligence of Greeks and the slow-wittedness of non-Greeks; for the later stereotype of the tricky and unreliable Greek, see Polybius 6.56.13–15, Petrochilos (1974) 40–5.

**802  σὺν θεῶι:** see 625n.

**803–5** Medea's scheme answers neatly to Jason's emphasis on the blending of his projected two sets of children (563–7, 596–7).

**803  γάρ** is postponed to the third position in the clause, for metrical convenience and to lend contrastive force to ἐξ ἐμοῦ. For such postponement, see Denniston 96.

**804  τὸ λοιπόν:** adv. acc. or acc. of duration of time, 'in the future', 'hereafter' (also 1128, 1383).

**805  νύμφης τεκνώσει:**  either plain gen. of source, 'will father from his new bride', or ἐξ is understood from its parallel use in the previous limb of the οὔτ'... οὔτε pair (Diggle (1981) 23–4).

**805–6  κακὴν κακῶς | θανεῖν:**  understand the participle οὖσαν with κακήν: 'being a wretch she must die wretchedly'; compare 1386 below (spoken to Jason by Medea) κατθάνηι κακὸς κακῶς. Both phrases are versions of a type of imprecation that draws strength from the juxtaposition of adj. and adv. from the same root: see LSJ s.v. κακός D.2; Watson (1991) 35 n. 152; for occurrences in inscriptions and a *defixio*, see Strubbe (1997) nos. 31, 155; Voutiras (1998) 8.

**807  κἀσθενῆ:**  crasis, καὶ ἀσθενῆ.

**808  θατέρου τρόπου**  'of the opposite temper', that is, fierce and aggressive. θατέρου is formed by crasis from τοῦ ἀτέρου, ἅτερος being a byform of ἕτερος that is seen in Attic only in crasis with the article (ἅτερος, ἅτεροι, θατέρωι, θάτερον, κτλ.).

**809  βαρεῖαν ἐχθροῖς καὶ φίλοισιν εὐμενῆ:**  a version of the familiar Greek ethical principle that it is the virtue of a man to help his friends and harm his enemies: Archilochus 23.14–15 West ἐπίσταμαί τοι τὸν φιλέοντα μὲν φιλεῖν, | τὸν δ' ἐχθρὸν ἐχθαίρειν τε καὶ κακο[στο-μεῖν?, Solon 13.5–6 West εἶναι δὲ γλυκὺν ὧδε φίλοις, ἐχθροῖσι δὲ πικ-ρόν, | τοῖσι μὲν αἰδοῖον, τοῖσι δὲ δεινὸν ἰδεῖν, Theognis 869–72, etc. See Blundell (1989) ch. 2, Dover (1974) 180–1.

**810  εὐκλεέστατος βίος:**  another aspect of Medea's assimilation of masculine values is her positive attitude here toward fame: whereas she had earlier bristled at Jason's claim to have benefited her by making her famous throughout Greece, she now seems to prize fame in the same way that Jason himself does (542–4).

**812–13  νόμοις βροτῶν | ξυλλαμβάνουσα**  'offering my assistance to the laws of mankind', with a mild personification of 'laws'; for this sense of συλλαμβάνω see LSJ s.v. VI.1 and compare 946 ξυλλήψομαι δὲ τοῦδέ σοι κἀγὼ πόνου. 'The laws of mankind' is a concept whose content varies with the context and speaker, but refers especially to major cultural sanctions related to incest, kin-murder, treatment of suppliants, burial of the dead, and the like. See *Cycl.* 299 (suppliants), *Supp.* 378 (burial), fr. 346 (parents' love for their children). Thus, τάδε probably refers entirely or predominantly to the killing of the children, as the follow-up in 816 and 818 suggests. The chorus does not object to the plot against the princess or the concept of revenge in general (indeed, the right of revenge against the person who harms one first is sometimes called a 'law of mankind', e.g. in Dem. 23.61).

**814** οὐκ ἔστιν ἄλλως 'it is not possible ⟨for me to do/for events to happen⟩ otherwise'.

**815** μὴ πάσχουσαν, ὡς ἐγώ, κακῶς: for the acc. participle after σοί in the previous line, see 57–8n. When a tragic character rejects the moderating advice of the chorus, the distance between the ambitions, excesses, experiences, and responsibilities of the elite character and the middling aspirations, caution, and relative safety of the humble collectivity is made clear. Compare *Hipp.* 722–4 (Phaedra); Aesch. *Sept.* 686–719 (Eteocles), Soph. *Trach.* 723–30 (Deianeira: esp. 729–30 τοιαῦτά τἂν λέξειεν οὐχ ὁ τοῦ κακοῦ | κοινωνός, ἀλλ' ὧι μηδὲν ἔστ' οἴκοι βαρύ).

**816** σπέρμα: the sense 'offspring' (without defining gen. as in 669 above) is characteristic of high-style poetry, e.g. (also of women's offspring) Aesch. *Supp.* 141, Soph. *Trach.* 204.

**818** δ' . . . γ': the addition of γε adds force to a lively rejoinder (Denniston 153).

**819** ἴτω 'so be it', 'let it happen' (798–9n.).

οὑν μέσωι λόγοι: (crasis, οἱ ἐν) 'the words in the interim', that is, from this moment to the moment when the planned action is complete. On unexpressed limits with ἐν μέσωι see Mastronarde on *Phoen.* 588–9.

**820** ἀλλ' εἶα: 401n. Medea turns to one of the silent attendants who entered by her side at 214 (and to whom she alluded in 774 ἐμῶν τιν' οἰκετῶν). For the argument that this faithful servant is not the nurse of the prologue, see Introd. 3.

**821** ἐς πάντα . . . τὰ πιστά 'for all matters that require special trust', an extended meaning of πιστός not accounted for by LSJ.

**823** δεσπόταις: poetic plural, referring to Medea alone (LS 33).

**γυνή τ᾽ ἔφυς:** Medea's initial appeal to the chorus and the chorus' first stasimon have already demonstrated the assumption of the
solidarity of women, and now Medea appeals to it explicitly in addressing her servant. Compare Iphigeneia's appeal to the chorus for
their silence, *IT* 1061–2 γυναῖκές ἐσμεν, φιλόφρον ἀλλήλαις γένος |
σώιζειν τε κοινὰ πράγματ᾽ ἀσφαλέστατα; the chorus-leader's statement to Helen, *Hel.* 329 γυναῖκα γὰρ δὴ συμπονεῖν γυναικὶ χρή; fr.
108 γυνὴ γυναικὶ σύμμαχος πέφυκέ πως.

**823** *Action:* the attendant goes off city-side. Medea stands before
the house, and the choral ode is addressed to her. Jason's first words
on entry at 866 indicate that Medea is standing before the door as he
approaches. See 789n. on the problem of when or whether Medea
prepares the poisoned gifts. One may wonder whether it would have
been possible for Medea to go indoors for a very short time to prepare them: Wilamowitz, for instance, supplies in his translation stage
directions for Medea to go in at this point and return from inside at
845, in time to be addressed in the second pair of stanzas of the stasimon. This certainly seems contrary to normal stage practice, and
although it is possible for a chorus to address a character who is not
present, a temporary absence during this stasimon consorts poorly
with the persuasive intention of the song. It is better to assume that
Eur. simply neglected this detail.

*824–65    Third stasimon*

Again the chorus does not start its song with any obvious close connection to the final tense words of the scene just ended; instead it
begins with an evocation of ideal beauty and calm. The Athenian
choristers behind the choral masks are praising their own city and its
culture, but this is not an obvious case of patriotic flattery of the audience. To the chorus in its Corinthian character, Athens is evoked
because of Aegeus' role in the previous scene, and the depiction of
the special blessings enjoyed by Athens is reminiscent of the prayer
for blessing that sometimes follows the reception or protection of a
suppliant (Aesch. *Supp.* 625ff., Soph. *OC* 668ff.; cf. Aesch. *Eum.* 916ff.).
On the one hand, the harmonious music and the moderate and safe
influence of Aphrodite in support of *sophia* and virtue present a clear

alternative to the disruptions in Corinth – a musical tradition in reversal (415–30), excessive Aphrodite (627–44), dangerous *sophia* (294–305, 580–3), and corrupted faith (410–14, 439–40, 659–62). On the other hand, there is the stark contrast between this idealized purity and the murderer who will be welcomed into it. Just as Aegeus is the truer friend and host who is also a dupe of Medea's scheme, so the glorious Athens of myth is exposed to irony by the collocation of a traditional source of Athenian pride (the protection of persecuted suppliants) with the disruptive pollution that will be carried there by Medea. The chorus is reluctant to believe that Athens will receive her or that she will in fact kill her sons, but the audience knows the tradition that Aegeus did receive her and probably also stories in which the sons died in Corinth (see Introd. 4).

## Metre

As in the previous stasimons, the rhythm of the first pair is dactylo-epitrite, and here the use of this metre is not only stately (in contrast to the intensity of the questions and appeals that follow in the second pair) but most directly reminiscent of its use in the praise-poetry of Pindar. The second pair begins in similar rhythm but soon shifts to the aeolic measures (already prepared for in aeolic clausula 834 = 845) that have also appeared in the second half of earlier stasimons.

The period structure of the first pair is hard to determine: there may be only two to four periods, with a long one 825–31 = 836–42 (or more extensive), or, at the other extreme, each line could be a separate period (but the repeated lack of rhetorical pause at period-end is somewhat unlikely). The second pair has perhaps six periods, with the longest at the start and then several short ones as the chorus envisions (and asks Medea to envision) the murder of the children. There is epic correption (PM 7) in 862 φόνου οὐ: for the correption coinciding with punctuation between the involved vowels compare *Hcld.* 768 ἔχει· οὔποτε, *Hec.* 449 ἀφίξομαι; ἤ.

U‒ UU ‒U   U‒U‒U‒ ||²

Ἐρεχθεῖδαι τὸ παλαιὸν ὄλβιοι         824 ×D×e

τοῦ καλλινάου τ' ἐπὶ Κηφισοῦ ῥοαῖς         835

‒ U‒ ‒‒ UU‒ UU‒ |

καὶ θεῶν παῖδες μακάρων, ἱερᾶς         825 e‒D

τὰν Κύπριν κλήιζουσιν ἀφυσσαμέναν         836

– – ◡ – – – ◡ ◡ – ◡◡ – |

χώρας ἀπορθήτου τ᾽ ἄπο, φερβόμενοι          826–7 – e – D
                                            (iambelegus)
χώρας καταπνεῦσαι μετρίους ἀνέμων           837–8

– ◡◡ – – ◡◡ – – – ◡ ◡ – ◡ ◡ – |

κλεινοτάταν σοφίαν, αἰεὶ διὰ λαμπροτάτου    828–9 D – D
ἡδυπνόους αὔρας· αἰεὶ δ᾽ ἐπιβαλλομέναν      839–40

– – ◡ – – – ◡ ◡ – ◡ ◡ – – ‖²

βαίνοντες ἁβρῶς αἰθέρος, ἔνθα ποθ᾽ ἁγνὰς    830–1 – e – D –
                                            (iambelegus
                                            extended)
χαίταισιν εὐώδη ῥοδέων πλόκον ἀνθέων        841–2

– ◡ ◡ – ◡ ◡ – – – ◡ – – ‖²

ἐννέα Πιερίδας Μούσας λέγουσι               832–3 D – e –
                                            (elegiambus)
τᾶι Σοφίαι παρέδρους πέμπειν Ἔρωτας,        843–4

– – – ◡ ◡ – ◡ – – ‖|

ξανθὰν Ἁρμονίαν φυτεῦσαι·                   834 hipponactean
παντοίας ἀρετᾶς ξυνεργούς.                  845

– – – – – – – – – –

◡̄ – ◡ ◡ – ◡ ◡ – |

πῶς οὖν ἱερῶν ποταμῶν                       846 ×D
πόθεν θράσος †ἢ φρενὸς ἢ                     856

– ◡ ◡ – ◡ – |

ἢ πόλις ἢ φίλων                             847 dodrans
χειρὶ τέκνων σέθεν†                         857

– ◡ – ◡ – – |

πόμπιμός σε χώρα                            848 ithyphallic
καρδίαι τε λήψηι                            858

– – ◡ ◡ – ◡ – – ‖²

τὰν παιδολέτειραν ἕξει,                     849 hagesichorean
δεινὰν προσάγουσα τόλμαν;                   859

– – ◡ – ◡ – ◡ – – ‖ᵇ

τὰν οὐχ ὁσίαν μετ᾽ ἄλλων;                   850 hagesichorean
πῶς δ᾽ ὄμματα προσβαλοῦσα                   860

– – ◡ ◡ – – – ‖²

σκέψαι τεκέων πλαγάν,                       851 telesillean
τέκνοις ἄδακρυν μοῖραν                      861

⏑ – ⏑ ⏑ – ⏑ – – ‖ʼ
σκέψαι φόνον οἷον αἴρηι.                    852 hagesichorean
σχήσεις φόνου; οὐ δυνάσηι                   862

⏑ – ⏑ ⏑ – ⏑ – – ‖ʼ
μή, πρὸς γονάτων σε πάνται                  853 hagesichorean
παίδων ἱκετᾶν πιτνόντων                     863

⏑ – ⏑ ⏑ – ⏑ – |
πάντως ἱκετεύομεν,                          854 telesillean
τέγξαι χέρα φοινίαν                         864

⏑ ⏑ ⏑ – – ‖|
τέκνα φονεύσηις.                            855 adonean
τλάμονι θυμῶι.                              865

**824–30** form a long nominal sentence (LS 30), with a series of predicate terms attached to subject Ἐρεχθεΐδαι: adj. ὄλβιοι, noun παῖδες,
ἀπό-phrase, two participles. Such a structure is typical of high-style
lyric poetry, and perhaps the form here implies the timeless truth or
the intrinsic quality of this characterization of the Athenians.

**824** Ἐρεχθεΐδαι 'sons of Erechtheus' is a poetic synonym for
'Athenians' in Pindar, Eur., Sophocles, and later poets (and the singular in a generic sense is used in mock oracles in Ar. *Knights* 1015 and
1030); it is honorific because it alludes to the autochthony on which
the Athenians prided themselves (825n.). In most passages the four-
syllable form is guaranteed by metre, but the five-syllable form (with
diaeresis of ει) seems secure here and in *Ion* 1056.

τὸ παλαιόν: adverbial acc., equivalent to πάλαι, 'from of old'.

**825** θεῶν παῖδες μακάρων: the Athenians claimed to be auto-
chthonous (and thus superior to other Greeks, who had experienced
migrations), and so they are in general children of the Earth (a goddess). Moreover, the titular founder of their line Erechtheus was,
through conflation with Erichthonius, considered the son of Hephaestus and Earth, and in some sense even the child of Athena, since
Hephaestus' seed was spilled in an unsuccessful assault on Athena
and she took an interest in the baby. See Loraux (1993) ch. 1.

**825–6** ἱερᾶς | ... ἀπορθήτου: Attica is sacred because of the
tutelage of Athena, while 'unconquered' alludes to the claim that
unlike almost all other Greek communities the Athenians were never

forced by invaders to abandon their original homeland or accept the domination of immigrant groups (Thuc. 1.2.1, 1.2.5).

**827–8  φερβόμενοι | κλεινοτάταν σοφίαν**  'feeding themselves on most glorious knowledge', with σοφίαν as a bold internal acc. giving the content of the nourishment (LS 12.a). Attic *sophia* includes the crafts sponsored by the patron gods Hephaestus and Athena (building, metalworking, sculpture, painting, weaving, seamanship) and poetry (the epic recitations established by the Peisistratids, the dramatic festivals and dithyrambic contests of the democracy) and all the other intellectual pursuits that had gathered themselves by preference in Athens by the last third of the fifth century. The encomium is thus anachronistic, or rather timeless, and properly comparable to the praise of Athens in Thucydides' Periclean Funeral Oration.

**829–30  διὰ λαμπροτάτου | . . . αἰθέρος**  'stepping with grace and luxury through the bright pure air', alluding to the notion that Attica has a wonderfully balanced and moderate climate, which was believed by earlier and contemporary philosophers and physicians to have the best possible effect on the health, vigour, and intelligence of the inhabitants. (The climate of modern Athens is not the same, partly perhaps because of climate shifts since antiquity and mainly because of modern urbanization, industrialization, and petroleum-powered transport.) For belief in the benefits of a moderate climate, see Hippocrates, *Airs, Waters, and Places* 5; for praise of the climate of Athens see Eur. fr. 971.3–4 οὐρανὸν ὑπὲρ γῆς ἔχομεν εὖ κεκραμένον, | ἵν' οὔτ' ἄγαν πῦρ οὔτε χεῖμα συμπίτνει, Plato, *Tim.* 24c 'so then, having at that time organized you [Athenians] in all this organization and arrangement, the goddess settled you on earth before other people, having selected the place in which you have been born, noting the temperateness (εὐκρασία) of the seasons in it and recognizing that this climate would bring forth men of supreme wisdom (φρονιμωτάτους)'. Further exx. of such praise are collected in Kienzle (1936) 14–18, 27–8.

**830  ἀβρῶς**  here perhaps combines an active sense ('gracefully') with a passive one ('with an experience of luxury', the sensuous feel of living in such an ideal atmosphere). Words from the stem ἀβρ-

traditionally had a positive connotation in the usage of the elite and in the high-style poetry they cultivated, but a negative connotation in the discourse of those devoted to egalitarian civic values (see Kurke (1992)). Eur. here is clearly drawing on the positive connotations, assimilating the whole populace of Attica to an elite dear to, and almost living like, the gods. Compare Pericles' confidence in defending the φιλοκαλία of the Athenians (Thuc. 2.40.1 φιλοκαλοῦμέν τε γὰρ μετ' εὐτελείας καὶ φιλοσοφοῦμεν ἄνευ μαλακίας).

**832–4 Μούσας . . | . Ἁρμονίαν φυτεῦσαι:** syntactically there is no way to tell which noun is subject and which object of 'begat, created'; but the genealogy of the Muses as daughters of Mnemosyne is so well known that Harmonia as subject seems unlikely, and with the Muses as subject we have a more pointed claim: not simply a genealogical fact, but an assertion that all artistic excellences come together perfectly in Athens. (For the opposite view, see Most (1999) 20 n. 1, who points to the epithet ξανθάν and makes a stricter distinction between concept and personification than seems appropriate for Greek lyric.) The Muses also feature in the praise of Athens in Soph. *OC* 691–2. Although Harmonia here verges on being a personification of an abstraction, Eur. is also relying on the mythological associations of Harmonia, daughter of Aphrodite and one of her attendants (*Hom. Hymn Apollo* 194–6, Aesch. *Supp.* 1041; *LIMC* s.v. Harmonia, nos. 12–15, vase-paintings from the late fifth century showing Harmonia in attendance upon Aphrodite along with Peitho, Eros, and similar figures).

**835 Κηφισοῦ:** praised also in Soph. *OC* 685–91, this is the major stream watering the plain west of Athens; it arises on Mt Parnes, is joined by tributaries from several directions, and empties into the Bay of Phaleron.

**836 Κύπριν:** Aphrodite likewise is mentioned as favouring Colonus and Attica in Soph. *OC* 692–3.

**κλήιζουσιν:** almost a synonym of λέγουσι, but this verb implies a sense of pride in the statement and the glory that results from the claim.

**ἀφυσσαμέναν** 'drawing water', 'filling her pail'; 'from the Kephisos' is understood with this from the locative phrase in the preceding verse (variants in some manuscripts show a mistaken effort to make the source more explicit).

**838–40 χώρας καταπνεῦσαι μετρίους ..|. αὔρας** 'wafts down over the land moderate sweet-smelling breaths of wind'; gen. χώρας goes with the κατα- of the compound (Smyth §1384) and is Reiske's emendation of χώραν, which would require a double acc. construction (external object and acc. of content) unparalleled for this verb. The form μετρίους adopted here is based on the ending surviving in a papyrus (for treatment of a three-ending adj. as of only two endings in tragedy, see LS 5.d), although it could be due to assimilation to the ending of ἡδυπνόους or to the presence of a noun other than αὔρας in the gap in the papyrus (the MSS' αὔρας involves an unusual responsion, contraction of biceps in the D element corresponding to κλεινοτάταν σοφίαν).

**840–2 ἐπιβαλλομέναν | χαίταισιν** 'putting upon her own hair' or 'dressing her hair with' (Kovacs): for this sense of the middle, LSJ s.v. III.2.

**844 παρέδρους ... Ἔρωτας:** the image suggests Sophia enthroned, with the Erotes seated beside her as powerful assistants; compare Soph. *OC* 1382 Δίκη ξύνεδρος Ζηνὸς ἀρχαίοις νόμοις (*Ant.* 796–9 describe Eros/Himeros as τῶν μεγάλων πάρεδρος ἐν ἀρχαῖς θεσμῶν, but the phrase is probably corrupt: see Griffith).

**845 παντοίας ἀρετᾶς ξυνεργούς** 'helpers in the creation of all manner of excellent achievement'; this positive assessment of Eros is in strong contrast to the image in the previous stasimon (627–9, excessive Eros hinders good repute and excellence).

**846–8 ἱερῶν ποταμῶν | ἢ πόλις ἢ φίλων | πόμπιμος ... χώρα:** the first ἢ is postponed by a licence of poetry (LS 35), and the sense is 'either a city of sacred rivers or a land that gives escort to friends'. The first alternative refers back to the previous stanza; the gen. is one of description (see Diggle (1994) 418–19). The second alternative alludes to the notion of Athens as protector of deserving suppliants and solver of their problems. In the two most famous cases of which the Athenians constantly boasted in their epideictic oratory, the Argives who died in the attack of the Seven on Thebes are granted their

burial after supplication of the mourners in Athens (Eur. *Supp.*), and
the children of Heracles, persecuted by Eurystheus, can go on their
way safely and with their goals met because of the help given by the
Athenians (*Hcld.*). There may also be an allusion to the incident
referred to by Aeschylus in *Eum.* 9–14: Apollo came from Delos to
Athens, and the Athenians built a road and pacified the wild countryside to escort the god to his new home in Delphi – Apollo too is
their φίλος. Kovacs emends to θεῶν πόμπιμος in order to make the
allusion to religious purity clearer.

**849 τὰν παιδολέτειραν:** the appositive is like an anticipated
quotation of what people will say of Medea (so Jason hurls παιδολέτορ at her in 1393). The fem. agent-noun may be a coinage of Eur.
for this passage (imitated in *Anth. Pal.* 4.138, of Medea, and by Non-
nus, *Dionys.* 48.748, of Procne).

**850 μετ᾽ ἄλλων:** this problematic phrase, if sound, is most likely
to mean 'in the company of others ⟨not similarly polluted⟩' (Bothe's
interpretation); some take it more closely with ἕξει and translate
'among its other inhabitants'; and Most (1999) provides a detailed
discussion of various approaches to the problem and argues (im-
probably) for 'along with the other suppliants ⟨that Athens is famous
for protecting⟩'. Diggle accepts the attractive emendation μέταυλον,
which would here be an *ad hoc* poetic synonym of μέτοικος, 'resident
alien' (cf. ξύναυλος, 'dwelling with' in Soph. *OT* 1126, *Ajax* 611). Kovacs accepts Jacobs' μετ᾽ ἀστῶν, but this is not so likely as the origin
of transmitted μετ᾽ ἄλλων.

**852 φόνον ... αἴρηι:** αἴρηι is a reinterpretation of MSS's αἰρῆι (a
common confusion), and φόνον αἴρεσθαι (apparently unique) is probably based on the more common πόλεμον (νεῖκος) αἴρεσθαι (LSJ s.v.
ἀείρω IV.4), 'stir up, set in motion, undertake war', but one cannot
rule out 'take upon yourself' (LSJ s.v. IV.5), as with ἄχθος in *Or.* 1–3
or πένθος in Soph. *OT* 1225.

**853–4 πάνται | πάντως:** πάνται is adverb πάντηι with Doric
vowel; the nearly synonymous adverbs, 'in every way entirely', make
a very strong expression, found about a dozen times in Plato and
Aristotle and once in Parmenides. The MSS have πάντες πάντως and
corruptions thereof.

**856–9**  The passage is corrupt and not convincingly cured by any suggested emendations. Assuming that the first ἤ is postponed and the corruption lies in τέκνων (e.g. μένος Kovacs), we may guess that the sense was approximately 'Whence will you acquire the daring of mind or the force for your hand or heart, executing a deed of dreadful daring?' Or, if the corruption is rather in ἢ φρενὸς ἤ, one might consider εἰς ὄλεθρον, yielding 'Whence will you acquire for your hand and heart the daring for the destruction of your children, applying dreadful boldness ⟨to the act⟩?' There is a thorough review of past interpretations in Most (1999), whose own defence of the transmitted text does not convince.

**861–2**  ἄδακρυν μοῖραν | σχήσεις φόνου:  from the context it is clear that this must mean something like 'how will you fail to weep at the prospect of murdering them?' and that the rhetorical question leads smoothly to the denial οὐ δυνάσηι, but it is not clear exactly how to construe the individual words of this phrase. Kovacs renders 'how will you behold their fate with tearless eyes?'. This is perhaps the most likely view: μοῖρα is then that of the children, and μοῖρα φόνου is almost a periphrasis for φόνος, as Elmsley proposed, with the not quite satisfactory parallel of 987 μοῖραν θανάτου; Page cites *El.* 1290, but that passage actually supports the next choice. Méridier's version gives (in English) 'how will you take on without tears the lot of a murderer?' (μοῖρα is that of Medea); Wecklein's gives 'how will you have a tearless participation in murder (participate tearlessly in murder)?'; and other less probable explications have been offered.

*866–975   Fourth episode*

As she had manipulated Creon and Aegeus, now Medea manipulates Jason. Her meeting with him is an apparent reversal of that in the second episode. Adopting the stance of the weak, irrational female (for this strategy, compare Clytemnestra's deception of Agamemnon in Aesch. *Ag.*), she now echoes Jason's own positions and appeals to his vanity and sense of superiority to entrap him. She admits to, criticizes, and apologizes for her anger: 870 ὀργάς, 878–9 οὐκ ἀπαλλαχθήσομαι θυμοῦ;, 883 μάτην θυμουμένη, answering to Jason's 447 τραχεῖαν ὀργὴν ὡς ἀμήχανον κακόν, 615 ὀργῆς. She refers to Jason's good sense and planning: 874 τοῖσι βουλεύουσιν εὖ, 884 σωφρονεῖν τέ μοι δοκεῖς, answering Jason's 548–9 σοφός ... σώφρων, 567 μῶν βεβούλευμαι κακῶς; She condemns her own folly: 873 μαίνομαι, 882 ἀβουλίαν, 885 ἄφρων, 891 νηπίων, 892 κακῶς φρονεῖν, answering Jason's 457 μωρίας, 600 ὡς ... σοφωτέρα φανῆι, 614 μωρανεῖς. She claims now to be changed and as prudent as Jason: 886 μετεῖναι τῶνδε τῶν βουλευμάτων, 893 ἄμεινον νῦν βεβούλευμαι τάδε. Jason swallows the bait entirely and replies with patronizing language about the expected behaviour of women and praises Medea for now acting like a 'sensible woman' (908–13). The silent children are brought forth again in this scene, and the secondary meanings of Medea's words and the momentary breakdown of her façade that result from their presence give a foretaste of the internal struggle to come in the next episode. Jason's hopes and prayers for his children create a stark contrast between his ignorance of the impending disaster and the knowledge of Medea, the chorus, and the audience. The fatal gifts form a significant prop in the scene, and Eur. teases the audience for a moment with the possibility that Medea's plot might be forestalled by Jason's objection to the offering of gifts, but this is of course soon overcome.

**866** *Action*: Jason enters, accompanied at minimum by the servant who was sent in the previous scene to fetch him and who now returns to Medea's side. See Introd. 3 for the unsolved problem of whether Jason has his own attendants in this scene.

**866 ἥκω κελευσθείς:** Jason begins abruptly, postponing the brusque vocative γύναι to the end of his short speech, while Medea here feigns a polite approach, beginning with the vocative 'Jason' in 869.

**867 τἄν:** crasis, τοι ἄν.

**τοῦδέ γ'** gets its sense from the whole previous sentence: 'my coming at your request'.

**871 νῷν ... ὑπείργασται:** νῷν is first person dual pronoun (LS 6.d), here dat. of agent or dat. of interest. ὑπείργασται is third sing. perfect mid.-pass. of ὑπεργάζομαι, 'many acts of affection have been done by us as preparation ⟨for reasonable behaviour between us now⟩' (both for this passage and for *Hipp*. 504 LSJ s.v. ὑπεργάζομαι wrongly creates separate rubrics; both are metaphorical applications of the normal sense of the verb, 'work to prepare ⟨for planting⟩').

**872 ἐμαυτῆι διὰ λόγων ἀφικόμην** 'I had a conversation with myself'; διά + abstract noun of emotion or activity + verb of motion is a favourite idiom of the tragedians as a periphrasis for the simple verb cognate with the noun (cf. 1081–2). For the variations and meaning of such idioms, see Barrett on *Hipp.* 542–4.

**873 κἀλοιδόρησα:** crasis, καὶ ἐλοιδόρησα.

**876 τὰ συμφορώτατα:** Medea now pretends to accede to Jason's evaluation of her own advantage: cf. Jason's claim that his actions show him to have been μέγας φίλος to Medea and their sons, 549–50; also 572–3 τὰ λῶιστα καὶ κάλλιστα, 601–2 τὰ χρηστά and εὐτυχοῦσα.

**877 τύραννον:** here fem., of the princess, as also in 957, 1066, 1125, 1356.

**877–8 κασιγνήτους .|.. φυτεύων:** cf. 563–7, 596–7.

**879 τί πάσχω** 'what's wrong with me?'; compare 1049 and *Ion* 1385 καίτοι τί πάσχω; this is a self-directed version of the more common colloquial τί πάσχεις; = 'what is the matter with you?' (Stevens (1976) 41).

**θεῶν ποριζόντων καλῶς:** Medea pretends to accept that what is happening is actually good fortune, as Jason claimed (εὐτυχοῦσα). The verb is used absolutely: 'when the gods are providing handsomely'.

**880 οὐκ** goes with οἶδα as well as with εἰσί, as the position of μέν shows: 'is it not the case that I have children and I know . . .'.

**882 ἐννοηθεῖσ'** is to be preferred to the variant ἐννοήσασ' because Eur. seems to favour treating this verb as deponent and because the familiarity of the active in other authors and in prose was likely to lead to the substitution of that form.

**886 ἧι χρῆν** 'who ought to have . . .'; imperfect of unfulfilled obligation (573n.).

**887 ξυμπεραίνειν:** 341n.

**παρεστάναι λέχει:** from a jealous rival, Medea transforms herself in this imagined scene into a virtual member of the bridal party, or servant of the groom's house. Sources say that the bride entered the marital bedchamber alone, leaving the νυμφεύτρια at the door: Erdmann (1934) 258–9; but some paintings show women at an earlier moment adorning the bed in preparation for the couple: Oakley and Sinos (1993) 35; Verilhac and Vial (1998) 324–5.

**888 νύμφην τε κηδεύουσαν ἤδεσθαι σέθεν:** in the final exaggeration of Medea's pretended attitude of compliance, she will not only attend the bride but enjoy it: 'to take delight in caring for your bride' (κηδεύουσαν governs νύμφην and agrees with understood με, subject of the inf.; for the shift of case from ἧι see 57–8n.). Verrall's emendation νύμφηι gives a much weaker climax ('take delight in contracting a tie with your bride').

**889 ἐσμὲν οἷόν ἐσμεν:** for this type of reticent euphemism, sometimes deprecatory, sometimes resigned in tone, refusing to go into specifics, compare 1011 ἤγγειλας οἷ' ἤγγειλας, *Tro.* 630 ὄλωλεν ὡς ὄλωλεν, *El.* 289 ἔκυρσεν ὡς ἔκυρσεν, Soph. *OT* 1376 βλαστοῦσ' ὅπως ἔβλαστε (further exx. in Denniston on *El.* 1141; see also Fehling (1969) 293 and Johnstone (1980)).

**οὐκ ἐρῶ κακόν:** parenthetic, 'I won't (go so far as to) say a bane', alluding to the Hesiodic discourse of woman as a necessary evil (*Theog.* 603–12) and Jason's wish for a world free of the bane of women (573–5).

**890 χρή:** this variant is more tactful than χρῆν and thus more suited to Medea's rhetoric here. χρῆν and χρή are constantly confused in the MSS, and the corruption may occur in either direction. The imperfect would imply 'ought not to do X, as you are now doing' (573n.), and Medea would then be suggesting that Jason has been behaving on the same level as she herself, an honesty that is less in tune with her pretence here.

**κακοῖς:** generalizing masc. pl., 'people who are bad ⟨like us women⟩'; some take it as neuter, giving the sense 'make yourself similar ⟨to me⟩ in faults'. Stadtmüller replaces κακοῖς with φύσιν in imitation of the closely similar passage in Andromache's speech to Menelaus in *Andr.* 352–4 οὐ χρὴ 'πὶ μικροῖς μεγάλα πορσύνειν κακὰ |

οὐδ', εἰ γυναῖκές ἐσμεν ἀτηρὸν κακόν, | ἄνδρας γυναιξὶν ἐξομοιοῦσθαι φύσιν (κἀξομοιοῦσθαι φύσιν also in Soph. *Aj.* 549).

**891 ἀντιτείνειν νήπι' ἀντὶ νηπίων** 'respond contentiously with foolish words in return for foolish words'; the verb involves a normal sense of τείνειν, 'stretch tightly, make forceful', and νήπια is object. (LSJ misleads.)

**892 παριέμεσθα:** middle of παρίημι, in the sense 'I ask for pardon' (LSJ s.v. VI.2; Soph. *OC* 1666 οὐκ ἂν παρείμην). Kovacs translates 'I give in', but the sense of 'yielding' requires an explicit object (cf. LSJ s.v. IV.1).

**φρονεῖν:** indirect form of imperfect ἐφρόνουν, as the adverb τότε makes clear.

**894** *Action*: Medea turns to the door and calls inside, and it is hard to guess how soon the children are actually visible: there could be a pause after 894 and they may emerge during 895; although Medea's words are meant as much for Jason as for the children, the emphasis in μεθ' ἡμῶν and μητρὸς μέτα fits better if they are already present. But it might be possible to play the scene with the boys emerging as late as 898 in time for the command in 899. Although he is not referred to here in the text, the tutor seen in the parodos must come out with the boys and accompany them to the palace with Jason, for he returns with them at 1002. (That the companion is the tutor is an inference from his being male – 1009 ἀγγέλλων – and from the command Medea gives him in 1020, παισὶ πόρσυν' οἷα χρὴ καθ' ἡμέραν.)

**894 δεῦρο** is Elmsley's emendation of transmitted δεῦτε, which is otherwise absent from tragedy (an epic word, also in Sappho and Pindar and Aeschylean satyr-play, and then common in late Greek, including *NT* – hence perhaps too colloquial for tragedy).

**896–7 διαλλάχθηθ' .|.. ἔχθρας ἐς φίλους:** the gen. ἔχθρας expresses separation, 'be reconciled, make your peace, abandoning the former enmity toward a dear one'; ἐς φίλους (generalizing pl. for Jason) goes with ἔχθρας.

**898 μεθέστηκεν:** perfect of μεθίστημι, intransitive, 'has changed its stance' (911), and so 'has departed' (here and 1295).

**899** λάβεσθε χειρὸς δεξιᾶς: the hand they are to grasp is Jason's, and this is of course a gesture of bonding and good faith, the same gesture that was exchanged with Medea in the past and violated by Jason's betrayal (see Introd. 2(*d*)). This reminder causes Medea's emotional outburst, threatening to break the illusion of her performance for Jason, but through ambiguous language she covers up the slip.

**899–900** κακῶν | ... τῶν κεκρυμμένων: for Medea, the reference is forward, to the concealed evils she intends; for Jason, the reference must be to the past, to the unexpected sufferings that come upon humans like Medea and Jason because the course of human fortunes is concealed by the gods.

**903** ἀρτίδακρυς: for the non-temporal sense of ἀρτι- in this compound ('close to tears', 'ready to weep easily'), compare ἀρτί-κολλος, 'close-glued', 'close-fitted', and ἀρτιεπής, 'ready of speech'.

φόβου πλέα: the same phrase was used in 263, in a striking concluding generalization in Medea's first speech. If the repetition is noticed, there is an interesting shift of meaning, from fear of facing violence and danger to fear of the consequences of her own violence against her children.

**904** χρόνωι 'after a time', 'at long last'.

νεῖκος πατρός 'my dispute with your father'; the gen. is objective.

**905** δακρύων: gen. pl. of δάκρυ/δάκρυον, since the upsilon must be short (participle δακρύων has long upsilon: *Or.* 950).

**906** κἀμοί: crasis, καὶ ἐμοί.

χλωρὸν ... δάκρυ: in the uses of χλωρός that do not clearly imply colour, the sense is usually 'fresh', that is 'moist' instead of 'dry' (see Irwin (1974) ch. 2, esp. 52–6); but it cannot be excluded that there is also a visual suggestion, either of 'glistening' surface or the swelling shape of droplets (cf. Pindar, *Nem.* 8.40 χλωραῖς ἐέρσαις and Soph. *Trach.* 847–8 ἀδινῶν χλωρὰν ... δακρύων ἄχναν).

**907** μὴ προβαίη μεῖζον ἢ τὸ νῦν κακόν 'may the trouble not proceed ⟨and become⟩ greater than the current one', if μεῖζον is taken as predicate adj. with κακόν as subject (another κακόν is supplied with τὸ νῦν, or the phrase could be adverbial like τὰ νῦν). The meaning is essentially the same if, alternatively, one takes μεῖζον as adverbial (or internal acc.) with the verb, 'proceed farther' (if so, προβαίνειν μεῖζον is an unusual phrase and perhaps carries a more vivid image, 'take a greater stride forward', as in Hippocrates, *De articulis* 60). Without betraying the plot to Jason, the chorus hopes Medea's plot will not be carried out.

**908** τάδ'... ἐκεῖνα   'your present attitude ... the way you reacted before'.

**909** ὀργὰς ... ποιεῖσθαι:   periphrasis for ὀργίζεσθαι, in a common use of the middle of ποιέω (LSJ s.v. A.II.5).

**910** γάμους παρεμπολῶντος ἀλλοίους †πόσει†   'when a husband smuggles in ⟨to the household⟩ another marriage/sexual liaison'; probably only the last word is corrupt, and the line was originally a gen. absolute with its subject substantive unexpressed (for this construction see refs. given by Mastronarde on *Phoen.* 70). Not understanding the construction, someone changed the last word to ἐμοῦ (the scholiast ascribes this reading to actors, but such ascriptions are not necessarily to be trusted); and in the medieval tradition a gloss specifying the husband has ousted the original final word and been adjusted to the dat. πόσει. For the lost word Diggle's suggestion δόμοις is attractive.

  **παρεμπολῶντος**   'trafficking improperly', hence, 'smuggling in'. ἐμπολάω itself can have a negative connotation in aristocratic discourse, and the παρα-prefix makes a pejorative sense utterly clear: here Jason uses language from the point of view (or 'focalization') of the angry woman. The compound is otherwise attested only in com. adesp. 771 K–A, of one who has falsely claimed citizenship. One can avoid the momentary shift of focalization and seek a different cure to the corruption by adopting γάμου ... ἀλλοίου πόσει from the MS V (a reading which could, however, be a mere accident) and assuming that a different verb originally stood here: so Kovacs, mentioning παρεμπεσόντος (probably too prosaic and bookish a verb for tragedy).

  **ἀλλοίους:**   although used by Homer and Pindar, this adj. is not found elsewhere in extant tragedy; here it seems little more than a metrical alternative to ἄλλους.

**911  λῶιον:** an archaic synomym for ἄμεινον/βέλτιον (127n.). For μεθέστηκεν see 898n.

**912  ἀλλὰ τῶι χρόνωι:** ἀλλά may here be translated 'at least' or 'at last', as if there is an ellipsis of 'not at first' or 'not previously'. See Denniston 13; LSJ s.v. ἀλλά 1.2.b.

**913  γυναικὸς ἔργα ταῦτα σώφρονος:** it is naturally the view of patriarchal males that prudence in a woman consists in meekly following the lead of a supervising male, but one also finds such sentiments put in the mouth of female characters (e.g. Andromache in *Andr.* 213–14 χρὴ γὰρ γυναῖκα, κἂν κακῶι πόσει δοθῆι, | στέργειν ἅμιλλάν τ' οὐκ ἔχειν φρονήματος).

**914  οὐκ ἀφροντίστως:** Jason returns to his claims of intelligent planning (548–50, 567).

**915  πολλὴν ἔθηκε σὺν θεοῖς σωτηρίαν** 'has created for you, with the favour of the gods, a high degree of security', spoken with terrible dramatic irony both in regard to the future safety of the children and in regard to the assumption of divine favour (which Medea seems to have preempted, 625, 802); see also 919. Note the poetic use of τίθημι in the sense 'make, create' (LS 31).

**917  τὰ πρῶτ'** 'the leading citizens', 'the primary powers', 'of the first rank' (LSJ s.v. πρότερος B.II.3). Most similar is Ar. *Frogs* 425 (the politician Archedemus) κἄστιν τὰ πρῶτα τῆς ἐκεῖ μοχθηρίας.

**918  ἐξεργάζεται:** probably a confident 'dynamic' or almost 'prophetic' use of the present tense (rather than a conative one).

**920–1  τέλος | μολόντας:** acc. without preposition with the verb of motion (LS 12.b).

**921  ἐχθρῶν τῶν ἐμῶν ὑπερτέρους:** the assumption that one's friendships and especially one's enmities will be carried on into the next generation is present in many heroic myths (e.g. the house of Atreus; Jason's own avenging of his father), but seems also to have been a fact of life in the competitive environment of Athenian families (esp. elite families). See Dover (1974) 182; Hunter (1997) 128–9. For superiority over one's enemies as essential to aristocratic success and reputation see 809n.

**922** *Action*:   the actor playing Medea perhaps showed some reaction as early as σωτηρίαν in 915, but to the accumulation of futile hopes in ἔτι, αὐξάνεσθε, εὐτραφεῖς, ἥβης τέλος Medea responds with a strong miming of a breakdown into tears, using the conventional gesture of turning the mask away to portray distress (923). Real tears are impossible with a mask (and would have been unseen in any case by most of the audience because of the size of the theatre), so they are made real for the audience in the words of Jason's question.

αὕτη:   a brusque address, 'you there!', indicating Jason's surprise that Medea has become self-absorbed and stopped paying attention to him and the children. For this quasi-vocative use, see LSJ s.v. οὗτος c.1.5; Stevens (1976) 37.

χλωροῖς δακρύοις:   906n.

**923** στρέψασα ... παρηίδα:   the turning of one's body or especially of one's head is a typical sign of withdrawal from, or refusal of, contact with someone else in one's presence: for this motif see 30 στρέψασα πάλλευκον δέρην, 1148 λευκήν τ' ἀπέστρεψ' ἔμπαλιν παρηίδα, 1151–2 οὐ μὴ ... πάλιν στρέψεις κάρα, *Hec.* 343–4 πρόσωπον ἔμπαλιν στρέφοντα, *IT* 801 μή μ' ἀποστρέφου, *Hel.* 78, *Or.* 720, Soph. *OT* 728, *OC* 1272.

**924** κοὐκ:   crasis, καὶ οὐκ.

**925–31**   When Jason asks why Medea is still visibly upset, her initial answer in 925 is not a full answer, but an evasion (see next n.). Jason replies to this in 926 with blithe confidence. Medea's double assurance in 927 may well be accompanied by a struggle to comply and some continued weeping during 927–8. This struggle to stop weeping prompts Jason's renewed question and the emphasis of λίαν in 929, and then Medea gives a fuller answer in 930–1. Some critics (Dyson (1988); Kovacs) have accepted Ladewig's transposition of 929–31 to a position between 925 and 926 in the belief that the sequence of dialogue is smoother or more logical. They feel that Jason's renewed question about the reason for Medea's tears is odd after she has already answered that she will heed his advice to 'take heart'. Although at first sight the changed order seems attractive, the repetition of τοῖσδ' ... τέκνοις in a line immediately after τέκνων τῶνδ' is (*pace* Dyson) unnatural idiom (τέκνοις should not be there: compare 926 after 925 for the normal usage), and the renewal of the question is not objectionable if the lines are played as just described.

**925** οὐδέν 'it is nothing', implying 'don't be concerned'; an attempt to defuse Jason's curiosity before she actually offers a vague answer in the participial phrase that follows.

**926** τῶνδ' ἐγὼ θήσω πέρι 'I will arrange things well concerning these ⟨boys⟩.' There is variation in the MSS, but the sense of the line is not in doubt. The reading printed here gives welcome emphasis to ἐγώ, the accidental loss of which could account for the other readings. The idiom 'arrange well' may feature εὖ or καλῶς and the active or middle of τίθημι, so these criteria give no help for choosing between the different readings: Diggle (1994) 262–5. It is, however, untypical (but not difficult to understand) that no object is expressed.

**927** δράσω τάδ': a formula of consent or agreement, 'I will do as you suggest.' Cf. 184, 267, 1019.

οὔτοι ... ἀπιστήσω: Medea continues to emphasize her new submission to Jason's guidance, but the emphasis of repetition and the use of the future may also reflect a struggle to stop crying (925–31n.).

**928** γυνὴ δὲ θῆλυ κἀπὶ δακρύοις ἔφυ 'but a woman is a soft, weak thing and is naturally prone to tears.' θῆλυς is from a root meaning 'suckle' and shares many of the denotations and connotations of γυνή; compounds of θηλυ- are often synonyms of compounds of γυναικ- (θηλύφρων/γυναικόφρων, θηλυμανέω/γυναικομανέω). The adj. is very readily applied to express qualities that the culture associates with the female. For connotation 'soft, weak' compare Soph. *Trach.* 1075 (of Heracles crying for the first time in his life) νῦν ... θῆλυς ηὕρημαι τάλας; LSJ s.v. II.2. ἐπί + dat. here expresses purpose (LSJ s.v. B.III.2).

**929** τί δῆτα λίαν: for τί δῆτα in a question (sometimes with exasperated tone) seeking fuller information after an evasive or incomplete answer, compare 678 above, *Alc.* 530, *Her.* 554. Some MSS have the reading τί δὴ τάλαινα, which would convey pity as well as curiosity, but the brusqueness of τί δῆτα fits Jason's attitude in 922 αὕτη,

959 ὦ ματαία); the test of which reading is more likely to have been corrupted into the other may also favour τί δῆτα λίαν.

**930 ἐξηύχου:** imperfect of ἐξεύχομαι, referring back to 921–2.

**931 εἰ γενήσεται τάδε:** an indirect question, following οἶκτος, 'pity ⟨aroused by uncertainty⟩ whether'.

**932 εἰς ἐμοὺς ἥκεις λόγους** 'you have come to speak with me'. Tragic idiom readily produces periphrases with a verb of motion and εἰς + abstract noun: compare *Or.* 998–9 ἐς κοινοὺς λόγους ἔλθωμεν, *Phoen.* 771 σοὶ ... ἐς λόγους ἀφίξεται, and see Mastronarde on *Phoen.* 194–5.

**938 ἀπαίρομεν:** the verb is intransitive in the sense 'depart' (a development of a military sense, ἀπαίρειν ναῦς or στρατόν); this is a 'dynamic' present equivalent to the future (esp. common with verbs of motion, as generally with Attic εἶμι). Elmsley tentatively proposed future ἀπαροῦμεν, adopted by some editors, which would make a stronger statement of Medea's intention to obey the edict.

**939 ἐκτραφῶσι:** aor. pass. subj. of ἐκτρέφω, 'raise'.

**940 αἰτοῦ ... μὴ φεύγειν:** παῖδας is understood as the subject of the infinitive from παῖδες in the previous line (where it is emphatically placed before the conjunction of the clause to which it belongs).

**941 οὐκ οἶδ' ἂν εἰ πείσαιμι:** in sense ἄν goes with πείσαιμι, a potential optative in an indirect question (almost the same phrase occurs in *Alc.* 48); its position is only partly conditioned by metrical need, since a similar displacement is found in prose (Plato, *Tim.* 26b4–5 οὐκ ἂν οἶδ' εἰ δυναίμην ἅπαντα ἐν μνήμηι πάλιν λαβεῖν). Here the tendency of ἄν to take the second position of the clause overrides the tendency to treat the clauses as independent speech-units (cola).

**942 δ' ἀλλά** introduces an alternative request after Jason has expressed a doubt about the efficacy of the first request: 'well, then, instead' or 'well, then, at least' (Denniston 10).

**κέλευσον:** here 'exhort, urge' rather than 'order', or at least Jason takes it thus, since he speaks of successfully persuading his bride.

**ἄντεσθαι:** this emendation is to be preferred to the MSS' αἰτεῖσθαι because the latter is not attested with a gen. of the person (cf.

940 αἰτοῦ Κρέοντα), while for a verb of supplication like ἄντομαι there is at least the analogy of δέομαι. For a similar corruption see 336n.; cf. Diggle (1994) 284.

**945** The MSS are split between making this the second line of Jason's speech and making it the first of Medea's reply (a scholion explains it as the latter). As the second line of Jason's speech, the line shows Jason holding the stereotypical notion that women are more given to pity and concern for children than men, and the irony in this is his blindness to Medea's plan and her potential to suppress the feminine qualities he is so sure about. As the opening of Medea's reply, it would show Medea playing on Jason's vanity and sense of male superiority by implying that any normal woman would listen to her husband's suasion (or that any woman would listen to Jason?). If Medea is adding this line as a supplement to Jason's, it would be more idiomatic to have γε in the line (Herwerden adds γ' after γυναικῶν). The former interpretation seems preferable (and the need to add γε weighs against the latter).

**946 κἀγώ:** crasis, καὶ ἐγώ.

**947–50 πέμψω γὰρ αὐτῆι δῶρ' κτλ.:** 947 is similar in phrasing to 784, 949 is identical to 786, and φέροντας is similarly placed in 950 and 785, and so many critics judge that there is interpolation in one or both places. The similarities are decreased if it is correct to delete 949 here and 785 in the earlier passage. Here 949 is less necessary than 786 in its context, and retaining 949 also makes the postponement of παῖδας φέροντας even harsher: the words αὐτῆι δῶρ' in 947 initially seem to be the indirect and direct objects of the adjacent verb πέμψω, but after the relative clause ἃ ... πολύ they are understood to be governed instead by φέροντας.

**947 καλλιστεύεται:** the verb is attested in classical times only in Hdt. (active only), Eur. and *TrGF* adesp. 625.7; here it is presumably passive in sense, 'are considered most beautiful' (cf. adesp. ἀγώνων τῶν κεκαλλιστευμένων).

**950 ὅσον τάχος** 'as quickly as possible' (105n.).

**951 κόσμον:** the gifts are repeatedly referred to as κόσμος, three times in the remainder of this scene (also 954, 972), and also at 787 (announcement of plan) and 982, 1156 (acceptance of gifts by the princess). For the relevance of this term to the Hesiodic theme of marriage and the Pandora story, see Mueller (2001).

**προσπόλων τινά:** the couplet 950–1 does not read like a shout directed indoors, so one of the silent attendants who came out with Medea at 214 either now goes indoors and very quickly reappears with the gifts, or goes to the door, gestures inside, and quickly receives the gifts from someone else. On Eur.'s apparent failure to show how the poisoned gifts were prepared, see 789n. and 823n. For the question of how visible the gifts were to the audience and the suggestion that they were carried on trays or in small chests, see Introd. 3.

**952 οὐχ ἕν ἀλλὰ μυρία:** internal accs., 'not in just one respect, but in countless ways'.

**953 ἀνδρός τ' ἀρίστου σοῦ τυχοῦσ' ὁμευνέτου** 'having received you, a peerless man, as her bedmate' (ὁμευνέτου predicative).

**955 δίδωσιν** is an historical present (note ποθ') or possibly a 'registering' present (LS 16–17).

**οἷς** 'his own', from epic possessive adj. ὅς (cf. ἑός, Latin *suus*), extremely rare in tragedy, extant only here in Eur.; the usage probably lends solemnity to Medea's description of her gift.

**956 λάζυσθε φέρνας:** although the boys could take the props from the servant in response to this command, it would better express Medea's control of the process (and more literally suit Jason's σὰς κενοῖς χέρας in 959) if (as M. Griffith suggests) she quickly conveys the items from the servants to her sons. Perhaps one son holds the robe, the other the crown (perhaps on trays or in chests: 951n.). λάζυμαι is a poetic synonym of λαμβάνω, and its use is an affectation of Eur. φέρνας indicates that these gifts are to be added to the bride's 'trousseau', the property she brings to the newly formed family.

**957 μακαρίαι νύμφηι:** an allusion to *makarismos* (509n.).

**958 οὔτοι ... μεμπτά:** litotes, 'no mean gifts', 'faultless gifts'; compare οὐ μεμπτός in *Phoen.* 425 and *IA* 712.

**959 ὦ ματαία:** 151–2n.

**κενοῖς:** second sing. pres. act. ind. of verb κενόω (dat. pl. masc./ neut. of the adj. κενός looks the same).

**960–1 δοκεῖς ... πέπλων, | δοκεῖς δὲ χρυσοῦ:** the anaphora adds vigour to the incredulous question.

**963 προθήσει χρημάτων** 'she will consider ⟨me, my desires⟩ more important than rich property.' For προτίθημι, 'rank ahead, rank in preference to' see LSJ s.v. iv.3. The gen. is one of comparison, as in Hdt. 3.53 πολλοὶ τῶν δικαίων τὰ ἐπιεικέστερα προτιθεῖσι.

**964 μή μοι σύ** 'please don't do that' (try to dissuade me); compare elliptical μὴ σύ γε (Mastronarde on *Phoen.* 532); μοι may be an ethic dative rather than the indirect object of an understood τοιαῦτα λέξῃς.

**πείθειν δῶρα καὶ θεοὺς λόγος** 'there is a saying that gifts persuade even the gods'; the assumption of reciprocity in relations between human and divine (honorific or pious action by mortals earns favours from the divine) is basic to traditional Greek religion (and many other religions), although it is attacked as fostering an unworthy image of divinity in the philosophical tradition. Plato, *Rep.* 390e3 quotes a hexameter proverb δῶρα θεοὺς πείθει, δῶρ' αἰδοίους βασιλῆας. See Yunis (1988) 50–8.

**966–7 κείνης ὁ δαίμων ... | νέα τυραννεῖ** 'to her belongs divine favour at this moment, her affairs god is now raising high, she in her youth [νέα with long alpha] enjoys kingly power'. The sequence of short cola, the anaphora κείνης ... κεῖνα, and the quasi-redundancy of the two halves of 966 are expressive of Medea's (feigned) earnestness. With the flexibility typical of the neuter demonstrative, κεῖνα means 'affairs over there, in the other, distant place' and can legitimately be translated into English as 'her affairs'. Nauck's deletion of 966b–7a is misconceived.

**968 ψυχῆς ἂν ἀλλαξαίμεθ'** 'I would take in exchange for my life' or (more naturally in English) 'for the ⟨release from⟩ exile of my sons, I would trade my life'; gen. of price or value (Smyth §1372). φυγὰς ἀλλάξασθαι has pregnant force here: either the abstract noun is given an extended meaning derived from the context (cf. *Hec.* 227 γίγνωσκε δ' ἀλκήν, where the noun means '⟨lack of⟩ defensive strength'), or the verb means 'buy off, ransom' rather than the usual 'buy, acquire', on the analogy of ἐξαιτεῖσθαι or παραιτεῖσθαι.

**969** **εἰσελθόντε:** the dual participle is metrically convenient here and is freely combined in the same sentence with plural forms (LS 9).

**πλουσίους δόμους:** the epithet must be spoken honorifically to deceive Jason, but Medea's insistence on gold (965, 968) and wealth (like the detailed reference in 970, 'your father's new wife, and my mistress') also reflects her resentment of the prosperity that Jason has sought in betraying her, and her confidence that her enemies will soon be brought low.

**973** **ἐς χεῖρ':** we cannot determine whether this is χεῖρα or χεῖρε; χεροῖν ἐδέξατ' is used in 1003–4, but singular χείρ often has a quasi-collective sense.

**974–5** **μητρὶ δ' ὧν ἐρᾶι τυχεῖν | εὐάγγελοι γένοισθε** 'may you prove to be bearers of good news for your mother about those things she yearns to obtain'. The unexpressed antecedent of ὧν is an objective gen. with εὐάγγελοι (cf. Aesch. *Ag.* 646 σωτηρίων δὲ πραγμάτων εὐάγγελον).

**975** **πράξαντες καλῶς** is intransitive, 'having been successful'.

### 976–1001    Fourth stasimon

The chorus ended the previous stasimon with the optimistic judgment that Medea would not be able to commit the murder she has planned. This optimism is abandoned from the first line of the fourth stasimon. The anticipation of the coming deaths in this ode may even induce an audience to expect that the next scene will bring a report of the princess' death and that the death of the children will quickly follow. Instead, the sequence of events is drawn out over two scenes, with Medea's monologue intervening before the messenger scene. The chorus' stance, however, contributes an air of inevitability to the coming horror, and this may affect how an audience reacts to Medea's own claim that the killing of her sons is now unavoidable (1061–2n., 1238–9n.).

The song is noteworthy for the shifts of focus, in the first pair starting with the children and then dwelling on the princess, and in the second pair dividing attention equally between Jason and Medea (both apostrophized). There is an even distribution of sympathy: the girl is δύστανος 979, 987, while Jason is invoked as τάλαν 990, δύστανε 995, and Medea as τάλαινα 997. The chorus' resignation is expressed in other verbal repetitions: οὐκέτι ... οὐκέτι and δέξεται ... δέξεται are most forceful, but also relevant are ἄταν 979 and 987, both times after δύστανος; νύμφα 978 and νυμφοκομήσει 985; ἀμφὶ ... θήσει 980 and περιθέσθαι 984; χρυσέων ἀναδεσμᾶν 978 and χρυσότευκτον ... στέφανον 984. The women acknowledge Jason's blindness to what is happening (990–5): in one sense Jason is already shown in the *agōn* to be blind in his faith in his own plans, but the preceding scene makes his ignorance of his circumstances thoroughly obvious, and the chorus will comment on his mistaken assumptions again in 1306–7. Eur. thus prepares for some shift of sympathy toward Jason in the final scene, but it is significant that the chorus refer again to his guilt here in 1000–1 and make his just suffering the chief point of their reaction to the messenger speech (1231–2).

*Metre*

The first pair of stanzas continues the motif of dactylo-epitrite rhythm (PM 27) seen in the previous odes. If it is correct to understand the ethos of this metre as stately, that may reinforce the air of the chorus' resigned acceptance. In this stasimon the second pair is more similar in rhythm to the first than in the previous odes, just as its subject matter and tone are similar. This probably likewise reflects regretful acceptance (in contrast to the intense emotion of the dochmiacs that accompany the actual moment of child-killing). There are no firm clues to the period-structure: the first pair seems to consist of four periods, the second pair could be one long period.

   – – ∪  ∪ – ∪ ∪  – – –  ∪  – |

νῦν ἐλπίδες οὐκέτι μοι παίδων ζόας,       976  – D – e

πείσει χάρις ἀμβρόσιός τ' αὐγὰ πέπλον      983

   – ∪ – – – ∪ ∪ – ∪ ∪  – – ‖

οὐκέτι· στείχουσι γὰρ ἐς φόνον ἤδη.      977  e – D –

χρυσότευκτόν ⟨τε⟩ στέφανον περιθέσθαι·    984

   – ∪ – – – ∪ ∪ – ∪  ∪ – –‖

δέξεται νύμφα χρυσέων ἀναδεσμᾶν      978  e – D –

νερτέροις δ' ἤδη πάρα νυμφοκομήσει.      985

$- \cup - - \ - \cup - - \|$
δέξεται δύστανος ἄταν·                       979 E −(2 tro)
τοῖον εἰς ἔρκος πεσεῖται                      986

$- - \ - \cup \cup - \ - - \cup \ - -$
ξανθᾶι δ' ἀμφὶ κόμαι θήσει τὸν Ἅιδα          980–1 e∧d¹ −e −
                                             (or D − e −,
                                             contracted
                                             elegiambus)
καὶ μοῖραν θανάτου δύστανος· ἄταν δ'         987–8
$- \cup - - \ \cup - \|||$
κόσμον αὐτὰ χεροῖν.                          982 2 cr
οὐχ ὑπεκφεύξεται.                            989

$- - - - - - - - - -$

$\cup - \cup \cup - \cup \cup - \cup - \cup - \cup - - \|^2$
σὺ δ', ὦ τάλαν ὦ κακόνυμφε κηδεμὼν           990–1 ∪D∪ +
    τυράννων,                                ithyphallic
                                             (erasmonidean
                                             + ithyphallic)
μεταστένομαι δὲ σὸν ἄλγος, ὦ τάλαινα         996–7
    παίδων
$- \cup - \ \cup - - \|^2$
παισὶν οὐ κατειδὼς                           992 ithyphallic
μᾶτερ, ἃ φονεύσεις                           998

$\cup \cup - \ \cup \cup - \ \cup \cup - \ \cup \cup -$
ὄλεθρον βιοτᾶι προσάγεις ἀλόχωι             993 2 anap (∪∪Dd²)
τέκνα νυμφιδίων ἕνεκεν λεχέων,               999

$\cup - \ \cup \cup - \cup \cup - \ |$
τε σᾶι στυγερὸν θάνατον.                     994 ∪D
ἃ σοι προλιπὼν ἀνόμως                        1000

$- - \cup - - \ \cup - \cup - - \|||$
δύστανε, μοίρας ὅσον παροίχηι.               995 ia, ithyphallic
ἄλλαι ξυνοικεῖ πόσις συνεύνωι.               1001

**976–9** οὐκέτι ... | οὐκέτι ... | δέξεται ... | δέξεται: for these
repetitions see LS 36, and for the latter type cf. the exx. given by
Diggle (1994) 370.

**978** ἀναδεσμᾶν is Doric gen. plural (LS 5.a). ἀναδέσμη is a rare epic term for 'headband', what Medea called πλόκος in 786. The word is defining gen. with ἄταν, 'the destruction caused/carried by the golden headband'.

**980–2** ἀμφὶ κόμαι θήσει ... | κόσμον: probably an instance of tmesis, as the verb is an epic one often featuring tmesis and this instance recalls Medea's κόσμον ἀμφιθῆι χροῖ (787).

τὸν Ἅιδα | κόσμον 'the finery of Death' (Kovacs), that is, 'the fatal adornment'; for this use of 'belonging to Hades' compare *Or.* 1398–9 ξίφεσιν σιδαρέοισιν Ἅιδα, *Cycl.* 396–7 τῶι θεοστυγεῖ Ἅιδου μαγείρωι; Aesch. *Ag.* 1235 Ἅιδου μητέρ'. For the Doric gen. ending of Ἅιδα, see LS 5.a.

**983–4** The MSS present a fault in responsion in 984 and the transmitted gen. πέπλων or πέπλου in 983 gives defective sense, as if the gleam of the robe makes the princess put on the crown. The best solution is to follow Reiske, who recognized that robe and crown should be in the same case and added τε, and Elmsley, who restored acc. sing. πέπλον (easily corrupted to gen. to go with χάρις or αὐγά).

**985** νερτέροις ... πάρα: anastrophe (LS 24).

νυμφοκομήσει: a rare verb, here only with the sense 'will wear her bridal apparel'. The image here evokes the idea of the death of an unmarried girl as a marriage to death: see Soph. *Ant.* 654 with Griffith's note; Seaford (1987) 110; Rehm (1994) *passim*. Eur. elsewhere extends the motif: death instead of hoped-for marriage for the sons of Heracles in *Her.* 484; death of long-married Helen in *Or.* 1109.

**986** ἕρκος 'net, snare, trap'.

**990** κακόνυμφε 'unhappily married', 'disastrously married' (206–7n.).

κηδεμών: in a stretching of language typical of tragic style (LS 31), Eur. uses a word that normally means 'guardian, protector' as a synonym for κηδεστής, 'kin by marriage', 'son-in-law'.

**992–3** παισὶν ..|. βιοτᾶι: both are dats. of disadvantage with ὄλεθρον ... προσάγεις, in a 'part and whole' construction typical of poetry (see Smyth §985, K–G 1.289). In English one may translate either 'to the life of your sons' or 'destruction of life for your sons'.

**995** μοίρας ὅσον παροίχηι   'how far you have gone aside from your destiny', that is, 'how thoroughly you have failed to understand what is about to happen'. This phrase thus restates the point of 992 οὐ κατειδώς. For the metaphor, compare Aesch. *Supp.* 452 ἦ κάρτα νείκους τοῦδ' ἐγὼ παροίχομαι, 'I am very far from understanding (knowing how to cope with) this strife' (where νείκους should be taken as gen. of separation, against the doubts of Friis Johansen and Whittle ad loc.). (LSJ s.v. παροίχομαι is misleading on these passages.)

**996** μεταστένομαι is taken by most to mean 'next, I lament', but Elmsley suggested that the meaning is rather 'I share with you in lamenting', an attractive possibility.

**999–1000** νυμφιδίων ἕνεκεν λεχέων, | ἅ σοι προλιπὼν ἀνόμως 'because of your marriage bed, which, hurting you [σοι, dat. of disadvantage], your husband lawlessly abandoned and ...'; the chorus recalls again the theme of Jason's betrayal.

**1001** ἄλλαι ξυνοικεῖ ... συνεύνωι perhaps recalls the mention of rivalry for the bed at the end of the first stasimon, 444–5 τῶν τε λέκτρων ἄλλα βασίλεια κρείσσων.

### *1002–80   Fifth episode*

The shortest episode of the play begins with rapid confirmation that Medea's plan has worked smoothly to this point: the princess has accepted the gifts and assurances have been given that the boys have been freed from the edict of exile. As in the previous scene with Jason, the dialogue plays upon the discrepant awareness of the tutor and Medea to hint at Medea's compunctions about her plan. Then Medea is left on stage with her children and engages in a long fare-well with veiled reference to her true plan. She comes close to breaking down and abandoning her plan, and she dismisses the boys and summons them back, but in the end they are sent in for the last time and their fate seems decided, although at the end of the scene Medea still stands before the door, holding the action in suspension.

The scene is dominated by Medea's famous monologue (1021–80). Although self-addressed speeches of deliberation in which two courses of action are contemplated and one finally chosen are already present in Homer (see e.g. Pelliccia (1995) ch. 2), the striking portrayal of competing impulses in this speech both goes beyond anything in the extant earlier tradition and was immensely influential on later Greek and Roman authors (e.g. Apollonius' Medea, Virgil's Dido, a large number of female characters in Ovid's *Heroides* and *Metamorphoses*). The speech is also controversial in the scholarly reception of the play, in terms of interpretation (see notes on 1051, 1053, 1059, 1060–1, 1064, 1078–80), authenticity (see Appendix), and originality (on Neophron see Introd. 5).

**1002** *Action:* the two boys are shepherded in from the direction of the palace by the tutor, who emerged with them at 894–8. Their empty hands already show visually that the gifts have reached their recipient.

ἀφεῖνται: third pl. perfect mid.-pass. of ἀφίημι.

**1004** τἀκεῖθεν 'the situation there', 'the attitude of the royal family', subject of the sentence, with ἐστί understood.

**1005a** ἔα: this exclamation (usually *extra metrum*, as here) generally expresses surprise at a new aspect of the situation that the speaker has just noticed. From it we can infer that, just as at 922, the actor playing Medea has mimed distress in stance or gesture, and as usual the words of the text also interpret this development for the audience. Medea's emotional distress is conveyed by her initial silence (and gesture), by her uttering an *extra metrum* exclamation in 1008a all by itself (that is, without following full trimeter, as with the tutor's ἔα), by the *antilabe* (1009n.), and by the postponement of full dialogue-contact with her interlocutor (Mastronarde (1979) 39).

**1005** συγχυθεῖσ': fem. sing. nom. aor. pass. participle of συγχέω, here 'upset, troubled, distraught'.

**[1006–7]** The second line is identical to 924 and the first very similar to 923; moreover, τρέπω is not elsewhere used in such phrases, where στρέφω is common (923n.), and the couplet is too explicit, spoiling the gradual development of the tutor's perplexity. Either this is an interpolation by actors, who padded this scene with a borrowing from the earlier one, or 923–4 were quoted in the margin by a reader and someone subsequently inserted them into the text and adapted the first line to the new context.

**1009 αἰαῖ μάλ’ αὖθις:** μάλ’ αὖθις is a formulaic combination appended to a repeated exclamation about a dozen times in tragedy: 'woe, I say again!' The sharing of a single iambic trimeter between two speakers is known as *antilabe*; in early Eur. it is quite uncommon and occurs only at points of great emotional turmoil (compare *Hipp.* 310, 352, crucial points in the nurse's uncovering of Phaedra's secret). On *antilabe* in general see Köhler (1913).

μῶν expresses the speaker's reluctance to believe his own surmise (567n.).

τύχην is here negative in connotation, 'misfortune'.

**1010 δόξης δ’ ἐσφάλην εὐαγγέλου** 'and have I been deceived in my expectation that I was bringing good news?'

**1011 ἤγγειλας οἷ’ ἤγγειλας:** spoken with euphemistic resignation; for this kind of phrase, see 889n.

**1012 τί δαί:** δαί is a very informal particle accompanying interrogatives (esp. πῶς, τίς, τί), common in Aristophanes but rare in tragedy; its colloquial tone is suitable here, as in the stichomythia at *Ion* 275 or *Helen* 1246. See 339n.

κατηφεῖς ὄμμα 'are you downcast in your gaze?' Diggle prints Cobet's κατηφὲς ὄμμα, 'why is your eye downcast and why are you crying?', but the resulting mixture of third-person phrase and second-person phrase is neither exactly like *Hcld.* 633 (τί χρῆμα κεῖσαι καὶ κατηφὲς ὄμμ’ ἔχεις;) nor more attractive than the MS text. Eur. is the only tragedian who uses epic root κατηφ-.

**1013 πολλή μ’ ἀνάγκη** 'there is a strong compulsion that I do so' (inf. δακρυρροεῖν or the like is understood), almost 'I have no other choice'; cf. *Alc.* 378 and Mastronarde on *Phoen.* 1674.

**1013–14 θεοὶ | κἀγώ:** the recognition of the co-responsibility of supernatural causes and human action is typical of traditional Greek theology and story-telling (including epic and tragedy); but here the reference to the gods' part in contriving events is also an index of Medea's growing inclination from this point on to portray herself as compelled by circumstances outside herself to carry her plan to its bitter conclusion. See also Introd. 2(e).

**1014 ἐμηχανησάμην:** the verb agrees in number with the closer subject (Smyth §§967–70); Page suggests that this agreement lays more emphasis on Medea's own responsibility, but see previous note.

**1015 κάτει:** second sing. of κάτειμι (εἶμι), 'you will return ⟨here from exile⟩', with a common meaning of the verbal prefix κατα- (compare LSJ s.v. κατάγω ii, s.v. κατέρχομαι ii).

**πρὸς τέκνων** 'through the influence of your sons' (26n.), with κάτει being treated as equivalent to a passive ('be brought back').

**1016 κατάξω:** to be interpreted by the tutor as 'I'll sooner bring others back ⟨from exile⟩' (a euphemism for 'I'll never return myself'), but understood by the audience and Medea herself as 'I'll first bring others (my children) down ⟨to the underworld⟩'.

**1017 οὔτοι μόνη:** it is a typical motif of rhetorical consolation to remind a sufferer that he or she is not the only one to experience such a loss (e.g. *Alc.* 892, *Hipp.* 834, *Andr.* 1041), but that it is the common fate of mankind, from which no one is entitled to except herself or himself.

**1018 θνητὸν ὄντα:** the masc. gender universalizes the statement ('anyone who is mortal'). For the commonplace sentiment, compare Soph. fr. 585.1–2 χρεὼν | τὰ θεῖα θνητοὺς ὄντας εὐπετῶς φέρειν, *Phoen.* [1763] τὰς γὰρ ἐκ θεῶν ἀνάγκας θνητὸν ὄντα δεῖ φέρειν, [Men.] *Sent.* 813 φέρειν ἀνάγκη θνητὸν ὄντα τὴν τύχην.

**1019 δράσω τάδ':** 927n.

**1020** *Action:* the tutor goes indoors, leaving the children on stage with Medea (for a different view, Burnett (1998) 210). There are presumably one or two silent (female) attendants standing nearby, as they have been throughout Medea's presence (see Introd. 3). Although Medea addresses the children for part of this speech and in other parts they may be still visible and, naturalistically, capable of hearing what she says, as child characters they do not, by convention, have full dramatic status, and it is not appropriate to inquire too closely into what they are making of Medea's cryptic words and shifting moods. See Battezzato (1991).

**1021  σφῶιν:**  second person dual pronoun (LS 6.d).

**1023  αἰεί:**  like λιπόντες in the previous line, which is not strictly appropriate to those who are staying while Medea departs, the adverb is a clue that Medea is thinking of her sons' death. Compare perhaps pathetic ἀεί in epitaphs, such as *IG* I³ 1261 σῆμα Φρασικλείας· κούρη κεκλήσομαι αἰεί, | ἀντὶ γάμου παρὰ θεῶν τοῦτο λαχοῦσ᾽ ὄνομα and *IG* I³ 1295 *bis*.5–8 μνήμην γὰρ ἀεὶ δακρυτὸν ἔχουσα, | ἡλικίας τῆς σῆς κλαίει ἀποφθιμένης.

**1025–7**  Although it is more common to speak of marriage as the *telos* of a girl (in contrast to serving as a warrior, the *telos* for a boy), female characters at least are often shown lamenting the loss of the fulfilment of seeing a son married and poised to carry on the family. Compare Megara's complaint in *Her.* 476–84, Hecuba's in *Tro.* 1167–9 and 1218–20. For the roles of mothers in weddings, see Erdmann (1934) 257–8, Oakley and Sinos (1993) 14–41 *passim*.

ὀνάσθαι is aor. mid. inf. of ὀνίνημι, (intrans.) 'benefit from, enjoy' (+ gen.).

**1026  λουτρά** is Burges' emendation of λέκτρα, which is too repetitious with the following terms; moreover, the prenuptial bath is one of the activities most often associated with the mother of the bride or groom, and is often paired with the carrying of torches in the procession. See Mastronarde on *Phoen.* 345, 347–8; Oakley and Sinos (1993) 15–16.

**1027  ἀγῆλαι:**  aor. act. inf. of ἀγάλλω, 'make splendid, adorn'.

**ἀνασχεθεῖν:**  ἔσχεθον is an alternative epic form of the aor. ἔσχον, occasionally convenient in tragedy. For the formation see Smyth §490D.

**1028  αὐθαδίας:**  103–4n.; gen. of cause with the exclamation (LS 10.c).

**1029  ἄλλως**  'in vain' (LSJ s.v. II.3).

**1030  κατεξάνθην:**  aor. pass. of καταξαίνω, lit. 'card (wool) thoroughly', but frequently used in metaphorical senses in poetry and late prose (here 'torn', 'shredded'). Note the almost identical line in *Tro.* 760, in Andromache's farewell to the doomed Astyanax, μάτην δ' ἐμόχθουν καὶ κατεξάνθην πόνοις, and for the motif of vain nurture compare also *Her.* 901–3, *Supp.* 918–24, *Tro.* 381. For the importance of the physical pains of labour or of the care of an infant in the emotional attachment of a woman to her child, see Mastronarde on *Phoen.* 30 and 355–6. Medea's complaint in 1029–30 and the lost hopes described in the following lines continue the ambiguity of 1025–7: they can be heard as the complaints of one who is to be permanently separated from her living children, but they are easily recognized by the audience as motifs of mourning for dead children. For complaints as a standard element of laments, see Alexiou (1974) ch. 8, esp. 182–4; Lattimore (1962) ch. 6.

**1033–4 γηροβοσκήσειν ..|. εὖ περιστελεῖν:** it is a fundamental tenet of the Greek social system that children are to pay back the nurture they received as children by caring for their parents in turn when the parents are burdened with old age (θρεπτήρια, τροφεῖα; Garland (1990) 261–2, Lacey (1968) 116–17), and that in a happy family the elders will receive all proper burial rituals from their living children. Compare *Alc.* 662–4 τοιγὰρ φυτεύων παῖδας οὐκέτ' ἂν φθάνοις, | οἳ γηροβοσκήσουσι καὶ θανόντα σε | περιστελοῦσι καὶ προθήσονται νεκρόν; *Tro.* 1182–6.

**1035 ζηλωτὸν ἀνθρώποισι** 'a thing that inspires men's envy/admiration'; neuter in apposition to the preceding inf. phrase (LS 12.a).

**1036 σφῷιν:** 1021n.

**1037 ἀλγεινόν τ' ἀεί:** the final word is uncertain, but F. W. Schmidt's τ' ἀεί is attractive. The transmitted text τ' ἐμοί produces a false emphasis: since the context makes it completely clear that the life and the pain are Medea's, there is no point in 'and painful *to me*'. Contrast *Bacch.* 1327–8 σὸς δ' ἔχει δίκην | παῖς παιδὸς ἀξίαν μέν, ἀλγεινὴν δὲ σοί, 'a punishment that *he* deserved, but painful *to you*'. Kovacs accepts Platnauer's emendation τ' ἐμόν, which is an easy change but still seems to provide a superfluous qualification so late in the sentence.

**1039** ἐς ἄλλο σχῆμ' ... βίου:   the surface meaning for the boys themselves is 'another form of life' (that is, one with Jason and a stepmother and without Medea), but the phrase is again easily understood as a euphemism for death (1016n.). Among the various, sometimes contradictory, beliefs the Greeks held about death are the ideas that the dead 'dwell' somewhere else forever and that at least some of the dead may enjoy some kind of blessed 'life' after death. See Vermeule (1979) ch. 1 and *passim*; Garland (1985) ch. 1 and *passim*; Rohde (1925). Compare *Ion* 1067 (Creusa will commit suicide and) εἰς ἄλλας βιότου κάτεισι μορφάς, *Hipp.* 195 δι' ἀπειροσύνην ἄλλου βιότου, 'for lack of experience of another ⟨form of⟩ life' (in the underworld).

**1040–8**   Medea's rehearsal of the motifs of mourning/separation has opened space for a softening of her resolve, and it is finally the simple glance and smile of her children that bring the first effort to step back from her plan. The shift is marked by the incorporation into her lines of the exclamations φεῦ φεῦ and αἰαῖ, by the deliberative question τί δράσω;, by the turn in these lines from the children as addressees to the women of the chorus, and by the emphatic repetition at a short interval of χαιρέτω βουλεύματα, forming a ring around a series of mostly short, asyndetic sentences. From 1021 to 1041 the actor playing Medea must engage the child-extras through stance and gesture and perhaps through some physical contact (nothing specific is referred to in the text itself), and the extras' response must not be very demonstrative or indicative of grief, only a fixity of attention on Medea, with an (implied) expression that can be understood as γέλως. This fits the notion that young children do not fully comprehend the concerns and words of adults (cf. 47–8) and conforms to the conventions of stage-children.

**1041** πανύστατον γέλων:   πανύστατος is consistently used in tragedy in connection with death, esp. last farewells and last sight of the sun (mocked by Ar. *Ach.* 1184), so its use here continues the pattern of transparent allusion to their death. For γέλων see LS 5.c.

**1042** καρδία ... οἴχεται   could be just 'my heart is undone, utterly distressed' but the chorus and the audience can also hear the sense 'my brave resolve ⟨to do murder⟩ is gone'; at this moment, Medea seems to be fulfilling the expectation the chorus expressed in 856–65 (note 858 καρδίαι and 865 τλάμονι θυμῶι). For the sense of οἴχεται see 226n.

**1044 οὐκ ἂν δυναίμην:** the following phrase shows that τέκνα φονεύειν is the action she now thinks impossible. Again, Medea seems to be echoing the chorus' hope, 862 οὐ δυνάσηι.

**1046 τοῖς τούτων κακοῖς** 'with their sufferings' alludes to the plan to kill the children without saying as much in their presence. If one worries about what the children are to make of the phrase, the phrase is simply unintelligible to them; but one should not be worried about this question.

**1047 αὐτήν** is here the emphatic pronoun: 'why should I, causing pain to their *father* ... *myself* acquire twice as much anguish?'

**1048 οὐ δῆτ᾽ ἔγωγε:** Medea answers her own question, apparently with great conviction, but this vehemence and the repetitions in the passage portray an intense struggle to convince herself, preparing for the shift in the next line.

**χαιρέτω βουλεύματα:** the scholiasts mention a variant reading παύσομαι βουλευμάτων, apparently a misguided attempt to eliminate the exact repetition from 1044.

**1049 καίτοι τί πάσχω:** 879n.

**γέλωτ᾽ ὀφλεῖν:** same phrase in Medea's self-exhortation in 404; for the importance of the theme of avoiding mockery see 383n. and Introd. 2(*b*); for the idiom with ὀφλεῖν 404n.

**1050 ἀζημίους** ignores the now-inevitable death of the princess, but this distortion is an intrinsic part of the representation of the situation that (one side of) Medea creates to exhort herself to action. For another distortion, see 1060–1n., 1238–9n.

**1051 τολμητέον τάδ᾽** 'I must have the daring courage to do this,' that is, to kill my children as planned. There is no difficulty in understanding τάδε in this sense since that is the underlying reference of the entire speech. As in 394–406 and elsewhere (see nn. on 11, 20, 316, 383, 394, 403, 438, 810, 1242–6, and Introd. 2(*b*) and (*f*)), Medea uses the language of masculine (often heroic/military) action and

values. With this phrase Medea has shifted back to her original plan;
then she reinforces the reversal by chastising the other position as
cowardice. Kovacs gives a more explicit reference to τάδ' by treating
these words as a question and giving the verb an unlikely 'passive'
interpretation: 'Must I put up with that (being laughed at, leaving my
enemies unpunished)?' For the dispute about 'active' vs 'passive'
sense of τολμάω, see further 1078n.

ἀλλὰ τῆς ἐμῆς κάκης  'oh, but what cowardice on my part!' The
conjunction marks objection to Medea's own previous softening
(referring back to 1040–8): Denniston 8. The gen. is exclamatory,
associated here with an exclamatory articular inf. phrase, perhaps a
colloquial combination: note *Alc.* 832 ἀλλὰ σοῦ τὸ μὴ φράσαι, Ar.
*Eccl.* 787–9 τῆς μωρίας, τὸ μηδὲ περιμείναντα . . . εἶτα τηνικαῦτ' ἤδη –
Χρ. τί δρᾶν; (cf. plain inf. in *Clouds* 818–19 τῆς μωρίας, τὸν [τὸ
Valckenaer] Δία νομίζειν ὄντα τηλικουτονί). The accent on κάκης
shows it is from noun κάκη, not adj. κακός.

**1052  προσέσθαι:** aor. mid. inf. of προσίημι, 'admit, allow in'.

**μαλθακοὺς λόγους:** these were the tools used against Medea's
enemies (316, 776), and to maintain her self-image as superior to
them she must not let them be applied to herself.

**1053  χωρεῖτε:** the movements of the boys are one of the problems most discussed in arguments about the authenticity of 1056–80.
The best solution (see Battezzato (1991)) is to have Medea shepherd
the boys toward the door herself, giving the appearance that she is
about to go inside too and do the deed forthwith (as the language of
ὅτωι δὲ μὴ θέμις . . . διαφθερῶ also implies). When she stops herself at
1056 she turns away from the boys and perhaps moves downstage
from them, and they simply wait on stage. Their awareness of what
she is saying is not a problem, because through placement and action
they are by convention out of dialogue-contact and because they are
children, of low dramatic status. In this scenario, the silent attendants may also approach the door and be left attending the boys
while Medea delivers 1056–68. See Appendix.

**1053–5  ὅτωι δὲ μὴ θέμις κτλ.:**  in a manner typical of tragedy,
ritual language and practice are used in a distorted way. Medea's
warning is like the traditional proclamation before a holy sacrifice

that any unsuitable (impure) witnesses should withdraw so as not to spoil the (pure) ritual and incur divine resentment. Compare Callimachus, *Hymn to Apollo* 2 ἑκὰς ἑκὰς ὅστις ἀλιτρός; Virg. *Aen.* 6.258 *procul o procul este, profani*. Here it is rather the ritual that is impure, and the pure who are warned to stay clear of it. Compare, for a ritually correct application of such a warning, *IT* 1226–9 ἐκποδὼν δ' αὐδῶ πολίταις τοῦδ' ἔχειν μιάσματος, | … | φεύγετ', ἐξίστασθε, μή τωι προσπέσηι μύσος τόδε.

**1055    αὐτῶι μελήσει** 'it will be a concern to him himself'; that is, let that person himself see to it that he does not witness what he would rather not see, since Medea herself will not forestall her deed to save anybody from distress.

**χεῖρα δ' οὐ διαφθερῶ** 'for I shall not spoil (weaken) ⟨the action of⟩ my hand'. For δέ as equivalent to γάρ, see Denniston 169.

**1056–80    More** than 100 years ago Bergk suggested that this passage was not part of the play as performed in 431, but an authorial alternative to the preceding passage. Several later scholars have assigned it to an interpolator. Other critics have continued to believe that the passage (or most of it) is original. Details about the dispute and the main proposed solutions are given in the Appendix. In the notes below, the passage is treated as genuine.

**1056    ἇ ἇ:** an exclamation often expressive of surprise or distress, sometimes in proximity to an implied or actual prohibition (as with ἇ ἇ, τί δράσεις, ὦ γεραιέ; μὴ πέσηις in *Andr.* 1076 (cf. *Cycl.* 565) or ἇ ἇ, μηδαμῶς δράσηις τάδε in *Or.* 1598). Thus, this is a first inarticulate sign that Medea is reversing position again, as she turns away from her children and the door. The exclamation is missing from a recently published Berlin papyrus (Luppe (1995)) that has the surrounding lines. It is more likely that the exclamation was lost by accident than that it is a false addition.

**θυμέ:** the address to one's own heart is a poetic tradition, from τέτλαθι δή, κραδίη in *Od.* 20.18 on (see Leo (1908); Schadewaldt (1926); Battezzato (1995); Pelliccia (1995)). Usually the heart is called upon for emotional or mental activity, but in Archilochus fr. 128 θυμέ, θύμ', ἀμηχάνοισι κήδεσιν κυκώμενε, the vocative is equivalent to a self-address and is followed by military and other metaphors (προσβαλὼν ἐναντίον στέρνον ... ἐχθρῶν πλησίον κατασταθείς and καταπεσών). Still, 'don't do this' is bold (Gibert (1995) 79 n. 49), and Aristophanes seems to have considered this extension of usage odd enough to deserve parody (*Ach.* 480–4).

μὴ σύ γ' 'please do *not*', an earnest appeal; in this common phrase γε often emphasizes the prohibition as a whole rather than σύ alone; see Mastronarde on *Phoen.* 532, Denniston 122.

**1057  φεῖσαι:**  aor. mid. imp. of φείδομαι, 'spare'.

**1058  ἐκεῖ μεθ' ἡμῶν** 'there in exile with us', that is, as the audience understands, in Athens.

**1059  μὰ τοὺς ... ἀλάστορας:**  reading a text, some critics find that it is not sufficiently clear which side of the debate Medea is expressing here; as performed by an actor on stage, however, the lines can unambiguously express a rejection of the appeal made in 1056–8. The shift back to the 'hard' viewpoint is marked both by the use of μά, which is very common in rejection of an alternative, and by the reference to the *alastores*, demons of punishment and revenge who are appropriately invoked only by the vengeful side of Medea, determined to bring violence against her enemies. On the concept of the *alastor*, see Barrett on *Hipp.* 877–90 and Mastronarde on *Phoen.* 1556 and below 1333n.

**1060–1  ἐχθροῖς ... | παῖδας παρήσω ... καθυβρίσαι** 'surrender/ abandon my children to my enemies to treat with outrage' (καθ-υβρίσαι is epexegetic inf.). Medea has in mind the fatal violence that the relatives of Creon and the princess could be expected to apply to the children of their murderer, a motif developed in more detail in the next scene (1236–41). Eur.'s manipulation of this motif seems to rely on the audience's awareness of the tradition that the children were killed by the Corinthians (Introd. 4). This phrase presents the most difficult problem for the interpretation of this passage as authentic.Why does Medea argue with herself as if the children cannot be taken out of Corinth (as she just seemed to assume in 1058)? As a character-based explanation one may suggest that the harsh side of Medea is here projecting a particular tendentious view of the situation in order to steel her own resolve to do the deed required by the desire for maximum vengeance. In that case, this is a tragic extension of Medea's rhetorical abilities, this time with herself as the victim, just as earlier she projected a view of women's life and her own disadvantages to win the chorus' favour, and similarly with Creon, Aegeus, and Jason. If a character-based (or rhetoric-based) explanation is not accepted, an alternative is to recognize a manipulation at the narrative or authorial level: that is, Eur., somewhat forcedly, makes Medea say this in order to prepare for her claim in 1236–41 and to make the murder seem inevitable for the audience. See Appendix.

**[1062–3]** This couplet is identical to 1240–1, so it is extremely unlikely that both are genuine. Here, the repetition of πάντως in 1062 and 1064 is clumsy, and the lines seem somewhat less dispensable in the later passage than here. Therefore, it seems best to regard 1062–3 as an interpolation. The Berlin papyrus (Luppe (1995)) presents a text without 1062–3, which may be regarded as helpful confirmation of the choice made here.

**1064** πάντως πέπρακται ταῦτα 'at all events these things have been completed'; ταῦτα is vague and in context means 'the elements of my scheme'; the perfect πέπρακται is prospective or anticipatory in sense, almost 'are as good as completed' (K–G 1.150; cf. Smyth §1950, Goodwin §51). Because this idiomatic use is less known and less obvious, the verb has been replaced by easier verbs in some parts of the tradition: πέπρωται is in some MSS, and the Berlin papyrus (Luppe (1995)) now offers the obvious δέδοκται (perhaps borrowed from 1236). The more difficult reading should be regarded as genuine.

κοὐκ ἐκφεύξεται: the princess is the subject, as is made clear retrospectively by κρατί (her head) even before she is explicitly named as a subject in ἐν πέπλοισι δὲ νύμφη. (For other views, see Appendix.) The vagueness of ταῦτα and the choppy style of the shift of subject within the line, while difficult for the silent reader, may in performance be played as signs of emotional pressure.

**1065** καὶ δή: Medea imagines the realization of the event (386n.). This idiomatic use is more likely to be authentic than ἤδη, found in the Berlin papyrus and approved by Luppe (1995).

**1067** ἀλλ' ... γάρ: the two particles have separate force here, ἀλλά marking the transition to action (βούλομαι) and γάρ explaining the new intention.

ὁδόν:   acc. of the space traversed (Smyth §1581), as also in the
next line, where ὁδόν is understood with τλημονεστέραν.

**1069** *Action*:   if the boys have never gone in (having stopped because their mother turned away), then the only action needed is for
Medea herself to turn back toward them during 1067–9 and approach
to embrace them (see Appendix). For those critics who have the
children go inside, Medea's statement προσειπεῖν βούλομαι is an im-
plicit order to a silent attendant, who quickly opens the door and
brings the children back out. This would seem to require a pause
within 1069. Dodds (1952) tries to ameliorate the situation by reading
δεῦτ', ὦ τέκνα, but this does not help very much, and δεῦτε is doubtful in tragedy (894n.).

**1070**   δότ' ἀσπάσασθαι μητρὶ δεξιὰν χέρα   'give your right hand to
your mother for her to hold fondly' (epexegetic inf.). The next several
lines would best be acted out with Medea kneeling to embrace and
kiss and stroke the children. She could rise again at 1076, when she
can no longer endure seeing them.

**1072**   σχῆμα:   not just 'form' or 'shape', but implying grace and
dignity of stature and stance, hence 'bearing'. See Mastronarde on
*Phoen.* 250–2.

**1073**   εὐδαιμονοῖτον:   second person dual present active opt.

ἐκεῖ ... ἐνθάδε:   for Medea, the chorus, and the audience, these
words mean 'there in the underworld' vs 'here in life'; at such an
emotional moment, an audience probably should not care what the
children might or might not make of the antithesis (1020n.), although
it is possible to supply the somewhat forced explication 'there at the
palace' vs 'here with me'.

**1074**   προσβολή   'touch, contact', hence 'embrace, kiss'; compare
*Supp.* 1138 φίλιαι προσβολαὶ προσώπων and *Hec.* 409–10 ἡδίστην
χέρα | δὸς καὶ παρειὰν προσβαλεῖν παρηίδι.

**1076** *action*:   by her words and probably by an accompanying gesture to the silent attendants, Medea directs the children indoors.
Medea is alone on stage from this point to the arrival of the messenger.

**1077** οἷά τε πρὸς σφᾶς: the text is uncertain, but the sense is not in doubt. Page's emendation is printed here: after the second-person plural imperatives in 1076, πρὸς σφᾶς could easily have been corrupted to unmetrical πρὸς ὑμᾶς, the reading that seems to be the basis of the other readings found in the MSS. Doubt arises, however, from the fact that in ten other instances in Sophocles and Eur. προσβλέπειν takes an acc. object and not a prepositional phrase; but προσβλέπειν πρός may mean 'look toward' as distinct from προσβλέπειν 'look in the face' (cf. the fourth-cent. Epidaurian (Doric) inscription cited in LSJ s.v.).

**κακοῖς:** the substantive κακά appears three times within the four lines 1077–80, and many different translations have been offered or argued for. It is not possible to use a single English translation in all three cases, and it is a false premise to insist that the meaning must be precisely the same in all, since κακόν is a general term that acquires precise connotations from its context and its function in its own sentence. Here in 1077 the sense is 'I cannot look upon my children any longer, but am overcome by the pains/sufferings ⟨that I feel⟩' – the pains deriving from seeing and touching the children who are soon to die at her hands. See 1078n.

**1078–80** have generated a great deal of discussion. For an overview of various interpretations, see Appendix.

**1078** μανθάνω: the notion that Medea will knowingly do evil has seemed to some critics to be significantly related to the Socratic doctrine that no man does evil knowingly. Snell (1948), for instance, has argued that this passage and the statement of Phaedra in *Hipp.* 375–87 (esp. 380–1 τὰ χρήστ' ἐπιστάμεσθα καὶ γιγνώσκομεν, | οὐκ ἐκπονοῦμεν δ') provide an indirect testimony to the emergence of Socrates' view, and that Socrates was directly inspired by Eur.'s portrayal of Medea. But to see a close relationship to Socrates here involves (1) the fallacy of treating the small amount of material surviving from the fifth century as the only material known to contemporaries, and of too readily assuming an intimate relationship between different extant testimonia (Plato, for instance, in *Prot.* 362d has Socrates ascribe a view like Phaedra's to 'the many'); (2) an oversimplification of Medea's situation (in which there is not one good and one bad, but various possibilities that all contain elements she regards as bad). On the debated relation to Socrates see Moline (1975), Irwin (1983), Rickert (1987).

**δρᾶν μέλλω:** most MSS have τολμήσω instead, while δρᾶν μέλλω is the reading of the many ancient authors (testimonia) who quote this famous passage (starting with the Stoic Chrysippus in the third century BCE) and is also in one MS. A familiar quotation often takes on a life of its own and suffers modification when repeated in isolation from its context, so it could be argued that the testimonia are wrong here; but if τολμήσω means 'will dare to do' (see below), then it seems to introduce an unwanted external 'focalizer' in these lines, while the more neutral 'am about to do' fits Medea's focalization better. Kovacs has accepted τολμήσω with the 'passive' meaning 'what pain I am about to undergo' (compare 1051n.), but in a context like this it seems inescapable that an audience will hear the 'active' sense 'dare to do'. Compare other contexts where kin-murder and similar violations are envisaged (*Or.* 827, *Med.* 816, *IA* 1257, *Ion* 976, *El.* 277) with the few places where a quasi-passive sense is present (*Hec.* 326, 333). Thus the meaning is not much changed by the choice of reading.

**κακά:** the difference in sense of this term between 1077 and 1078 is not a problem requiring drastic solutions (1077n.). οἷα δρᾶν μέλλω κακά is best taken as 'what harmful things I am about to do'; 'what evil I am about to do' is possible, so long as one does not over-emphasize the modern moralistic sense of 'evil'. Medea is primarily concerned with the harm she will do to her sons and to herself: this is based principally on a calculation of pain and suffering, but concerns that some moderns might call 'moral' are not excluded, since Medea herself criticizes the killing as unholy (796, 1383). See Rickert (1987).

**1079 θυμὸς δὲ κρείσσων τῶν ἐμῶν βουλευμάτων:** a controversial line; the choice is essentially between 'my angry passion controls my plans' and 'my angry passion is stronger than my deliberations'. In the former, the sense of κρείσσων is unusual, but βουλευμάτων refers to what it has previously referred to, Medea's calculations of how she can get revenge on her enemies and cause the greatest pain to Jason. In the latter, κρείσσων has an ordinary sense, but βουλευμάτων now refers either to Medea's brief considerations of the pref-

erability of letting her children live or to the entire complex of deliberations on both sides. The narrower reference is perhaps problematic
because of the epithet ἐμῶν: it is in the interest of Medea's winning
vengeful side to dissociate from herself the soft considerations made
on behalf of the children, and ἐμῶν would do just the opposite if it
refers only to 1044–8 and 1056–8. βουλεύματα cannot mean 'rationality' or 'reason'; nor is the interpretation 'considerations' (of the pain
my course will cause me) convincing.

In the Greek philosophical tradition, in which partition of the
soul into rational and irrational elements was a basic strategy for
many thinkers and schools from Socrates and Plato onward, Medea
was treated as an example of a person dominated by her emotions,
and this line was read as, in essence, 'my emotion (anger) is stronger
than my reason'; see Gill (1983) and (1996) 226–39; Dillon (1997).
This treatment conforms with the (non-tragic or anti-tragic) faith in
reason that is a hallmark of the Greek philosophical tradition: that
is, philosophers needed to see Medea's action in this starkly dualistic
light. In the play itself, we are actually shown a mixture and alternation of rational and emotional elements at work, and Medea's revenge scheme involves not only her sense of outrage and attachment
to 'heroic honour' but also a calculating rationality and manipulative rhetoric. In addition to the theme of planning and wisdom/
cleverness that runs throughout the play, Medea's own use of ἐμηχανησάμην in 1014 and the striking conclusive generalization of the
messenger in 1224–30 point to the importance of calculating and rational elements in Medea's action.

**1080 ὅσπερ μεγίστων αἴτιος κακῶν βροτοῖς** 'the very thing
which causes mankind the greatest harm/suffering' (see 1077n, 1078n.
on κακά). In later times there was a genre of philosophical and moralistic literature *de ira* (Diogenes Laertius ascribes a book Περὶ παθῶν
⟨ἢ περὶ⟩ ὀργῆς to Aristotle; the title περὶ ὀργῆς is also attested for
works of Posidonius, Philodemus, Sotion (teacher of Seneca), and
Plutarch); but it was already a commonplace in archaic and classical
times that anger is detrimental to good judgment. Compare the references to wrath throughout *Iliad* Book 9 and Achilles' curse in
18.107–10 ὡς ἔρις ἔκ τε θεῶν ἔκ τ' ἀνθρώπων ἀπόλοιτο | καὶ χόλος, ὅς
τ' ἐφέηκε πολύφρονά περ χαλεπῆναι, | ὅς τε πολὺ γλυκίων μέλιτος

καταλειβομένοιο | ἀνδρῶν ἐν στήθεσσιν ἀέξεται ἠΰτε καπνός; Theognis 1223–4 οὐδέν, Κύρν', ὀργῆς ἀδικώτερον, ἢ τὸν ἔχοντα | πημαίνει θυμῶι δειλὰ χαριζομένη; Thuc. 2.11.7 καὶ οἱ λογισμῶι ἐλάχιστα χρώμενοι θυμῶι πλεῖστα ἐς ἔργον καθίστανται, 2.22.1 τοῦ μὴ ὀργῆι τι μᾶλλον ἢ γνώμηι ξυνελθόντας ἐξαμαρτεῖν, 3.42.1 νομίζω δὲ δύο τὰ ἐναντιώτατα εὐβουλίαι εἶναι, τάχος τε καὶ ὀργήν, ὧν τὸ μὲν μετὰ ἀνοίας φιλεῖ γίγνεσθαι, τὸ δὲ μετὰ ἀπαιδευσίας καὶ βραχύτητος γνώμης; Eur. fr. 31 N² ὀργῆι γὰρ ὅστις εὐθέως χαρίζεται, | κακῶς τελευτᾶι· πλεῖστα γὰρ σφάλλει βροτούς, fr. 760 ἔξω γὰρ ὀργῆς πᾶς ἀνὴρ σοφώτερος; Soph. *OT* 523–4 ἀλλ' ἦλθε μὲν δὴ τοῦτο τοὔνειδος τάχ' ἂν | ὀργῆι βιασθὲν μᾶλλον ἢ γνώμηι φρενῶν, *OC* 855 ὀργῆι χάριν δοὺς ἤ σ' ἀεὶ λυμαίνεται.

**1080**   *Action:*   Medea's first words in the next episode (1116) sound like those of a character who has been waiting on stage. Thus, after the apparent conclusiveness of 1055 (esp. if Medea was heading toward the door herself with the children), Medea has reached a moment of stasis: she seems determined to do the terrible deed, but as long as she has not yet gone inside there is still room for suspense and the possibility that she will waver again. A much different effect will be produced if Medea does go inside at 1080 and then reemerges at 1116, for the audience would then believe that the killings are about to take place and be surprised at 1116 when Medea says that she is waiting to learn what happened at the palace.

### *1081–1115   Anapaestic interlude*

This anapaestic interlude serves in place of the stasimon that usually precedes the entrance of a messenger (for anapaestic passages with act-dividing function see Taplin (1977) 225–6). What is remarkable is the contrast between the anguish and tension of Medea's monologue and the relative calmness and displacement of the choral intervention (quite different from the tense expectation projected by shorter anapaestic interludes like Aesch. *Ag.* 1331–42, *Cho.* 719–29, 855–68). As a chorus sometimes does, the Corinthian women deflect attention from the particular to the general or from the individual to the group, but here without the concluding apostrophe or application that characterizes many other examples. The choral voice does not respond to the divided impulses just expressed by Medea or object to the victory of the revenge impulse over the maternal bond; rather it avoids personal engagement or dissuasion and instead deflects its emotional response to a resigned and generalized regret for the condition of human parenthood. The opening stakes claim to female *mousa* and *sophia*, thus recalling the gender-competition of the first stasimon, but it is significant that the judgment that follows is generalized so as to apply to parents of both sexes, using the universalizing masculine plural and terms that suggest both the mother's effort in childbirth and nurture (*mochthos, mochthein*) and the father's economic responsibility (finding and leaving behind a livelihood, *biotos*). Thus there is created an emotional resonance between everyday experience of the loss of children and the loss about to be felt by Medea and Jason, yet this resonance has a curious effect of helplessness and resignation, and one might even say irrelevance, since the choral generalization at its end emphasizes (indeed complains of) the role of the gods in taking children from their parents (1109–15), whereas the deaths of children in this play arise largely from human decisions and actions. Perhaps one major effect of the abstraction and subdued emotion of this interlude at this point is to lull the audience into a sense of resignation and inevitability in regard to the killing of the children, to add plausibility to Medea's certainty in 1236ff. that the children must die. Another possible effect is to bear witness to the claim made earlier by the nurse that poetry has failed to deal with grief and woe. Although the women here lay claim to a poetic gift, their song is still incommensurate with the horror that faces them.

The passage consists of chanted anapaests, with paroemiacs at 1089, 1097, 1104, 1115. This produces at minimum four periods of 15, 13, 13, and 19 metra before the paroemiac. One could also postulate period-end at full metron at one or more other locations such as 1084, 1093, 1100, 1106, or 1111, but these are unverifiable (see 184–204n.).

**1081–9** provide a warrant for the generalizations to be made in the interlude, emphasizing that they are not a spur-of-the-moment evaluation but the product of long consideration; they also carry on the theme of male-female competition by asserting the right to offer wisdom. Compare the opening of the gnomic observations of the (male) chorus at *Alc.* 962–6 ἐγὼ καὶ διὰ μούσας | καὶ μετάρσιος ᾖξα, καὶ | πλείστων ἀψάμενος λόγων | κρεῖσσον οὐδὲν Ἀνάγκας | ηὗρον κτλ., and Phaedra's proem in *Hipp.* 375–6 ἤδη ποτ' ἄλλως νυκτὸς ἐν μακρῶι χρόνωι | θνητῶν ἐφρόντισ' ἧι διέφθαρται βίος.

**1081–2   διὰ λεπτοτέρων μύθων ἔμολον** 'I engaged in discourses (thoughts) of a more subtle nature'; the comparative may not be pointing forward to ἢ χρή, but simply mean 'more subtle than the average' (for this use of comparatives see Smyth §1082a). For the idiomatic use of διά-phrase and verb of motion, see 872n.

**1082–3   πρὸς ἁμίλλας ἦλθον** 'I entered into intellectual struggles.'

**1085   ἀλλὰ γάρ:** elliptical in sense (cf. 252n.), 'but ⟨my opinion is still worth hearing⟩, for . . .' See Denniston 102.

**1087–8   πάσαισι μὲν οὔ, παῦρον δὲ γένος κτλ.** 'not to all women, but small is the group of women (you could find one among many) that is not lacking in inspiration': the μέν-limb is a correction-in-stride, in apposition to ἡμῖν, while the δέ-limb becomes an independent clause (with ἐστι understood; also understand ὄν with ἀπόμουσον). The MSS have an unmetrical text, lacking Elmsley's μίαν and having either τι or δή before γένος. A Berlin papyrus now presents both words in a reading that had been proposed by Schoemann (δέ τι δὴ γένος). This is metrical and could be translated 'not to all women, but you could find among many some quite small group of women that is not lacking in inspiration'. But the word order δέ τι δή is unparalleled (whereas both δή τι and δὲ δή τι are found, not only in iambic poetry, but in prose).

**1092–3   προφέρειν εἰς εὐτυχίαν | τῶν γειναμένων** 'are superior in happiness to those who have begotten children'; for this intransitive sense of προφέρω, see LSJ s.v. IV.2; the gen. of comparison is normal with this sense, but εἰς εὐτυχίαν is a poetic alternative to the dat. of respect seen in other authors.

**1094–6   δι' ἀπειροσύνην | . . . οὐχὶ τυχόντες** 'through their inexperience not finding out'; on this view, the whole phrase and not just δι' ἀπειροσύνην governs the intervening indirect question, and τυχόντες is understood in the common sense of 'receive or experience a certain fortune', as a (typically) redundant clarification of δι' ἀπειροσύνην (compare the gloss μαθόντες in MS B). Another view takes οὐχὶ τυχόντες as restating ἄτεκνοι, 'not having obtained ⟨children⟩'.

**1103** ἔτι δ' ἐκ τούτων 'and furthermore, after that'; again the δέ-limb turns into an independent clause (1087n.).

**1103–3a** ἐπὶ φλαύροις | ... χρηστοῖς: understand τοῖς παισί or τοῖς τέκνοις; we may translate 'on behalf of children who will turn out bad or good' (ἐπί + dat. of occasion or cause); but some suggest instead ἐπί + dat. of the price or wage (Page: 'whether good children or bad will be the wages of their toil').

**1107** καὶ δὴ γάρ: the first two particles present a supposition as real (386n., 1065), while γάρ introduces the exposition of the 'one thing' just promised.

ἅλις βίοτόν θ' ηὗρον: ἅλις, which logically goes only with ηὗρον, receives extra prominence from the delayed position of θ' (unless θ' is to be regarded as a misguided metrical supplement and the true solution to the unmetrical text of most MSS is to read βιοτὴν ηὗρον with Lenting).

**1108** ἤλυθε: Eur. uses the epic alternative to ἦλθον over a dozen times, usually in lyrics or anapaests, but also in trimeters (*Tro.* 374, *El.* 598).

**1109** κυρήσαι: third sing. aor. optative (as the accent shows) of κυρέω. Translate 'if fate should befall thus' or 'if fortune should come to pass thus' (cf. LSJ s.v. κυρέω I.1.b and II.1), euphemistic for 'if bad fortune befalls one'.

**1110** φροῦδος ἐς Ἅιδου: the predicate adj. (without copula: LS 30) is here equivalent to a verb, 'flies off, disappears'. By its position, 'to Hades' will inevitably be taken initially with φροῦδος, but it complements προφέρων as well.

**1111** Θάνατος is strongly personified here, since φροῦδος is most commonly used of persons and there was an established iconography of the winged demon Thanatos carrying off the dead (originally paired with Hypnos carrying the corpse of Sarpedon, but by the middle of the fifth century also depicted carrying anonymous dead and sometimes shown without Hypnos: see *LIMC* s.v. Thanatos).

Thus it is probably justified to print the noun with a capital letter here, as in Paley's edition and a few others.

**1112** λύει: impersonal, 'is it profitable' (566n.), with θεοὺς ἐπιβάλλειν as subject. The chorus implies criticism of the way the gods operate the world: see 190–204n.

### *1116–1250    Sixth episode*

This episode is taken up almost entirely by the report of the 'messenger', a conventional term for the minor character who brings news of a major event that has taken place out of the sight of the audience and chorus (usually offstage at another location, but sometimes within the house). In Sophocles and Eur. these scenes stereotypically feature a brief relaying of the essential facts in a dialogue and then an extended rhesis giving the narrative in full detail (SE 3a). The messenger-rhesis is a *tour-de-force* of narrative skill, often tinged with reminiscences of epic (quoted direct speech, more frequent use of epithets, omission of temporal augment, and (rarely) short third-person plural forms like ἔκρυφθεν in *Hipp.* 1247 (LS 7c)), and affords the actor an opportunity for virtuoso performance highlighting shifting emotions. See de Jong (1991) on narrative in Eur.'s messenger-speeches and Goward (1999) on narrative in tragedy in general. The narrative here is typically circumstantial: the sequence of events is carefully marked (1136, 1145, 1147, 1156, 1157, 1163, 1167, 1173, 1176, 1181, 1205, 1211, 1218); not only are the changing moods and movements of the major figure, the princess, detailed, but there is also attention to the emotions and actions of subsidiary figures and extras in the scenario (1138–42, 1142–3, 1171–7, 1177–80, 1202–3); quoted speeches are included (1151–5, 1207–10); gruesome physical details are made explicit; and similes (1200, 1213) and other imagistic language are frequent. This speech also plays repeatedly on the superior retrospective knowledge of the speaker (shared by the audience), in contrast to the mistaken joy and belief of the servants (1138–40), the speaker's own earlier satisfaction (1142), the delight of the princess in trying on the gifts (with the ominous phrase 'lifeless likeness': 1162n.), the old woman's false inference of a divine visitation (1171–3), and Creon's ill-omened wish συνθάνοιμι. The messenger concludes with a moralizing generalization: the expression of traditional wisdom and the rejection of the position of an elite group (1225 τοὺς σοφοὺς βροτῶν) align him with the nurse as a humble anonymous figure distinct in aspirations and experience from the princely main characters. After the messenger's departure, the chorus-leader delivers a conventionally required reaction to the long rhesis, and then Medea makes her last declaration of intention and self-exhortation before going in to do the deed so long expected.

**1116** **τοι:** the particle expresses emotional involvement (Denniston 541).

**1117** **καραδοκῶ:** this verb implies waiting with nervous expectation for an outcome, often in a military context with the notion of determining one's behaviour according to who wins a battle. So here it once again raises some suspense whether Medea will go through with the murder or not.

τἀκεῖθεν is both proleptic object of the verb (37n.) and subject of the clarifying indirect question that follows, as in the similar phrase in Hdt. 7.163 καραδοκήσοντα τὴν μάχην τῆι πεσέεται.

**1118** **καὶ δή** marks perception of the newly entering character: Denniston 251.

**1118–19** **τόνδε τῶν Ἰάσονος | ... ὀπαδῶν** 'this man [with gesture], one of Jason's attendants'; although Jason may have been accompanied by silent attendants in his earlier visits to the stage, the messenger is not to be identified as one of them, but as an attendant who has until now been at Jason's new home. The viewpoint in 1136–43 is that of those in the house, just learning of the 'truce' between Jason and Medea.

πνεῦμα δ' ἠρεθισμένον: entrance-announcements may be used both to call attention to the haste of an entrance (which can actually be conveyed by the actor) and to interpret the mood of the newcomer for those who cannot see the mask well or in cases where the expression may not be obvious on the mask. Thus σπουδή is often mentioned (e.g. Aesch. *Sept.* 371, 374; *Hcld.* 1118, *Hipp.* 1152, *Andr.* 546, *Bacch.* 212), and expressions of anxiety or grief are remarked upon (e.g. *Hcld.* 381, *Hipp.* 1152, *Phoen.* 1333). ἠρεθισμένον is perf. mid.-pass. part. of ἐρεθίζω, 'agitate, excite'.

**1120 καινόν:** news from a messenger-figure is often anticipated by reference to revealing (σημαίνειν) or reporting (ἀγγέλλειν, λέγειν) something καινόν or νέον: e.g. *Prom.* 943, *Tro.* 238, *Phoen.* [1075], *Hec.* 217, *IT* 237, *Bacch.* 1029.

**[1121]** This line is absent from one branch of the medieval tradition: this may be a reflection of uneven attestation in ancient copies, which is sometimes a sign of interpolation. The explicitness of δεινὸν ἔργον παρανόμως is oddly followed by Medea's question in 1124, so the sequence of dialogue also points to a text without 1121. The line seems to have been added to heighten the emotion of the address and to make the messenger's moral disapproval of Medea's action more apparent. For this type of expansion see Haslam (1979).

**1122–3 μήτε ναῖαν | λιποῦσ᾽ ἀπήνην μήτ᾽ ὄχον πεδοστιβῆ** 'neglecting neither ship-formed carriage nor vehicle that travels the ground', a grandiloquent circumlocution for 'whether by sea or by land' or 'by any available means'. The markedly heightened language is perhaps expressive of the inspiration that the humble messenger-figure receives from witnessing tragic events. The sense of λιποῦσα is one seen more often in παραλείπω or ἐκλείπω, but cf. LSJ s.v. λείπω A.I.3. For the extended use of ἀπήνη compare *Tro.* 517–18 τετρα-βάμονος ὡς ὑπ᾽ ἀπήνης Ἀργείων (the Trojan horse), *Phoen.* 328 with Mastronarde's note.

**1124 τυγχάνει** 'befalls'; compare *Or.* 1326 ἄξι᾽ ἡμῖν τυγχάνει στεναγμάτων.

**1126 ὕπο:** anastrophe (LS 24).

**1128 τὸ λοιπόν** 'hereafter' (804n.).

**1130 ἥτις:** 589n.
      **ἠικισμένη:** perf. mid.-pass. part. of αἰκίζω, in middle sense (same as active) 'having damaged outrageously' (cf. epic ἀεικίζω, ἀεικέλιος).

**1133 μὴ σπέρχου:** the recipients of a climactic report often insist on their need or desire to hear all the details and sometimes give a motivation (for delight at good news compare *Supp.* 649, *Phoen.* 1088–9); but as usual in Greek tragedy there is a mixture of naturalistic motivation and non-naturalistic theatrical convention, for time stands still during a messenger rhesis and any pressure to act quickly is suspended or ignored until the narrative is over.

**1138** ἤσθημεν: aor. pass. ind. of ἥδομαι, 'we felt delight'.

**1138–9** οἵπερ σοῖς ἐκάμνομεν κακοῖς | δμῶες provides another clue to the sympathy of others for the way Medea had been treated by Jason and Creon (see 17n., 663–823n., 707).

**1140** νεῖκος ἐσπεῖσθαι 'have reached a truce to end your previous dispute' involves a somewhat bold extension of the construction of σπένδομαι (ἐσπεῖσθαι is perf. mid.-pass. inf.). Usually the object is internal or an object of the product produced: peace, an opportunity to pick up the dead (Thuc. 3.24), safe passage for retreat (Thuc. 3.109). Here it is an external object affected by the truce, for which parallels are found in later prose (object πόλεμον in Dionysius Hal. 4.52.2, 9.36.3, 19.13.4).

**1142** καὐτός: crasis, καὶ αὐτός.
ὕπο: anastrophe (LS 24).

**1143** στέγας γυναικῶν 'into the women's chambers', acc. of goal of motion without preposition (LS 12.b). Many texts speak of a separate area of the Greek house in which women might be confined and into which outside males would not normally be allowed, but archaeological evidence does not show any fixed arrangement in domestic architecture to provide such separation. See Jameson (1990a), esp. 186–91, and (1990b), esp. 104; Nevett (1999), esp. 154–6.

**1146** πρόθυμον εἴχ' ὀφθαλμὸν εἰς Ἰάσονα 'looked with loving anticipation toward Jason'.

**1147** προυκάλυψατ': crasis, προεκαλύψατο.

**1148** ἀπέστρεψ' ἔμπαλιν παρηίδα: the gesture has previously been ascribed to Medea (30, 923n.), and perhaps the repetition makes the point that Medea is imposing her own experiences in turn upon her enemies.

**1149** μυσαχθεῖσ': aor. pass. part. of μυσάττομαι, 'feel disgust at'; a very rare verb in classical authors (elsewhere only Xen. *Cyrop.* 1.3.5; cf. Aesch. *Supp.* 955 μύσαγμα).

**1151** οὐ μή introducing a question with the fut. ind. ἔσηι is equivalent to a prohibition, and after ἀλλά or δέ (as here) οὐ alone is carried forward to the following futures παύσηι ... παραιτήσηι, making them equivalent to positive commands (see Barrett on *Hipp.* 212–14). Imperatival questions of this form often express shock, exasperation or peremptory superiority, but in a few places perhaps a tone of gentler remonstrance or appeal may be detected (*Andr.* 757, *Supp.* 1066), so a wheedling tone rather than a peremptory one may be possible here.

**1153** οὕσπερ ἄν: sc. νομίζηι (subj. in relative clause with present general force).

**1154** παραιτήσηι πατρός 'request from your father that he remit ...', with the gen. of the person asked on the analogy of δέομαι.

**1156** ἠνέσχετο: aor. middle of ἀνέχω, with double augment (Smyth §451); cf. 1159 ἠμπέσχετο from ἀμπέχω.

**1157** ἤινεσ' ἀνδρὶ πάντα: the bride's compliance matches Jason's expectation (940) and also recalls the happier former days of Medea's marriage (13 αὐτῶι τε πάντα ξυμφέρουσ').

ἐκ δόμων: as the audience knows, the children returned to Medea's house from the palace; Jason's absence from the house is necessary to the plot, and no reason is given for it here.

**1158** πατέρα: in the context, an audience will easily interpret this as 'the father ⟨of the boys⟩', Jason, not as 'her father'.

**1161** κατόπτρωι: Greek mirrors were disks of burnished metal, usually bronze (for examples see Lamb (1969) 125–9 and plate LX, Congdon (1981) plates 4a, 5a, 11a, 16a, etc.), and they could be designed for holding by hand or mounted on a stand. Through association with personal adornment they were considered emblematic of femininity (hence the exasperated question of Euripides' boorish kinsman to the androgynous Agathon in Ar. *Thesm.* 140 τίς δαὶ κατόπτρου καὶ ξίφους κοινωνία;).

**1162** ἄψυχον εἰκώ: the 'lifeless likeness' is an ominous portent of her impending death. εἰκώ is alternative (poetic) acc. sing. of εἰκών, instead of εἰκόνα: see LS 5.c.

**1163**  κἄπειτ':  crasis, καὶ ἔπειτα.

**1164**  ἁβρὸν βαίνουσα:  a grim echo of the encomiastic βαίνοντες ἁβρῶς in 829.

**1165**  πολλὰ πολλάκις:  a rhetorical intensification, 'very often', 'again and again'; elsewhere πολλά has a separate force, as *Tro.* 1015 καίτοι σ' ἐνουθέτουν γε πολλὰ πολλάκις. Compare 579 πολλὰ πολλοῖς with n.

**1166**  τένοντ' ἐς ὀρθόν  'at the back of her straightened leg'; the tendon referred to is the Achilles' tendon at the back of the ankle, and ὀρθόν refers to the flexing of the foot as one leg is stretched backwards to display the hang of the dress (compare Pentheus' examination of his dress in *Bacch.* 935–8).

**1167**  τοὐνθένδε:  crasis, τὸ ἐνθένδε, adv. acc., 'then, next'.
     δεινὸν ... ἰδεῖν  'terrible to behold', epexegetic inf. (LS 18).

**1168**  λεχρία may mean 'moving sideways' or 'bent over, off-balance' or may suggest both together.

**1169**  τρέμουσα κῶλα:  acc. of specification, as also in *IT* 283 ὠλένας τρέμων ἄκρας.

**1170**  ἐμπεσοῦσα μὴ χαμαὶ πεσεῖν:  the participle is supplementary with φθάνει (Smyth §2096d), while the inf. is epexegetic (LS 18), 'so as to avoid falling on the ground'.

**1172**  Πανὸς ὀργάς:  the old woman (her age may hint at a heightened sensitivity to religious matters) suspects that the princess' odd behaviour is caused by divine possession (see 1208n.). Pan is associated with sudden mental disturbance of various kinds, including the 'panic' of an army.

**1173**  ἀνωλόλυξε:  the ululation (ὀλολυγή) is a (sometimes spontaneous) cry of women reacting to or accompanying an emotionally or ritually powerful event (e.g. victory, sacrifice, birth): it seems to greet or acknowledge the presence of divine power or an epiphany (and thus lessen the danger from such power). So here there is a contrast between the initial cry of the old woman and the lamentation into which it is converted as she observes the girl further (ἀντίμολπον ...

κωκυτόν). See Rudhardt (1958) 178–80; Pulleyn (1997) 178–81; Diggle (1994) 477–80; Eitrem (1927) 48; Deubner (1941).

**πρίν γ' ὁρᾶι:** πρίν is here equivalent to ἕως, 'until', and is here used after an affirmative verb (in prose the main verb is usually negative: Smyth §2441, Goodwin §§632–3).

**1174–5** ὀμμάτων τ' ἄπο | κόρας στρέφουσαν 'twisting her pupils away from her eyes', that is, making her eyes stand out from their sockets, a symptom of great pain; but perhaps also implying the twisting and fluttering of the eyes that is associated with madness and possession elsewhere (cf. LSJ s.v. διαστρέφω, διάστροφος). ἄπο by anastrophe (LS 24).

**1175** ἐνόν is neuter sing. acc. part. of ἔνειμι.
     **χροΐ:** 787n.

**1177–8** ἡ μὲν ..|. ἡ δέ 'one of the (women) servants ... another ...'

     ἐς πατρὸς δόμους 'to her (the princess') father's rooms/ apartment' within the same royal palace. There is nothing earlier that would lead an audience to think that there are two separate off-stage houses. Rather, they will assume one royal palace in which Creon, Jason, and the princess all live (cf. 327, Medea's plotting to invade one house to kill her enemies in 375–94, 960, 969).

**1178** ἀρτίως 'recently ⟨married⟩'.

**1181–4** form a paratactic comparison, equivalent to 'as quickly as a swift runner ... so swiftly the princess ...' The idiomatic construction is eliminated in the reading of a papyrus which offers ὅτ' ('when') in place of ἡ δ' in 1183, probably a deliberate simplification and thus to be rejected.

**1181–2** 'And already a swift runner going up along the six-plethron leg of the race-course would be reaching the goal.' (The text is disputed: for a thorough treatment see Diggle (1994) 285–8.) The plethron is 100 Greek feet, and six plethra make a stade, the normal length of a stadium and the shortest length of a normal footrace (στάδιον, 'stade-race', more or less a 200-yard dash). It is less likely that the meaning with ἀνελθών would be 'come back along the six-plethron return-leg of the (double-legged) race course', since this sense of ἀνελθών is doubtful (see Diggle) and it is less to the point to refer to the longer race (δίαυλος). κῶλον is acc. of the space traversed (1067n.); ἂν ἥπτετο is an unreal indicative (Smyth §1786).

**1183** ἡ δ᾽ is again the princess.

ἐξ ἀναύδου καὶ μύσαντος ὄμματος  '⟨changing⟩ from a state of silence and from tight-closed eyes', that is, 'breaking her silence and opening her eyes'.

**1184** ἠγείρετο:  imperfect of ἐγείρω, 'rouse, stir', middle 'awaken, stir oneself'.

**1188** σῶν τέκνων δωρήματα:  like many messengers, the servant incorporates second-person references in the narrative to underline the relation of the event to the addressee (seven times in 1136–58); the return of the second person here after a long interval (and for the last time before 1222–3) is especially effective as a reminder that the children have been made the tools of the murder and are accordingly at risk for revenge.

**1194** μᾶλλον δὶς τόσως  'twice as much more than before'; compare *Rhesus* 160 δὶς τόσως ἔθηκας εὐκλεέστερον, 'you made (your house) twice as glorious as before'; *El.* 1092. These are the only extant occurrences of adverb τόσως. δὶς τόσως and δὶς τόσον (1134) are metrical alternatives.

**1196** δυσμαθὴς ἰδεῖν  'hard to recognize at sight/by looking' (epexegetic inf.; LS 18).

**1197** κατάστασις  'the set form'.

**1200** πεύκινον δάκρυ  'dripping resin'.

**1201** γνάθοις:  in favour of this normal tragic form against the epic γναθμοῖς see Diggle (1994) 265.

**1202** πᾶσι δ᾽ ἦν φόβος θιγεῖν:  the inf. is used as if after πάντες ἐφοβούμεθα; for a somewhat different construction see 1256–7n.

**1203** τύχην  'what had happened'.

**1204** συμφορᾶς ἀγνωσίαι  'in his ignorance of the terrible thing that had happened' (dat. of manner or cause).

**1205** παρελθὼν δῶμα: probably 'entering the room' rather than 'entering the house'; see 1177n.

**1208** τίς ... δαιμόνων ἀπώλεσεν: in traditional Greek belief, any extraordinary event or affliction that cannot readily be attributed to a visible cause is viewed as the intervention of a divine force, and it is in the nature of tragic story-telling that characters are quick to assume a demonic cause (not always entirely correctly: see Theseus' misrecognition of the force behind Phaedra's death in *Hipp.* 831–3).

**1209** τὸν γέροντα τύμβον 'the old man so close to the grave' (lit. 'old man who is a grave'; probably a colloquial usage). The same phrase is used insultingly in *Hcld.* 166–7 (by the Theban herald of Iolaos); compare Ar. *Lys.* 372, where the old women address the old men as ὦ τύμβ', and LSJ s.v. τυμβογέρων.

**1210** συνθάνοιμί σοι: the wish to join another in death is a conventional mark of extreme love/loyalty or extreme grief (e.g. *Hec.* 396, *Supp.* 769, 1007 (Evadne) ἥδιστος γάρ τοι θάνατος συνθνήισκειν θνήισκουσι φίλοις, Soph. *OC* 1690, fr. 953); it is an ironic distortion of the motif to have Creon's wish here come true against his will.

**1217** ἐσπάρασσ': the subject is presumably Creon himself, who is also the subject of preceding ἄγοι and following ἀπέστη.

**1218** ἀπέστη 'he gave up on his effort'; for the sense cf. LSJ s.v. B.5, but this instance is somewhat harsh, since Creon has been trying to separate himself from his daughter and 'separate from' is a possible meaning of ἀφίστασθαι. Scaliger's emendation ἀπέσβη (intrans. second aor. of ἀποσβέννυμι, here 'his strength was extinguished') is attractive, but then μεθῆχ' ... ψυχήν is perhaps somewhat anticlimactic and redundant, although it could be taken as a plainer explication of the figurative term just used.

**1220–1** The concluding phrase in 1221 is very doubtful: perhaps 'a disaster arousing longing ⟨to mourn⟩ with tears', but this involves an odd use of both ποθεινή and the dative δακρύοισι (the variant δακρύουσι, 'for those weeping', will not scan because the upsilon of the verb is long everywhere else in classical poetry). If 1220 can stand on its own ('and so they lie as corpses, child and aged father'), then it is best to delete 1221 (Reeve): πέλας may have been added as a gloss, and this gloss could then have been supplemented incompetently into a complete line. But in parallel passages with phrases like κεῖται νεκρός or κεῖται θανών, there is some additional phrase to evoke pathos (e.g. Aesch. *Pers.* 325, Soph. *Ant.* 1240, Eur. *Phoen.* 1459, *Or.* 366), so it is doubtful whether 1220 can stand by itself. There is probably an uncured corruption in the following words. Deleting both 1220 and 1221 with West leaves a weak conclusion to the narrative.

**1222  ἐκποδὼν ... λόγου:**  (adv. as predicate) '⟨left⟩ out of account', 'out of the reckoning', or perhaps just 'without mention'; cf. Libanius *or.* 32.27 ἔξω λόγου καὶ ἀριθμοῦ κείμενοι, 'left out of account and consideration'.

**1223  ζημίας ἐπιστροφήν**  'the visitation of punishment'. The MSS have ἀποστροφήν, 'refuge, escape', but the scholiasts' explanation of the line shows that they did not read this, but either ἐπιστροφήν (Lenting) or ἀντιστροφήν (Kirchhoff), 'the balancing return of punishment' (Diggle (1994) 288–91).

**1224–30**  The conclusive reflection by the humble messenger is similar to what the messenger in Soph. *Ant.* says as prelude to his report of the disaster (1155–71); compare also *Ant.* 1242–3, Eur. *Hcld.* 863–5, *Supp.* 726–30, *Bacch.* 1150–2. The generalization about 'those who seem to be wise/clever' and 'practitioners of speeches' should be taken to be a direct comment on both Medea and Jason.

**1224  τὰ θνητὰ ... σκιάν:**  for the notion that mortal life/fortune is as insubstantial as a shadow, compare Pindar *Pyth.* 8.95–6 σκιᾶς ὄναρ ἄνθρωπος, Aesch. frr. 154a.9, 399.2, Soph. *Ajax* 126, fr. 13 ἄνθρωπός ἐστι πνεῦμα καὶ σκιὰ μόνον.

**1225  οὐδ' ἂν τρέσας εἴποιμι**  'I'd say without fear', 'I would not hesitate to say'.

**1227  τούτους** emphatically (perhaps contemptuously) restates the long subject phrase τοὺς σοφοὺς ... λόγων before the harsh predicate.

μωρίαν ὀφλισκάνειν: in this development of the idiomatic phrase (404n., 581n.), the object is not the penalty incurred, but the grounds or charge on which blame is incurred: ἀμαθίαν *Hec.* 327, σκαιότητα Soph. *Ant.* 1028, μωρίαν in four other passages of tragedy. The MSS have ζημίαν by contamination with 581.

**1229 ἐπιρρυέντος:** aor. pass. participle (in gen. absolute) of ἐπιρρέω, intransitive in sense, 'flowing in, accumulating'.

**1231–2** After the messenger's virtuoso performance, the chorus-leader's couplet allows a pause before the resumption of the murderous action. The reference to divine dispensation, many evils, and 'this day' (the one day on which the action of a tragedy is normally concentrated) are conventional features. It is significant that the chorus-leader keeps alive here the theme of Jason's injustice by declaring his sufferings to be justly imposed, and that the focus is immediately (and solely, if 1233–5 are correctly deleted) placed on Jason, not on the princess or king. The chorus thus follows Medea's vindictive perspective, but the tone of this couplet is probably resigned and objective (ἔοιχ') rather than rejoicingly vengeful. The audience may well feel some sympathy for the victims after the shocking details of their sufferings, but the chorus is apparently not here used to prompt that feeling.

**[1233–5]** The articulating intervention of the chorus-leader after most long rheseis, including messenger-speeches, is normally a couplet and no more. This consideration, the sentimentality of the address to the dead princess in contrast to the resignation of 1231–2, and the lack of connection between the couplet and the following lines (one could easily imagine something antithetic like 'justly has Jason been punished, but I pity the poor princess') have led many editors to regard these lines as a later addition.

**1234 ἥτις:** 589n.

**1236–50** In this whole speech, Medea blurs the issues of responsibility and motivation: δέδοκται τοὔργον points to the decision to use the children's death to punish Jason, and πάντως ... ἀνάγκη can initially be heard as including the internal 'necessity' of completing the revenge-plot, even though the following clause looks to the external compulsion. Likewise, words like ὁπλίζου and κακισθῆις are reminders of the internal motivations explicated in earlier speeches. Yet Medea does not openly repeat here that she acts to hurt Jason, and she indulges several times in impersonal terms and self-pitying language.

**1236 δέδοκται τοὖργον:** τοὖργον (crasis, τὸ ἔργον) is subject of δέδοκται ... μοι, with the participle + inf. phrase in apposition to it (cf. the more normal construction with a demonstrative in Plato, *Symp.* 176e τοῦτο μὲν δέδοκται, πίνειν ὅσον ἂν ἕκαστος βούληται). The interlaced word order (μοι placed after ὡς τάχιστα) seems to reflect the fact that the 'deed' is primarily the killing rather than the departure. The perfect δέδοκται contributes an air of finality: cf. *Hel.* 982, *Bacch.* 982, Soph. *Trach.* 719, *El.* 1049, *Phil.* 990, etc.

**1237–8 κτανούσηι .|.. ἄγουσαν:** for the shift in case, see 57–8n.

**1238–9** Medea's conviction that the children will be killed by others if she does not do so herself is not motivated in detail (it is logically justified only with the unstated premise that there is no way to take them away with her). But it has been prepared for by the attitude she adopted in her monologue (1059–61). Moreover, the playwright has manipulated the audience to accept this attitude more readily, because he has (apparently) reminded them at various points of the tradition about the murder of the children by the Corinthians (Introd. 4), and he has used the chorus to create a mood of resignation and inevitability.

**1239 φονεῦσαι:** inf. of purpose after ἐκδοῦναι (Smyth §2008).

**1240–1** are the same as 1062–3 (n.). The couplet seems more integral here, where ἡμεῖς ... οἵπερ ἐξεφύσαμεν follows well in contrast to ἄλλη ... δυσμενεστέραι χερί.

**1242–6** As earlier (403n., 1051n.), Medea uses military and athletic terms from the masculine spheres: ὁπλίζου, τὰ δεινά, ξίφος, βαλβῖδα, μὴ κακισθῆις.

**1242–3 τί μέλλομεν | ... μὴ οὐ πράσσειν:** μέλλω here has the sense 'delay', and the negative implicit in the form of question τί μέλλομεν; accounts for the idiomatic use of μὴ οὐ with the inf.

(pleonastic and not to be translated): cf. *Prom.* 627, Soph. *Ajax* 540 (Smyth §2742). (μὴ οὐ is restored by Elmsley for transmitted μή, a common corruption; the two negatives form one syllable by crasis.)

**1244** χείρ: almost the last reference by Medea to her own hand (see 1378); for the importance of the motif of the hand, see Introd. 2(*d*).

**1245** ἕρπε πρὸς βαλβῖδα λυπηρὰν βίου: like a competitor entering a race very reluctantly, Medea exhorts herself to 'step up to the painful starting-line of your ⟨future, remaining⟩ life', that is, (Page) 'where life's misery begins'. The *balbides* were grooves in the stone starting-blocks of the ancient stadium; athletes fitted their toes into the grooves to position themselves in readiness for the start of a race. Most metaphorical uses of the term connote 'starting-point' (*Her.* 867 βαλβίδων ἄπο, Ar. *Wasps* 548 ἀπὸ βαλβίδων), but the same line was also the finish of the *diaulos* and longer races, so occasionally the word is also a metaphor for the goal (Soph. *Ant.* 131 βαλβίδων ἐπ' ἄκρων of the top of the walls as the goal of an attacker). 'Starting-point' is more apposite here, where Medea urges herself to forget for one day then mourn thereafter. Kovacs' 'go to your life's miserable goal' introduces a false note: in her own eyes, Medea's life-goal is not infanticide, but revenge on Jason and the maintenance of the respect and fear she deserves.

**1246–50** Medea's self-exhortation is less ferocious and less dismissive of soft feelings than in her earlier speech, as Eur. takes pains to indicate the suffering her action causes her now and will cause her in the future. She has not fully succeeded in conceiving of the children as solely Jason's, but admits that they are precious to her and are indeed her φίλοι (Introd. 2(*d*)). Her present expedient is to temporarily 'forget' the relationship while she completes her revenge, but to acknowledge it thereafter in mourning.

**1250** δυστυχὴς δ' ἐγὼ γυνή: after the stength she has shown in her confrontations with her male interlocutors, Medea is momentarily back in the wretched condition in which she began the play and in which she envisioned all women (230–51). Her closing word recalls once more the theme of gender-conflict, which will be continued in the final scene, although Medea then appears and acts as more than a mortal woman.

## *1251–92    Fifth stasimon*

As Medea finally goes in to do the terrible deed, the chorus succumbs at last to the intensity of the situation. After the stately dactylo-epitrites of the previous stasimons and the detached contemplation of the anapaests before the messenger-scene, the dochmiacs (see PM 28) of this song clearly mark the desperate climax of the action. The first pair of stanzas presents a familiar pattern: the strophe appeals to divine powers, especially Medea's grandfather Helios, a symbol of light and purity, evoking the opposite forces that the women hope will stop Medea (cf. the invocation of the purity and divine excellence of Athens in 824–45); the antistrophe brings another direct address to Medea, not so much dissuading her from action as foreseeing the result. The invocation of Earth and Light here produces no welcome response from the gods (although shortly Helios' assistance to Medea will be revealed) but reminds us of the chorus' exclamatory address in 148. As with Aegeus' opportune arrival, it is as if the gods did listen earlier to Medea's complaints and recognized their justification: see Introd. 2(*e*).

The second pair of stanzas is unusual in incorporating in the strophe iambic trimeters spoken by the children from within (the corresponding verses in the antistrophe are a seamless part of the chorus' own utterance). Cries from within are a conventional way of staging the ultimate violence of murder (1270a n.). Also conventional is the chorus' brief consideration of entering the house to intervene in the event (1275n.), but the idea is dropped very quickly, as if it is evoked only to emphasize again the chorus' detachment from the action and the untenable moral position in which they have found themselves. In the second antistrophe, the only thing left to do is to react to the completed event. The mythological exemplum (Ino) is somewhat off-key (see 1284n.): the women are again unable to make their song commensurate to the event before them.

### *Metre*

Like anapaestic metra, dochmiacs run in long sequences, often conveniently laid out as dimeters with an occasional monometer, but with periods of indeterminate length. The period-ends posited at 1254 = 1264 and 1257 = 1267 are suggested by punctuation but cannot be proved. Word overlap between metra (especially by one syllable) is common. There are several instances of long in correspondension with short in the first anceps of the dochmiac, and therefore Ἐρινύν in 1260 may be scanned with long upsilon (see Mastronarde on *Phoen.*, p. 437), against LSJ. On the two possible ways of articulating 1255 = 1265 see Diggle (1994) 373–6, who doubts cretic between dochmiacs.

| | |
|---|---|
| ∪ – – ∪ – – ∪ – \| | |
| ἰὼ Γᾶ τε καὶ παμφαὴς | 1251 ba, dochm |
| μάταν μόχθος ἔρρει τέκνων, | 1261 |
| | |
| ‾ – ‾∪ ∪ – ∪ ∪͡ ∪͡ ∪ – | |
| ἀκτὶς Ἀλίου, κατίδετ' ἴδετε τὰν | 1252 2 dochm |
| μάταν ἄρα γένος φίλιον ἔτεκες, ὢ | 1262 |
| | |
| ∪ ∪͡ – ∪ – ∪ – – ∪ – \| | |
| ὀλομέναν γυναῖκα, πρὶν φοινίαν | 1253 2 dochm |
| κυανεᾶν λιποῦσα Συμπληγάδων | 1263 |
| | |
| ∪ – – ∪ – ∪ – –∪ – ‖ | |
| τέκνοις προσβαλεῖν χέρ' αὐτοκτόνον· | 1254 2 dochm |
| πετρᾶν ἀξενωτάταν ἐσβολάν. | 1264 |
| | |
| – – – ∪ – ∪͡ ∪ – \| | |
| σᾶς γὰρ χρυσέας ἀπὸ γονᾶς | 1255 dochm, cr |
| δειλαία, τί σοι φρενοβαρὴς | 1265 (or molossus, dochm?) |
| | |
| ‾ – – ∪ – – ∪͡ –∪ – \| | |
| ἔβλαστεν, θεοῦ δ' αἷμα ⟨χαμαὶ⟩ πίτνειν | 1256 2 dochm |
| χόλος προσπίτνει καὶ ζαμενὴς ⟨φόνου⟩ | 1266 |
| | |
| ∪ ∪͡ – ∪ – ‖ | |
| φόβος ὑπ' ἀνέρων. | 1257 dochm |
| φόνος ἀμείβεται; | 1267 |
| | |
| ‾ ∪͡ – ∪ – ∪ ∪͡ – ∪ – | |
| ἀλλά νιν, ὦ φάος διογενές, κάτειρ- | 1258 2 dochm |
| χαλεπὰ γὰρ βροτοῖς ὁμογενῆ μιά- | 1268 |
| | |
| ∪ ∪͡ – ∪ – ∪ – –∪– | |
| γε κατάπαυσον, ἔξελ' οἴκων τάλαι- | 1259 2 dochm |
| σματ' †ἐπὶ γαῖαν† αὐτοφόνταις ξυνωι- | 1269 |
| | |
| ‾ ∪͡ – ∪ – ‾∪͡ –∪ – ‖‖ | |
| νάν φονίαν τ' Ἐρινὺν †ὑπ' ἀλαστόρων†. | 1260 2 dochm |
| δὰ θεόθεν πίτνοντ' ἐπὶ δόμοις ἄχη. | 1270 |
| – – – – – – – – – – | |
| ἰώ μοι. | 1270a (extra metrum) |

⏑ – – ⏑ –   ⏑ – – ⏑ –|
ἀκούεις βοὰν ἀκούεις τέκνων;   1273 2 dochm
μίαν δὴ κλύω μίαν τῶν πάρος   1282

⏑ – – ⏑ –   ⏑ ⌢⌣ – ⏑ – ||ʰ
ἰὼ τλᾶμον, ὦ κακοτυχὲς γύναι.   1274 2 dochm
γυναῖκ' ἐν φίλοις χέρα βαλεῖν τέκνοις,   1283

– – ⏑– –⏒ ⋮ – ⏑ – –⏒ – ⏑ –||
οἴμοι, τί δράσω; ποῖ φύγω μητρὸς χέρας;   1271 ia trimeter
Ἰνὼ μανεῖσαν ἐκ θεῶν, ὅθ' ἡ Διὸς   1284

–⏒ – ⏑ – ⏑  – ⏑ ⋮ – ⏑ – ⏑ – ||
οὐκ οἶδ', ἄδελφε φίλτατ'· ὀλλύμεσθα γάρ.   1272 ia trimeter
δάμαρ νιν ἐξέπεμπε δωμάτων ἄλαις·   1285

⏑ – – ⏑ –   ⏑ – – ⏑ –|
παρέλθω δόμους; ἀρῆξαι φόνον   1275 2 dochm
πίτνει δ' ἁ τάλαιν' ἐς ἅλμαν φόνωι   1286

⏑ – – ⏑ – ||ʰ
δοκεῖ μοι τέκνοις.   1276 dochm
τέκνων δυσσεβεῖ,   1287

– – ⏑ – ⏝  – ⏑ ⋮ – ⏑ – ⏑ – ||
ναί, πρὸς θεῶν, ἀρήξατ'· ἐν δέοντι γάρ.   1277 ia trimeter
ἀκτῆς ὑπερτείνασα ποντίας πόδα,   1288

–⏒ – ⏑ – –  ⋮ – ⏑ – ⏑ – ⏑ – ||
ὡς ἐγγὺς ἤδη γ' ἐσμὲν ἀρκύων ξίφους.   1278 ia trimeter
δυοῖν τε παίδοιν ξυνθανοῦσ' ἀπόλλυται.   1289

⏑ – – ⏑–  ⏑⌢⌣ – ⏑ –
τάλαιν', ὡς ἄρ' ἦσθα πέτρος ἢ σίδα-   1279 2 dochm
τί δῆτ' οὐ γένοιτ' ἂν ἔτι δεινόν; ὦ   1290

⏑ – – ⏑ –|
ρος, ἅτις τέκνων   1280 dochm
γυναικῶν λέχος   1291

⏑ ⌢⌣ ⏑ ⌢⌣ ⏑ – ⏑ –
ὃν ἔτεκες ἄροτον αὐτόχει-   1281 2 ia
πολύπονον, ὅσα βροτοῖς ἔρε-   1292

⏑ – – ⏑ – |||
ρι μοίραι κτενεῖς.   1281 dochm
ξας ἤδη κακά.   1292

**1251–2**  ἰὼ Γᾶ τε καὶ παμφαὴς ἀκτὶς Ἀλίου:  for the pairing, see 148n.

**1252 κατίδετ᾽ ἴδετε:** the simple verb follows on the compound in a rhetorical reinforcement similar to the exact doubling of a word; for this mannerism of Euripides' lyrics see the references in Willink on *Or.* 181 and Diggle (1994) 389.

**1253 ὀλομέναν:** this participle is sometimes used in a 'modal' sense, reflecting the curse optative ὄλοιο/ὄλοιτο, and hence to be translated as 'accursed'; see Mastronarde on *Phoen.* 1529.

**1253–4 πρὶν .|.. αὐτοκτόνον:** again the chorus imagines the shockingly murderous mother's hand (856–65). 'Kin-murdering hand' is probably a reminiscence of Aesch. *Sept.* 805 (Eteocles and Polynices) τεθνᾶσιν ἐκ χερῶν αὐτοκτόνων, although it cannot be excluded that the adj. here goes not with χέρ᾽ but with the understood subject of the inf., 'carrying out kin-murder'. For the use of αὐτο- in Greek compounds to convey kin-murder rather than self-murder, compare αὐτοφόνταις in 1269 and LSJ s.vv. αὐθέντης, αὐτοφόνος, αὐτόχειρ (but see 1281n.); see Fraenkel on *Ag.* 1091ff., Hutchinson on *Sept.* 734–41. For the problem of the etymological origin of this sense, see Chantraine and Frisk s.vv. αὐθέντης, αὐτός.

**1255 χρυσέας ἀπὸ γονᾶς** 'golden' is always suitable in reference to the Olympian gods and their accoutrements, and the notion fits the sun-god in particular (*Hec.* 636 χρυσοφαής; *Phoen.* [2] χρυσο-κολλήτοισιν ἐμβεβὼς δίφροις; Pindar, *Pyth.* 4.133 σθένος ἀελίου χρύσεον); here the chorus wishes to emphasize how precious the children are and how much they deserve divine intervention. (The word-order of the MSS has been adjusted by editors since Musgrave to restore responsion.)

**1256–7 θεοῦ ..|. ὑπ᾽ ἀνέρων** 'it is a cause of fear (a terrible outrage) that the blood of a god should be spilled by humans'; for this sense of φόβος compare the more concrete uses in *Tro.* 1136, Soph. *OC* 1651–2, LSJ s.v. II.2. 'Blood of a god' is a brachylogy for 'blood of a descendant of a god'; but the chorus is tendentious (in the interest of their appeal) in emphasizing the portion of divine blood in the children while referring to Medea herself, who has a greater portion, under the generalizing plural 'humans'. With the contrast god/human the chorus perhaps wishes to suggest – again in the interest of their appeal – there is something impious in the action of killing a descendant of a god, but in myth the point is usually rather that a god may be angry at anyone who harms his or her protegé, whether an offspring or not: for instance, Apollo's anger at Agamemnon and the Greeks for Agamemnon's treatment of his priest Chryses, Poseidon's anger against Odysseus because of what he did to Polyphemus, the wrath of Ares and Earth against Cadmus and the Thebans for the death of the guardian serpent (*Phoen.* 934). Even in the stories of Heracles fighting Cycnus and his father Ares or Neleus and his father Poseidon (Gantz (1993) 421–2, 455), the conflict is simply a matter of solidarity of kinship.

**1256** ⟨χαμαί⟩: the supplements added here and 1266 are designed to restore the simple dochmiac metre: without them we have an isolated choriamb (− ∪ ∪ −) between dochmiacs, an unlikely phenomenon. Moreover, Diggle (1994) 291–4 has shown that πίτνειν without the addition of 'onto the ground' is abnormal and ἀμείβεται in 1267 is likewise harsh without a supplement.

**1257** ἀνέρων: the alpha is long in the trisyllabic epic forms ἄνερι, ἄνερες, etc. (for ἀνδρί, ἄνδρες, etc.), which are occasionally used in tragic lyric for metrical convenience.

**1258** διογενές 'Zeus-born' either because Helios is identified with Apollo (Diggle on *Phaethon* 225), son of Zeus and Leto, or because the brightness of the sky is a manifestation of Zeus. There is no need to give the adj. (here only) the vague sense 'divine' (LSJ).

**1258–9** κάτειρ | γε κατάπαυσον ἔξελ': the asyndeton and the anaphora of κατ- are expressive of strong emotion (LS 28).

**1260** †ὑπ' ἀλαστόρων†: this would have to mean 'remove her through the agency of avenging divinities' (on *alastor* see 1333n.), but since Medea herself is being portrayed as an Erinys and thus is being identified with just such a divinity, this would be a very odd sense. Page proposed the unattested epithet ὑπαλάστορον, meaning 'Fury driven by an avenging demon', while Eden (1988) suggests ὑπαλαστόρων ('infested with avenging demons') to agree with οἴκων, a noun that doesn't need an epithet, much less one so distant and so emphatically placed at the end of the stanza.

**1261–2** μάταν … | μάταν: the chorus echoes Medea's own complaint in 1029–30 ἄλλως ἄρ' ὑμᾶς, ὦ τέκν', ἐξεθρεψάμην | ἄλλως δ' ἐμόχθουν κτλ. as well as their own generalizations about the μόχθος of parenthood (1090–1115).

**1263–4** κυανεᾶν λιποῦσα ..|. ἀξενωτάταν ἐσβολάν: at this point of greatest revulsion, the chorus reminds the audience of Medea's foreignness and of the fatal mixing of ethnicities and realms symbolized by the crossing of the famous boundary ('most inhospitable entryway marked by the dark clashing rocks'): Introd. 2(*c*).

**1265** φρενοβαρής: (not in LSJ ) 'heart-oppressing' or 'mind-oppressing'; the epithet is an emendation of Seidler to restore dochmiac metre and to sharpen the sense of transmitted φρενῶν βαρὺς χόλος ('heavy wrath of mind').

**1266–7** ζαμενὴς ⟨φόνου⟩ | φόνος ἀμείβεται 'frenzied murder (of the children) follows on murder (of the princess and king)'; see Diggle (1994) 293–4. For the gen. of exchange φόνου and the sense of the verb, compare *Hipp.* 1108 ἄλλα … ἄλλοθεν ἀμείβεται, 'different things succeed from different sources', that is, 'one kind of fortune follows another'.

**1268–70** As transmitted, the text contains no finite verb, leaving too many apparent nominatives, and ἐπὶ γαῖαν is senseless. The most likely solution is that one sentence ends at μιάσματ' ('difficult for mortals is the pollution of kin-murder') and that a verb (and perhaps a conjunction) has been corrupted to ἐπὶ γαῖαν (for instance, 'and it brings to kin-murderers woes consonant ⟨with their crime⟩, falling upon their house by the will of the gods').

**1270a–75** The MSS lack the exclamation of 1270a and present the iambic trimeters of the children (1271–2) before the first dochmiacs of the chorus. As Seidler saw, the iambic trimeters should have the same position in the strophe as in the antistrophe, and some other exclamation is needed before the chorus' initial ἀκούεις. The Strasbourg papyrus (third cent. BCE) shows the expected initial exclamation and also has the couplet of trimeters both before and after 1273–4, a confirmation of Seidler's corrections and an indication of the very early origin of the corruption in the MSS.

**1270a** (ἔσωθεν):  cries from within are a standard signal of murder or the discovery of suicide taking place beyond the view of the audience. The cries often evoke a reaction from the chorus, including the idea that the chorus might go inside to intervene or to find out what is wrong, and may lead an audience to expect that the results of the violence will soon be displayed to them by the use of the *ekkyklēma*. See Hamilton (1987).

**1273** ἀκούεις βοὰν ἀκούεις τέκνων:  the repeated word at the beginning of successive dochmiac metra is a fairly common structure for intensification and is matched in the corresponding line 1282 (see Diggle (1994) 296–7, 376–8; Tessier (1975); Fehling (1969) 177).

**1275** παρέλθω:  prospective/deliberative subjunctive question, 'shall I enter the house?' It is conventional for the chorus to contemplate such an intervention, but equally conventional that the intervention is avoided, either by a hesitation or lack of resolve on the chorus' part or because the entry is forestalled by the appearance of a character or by certainty that it is too late for action (compare *Hipp.* 776–89; see Arnott (1982) and (1984–85), Pöhlmann (1995b)). This instance is remarkable for the rapidity with which the idea of intervention is dropped and for the lack of explicit motivation for dropping it. There is also no other example extant in which the speaker inside replies to something said by those outside, as here in 1277.

**1277–8**  The MSS treat this as a continuous speech of both boys in unison, but it is better to match the division seen in 1271–2, and the presence of γ' in 1278 is also a clue that the second boy is adding confirmation to what the first boy has just said.

ἐν δέοντι  'at the needed moment', 'at the time it is critically needed'; the phrase (sometimes ἐν τῶι δέοντι) is prosaic (several times in Eur., once in Ar. *Peace* 272, and many prose exx. from Herodotus to late authors).

ἀρκύων ξίφους  'the net/snare of the sword', that is, 'the inescapable assault of our mother's sword' or (Kovacs) 'the murderous snare'.

**1279** ὡς ἄρ' ἦσθα:  ὡς is to be taken as exclamatory, 'how, how truly', and imperfect ἦσθα expresses a new or sudden realization of a truth that had not been recognized before (703n.) 'this *was* the case all along, but I didn't see it or believe it'.

**1279–80** πέτρος ἢ σίδα | ρος: 28–9n.

**1280** ἄτις: 589n.

**1281** ἄροτον 'crop'; the metaphor of ploughing and sowing is common in poetry for procreation (cf. LSJ s.vv. ἀρόσιμος, ἀροτήρ, ἄροτρον, ἄρουρα, ἀρόω), but was also a standard part of the Greek betrothal formula (Men. *Dysc.* 842 ἐγγυῶ παίδων ἐπ' ἀρότωι γνησίων, *Sam.* 727 δίδωμ' ἔχειν γνησίων παίδων ἐπ' ἀρότωι, etc.).

αὐτόχειρι μοίραι 'with a doom accomplished by your own (kindred) hand'; for the connotation of kin-murder in αὐτο-compounds see 1253–4n. The use here seems to play upon the different etymological connotations of αὐτο-, both 'very own' and 'same/kindred'.

**1282** μίαν: a rhetorical exaggeration, since the legend of Tereus, Procne, and Itys was well known to the Athenian audience (most similar because the mother uses the death of the child to punish her faithless husband), and the pairs Agave-Pentheus and Althaea-Meleager were also well known. The exemplum does not here provide consolation or mitigation, as often when a series of exempla are cited; rather, rarity or deficiency of the comparandum marks the superlative quality of the present event (compare *Her.* 1016–18, 1021–2: Heracles' murder spree outdoes the Danaids' famous crime and surpasses Procne's slaughter of a single child). The mythological comparandum is not exactly apposite, since Ino is clearly described as driven insane by the gods' intervention, whereas we have observed Medea choosing quite consciously to kill her sons, although the chorus suggests that such extremity must indicate derangement (1260, 1265–7), and some might regard Medea as in fact under the influence of the gods (Introd. 2(e)). For more on the possible relevance of Ino, see Newton (1985).

**1283** ἐν φίλοις χέρα βαλεῖν τέκνοις: ἐν goes with βαλεῖν (= ἐμβαλεῖν, tmesis, Smyth §§1650–1); it is perhaps significant that ἐμβάλλειν χεῖρα normally means to confirm a pledge or promise by a handshake, whereas in this context the phrase has a hostile meaning, like other phrases with χεῖρα(ς) (LSJ s.v. ii.5.d) and like ἐμβαλεῖν ξίφος (1325).

**1284** Ἰνὼ μανεῖσαν: Ino earned the enmity of Hera by nursing the baby Dionysus. At least three versions of the deaths of Learchus and Melicertes, the two sons of Ino and Athamas, are extant. In the most common version, Athamas (either maddened by Hera or angry because he has discovered the treachery of Ino that led to the loss of Athamas' previous children Phrixos and Helle) killed one son and Ino snatched the other son to save him, but when pursued by Athamas leapt with Melicertes into the sea. Eur. seems to allude here to a version in which Ino, in madness (compare Heracles), kills both her children, but then leaps into the sea (or kills them by taking them with her in her leap). Pseudo-Apollodorus tells a version in which both Athamas and Ino are driven mad by Hera and each kills one son before Ino jumps into the sea. Newton (1985) suggests that the version here is Eur.'s invention: if it is, the audience presumably accepted it as a poetic licence (and did not think, as Newton proposes, that the chorus cites an event that never occurred).

ἐκ θεῶν: equivalent to prosaic ὑπὸ θεῶν, 'driven mad by the gods'.

**1285** ἄλαις 'in wandering' (dat. of manner or circumstance), but this is not a case of long exile such as that imposed upon Io by Hera, but of uncontrolled movement that quickly led to the fatal fall into the sea; hence there may be a suggestion of mental distraction in the word, and perhaps it is actually metaphorical (as claimed by LSJ s.v.). (In Aesch. *Ag.* 194 ἄλαι has been taken by some as '⟨cause of⟩ mental distraction', but a literal meaning is possible.)

**1286–7** φόνωι | τέκνων δυσσεβεῖ: the sense is ambiguous to us since we do not know what version Eur. is alluding to. The dat. is either causal ('because of her impious murder of her children') or of circumstance ('while impiously murdering her children').

**1288–9** contain details that may anticipate, through the opposite, what happens with Medea: Ino leaves the ground, but falls into the sea, Medea rises and flies successfully away; Ino dies with her two children, Medea lives on after them. Cf. Newton (1985).

**1289   δυοῖν τε παίδοιν:**   dat. dual (the accent of παίδοιν follows the pattern of παίδων).

**1290   τί δῆτ' οὐ γένοιτ' ἂν ἔτι δεινόν:**   in view of Medea's almost unparalleled action, the chorus asks 'what terrible deed then would any longer be impossible?' (οὐ is to be taken closely with the verb, 'would fail to happen'). The negative is found in a papyrus of the second century CE. The MSS have οὖν (as well as δή ποτ' for δῆτ', from a common tendency to corrupt dochmiacs into iambic metra; δήποτ' οὖν is a prosaic combination). This would have to mean 'Then what ⟨additional⟩ terrible deed could any longer occur?', a sense for which either δεινότερον or ἄλλο ... δεινόν would be better. In addition, δῆτ' οὖν is an order of these particles not attested except here and in some MSS of Ar. *Clouds* 423, where δῆτ' οὐ is again superior.

**1291–2   γυναικῶν λέχος | πολύπονον:**   the phrase is richly ambiguous between 'bed (sexual nature) of women, cause of many sufferings', directly echoing the misogynistic tradition that the chorus earlier (410–30) thought was being overturned, and 'marriage of women, full of many woes', which is more neutral; but the following phrase 'you have done harm' tilts the interpretation toward the former sense.

### *1293–1419   Exodos*

After the cries from within, the audience may expect to see the bodies of the boys on the *ekkyklēma* (1270a n.), and this expectation would probably increase when Jason appears and has to be told of the killing of his sons. Yet an audience will also be uncertain once Jason has appeared how Medea is going to depart from the palace and make her way to her planned refuge in Athens. It will be a major theatrical surprise when the crane suddenly lifts into view above the roof a chariot holding Medea and the corpses of her sons. Since the higher position of the roof and crane is normally reserved for divine figures, and since Medea's initial utterance is a stopping action similar to that performed by many *dei ex machina*, the scenic arrangement raises Medea to a quasi-divine status, which may have multiple meanings (for instance, Medea as divine retribution incarnate punishing Jason's betrayal of oaths taken in the name of the gods; or Medea as a vengeful individual who has lost her humanity by her cruel action against her own offspring). See Cunningham (1954); Collinge (1962); Knox (1977) 206–11; Mastronarde (1990) 264–6.

This scene presents many elements of reversal in the positions of Jason and Medea. The accusations of Jason are reminiscent of Medea's charges in the *agōn*-scene, and the structure of the interchange is a kind of reduced *agōn* (a rhesis by Jason, then a much briefer rhesis by Medea, who contemptuously refuses to answer at equal length, then a recapitulation of the opposition in angry stichomythia). Jason's appeals to the gods and curses are similar to those that Medea uttered earlier, in prologue and parodos. Medea has thus risen from her lowest point of dejection and distraction to triumph over her enemy, and placed her enemy in the position of helplessness she seemed to be in at the start. She also has control of the lamentation and funeral rites of her sons, blocking Jason's efforts at verbal lament and physical contact (cf. Battezzato (1995) 172–6). Among the thematic and verbal echoes are: 'most hateful', 1323, 467; 'look upon after doing evil', 1327, 470; 'now have sense, but didn't before when marriage was made', 1329, 800–1; shameless boldness (*thrasos*), 1345, 469; call on Dike/Themis, 1390, 160; call to Zeus, 1405, 169; 'how/what I suffer', 1406, 161; not 'benefiting from, taking delight in the children', 1348, 1025; 'concerned less about Medea than about the children', 1301, 346–7; nurtured sons in vain, 1349–50, 1029. Compare also the ironic contrasts of 1413–14 'I wish I had not seen destroyed' with 163–4 'may I see destroyed', and of 1375 'easy separation' with 226 'no respectable separation/divorce'.

**1293** *Action*: Jason enters in haste and immediately addresses a question to the chorus. On the problem of whether he is alone or accompanied, see Introd. 3 and also 1314–15n. and 1317n.

In Sophocles and Eur. entering characters normally acknowledge a present actor in preference to addressing the chorus, and even when the chorus alone is present an entering character may address the house or call/knock at the door without addressing the chorus (Taplin (1977) 86–7; Mastronarde (1979) 20–3). Sometimes the chorus is addressed as the logical source of information (*Alc.* 477, Soph. *El.* 660, *OT* 924), but the technique of address employed here also seems to be intended to show some caution in Jason or at least to allow a build-up toward the terrible revelation by showing his mistaken certainty that Medea will be punished and his pathetic intention to save his children. Menelaus enters with a bolder attitude in *Or.* 1554–66, ignoring the chorus and attacking the door; more comparable to Jason's approach is the caution of Polyneices in *Phoen.* 261–79, who chooses to address the chorus rather than approach the palace door.

γυναῖκες, αἳ τῆσδ' ἐγγὺς ἕστατε στέγης: this is an unusually explicit reference to the chorus as bystanders; only *Phoen.* 277 is partly comparable (καὶ τάσδ' ἔρωμαι τίνες ἐφεστᾶσιν δόμοις).

**1294–5** contain a question that is not immediately answered. Jason's own comments shift the course of the dialogue from interest in Medea to concern about his sons. Eventually, when he reframes his question in 1312 to learn where his sons' bodies are, Medea's whereabouts is also revealed: Mastronarde (1979) 36.

**1295** τοισίδ' is separated from its noun and in a weak position in its clause because the initial phrase ἆρ' ἐν δόμοισιν is already sufficiently clear and because of the weight given to the indignant attributive phrase ἡ τὰ δείν' εἰργασμένη.

μεθέστηκεν 'has she departed' (898n.).

**1296–7** ἤτοι γῆς γε κρυφθῆναι κάτω | ἢ πτηνὸν ἆραι σῶμ' ἐς αἰθέρος βάθος 'either be hidden down under the earth or raise her body aloft on wings to the distant heights of the sky'; for this conventional opposition of underworld and sky as two locations for impossible escape-wishes, see Barrett on *Hipp.* 1290–3. Winged flight, which Jason views as impossible, soon turns out to be within Medea's power. ἆραι is aor. act. inf. of αἴρω; πτηνόν should be taken as predicative. βάθος and βαθύς may refer to height as well as depth, depending on the viewpoint from which the vertical dimension is viewed, although the downward viewpoint is the more common. The combination ἤτοι ... γε lends liveliness and emphasis to the whole first alternative (Denniston 119).

**1300** ἀθῷος has a legalistic flavour, 'free of legal sanction or penalty', following up on δώσει δίκην in 1298 and in conformity with Jason's assumption (now that he is the injured party) that the legal

mechanisms he values as essentially 'Greek' (536–8n., 1330–2) will be
in force against Medea.

**1301** ἀλλ' οὐ γάρ: the particles mark a breaking off to turn to
what is essential (252n.); so too in 1344. It is also possible to view οὐ
γὰρ ... ἔχω as parenthetic and ἀλλά as introducing the sentence
1302–3 (where the δέ-limb carries the real emphasis).

ὡς: here 'as much as'.

**1302** κακῶς: the adverb is to be taken with both verbs: 'as for
her, those to whom she has done harm will harm her'.

**1304** μή μοί τι δράσωσ' 'lest they do something ⟨to the boys⟩
that would cause me grief'; the personal object has to be understood
(μοι is ethic dat. or dat. of disinterest/disadvantage), and τι is a eu-
phemistically vague substitute for 'some harm'.

οἱ προσήκοντες γένει: this seems to be a clear allusion to the
versions in which the children were killed by the kinsmen of Creon
(see Introd. 4).

**1305** μητρῶιον ἐκπράσσοντες ... φόνον: note the idiomatic
contextual definition of μητρῶιον, here 'committed by the boys'
mother'; ἐκπράσσω is here extended from the prosaic sense 'execute
a punishment, exact a penalty' to the sense 'extract punishment/
retribution for' with the crime as object (compare Hdt. 7.158).

**1306** οἵ κακῶν 'to what point (extremity) of woes/evils' (partitive
gen. depending on the adverbial relative: Smyth §§1439–40).

**1308** ἤ που probably carries a tone of sarcasm here, or possibly a
tone of bewilderment; the alternative reading οὔ που (in a papyrus)
would be preferable only if one wishes Jason to adopt a tone of lively
concern and fear. On the alternation of these two combinations in
MSS, see Mastronarde on *Phoen.* 1072, with refs.

κἄμ': crasis, καὶ ἐμέ, as also in 1318 κἀμέ, 1324 κἀμοί, 1326 κἄμ'.

**1309** παῖδες ... σέθεν: for the separation of the modifier from its
noun, see LS 35.

**1310** τί λέξεις: a horrified 'what do you mean to say?', expressing
reluctance to credit the bad news just heard and awaiting elaboration; for this Euripidean idiom see Barrett on *Hipp.* 353.

**1311** ὡς ... ὄντων: the gen. absolute introduced by ὡς may express an assumption or belief as an alternative to other indirect-discourse constructions; see Smyth §2122.

**1312** γάρ here reflects the progressive use in question-and-answer stichomythia (Denniston 81–5) and apparently implies that Jason has now accepted that the children are dead and wants to locate and see their bodies.

**1313** πύλας ἀνοίξας ... ὄψηι: this is close to a metatheatrical allusion to the expectation that the interior scene will be revealed for all to see, on the *ekkyklēma*, once the door is opened; but the door is not opened and the *ekkyklēma* is not used.

**1314–15** χαλᾶτε κλῆιδας ... πρόσπολοι, | ἐκλύεθ' ἁρμούς: two interpretations are possible, related to the question whether silent attendants have entered with Jason (Introd. 3). Probably (against the view expressed in Mastronarde (1990) 266: 'Jason with his attendants'), Jason is alone: he calls to servants inside the house and the intended meaning is 'unfasten the bars at once, servants, undo the closure of the doors'. The bars are inside and can be undone from there. Jason also attacks the door himself from outside, as is evident from Medea's address to him in 1317–19. Very similar lines occur in *Hipp.* when Theseus calls for the doors to be opened so that he may see his wife's corpse (which is then rolled out on the *ekkyklēma*): 809–11 χαλᾶτε κλῆιθρα, πρόσπολοι, πυλωμάτων, | ἐκλύεθ' ἁρμούς, ὡς ἴδω πικρὰν θέαν | γυναικός (on which see Barrett). This is the view favoured by Stanley-Porter (1973) 86 n. 53. Alternatively, if Jason is not alone, then the address πρόσπολοι is made to those outside with him, and we may translate 'loosen the locked doors, servants, break the fastenings', and Jason joins in on the assault. The singular verbs in Medea's question and command at 1317–19 do not decide the issue, since at *Or.* 1567–8 Orestes addresses only Menelaus although there are clearly servants pushing against the door with him.

**1316** If the line is both genuine and sound, then there is a strong break in the construction (anacoluthon). Instead of balancing 'first, my sons dead' with 'and, secondly, the murderous woman', Jason, in his eagerness for revenge, promotes the next or subordinate thought ('whom I intend to punish') to coordinate status. For this kind of

anacoluthon with μέν and δέ see K–G ΙΙ.100. Since the phrase begins
as a simple partitive apposition, however, this shift is particularly
harsh and not well supported by the accepted examples. Apart from
recognizing this harsh construction (or assuming an uncured corruption in the text), two other approaches are possible. (1) 'double evil'
could be taken as referring to the sight of *two* dead children: someone
who was bothered by διπλοῦν and who perhaps looked forward to
1318 ('seeking dead bodies and me who did the deed') could have
added 1316 as a clumsy supplement to specify something double (thus
Schenkl, followed by Diggle). But διπλοῦν κακόν is plausibly deemed
by most critics to be rhetorically incomplete on its own: it needs a
defining gen., some preparation for the idea of twoness in the context, or an apposition such as 1316 seems to offer (compare μέν-δέ
limbs after 1185 above, *Supp.* 1035, Aesch. *Supp.* 1009, *Ag.* 325). (2)
Kovacs assumes a lacuna in which τὴν δέ is completed in proper
balance, and then the threat of vengeance is added. Retaining the
line also produces a smoother transition to Medea's speech, as she
takes up the pairing in 1318 and declares that Jason will not be able
to take vengeance on her.

**1317**   *action*:   above the centre of the *skēnē* a prop-chariot carrying
Medea and dummy-corpses of the children comes into view, carried
by the rising arm of the crane. The chariot is not described in the
text, but is clearly capable of flight, so is in some way winged. The
hypothesis of the play says she is 'riding a chariot drawn by winged
serpents' and South Italian vases from around 400 BCE do indeed
show a serpent-chariot (Taplin (1993) plates 1.101, 2.103; *LIMC* s.v.
Medeia nos. 35–6, cf. nos. 37–9 from mid and late fourth century,
and see M. Schmidt's commentary in *LIMC*). But those illustrations
also feature different treatments of the sons' corpses (see Introd. 6),
and the serpent-chariot may be an iconographic borrowing from
the tradition of images of Triptolemus. That hero is depicted with
a flying serpent-chariot in Attic vases from *c.* 480 and 470 (*LIMC*
s.v. Demeter nos. 344, 346) and was shown or described thus in
Sophocles' early eponymous play (fr. 596). Moreover, serpents, as
chthonic creatures, make sense with a chariot of the earth-goddess
Demeter, but less sense with a chariot supplied by Helios, whose own
chariot is always shown with horses or winged horses. On the other

hand, serpents are associated very early with Medea herself as a figure (or goddess) with magical powers: an unexplained Etruscan representation from the seventh century appears to show her confronting a three-headed serpent, with another serpent behind her (*LIMC*
s.v. Medeia, no. 2); and a series of four Attic black-figure vases from
the period 530–500 show a woman's bust flanked by serpents, and
one of the four vases labels the woman Medea (*LIMC* s.v. Medeia,
nos. 3–6). This does not prove that a serpent-chariot was already associated with Medea, but it does indicate why a serpent-chariot is
appropriate to her. Thus it is possible that the prop used in 431 was
already a serpent-chariot, but it is also possible that this was the
iconographic choice of a subsequent production of the play in South
Italy or of the vase-painters themselves.

On the theory that Medea's changed status is also marked by a
change in her costume in this scene, see Introd. 3.

**1317  κἀναμοχλεύεις:**  crasis καὶ ἀναμοχλεύεις. This verb is extant
here alone in classical Greek, and it is uncertain whether it means
'try to pry open (as if with a lever)' (virtually ἀνοίγειν μοχλῶι) or 'try
to undo the bars'. The former is perhaps more probable in view of
*Her.* 990 σκάπτει μοχλεύει θύρετρα and Antiphanes fr. 193 K–A θύρας
μοχλεύειν (cf. Aelian fr. 252 τὰς θύρας ἀναμοχλευόντων), Ar. *Lys.*
428–30 οὐχ ὑποβαλόντες τοὺς μοχλοὺς ὑπὸ τὰς πύλας | ἐντεῦθεν ἐκ-
μοχλεύσετ'; κτλ. In about 70 instances in post-classical authors ἀνα-
μοχλεύω means 'lever up' or 'force open' or (rarely) simply 'force'. In
the imitations of this passage in Heliodorus 1.8.7 and *Christus Patiens*
121 and 437 κἀναμοχλεύεις is treated simply as an intensifying synonym of κινεῖς.

**1318  τὴν εἰργασμένην:**  an object such as 'the murder' or 'the
deed' is easily understood from the context.

**1319  παῦσαι**  is here second sing. aor. mid. imperative.

**1322**  contains two resolutions, both in the middle metron. Whereas
in 324 and 710 the double resolutions occur in lively appeals, here
they perhaps do not carry any particular force (unless the unusual
rhythm is meant to match Medea's translation to a different dimen-
sion). See PM 19.

**1325** ἥτις: 589n.

**1326** τεκοῦσα: concessive participle, concise and indignant; in English we might be more explicit: 'the very children you yourself gave birth to'.

ἄπαιδ' is predicative in sense, '(by) making me childless'.

**1328** ἔργον τλᾶσα δυσσεβέστατον: Medea had already judged herself in the same terms at 796 τλᾶσ' ἔργον ἀνοσιώτατον; Aegeus uses similar terms of Jason's betrayal in 695 τετόλμηκ' ἔργον αἴσχιστον, but with a term connoting loss of social face rather than impiety.

**1329** τότ' οὐ φρονῶν: the so-called 'imperfect participle', that is, a use of the participle in its present-stem aspect of continuation but with past time indicated by an accompanying adverb (Smyth §1872a1, Goodwin §140).

**1330–1** ἐκ δόμων σε βαρβάρου τ' ἀπὸ χθονὸς | Ἕλλην' ἐς οἶκον: the theme of non-Greek vs Greek returns again in this balanced phrase: see Introd. 2(c). From βαρβάρου in the conjoined phrase βαρβάρων is to be understood with δόμων.

**1333** τὸν σὸν δ' ἀλάστορ' 'the avenging demon that was sent after you' (for your murder of your brother). The *alastor* (1059n.) is an embodiment of the pollution or curse that attaches to murder: see Parker (1983) ch. 4 and 315.

**1334** παρέστιον 'by the hearth' implies that Apsyrtus was killed in his own home; on the mythic variants see Introd. 4.

**1335** καλλίπρωιρον: the rare ornamental epithet (otherwise only in Aesch. *Sept.* 533, *Ag.* 235, metaphorically of lovely youthful faces) is included to sharpen the contrast between the guilty passenger and the glorious vessel of heroic fame.

**1337** παρ' ἀνδρὶ τῶιδε is equivalent to 'with me'; for such first-person reference in ὅδε see Smyth §1242.

**1338** εὐνῆς ... καὶ λέχους is emphatic through fullness; we might translate 'the marriage-bed and sex' or 'sex and the marriage-bed', but there is no way to claim that one word bears a meaning distinct from the other.

**1339**  οὐκ ἔστιν ἥτις τοῦτ' ἂν Ἑλληνὶς γυνή:  either Ἑλληνὶς γυνή may be regarded as an antecedent incorporated into the relative clause (Smyth §2536), or οὐκ ἔστιν ἥτις may be regarded as a fixed phrase, a stronger alternative of οὐδεμία (171n.).

**1340**  ὧν γε πρόσθεν:  gen. of comparison with πρόσθεν in the sense 'in preference to'. The plural of the relative is used after the singular antecedent because 'no Greek woman' implies the whole class of Greek women: Smyth §2502b.

**1341**  κῆδος is in apposition to the action of inf. γῆμαι σέ, 'a marriage hateful and destructive for me' (LS 12.a), while the nouns in 1342 are in apposition to σέ.

**1342–3**  λέαιναν:  for Medea as wild beast and specifically lioness see Introd. 2(ƒ) and 187–8n. Medea accepts the term in 1358 and Jason repeats it in 1407.

Τυρσηνίδος | Σκύλλης  'Tyrrhenian' (Etruscan) was in the sixth and fifth centuries a general term for non-Greek Italians, by extension from the major power of that time. The Tyrrhenian Sea is the sea north of Sicily and west of Italy, ending at the Straits of Messene. Thus, for those who localized Scylla and Charybdis in the Straits of Messene, Scylla was at least on the edge of Tyrrhenian territory and the Tyrrhenian Sea. Circe's island was sometimes located in the Tyrrhenian Sea, and this assumption too would lead to describing Scylla as Tyrrhenian. See Hes. *Theog.* 1011–16 with West's notes.

**1344**  ἀλλ' οὐ γάρ:  1301n.

**1347**  πάρα = πάρεστι, here impersonal: 'what is left for me is to bewail my fate'.

**1348**  ὀνήσομαι:  1025–7n.

**1349**  οὐ is used instead of the expected οὔτε because Jason's emotion causes him to break the smoothness of his syntax (Denniston 510).

κἀξεθρεψάμην:  crasis, καὶ ἐξεθρεψάμην.

**1351–60**  Enjoying her superiority in the contest, Medea does not deign to answer Jason's long rhesis in detail and simply cites Zeus as the authority who is aware of the truth of the situation. Her use of 'father Zeus' suggests the god as witness and highest judge of human actions, but the reference also recalls the earlier appeals to Zeus as witness of oaths and punisher of perjurers, and the neat pairing in 1353 'how you were treated by me and how you treated me' evokes again the crucial matter of Jason's failure of reciprocity. Part of the tragic effect for the audience is their confronting the unpalatable and unsettling conclusion that Medea's position is justified and yet appalling, that the murder of her own children can be summarized in ὡς χρῆν. See Introd. 2(e).

**1351** **μακρὰν ἂν ἐξέτεινα** 'I could have spoken at length'. The fem. adj. is idiomatically used in some adverbial words and phrases (e.g. ἐξ ἴσης, ἐξ ἐναντίας, διὰ κενῆς); sometimes the usage derives from omission of a noun, sometimes no particular noun is understood. See Fraenkel on *Ag.* 916 μακρὰν γὰρ ἐξέτεινας, LSJ s.v. μακράν I.2.

**1353** **ἠργάσω** is aor. mid. of ἐργάζομαι: MSS and editions often print the aor. ind. as εἰργασ-, but inscriptional evidence suggests that the augment was in eta.

**1354** **σὺ δ᾽ οὐκ ἔμελλες:** for this almost gloating declaration that an enemy was not destined to get away with evil behaviour, compare *Cycl.* 693 δώσειν δ᾽ ἔμελλες ἀνοσίου δαιτὸς δίκας (based on *Od.* 9.477), *Hcld.* 285–6 ἐνθένδε δ᾽ οὐκ ἔμελλες αἰσχύνας ἐμὲ ἄξειν βίαι τούσδ᾽.

**τἄμ᾽:** crasis, τὰ ἐμά.

**1354–5** **ἀτιμάσας .|.. ἐγγελῶν:** for the themes of dishonour and the laughter of one's enemies, see 20n., 383n., Introd. 2(b).

**1358** **πρὸς ταῦτα** and πρὸς τάδε often introduce imperatives with a defiant tone; see Mastronarde on *Phoen.* 521 (with refs.); the import is 'that's the way it is, whether you like it or not, so go ahead and . . .'

**1358–9** **καὶ λέαιναν ... | καὶ Σκύλλαν:** Medea casts back in Jason's face and willingly accepts both creatures he referred to in 1342 (1342–3n.). Diggle accepts Verrall's suggestion that 1359 is an interpolation, an expansion imitating 1342–3 or responding to the feeling that καὶ λέαιναν in 1358 needed to be followed by another term (but the first καί could be adverbial).

**πέδον** 'plain, ground', seems rather flat, and perhaps the word is corrupt: Musgrave's σπέος and Elmsley's πέτραν are attractive.

**1361–78** present a good example of violently argumentative stichomythia (SE 3b) with a characteristic echoing and contrasting of specific words in successive lines: 1361 λυπῆι, 1362 ἄλγος; 1363 ὦ τέκνα, μητρός, 1364 ὦ παῖδες … πατρώιαι; 1370 οἶδ᾽ οὐκέτ᾽ εἰσί, 1371 οἶδ᾽ εἰσίν; 1372 ἴσασιν, 1373 ἴσασι δῆτα; 1377 θάψαι, 1378 οὐ δῆτ᾽ … θάψω. The use of particles is also typical: 1369 γε (marking ellipse and limitation: Denniston 135), 1373 δῆτα (marking defiant echo: Denniston 276), 1375 καὶ μήν (marking tit-for-tat reversal: Denniston 352); 1378 οὐ δῆτα (refusing request: Denniston 275).

**1361 καὐτή:** crasis, καὶ αὐτή.

**1362 λύει δ᾽ ἄλγος** 'the pain is worthwhile' (compare the impersonal use, 566n.).

**μὴ ᾽γγελᾶις:** prodelision (PM 10), μὴ ἐγγελᾶις.

**1365 ἡμή:** crasis, ἡ ἐμή.

**1367 κἠξίωσας:** that is, καὶ ἠξίωσας, 'you *actually* thought it proper to kill them because of your bed?' (Denniston 316). Jason persists in his perception that Medea's action is simply a result of sexual jealousy, despite Medea's use once again of the language of reciprocity and honour and divine justice (1352–5).

**1369 ἥτις γε σώφρων** 'yes, ⟨it is a slight thing⟩ to any woman who has good sense and self-control'.

**σοὶ δὲ πάντ᾽ ἐστὶν κακά:** the meaning is disputed. Probably 'but you (as opposed to a sensible woman) have all wicked qualities' (with ἐστι in the sense of ἔνεστι), more or less 'you are utterly base'. Page wants to understand 'but your (neglected/insulted) bed is to you all evils', while Kovacs offers 'but you find everything a disaster'.

**1370 γάρ** gives the reason for saying 'These sons are dead!' (Denniston 60).

**1371 μιάστορες:** the etymology of this word (cf. μιαίνω, μιαρός) shows the connection between the pollution of murder and notion of curse or avenging demon; see 1333n.

**1375 ἐγὼ σήν:** understand βάξιν ἐχθαίρω.

**1376** πῶς οὖν;   is a shortening of πῶς οὖν ποιήσομεν; or πῶς οὖν ποιήσεις; and Eur. uses it several times at points of transition, often to reinforce a following τί δράσεις; or the like: *Hipp.* 598, 1261, *Hec.* 876, *Hel.* 1228, 1266.

   **κἀγὼ θέλω:**   crasis, καὶ ἐγώ; with θέλω, understand ἀπαλλαχθῆναι from 1375 ἀπαλλαγαί.

**1377** πάρες is aor. act. imperative of παρίημι, here 'permit, allow' (LSJ s.v. IV.2).

**1379–83**   It is very common for Eur. to include a prediction or cultic aetiology at the end of his plays, commonly in the mouth of an omniscient *deus ex machina* (thus we have here another 'divine' aspect to Medea's final appearance), but occasionally spoken with temporary prophetic power by a human on the point of death or in a desperate position (Eurystheus in *Hcld.* and Polymestor in *Hec.*). This gesture is in part a claim by the poet to the *sophia* required to integrate the plot just presented (often containing novel features) with the larger matrix of myth and cult by connecting it to, or re-explaining, details with which the audience is familiar. Here, if Eur. has invented the child-killing by Medea herself (see Introd. 4), then these lines allow him to explain and appropriate the alternative tradition that the children were killed by the Corinthians and that the rites performed for them were an expiation of that communal crime. Dunn (1994) and Scullion (2000) have recently emphasized the degree of invention in Euripidean aetiologies, and Dunn argues that there is no reason to believe there was a tomb of Medea's children in the precinct of Hera Akraia. What is noteworthy, however, is not the dissonance between Eur.'s aetiologies and what can be known from other sources, but the skill with which the poet appropriates and integrates some known feature of cultic activity into a novel context, thus asserting the power of his (re)interpretation.

**1379**   Ἥρας τέμενος Ἀκραίας θεοῦ:   Pausanias locates a tomb of the sons of Medea in the town of Corinth itself (the town he visited was the reconstructed Roman colony founded in 44 BCE, the original city having been destroyed in 146 BCE). Some have assumed that Hera Akraia was worshipped on Acrocorinth. But archaeology (see Sinn (1990)) has shown that in classical times Akraia was an epithet of

Hera in a sanctuary at Perachora, so that Akraia means 'on a prom-
ontory' rather than 'on a peak'.

**1380** **καθυβρίσηι** recalls Medea's earlier concern that enemies
would kill her sons to avenge themselves on her (782, 1061, cf. 1238–
9).

**1381** **τύμβους ἀνασπῶν:** desecration of tombs is infrequently attested in Greek sources (but note the fear that a mocking Trojan will
one day leap on Menelaus' tomb in *Il.* 4.176–7, Aegisthus' dancing on
Agamemnon's tomb in *El.* 326–31 and Cambyses' opening of Egyptian tombs in Hdt. 3.37.1; also *Tro.* 95–7, the text and sense of which
are disputed), but the insult is analogous to the refusal of burial.

**1383** **ἀντὶ τοῦδε δυσσεβοῦς φόνου:** this detail is anomalous in
cultic terms (Medea committed the impiety, but the Corinthians are
charged to atone) and is most reasonably explained on the grounds
that such a cult practice did exist but was explained as expiation for
the killing of the children by the Corinthians. See Introd. 4.

**1385** **συνοικήσουσα** is often used of the cohabitation of marriage,
so this detail will suggest to the audience a future in which Medea
becomes Aegeus' wife. See Introd. 4 and 663–823n.

**1386** **κατθανῆι κακὸς κακῶς:** 805–6n.

**1387** **κάρα ... λειψάνωι πεπληγμένος:** for this detail, which
might be an *ad hoc* invention, see Introd. 4.

**1388** **πικρὰς ... ἰδών:** 399–400n.

**1389–1414** The transition to chanted anapaests marks, as often,
the approaching end of the drama (SE 1). Sometimes processional
exits or the exiting movement of the crane are accompanied by the
anapaests, but the anapaests may start well before the movements, so
we cannot say whether the chariot begins to rise at about 1389 or
somewhat later. Noteworthy here is the accelerating pace of the dialogue in 1389–98, with the shortening of individual speeches (down
to two metra, and then one) and borrowing of syntax in 1397–8. This
run features period-end after 15 full metra (proven by *brevis in longo* at
1396) and then 34 metra followed by final paroemiac (there may be

undetectable period-end elsewhere (184–204n.), esp. at change of speaker, but it is noteworthy that synapheia between utterances is certain in the 1397 and 1399).

**1391–2**  τίς δὲ κλύει σοῦ ... | τοῦ ψευδόρκου καὶ ξειναπάτου:  for this taunting repartee, denying the opponent a hearing from the gods, compare *Phoen.* 605 ΠΟΛ. κλύετέ μου ΕΤ. τίς δ᾽ ἂν κλύοι σου πατρίδ᾽ ἐπεστρατευμένου;. Medea continues to point to the institutional violations committed by Jason: ψεύδορκος is a very rare poetic synonym for the somewhat more common ἐπίορκος, and ξεναπάτης is also poetic (the meaning here is 'deceiver of a stranger/foreigner with whom one has contracted a sacred bond of guest-friendship', not (as LSJ) 'one who betrays his host').

**1396**  μένε καὶ γῆρας:  in the Hesiodic view (*Theog.* 602–7), men must put up with women in order to have offspring, so that the offspring may care for one in one's old age; Medea has stripped Jason of that hope (see Mueller (2001)).

**1397–8**  for the continuity of syntax from Jason's speeches to Medea's (marked by idiomatic γε) see LS 29, 698n.

**1398**  κἄπειτ᾽:  crasis, καὶ ἔπειτα.

**1399–1400**  φιλίου χρῄζω στόματος | ... προσπτύξασθαι:  syntactically, since προσπτύσσομαι elsewhere takes an acc., the gen. is the object of χρῄζω, 'long for', and the inf. is epexegetic, although the sense is equivalent to 'I long to hold close to me the dear mouths of my sons.'

**1402–3**  δός .. | . ψαῦσαι  'permit me to touch', LSJ s.v. δίδωμι III.1. For Jason as suppliant of Medea in this scene (with πρὸς θεῶν here and ἀπελαυνόμεθ᾽ in 1405), see Introd. 2(*d*).

**1404**  οὐκ ἔστι· μάτην ἔπος ἔρριπται:  with this simple dismissive line Medea flies away, saying no more, leaving the last words to the pathetic Jason. Compare the departure of Artemis just before the end of *Hipp.*, leaving the mortals alone to express pity, forgiveness, and grief, or the refusal of Dionysus at the end of *Bacch.* to express any sympathy for the sufferings of Cadmus and Agave. ἔρριπται is third sing. perf. mid.-pass. of ῥίπτω, 'throw, cast'.

**1405–14**  Jason makes a futile appeal to Zeus, but then returns to address his tormentor. He is now in the position of abjection in which Medea had been at the outset (on motifs of reversal see 1293–1419n, Introd. 2(*a*) and (*d*)). His weakness (1408) and his frustrated longing to perform the rituals of mourning here make him at last an object of strong sympathy from the audience. The triple repetition of child-killing (1407 παιδοφόνου, 1411 τέκνα κτείνασ', 1414 φθιμένους) keeps the shock of this crime prominent in the audience's mind.

**1408**  πάρα = πάρεστι, 'it is possible'.

**1409**  τάδε is best taken as internal object of the two verbs, 'I both make this lament and utter this invocation of the gods.' κἀπιθεάζω is crasis, καὶ ἐπιθεάζω.

**1410**  μοι: virtually possessive, 'my sons', but strictly dat. of disadvantage.

**1412**  χεροῖν 'with my hands' (370n.).

**1413**  ὄφελον: the augment is omitted for metrical convenience (LS 7.a); the construction is as in 1–6, equivalent to contrary-to-fact wish.

**[1415–19]**  Chanted anapaests (8 metra plus final paroemiac). With the substitution of πολλαὶ μορφαὶ τῶν δαιμονίων for 1415, almost the same choral anapaests appear at the end of *Alc.*, *Andr.*, *Hel.*, and *Or.* It is probable that the formulaic passages have been added in most or all of these places by actors or book-editors: see Barrett on *Hipp.* 1462–6; or if it is genuine, it is so generic that that no great significance should be ascribed to it (that is, the play really ends at 1414). In favour of retaining the lines here see Roberts (1987), Kovacs (1987). The specific reference to Zeus in 1415 has been taken to show that the passage in this form is designed to go with this play, and ταμίας could be a faint echo of 169–70 ὅρκων ... ταμίας. Zeus is, to be sure, very relevant in this play (see Introd. 2(*e*)), but as dispenser of justice against one who has violated his oath and his bond of *xenia*, not as the controller of the unforeseeable vicissitudes of human fortune, and it is the latter generalized aspect that 1415–18 emphasize. The contrast between the expected and the unexpected fits a play like *Alc.* better than one like *Medea*.

**1416–18**  A basic traditional Greek distinction between gods and men is the notion that gods can see and/or control the fulfilment (τέλος) of events, while mortals cannot. To recognize this limitation is for some authors a part of piety toward the gods, and thus acknowledging the power of the gods to turn affairs unexpectedly on their head may be both a praise of the divine and a consolation to mortals for their lot. Compare Semonides 1 West, Solon 13.63–70 West, Theognis 132–42, 161–4, 639–40, 657–66.

**1417  δοκηθέντ':**  this alternative form of the aor. pass. of δοκέω occurs very rarely outside of this repeated tailpiece and various quotations and imitations of it in late Greek authors. Compare δε-δόκησαι (763n.).

# APPENDIX: *MEDEA* 1056–80

---

## A. Authenticity of 1056–80

Long before anyone suggested that *Medea* 1056–80 were interpolated, that is, added by an actor/director other than Eur. in a performance later than 431 BCE, there had been scholarly speculation about two recensions of the play by Eur. himself. This theory derived from Paolo Manuzio's observation of the absence in our text of a line of Ennius' *Medea* (fr. CV Jocelyn: *qui ipse sibi sapiens prodesse non quit nequiquam sapit*) that he wrongly identified as an exact version of Eur. fr. 905 (Cicero, *ad Fam.* 13.15.2: μισῶ σοφιστὴν ὅστις οὐχ αὑτῶι σοφός), and it received some support from remarks by Porson, Boeckh, and others, but by 1875 most of the passages referred to this Euripidean revision were satisfactorily explained in other ways.[1] Already in the first edition of his school commentary[2] Wecklein had developed the theory that Eur., some years earlier than 431, wrote a version of *Medea* fundamentally similar in conception to the play of 431, and that this earlier version inspired Neophron's imitation, produced before 431 as well (and thus in the festival records as earlier than Eur.'s play, misleading Aristotle and Dicaearchus: see Introd. 5). It was in the context of such theories that Bergk[3] proposed that lines 1056–80 were to be regarded as a (Euripidean) doublet of 1040–55. Pointing to Medea's inconsistency about whether the children can be taken away with her or not, Bergk judged that the contradiction could be explained by her emotional agitation, but then opined that 1056–80 simply repeat the thoughts of the earlier lines, a repetition he thought weakened rather than heightened the effect. Bergk could not decide which variant was the original. Soon thereafter, Wecklein, in

---

[1] See Wecklein's comm., 26 n. 1, and Klette (1875).

[2] The dates of the four editions of Wecklein's *Medea* are apparently 1873, 1880, 1891, and 1909; of these only the third and fourth have been accessible, but Klette (1875) indicates that Wecklein's first edition contained this theory (but apparently without reference to 1056–80).

[3] Bergk (1884) 512 n. 140. Bergk died in 1881 and this volume was a posthumous edition.

the introduction to the third edition of his commentary, modified his view of two Euripidean recensions to include 1056–80 as part of the evidence. On this view, passages from the first version survived in the written text, although not part of the play as performed in 431, and 1056–80 derived from the first version.[4] Bethe (1918) argued for a hypothesis by which Euripides himself created confusions in the monologue after a change in his conception of the plot involving insertion of the Aegeus scene and Medea's escape to Athens; he too posited that at least part of the text after 1055 was from an earlier version.

Such analysis of layers of conception and composition is no longer given much credence. Reacting to the same objections raised by Bergk, Wecklein, and Bethe, however, some have judged that the passage 1056–80 is not by Euripides at all, beginning with a brief condemnation of it as a monstrosity by Jachmann (1936) 193 n. 1. Müller (1951) made a more thorough argument, but it was the essay of Reeve (1972) that earned the most attention and respect, including the bracketing of the lines in Diggle's OCT. In reaction, a few shorter deletions have been contemplated and strained interpretations of some lines have been suggested. But as shown by Seidensticker (1990) (the clearest exposition of the problem in English) and Battezzato (1991), the most serious charges against the passage come down to three points: (1) the movements of the children and their awareness or lack of awareness of what Medea is saying at various moments; (2) the new appearance of the motif of 'external compulsion' at 1060–3 – the threat to the children from those angered by Medea's murder of the princess, as opposed to the 'internal compulsion' of Medea's urge to assert her status by hurting Jason in the

---

[4] Wecklein also considered 38–9, 1233–5, part of 723–30, 798–810, and 1299–1300 to be candidates for remnants of the first recension, but did not always arrive at consistency between what he said in his introduction and what appeared in the notes in the commentary. Neither in his 1899 *editio maior* of Eur. nor in the third or fourth edition of his school commentary did he bracket 1056–80. In the fourth edition, the discussion of Neophron was omitted, as Wecklein by that time took the view that the claim about Neophron's precedence was false; otherwise he maintained the view of the third edition that 1056–80 are a Euripidean doublet and that the other passages listed above may derive from an earlier version.

most extreme way; (3) the integration of 1078–80 into the overall context of the speech and of all Medea's earlier statements.

The first two points are discussed in this section, the third in section B. But first brief reference may be made to a series of minor points raised by critics that have been answered in the commentary: 1058 the reference of ἐκεῖ is considered unclear by Reeve, but others accept that it means 'there in exile (Athens)';[5] 1059 the transition from pleading 'soft' view to determined 'hard' view seems unclear to many, but linguistic clues and performance make the situation clear; 1064 objection has been made to the future sense of the perfect πέπρακται (but this is idiomatic) and to the vagueness of ταῦτα (but the demonstrative takes its sense from the overall context, as often); 1064 the change of subject between the two verbs of this line has been doubted, but the princess should be accepted as the subject of ἐκφεύξεται;[6] 1073 Reeve again finds the sense of ἐκεῖ unclear; 1077 κακοῖς is considered unclear by some, and others insist it ought to have precisely the same meaning as in the following line (1078n.).

The children's movements have been explained in two ways. For some, they are sent in at 1053 (χωρεῖτε, παῖδες) and summoned out again at 1069 (παῖδας προσειπεῖν βούλομαι), but to this it has correctly been objected that there is no time for the command to be carried out and that it is implausible to posit a significant pause in the middle of 1069 or between 1069 and 1070 (contrast the summons

---

[5] Burnett (1998) 284 n. 42 is the latest scholar to accept Hermann's κεῖ μὴ μεθ' ἡμῶν for ἐκεῖ μεθ' ἡμῶν in 1058. This reading implies a momentary assumption that the children would be safe in Corinth despite their role in carrying the fatal gifts, followed by a realization that they would not be safe. Both the chorus (976–7) and Medea (1008–16) have already assumed that the children are doomed, and having Medea momentarily fantasize about their living on in Corinth is not an improvement over having her think briefly of taking them, as ἐκεῖ μεθ' ἡμῶν implies.

[6] The rejected alternatives, with ταῦτα continuing as subject, are: (1) ἐκφεύξεται is taken to be passive, 'these things will not be avoided' (φεύγω and compounds are not used as passive in classical Greek, and in post-classical Greek apparently only in Epicurus (or Plutarch paraphrasing him: *Mor.* 1091B) and in Josephus, who invents aor. pass. ἐφεύχθην); (2) ἐκφεύξεται is taken by Dyson (1987) to mean 'will get away ⟨from my control or from the course of my plan⟩' (the parallels are all from Demosthenes, in an idiom with πράγματα as subject and an explicit person as object).

in 895–9, with 894n.). For others, the children do not actually go in after 1053, but linger near the door and so are readily addressed again in 1069 and quickly embraced when Medea turns towards them. The proponents of deletion argue that it is not proper Euripidean dramatic technique for the command in 1053 to be left unobeyed (see Bain (1977) 24–7 and (1981) 33). But if attendants are present to guide the children (as argued in Introd. 3), there are sufficient near-parallels for their delaying execution of the command because of Medea's behaviour as she continues to speak. She herself seems to be heading toward the door, but at 1056 turns back downstage with the sharp exclamation ἃ ἅ.[7] If, on the other hand, there are no attendants left with Medea at this point, then Medea herself is the one guiding them toward the door, and her halting and moving away leaves them waiting for her to complete the action of escorting them. 1053–5 are correctly read as exit lines by the proponents of deletion: the audience does receive the impression that Medea is about to go in and carry out the killings. But just as there are retarding moments when Medea earlier thinks of poisoning her victims but postpones the action while waiting for a secure haven and when Medea offers the gifts but Jason initially objects to their being sent, so here Eur. brings the action right to the brink and then postpones Medea's entrance. She pulls away with her cry ἃ ἅ and then when the children finally are sent in she lingers on the stage, awaiting the news from the palace (1080n., 1117n.).

The children's understanding or lack of understanding of what Medea is saying should not be a serious issue. Drama is not equivalent to a documentary record of real people speaking and acting without awareness of being watched by an audience. The speeches of drama do more than communicate from one character to another. Through various non-naturalistic conventions they communicate to the audience as well, and the goals of this communication may take precedence over other goals. Moreover, children on the tragic stage are not figures of full dramatic status.[8] Eur. can thus have it both

[7] Mastronarde (1979) 110. Battezzato (1991) 429 n. 2 objects that 1056 is not addressed to the children; but it is still possible for the children, or children and attendant(s), to turn in response to the cry (the application of the dictum 'one thing at a time' by Bain (1977) 27 does not seem compelling).

[8] See especially Battezzato (1991).

ways: he can put in Medea's mouth phrases with double meanings (as in 1021–3, 1038–9, when she is directly addressing the boys), and he can have her speak less cryptically when she has turned from them, without expecting his audience to be concerned about what they hear or what they understand.

There is no denying the illogicality of the introduction at 1060–1 of the notion that the threat to the children's lives from the kinsmen of Creon is inescapable, after 1045 ἄξω παῖδας ἐκ γαίας ἐμούς and 1058 ἐκεῖ μεθ᾽ ἡμῶν. Yet this motif is firmly embedded in Medea's speech at the end of the next episode (1236–41) and recurs in Jason's mouth (1301–5). Audiences and critics are not entitled to make *a priori* assumptions that no illogicality will be committed by the playwright or that Medea is such a clear-headed and single-minded individual that it is ruinous to put this illogicality in her mouth. What we have here is at least an authorial manipulation, as Seidensticker has well explained, declining to accept a psychological interpretation.[9] It is open to an audience-member, however, to construct a character-based interpretation of the illogicality as well, and in 1061–2n. it is suggested that the harsh side of Medea is as it were rejecting the premise assumed by the soft side of Medea, projecting a tendentious view of the circumstances in an effort at self-persuasion or self-delusion. In any case, the inevitability of the children's deaths posited here prepares for the resigned attitude of the chorus in the anapaestic interlude (1081–1115) that follows Medea's monologue and facilitates the rapid movement toward action in Medea's last speech before the murders.

Some efforts have been made to overcome these difficulties by a shorter deletion than that proposed by Jachmann and Reeve. Lloyd-Jones (1980) contemplates removing 1059–63, but as Seidensticker points out there is still a transition from the inner motivation of 1049–51 to the external compulsion in 1064–5 (but not so clearly expressed as with 1059–61 preceding). Kovacs (1986) argues for removing 1056–64, leaving a bald transition from 1055 to 1065 and a clumsily brief interval between Medea's sending the children in and saying she wants to address them. Another proposed remedy for the illogicality is a reinterpretation of 1060–1 by Dyson (1987) as 'I will

---

[9] See also Scodel (1999) 161–6.

not expose my children to hostile persons (in general) to treat with dishonour (as orphaned boys in exile).' But this requires unstated assumptions that are not obvious and gives a poor sequence from 1061 to 1064.

## B. Medea *1078–80: interpretations*

Because of the history of Greek philosophy after Socrates and because of the history of reception and imitation of Euripides' play, it has often been an over-simplified commonplace of criticism that Medea is an example of the overwhelming of reason by emotion. Thus a common translation or paraphrase of 1079 θυμὸς δὲ κρείσσων τῶν ἐμῶν βουλευμάτων has been 'anger (spirit, spirited emotion) is stronger than my reason'. This is unsatisfactory for at least two reasons. First, as many critics have noted, Medea is characterized by σοφία and shows great adeptness in calculating the steps of her revenge and outwitting her opponents – she is not merely striking out at her enemies in an excess of emotion. Second, the noun βουλεύματα does not mean 'reason' or 'better judgment', but generally refers to specific plans or resolutions (as elsewhere in the play) or to the process of deliberation. In the narrower context of the monologue itself (1044, 1048) and in the broader context of the motif of Medea's cunning and planning (Introd. 2(a) and (b)), βουλεύματα ought to be associated with the plan to exact revenge from her enemies, the plan that entails the killing of her children in order to harm Jason in the extreme. Thus a sense that is consonant with the developments to this point is 'my angry passion controls my (revenge-)plans'. This meaning was advocated by Diller (1966) and has been supported by Di Benedetto (1971), Stanton (1987), Foley (1989) (also in Foley (2001)), and Gill (1996). It requires that κρείσσων be taken in the sense 'master of', 'in control of' (so that the gen. is virtually objective) rather than simply 'stronger than' with a more obvious use of the gen. of comparison (as in 965 χρυσὸς δὲ κρείσσων μυρίων λόγων βροτοῖς).

Although this interpretation has great attractions, it must be conceded that the proposed construction is hard to establish by parallels. Some parallels cited by supporters are unhelpful. Aesch. *Ag.* 60 has ὁ κρείσσων (with no gen.) used of Zeus, but this can be taken as 'master' only in the sense that Zeus is indeed stronger than all others (as the gods in general are more powerful than mortals: see Fraenkel's note, referring to the term οἱ κρείττονες used of the gods). The instance cited from *Med.* 444–5, λέκτρων ... κρείσσων, is itself subject to divergent interpretations (444–5n.) as well as differences in choice of reading. The notion that κρείσσων there means 'in control of, ruling' apparently originates in Wecklein's comment ('κρατοῦσα (im Besitze)') and is accepted by Diller (1966). But τῶν λέκτρων can be adequately explained as gen. of comparison with the normal sense 'stronger than', and this interpretation is even more secure for those who adopt Porson's σῶν λέκτρων. In *Bacch.* 879–80 χεῖρ᾽ ὑπὲρ κορυφᾶς τῶν ἐχθρῶν κρείσσω κατέχειν, 'more powerful' or 'stronger' is an adequate sense and there is no need to translate 'controlling arm' (with Diller and Stanton). Initially more promising is what may be called the 'enkratic' use of κρείσσων implying self-mastery through resistance to temptations, found especially in philosophers and moralists. Cf. Democritus 68 B 214 D–K ἀνδρεῖος οὐχ ὁ τῶν πολεμίων μόνον, ἀλλὰ καὶ ὁ τῶν ἡδονῶν κρέσσων. ἔνιοι δὲ πολίων δεσπόζουσι, γυναιξὶ δὲ δουλεύουσιν; Gorgias *Palamedes* 82 B 11a.15 D–K οὐχ οἱ κρείττονες τῶν τῆς φύσεως ἡδονῶν, ἀλλ᾽ οἱ δουλεύοντες ταῖς ἡδοναῖς; Protagoras 80 B 9 D–K μεγαλόφρονα τε καὶ ἀνδρεῖον ... καὶ ἑαυτοῦ κρείσσω; Plato *Phaedr.* 232A τοὺς δὲ μὴ ἐρῶντας, κρείττους αὑτῶν ὄντας, τὸ βέλτιστον ἀντὶ τῆς δόξης τῆς παρὰ τῶν ἀνθρώπων αἱρεῖσθαι.[10] These are unfortunately not exact parallels for *Medea* 1079 because, as Plato clearly explains in *Rep.* 430E–431B, the expression κρείττων αὑτοῦ refers to ἡδονῶν τινων καὶ ἐπιθυμιῶν ἐγκράτεια and both κρείττων αὑτοῦ and ἥττων αὑτοῦ imply a division of the person into a better and worse part and resistance to or surrender to the impulses of the inferior portion. Thus, in these phrases, 'master of' appears in the sense 'quelling the bad impulses of' (because strong enough to defeat them), which is not the sense needed in *Medea* 1079 (strong enough to determine the plans). The argument for Diller's interpretation would instead have to be that on the basis of this common usage the author of 1079 extended the meaning in a new direction, uniquely, to encompass ruling and guiding without the connotation of suppression and coercion.

---

[10] For more exx. see LSJ s.v. κρείσσων III, Ast, *Lex. Plat.* s.vv. ἥττων, κρείττων.

If 'controlling/guiding my plans' is rejected, then the sense is 'stronger than my *bouleumata*' and two options are open. For those who suspect 1056–80, the evident difference between the *bouleumata* in 1079 and those mentioned earlier by Medea is a trace of the incoherence produced by the joining of a post-Euripidean passage to a speech that originally ended at 1055. For those who deem the whole speech to be Euripidean (and not a conflation of alternative Euripidean versions), the *bouleumata* of 1079 need to be defined. Some suggest that 1044–5 βουλεύματα τὰ πρόσθεν may be taken to imply βουλεύματα τὰ νῦν, the plan to spare the children and take them with her into exile, and that at 1079 we should understand 'stronger than my plan ⟨to spare my children⟩'. Unfortunately, what has been most prominent for the past 20 lines is the other plan, the revenge plan, so it is difficult for an audience to supply this reference to τῶν ἐμῶν. Lloyd-Jones (1980) insists that the word *bouleumata* itself is 'colourless' and that here the immediate context provides its 'colour': thus, 'my calculations' in this context is a reference to 1078, Medea's awareness that she knows what harm she is about to do (and that this knowledge should in most circumstances dissuade her from action). This has been approved by Seidensticker and Kovacs,[11] but it is hard to believe that *bouleumata* can be heard as such a 'colourless' word given the wider context of the speech and Medea's earlier speeches. Another approach is to refer *bouleumata*, 'deliberations', to the entire process of internal debate carried on in the monologue, not to just one side or the other,[12] so that Medea is almost acknowledging an impasse between the two sides but saying that her angry spirit makes this impasse and the process of debate irrelevant.

---

[11] Kovacs, however, takes a different view of the context. He takes the κακά of 1077 and 1078 as Medea's pains, he accepts τολμήσω as the reading in 1078 and gives it the quasi-passive sense 'endure, undergo' instead of active 'dare to do' (as he had also done in 1051, taking τολμητέον τάδε as interrogative). Then τῶν ἐμῶν βουλευμάτων is 'my calculation ⟨of the pains I am about to cause myself⟩' and is more tightly defined by its immediate context. The translation in the Loeb is: '. . . but am overwhelmed with my pain. And I know well what pain I am about to undergo, but my wrath overbears my calculation, wrath that brings mortal men their gravest hurt'. Against this treatment of κακά and τολμήσω see 1077n., 1078n., 1051n.

[12] As argued by Alex Kozak in an unpublished paper.

Whichever of the above views is preferred, two further points deserve consideration. First, is the general assumption that Medea is clear minded and accurately self-critical at this moment justified, or could the near incoherence, or sudden shift, of the reference of τῶν ἐμῶν βουλευμάτων be a sign of psychological pressure and a form of self-delusion, a conscience-saving effort to identify the abandoned course of mercy as more essentially 'my plans' than the path to revenge? Second, would any of these interpretations be easier if the reading were τῶνδε τῶν βουλευμάτων[13] (which could easily have been corrupted in the tradition of quotation of the passage to make the lines self-standing and more widely applicable: we already have evidence of such variation in 1078)?

A completely different approach to the problems posed by 1079 was put forward by Dihle (1976)/(1977) and has been advocated strongly by Burnett (1998). On this view it is θυμός that is reinterpreted, while *bouleumata* is referred unequivocally to the revenge-plan. Dihle argues that *thumos* here is the soft emotion of Medea's love for her children, and that at the end of her speech Medea has in fact abandoned her intention to kill the children: overcome by her sufferings, she says she knows what evils she is about to suffer, but her emotion is stronger than her revenge-plans.[14] The argument that *thumos* refers to maternal love requires much special pleading with regard to this passage and others in the play,[15] but it is already refuted by the fact that 1080 'the very thing that is the cause of the greatest evils for mankind' makes no sense except with a harsh meaning of *thumos* (see 1080n. for parallels commenting on the harmfulness

---

[13] For this line-ending see *Medea* 886, Soph. *El.* 1381.

[14] On this view, the chorus' calm contemplation in the anapaestic interlude 1081–1115 reflects their understanding that Medea has given up her plan to kill her children. See 1081–1115n. for a different explanation of the lack of passionate dissuasion from the chorus at this moment. Medea's immobility at 1080, her use of καραδοκῶ in 1117, and the brevity of her rhesis at 1236–50 all work best dramatically if the audience understands at 1080 that Medea's insistence on revenge has won out in the speech just concluded.

[15] For instance, Dihle takes 1056 μὴ σύ γ' as 'don't *you* ⟨of all possible agents, since you are naturally the seat of gentle maternal love⟩', but in this idiom there is no need to give limitative force to γε and attach its force strongly to the pronoun (1056n.).

of anger). Dihle's interpretation also involves an unlikely sense of δρᾶν κακά: although the idiomatic reply δράσω τάδε may convey in certain contexts submission to a behaviour recommended by an interlocutor, even in such passages as 927 and 1019 the sense is 'I'll do this', not 'I'll endure/suffer this'; and neither this idiom nor the other usages cited in Dihle (1977) 37 n. 22 justify his claim about δρᾶν κακά. Burnett modifies Dihle's approach to the extent of interpreting θυμός not as maternal love but as the container for whatever emotion is dominant, in this case pity, which induces cowardice. She takes the meaning to be 'I understand that giving up the vengeance programme is cowardly, but my passionate heart (now filled with pity) is stronger than my plans.' Apart from doubts about taking δρᾶν κακά and θυμός in the proposed sense, this interpretation still founders on the generalization in 1080. Burnett translates the line as '– such is the cause of men's worst disasters' and cites maxims about the bane of ἀβουλία, which she takes any domination of θυμός over νοῦς or well-considered thought to be. For such a sense, we would need to emend ὅσπερ to ὅπερ.

# BIBLIOGRAPHY

The following editions and commentaries are referred to by editor's name only:

Barrett, W. S., Euripides, *Hippolytos*. Oxford 1964

Bond, G. W., Euripides, *Heracles*. Oxford 1981

Bury, R. G., Plato, *Philebus*. Cambridge 1897

Collard, C., Euripides, *Supplices*. Groningen 1975

Cropp, M., Euripides, *Electra*. Warminster 1988

Dodds, E. R., Euripides, *Bacchae*. 2nd edn, Oxford 1960

Dover, K. J., Aristophanes, *Frogs*. Oxford 1993

Diggle, J., Euripides, *Phaethon*. Cambridge 1970

Diggle, J., *Euripidis fabulae*, 3 vols., Oxford 1981–94

Easterling, P. E., Sophocles, *Trachiniae*. Cambridge 1982

Fraenkel, E., Aeschylus, *Agamemnon*. Oxford 1950

Friis Johansen, H., and Whittle, E.W., Aeschylus, *The suppliants*. Copenhagen 1980

Garvie, A. F., Aeschylus, *Choephori*. Oxford 1986

Gow, A. S. F., Theocritus. 2nd edn, Cambridge 1952

Griffith, M., Aeschylus, *Prometheus bound*. Cambridge 1983

Griffith, M., Sophocles, *Antigone*. Cambridge 1999

Heubeck, A., Homer, *Odyssey 9–12*, in Heubeck, H., West, S., and Hainsworth, J. B., *A commentary on Homer's Odyssey*, 3 vols., Oxford 1988–92

Hollis, A., Callimachus, *Hecale*. Oxford 1990

Hunter, R., Eubulus, *The fragments*. Cambridge 1983

Hunter, R., Apollonius of Rhodes, *Argonautica, Book III*. Cambridge 1989

Hutchinson, G. O., Aeschylus, *Septem contra Thebas*. Oxford 1985

Jocelyn, H. D., *The tragedies of Ennius: the fragments*. Cambridge 1967

Kovacs, D., Euripides, vol. 1 (Loeb Classical Library), Cambridge, Mass. 1994

Mastronarde, D. J., Euripides, *Phoenissae*. Cambridge 1994

Méridier, L., Euripide, tome 1: *Le Cyclope, Alceste, Médée, les Héraclides* [Budé edn]. Paris 1925

Olson, S. D., Aristophanes, *Peace*. Oxford 1998

Page, D. L., Euripides, *Medea*. Oxford 1938

Paley, F. A., Euripides, 2nd edn, 3 vols., London 1872–74

Rusten, J., Thucydides, *The Peloponnesian war, Book II*. Cambridge 1988

Sandbach, F. H., *Menandri reliquiae selectae*. Rev. edn, Oxford 1990

Seaford, R., Euripides, *Cyclops*. Oxford 1984

Stevens, P. T., Euripides, *Andromache*. Oxford 1971

Van Looy, H., Euripides, *Medea* (Teubner). Stuttgart and Leipzig 1992

Wecklein, N., Euripides, *Medea*, in *Ausgewählte Tragödien des Euripides*, 1. Bändchen, 3rd edn, Leipzig 1891

Weil, H., Euripides, *Medea*, in *Sept tragédies d'Euripide*. Paris 1879

West, M. L., Hesiod, *Theogony*. Oxford 1966

West, M. L., Hesiod, *Works and days*. Oxford 1988

Wilamowitz = Wilamowitz-Moellendorff, U. von, Euripides, *Herakles*. Berlin 1889

Willink, C. W., Euripides, *Orestes*. Oxford 1986

List of books and articles cited (in general, scholars mentioned simply as the proposers of emendations or deletions are not included in this list):

Aerts, W. J. (1965) *Periphrastica. An investigation of the use of* εἶναι *and* ἔχειν *as auxiliaries or pseudo-auxiliaries in Greek from Homer up to the present day*. Amsterdam

Alexiou, M. (1974) *The ritual lament in the Greek tradition*. Cambridge

Allan, W. (2000a) 'Euripides and the sophists: society and the theatre of war', in Sansone et al. (2000) 145–56

Allan, W. (2000b) *The* Andromache *and Euripidean tragedy*. Oxford

Andronikos, M. (1984) *Vergina: the royal tombs and the ancient city*. Athens

Arnott, W. G. (1982) 'Off-stage cries and the choral presence. Some challenges to theatrical conventions in Euripides', *Antichthon* 16: 35–43

Arnott, W. G. (1984–85) 'Alcuni osservazioni sulle convenzioni teatrali dei cori Euripidei', *Dioniso* 55: 147–55

Bain, D. (1977) *Actors and audience. A study of asides and related conventions in Greek drama*. Oxford

Bain, D. (1981) *Masters, servants and orders in Greek tragedy. A study of some aspects of dramatic technique and convention*. Manchester

Barlow, S. A. (1971) *The imagery of Euripides: a study in the dramatic use of pictorial language*. London

Battezzato, L. (1991) 'Scena e testo in Euripide, Med. 1053–1080', *RIFC* 119: 420–36

Battezzato, L. (1995) *Il monologo nel teatro di Euripide* [Scuola Normale Superiore, Pubblicazioni della classe di lettere e filosofia]. Pisa

Bergk, T. (1884) *Griechische Literaturgeschichte*, Bd. 3. Berlin

Bers, V. (1984) *Greek poetic syntax in the Classical age*. New Haven and London

Bessone, F. (1997) *P. Ovidii Nasonis Heroidum Epistula XII: Medea Iasoni* (Serie dei classici greci e latini (Biblioteca nazionale centrale di Firenze). Testi con commento filologico; nuova ser., 6). Florence

Bethe, E. (1918) *Medea-Probleme* [Berichte über die Verhandlungen der königlichen Sächsischen Gesellschaft der Wissenschaften zu Leipzig, 70, Heft 1]. Berlin

Bierl, A., Calder, W. M., and Fowler, R. L., eds. (1991) *The Prussian and the poet. The letters of Ulrich von Wilamowitz-Moellendorff to Gilbert Murray (1894–1930)*. Hildesheim

Blackman, D. (1998) 'Archaeology in Greece 1997–1998', *Archaeological Reports* 44: 1–128

Blanchard, A. (1989a) *Les débuts du codex* (Bibliologia. Elementa ad librorum studia pertinentia, 9). Turnhout

Blanchard, A. (1989b) 'Choix antiques et codex', in Blanchard (1989a) 181–90

Blundell, M. W. (1989) *Helping friends and harming enemies. A study in Sophocles and Greek ethics*. Cambridge

Boedeker, D. (1991) 'Euripides' Medea and the vanity of ΛΟΓΟΙ', *CP* 86: 95–112

Boedeker, D. (1997) 'Becoming Medea: assimilation in Euripides', in Clauss and Johnston (1997) 127–48

Bogaert, R. (1976) 'L'essai des monnaies dans l'antiquité', *Revue Belge de numismatique et de sigilographie* 122: 5–34

Bolkestein, H. (1949) 'Varia Tragica', *Mnemosyne* ser. 4, 2: 177–93

Bongie, E. B. (1977) 'Heroic elements in the *Medea* of Euripides', *TAPA* 107: 27–56

Breitenbach, W. (1934) *Untersuchungen zur Sprache der Euripideischen Lyrik* (Tübinger Beiträge zur Altertumswissenschaft, Heft 20). Stuttgart

Burnett, A. P. (1971) *Catastrophe survived. Euripides' plays of mixed reversal*. Oxford

Burnett, A. P. (1973) 'Medea and the tragedy of revenge', *CP* 68: 1–24

Burnett, A. P. (1998) *Revenge in Attic and later tragedy*. Berkeley and Los Angeles

Burnett, A. P. (1985) '*Rhesus*: are smiles allowed?', in P. Burian, ed., *Directions in Euripidean criticism* (Durham N.C.) 13–51

Buttrey, T. V. (1958) 'Accident and design in Euripides' *Medea*', *AJP* 79: 1–17

Caiazza, A. (1989–93) 'Medea: fortuna di un mito' (parti 1–4), *Dioniso* 59: 9–84, 60: 82–118, 63: 121–41, 64: 155–66

Cairns, D. L. (1993) *Aidos: the psychology and ethics of honour and shame in ancient Greek literature*. Oxford

Cameron, A. (1995) *Callimachus and his critics*. Princeton

Canter, H. V. (1930) 'The figure ΑΔΥΝΑΤΟΝ in Greek and Latin Poetry', *AJP* 51: 32–41

Carden, R. (1974) *The papyrus fragments of Sophocles: an edition with prolegomena and commentary* [Texte und Kommentare, Bd. 7]. Berlin and New York

Carter, L. B. (1986) *The quiet Athenian*. Oxford

Casson, L. (1971) *Ships and seamanship in the ancient world*. Princeton

Cavallo, G. (1989) 'Codice e storia dei testi greci antichi. Qualche riflessioni sulla fase primitiva del fenomeno', in Blanchard (1989a) 169–80

Clauss, J., and Johnston, S. I. (1997) *Medea. Essays on Medea in myth, literature, philosophy, and art*. Princeton

Clay, D. M. (1958–60) *A formal analysis of the vocabularies of Aeschylus, Sophocles and Euripides*, Part 1 (Minneapolis 1960) and Part 2 (Athens 1958)

Clayman, D. L. (1987) 'Sigmatism in Greek poetry', *TAPA* 117: 69–84

Cohen, D. (1989) 'Seclusion, separation, and the status of women in classical Athens', *Greece and Rome* 36: 3–15

Cohn-Haft, L. (1995) 'Divorce in classical Athens', *JHS* 115 (1995) 1–14

Collard, C., Cropp, M. J., and Lee, K. H., eds. (1995– ) *Euripides. Selected fragmentary plays*, with introductions, translations, and commentaries. Warminster

Collinge, N. E. (1962) 'Medea ex machina', *CP* 57: 170–2

Conacher, D. J. (1998) *Euripides and the sophists. Some dramatic treatments of philosophical ideas*. London

Congdon, L. O. K. (1981) *Caryatid mirrors of ancient Greece*. Mainz am Rhein

Croally, N. T. (1994) *Euripidean polemic: the* Trojan Women *and the function of tragedy*. Cambridge

Cropp, M., and Fick, G. (1985) *Resolutions and chronology in Euripides. The fragmentary tragedies* [BICS Suppl. 43]. London

Csapo, E., and Slater, W. J. (1995) *The context of ancient drama*. Ann Arbor

Cunningham, M. P. (1954) 'Medea ἀπὸ μηχανῆς', *CP* 49: 151–60

Dale, A. M. (1968) *The lyric metres of Greek drama*. 2nd edn, Cambridge

Dearden, C. (1999) 'Plays for export', *Phoenix* 53: 222–48

Demand, N. H. (1994) *Birth, death, and motherhood in classical Greece*. Baltimore

Denniston, J. D. (1936) 'Pauses in the tragic senarius', *CQ* 30: 73–9

Detienne, M., and Vernant, J.-P. (1978) *Cunning intelligence in Greek culture and society*. Atlantic Highlands, N.J.

Deubner, L. (1941) *Ololyge und Verwandtes* (Abhandlungen der Preussischen Akademie der Wissenschaften, Philosophisch-historische Klasse, 1941, Nr. 1)

Devine, A. M., and Stephens, L. D. (1984) *Language and metre. Resolution, Porson's bridge and their prosodic basis* [American Classical Studies, 12]. Chico, Calif.

Devine, A. M., and Stephens, L. D. (1994) *The prosody of Greek speech*. Oxford

Devine, A. M., and Stephens, L. D. (2000) *Discontinuous syntax: hyperbaton in Greek*. Oxford

Di Benedetto, V. (1971) *Euripide: teatro e società*. Turin

Di Benedetto, V., and Medda, E. (1997) *La tragedia sulla scena: la tragedia greca in quanto spettacolo teatrale*. Turin

Diggle, J. (1981) *Studies on the text of Euripides*. Oxford

Diggle, J. (1983) 'The manuscripts and text of *Medea*: 1. The manuscripts', *CQ* 33: 339–57

Diggle, J. (1994) *Euripidea. Collected essays*. Oxford

Dihle, A. (1976) 'Euripides' Medea und ihre Schwestern im europäischen Drama', *Antike und Abendland* 22: 175–84

Dihle, A. (1977) *Euripides' Medea* [Sitzungsber. Heidelb. Akad. der Wissenschaften, 5]. Heidelberg

Diller, H. (1966) 'θυμὸς δὲ κρείσσων τῶν ἐμῶν βουλευμάτων', *Hermes* 94: 267–75 [= *Kleine Schriften zur antiken Literatur* (Munich 1971) 359–68]

Dillon, J. M. (1997) 'Medea among the philosophers', in Clauss and Johnston (1997) 211–18

Dodds, E. R. (1952) 'Three notes on the Medea', *Humanitas* (Coimbra) 4: 13–18

Dover, K. J. (1974) *Greek popular morality in the time of Plato and Aristotle*. Oxford and Berkeley

Dräger, P. (1993) *Argo pasimelousa. Der Argonautenmythos in der griechischen und römischen Literatur.* Teil I: Theos aitios [Palingenesia 43] Stuttgart

Duchemin, J. (1945) *L'agōn dans la tragédie grecque*. Paris

Dunkle, J. R. (1969) 'The Aegeus episode and the theme of Euripides' *Medea*', *TAPA* 100: 97–107

Dunn, F. M. (1994) 'Euripides and the rites of Hera Akraia', *GRBS* 35: 103–15

Dutoit, E. (1936) *Le thème de l'adynaton dans la poésie antique*. Paris

Dyson, M. (1987) 'Euripides, *Medea* 1056–80', *GRBS* 28: 23–34

Dyson, M. (1988) 'Euripides, *Medea* 926–31', *CQ* 38: 324–7

Easterling, P. E. (1977) 'The infanticide in Euripides Medea', *Yale Classical Studies* 25: 177–91

Easterling, P. E. (1985) 'Anachronism in Greek tragedy', *JHS* 105: 1–10

Easterling, P. E. (1987) 'Women in tragic space', *BICS* 34: 15–26

Easterling, P. E. (1994) 'Euripides outside Athens: a speculative note', *ICS* 19: 73–80

Easterling, P. E., ed. (1997a) *The Cambridge companion to Greek tragedy*. Cambridge

Easterling, P. E. (1997b) 'From repertoire to canon', in Easterling (1997a) 211–27

Eden, P. T. (1988) 'Two notes on Euripides', *CQ* 38: 560–1

Ehrenberg, V. (1947) 'Polypragmosyne', *JHS* 67: 46–67

Eitrem, S. (1927) *Beiträge zur griechischen Religionsgeschichte* 3 vols. Kristiania

Erdmann, W. (1934) *Die Ehe im alten Griechenland* (Münchener Beiträge zur Papyrusforschung und antiken Rechtsgeschichte, Heft 20). Munich

Ewans, M. (1995) *Aeschylus: Oresteia*. London

Fairweather, J. A. (1974) 'Fiction in the biographies of ancient writers', *Ancient Society* 5: 231–75

Fantham, E., et al. (1994) *Women in the classical world: image and text.* Oxford

Fehling, D. (1969) *Die Wiederholungsfiguren und ihr Gebrauch bei den Griechen vor Gorgias*. Berlin

Finley, J. H. (1967) *Three essays on Thucydides*. Cambridge, Mass.

Fisher, N. R. E. (1992) *Hybris: a study in the values of honour and shame in ancient Greece*. Warminster

Flory, S. (1978) 'Medea's right hand. Promises and revenge', *TAPA* 108: 69–74

Foley, H. P. (1981) 'The conception of women in Athenian drama', in Foley, H. P., ed., *Reflections of women in antiquity* (New York 1981) 127–67

Foley, H. P. (1985) *Ritual irony. Poetry and sacrifice in Euripides*. Ithaca, N.Y.

Foley, H. P. (1989) 'Medea's divided self', *Classical Antiquity* 8: 61–85

Foley, H. P. (2001) *Female acts in Greek tragedy*. Princeton

Fontenrose, J. (1978) *The Delphic oracle: its responses and operations with a catalogue of responses*. Berkeley

Fraenkel, E. (1965) Review of Ritchie (1964) in *Gnomon* 37: 228–41

Fraser, P. M. (1972) *Ptolemaic Alexandria*, 3 vols. Oxford

Friedrich, W.-H. (1968) 'Medeas Rache', in Schwinge, E.-R., ed., *Euripides* [Wege der Forschung, 89] (Darmstadt) 177–237

Friis Johansen, H. (1959) *General reflection in tragic rhesis*. Copenhagen

Gantz, T. (1993) *Early Greek myth. A guide to literary and artistic sources*. Baltimore

Garlan, Y. (1988) *Slavery in ancient Greece*. Ithaca

Garland, R. (1985) *The Greek way of death*. London and Ithaca, N.Y.

Garland, R. (1990) *The Greek way of life from conception to old age*. London and Ithaca, N.Y.

Gentili, B. (1972) 'Il 'letto insaziato' di Medea e il tema dell' *adikia* a livello amoroso nei lirici (Saffo, Teognide) e nella *Medea* di Euripide', *Studi classici e orientali* 21: 60–72

Gibert, J. (1995) *Change of mind in Greek tragedy* [Hypomnemata 108] Göttingen

Gibert, J. (1997) 'Euripides' "Hippolytus" plays: which came first?', *CQ* 47: 85–97

Gigon, O. (1987) *Aristotelis Opera, volumen tertium: librorum deperditorum fragmenta*. Berlin and New York

Gill, C. (1983) 'Did Chrysippus understand Medea?', *Phronesis* 28: 136–49

Gill, C. (1996) *Personality in Greek epic, tragedy, and philosophy: the self in dialogue*. Oxford

Goheen, R. F. (1951) *The imagery of Sophocles'* Antigone. Princeton

Goldhill, S. (1986) *Reading Greek tragedy*. Cambridge

Gould, J. (1973) 'Hiketeia', *JHS* 93: 74–103 [reprinted in his *Myth, ritual, memory, and exchange: essays in Greek literature and culture*, Oxford 2001, 22–77]

Gould, J. (1980) 'Law, custom and myth: aspects of the social position of women in classical Athens', *JHS* 100: 38–59 [reprinted in his *Myth, ritual, memory, and exchange: essays in Greek literature and culture*, Oxford 2001, 112–73]

Gow, A. S. F., and Page, D. L. (1968) *The Greek anthology: the Garland of Philip*, 2 vols. Cambridge

Goward, B. (1999) *Telling tragedy: narrative technique in Aeschylus, Sophocles and Euripides*. London

Graf, F. (1997) 'Medea, the enchantress from afar: remarks on a well-known myth', in Clauss and Johnston (1997) 21–43

Griffith, M. (1977) *The authenticity of* Prometheus Bound. Cambridge

Griffith, M. (1978) 'Euripides' *Alkestis* 636–41', *HSCP* 82: 83–6

Griffith, M. (1990) 'Contest and contradiction in early Greek poetry', in Griffith and Mastronarde (1990) 185–207

Griffith, M. (1995) 'Brilliant dynasts: power and politics in the *Oresteia*', *Classical Antiquity* 14: 62–129

Griffith, M. (1998) 'The king and eye: the rule of the father in Greek tragedy', *PCPS* 44: 20–84

Griffith, M. (2001) 'Antigone and her sister(s): embodying women in Greek tragedy', in Lardinois and McClure (2001) 117–36

Griffith, M., and Mastronarde, D. J., eds. (1990) *Cabinet of the muses. Essays on classical and comparative literature in honor of Thomas G. Rosenmeyer*. Atlanta

Guiraud, C. (1962) *La phrase nominale en grec d'Homere à Euripide* [Études et commentaires 42]. Paris

Günther, H.-C. (1996) *Exercitationes Sophocleae* [Hypomnemata 109]. Göttingen

Hall, E. (1989) *Inventing the barbarian: Greek self-definition through tragedy*. Oxford

Hall, E. (1997) 'The sociology of Athenian tragedy', in Easterling (1997a) 93–126

Hall, E. (2000) '*Medea* on the eighteenth-century London stage', in Hall, Macintosh, and Taplin (2000) 49–74

Hall, E., Macintosh, F., and Taplin, O., eds. (2000) *Medea in performance 1500–2000*. Oxford

Hamilton, R. (1987) 'Cries within and the tragic skene', *AJP* 108: 585–99

Harrison, A. R. W. (1968) *The law of Athens. The family and property*. Oxford

Harrison, S. J. (1986) 'A note on Euripides, *Medea* 12', *CQ* 36: 260

Haslam, M. W. (1979) 'O suitably-attired-in-leather-boots. Interpolations in Greek tragedy', in Bowersock, G. W., et al., eds., *Arktouros. Hellenic studies presented to Bernard M. W. Knox on the occasion of his 65th birthday* (Berlin) 91–100

Hill, B. H. (1964) *Corinth*, vol. I, part 3: *The Springs*. Princeton

Hunter, R. L. (1981) 'P. Lit. Lond. 77 and tragic burlesque in Attic comedy', *ZPE* 41: 19–24

Hunter, V. J. (1997) *Policing Athens: social control in the Attic lawsuits, 420–320 B.C.* Princeton

Huxley, G. (1969) *Greek epic poetry from Eumelos to Panyassis*. London

Irwin, E. (1974) *Colour terms in Greek poetry*. Toronto

Irwin, T. H. (1983) 'Euripides and Socrates', *CP* 78: 183–97

Itsumi, K. (1984) 'The glyconic in tragedy', *CQ* 34: 66–82

Itsumi, K. (1991–93) 'Enoplian in tragedy', *BICS* 38: 242–61

Jachmann, G. (1936) 'Binneninterpolationen II', *Nachrichten von der Gesellschaft der Wissenshaften zu Göttingen*, Philologisch-historische Klasse, Fachgruppe I, n. F., Bd. I, Nr. 9 (pp. 185–215)

Jameson, M. (1990a) 'Private space and the Greek city', in Murray, O., and Price, S., eds., *The Greek city from Homer to Alexander* (Oxford) 171–95

Jameson, M. (1990b) 'Domestic space in the Greek city-state', in Kent, S., ed., *Domestic architecture and the use of space: an interdisciplinary cross-cultural study* (Cambridge) 92–113

Johnston, S. I. (1997) 'Corinthian Medea and the cult of Hera Akraia', in Clauss and Johnston (1997)

Johnstone, H. W. (1980) 'Pankoinon as a rhetorical figure in Greek tragedy', *Glotta* 58: 49–62

Jong, I. J. F. de (1991) *Narrative in drama: the art of the Euripidean messenger-speech* [Mnemosyne Suppl. 116]. Leiden and New York

Jouan, F., and Van Looy, H. (1998) *Euripide*. Tome VIII Fragments Ire Partie. Paris

Jouan, F., and Van Looy, H. (2000) *Euripide*. Tome VIII Fragments 2e Partie. Paris

Just, R. (1989) *Women in Athenian life and law*. New York and London

Kaimio, M. (1970) *The chorus of Greek drama within the light of the person and number used* (Commentationes Humanarum Litterarum 46). Helsinki

Kaimio, M. (1988) *Physical contact in Greek tragedy: a study of stage conventions* (Annales Academiae Scientiarum Fennicae, ser. B, tom. 244). Helsinki

Kerrigan, J. (1996) *Revenge tragedy: Aeschylus to Armageddon*. Oxford

Kienzle, E. (1936) *Der Lobpreis von Städtern und Ländern in der älteren griechischen Dichtung*. Basle

Klette, T. (1875) *Quid de iterata Medeae Euripideae editione sit iudicandum*. Leipzig

Knox, B. M. W. (1964) *The heroic temper: studies in Sophoclean tragedy*. Berkeley and Los Angeles

Knox, B. M. W. (1977) 'The *Medea* of Euripides', *Yale Classical Studies* 25: 193–225 [reprinted in his *Word and action: essays on the ancient theater* (Baltimore 1979) 295–322]

Köhler, W. (1913) *Die Versbrechung bei den griechischen Tragikern.* Darmstadt

Kovacs, D. (1986) 'On Medea's great monologue (E. *Med.* 1021–80)', *CQ* 36: 343–52

Kovacs, D. (1987) 'Treading the circle warily. Literary criticism and the text of Euripides', *TAPA* 117: 257–70

Kovacs, D. (1993) 'Zeus in Euripides' *Medea*', *AJP* 114: 45–70

Kovacs, D. (1994) *Euripidea* [Mnemosyne Suppl. 132]. Leiden

Kullmann, W. (1987) 'Deutung und Bedeutung der Götter bei Euripides', in W. Kullmann et al., *Mythos. Deutung und Bedeutung* [Innsbrucker Beitr. zur Kulturwissenschaft. Dies Philologici Aenipontani, 5] (Innsbruck) 7–22

Kurke, L. V. (1992) 'The politics of ἁβροσύνη in archaic Greece', *Classical Antiquity* 11: 91–120

Kurke, L. V. (1999) *Coins, bodies, games and gold: the politics of meaning in archaic Greece.* Princeton

Kurtz, W. (1985) *Die bildliche Ausdrucksweise in den Tragödien des Euripides* [Heuremata, 8]. Amsterdam

Labarbe, J. (1980) 'La prière "contestataire" dans la poésie grecque', in Limet, H., and Ries, J. eds., *L'expérience de la prière dans les grandes réligions* [Homo religiosus, 5]. Louvain-la-neuve

Lacey, W. K. (1968) *The family in classical Greece.* London and Ithaca, N.Y.

Lamb, W. (1969) *Ancient Greek and Roman bronzes*, rev. L. K. Congdon. Chicago

Lanérès, N. (1994) *La phrase nominale en grec ancien: étude sur la langue de l'*Iliade. Lille

Lardinois, A., and McClure, L., eds. (2001) *Making silence speak: women's voices in Greek literature and society.* Princeton

Lattimore, R. (1962) *Themes in Greek and Latin epitaphs.* Urbana

Lebeck, A. (1971) *The* Oresteia: *a study in language and structure.* Cambridge, Mass.

Lee, K. H. (1968) 'Influence of metre on tragic vocabulary', *Glotta* 46: 54–6

Lee, K. H. (1971) 'ΒΑΛΛΩ compounds in the tragedians', *AJP* 92: 312–15

Lefkowitz, M. R. (1979) 'The Euripides Vita', *GRBS* 20: 187–210

Lefkowitz, M. R. (1981) *The lives of the Greek poets*. Baltimore and London

Lefkowitz, M. R. (1987) 'Impiety and atheism in Euripides' dramas', *CQ* 39: 70–82

Lefkowitz, M. R. (1989) 'Was Euripides an atheist?', *SIFC* 5: 149–66

Lendle, O. (1995) 'Überlegungen zum Bühnenkran', in Pöhlmann (1995a) 165–72

Leo, F. (1908) *Der Monolog im Drama: Ein Beitrag zur griechisch-römischen Poetik*. Berlin

Leo, F. (1912) *Plautinische Forschungen zur Kritik und Geschichte der Komödie*. 2. Aufl. Berlin

Lesky, A. (1948) 'Aia', *Wiener Studien* 63: 22–68

Ley, G., and Ewans, M. (1985) 'The orchestra as acting area in Greek tragedy', *Ramus* 14: 75–84

Lloyd, G. E. R. (1962) 'Right and left in Greek philosophy', *JHS* 82: 56–66

Lloyd, G. E. R. (1966) *Polarity and analogy*. Cambridge

Lloyd, M. (1992) *The agon in Euripides*. Oxford

Lloyd, M. (1999) 'The tragic aorist', *CQ* 49: 24–45

Lloyd-Jones, H. (1980) 'Euripides, *Medea* 1056–1080', *Würzburger Jahrbücher für die Altertumswissenschaft*, n.F. 6a: 51–9

Lloyd-Jones, H. (1983) *The justice of Zeus*. Rev. edn, Berkeley and Los Angeles

Long, A. A. (1968) *Language and thought in Sophocles; a study of abstract nouns and poetic technique*. London

Loraux, N. (1993) *The children of Athena. Athenian ideas about citizenship and the division between the sexes*, transl. by C. Levine. Princeton

Lord, L. E. (1936–37) 'The touchstone', *CJ* 32: 428–31

Luppe, W. (1995) 'Ein neuer früher "Medeia"-Papyrus P. Berol. 21 257', *Archiv für Papyrusforschung* 41: 34–9

Macintosh, F. (2000) 'Introduction: the performer in performance', in Hall, Macintosh, and Taplin (2000) 1–31

Manuwald, B. (1983) 'Der Mord an den Kindern', *Wiener Studien* 19: 27–61

Marshall, F. H. (1911) *Catalogue of the jewellery, Greek, Etruscan, and Roman, in the Departments of Antiquities, British Museum*. London

Mastronarde, D. J. (1979) *Contact and discontinuity. Some conventions of speech and action on the Greek tragic stage* (University of California Publications: Classical Studies, 21). Berkeley and Los Angeles

Mastronarde, D. J. (1986) 'The optimistic rationalist in Euripides: Theseus, Jocasta, Teiresias', in M. Cropp et al., eds., *Greek tragedy and its legacy: Essays presented to Desmond Conacher* (Calgary) 201–11

Mastronarde, D. J. (1990) 'Actors on high: the skene roof, the crane, and the gods in Attic drama', *Classical Antiquity* 9: 247–94

Mastronarde, D. J. (1998) 'Il coro euripideo: autorità e integrazione', *Quaderni Urbinati di Cultura Classica* 60: 55–80

Mastronarde, D. J. (1999) 'Knowledge and authority in the choral voice of Euripidean tragedy', *Syllecta Classica* 10: 87–104

Mastronarde, D. J. (2000) 'Euripidean tragedy and genre: the terminology and its problems', in Sansone et al. (2000) 23–39

Mastronarde, D. J. (forthcoming) 'Euripidean tragedy and theology', *Seminari romani di cultura greca*

McClure, L. (1999a) *Spoken like a woman: speech and gender in Athenian drama.* Princeton

McClure, L. (1999b) ' "The worst husband": discourses of praise and blame in Euripides' *Medea*', *CP* 94: 373–94

McDermott, E. (1989) *Euripides' Medea: the incarnation of disorder.* University Park, Pennsylvania

McDonald, M. (1983) *Euripides in cinema: the heart made visible.* Philadelphia

McDonald, M. (1992) *Ancient sun, modern light: Greek drama on the modern stage.* Columbia

McDonald, M. (1997) 'Medea as politician and diva: riding the dragon into the future', in Clauss and Johnston (1997) 297–323

Meridor, R. (1986) 'Euripides, *Medea* 639', *CQ* 100: 95–100

Mezzabotta, M. R. (1994) 'Jason and Orpheus; Euripides *Medea* 543', *AJP* 115: 47–50

Michelini, A. N. (1989) 'Neophron and Euripides' *Medeia* 1056–80', *TAPA* 119: 115–35

Mikalson, J. D. (1989) 'Unanswered prayers in Greek tragedy', *JHS* 109: 81–98

Mikalson, J. D. (1991) *Honor thy gods: popular religion in Greek tragedy.* Chapel Hill and London

Miller, S. G. (2000) 'Naked democracy', in Flensted-Jensen, P., Nielsen, T. H., and Rubinstein, L., eds., *Polis and politics: studies in ancient Greek history presented to Mogens Herman Hansen* (Copenhagen 2000) 277–96

Mimoso-Ruiz, D. (1982) *Médée antique et moderne: aspects rituels et socio-politiques d'un mythe*. Paris

Moline, J. (1975) 'Euripides, Socrates, and virtue', *Hermes* 103: 46–67

Moretti, J.-C. (2000) 'The theater of the sanctuary of Dionysus Eleuthereus in late fifth-century Athens', in Sansone et al. (2000) 377–98

Moreau, A. (1994) *Le mythe de Jason et Médée. Le va-nu-pied et la sorcière.* Paris

Most, G. W. (1999) 'Two problems in the third stasimon of Euripides' *Medea*', *CP* 94: 20–35

Mueller, M. (2001) 'The language of reciprocity in Euripides' *Medea*', *AJP* 123: 471–504

Müller, G. (1951) 'Interpolationen in der Medea des Euripides', *Studi italiani di filologia classica* 25: 65–82

Nevett, L. C. (1999) *House and society in the ancient Greek world.* Cambridge

Newton, R. M. (1985) 'Ino in Euripides' *Medea*', *AJP* 106: 496–502

Oakley, J. H., and Sinos, R. H. (1993) *The wedding in ancient Athens.* Madison

O'Neal, J. L. (1986) 'The semantic usage of τύραννος and related words', *Antichthon* 20: 26–40

Pack, R. A. (1967) *The Greek and Latin literary texts from Greco-Roman Egypt.* 2nd edn, Ann Arbor

Padel, R. (1992) *In and out of mind. Greek images of the tragic self.* Princeton

Page, D. L. (1934) *Actors' interpolations in Greek tragedy.* Oxford

Page, D. L. (1955) *Sappho and Alcaeus.* Oxford

Parke, H. W., and Wormell, D. E. W. (1956), *The Delphic oracle*, 2 vols. Oxford

Parker, R. (1983) *Miasma: pollution and purification in early Greek religion.* Oxford

Pelliccia, H. (1995) *Mind, body, and speech in Homer and Pindar* [Hypomnemata 107]. Göttingen

Petrochilos, N. (1974) *Roman attitudes to the Greeks.* Athens

Pfeiffer, R. (1934) *Die neuen ΔΙΗΓΗΣΕΙΣ zu Kallimachosgedichten* [Sitzungsberichte der Bayerische Akademie der Wissenschaften, Philosophisch-historische Abt., 1934, Heft 10]. Munich

Pfeiffer, R. (1968) *History of classical scholarship from the beginnings to the end of the Hellenistic age.* Oxford

Pfister, M. (1988) *The theory and analysis of drama.* Cambridge

Pickard-Cambridge, A. W. (1968) *The dramatic festivals of Athens.* 2nd edn, revised by J. Gould and D. M. Lewis. Oxford

Pöhlmann, E., et al. (1995a) *Studien zur Bühnendichtung und zum Theaterbau der Antike* (Studien zur klassichen Philologie, Band 93). Frankfurt am Main

Pöhlmann, E. (1995b) 'Der Chor der Tragödie an den Grenzen der Bühnenkonventionen des 5. Jh.', in Pöhlmann (1995a) 63–72

Pulleyn, S. (1997) *Prayer in Greek religion.* Oxford

Rabinowitz, N. (1993) *Anxiety veiled: Euripides and the traffic in women.* Ithaca

Race, W. H. (1981) 'The word καιρός in Greek drama', *TAPA* 111: 197–213

Reeve, M. D. (1972) 'Euripides, *Medea* 1021–1080', *CQ* 22: 51–61

Rehm, R. (1989) 'Medea and the λόγος of the heroic', *Eranos* 87: 97–115

Rehm, R. (1994) *Marriage to death: the conflation of wedding and funeral rituals in Greek tragedy.* Princeton

Reid, J. D. (1993) *The Oxford guide to classical mythology in the arts, 1300–1990s.* Oxford

Reinhardt, K. (1957) 'Die Sinneskrise bei Euripides', *Die neue Rundschau* 68: 615–46

Renehan, R. (1976) *Studies in Greek texts: critical observations to Homer, Plato, Euripides, Aristophanes and other authors* (Hypomnemata 43). Göttingen

Revermann, M. (2000) 'Euripides, tragedy and Macedon: some conditions of reception', in Sansone et al. (2000) 451–67

Rickert, G. A. (1987) 'Akrasia and Euripides' *Medea*', *HSCP* 91: 91–117

Ritchie, W. (1964) *The authenticity of the* Rhesus *of Euripides.* Cambridge

Roberts, D. (1987) 'Parting words. Final lines in Sophocles and Euripides', *CQ* 37: 51–64

Rohde, E. (1925) *Psyche; the cult of souls and belief in immortality among the Greeks.* (translation of *Psyche: Seelencult und Unsterblichkeitsglaube der Griechen*, 2nd edn 1898) London

Rose, V. (1863) *Aristoteles pseudepigraphus.* Leipzig

Rosen, R. (1988) *Old comedy and the iambographic tradition* [American Classical Studies, 19]. Atlanta

Roux, G. (1972) 'Notes en marge de Médée', REG 85: 39–46

Rudhardt, J. (1958) *Notions fondamentales de la pensée religieuse et actes constitutifs du culte dans la Grèce classique.* Geneva

Sansone, D. (1984) 'On hendiadys in Greek', *Glotta* 62: 16–25

Sansone, D., et al., eds. (2000) *Euripides and tragic theatre in the late fifth century* [= *Illinois Classical Studies* 24–5 (1999–2000)]. Champaign, Illinois

Schadewaldt, W. (1926) *Monolog und Selbstgespräch* [Neue Philologische Untersuchungen 2]. Berlin

Schein, S. L. (1990) '*Philia* in Euripides' *Medea*', in Griffith and Mastronarde (1990) 57–73

Schiassi, G. (1955) 'Parodia e travestimento mitico nella commedia attica di mezzo', *Rendiconti dell' Istituto Lombardo de scienze e lettere* 88: 99–120

Schmid, W. (1940) *Die griechische Literatur zur Zeit der attischen Hegemonie nach dem Eingreifen der Sophistik* [= Schmid, W., and Stählin, O., *Geschichte der griechischen Literatur*, 1. Teil, 3. Band]. Munich

Scodel, R. (1999) *Credible impossibilities: conventions and strategies of verisimilitude in Homer and Greek tragedy* [Beiträge zur Altertumskunde, 122]. Stuttgart and Leipzig

Scodel, R. (2000) 'Verbal performance and Euripidean rhetoric', in Sansone et al. (2000) 129–44

Scullion, S. (1994) *Three studies in Athenian dramaturgy* (Beiträge zur Altertumskunde 25). Stuttgart

Scullion, S. (2000) 'Tradition and invention in Euripidean aetiology', in Sansone et al. (2000) 217–33

Seaford, R. (1987) 'The tragic wedding', *JHS* 107: 106–30

Seaford, R. (1998) 'Tragic money', *JHS* 118: 119–39

Séchan, L. (1926) *Études sur la tragédie grecque dans ses rapports avec la céramique.* Paris

Seidensticker, B. (1990) 'Euripides, *Medea* 1056–1080', in Griffith and Mastronarde (1990) 89–102

Sentieri, A. de Cavazzani (1919) 'Sulla figura dell' ἀδύνατον', *Athenaeum* 7: 179–84

Sfyroeras, P. (1994) 'The ironies of salvation: the Aigeus scene in Euripides' *Medea*', *CJ* 90: 125–42

Simon, E. (1954) 'Die Typen der Medeadarstellung in der antiken Kunst', *Gymnasium* 61: 203–27

Sinn, U. (1990) 'Das Heraion von Perachora. Eine sakrale Schutzzone in der korinthischen Peraia', *Mitteilungen des deutschen archäologischen Instituts. Athenische Abteilung* 105: 53–116

Snell, B. (1948) 'Das frühste Zeugnis über Sokrates', *Philologus* 97: 125–34

Snyder, J. M. (1989) *The woman and the lyre: women writers in classical Greece and Rome*. Carbondale, Illinois

Sourvinou-Inwood, C. (1979) *Theseus as son and stepson. A tentative illustration of Greek mythological mentality* [BICS Supplement 40]. London

Sourvinou-Inwood, C. (1997) 'Medea at a shifting distance: images and Euripidean tragedy', in Clauss and Johnston (1997) 253–96

Stanley-Porter, D. P. (1973) 'Mute actors in the tragedies of Euripides', *BICS* 20: 68–93

Stanton, G. R. (1987) 'The end of Medea's monologue: Euripides, *Medea* 1078–1080', *Rheinisches Museum* 130: 97–106

Stevens, P. T. (1956) 'Euripides and the Athenians', *JHS* 76: 87–94

Stevens, P. T. (1976) *Colloquial expressions in Euripides* [Hermes Einzelschriften 38]. Wiesbaden

Stewart, A. (1998) 'Nuggets: mining the texts again', *AJA* 102: 271–82

Stillwell, R. (1930) *Corinth*, vol. III, part 1: *Acrocorinth*. Cambridge, Mass.

Stinton, T. C. W. (1990) *Collected papers on Greek tragedy*. Oxford

Stroud, R. S. (1974) 'An Athenian law on silver coinage', *Hesperia* 43: 157–88

Strubbe, J. (1997) ΑΡΑΙ ΕΠΙΤΥΜΒΙΟΙ: *Imprecations against desecrations of the grave in the Greek epitaphs of Asia Minor. A catalogue* [Inschriften griechischer Städte aus Kleinasien, Bd. 52]. Bonn

Synodinou, K. (1977) *On the concept of slavery in Euripides*. Ioannina

Szlezák, T. A. (1990) 'Hikesie und Bitte in Euripides' *Medea*', *Orientalia* 59: 280–97

Taplin, O. (1977) *The stagecraft of Aeschylus. The dramatic use of exits and entrances in Greek tragedy*. Oxford

Taplin, O. (1993) *Comic angels and other approaches to Greek drama through vase-paintings*. Oxford

Tessier, A. (1975) 'Per un inventario di docmi ripetitivi in Euripide', *Bolletino dell' Istituto di Filologia Greca* (Padova) 2: 130–43

Thompson, E. A. (1944) 'Neophron and Euripides' *Medea*', *CQ* 38: 10–14

Thomson, G. (1939) 'The postponement of interrogatives in Attic drama', *CQ* 33: 147–52

Tozer, F. (1893) *Selections from Strabo*. Oxford

Turner, E. G. (1987) *Greek manuscripts of the ancient world*. 2nd edn, revised and enlarged by P. J. Parsons (BICS Suppl. 46). London

Verilhac, A.-M., and Vial, C. (1998) *Le mariage grec du VIe siècle av. J. C. à l'époque d'Auguste* [BCH Suppl. 32]. Athens and Paris

Vermeule, E. (1979) *Aspects of death in early Greek art and poetry*. Berkeley and Los Angeles

Vernant, J.-P. (1981) 'Tensions and ambiguities in Greek tragedy', in Vernant, J.-P. and Vidal-Naquet, P., *Tragedy and myth in ancient Greece* (Atlantic Heights, N.J. 1981) 6–27 [translated from *Mythe et tragédie en Grèce ancienne* (Paris 1972)]

Vogt, J. (1965) *Sklaverei und Humanität. Studien zur antiken Sklaverei und ihrer Erforschung* [Historia Einzelschriften, 8]. Wiesbaden

von Fritz, K. (1959) 'Die Entwicklung der Iason-Medea-Sage und die Medea des Euripides', *Antike und Abendland* 8: 33–106 [reprinted in his *Antike und moderne Tragödie: neun Abhandlungen* (Berlin 1962) 322–429]

Voutiras, E. (1998) *ΔΙΟΝΥΣΟΦΩΝΤΟΣ ΓΑΜΟΙ. Marital life and magic in fourth century Pella*. Amsterdam

Watson, L. (1991) *Arae. The curse poetry of antiquity*. Leeds

West, M. L. (1974) *Studies in Greek elegy and iambus* [Untersuchungen zur antiken Literatur und Geschichte, 14]. Berlin and New York

West, M. L. (1982) *Greek metre*. Oxford

West, M. L. (1984) 'Tragica VII,' *BICS* 31: 171–92

West, M. L. (1987) *Introduction to Greek metre*. Oxford

West, M. L. (1990) 'Dating Corinna', *CQ* 40: 553–7

Wilamowitz-Moellendorff, U. von (1921) *Griechische Verskunst*. Berlin

Wiles, D. (1997) *Tragedy in Athens. Performance space and theatrical meaning.* Cambridge

Willink, C. (1988) 'Eur. *Medea* 1–45, 371–85', *CQ* 38: 313–23

Wohl, V. (1998) *Intimate commerce: exchange, gender, and subjectivity in Greek tragedy.* Austin

Yunis, H. (1988) *A new creed: fundamental religious beliefs in the Athenian polis and Euripidean drama* (Hypomnemata 91). Göttingen

Zeitlin, F. (1996) *Playing the other: gender and society in classical Greek literature.* Chicago

Zuntz, G. (1955) *The political plays of Euripides.* Manchester

# INDEXES

Numbers in italics refer to pages of the Introduction or Appendix, non-italic to line numbers of the commentary.

## 1 Subject

The names Medea and Jason are not indexed.

417

## 2 Greek words